MARKETING ESSENTIALS

SALLY DIBB AND LYNDON SIMKIN

SOUTH-WESTERN
CENGAGE Learning

Australia • Brazil • Japan • Korea • Mexico • Singapore • Spain • United Kingdom • United States

SOUTH-WESTERN
CENGAGE Learning

Marketing Essentials
Sally Dibb and Lyndon Simkin

Publisher: Charlotte Loveridge

Project Content Editor: Leonora Dawson-Bowling

Manufacturing Manager: Jane Glendening

Production Controller: Eyvett Davis

Marketing Manager: Vicky Fielding

Typesetter: ICC Macmillan Inc.

Cover Design: Adam Renvoize

For product information and technology assistance,
contact **emea.info@cengage.com**.

For permission to use material from this text or product,
and for permission queries,
email **clsuk.permissions@cengage.com**

The Author has asserted the right under the Copyright, Designs and
Patents Act 1988 to be identified as Author of this work.

This work is adapted from *Marketing Concepts and Strageties*, 5th Edition, published by Houghton Mifflin © 2006.

British Library Cataloguing-in-Publication Data
A catalogue record for this book is available from the
British Library.

ISBN: 978-1-4080-1150-8

Cengage Learning EMEA
Cheriton House, North Way, Andover, Hampshire. SP10 5BE. United
Kingdom

Cengage Learning products are represented in Canada by Nelson
Education Ltd.

For your lifelong learning solutions, visit
www.cengage.co.uk
Purchase your next print book, e-book or e-chapter at
www.ichapters.co.uk

Printed by Seng Lee, Singapore
3 4 5 6 7 8 9 10 – 11 10 09

Marketing Essentials is dedicated to
Rosalie Alice, Samantha, Mae, Abby, James
and Becky – the 'Simkin clan'

Brief Contents

Contents

Note: Each chapter contains a Summary, Key Links, a list of Important Terms, Discussion and Review Questions, Recommended Readings, an Internet Exercise, an Applied Mini-Case and a Case Study.

Preface

Marketing affects everyone – we are all consumers. Most of the brands, products and services that we buy and consume have been nurtured by their marketers. Away from consumer markets, the majority of organisations also use the marketing toolkit to stay ahead of market developments, identify and satisfy stakeholders, manage relationships, develop persuasive propositions and maximise their budgets. Organisations depend on their marketing colleagues to provide an understanding of the marketplace, identify opportunities, ensure their products and services satisfy the needs of customers and compete effectively. Even in organisations without a marketing department, there will be personnel tasked with seeking new opportunities, addressing strengths and weaknesses, monitoring competitors, building understanding of customers, selecting target markets, creating brand positionings, managing sales and marketing programmes, budgeting and assessing performance – all of which are marketing activities.

There is little doubt that marketing is an important part of today's society and activities of most organisations. In order to provide the necessary market insights, create a compelling marketing strategy and deliver effective marketing programmes in the marketplace, there is a required process of marketing analysis, marketing strategy formulation and then the operationalisation of the agreed target market strategy with appropriate marketing programmes. This marketing process – its core analysis, strategy and programme stages – and the essential concepts which under-pin its success, are explored in *Marketing Essentials*.

In the majority of business schools and colleges in the UK, Eire, Benelux and Scandinavia, the authors' *Marketing: Concepts and Strategies*, now in its 5th edition, is used to introduce undergraduate and MBA students to the nature and scope of marketing. However, not all modules and courses – particularly shorter ones – require a book with nine hundred pages and twenty-six chapters. Sally Dibb and Lyndon Simkin have, therefore, selected the most important chapters and the essential concepts in order to produce this more concise overview of the essentials of marketing, *Marketing Essentials*. As senior marketing academics at the Open University Business School, Warwick Business School and Oxford Brookes familiar with undergraduate and postgraduate audiences, this book is up to date in terms of academic content. Owing to the authors' wide ranging consultancy and research experiences outside lecture theatres, in addition *Marketing Essentials* offers students the all-important practitioner perspective.

The first edition of *Marketing: Concepts and Strategies* appeared in 1991. Since then, that text has become the leader in its market. Whether for undergraduates seeking a comprehensive introduction to marketing, MBAs requiring a grounding in marketing analysis or marketing management, or students in colleges wishing to pass degrees and diplomas, *Marketing: Concepts and Strategies* is used by lecturers and teaching staff to provide an accessible, topical and enlightening insight into the world of marketing. *Marketing: Concepts and Strategies* is also recommended by the Chartered Institute of Marketing and the Marketing Institute of Ireland. The new and more concise *Marketing Essentials* has retained the values of its bigger sister, while offering an accessible and topical overview of the discipline of marketing and its essential components.

The Authors

Sally Dibb is Professor of Marketing at the Open University Business School. Formerly she was Associate Dean at Warwick Business School. After over 20 years at Warwick Business School, Lyndon Simkin recently joined Oxford Brookes University as Professor of Marketing. They also co-chair the Academy of Marketing's special interest group in Market Segmentation. They have been teaching undergraduates, MBAs and executives the basics of marketing, advanced strategic marketing, marketing management, buyer behaviour, marketing communications and marketing research for more than two decades. Sally and Lyndon's research focuses on market segmentation, marketing planning, marketing strategy operationalisation and teaching methods, in which areas they have published extensively in the academic journals in the UK and USA. They also operate a strategy consultancy, with an impressive list of UK and international clients. Lyndon is a recognised expert witness in high court business planning and marketing litigation cases. Both Sally and Lyndon are reviewers for the main European marketing conferences and the leading global marketing and strategy journals.

In addition to being joint authors of *Marketing Essentials*, they co-authored *Marketing: Concepts and Strategies,* (published by Houghton Mifflin, 2006), the innovative *The Marketing Casebook: Cases and Concepts* (Thomson) in 1994 and 2001, mixing real-world cases with overviews of theory, and in 1996 and 1998 *The Market Segmentation Workbook* and *The Marketing Planning Workbook* (both Thomson), aimed at assisting marketing practitioners to reassess their target markets and understand the complexities of marketing planning. These workbooks were based on their consultancy experiences with organisations as diverse as Accenture, AstraZeneca, Calor, Cap Gemini, Conoco, DERA (MoD), EDF Energy, E.on, Fintur, Fujitsu, GfK, ICI, JCB, McDonald's, Raytheon, Royal & Sun Alliance, Standard Chartered, Tesco, Tilda, Willis and various public sector bodies. The *Workbooks* have been translated and published in China and Russia. In 2001, Sally and Lyndon published the revision aid, *Marketing Briefs* (Elsevier Butterworth-Heinemann), revised in its second edition in 2004. While primarily targeted at students preparing for examinations in marketing, *Marketing Briefs* is ideal for providing time-pressured managers with concise and topical insights into the core concepts and tools of strategic marketing. In addition to *Marketing Essentials*, 2008 has seen the publication of two advanced marketing management texts aimed at MBAs and senior practitioners, *Market Segmentation Success: Making It Happen!* (The Haworth Press) in the USA and *Marketing Planning* (Cengage). Both feature the experiences of many of their well known consultancy clients.

Running Order and Key Features
of *Marketing Essentials*

The principal aim of *Marketing Essentials* is to provide a book which students find easy to use and which reflects accurately the current thinking in the world of marketing. The Parts follow a logical structure which adheres to the premise that for effective marketing there first must be analysis of the marketplace, then the recommendation of a marketing strategy, and finally the production of marketing programmes with control processes to facilitate implementation of the desired strategy. Every chapter is up-to-date in terms of the current research and thinking in the area, the latest statistics and industry figures where relevant, and to reflect the views of leading academics and practitioners who have kindly reviewed the chapters, provided thought-provoking quotes and suggested the key readings in their area of expertise as additional references. Chapter openers are designed to build understanding from the word go and the concluding pages of each chapter provide an applied case, a case study, an Internet exercise, key links to related chapters, recommended readings and questions for discussion. Further materials – for students and faculty – are available on the accompanying web site, located at www.dibbmarketing.com.

Part I: Marketing Defined and Marketing in Context. An introduction to the nature and scope of marketing and the marketing process, marketing strategy and competitive forces. Placing marketing in context.

Part II: Understanding Markets. The marketing environment, consumer and business-to-business buying behaviour, target marketing, brand positioning, and marketing research. Marketing analyses and target market strategy.

Part III: Developing Marketing Programmes. Products and services, marketing channels, pricing, marketing communications and branding. Creating and managing the marketing mix.

Key features include:

- Full-length strategic case studies to aid understanding of key concepts.
- Coverage of the issues relating to marketing in consumer goods markets, services and business-to-business markets.
- Extensive cross-referencing between chapters, Parts and key concepts.
- The inclusion of the insights of leading marketing practitioners.
- The thoughts of the leading academic 'gurus', their recommended further readings and quotes.
- Chapter opening vignettes, in-chapter boxes illustrating current developments, and end of chapter cases for discussion.
- The inclusion of applied cases and Internet exercises at the ends of each chapter.
- Up-dated industry/market statistics, figures and examples for the EU and leading brands.

Companion Website

Visit the *Marketing Essentials* companion website at **www.cengage.co.uk/dibb_essentials** to find valuable teaching and learning materials including:

For students
- Testbank
- Web links
- Financial analyses in marketing
- Full glossary of key terms
- Applied help to students examining how to:
  - Tackle case studies
  - Write reports
  - Make presentations
  - Revise and prepare for examinations
  - Handle job interviews
  - Produce CVs

For lecturers
- PowerPoint visual aids
- Extra cases
- Suggested examination formats and questions
- Selected course outlines and syllabus proposals
- Q&A topics and solutions

Acknowledgements

This text would not have happened without the support and encouragement of the original American co-authors Bill Pride and O.C. Ferrell, Andrew Nielsen and Susan Kahn at Houghton Mifflin, the team in Cambridge, everyone at Cengage, the comments and enthusiasm from fellow marketing lecturers at Warwick University and the Open University, our numerous consultancy clients, and above all the feedback from our students past and present.

Above all, we owe thanks to our wonderful children: Rosalie Alice, Samantha, Mae, Abigail, James and Becky.

Sally Dibb & Lyndon Simkin
Kenilworth, Summer, 2008

Marketing Matters . . . to All Types of Organisations

Experian

The first important thing is to have a clear vision of what you want to be – particularly when you provide a diverse and complex range of products to an equally diverse range of customers and markets. It becomes vital that *all* marketing activities, including pricing, have a predefined consistency, and contribute to an overall clear and simple set of messages that effectively communicate the company's vision to business customers, consumers, colleagues, investors and communities alike.

It's a given that all marketing activity must involve *robust* market planning, rigorous product management – internally and externally – and the development of consistent simple messages, for all relevant audiences. Even before that starts though, there has to be a clear business strategy that evaluates macro-economic and market trends and competitive activity, and that can still deliver sustainable market advantage.

David Coupe, managing director, international marketing services, Experian

Experian is a global leader in providing information solutions to organisations and consumers. Experian helps organisations find, develop and manage profitable customer relationships by providing information, decision-making solutions and processing services. Experian empowers consumers to understand, manage and protect their personal information and assets.

Tesco

Marketing – it's fundamental. But our definition of marketing is perhaps different to many other companies. First and foremost we think of marketing as looking after our customers. Our core purpose is to create value for customers to earn their lifetime loyalty. We do this by responding to the different and constantly changing needs of all of our customers to deliver what they want, when they want it. Marketing sets the customer priorities for the business and keeps us on track to deliver. It also guides our entry into new product areas and markets. From simplifying phone tariffs to opening convenience shops in Japan, we always start with understanding the customer.

The marketing discipline is absolutely vital to implementing and executing effective marketing strategies. Because the customer leads our business, marketing has to provide the insight and independence to help make the right decisions for them. In the last year alone, we have held over 200 'Customer Question Time' sessions in our stores, helping us to learn and understand what is important for customers. We would like all our customers to say that they feel welcome at Tesco, that they trust us and that we give them the best all-round shopping trip of all our competitors.

Tim Mason, marketing director and head of US operations, Tesco

Tesco is the market-leader supermarket retailer in the UK, with a significant presence in eastern Europe and South-east Asia.

St Andrew's Healthcare

As a not-for-profit charitable healthcare provider, marketing is key to determining the charity's strategic direction. St Andrew's Healthcare operates in a complex healthcare market environment and therefore effective marketing planning is essential for ensuring that the organisation delivers clinical services ('products') that are required by the healthcare sectors the Charity operates in, at affordable prices. Marketing also ensures that St Andrew's effectively communicates the core messages about what the St Andrew's brand stands for to its key stakeholders. Part of St Andrew's charitable purpose is to develop new and improved services. An effective analysis of their markets is critical to making sure that the charity makes successful investment and new service decisions.

The marketing discipline drives St Andrew's business planning processes by ensuring that the charity follows a systematic approach to analysing its external market environment; determining a sensible strategic response to this environment; and implementing effective promotional and communication strategies. The marketing planning approach provides a common framework and language, for both clinical and commercial staff, to review the Hospital's clinical services and make well-informed decisions about where the charity should be investing in future services in order to best meet its charitable objectives.

James Watkins, group director of strategic development and marketing, St Andrew's Healthcare

St Andrew's Healthcare is the UK's leading charitable provider of specialist mental health, learning disabilities and acquired brain injury services, working in partnership with the NHS in serving these patient groups.

Calor

At Calor, marketing is the essential, dynamic process through which we maximise shareholder value, by profiling, identifying and locating individuals or companies, enabling us to establish intimate, relevant, long-term relationships that bring continuous mutual satisfaction and tangible financial benefit. Marketing has banished the historical darkness of prejudice, arrogance and self-interest, providing insight and enlightenment, which beams on the customer as our sole and ultimate focus.

Marketing strategy should not remain the property of the Marketing Department, but must be both 'understood' and 'owned' company-wide. At Calor, cross-functional business planning is directed by our marketing strategy and all action plans delivered 'in concert' with it. Successful deployment of actions arising from the marketing strategy requires 'buy-in' from all functional departments and reinforcement via unambiguous direction from the board room. Having said that, markets are dynamic, and therefore assumptions and strategies must be continually and constructively challenged, to ensure ongoing relevance and effectiveness in their deployment. Communication of marketing strategy must cascade down through the organisation and, within the boundaries of commercial sensitivity, future intentions must be shared across the spectrum of stakeholders, who individually impact directly on customer relationships.

Alex Davis, managing director, Calor

Calor, part of the Dutch SHV Group, is the UK's leading supplier of LPG with over 65 years' experience in this flexible and environmentally sensitive energy market. Around 4 million homes and organisations rely on Calor for an enormous variety of applications. Calor's own depots deal directly with many of these customers, but dealers and agents are also important channel members for Calor.

Fujitsu

Marketing lies at the heart of business decision-making in driving profitable growth. There are three primary elements to this: go-to-market strategy, innovation and brand.

> Go-to-market strategy: we help our business units prioritise who to talk to, about what and when; we provide them with the customer and competitor intelligence to engage with priority target customers in the most compelling manner; and we help them to powerfully position our business with this customer.

> Innovation: we lead cross-functional teams from every part of our business in developing distinctive new-thinking that challenges the accepted norms; we package and communicate the new value propositions that emerge from this work; and we ensure that our sales and account teams understand and connect with it, so they can actively use these propositions to better engage with their customers.

> Brand: we define our brand positioning, and how this positioning will develop over time; we make this positioning manifest in our internal and external communications; and we work with others across the business to ensure that the positioning translates into a coherent employee and customer experience.

Marketing strategy is critical to our business. Without it we are left behaving in an utterly responsive manner to the latest new business opportunity, whether or not it is well suited to our goals, talents and current market positioning. With it we can maximise the return from our marketing, sales and account management effort through targeting only those customers whose business we really want – and that we can realistically expect to win. Understanding the external trading environment is very important because this helps us to determine the nature and the scale of our resourcing requirements, and how we can best deploy these resources to generate the maximum business value.

George Miller, formerly group marketing director, Fujitsu Services

Fujitsu is the world's third largest IT services group and works closely with large government and commercial organisations to help them seize the possibilities of effective, innovative IT.

Tilda

Over a number of years Tilda has built a brand-leading position across numerous international markets for its Pure Basmati rice brand. The success of this premium brand has been founded on the basic marketing principle of superior product quality, namely Pure Basmati, allied to tight targeting of consumers who demand real food quality and authentic values. In short, delicious food.

This market segmentation approach has recently been applied to a brand new market opportunity: two-minute microwaveable rice. Whereas 'scratch cooks' form the basis of the Basmati market the microwaveable rice market is one for 'convenience cooks', a massive and growing segment of consumers who are time-pressured but prepared to pay for convenience.

Tapping into this market trend, the Tilda Steamed brand is targeted at the same type of Tilda consumer, who demands better food quality, but this time wants it in a convenient modern form. The Steamed brand has all the superior food values of its sister brand, with Basmati rice as the key ingredient for the sixteen cosmopolitan recipe rices in the range, from pilau rice, through egg fried rice to Thai lime and coriander rice.

Originally launched in 2001 with a comprehensive TV advertising and promotional sampling campaign, the Tilda Steamed brand is already worth nearly £10 million at retail selling prices and is still growing at over 50 per cent per annum. The success of Tilda's marketing can be measured in the fact that Tilda Steamed's consumer base is totally separate from that of Tilda Basmati (dry rice) – and Tilda Basmati sales are as high as ever.

Stephen von Speyr,
Tilda Mainstream Marketing

Led by a powerfully strong brand, UK-based Tilda is now a prominent player in many international markets, including Australia and the USA. Tilda only produces rice. Its marketers maintain its successful standing.

Raytheon

Marketing has played a major part in enabling our business to make fact-based decisions, which have seen a successful change in our strategy. Previously we were the type of business that spread itself 'too thinly', meaning we did not achieve the results we should in our real areas of expertise. By using tried and tested marketing tools, we have identified the attractive markets and equally those not so attractive, to enable us to focus on successfully moving towards the achievement of our vision. Currently we are achieving and forecasting major growth in turnover and profit, which is the result of implementing marketing processes in our business.

The global markets in which our business competes are increasingly competitive and the need for a marketing discipline in implementing marketing strategies is extremely important. Systematically analysing key developments in constantly changing markets and capturing customer needs is vital in providing us with a competitive advantage. Providing key decision-makers with the toolkit, and more importantly the information, to execute winning plans increases the effectiveness of the plans. The value and effectiveness of having the discipline is reflected in the continued success of this business.

Jim Trail, chief operating officer, Raytheon Systems Limited

Power & Control Systems is a business within Raytheon Systems Limited, a wholly owned subsidiary of Raytheon Company, and was established in Glenrothes, Fife, in 1960. Core capabilities of the company are the design, development and manufacture of power products for international aerospace, industrial and defence markets.

A Career in Marketing

Marketing is the most fun you can have in business, with your clothes on.

Marketing is the most fascinating aspect of business because it is about creating a profit out of studying and satisfying the needs of endlessly unpredictable customers.

You can make a million in marketing by becoming the Marketing Director of Tesco, or by starting your own consultancy, or by coming up with your own business idea and becoming an entrepreneur yourself. You can help change the world by becoming the Marketing Director of a leading charity.

Some companies have lots of marketing executives, some have very few. The company that you should try to work for does not just have a marketing department but is one where the customer is truly placed at the heart of the organisation.

Hugh Burkitt, Chief Executive of The Marketing Society

The Marketing Society is a professional association dedicated to raising the stature of marketing in business. It champions marketing excellence by providing the best network for senior marketers to exchange ideas and share best practice.

MARKETING ESSENTIALS

**SALLY DIBB
AND
LYNDON SIMKIN**

I Marketing Defined and Marketing in Context

©iStockphoto.com/RichMatts

Marketing consists of individual and organisational activities that facilitate and expedite satisfying exchange relationships in a dynamic environment through the creation, distribution, promotion and pricing of goods, services and ideas. The simple premise of marketing is that to be successful, any organisation must understand its customers' requirements and satisfy them in a manner that gives the organisation an edge over its competitors. This involves offering the 'right' mix of product, people, service, pricing, promotion and distribution channel. Marketing also depends on constant up-dating of ideas and market insights. Customers are often surprisingly fickle and modify their needs and wants, rivals alter their strategies and forces in the marketplace regularly change. Marketing is an organisational function and a set of processes for creating, communicating and delivering value to customers and for managing customer relationships in ways that benefit the organisation and its stakeholders.

Part I of *Marketing Essentials* introduces the nature and scope of marketing and the marketing process, marketing strategy and competitive forces. The aim of Part I is to define marketing and enable readers to appreciate its context.

Chapter 1, 'The Marketing Concept', defines marketing; establishes its importance to organisations and to consumers; and outlines the major components of marketing strategy – notably marketing opportunity analysis, target market selection, competitive advantage, and the development of marketing programmes that implement the marketing strategy. The discussion also examines the concept of marketing orientation within an organisation. The chapter also establishes the ethos of *Marketing Essentials,* describes the structure of the text and presents an overview of the marketing process. Important concepts presented in Chapters 1 and 2 are deliberately repeated throughout the text. It is important for the reader to understand and accept them before progressing to the following chapters.

Chapter 2, 'Marketing Strategy', presents an overview of marketing strategy and the strategising process. This chapter aims to highlight which strategic marketing considerations help to ensure that a product or service is marketed for the benefit of the organisation as well as its targeted customers. The product or service should be marketed differently enough from competitors' marketing programmes to provide the organisation's product or service with a perceived advantage over these competitors. The chapter first explores what is marketing strategy and the importance of organisational mission, goals and corporate strategy. The discussion next turns to assessing organisational opportunities, capabilities and SWOT issues, as well as identifying strategic objectives. The chapter addresses the all-important role of identifying market segments, targeting and brand positioning in marketing strategy: the development of clear target market priorities. The chapter then focuses on competitive strategies for marketing: the role of competition, its ramifications for strategy, competitive positions and warfare strategies. The link between marketing objectives and marketing mix programmes is examined, along with implementation and performance monitoring.

By the conclusion of Part I of *Marketing Essentials,* readers should understand what is meant by the terms *marketing*, *marketing orientation*, *marketing strategy* and the *marketing process*. The essential themes in Part I are developed further as the text continues.

1

The Marketing Concept

"**Marketing is concerned with the establishment and maintenance of mutually satisfying exchange relationships.**"

Michael Baker, formerly of the University of Strathclyde

Objectives

- To understand the definition of marketing

- To appreciate the context of marketing and marketing orientation

- To explain the marketing process

- To understand the importance of marketing

- To gain insight into the basic elements of the marketing concept and its implementation

- To understand the major components of a marketing strategy and the marketing mix

- To gain a sense of general strategic marketing issues, such as market opportunity analysis, target market selection and marketing mix development

- To grasp the ethos and structure of this book

Introduction

Marketing's aim is the identification of target markets and the satisfaction of these customers, now and in the future. In most organisations, marketing fulfils an analytical function, provides strategic direction and facilitates a set of tactical activities designed to attract the targeted customers to the organisation's products or services.

Organisations with a marketing orientation have more than a few staff engaged in marketing activities. Such organisations have a sound awareness of customers' needs and buying behaviour, of competitors' offerings and strategies, and of market trends. They take steps to ensure they know how these market conditions will evolve. In addition, they orientate their operational practices and coordinate their inter-functional thinking around these market conditions.

To be truly effective, marketing needs to be an analytical process combining marketing analysis, strategising, and the creation of marketing programmes designed to implement the designated marketing strategy. Marketing opportunity analysis is a pivotal part of marketing: the determination of emerging and existing market opportunities and the choice of which to address. At the heart of a marketing strategy is the formation of a target market strategy and a basis for competing in order to focus on the opportunities prioritised by the organisation.

Most members of the general public think of 'advertising', 'marketing research' or 'sales persuasion' when the term 'marketing' is mentioned. These brief introductory comments alone demonstrate that there is in fact much more to marketing. This first chapter of *Marketing Essentials* is designed to define marketing and explain its role.

Opener

Even Condoms Need Marketing

Not too long ago, no one would have seen advertisements for condoms. A mix of changing social attitudes, concerns about sexually transmitted diseases and campaigns to combat teenage pregnancies have led to a range of brands turning to mainstream TV and press advertising. This surge in marketing activity has not been without its critics, however.

Mates Condoms used agency Real Adventure for its £2 million account. Mates, launched by Richard Branson in the 1980s, is now part of Ansell Healthcare and has made significant market share gains against long-standing market leader Durex. A recent ploy by Mates was to target women with a separate range of condoms, branded Pleasure. This new brand launch was placed next to cosmetics and haircare products in supermarkets and pharmacies, rather than among other condom lines. In targeting women, Mates is moving away from the traditional target audience, male purchasers. By persuading retailers to display the range among beauty products, the company is striving to achieve an edge over its competitors while demonstrating an affinity with the purchasing behaviour of its target customers. Mates' marketers are seeking to grow market share and to take advantage of changing attitudes to condoms.

A real storm was created when US brand Trojan broadcast TV advertisements for its Shared Pleasure brand, showing a couple having sex. The first adverts ran in the commercial breaks of TV reality show *Big Brother*, which attracted a viewing profile similar to the target market profile for the brand. Trojan attained approval from the UK's Broadcast Advertising Clearance Centre for a post-9.00 p.m. watershed showing of the 20-second adverts. Trojan claimed that this marked the first time an orgasm had been shown in a UK television advert. The advert, made by agency Media Therapy, apparently showed people captured at the height of pleasure, linking to the Shared Pleasure brand name. Building on the back of a poster campaign, this advertising was bound to court controversy, receiving complaints to the Advertising Standards Authority that the campaign was offensive, demeaning to women, pornographic and not suitable for television audiences. While the brand-building creativity may have been clever, Trojan's marketers nevertheless caused uproar in certain circles.

Sources: 'Trojan under fire for "her pleasure" ad', *Marketing Week*, 4 April 2004, p. 8; 'Trojan to screen first orgasm ad', *Marketing*, 26 April 2004, p. 6; 'Mates', *Marketing Week*, 3 June 2004, p. 10; 'Why is safe sex unpalatable?', *Marketing*, 8 April 2004, p. 15. Photo: Courtesy of Mates Healthcare

This chapter first overviews the concept of marketing orientation before developing a definition of marketing. The focus then moves on to some of the reasons people should study marketing and why marketing is important. The chapter proceeds to explore the marketing concept and examines several issues associated with successful implementation. The chapter explains the importance of an analytical process to effective marketing, from analysis to strategy formulation to the creation of marketing programmes. Mates – see 'Opener' box – analysed the purchasing behaviour of its targeted consumers before developing the marketing strategy for its new Pleasure range of condoms. The chapter concludes by discussing the organisation and running order of this text. The concepts and strategies discussed throughout this book are applicable to consumer goods and services, business-to-business products and services, as well as to not-for-profit and public-sector organisations.

Like all the chapters in *Marketing Essentials*, this one contains detailed topical illustrative examples in highlighted boxes, presents cases for discussion, suggests Internet exercises at its conclusion, lists at the end all the key terms presented in the chapter, provides discussion and review questions to emphasise the key themes and offers suggested further reading choices. In addition, as the principal definitions are introduced in the text, they are repeated in the margins for ease of understanding, glossary-style. If you have not yet done so, *before* tackling the chapters you should read the Preface to this book in order to understand the perspective, structure and chapter components of *Marketing Essentials*.

Marketing Explained and Defined

Marketing Orientation

Marketing orientation
A marketing-oriented organisation devotes resources to understanding the needs and buying behaviour of customers, competitors' activities and strategies, and of market trends and external forces – now and as they may shape up in the future; inter-functional coordination ensures that the organisation's activities and capabilities are aligned to this marketing intelligence

An organisation exhibiting a **marketing orientation** is said to have a sound understanding of customer needs, buying behaviour and the issues influencing the purchasing choices of customers. A marketing-oriented organisation also has a shrewd appreciation of competitors and external marketing environment forces and trends.[1] In addition to comprehending these customer, competitor and marketing environment issues, a marketing-oriented organisation ensures its operations, personnel and capabilities are aligned to reflect these external drivers. A truly marketing-oriented organisation understands these current issues, but is also focused on identifying how they will evolve, so ensuring that the organisation's strategy and capabilities are modified to reflect not just current market requirements but also future market conditions.

A marketing-oriented organisation, therefore, devotes resources to understanding the needs and buying behaviour of customers, competitors' activities and strategies, and market trends and external forces (now and as they may shape up in the future). Inter-functional coordination ensures that the organisation's activities and capabilities are aligned to this marketing intelligence.

Not all organisations can claim to have a marketing orientation. For example, some are purely sales led, concentrating on short-term sales targets, whereas other organisations are production oriented, choosing to emphasise product development and production efficiency in their business strategy. Few experts would argue against maximising sales or seeking leading-edge production practices, or indeed the adoption of best-practice financial and human resource approaches. Similarly, the adoption of a marketing orientation is also highly desirable. A marketing orientation is of significant benefit to an organisation, as it facilitates a better understanding of customers and helps a business to prepare for external market developments, threats and opportunities. It is difficult to contemplate a scenario where a marketing orientation would not be beneficial to an organisation.

An organisation practising the concepts explained in *Marketing Essentials* is well on the way to having a marketing orientation; but it is important that inter-functional coordination aligns the activities within the organisation to the marketplace, and specifically to customer buying behaviour, competitive pressures and marketing environment forces, and to the evolving nature of these market conditions. The use of some of marketing's concepts and an understanding of the role of marketing in attracting and satisfying customers, are not enough on their own to establish what is termed a *marketing orientation*. However, failure to comprehend the core concepts of marketing will make a marketing orientation impossible to achieve. The focus of this text, therefore, is on explaining the core concepts of marketing.

It is possible for an organisation lacking a full marketing orientation to nevertheless deploy aspects of the marketing toolkit as described in the following chapters. Indeed, it is common for a business to understand its customers adequately, but not its competitors' strategies or the external marketing environment forces. Obviously, it is better not to operate in ignorance of these external pressures, which may create threats or opportunities. The definition of marketing *per se* is not, therefore, the same as the definition of marketing orientation.

Marketing Defined

Asking members of the public to define marketing is an illuminating experience. They will respond with a variety of descriptions, including 'advertising', 'selling', 'hype', 'conning people', 'targeting' and 'packaging'. In reality, marketing encompasses many more activities than most people realise and depends on a wealth of formal concepts, processes and models not implied by the soundbites just listed. Since it is practised and studied for many different reasons, marketing has been, and continues to be, defined in many different ways, whether for academic, research or applied business purposes. This chapter examines what is meant by the term **marketing**.

Marketing

Individual and organisational activities that facilitate and expedite satisfying exchange relationships in a dynamic environment through the creation, distribution, promotion and pricing of goods, services and ideas

> Marketing consists of individual and organisational activities that facilitate and expedite satisfying exchange relationships in a dynamic environment through the creation, distribution, promotion and pricing of goods, services and ideas.
>
> *Dibb, Simkin, Pride and Ferrell in Marketing: Concepts and Strategies*

The basic rationale of marketing is that, to succeed, an organisation requires satisfied and happy customers who return to the organisation to provide additional custom. In exchange for something of value, typically payment or a donation, the customers receive a product or service that satisfies their needs. Such a product has an acceptable level of quality, reliability, customer service and support, is available at places convenient for the customer at the 'right' price and is promoted effectively by means of a clear message that is readily comprehended by the customers in question. For example, in return for quenching thirst at affordable prices with a reliable product that is widely available in easy-to-use containers, Coca-Cola receives a great deal of money from customers. Unfortunately for companies and their marketers, customers' requirements change as their needs alter, marketing messages infiltrate their thinking, friends and colleagues discuss purchases, and competing products are pushed by rival organisations. In the dynamic world of marketing, an effective solution to satisfying customer needs rarely has longevity. High-specification cassette decks no longer satisfy the majority of music lovers' needs: compact disc players and mp3 players, therefore, have taken over the dominant share of Sony's range. Marketers must constantly assess their customers' requirements and be prepared to modify their marketing activity accordingly. An assessment of marketing opportunities is an ever evolving process requiring regular revision and updating.

> Marketing is the management process responsible for identifying, anticipating and satisfying customer requirements profitably.
>
> *Chartered Institute of Marketing*

Understanding customers and anticipating their requirements is a core theme of effective marketing.[2] So, too, is understanding general market trends and developments that may affect both customers' views and the activities of organisations operating in a particular market. These factors may include social trends, technological enhancements, economic patterns, and changes in the legal and regulatory arena, as well as political influences. These forces are often termed the **marketing environment**. Compared with five years ago, for example, look at how many companies now produce products in 'environmentally friendly' packaging in line with the social trend of the 'greening consumer'. An organisation does not have a marketplace to itself. There are direct competitors, new entrant rivals, substitute products with alternative solutions to a customer's specific need. Construction-equipment giant JCB markets trench-digging equipment to utilities and local authorities. The growth of subterranean tunnelling robotic 'moles' for pipe laying, requiring no trench digging, is a substitute for the traditional JCB backhoe loader and a major competitive threat. The competitive context is of fundamental importance to marketers of any good or service. So, too, are the internal resource base, and the strengths and weaknesses within the business that will determine which market opportunities are in fact viable for the organisation to pursue. Marketing, therefore, depends on the successful analysis of customers, the marketing environment, competition and internal capabilities.

> The aim of marketing is to make selling superfluous. The aim is to know and to understand the customer so well that the product or service fits him/her and sells itself!
>
> *US management guru Peter Drucker*

With an understanding of these aspects of the marketplace, an organisation must then develop a marketing strategy. Even the mighty global organisations such as GM/Vauxhall, DuPont or Unilever choose not to offer a product for every type of consumer or customer need. Instead, they attempt to identify groups of customers where each separate group, or 'market segment', has 'similar' needs. Each group of customers may then be offered a specifically tailored product or service proposition and a 'marketing mix' programme. The Ford Kuga off-roader appeals to a separate group of customers than does the Ford Focus town car, and it is marketed totally differently. In developing unique marketing programmes for individual market segments – groups of customers – an organisation must prioritise which particular groups of customers it has the ability to serve and which will provide satisfactory returns. Resources will not permit all segments in a market to be targeted. In deciding on which segments to target, an organisation must be clear about the message – or *positioning* – it intends to offer to each group of customers. The organisation should endeavour to serve those customers it targets in a manner that gives it an edge over its competitors. Knowing how to group customers sensibly into homogeneous market segments; determining which, ultimately, to target; selecting a suitable positioning platform; and seeking superiority over rivals, are some of the core elements of marketing strategy.

> The marketing concept holds that the key to achieving organisational goals lies in determining the needs and wants of target markets and delivering the desired satisfaction more efficiently and effectively than the competition.
>
> *US marketer Philip Kotler*

Once a company has devised a marketing strategy, its attention must switch to marketing mix programmes.[3] As consumers of food brands, audio products or banking services, all readers of this text will have experienced the marketing mix programmes of major companies such as Cadbury's, Sony or Lloyds TSB. These are the tactical actions of marketing departments, which are designed to implement the desired marketing strategy. The product or offer must be clearly defined in line with target customer needs; service levels and guarantees must be determined; pricing and payment issues decided; channels of distribution established to make the product or service available; and promotional strategies devised and executed to communicate with the targeted customers. These tactical aspects of marketing programmes – the marketing mix – must be supported with carefully managed controls in an organisation to ensure their effective execution and the monitoring of their effectiveness.

Marketing environment
External changing forces within the trading environment: laws, regulations, political activities, societal pressures, economic conditions and technological advances

Marketers must understand their markets – customers, competitors, market trends – and their own capabilities before developing marketing programmes. A marketing strategy must be determined that reflects the analyses, before the marketing programmes required to action the recommended strategy are specified. **A**nalysis first, then **S**trategy decisions with, finally, the formulation of marketing **P**rogrammes: ASP. The focus must be on providing customer satisfaction, but in a manner that leads to the organisation's successful performance. For example, by addressing customers' needs and adopting a marketing culture incorporating clear controls, construction equipment manufacturer JCB has enjoyed the most successful financial returns in the company's history.

The intention of this introductory marketing text is to explore these facets of marketing comprehensively and thus provide a sound conceptual basis with which to understand the nature and activities of marketing. There are many definitions of marketing, since it is not a pure science. However, certain core ingredients of the various definitions collectively indicate the basic priorities of marketing:

- satisfying customers
- identifying/maximising marketing opportunities
- targeting the 'right' customers
- facilitating exchange relationships
- staying ahead in dynamic environments

- endeavouring to beat and pre-empt competitors
- utilising resources/assets effectively
- increasing market share
- enhancing profitability or income
- satisfying the organisation's stakeholders.

These aims form the objectives for many marketing directors and marketing departments. They are featured throughout this book, which adopts the definition below of marketing by the American Marketing Association, and the Association's more recent explanation. (See also the marginal definition on page 7.)

> **Marketing.** Noun. An organisational function and a set of processes for creating, communicating and delivering value to customers and for managing customer relationships in ways that benefit the organisation and its stakeholders.

Marketing indeed must be viewed as a process, of analysis to gain market insights, strategy decisions and the management of marketing programmes in order to implement the desired marketing strategy. A definition of marketing must acknowledge that it relates to more than just tangible goods, that marketing activities occur in a dynamic environment and that such activities are performed by individuals as well as organisations.[4] The ultimate goal is to satisfy targeted customers and stakeholders, seeking their loyalty and consumption, in a way that adds value for the organisation and its stakeholders. This should be achieved in a manner that is differentiated in the view of customers and stakeholders vis-à-vis competitors' marketing mixes, that provides an organisation with a competitive edge over rivals and that is updated regularly to reflect market forces and developments. To be in a position to satisfy targeted customers or stakeholders, much work is required by those tasked within the organisation and their external partners to conduct the required marketing analyses, develop sensible marketing strategies, and create appropriate marketing programmes to take to market.

The Definitions of Marketing Explored

> Marketing consists of individual and organisational activities that facilitate and expedite satisfying exchange relationships in a dynamic environment through the creation, distribution, promotion and pricing of goods, services and ideas.

Marketing Consists of Activities

The marketing of products or services effectively requires many activities. Some are performed by producers; some are accomplished by intermediaries, who purchase products from producers or from other intermediaries and resell them; and some are even performed by purchasers. Marketing does not include all human and organisational activities, only those aimed at facilitating and expediting exchanges. Table 1.1 lists several major categories and examples of marketing activities, as ultimately encountered by the consumer or business customer, who remains at the 'sharp end' of such decisions and marketing programmes. Note that this list is not all-inclusive. Each activity could be sub-divided into more specific activities.

Marketing is Performed by Individuals and Organisations

All organisations perform marketing activities to facilitate exchanges. Businesses as well as not-for-profit and public-sector organisations, such as colleges and universities, charitable organisations, community theatres and hospitals, perform marketing activities. For example, colleges and universities and their students engage in exchanges. To receive instruction, knowledge, entertainment, a degree, the use of facilities and sometimes room and board, students give up time, money and perhaps services in the form of labour; they may also give up opportunities to do other things! Many organisations engage in marketing activities. Various police forces have surveyed their communities in order to prioritise services and reassure the general public that people's concerns will be addressed. Politicians now conduct analyses before determining strategies; they think of target markets rather than just the electorate. Even the sole owner of and worker in a small corner shop decides which products will sell, arranges deliveries to the shop, prices and displays products, advertises and serves customers.

TABLE 1.1 POSSIBLE DECISIONS AND ACTIVITIES ASSOCIATED WITH MARKETING MIX VARIABLES

Marketing Mix Variables	Possible Decisions and Activities
Product	Develop and test-market new products; modify existing products; eliminate products that do not satisfy customers' desires; formulate brand names and branding policies; create product guarantees and establish procedures for fulfilling guarantees; plan packages, including materials, sizes, shapes, colours and designs
Place/distribution	Analyse various types of distribution channels; design appropriate distribution channels; select appropriate channel members and partners; design an effective programme for dealer relations; establish distribution centres; formulate and implement procedures for efficient product handling; set up inventory controls; analyse transportation methods; minimise total distribution costs; analyse possible locations for plants and wholesale or retail outlets
Promotion (marketing communications)	Set promotional objectives; determine major types of promotion to be used; select and schedule advertising media; develop advertising messages; measure the effectiveness of advertisements; recruit and train salespeople; formulate payment programmes for sales personnel; establish sales territories; plan and implement sales promotion efforts such as free samples, coupons, displays, competitions, sales contests and cooperative advertising programmes; prepare and disseminate publicity releases; evaluate sponsorships; provide direct mail; and establish websites or Internet facilities
Price	Analyse competitors' prices; formulate pricing policies; determine method(s) used to set prices; set prices; determine discounts for various types of buyer; establish conditions and terms of sales; determine credit and payment terms; understand the consumers' notion of value
People	Manipulate the marketing mix and establish service levels, guarantees, warranties, expertise, sales support, after sales back-up, customer handling requirements, personnel skills training and motivation (people as marketers); make products and services available (people as intermediaries); provide a market for products (people as consumers)

Marketing Facilitates Satisfying Exchange Relationships

For an **exchange** to take place, four conditions must exist.

1 Two or more individuals, groups or organisations must participate.
2 Each party must possess something of value that the other party desires.
3 Each party must be willing to give up its 'something of value' to receive the 'something of value' held by the other party. The objective of a marketing exchange is to receive something that is desired more than that which is given up to get it – that is, a reward in excess of costs.
4 The parties to the exchange must be able to communicate with each other to make their 'something of value' available.[5]

Exchange
The provision or transfer of goods, services and ideas in return for something of value

Figure 1.1 illustrates the process of exchange. The arrows indicate that the parties communicate and that each has something of value available to exchange. Note, though, that an exchange will not necessarily take place just because these four conditions exist. Nevertheless, even if there is no exchange, marketing activities have still occurred. The 'somethings of value' held by the two parties are most often products and/or financial resources, such as money or credit. When an exchange occurs, products are traded for other products or for financial resources.

An exchange should be *satisfying* to both the buyer and the seller. In fact, in a study of marketing managers, 32 per cent indicated that creating **customer satisfaction** was the most important concept in a definition of marketing.[6] Marketing activities should be oriented towards creating and maintaining satisfying exchange relationships. To maintain an exchange relationship, the buyer must be satisfied with the goods, service or idea obtained in the exchange; the seller must be satisfied with the financial reward or something else of value received in the exchange.

Customer satisfaction
A state that results when an exchange meets the needs and expectations of the buyer

Maintaining a positive relationship with buyers is an important goal for a seller, regardless of whether the seller is marketing cereal, financial services or construction plant. Through buyer–seller interaction, the buyer develops expectations about the seller's future behaviour. To fulfil these expectations, the seller must deliver on promises made. Over time, a healthy buyer–seller relationship results in interdependencies between the two parties. The buyer depends on the seller to furnish information, parts and service; to be available; and to provide satisfying products in the future.

Marketing Occurs in a Dynamic Environment

The marketing environment consists of many external changing forces within the trading environment: laws, regulations, political activities, societal pressures, changing economic conditions and technological advances. Each of these dynamic forces has an impact on how effectively marketing activities can facilitate and expedite exchanges. For example, the development and acceptance of the Internet in home PCs has given organisations another vehicle through which to promote their products. Another example is the impact EU regulations have had on reducing distribution headaches within much of Europe, along with recent strides towards economic monetary union and the launch of the euro.

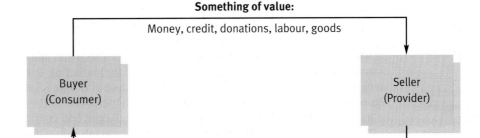

Figure 1.1
Exchange between buyer and seller

Marketing Involves Products, Distribution, Promotion, Pricing and People

Marketing Focuses on Goods, Services and Ideas

Product
A good, service or idea

Good
A physical entity that can be touched

Service
The application of human and mechanical efforts to people or objects in order to provide intangible benefits to customers

Idea
A concept, philosophy, image or issue

Marketing means more than simply advertising or selling a product; it involves developing and managing a product that will satisfy certain needs. It focuses on making the product available at the right place, at the right time, at a price that is acceptable to customers and with appropriate people and service support. It also requires transmitting the kind of promotional information that will help customers determine whether the product will in fact be able to satisfy their needs.

The word 'product' has been used a number of times in this chapter. For purposes of discussion in this text, a **product** is viewed as being a good, a service or an idea. A **good** is a physical entity that can be touched. A Ford Focus, a Sony compact disc player, Kellogg's Cornflakes, a bar of Lux soap and a kitten in a pet shop are examples of goods. A **service** is the application of human and mechanical efforts to people or objects in order to provide intangible benefits to customers. Services such as air travel, dry cleaning, hairdressing, banking, medical care and childcare are just as real as goods, but an individual cannot actually touch or stockpile them. Marketing is utilised for services but requires certain enhancements in order to be effective (see Part III). **Ideas** include concepts, philosophies, images and issues. For instance, a marriage counsellor gives couples ideas and advice to help improve their relationships. Other marketers of ideas include political parties, charities, religious groups, schools and marketing lecturers.

> An organisational function and a set of processes for creating, communicating and delivering value to customers and for managing customer relationships in ways that benefit the organisation and its stakeholders.

The more recent definition suggested by the American Marketing Association came as a welcome addition to these authors, who for two decades have presented marketing to their students as an analytical process of analysis, strategising and then programmes for implementation in their *marketing process*. This process is relevant to not only those organisations with consumers or business customers. In the context that all organisations have stakeholders to influence and satisfy, this process is suitable for any organisation.

The Marketing Process

Marketers spend much of their time managing existing products, target markets and marketing programmes. Even with such so-called 'steady-state' operations, the dynamic nature of marketing leads to continual changes in the marketing environment, competitors and their activities, as well as in customers' needs, expectations, perceptions and buying behaviour. Without a sound understanding of these issues, marketing strategies and their associated marketing programmes cannot be truly effective. Marketers must, therefore, undertake analyses of these market conditions. As changes in the marketplace occur, marketers should revise their marketing strategies accordingly. Any strategy modifications will necessitate changes to the organisation's marketing programmes.

This analytical process of marketing analyses, strategy formulation and the creation or modification of marketing programmes is necessary for existing activities and target markets. This marketing process is also required when an organisation contemplates entering new markets, launching new or replacement products, modifying the brand strategy, changing customer service practices, rethinking advertising and promotional plans, altering pricing or evaluating distribution policies. Unexpected sales patterns also require such a process of understanding, thinking and action. This is the **marketing process**: analysis of market conditions, the creation of an appropriate marketing strategy, and the development of marketing programmes designed to action the agreed strategy, as depicted in Figure 1.2. Finally, as part of this process, the implementation of the marketing strategy and its associated marketing programmes must be managed and controlled.

With an understanding of customers' needs, buying behaviour, expectations and product or brand perceptions, marketers are able to create marketing programmes likely to attract, satisfy and retain customers. With an appreciation of competitors' activities and plans, the marketing programmes are more likely to combat rivals' marketing programmes and to differentiate an organisation's product. Without an awareness of changes in the marketing

Marketing process
Analysis of market conditions, the creation of an appropriate marketing strategy, the development of marketing programmes designed to action the agreed strategy and, finally, the implementation and control of the marketing strategy and its associated marketing programmes

Figure 1.2
The marketing process
Source: © Sally Dibb
& Lyndon Simkin

Corporate goals/objectives

The marketing process

Marketing analysis
• Customers
• Competition
• Trends/marketing environment
• Internal capabilities

Marketing strategy
• Market opportunity identification
• Target market priorities
• Brand positioning
• Basis for competing
• Marketing objectives

Marketing programmes
• Products
• Pricing
• Place/distribution
• Promotion/communication
• People, processes, physical environment

Marketing controls
• Budgets and schedules
• Personnel and responsibilities
• Benchmarking and monitoring progress

environment, it is unlikely that the specified marketing programme will be sustainable in the longer term. As trading environment changes occur, it is important that an organisation's capabilities are modified in order to reflect market conditions and likely demands. The marketing analysis stage of the marketing process is, therefore, of fundamental importance.

Equipped with an awareness of the marketplace made possible through marketing analyses, a marketing strategy may be derived. This involves selecting the opportunities to be pursued and devising an associated target market strategy. Few organisations have adequate financial, managerial and employee resources to address all of the possible marketing opportunities that exist: there must be some trade-offs. This generally involves selecting only some of the opportunities to pursue and focusing on specific target markets. Having made these decisions, marketers must ensure that they develop a compelling brand positioning and that they create a strong basis for competing versus their rivals, aimed specifically at attracting customers in the prioritised target markets. These strategic recommendations should then translate into specific marketing objectives, designed to hone the creation of marketing programmes.

In most organisations the majority of the budget, time and effort within the marketing function is devoted to creating and managing marketing programmes. These programmes revolve around specifying product, people, promotion (communication), pricing and place (distribution channel) attributes and policies, designed to appeal to and serve those customers identified as being in the priority target market(s). In addition to these ingredients of the marketing mix, marketers of services include other ingredients, as detailed in Chapter 10. Finally, the marketing programmes must be rolled out and controlled.

13

Part III of *Marketing Essentials* addresses the creation of marketing programmes. Chapters 8 to 14 examine extensively each of the ingredients of the marketing mix, which are the essentials for a marketing programme. However, the marketing programmes should not be created before marketers have fully analysed the market and then devised a marketing strategy. These aspects of marketing analysis and marketing strategy are, therefore, explored in the early stages of *Marketing Essentials,* in Parts I and II. The chapter running order is also structured to reflect the syllabus content popular on most mainstream marketing modules and courses at diploma and degree level.

The Importance of Marketing

Marketing Activities are Used in Many Organisations

The commercial importance of marketing and its relevance as a topic worth studying are apparent from the definitions of marketing just presented. The use of marketing techniques and the development of a marketing orientation should enable an organisation to understand its customers and stakeholders better, address competitors' activities and market developments, and effectively harness its capabilities. The results should be enhanced customer satisfaction and retention, improved market share in key target markets and stronger financial performance. This section discusses several less obvious reasons why marketing should be studied.

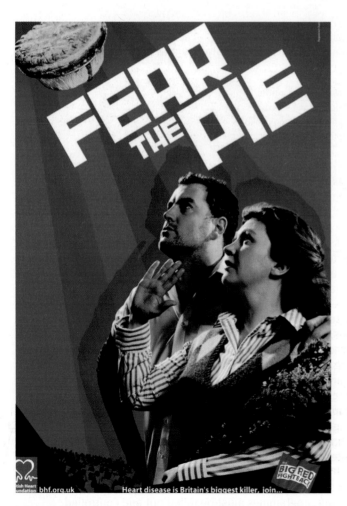

In Europe and the United States between 25 per cent and 33 per cent of all civilian workers perform marketing activities. The marketing field offers a variety of interesting and challenging career opportunities, such as strategic planning, personal selling, advertising, packaging, transport, storage, marketing research, product development, creative design, wholesaling, retailing, marketing planning and consultancy. In addition, many individuals who work for not-for-profit organisations – such as charities or health agencies – engage in marketing activities. Marketing skills are used to promote political, cultural, religious, civic and charitable activities. The advertisement in Figure 1.3 encourages support of the British Heart Foundation, a non-profit organisation. Whether a person earns a living through marketing activities or performs them without reward in non-business settings, marketing knowledge and skills are valuable assets. For both commercial and non-profit organisations there are needs to satisfy, exchanges to expedite, changing circumstances to monitor and decisions to make. Even a country benefits from marketing, as described in the Marketing Insight box on page 15.

Figure 1.3
Promotion of a non-profit organisation. The British Heart Foundation uses marketing to communicate its message
Source: Courtesy of the British Heart Foundation, Heart Week 2004 campaign

○ Marketing Insight

Ireland: Marketing a Country

How do you develop a marketing strategy for a country? This was a question faced by the Irish government during difficult times in the 1960s and 1970s. The challenge was to build the Irish economy to match the affluence enjoyed by some of its European neighbours. At the time, Ireland was viewed as being backward and unattractive for investment by international corporations. The Industrial Development Authority (IDA) played an important role in developing the country's economy, moving it away from its traditional overreliance on agriculture. Today, with well over a third of the country's GDP coming from industry, and services also accounting for approaching a third, agriculture's contribution has fallen to just 10 per cent.

Marketing and good promotion alone were not responsible for this turnaround. The Irish government realised that to attract investment from overseas it had to provide a stable economy, desirable residential suburbs, modern road and air infrastructure, state-of-the-art telecommunications and, crucially, a well-qualified, dynamic and motivated workforce. These improvements took some time to achieve, but today the companies located in Dublin and around Ireland's airports testify readily to the excellent infrastructure, communications, workforce and tax breaks. The Irish workforce is one of the best educated and most highly prized in Europe.

Having improved the amenities, infrastructure and the workforce, the perceptions of investors overseas had to be addressed. In order to instigate this change, the IDA established a clear strategy by pinpointing attractive sectors for growth and actively encouraging growth businesses in those areas. Consumer products, electronics, healthcare and financial services were some of the key targets. Once decisions about growth priorities had been made, the aim was to develop a marketing programme based around the particular assets that Ireland was able to offer. For example, promotional material focused on – among other things – the young, highly educated workforce, the low rates of corporate taxation, excellent digital and satellite telecommunications systems, and a stable currency with low inflation. The attractive countryside and vibrant cultural scene also featured prominently in the IDA's branding of Ireland.

Considerable care was taken to ensure that the propositions developed matched the requirements of the businesses targeted. This provided many overseas businesses with substantial, tangible reasons for establishing a base in Ireland, bringing with it the investment the country so badly craved. Leading computer manufacturers, pharmaceutical businesses, financial corporations and telecommunications businesses are just some of those who have located facilities in the country: over 1,000 well-known organisations have chosen Ireland ahead of other locations for their European operations.

Sources: Irish Embassy, London; Industrial Development Authority (IDA); 'Facts about Ireland', IDA, 1995, 1996, 1999, 2003, 2008.

Marketing Activities are Important to Organisations and the Economy

An organisation must sell products in order to survive and grow. Directly or indirectly, marketing activities help sell an organisation's products. By doing so, they generate financial resources that can be used to develop innovative products. New products allow a company to satisfy customers' changing needs more efficiently, which in turn enables the company to generate more profits. Charities and other not-for-profit organisations use marketing to generate revenues and funds.

Europe's highly complex economy depends heavily on marketing activities. These help produce the profits that are essential not only to the survival of individual organisations but also to the health and ultimate survival of the economy as a whole. Profits are essential to economic growth because without them organisations find it difficult, if not impossible, to buy more raw materials, recruit more employees, attract more capital and create the additional products that in turn lead to more profits.

Marketing Knowledge Enhances Consumer Awareness

Besides contributing to a country's economic well-being, marketing activities permeate everyone's lives. In fact, they help to improve quality of life. Studying marketing activities enables the costs, benefits and flaws of marketing to be evaluated. The need for improvement and ways to accomplish changes can be determined. For example, an unsatisfactory experience with a guarantee may lead consumers to demand that laws be enforced more strictly to make sellers fulfil their promises. Similarly, there may be the desire for more information about a product – or more accurate information – before purchase. Understanding marketing leads to the evaluation of the corrective measures – such as laws, regulations and industry guidelines – that may be required to stop unfair, misleading or unethical marketing practices. The results of the survey presented in Table 1.2 indicate that there is a considerable lack of knowledge about marketing activities, as reflected by the sizeable proportion of respondents who agree with the myths in the table.

Marketing Costs Consume a Sizeable Proportion of Buyers' Incomes

The study of the marketing discipline emphasises that many marketing activities are necessary to provide people with satisfying goods and services. Obviously, these marketing activities cost money. A family with a monthly income of £1000, of which £300 goes towards taxes and savings, spends about £700 on goods and services. Of this amount, typically £350 goes towards marketing activities. Clearly, if marketing expenses consume that much income, it is necessary to know how this money is used.

Business Performance

Marketing puts an emphasis on satisfying customers. Marketing analyses should lead an organisation to develop a marketing strategy that takes account of market trends, aims to satisfy customers, is aware of competitive activity and targets the right customers with a clear positioning message. In so doing, an organisation should benefit from customer loyalty and advantages over its rivals, while making the most efficient use of resources to effectively address the specific requirements of those markets it chooses to target. Hence, marketing should provide both a financial benefit and a greater sense of well-being for the organisation.

The Marketing Concept and its Evolution

Some organisations have tried to be successful by buying land, building a factory, equipping it with people and machines, and then making a product that they believe consumers need. However, these organisations frequently fail to attract buyers with what they have to offer because they defined their business as 'making a product' rather than as 'helping potential customers satisfy their needs and wants'. Such organisations have failed to implement

TABLE 1.2 POPULAR MARKETING MYTHS					
Myths	Strongly Agree	Somewhat Agree	Neither Agree nor Disagree	Somewhat Disagree	Strongly Disagree
Marketing is selling	14%	34%	26%	18%	8%
Marketers persuade	21%	25%	20%	11%	23%
Dealers' profits significantly increase prices consumers pay	21%	32%	12%	8%	27%
Marketing depends on advertising	17%	44%	12%	9%	18%
Strategic planning has nothing to do with marketing	19%	19%	21%	17%	24%
Sources: Student surveys.					

the marketing concept. It is not enough to be product-led, no matter how good the product. An organisation must be in tune with consumer or business customer requirements.

According to the **marketing concept**, an organisation should try to provide products that satisfy customers' needs through a coordinated set of activities that also allows the organisation to achieve its goals. Customer satisfaction is the major aim of the marketing concept. First, an organisation must find out what will satisfy customers. With this information, it then attempts to create satisfying products. But the process does not end there. The organisation must continue to alter, adapt and develop products to keep pace with customers' changing desires and preferences. The marketing concept stresses the importance of customers, and emphasises that marketing activities begin and end with them.[7]

In attempting to satisfy customers, organisations must consider not only short-term, immediate needs but also broad, long-term desires. Trying to satisfy customers' current needs by sacrificing their long-term desires will only create future dissatisfaction. For instance, people want efficient, low-cost energy to power their homes and cars, yet they react adversely to energy producers that pollute the air and water, kill wildlife, or cause disease or birth defects. To meet these short- and long-term needs and desires, a company must coordinate all its activities. Production, finance, accounting, personnel and marketing departments must work together.

The marketing concept is not another definition of marketing. It is a way of thinking: a management philosophy guiding an organisation's overall activities. This philosophy affects all the efforts of the organisation, not just marketing activities, and is strongly linked to the notion of marketing orientation. However, the marketing concept is by no means a philanthropic philosophy aimed at helping customers at the expense of the organisation. A company that adopts the marketing concept must not only satisfy its customers' objectives but also achieve its own goals, or it will not stay in business long. The overall goals of an organisation may be directed towards increasing profits, market share, sales or a combination of all three. The marketing concept stresses that an organisation can best achieve its goals by providing customer satisfaction. Thus, implementing the marketing concept should benefit the organisation as well as its customers.

Marketing concept
The philosophy that an organisation should try to provide products that satisfy customers' needs through a coordinated set of activities that also allows the organisation to achieve its goals

The Evolution of the Marketing Concept

The marketing concept may seem an obvious and sensible approach to running a business. However, business people have not always believed that the best way to make sales and profits is to satisfy customers. A famous example is the marketing philosophy for cars widely attributed to Henry Ford in the early 1900s: 'The customers can have any colour car they want as long as it's black.' The philosophy of the marketing concept emerged in the third major era in the history of business, preceded by the **production era** and the **sales era**. Surprisingly, it took nearly 40 years after the **marketing era** began before many organisations started to adopt the marketing concept. The more advanced marketing-led companies have now entered a spin-off from the marketing era: the **relationship marketing era**.

Production era
The period of mass production following industrialisation

Sales era
The period from the mid-1920s to the early 1950s when competitive forces and the desire for high sales volume led a company to emphasise selling and the sales person in its business strategy

The Production Era During the second half of the nineteenth century, the Industrial Revolution was in full swing in Europe and the United States. Electricity, railways, the division of labour, the assembly line and mass production made it possible to manufacture products more efficiently. With new technology and new ways of using labour, products poured into the marketplace, where consumer demand for manufactured goods was strong. This production orientation continued into the early part of the last century, encouraged by the scientific management movement that championed rigidly structured jobs and pay based on output.

The Sales Era In the 1920s, the strong consumer demand for products subsided. Companies realised that products, which by this time could be made quite efficiently,

Marketing era
The period in which product and aggressive selling were no longer seen to suffice if customers either did not desire a product or preferred a rival brand, and in which customer needs were identified and satisfied

Relationship marketing era
The current period, in which the focus is not only on expediting the single transaction but on developing ongoing relationships with customers

would have to be 'sold' to consumers. From the mid-1920s to the early 1950s, companies viewed sales as the major means of increasing profits. As a result, this period came to have a sales orientation. Business people believed that the most important marketing activities were personal selling and advertising.

The Marketing Era   By the early 1950s, some business people began to recognise that efficient production and extensive promotion of products did not guarantee that customers would buy them. Companies found that they first had to determine what customers wanted and then produce it, rather than simply making products first and then trying to change customers' needs to correspond to what was being produced. As organisations realised the importance of knowing customers' needs, companies entered into the marketing era – the era of customer orientation.[8]

The Relationship Marketing Era   By the 1990s, many organisations had grasped the basics of the marketing concept and had created marketing functions. However, their view of marketing was often largely transaction based. The priority for marketing was to identify customer needs, determine priority target markets and achieve sales through marketing programmes. The focus was on the individual transaction or exchange. It should be recognised that long-term success and market share gains depend on such transactions, but also on maintaining a customer's loyalty and on repeatedly gaining sales from existing customers. This requires ongoing, committed, reassuring and tailored relationship-building marketing programmes.

Relationship marketing refers to 'long-term, mutually beneficial arrangements in which both the buyer and seller focus on value enhancement through the creation of more satisfying exchanges'.[9] Relationship marketing continually deepens the buyer's trust in the company and, as the customer's confidence grows, this in turn increases the company's understanding of the customer's needs. Successful marketers respond to customers' needs and strive to increase value to buyers over time. Eventually this interaction becomes a solid relationship that allows for cooperation and mutual dependency.

As the era of relationship orientation has developed, it has been suggested that it is not only relationships with customers that are important. Suppliers, agents, distributors, recruiters, referral bodies (such as independent financial advisers recommending financial services companies' products), influencers (such as government departments, national banks or the EU), all should be 'marketed to' in order to ensure their support, understanding and resources. The internal workforce must be motivated and provided with a clear understanding of a company's target market strategy, marketing mix activities and, indeed, of the corporate strategy and planned direction. Hence, the current era is moving away from transaction-based marketing and towards nurturing ongoing relationships.[10]

Implementing the Marketing Concept

A philosophy may sound reasonable and look good on paper, but that does not mean it can be put into practice easily. The marketing concept is a case in point. To implement it, an organisation must focus on some general conditions and recognise several problems. Because of these conditions and problems, the marketing concept has yet to be fully accepted by some organisations.

Because the marketing concept affects all types of business activities, not just marketing activities, the top management of an organisation must adopt it wholeheartedly. High-level executives must incorporate the marketing concept into their philosophies of business management so completely that it becomes the basis for all the goals and decisions that they set for their companies. They should also convince other members of the organisation to accept the changes in policies and operations that flow from their acceptance of the marketing concept. Costs and budgetary controls are important, products and manufacturing essential, and personnel management necessary; but all are to no avail if the organisation's products or services are not desired by the targeted customers.

As a first step, management must establish an information system that enables it to discover customers' real needs and to use the information to create satisfying products. Because such a system is usually expensive, management must be willing to commit money and time for development and maintenance. Without an adequate information system, an organisation cannot be customer oriented.

Management's second major task is to restructure the organisation. If a company is to satisfy its customers' objectives as well as its own, it must coordinate all its activities. To achieve this, the internal operations and the overall objectives of one or more departments may need restructuring. If the head of the marketing unit is not a member of the organisation's top-level management, he or she should be. Some departments may have to be abolished and new ones created. Implementing the marketing concept demands the support not only of top management but also of managers and staff at all levels within the organisation.

Even when the basic conditions of establishing an information system and reorganising the organisation are met, the organisation's new marketing approach may not work perfectly, for the following reasons.

- There is a limit to a company's ability to satisfy customers' needs for a particular product. In a mass-production economy, most business organisations cannot tailor products to fit the exact needs of each customer.
- Although a company may attempt to learn what customers want, it may be unable to do so, and when the organisation does identify customers' needs correctly, it often has a difficult time developing a product that satisfies those needs. Many companies spend considerable time and money researching customers' needs and yet still create some products that do not sell well.
- By striving to satisfy one particular segment of society, a company sometimes dissatisfies other segments. Certainly, government and non-business organisations also experience this problem.
- An organisation may have difficulty maintaining employee morale during any restructuring needed to coordinate the activities of various departments. Management must clearly explain the reasons for the various changes and communicate its own enthusiasm for the marketing concept.

Adoption of the marketing philosophy takes time, resources, endurance and commitment.

The Essentials of Marketing

Marketing Analyses

Already, from these brief introductory comments, it should be evident that marketing can enhance an organisation's understanding of its customers, competitors, market trends, threats and opportunities. Marketing should, therefore, be able to direct an organisation's target market strategy, product development and communication to its distribution channels and customers. However, in order to contribute in these ways, marketing personnel must have marketing intelligence about these issues, which inevitably leads to marketing analysis.

The core aspects of marketing analysis should be:

- customers
- competitors
- marketing environment forces
- the organisation's capabilities and marketing assets.

As will be seen later in this book, there are many additional marketing analyses, but these are the essential building blocks for the development of marketing strategies and the creation of marketing programmes. The majority of the chapters in Part II of *Marketing*

Essentials address these marketing analyses, which are the foundation of the marketing process.

Marketing Strategy

Marketing strategy
The selection of which marketing opportunities to pursue, analysis of target market(s), and the creation and maintenance of an appropriate marketing mix that will satisfy those people in the target market(s)

Marketing mix
The tactical 'toolkit' of the marketing programme; product, place/distribution, promotion, price and people variables that an organisation can control in order to appeal to the target market and facilitate satisfying exchange

To achieve the broad goal of expediting desirable exchanges, an organisation's marketing managers are responsible for developing and managing marketing strategies. Specifically, a **marketing strategy** encompasses selecting opportunities to pursue, analysing a target market (the group of people the organisation wants to reach), developing a competitive edge, and creating and maintaining an appropriate **marketing mix** (the tactical 'toolkit' of product, place [distribution], promotion, price and people) that will satisfy those customers in the target market. A marketing strategy articulates a plan for the best use of the organisation's resources and directs the required tactics to meet its objectives.

When marketing managers attempt to develop and manage marketing activities, they must deal with three broad sets of variables:

1 those relating to the marketing mix
2 those inherent in the accompanying target market strategy
3 those that make up the marketing environment.

The marketing mix decision variables – product, place/distribution, promotion, price and people – and the target market strategy variables are factors over which an organisation

Figure 1.4
The marketing environment, marketing strategy, the marketing mix and customer satisfaction; consumers and organisations are affected by the forces of the marketing environment; organisations must determine a marketing strategy, implemented through the ingredients of the marketing mix, which aims to satisfy targeted customers

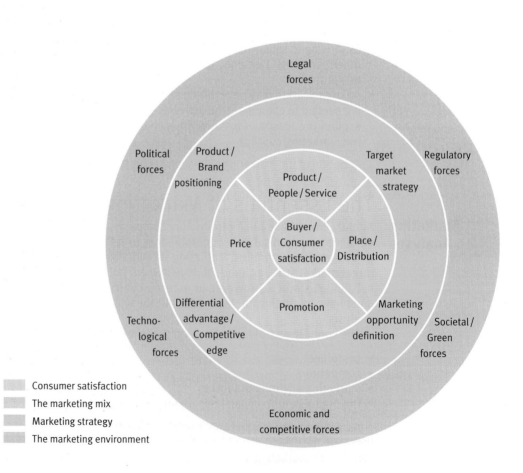

has control. As Figure 1.4 shows, these variables are constructed around the buyer or consumer. The marketing environment variables are political, legal, regulatory, societal/green, technological, and economic and competitive forces. These factors are subject to less control by an organisation, but they affect buyers' needs as well as marketing managers' decisions regarding marketing mix variables.

To develop and manage marketing strategies, marketers must focus on several marketing tasks: marketing opportunity analysis and marketing analyses, the determination of a marketing strategy and target market selection, marketing mix development and management of the programmes that facilitate implementation of the marketing strategy. Figure 1.5 lists these tasks, along with the chapters of this book in which they are discussed.

Marketing opportunity
One that exists when circumstances allow an organisation to take action towards reaching a particular group of consumer or business customers

Marketing Opportunity Analysis   A **marketing opportunity** exists when circumstances allow an organisation to take action towards reaching a particular group of customers. An opportunity provides a favourable chance or opening for a company to generate sales from identifiable markets for specific products or services. For example, during a heatwave, marketers of electric fans have a marketing opportunity – an opportunity to reach customers who need electric fans. Various 'no frills' airlines have entered the rapidly growing market for low-priced scheduled air travel, as consumers have demonstrated their liking for this alternative to high-priced full-service airlines or charters. Bluetooth and wireless connectivity is creating numerous opportunities for computer manufacturers and online service providers, as wireless access to the Internet offers users greater flexibility. Most new products or services reflect the identification by marketers of a marketing opportunity.

Marketers should be capable of recognising and analysing marketing opportunities. An organisation's long-term survival depends on developing products that satisfy its customers. Few organisations can assume that products popular today will interest buyers ten years from now. A marketing-led organisation can choose among several alternatives for continued product development through which it can achieve its objectives and satisfy buyers. It can modify existing products (for example, by reducing salt content and additives in foods to address increasing health consciousness among customers), introduce new products (such as Windows Vista, pay-as-you-talk mobile phone packages or digital flat-screen TVs) and delete some that customers no longer want (such as disc cameras or cassette decks). A company may also try to market its products to a greater number of customers, persuade current customers to use more of a product, or perhaps expand marketing activities into additional countries. Diversification into new product offerings through internal efforts or through acquisitions of other organisations may be viable options for a company. For example, Sony has established itself as a major supplier of business laptop and desktop computers, diversifying from its base of consumer home entertainment products; while Virgin has entered financial services. An organisation's ability to pursue any of these alternatives success-fully depends on its internal characteristics and the forces within the marketing environment. These strategic options are discussed further in Chapter 2 of *Marketing Essentials*.

Internal Organisational Factors   The primary factors inside an organisation that should be considered when analysing marketing opportunities and devising target market strategies are organisational objectives, financial resources, managerial skills, organisational strengths and weaknesses, and cost structures. Most organisations have overall organisational objectives. Some marketing opportunities may be consistent with these objectives; others may not, and to pursue them is hazardous. Frequently, the pursuit of such opportunities ends in failure, or forces the company to alter its long-term objectives. The links with corporate strategy and an organisation's mission are discussed in Chapter 2.

Figure 1.5
*Marketing tasks:
analysis, strategy and
programmes for
implementation and
control*

Marketing Opportunity Analysis	Chapters
• The marketing environment	3
• Consumer buying behaviour	4
• Business markets and business-to-business buying behaviour	5
• Marketing research and information systems	7

Target Market Strategy	Chapters
• Marketing strategy	2
• Market segmentation and targeting	6
• Product and brand positioning	6, 14
• Competitive advantage	2, 6

Marketing Mix Development	Chapters
• Product, branding, packaging and service decisions	8, 9, 10, 14
• Place (distribution and marketing channel) decisions	11
• Promotion (marketing communications) decisions	13
• Pricing decisions	12

Obviously, an organisation's financial resources constrain the type of marketing opportunities it can pursue. Typically, an organisation does not develop projects that can bring economic catastrophe. In some situations, however, a company must invest in a high-risk opportunity, because the costs of not pursuing the project are so great. Thus, despite an economic recession and reduced house and road building, construction equipment manufacturer JCB continued to launch new ranges and enter new markets. It developed and launched its Compact Division, emphasising mini excavators, at a cost of millions, to respond to changing market requirements. As the market for construction equipment became more buoyant JCB, with its new ranges, was well placed to take advantage of this.

The skills and experience of management also limit the types of opportunity that an organisation can pursue. A company must be particularly cautious when exploring the possibility of entering unfamiliar markets with new products. If it lacks appropriate managerial skills and experience, the business can sometimes acquire them by recruiting additional managerial personnel. Most organisations at some time are limited in their growth plans by a lack of sufficient managers with suitable skills and market insights.

Like people, most organisations have strengths and weaknesses. Because of the types of operation in which a company is engaged, it will normally have employees with specialist skills and technological information. Such characteristics are a strength when launching marketing strategies that require them. However, they may be a weakness if the company tries to compete in new, unrelated product areas. A major IT services company altered its strategy to focus on winning more business for IT infrastructure management from existing clients rather than from attracting new clients. This required a different set of selling skills, and managers with the ability to nurture relationships and exploit emerging sales opportunities within a client company. The revised target market strategy resulted in redundancies among the existing salesforce, and the recruitment of account managers with the requisite skills and interpersonal abilities.

An organisation's cost structure may be an advantage if the company pursues certain marketing opportunities, and a disadvantage if it pursues others. Such factors as geographic location, employee skills, access to raw materials, and type of equipment and facilities can all affect cost structure. Previous investment levels and priorities will have ramifications for the current cost structure. As discussed in Chapter 2, the cost structure of an organisation may provide a competitive advantage over rivals, or may place a business at a competitive disadvantage.

Marketing Environment Forces   The marketing environment, which consists of political, legal, regulatory, societal/Green, technological, and economic/competitive forces, surrounds the buyer (consumer) and the marketing mix (see Figure 1.4). Each major environmental force is explored in considerable depth in Chapter 3. Marketers know that they cannot predict changes in the marketing environment with certainty. Even so, over the years marketers have become more systematic in taking these forces into account when planning their competitive actions.[11] An organisation that fails to monitor the forces of the marketing environment is likely to miss out on emerging opportunities at the expense of rivals with the foresight to examine these market drivers.

Marketing environment forces affect a marketer's ability to facilitate and expedite exchanges, in four general ways.

1 They influence customers by affecting their lifestyles, standards of living, preferences and needs for products. Because a marketing manager tries to develop and adjust the marketing mix to satisfy consumers or business customers, the effects of environmental forces on customers also have an indirect impact on the marketing mix components.
2 Marketing environment forces help determine whether and how a marketing manager can perform certain marketing activities. They may force marketers to cease certain practices or to adopt new strategies.
3 Environmental forces may affect a marketing manager's decisions and actions by influencing buyers' reactions to the company's marketing mix.
4 Marketing environment forces may provide an organisation with a window of opportunity over rivals that fail to notice the market development or that take no action themselves. Equally, market drivers may provide competitors with such an opportunity ahead of a marketer's own organisation.

Although forces in the marketing environment are sometimes viewed as 'uncontrollables', a marketing manager may be able to influence one or more of them. However, marketing environment forces fluctuate quickly and dramatically, which is one reason marketing is so interesting and challenging. Because these forces are highly interrelated, a change in one may cause others to change. For example, from Freons in fridges to additives in foods, most consumers have become increasingly aware of health and environmental issues. Manufacturers have altered product specifications and production methods. Legislators and regulatory bodies have also responded to expert and consumer opinions with new regulations and informal agreements, forcing companies to rethink their manufacturing and marketing policies.

Even though changes in the marketing environment produce uncertainty for marketers and at times impede marketing efforts, they can also create opportunities. After the 1989 oil spills, for example, more companies began developing and marketing products designed to contain or dissipate spilled oil. The BSE beef crisis gave producers of other meats significant opportunities. Environmental concerns have encouraged car manufacturers to develop emission-free engines. The growth in mobile phone use and improvements to network technology have enabled various information providers to tailor services to sports fans or stock-market investors. Thus a marketer must be aware of changes in environmental forces not only to adjust to and influence them but also to capitalise on the opportunities they provide. The marketing environment is discussed more fully in Chapters 2 and 3 of *Marketing Essentials*. The Marketing Insight box below illustrates the impact of the marketing environment, in this case upon food products.

♻ Marketing Insight

The Marketing Environment Offers Threats and Opportunities: Miller Lite Versus Slimfast

During the early part of the decade, the Atkins diet hit the bookshelves, colour supplements and couches of day-time television. Thousands of consumers opted to try this new approach to losing weight and feeling healthier. While some experts are concerned about the longer-term impact of such an approach to dieting, other reports seem to support the loss of weight from cutting the intake of carbohydrates. Manufacturers have been quick to capitalise on this trend, with low-carb beers, breads and other foods quickly appearing on supermarket shelves. This diet grew in popularity at a time when there was growing concern among policy-makers and health workers, widely publicised by the media, into childhood and adult obesity, increasing diabetes and heart disease, and the likely implications for the future provision of healthcare.

While certain fast-food chains and food brands have reacted by launching healthier menus or bringing out low-carb versions of popular brands, for other companies commercial prospects are not looking good. McDonald's has reduced the size of its portions, added fruit and salads and even Quorn burgers. Coca-Cola has launched a low-carb cola called C2 and Nestlé has created low-carb Rolos and Kit-Kats. For Krispy Kreme, however, there was a profits warning to investors as a result of consumers avoiding the carbohydrates in its doughnuts. By contrast, at Tiffin Bites, the Indian fast-food chain, its low-carb meal has become a best-seller, generating gratefully received positive publicity for the company. The Miller beer brand has been rejuvenated thanks to the low-carb content of Miller Lite, leading to significant increases in profitability.

Atkins is a health-driven diet phenomenon, so perhaps one of its biggest victims may come as something of a surprise. A leading brand for dieters for many years has been Slimfast, with its range of slimming food aids and supplements. Slimfast had become one of Unilever's leading brands. Sales of Slimfast plummeted as slimmers viewed the benefits of Atkins with glee. For Slimfast's marketers the social and regulatory trends had been very supportive, and the growth prospects for the brand appeared to be strongly encouraged by the forces of the marketing environment. The popularity of an alternative way of thinking for dieters offered by Atkins led to social and competitive marketing environment forces that seriously damaged the Slimfast brand and its market potential.

Sources: Unilever plc, 2004; Boots, 2004; 'Nestlé gambles on low-carb craze', *Marketing*, 3 June 2004, p. 16; Emily Rogers in *Marketing*, 8 January 2004, p. 4; Ben Bold in *Marketing*, 11 December 2003, p. 8.

Target market
A group of people for whom a company creates and maintains a marketing mix that specifically fits the needs and preferences of that group

Target Market Selection   A **target market** is a group of people for whom a company creates and maintains a marketing mix that specifically fits the needs and preferences of that group.[12] When choosing a target market, marketing managers try to evaluate possible markets to see how entering them would affect the company's sales, costs and profits. Marketers also attempt to determine whether the organisation has the resources to produce a marketing mix that meets the needs of a particular target market, and whether satisfying those needs is consistent with the company's overall objectives and mission. The size and number of competitors already marketing products in possible target markets are also of concern.

Marketing managers may define a target market as a vast number of people or as a relatively small group. For example, Ford produces cars suitable for much of the population – although specific models are quite narrowly targeted, such as the family runaround Focus or the executive Mondeo. Porsche focuses its marketing effort on a small proportion of the population, believing that it can compete more effectively by concentrating on an affluent target market desiring sports coupés. Although a business may concentrate its efforts on one target market through a single marketing mix, organisations often focus on several target markets by developing and deploying multiple marketing mixes. Reebok, for example, markets different types of shoes to meet the specific needs of joggers, walkers, aerobics enthusiasts and other groups.

Target market selection is crucial to generating productive marketing efforts. At times, products and organisations fail because marketers do not identify the appropriate customer groups at which to aim their efforts. Organisations that try to be all things to all people typically end up not satisfying the needs of any customer group very well. It is important for an organisation's management to designate which customer groups the company is trying to serve and to have adequate information about these customers. The identification and analysis of a target market provide a foundation on which a marketing mix can be developed. As will be explored in the next chapter, it is important to strive to develop an advantage over competitors in the markets targeted.

Marketing Programmes   In order to make the devised marketing strategy a reality, marketers must specify a set of marketing mix ingredients that, collectively, become the marketing programme designed to implement the agreed marketing strategy. These marketing mix decisions occupy the majority of marketing personnel for most of their time, and account for most of a marketing department's budget. However, as previously explained, before the marketing mix is specified, marketers should undertake sufficient marketing analyses and reflect the findings of these analyses in their marketing strategy.

Marketing Mix Development   Traditionally, the marketing mix was deemed to consist of four major components: product, place (distribution), promotion and price. Increasingly, a fifth component is viewed as 'people', who provide customer service and interact with customers and organisations within the supply chain. These components are called 'marketing mix decision variables' because a marketing manager decides which type of each component to use and in what amounts. A primary goal of a marketing manager is to create and maintain a marketing mix that satisfies consumers' needs for a general product type. Note that in Figure 1.4, the marketing mix is built around the buyer – as is stressed by the marketing concept and definition of marketing. Bear in mind, too, that the forces of the marketing environment affect the marketing mix variables in many ways.

Marketing mix variables are often viewed as controllable variables because they can be changed. However, there are limits to how much these variables can be altered. For example, because of economic conditions or government regulations, a manager may not be free to adjust prices daily. Changes in sizes, colours, shapes and designs of most tangible goods are expensive; therefore such product features cannot be altered very often. In addition, promotional campaigns and the methods used to distribute products ordinarily cannot be changed overnight. People, too, require training and motivating, and cannot be recruited or sacked overnight.

Marketing managers must develop a marketing mix that precisely matches the needs of the people – or organisations in business-to-business marketing – in the target market. Before they can do so, they have to collect in-depth, up-to-date information about those needs. The information might include data about the age, income, ethnic origin, sex and educational level of people in the target market; their preferences for product features; their attitudes towards competitors' products; and the frequency and intensity with which they use the product. Armed with these kinds of data, marketing managers are better able to develop a product, service package, distribution system, promotion programme and price that will satisfy the people in the target market.

This section looks more closely at the decisions and activities related to each marketing mix variable (product, place/distribution, promotion, price and people – the '5Ps' of the marketing mix). Table 1.1 contains a list of the decisions and activities associated with each marketing mix variable.

Product variable
The aspect of the marketing mix that deals with researching consumers' product wants and designing a product with the desired characteristics

The Product Variable   A product can be a good, a service or an idea. The **product variable** is the aspect of the marketing mix that deals with researching consumers' product wants and designing a product with the desired characteristics. It also involves the creation or alteration of packaging and brand names, and may include decisions about guarantees, repair services and customer support. The actual manufacturing of products is not a marketing activity, but marketing-oriented businesses look to marketers to specify product development requirements that reflect customer needs and evolving expectations.

Product-variable decisions and related activities are important because they directly involve creating products and services that satisfy consumers' needs and wants. To maintain a satisfying set of products that will help an organisation achieve its goals, a marketer must be able to develop new products, modify existing ones and eliminate those that no longer satisfy buyers or yield acceptable profits. For example, after realising that competitors were capturing large shares of the low-calorie market, Heinz introduced new product items under its Weight Watchers name. To reflect greater use of microwave ovens, rice company Tilda introduced its steam-in-a-pouch range of quick-cook microwavable sachets.

Place/distribution variable
The aspect of the marketing mix that deals with making products available in the quantities desired to as many customers as possible and keeping the total inventory, transport and storage costs as low as possible

The Place/Distribution Variable   To satisfy consumers, products must be available at the right time and in a convenient location. In dealing with the **place/distribution variable**, a marketing manager seeks to make products available in the quantities desired to as many customers as possible, and to keep the total inventory, transport and storage costs as low as possible. A marketing manager may become involved in selecting and motivating intermediaries (wholesalers, retailers and dealers), establishing and maintaining inventory control procedures, and developing and managing transport and storage systems.

Promotion variable
The aspect of the marketing mix that relates to activities used to inform one or more groups of people about an organisation and its products

The Promotion Variable   The **promotion variable** relates to communication activities that are used to inform one or more groups of people about an organisation and its products. Promotion can be aimed at increasing public awareness of an organisation and of new or existing products. In addition, promotion can serve to educate consumers about product features or to urge people to take a particular stance on a political or social issue. It may also be used to keep interest strong in an established product that has been available for decades. The advertisement in Figure 1.6 is an example. Marketers increasingly refer to the promotion variable in the marketing mix as 'marketing communications'.

Price variable
The aspect of the marketing mix that relates to activities associated with establishing pricing policies and determining product prices

The Price Variable   The **price variable** relates to activities associated with establishing pricing policies and determining product prices. Price is a critical component of the marketing mix because consumers and business customers are concerned about the value

Figure 1.6
Promoting an established brand. Champagne house Moët & Chandon uses its heritage in its advertising to reinforce its brand appeal
Source: Courtesy of Moët Hennessy UK Ltd

obtained in an exchange. Price is often used as a competitive tool; in fact, extremely intense price competition sometimes leads to price wars. For example, airlines like Aer Lingus, British Airways and Virgin Atlantic are engaged in ruthless price cutting in the battle for transatlantic routes. Price can also help to establish a product's image. For instance, if Chanel tried to sell Chanel No. 5 in a two-litre bottle for £3 or €4, consumers would probably not buy it because the low price would destroy the prestigious image of this deluxe brand.

The People Variable Product, place/distribution, promotion and price are traditionally the principal elements of the marketing mix: the '4Ps'. Marketers of services include *people* as a core element, along with other ingredients (see Chapter 10). Whether part of the product element or a separate element of the marketing mix, there is no doubt that people are important. As marketers, they manipulate the rest of the marketing mix. As intermediaries in the marketing channel, they help make products and services available to the marketplace. As consumers or organisational purchasers, they create the need for the field of marketing. In the marketing mix, the **people variable** reflects the level of customer service, advice, sales support and after-sales back-up required, involving recruitment policies, training, retention and motivation of key personnel. For many products and most services, personnel interface directly with the intended purchaser and are often perceived by such consumers as being part and parcel of the product offering.

Developing and maintaining an effective marketing mix is a major requirement for a strong marketing strategy. Thus, as indicated in Figure 1.5, a large proportion of this book

People variable
The aspect of the marketing mix that reflects the level of customer service, advice, sales support and after-sales back-up required, involving recruitment policies, training, retention and motivation of key personnel

27

(Chapters 8 to 14) focuses on the concepts, decisions and activities associated with the components of the marketing mix. It is the marketing mix that readers, as consumers, will most frequently have experienced for products and services purchased. It is important to remember, however, that analysis must precede the development of a marketing strategy, which in turn must be formulated before the marketing mix is determined for a product or a service.

Marketing Management

Marketing management
A process of planning, organising, implementing and controlling marketing activities to facilitate and expedite exchanges effectively and efficiently

Marketing management is the process of planning, organising, implementing and controlling marketing activities to facilitate and expedite exchanges effectively and efficiently. Effectiveness and efficiency are important dimensions of this definition. *Effectiveness* is the degree to which an exchange helps achieve an organisation's objectives. *Efficiency* is the minimisation of resources an organisation must spend to achieve a specific level of desired exchanges. Thus the overall goal of marketing management is to facilitate highly desirable exchanges and to minimise as much as possible the costs of doing so.

Marketing planning is a systematic process of assessing opportunities and resources, determining marketing objectives, developing a marketing strategy and developing plans for implementation and control. Planning determines when and how marketing activities will be performed and who is to perform them. It forces marketing managers to think ahead, to establish objectives and to consider future marketing activities. Effective marketing planning also reduces or eliminates daily crises.

Organising marketing activities refers to developing the internal structure of the marketing unit. The structure is the key to directing marketing activities. The marketing unit can be organised by function, product, region, type of customer or a combination of all four.

Proper implementation of marketing plans hinges on the coordination of marketing activities, motivation of marketing personnel and effective communication within the unit. Marketing managers must motivate marketing personnel, coordinate their activities and integrate their activities, both with those in other areas of the company and with the marketing efforts of personnel in external organisations, such as advertising agencies and marketing research businesses. An organisation's communication system must allow the marketing manager to stay in contact with high-level management, with managers of other functional areas within the company and with personnel involved in marketing activities both inside and outside the organisation.

The marketing control process consists of establishing performance standards, evaluating actual performance by comparing it with established standards, and reducing the difference between desired and actual performance. An effective control process has the following four requirements.

1 The control process should ensure a rate of information flow that allows the marketing manager to quickly detect differences between actual and planned levels of performance.
2 The control process must accurately monitor different kinds of activities and be flexible enough to accommodate changes.
3 The control process must be economical so that its costs are low relative to the costs that would arise if there were no controls.
4 Finally, the control process should be designed so that both managers and subordinates can understand it. To maintain effective marketing control, an organisation needs to develop a comprehensive control process that evaluates marketing operations at regular intervals. The authors' other titles, including *Marketing Planning* (Cengage), *Market Segmentation Success: Making It Happen!* (The Howarth Press) and *Marketing: Concepts and Strategies* (Houghton Mifflin) explore the operationalisation of marketing strategies and marketing control processes in more detail.

The Organisation of This Book

The structure of this book adheres to the principle that it is important to analyse markets and marketing opportunities, then develop marketing strategies and construct marketing programmes that implement the desired marketing strategy, before ensuring suitable controls are in place to manage the roll-out of the strategy and programmes: the marketing process. Marketing analyses develop a thorough understanding of the marketplace – particularly customers, competitors and market trends. This knowledge of the marketplace provides a sound basis from which to devise marketing strategies. These strategies should determine marketing opportunities to pursue, identify attractive target markets, and develop a clear brand positioning and basis for competing. In order to implement the recommended target market strategy, marketing programmes must be designed with marketing mix combinations and control processes to ensure effective implementation. This marketing process, as presented in Figure 1.2, is fundamental to sound marketing practice.

What Does Each Part of This Book Cover?

The first Part of *Marketing Essentials* provides an explanation of the marketing concept, presents the marketing process and overviews the principles of marketing strategy:

- Part I: Marketing Defined and Marketing in Context

The second Part explores the essential marketing analyses, marketing opportunity assessment, target market selection, brand positioning and establishing a basis for competing:

- Part II: Understanding Markets

The final Part examines in detail the core ingredients of the marketing mix, which are used by marketers to develop marketing programmes in order to operationalise the marketing strategy:

- Part III: Developing Marketing Programmes

Marketing Essentials also offers:

- an indexed margin/glossary of key terms
- full subject and name indexing
- extended cases to enhance readers' understanding of key topics
- internet-based exercises
- questions for discussion
- recommended further reading on each topic
- detailed illustrative examples in every chapter
- up-to-date statistics for the marketing industry
- support material on its own website: www.dibbmarketing.com

Various auxilliaries are also available to tutors on the companion website at **www.cengage.co.uk/dibb_essentials**.

Further Reading   Readers may find the following books useful.

Marketing Briefs: a Study and Revision Guide, Sally Dibb and Lyndon Simkin (Oxford: Elsevier Butterworth-Heinemann), 2004.

As implied in the title, this is a revision aid, complete with brief overviews of concepts, illustrative examples and cases, trial questions and revision guidance.

The Marketing Casebook, Sally Dibb and Lyndon Simkin (London: Thomson), 2001.

For readers requiring concise summaries of essential concepts and explanatory applied cases.

Marketing Planning, Sally Dibb and Lyndon Simkin (London: Cengage), 2008.

Aimed at marketing practitioners and offering a step-by-step guide to undertaking marketing planning.

Market Segmentation Success: Making It Happen!, Sally Dibb and Lyndon Simkin (New York: The Haworth Press), 2008.

Aimed at marketing practitioners undertaking market segmentation and devising a target market strategy.

Summary

Organisations that practise marketing do not necessarily have a *marketing orientation*. Organisations with a marketing orientation have a sound awareness of customers' needs and buying behaviour, of competitors' offerings and strategies, and of market trends. They also take steps to ensure they know how these market conditions will evolve. In addition, they orientate their operational practices and coordinate their inter-functional thinking around these market conditions. In order to have a marketing orientation, it is necessary to adopt the concepts and techniques described in *Marketing Essentials*. To practise marketing and to benefit from the activities of marketing, however, it is not necessary for an organisation to have a fully developed marketing orientation. A few managers, whether or not in an organisation's marketing function, utilising the concepts described in this book, will make a significant contribution to the organisation's fortunes and its understanding of its marketplace.

» *Marketing* consists of individual and organisational activities that facilitate and expedite satisfying exchange relationships in a dynamic environment through the creation, distribution, promotion and pricing of goods, services and ideas.

» Marketing opportunity analysis involves reviewing both internal factors (organisational objectives and mission, financial resources, managerial skills, organisational strengths, organisational weaknesses and cost structures) and external ones in the *marketing environment* (the political, legal, regulatory, societal/Green, technological, and economic/competitive forces).

» An *exchange* is the provision or transfer of goods, services and ideas in return for something of value. Four conditions must exist for an exchange to occur: (1) two or more individuals, groups or organisations must participate; (2) each party must have something of value desired by the other; (3) each party must be willing to give up what it has in order to receive the value held by the other; and (4) the parties to the exchange must be able to communicate with each other to make their 'somethings of value' available. In an exchange, products are traded either for other products or for financial resources, such as cash or credit. Through the exchange, the recipient (the customer) and the provider (the organisation) must be satisfied (leading to *customer satisfaction*). *Products* can be *goods, services or ideas.*

» The *marketing process* is the analysis of market conditions, the creation of an appropriate marketing strategy, the development of marketing programmes designed to action the agreed strategy and, finally, the implementation and control of the marketing strategy and its associated marketing programme(s). Organisations contemplating entering new markets or territories, launching new products or brands, modifying their strategies or manipulating their marketing programmes, should use this sequential analytical process. Even steady-state markets and products encounter changing market conditions, and marketers should continually analyse and then modify their marketing strategies and marketing programmes accordingly.

» It is important to study marketing because it permeates society. Marketing activities are performed in both business and non-business organisations. Moreover, marketing activities help business organisations generate profits and income, the life-blood of an economy. Even organisations without 'customers' have to maximise the deployment of their resources, address trends, identify stakeholders and develop compelling propositions to satisfy these stakeholders. The study of marketing enhances consumer awareness. Marketing costs absorb about half of what the consumer spends. Marketing, practised well, improves business performance.

» The *marketing concept* is a management philosophy that prompts an organisation to try to satisfy customers' needs through a coordinated set of activities that also allows the organisation to achieve its goals. Customer satisfaction is the major objective of the marketing concept. The philosophy of the marketing concept emerged during the 1950s, as the *marketing era* succeeded the *production era* and the *sales era*. As the 1990s progressed into the *relationship marketing era*, a focus on transaction-based marketing was replaced by relationship marketing. To make the marketing concept work, top management must accept it as an overall management philosophy. Implementing the marketing concept requires an efficient information system and sometimes the restructuring of the organisation.

» The essentials of marketing are that there are marketing analyses, a marketing strategy, marketing programmes centred around well-specified marketing mixes, plus marketing management controls and implementation practices. *Marketing strategy* involves selecting which marketing opportunities to pursue and analysing a target market (the group of people the organisation wants to reach), and creating and maintaining an appropriate *marketing mix* (product, place/distribution, promotion, price and people) to satisfy this target market. Effective marketing requires that managers focus on four tasks to achieve set objectives:
(1) marketing opportunity analysis, (2) target market selection, (3) marketing mix development, and (4) marketing management.

» Marketers should be able to recognise and analyse *marketing opportunities*, which are circumstances that allow an organisation to take action towards reaching a particular group of customers.

» A *target market* is a group of people for whom a company creates and maintains a marketing mix that specifically fits the needs and preferences of that group. It is important for an organisation's management to designate which customer groups the company is trying to serve and to have some information about these customers. The identification and analysis of a target market provide a foundation on which a marketing mix can be developed.

» The five principal variables that make up the marketing mix are product, place/distribution, promotion, price and people: the '5Ps'. The *product variable* is the aspect of the marketing mix that deals with researching consumers' or business customers' wants and designing a product with the desired characteristics. A marketing manager tries to make products available in the quantities desired to as many customers as possible, and to keep the total inventory, transport and storage costs as low as possible – the *place/distribution variable*. The *promotion variable* relates to activities used to inform one or more groups of people about an organisation and its products. The *price variable* refers to establishing pricing policies and determining product prices. The *people variable* controls the marketing mix; provides customer service and often the interface with customers, facilitates the product's distribution, sale and service; and – as consumers or buyers – gives marketing its rationale. Marketing exists to encourage consumer satisfaction.

❯❯ *Marketing management* is a process of planning, organising, implementing and controlling marketing activities to facilitate and expedite exchanges effectively and efficiently. Marketing planning is a systematic process of assessing opportunities and resources, developing a marketing strategy, determining marketing objectives and developing plans for implementation and control. Organising marketing activities refers to developing the internal structure of the marketing unit. Properly implementing marketing plans depends on coordinating marketing activities, motivating marketing personnel and communicating effectively within the unit. The marketing control process consists of establishing performance standards, evaluating actual performance by comparing it with established standards, and reducing the difference between desired and actual performance.

⊙ *Key Links*

At the end of each chapter summary, a 'Key Links' box will steer readers to any chapters that are directly related.

- Obviously, given that this is an introductory chapter, the other chapters of *Marketing Essentials* are all relevant links.
- Specifically, Chapters 2 and 3 are required reading associated to this chapter.

Important Terms

Marketing orientation
Marketing
Marketing environment
Exchange
Customer satisfaction
Product
Good
Service
Idea
Marketing process
Marketing concept
Production era
Sales era
Marketing era
Relationship marketing era
Marketing strategy
Marketing mix
Marketing opportunity
Target market
Product variable
Place/distribution variable
Promotion variable
Price variable
People variable
Marketing management

Discussion and Review Questions

1   What is meant by marketing orientation?
2   What is marketing? How did you define marketing before you read this chapter?
3   Why should someone study marketing?
4   What is the marketing process? Why should the process be so sequenced?
5   Discuss the basic elements of the marketing concept. Which organisations use this concept? Have these organisations adopted the marketing concept? Explain your views.
6   Identify several organisations that obviously have not adopted the marketing concept. What characteristics of these organisations indicate non-acceptance of the marketing concept?
7   Describe the major components of a marketing strategy. How are these major components related?
8   Identify the tasks involved in developing a marketing strategy.
9   What are the primary issues that marketing managers consider when conducting a market opportunity analysis?
10   What are the variables in the marketing environment? How much control does a marketing manager have over environmental variables?
11   Why is the selection of a target market such an important issue?
12   Why are the elements of the marketing mix known as variables? What are these variables?
13   What type of management activities are involved in marketing management?
14   Why is it important to adhere to the principle of analyses first, then marketing strategy development, followed ultimately by programmes for implementing the recommended marketing strategy?

Recommended Reading

- Baker, M., 'What is Marketing?', in M. Baker (ed.), *The Marketing Book* (Oxford: Butterworth-Heinemann, 2002).
- Baker, M., *Marketing: An Introductory Text* (Westburn: Helensburgh, 2007).
- Day, G.S., *The Market Driven Organization: Attracting and Keeping Valuable Customers* (New York: Free Press, 1999).
- Hart, S., *Marketing Changes* (London: Thomson Learning, 2003).
- Kotler, P., *Marketing Insights from A to Z: 80 Concepts Every Manager Needs to Know* (Hoboken, NJ: Wiley, 2003).

🕸 Internet Exercise

Seat cars used to be cheap and cheerful. Under VW's ownership the marque has been repositioned as sporty but good value. The range of cars is well specified, produced to VW's high standards, reasonably quick, but keenly priced. Take a look at Seat's website at: www.seat.co.uk or www.seat.com

1 How user-friendly is the site?
2 To what extent does the site provide the information required by someone seeking additional product information in order to construct a shortlist of possible models to purchase?
3 Consider the decision-making process of a car buyer: to what extent is this website reflecting the issues considered by car buyers?

⊛ Applied Mini-Case

The market for crisps (potato chips) is dominated by global giants such as P&G and PepsiCo. Brands including Pringles, Walkers and KP are household names. So what of Salty Dog? Never heard of these hand-cooked crisps? They are produced by a very small-scale operation, run from a barn deep in the Chiltern hills in the UK. Since their launch in 2002, sales have been way ahead of forecasts and exports are heading to France, Germany, Norway, Belgium and even China. So far so good, but in order to grow, the company has to attract major retailers and pub/bar chains, and broaden the brand's appeal among consumers – not easy tasks. Worse, the company is now attracting the attention of the major players in this market, which are unlikely to stand back and permit Salty Dog to steal their market shares.

❓ Question

As a newly recruited marketing manager for Salty Dog, what would be your priorities? How would you explain these to the owners of Salty Dog?

⊛ Case Study

Sweden's IKEA Marches On

When Swedish home furnishings retailer IKEA opened its first store in the UK, a retail shed near the M6 at Warrington, curious shoppers found queues jamming nearby roads, parking spaces at a premium and retailing analysts by the score. With just one store, IKEA had the UK furniture industry on its toes: large retail groups and manufacturers alike feared large market share losses. With its acquisition of the UK's Habitat and the opening of a national network of 17 stores, IKEA has conquered yet another territory. Such an impact is not confined to the UK market. The leading five countries for IKEA are Germany, the UK, the USA, France and Sweden.

IKEA has grown from one store in 1958 to 260 stores in 45 countries; with sales of 20,685,000,000 Euros and 583,000,000 customer visitors each year. 191,000,000 copies of the famous IKEA catalogue are distributed annually. Close to 80 per cent of sales are from within Europe, but expansion in North America, South-east Asia and Australasia is now increasing sales in the rest of the world – despite some initial franchising difficulties in certain territories. IKEA's distinctive catalogue is produced in-house and now printed in nearly 50 languages. IKEA is perhaps one of the world's most successful retailers, with a brand name that is known, recognised and discussed; a retail concept that stands for value, style and quality; everything for the home under one roof, with easy parking, children's play areas and cafés – in fact, 'a day out'!

As the company succinctly states in its advertising:

IKEA: the furnishings store from Sweden
More for your money
IKEA is more than just furnishing ideas. It's a day out for all the family.
Most of the time, beautifully designed home furnishings are created for a small part of the population – the few who can afford them. From the beginning, IKEA has taken a different path. We have decided to side with the many.
That means responding to the home furnishing needs of people throughout the world. People with many different needs, tastes, dreams, aspirations ... and wallets. People who want to improve their home and create a better everyday life.
For IKEA, helping create a better everyday life means offering a wide range of home furnishings in IKEA stores. Home furnishings that combine good design, good function and good quality with prices so low that as many people as possible can afford them.
Source: IKEA

IKEA's huge volumes – 10,000 items in a typical store – cheap out-of-town sites and dedication to keeping costs low through self-assembly packs mean that, unlike many competitors, the company can cope with any troughs in consumer spending. Low prices have been the key to IKEA's success, but price alone cannot create an international long-term marketing success story. Products are updated consistently to match consumers' expectations and lifestyles. In-store service and staff training are integral to the IKEA shopping experience. Sites are chosen to maximise catchment areas, to make access easy for shoppers and to bring the brand name to the attention of the whole community. Logistics give IKEA an edge, with carefully managed ordering and delivery reducing both stock holdings and stock-outs. Promotion emphasises the 'style without expense' philosophy and the IKEA name. The result has been a country-by-country revolution as staid furniture markets have been rejuvenated with the entry of IKEA. Shoppers intending to buy just a sofa return home with a sofa, a chair, some lamps and a general excitement about a new store where they can buy home furnishings at unbelievable prices. The IKEA vision is simple: 'Good design and function at low prices.'

The latest strategic developments for IKEA include entering eastern European markets, developing a new IKEA format and expanding its mail-order/electronic ordering. Eastern Europe has been a recent target for expansion, with IKEA stores opening in Poland, the Czech Republic and Hungary. The company is also sourcing furniture from eastern European manufacturers, which now supply 15 per cent of its range. The standard 'big box' IKEA concept was brought to a smaller stage with the New York opening in Manhattan of the first IKEA Marketing Outpost, a 720-square-metre (7500-square-foot) 'boutique', significantly smaller than the normal 19,000-square-metre (200,000-square-foot) IKEA superstore. Even more unusual was the decision to offer only a selected, themed, reduced range at any point in time. For example, IKEA Cook showcases the company's kitchen-related merchandise. In early 2008, Coventry in the UK saw the opening of IKEA's first ever 'vertical store': built on the city centre site of a former grocery superstore, the constrained site has led IKEA to develop a new-look format that retails on three levels with parking on three others. IKEA is also recognising the growing use of the Internet and is developing sales tools to utilise this new technology.

IKEA has its ideals and operating philosophies: standards matter. IKEA has a forceful, well-directed marketing strategy actioned through primarily one tightly developed marketing mix for the core superstore operation. The result is a successful, expanding company, satisfied target customers highly motivated personnel and unhappy competitors.

Sources: www.ikea.co.uk, 2004; Helen Jones, 'IKEA's global strategy is a winning formula', *Marketing Week*, 15 March 1996, p. 22; Jennifer Pellet, 'IKEA takes Manhattan!', *Discount Merchandiser*, October 1995, pp. 22–3; 'IKEA', *Retail Business*, March 1995, pp. 78–81; Jonathan Pell, 'IKEA successfully penetrates east European consumer markets', *Central European*, June 1994, pp. 13–14; *IKEA Facts*, 1990 and 1992; B. Solomon, 'A Swedish company corners the business: worldwide', *Management Review*, 80 (4), 1991, pp. 10–13; IKEA HQ, 1998; www.ikea.com, 2007; IKEA Coventry store, 2008.

❷ *Questions for Discussion*

1 Explain why IKEA is successful.
2 To whom did the Marketing Outpost concept appeal? Why did IKEA developed this novel format?
3 In what ways does IKEA deploy the marketing concept?

2
Marketing Strategy

" **A proper analysis of the strategic aspects of any competitive marketplace may not result in certain success, but it almost always helps to avoid failures.** "

Robin Wensley, Warwick Business School

Objectives

- **To define marketing strategy and explore the relationship with a company's organisational mission, goals and corporate strategy**

- **To assess organisational opportunities, capabilities and the SWOT analysis**

- **To consider strategic objectives**

- **To appreciate the role of target market strategy and brand positioning in marketing strategy**

- **To examine competitive advantage, competitive positions and differential advantage**

- **To explore marketing objectives and marketing mix programmes in marketing strategy**

- **To understand the importance of implementation and performance monitoring in marketing strategy**

Introduction

Marketing strategy involves planning and decision-making over the longer term, with the aim of effectively selecting and pursuing marketing opportunities and establishing a competitive advantage. This requires an awareness of the external trading environment and market trends, an appreciation of the organisation's capabilities and resource base, and the ability to develop appropriate target market strategies. Marketing mix programmes must be developed to reflect these market conditions, organisational characteristics and target market strategies.

Market-oriented organisations have a marketing strategy that clearly articulates the opportunities the organisation has decided to address, and focuses the organisation on a specific set of target markets. These decisions will have been made with the knowledge of market drivers and marketing environment forces; an understanding of customer needs, expectations and buying behaviour; and with full knowledge of competitors' activities and their likely impact in target markets. The strategy will reflect, too, the marketing assets and capabilities of the organisation. This mix of external and internal awareness is pivotal to effective marketing strategy development. An organisation's marketing plan will then specify marketing programmes designed to achieve this marketing strategy.

Opener

Diversification of a Brand: Coca-Cola's Move into Clothing

L eading online retailer of designer men's clothing and shoes, Otoko, states:

Probably the best-known individual brand in the world today, Coca-Cola is also much more than a soft drink. Coca-Cola Ware is produced in Italy, under licence from Coca-Cola, using the same fabrics and design processes as its sister company Replay.

Building on the heritage of the label, and using designs from the original bottle labels, Coca-Cola Ware is one of the most up-and-coming clothing labels ...

This is an impressive endorsement from a fashion retailer stocking brands such as 4:45, Armand Basi, Buckler, DiSanto, Junk de Luxe, Klaus Samsoe, Legless Horse, Marshall Artist, Moschino, Pepé and Ra:Re.

So why has Coca-Cola extended the well-known brand for soft drinks into new territory? In general, Coca-Cola has enjoyed the effects of massive growth in global soft drinks sales. However, towards the end of 1998, for the first time in many years, the company failed to hit its expected 7–8 per cent volume growth. Following this disappointing performance, senior managers were quick to deny that the core soft drinks business had reached maturity, blaming economic problems in key markets for the difficulties. The launch of Coca-Cola Ware was not, they stated, because of difficulties with the core business. Instead, the company sees the clothing as a promotional activity, an extension of

Coca-Cola's licensing programme, which raises the profile of the brand around the world and is a core ingredient of the brand's strategy. The new clothing range certainly added an extra dimension to the company's existing licensing activities. With 250 licensees offering some 10,000 different items in 40 different countries, the precedent for such an arrangement was well established.

The clothing range, which comprises casual clothing and accessories, was test marketed prior to being launched globally. The target market for the jeans, woven clothing and knitwear is teenagers and young adults, but in future may include other age groups. According to US spokeswoman Susan McDermott, 'This is an integrated approach to create a fashion line with a cohesive feel and a sense of lifestyle.' Coca-Cola Ware is sold through department stores, fashion boutiques and specialist 'active' wear shops. The company has been quick to stress that the range is used to support and communicate Coca-Cola brand values, rather than to detract from the company's core products of soft drinks. This is a similar brand-building approach to that adopted by construction equipment giants CAT and JCB, whose footwear and clothing ranges have done much to raise the profile of their brands. However, some industry experts warn about the dangers of devaluing the core brand, suggesting that the fashion market is notoriously difficult to enter.

Jaguar also entered the fray, with a range of men's clothing competing with the likes of Boss and Armani. The appearance of Jaguar suits, shirts, ties, shorts and sweaters coincided with the launch of the Jaguar S-Type car. The clothing is sold through department stores and is supported by an advertising campaign. The rationale for the move was linked to the company's desire to target its cars at younger consumers. The Jaguar S-Type was the first of a series of models that Jaguar intended to appeal to the younger market, and the company believes that this appeal may be reflected in a desire to purchase fashion items carrying the same brand.

The extension of familiar brands into clothing is not a new trend. However, in a highly competitive market already saturated with well-known fashion house labels, success is difficult to achieve. One brand extension expert believes that brands seeking such a move must exhibit three crucial strengths: expertise, image and reputation. Few would deny that the classic and timeless brand of Coca-Cola possesses these qualities. Certainly Otoko's endorsement implies that Coca-Cola Ware is already creating the right impression. All marketers strive to promote their brands. Coca-Cola's marketers hope Coca-Cola Ware

will lead to thousands of walking 'adverts', raising the profile of this already ubiquitous and successful brand. Nevertheless, the move into clothing was a significant diversification from the company's soft drinks business.

Sources: www.Coca-Cola.com, 2004 and 2007; Amanda Wilkinson, 'Is Coke hip?', *Marketing Week*, 28 January 1999, pp. 26–9; Julia Day, 'Coke plans global clothing brands', *Marketing Week*, 21 January 1999, pp. 37–42; 'Jaguar drives in UK men's clothing market', *Marketing Week*, 18 March 1999, p. 7.

This chapter aims to highlight which strategic marketing considerations help to ensure that a product or service is marketed for the benefit of the organisation as well as its targeted customers. The product or service should be marketed differently enough from competitors' marketing programmes to provide the organisation's product or service with a perceived advantage over these competitors for priority target markets. These core components of marketing strategy are illustrated in Figure 2.1 and are clearly of great concern to the business described in this chapter's opener, Coca-Cola, as it chose to diversify into clothing.

The chapter first explores how to develop marketing strategies and then discusses strategic market planning, stressing the importance of organisational mission, goals and corporate strategy. The discussion next turns to assessing organisational opportunities and resources, as well as identifying strategic objectives and strategic focus. The chapter addresses the all-important role of identifying market segments, targeting and brand positioning in marketing strategy: the development of clear target market priorities. The chapter then focuses on competitive strategies for marketing: the role of competition, its ramifications for strategy, competitive positions and warfare strategies. The link between marketing objectives and marketing mix programmes is examined, along with implementation and performance monitoring.

Marketing Strategy Defined

Marketing strategy
A strategy indicating the opportunities to pursue, specific target markets to address, and the types of competitive advantages that are to be developed and exploited

Marketing strategy articulates the best uses of an organisation's resources and tactics to achieve its marketing objectives. It states which opportunities are to be pursued by an organisation, indicates the specific markets towards which activities are to be targeted, and identifies the types of competitive advantage that are to be developed and exploited.[1] Implicitly, as described in Figure 2.1, the strategy requires clear objectives and a focus in line with an organisation's corporate goals; the 'right' customers must be targeted more effectively than they are by competitors, and associated marketing mixes should be developed as marketing programmes to implement the marketing strategy successfully.[2]

Strategic market plan
An outline of the methods and resources required to achieve an organisation's goals within a specific target market

A **strategic market plan** is an outline of the methods and resources required to achieve an organisation's goals within a specific target market. It takes into account not only marketing but also all the functional aspects that must be coordinated, such as production, IT, logistics, finance and personnel. Environmental issues are an important consideration too. The concept of the strategic business unit is used to define areas for consideration in a specific strategic market plan. Each **strategic business unit (SBU)** is a division, product line or other profit centre within a parent company. Each sells a distinct set of products to an identifiable group of customers, and each competes with a well-defined set of competitors. Each SBU's revenues, costs, investments and strategic plans can be separated from those of the parent company and evaluated. SBUs operate in a variety of markets, which have differing growth rates, opportunities, degrees of competition and profit-making potential. Construction giant JCB, for example, includes the Compact Division for smaller machines, which is a strategic

Strategic business unit (SBU)
A division, product line or other profit centre within a parent company

Figure 2.1
*The components of
marketing strategy*

Organisational mission, goals and corporate strategy

Organisational opportunities and capabilities
- Environmental scanning
- Customer and competitor analysis
- Marketing opportunities
- Capabilities and resources

Strategic objectives
- Intense growth
- Diversified growth
- Integrated growth
- Maintenance

Target market strategy and brand positioning
- Market segmentation
- Priority target markets
- Brand positioning
- Differential advantage

Marketing objectives

Marketing programmes for implementation
- Marketing mix tactics
- Operational controls

Performance assessment and benchmarking

Strategic market planning
A process that yields a marketing strategy that is the framework for a marketing plan

Marketing plan
The written document or blueprint for specifying, implementing and controlling an organisation's marketing activities and marketing mixes

business unit. Figure 2.2 illustrates one of Magnet's SBUs. Strategic planners, therefore, must recognise the different performance capabilities of each SBU and allocate resources carefully. They must also ensure that the SBUs complement each other for the greater good of the overall business.

The process of **strategic market planning** yields a marketing strategy that is the framework for a marketing plan. The planning process should be guided by a marketing-oriented culture and processes in the organisation.[3] A **marketing plan**, includes the framework and entire set of marketing activities to be performed; it is the written document or blueprint for specifying, implementing and controlling an organisation's marketing activities and marketing mixes. Thus a strategic market plan is not the same as a marketing plan – it is

Figure 2.2
Magnet's kitchen business unit strives to market the appeal of its range and services
Source: Courtesy of Magnet Kitchens

it's gorgeous on the inside, too

When we design a kitchen for you at Magnet, it goes without saying that it will be drop-dead-gorgeous to look at. But any kitchen worth its salt has to be practical, too. That's why we've introduced something called Smart Space Solutions. A range of innovative storage options that can significantly increase the internal space of your kitchen, from plate and pan drawers that extend fully so you can access every single millimetre of space to wine racks that pull out of base units. Ask your designer for details, who will happily recommend a variety of solutions designed around you and your needs. And pretty soon you'll find yourself getting just as excited about the inside of your new kitchen as the outside.

Magnet
designed around you

call 0845 123 6789 for details of your nearest showroom, quoting H856 or visit www.magnet.co.uk

a plan of all aspects of an organisation's strategy in the marketplace.[4] A marketing plan, in contrast, deals primarily with implementing the marketing strategy as it relates to target markets and marketing programmes.[5] The marketing plan states which are priority target markets and details the marketing programmes, specifying also timeframes, budgets and responsibilities.

Figure 2.3 shows the components of strategic market planning. The process is based on the establishment of an organisation's overall goals, and it must stay within the bounds of the organisation's opportunities and resources. When the business has determined its overall goals and identified its resources, it can then assess its opportunities and develop a corporate strategy. Marketing objectives must be designed so that their achievement will contribute to the overall corporate strategy and so that they can be accomplished through efficient use of the company's resources. For example, IT service company Fujitsu wants to be the dominant provider of IT solutions and outsourcing to government and the public sector, along with certain commercial sectors such as financial services. The marketing

Figure 2.3
The components of strategic market planning

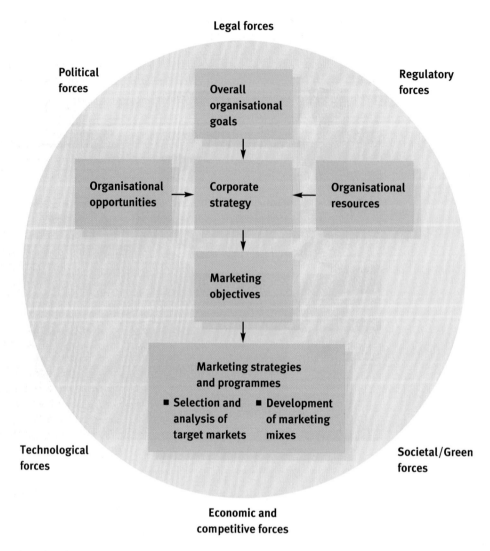

Legal forces

Political forces

Regulatory forces

Overall organisational goals

Organisational opportunities → **Corporate strategy** ← **Organisational resources**

Marketing objectives

Marketing strategies and programmes

■ **Selection and analysis of target markets**
■ **Development of marketing mixes**

Technological forces

Societal/Green forces

Economic and competitive forces

function in Fujitsu must identify opportunities to pursue in these sectors, specifying target market prospects, developing appropriate services and marketing messages, engaging with potential clients, and helping to win individual pieces of business within the organisation's priority sectors. In some organisations, marketers steer the development of the strategic market plan because they are the holders of market knowledge. In other organisations, the board of directors develops the strategic market plan and marketers focus on devising marketing strategies capable of achieving the aims of the top-line strategic market plan.

To achieve its marketing objectives, an organisation must develop a marketing strategy, or a set of marketing strategies, as shown in Figure 2.3. To operationalise a marketing strategy, a marketing mix must be developed. Most marketers refer to their marketing strategy and associated marketing mix activities as their **marketing programme**. Marketing programmes centre around a detailed marketing mix specification and include internal controls and procedures to ensure that they are implemented effectively. Through the process of strategic market planning, an organisation can develop marketing strategies that, when properly implemented and controlled, will contribute to the achievement of its marketing objectives and its overall goals. To formulate a marketing strategy, the marketer identifies and analyses opportunities and the associated target market, and develops a marketing

Marketing programme
A marketer's marketing mix activities and implementation processes designed to operationalise the marketing strategy

mix to satisfy individuals in that market. Marketing strategy is best formulated when it reflects the overall direction of the organisation and is coordinated with all the company's functional areas.

As indicated in Figure 2.3, the strategic market planning process is based on an analysis of the broader marketing environment. As detailed in Chapter 3, marketing environment forces can place constraints on an organisation and possibly influence its overall goals; they also affect the amount and type of resources that a business can acquire. However, these forces can create favourable opportunities as well – opportunities that can be translated into overall organisational goals and marketing objectives. For example, when oil prices declined during the second half of the 1980s, consumers viewed cars with high petrol consumption more favourably. This situation created an opportunity for manufacturers of large vehicles, such as BMW and Volvo. Political uncertainty in the Middle East resulted in higher fuel prices, creating opportunities for alternative energies and vehicle manufacturers with capabilities in these areas.

Marketers differ in their viewpoints concerning the effect of marketing environment variables on planning and strategy development. Some take a deterministic perspective, believing that companies must react to external conditions and tailor their strategies and organisational structures to deal with these conditions. According to others, however, companies can influence their environments by choosing in which markets to compete, lobbying regulators and politicians, striving to modify social views, joining forces with trade bodies for campaigning purposes, and so forth. They can also change the structures of their industries, engaging in activities such as mergers and acquisitions, demand creation or technological innovation.[6]

Regardless of which viewpoint is adopted, marketing environment variables play a part in the creation of a marketing strategy. When environment variables affect an organisation's overall goals, resources, opportunities or marketing objectives, they also affect its marketing strategies, which are based on these factors. Marketing environment forces more directly influence the development of a marketing strategy through their impact on consumers' needs and desires, as well as their effect on competitors' plans. In addition, these forces have a bearing on marketing mix decisions. For instance, competition strongly influences marketing mix decisions. The organisation must diagnose the marketing mix activities it performs, taking into account competitors' marketing mix decisions, and develop a differential advantage to support a strategy. Thus as Honda and Toyota entered the luxury car market with the Acura and Lexus models, European car makers BMW, Mercedes and Jaguar had to change their marketing strategies to maintain their market shares. They did so by lowering prices, introducing new models and creating brand-building marketing communications campaigns to compete with the new Japanese models.

Organisational Mission, Goals and Corporate Strategy

Mission
The broad, long-term tasks that the organisation wants to accomplish

Central to the strategic market plan is a clear view of the organisational mission, goals and corporate strategy. A company's organisational goals should be derived from its **mission** – the broad, long-term tasks that the organisation wants to accomplish. IBM, for example, has stated that its mission is helping business people make decisions in a connected world on demand. When a company decides on its mission, it really answers two questions.

1 What is the company's core business/area of activity?
2 What should this be?[7]

Although these questions seem very simple, they are in fact two of the hardest, yet most important, for any organisation to answer.

41

Creating or revising a mission statement is very difficult because of the many complex variables that must be examined. However, having a mission statement can greatly benefit the organisation in at least five ways.[8] A mission statement:

1 gives the organisation a clear purpose and direction, keeping it on track and preventing it from drifting
2 describes the unique aim of the organisation that helps to differentiate it from similar competing organisations
3 keeps the organisation focused on customer needs rather than its own abilities. This ensures that the organisation remains externally rather than internally focused
4 provides specific direction and guidelines to top managers for selecting alternative courses of action. It helps them decide which business opportunities to pursue, as well as which opportunities not to pursue
5 offers guidance to all employees and managers of an organisation, even if they work in different parts of the world. As a result, the mission statement acts like 'glue' to hold the organisation together.

A company's mission and overall organisational goals should guide all its planning efforts. Its goals should specify the ends, or results, that are sought. Examples of organisational goals include profit, return on investment, an increase in market share, an increase/decrease in the number of active markets, the desire to enter specific market sectors, to develop a particular reputation and track record. Organisations can also have short-term and long-term goals. Companies experiencing financial difficulty may be forced to focus solely on the short-term results necessary to stay in business, such as increasing cash flow by lowering prices or selling off parts of the business. Other organisations may have more optimistic long-term goals. In many cases, companies that pursue long-term goals have to sacrifice short-term results to achieve them. Businesses that are successful over time tend to have a longer-term, market share-driven strategy, rather than a short-term, 'profits only' sales-led emphasis.

An organisation in serious financial trouble may be concerned solely with short-run results needed for remaining viable and fending off creditors. There is usually, for example, an airline or major retailer being forced by cash shortages to take drastic action to stay in business. Lowndes Queensway, once the UK's largest retailer of carpets and furniture, had to renegotiate its financing several times with city institutions, alter payment and credit lines and terms with its suppliers, and ultimately identify which of its 500 superstores should be closed to save costs. The company went into receivership despite all its efforts. BA had to cut costs drastically in order to return to profitability and regain the faith of investors. Sainsbury's and Marks & Spencer are still trying to find strategies that appease the financial analysts and journalists. On the other hand, some companies have more optimistic goals. Often manufacturers, such as General Motors, have goals that relate to return on investment. A successful company, however, may want to sacrifice the current year's profits for the long run and at the same time pursue other goals, such as increasing market share.

Corporate strategy
A strategy that determines how resources are to be used to meet the organisation's goals in the areas of production, logistics, finance, research and development, human resources, IT and marketing

Corporate strategy determines the means for utilising resources in the areas of production, logistics, finance, research and development, human resources, IT and marketing to reach the organisation's goals. A corporate strategy determines not only the scope of the business but also its resource deployment, differential advantages and overall coordination of R&D, production, finance, distribution, sales, marketing and the other functional areas. The term 'corporate' in this context does not apply only to corporations: corporate strategy is used by all organisations, from the smallest sole proprietorship to the largest multinational corporation.

Corporate strategy planners are concerned with issues such as diversification, competition, differentiation, interrelationships among business units, and environmental issues. Strategic planners attempt to match the resources of the organisation with the various opportunities and risks in the external environment. Corporate strategy planners are also concerned with defining the scope and role of the strategic business units of the organisation so that they are coordinated to reach the ultimate goals desired.

While not the focus of *Marketing Essentials*, it is important to recognise that the marketing strategy, marketing plan and marketing mix programmes actioned by an organisation's marketers must reflect the aims and ethos of the overall corporate plan. Unfortunately, in some instances those empowered to deliver marketing programmes are unaware of or are unconcerned about the nuances of the organisation's overall corporate plan, and may even be pursuing a course of action that is at odds with the Board's sense of purpose. In some businesses, this reflects the paucity of analysis behind corporate planning, and the failure to involve senior marketers in such strategy development. In most organisations, the forces of the external marketing environment, competitors' strategies and evolving customer expectations are poorly assessed. In other cases, only an organisation's marketers are aware of these issues and have the relevant marketing intelligence to be able to suggest likely scenarios. It is therefore essential that those responsible for establishing corporate plans tap into this expertise and knowledge within the marketing function, just as it is essential for marketers to devise target market strategies and marketing programmes that properly reflect the direction desired by the corporate strategy.

Organisational Opportunities and Resources

There are three major considerations in assessing opportunities and resources:

1 evaluating marketing opportunities
2 environmental scanning (discussed in Chapter 3)
3 understanding the organisation's capabilities and assets.

An appreciation of these elements is essential if an organisation is to build up a sustainable differential advantage or competitive edge.

Marketing Opportunities

Marketing opportunity
Circumstances and timing that allow an organisation to take action towards reaching a target market

A **marketing opportunity** arises when the right combination of circumstances occurs at the right time to allow an organisation to take action towards reaching a target market. Government concerns about energy supplies have provided the turbine makers for wind farms with an opportunity that a few years ago did not exist. An opportunity provides a favourable chance or opening for an organisation to generate sales from identifiable markets. For example, in reaction to the overwhelming growth in cereals and other foods containing oat bran – which some researchers believe helps lower cholesterol levels – the Quaker Oats Company developed an advertising campaign to remind consumers that Quaker porridge oats have always contained oat bran. The advertisements told consumers that eating porridge is 'the right thing to do' and helped boost sales of Quaker Oats dramatically.[9] Increasing concerns about cancer and heart disease gave Quaker a marketing opportunity to reach consumers who are especially health-conscious by touting the health benefits of its oats. Kellogg's also took advantage of the popularity of oat bran by creating its Common Sense™ Oat Bran cereal. Interestingly, in 1990 a study published in a leading medical journal questioned the effectiveness of oat bran in lowering cholesterol, concluding that it was the elimination of high cholesterol animal products that really lowered cholesterol. Therefore, some of the oat bran mystique vanished overnight. The term **strategic window** has been used to describe what are often temporary periods of optimum fit between the key requirements of a market and the particular capabilities of a company competing in that market.[10]

Strategic window
A temporary period of optimum fit between the key requirements of a market and the particular capabilities of a company competing in that market

The attractiveness of marketing opportunities is determined by market factors such as size and growth rate; by political, legal, regulatory, societal/Green, economic and competitive, and technological marketing environment forces; and by internal capital, plant, and human and financial resources.[11] Because each industry and each product is somewhat different, the factors that determine attractiveness tend to vary.

43

Market requirements
Requirements that relate to customers' needs or desired benefits

Market requirements relate to customers' needs or desired benefits. Market requirements are satisfied by components of the marketing mix that provide buyers with these benefits. Of course, buyers' perceptions of what requirements fulfil their needs and provide the desired benefits determine the success of any marketing effort. Marketers must devise strategies to out-perform competitors by finding out what product attributes buyers use to select products. An attribute must be important and differentiating if it is to be useful in strategy development. As discussed in Chapters 4 and 5, when marketers fail to understand buyers' perceptions and market requirements, the result may be failure. Toyota had failed to attract prestige-led car purchasers, even though it produced well-specified executive cars. The brand image was not attractive enough to these target customers. As a result, Toyota created its highly successful Lexus marque, focusing on the brand values desired by these customers.

Environmental Scanning

Environmental scanning
The process of collecting information about the marketing environment to help marketers identify opportunities and threats, and assist in planning

Environmental scanning is the process of collecting information about the marketing environment to help marketers identify opportunities, prepare for impending threats, and assist in planning. Some companies have derived substantial benefits from establishing an 'environmental scanning (or monitoring) unit' within the strategic planning group, as part of their marketing planning activity, or by including line management in teams or committees to conduct environmental analysis. This approach engages management in the process of environmental forecasting and enhances the likelihood of successfully integrating forecasting efforts into strategic market planning.[12] Results of forecasting research show that even simple quantitative forecasting techniques out-perform the unstructured intuitive assessments of experts.[13]

Environmental scanning to detect changes in the environment is extremely important if an organisation is to avoid crisis management. A change in the external marketing environment can suddenly alter an organisation's opportunities or resources. Reformulated strategies may then be needed to guide marketing efforts. For example, after the UK government legislated against heavy emissions from cars and gave unleaded fuel tax advantages, petrol suppliers and vehicle manufacturers had to reformulate their strategies and marketing programmes.[14] Because car manufacturers had engaged in environmental scanning and were aware that such legislation might indeed be enacted because of social and political concerns, most had already begun developing plans for cars powered by clean fuel. Environmental scanning should identify new developments and determine the nature and rate of change.

Capabilities and Assets

Capabilities
A company's distinctive competencies to do something well and efficiently

Marketing assets
Customer, distribution and internal capabilities that managers and the marketplace view as beneficially strong

A company's **capabilities** relate to *distinctive competencies* that it has developed to do something well and efficiently. A company is likely to enjoy a differential advantage over its rivals in an area where its competencies out-do those of its potential competitors.[15] Often a company may possess manufacturing or technical skills that are valuable in areas outside its traditional industry. For example, BASF, known for the manufacture and development of audio and video tapes, produced a new type of lightweight plastic that has uses in other industries. Capabilities can be classified in terms of **marketing assets**, highlighting capabilities that managers and the marketplace view as beneficially strong. These capabilities can then be stressed to the company's advantage. Marketing assets are commonly classified as either customer based, distribution based or internal. *Customer-based assets* include capabilities that are customer-facing, such as brand image and reputation, product quality and customer service expertise; *distribution-based assets* relate to marketing channel issues and may involve density of dealers and geographic coverage, the responsiveness of distributors, after-sales support and logistical capabilities; *internal marketing assets* are operational, process and resource capabilities, including skills, experience, economies of scale, technology, working practices and people resources.[16] It is essential for a business to take time to assess its capabilities and assets, and to map these alongside identified opportunities. Research findings suggest that the mix of these capabilities and assets affects the types of strategy that should be pursued.[17]

SWOT analysis
The examination of an organisation's strengths and weaknesses, opportunities and threats, usually depicted on a four-cell chart

SWOT Analysis   **SWOT analysis** (strengths, weaknesses, opportunities, threats) is one of the most simplistic used by marketers; fundamentally it is little more than a set of checklists. However, it cannot be ignored in a book such as this owing to its popularity and widespread use. The strengths it refers to relate to those internal operational, managerial, resource and marketing factors that managers believe provide a strong foundation for their organisation's activities and for their ability to compete effectively in the marketplace. Many marketers treat the notion of marketing assets as a means for classifying strengths. Weaknesses are those aspects of the organisation, its products and activities in the marketplace that place the organisation at a disadvantage vis-à-vis competitors and in the view of targeted customers. Best practice indicates that an organisation should strive to remedy such faults, particularly those that may be exploited by rivals. An analysis of strengths and weaknesses is a fundamental aspect for developing a marketing strategy as an organisation must have an awareness of its capabilities and how these map out against competitors' strengths and weaknesses.

The other elements of the SWOT analysis are opportunities and threats, which are external-facing issues of the trading environment. As explained in Chapter 1, at the forefront of the marketing concept is marketing opportunity analysis. A sound appreciation of marketing environment forces and evolving market trends is essential for a marketing-oriented organisation. It is difficult to contemplate a scenario in which an organisation lacking such an external awareness is able to develop a truly meaningful marketing strategy. As described above, marketing environmental scanning identifies numerous issues that marketers must consider when developing marketing strategies. These market developments may offer opportunities for marketers to exploit or they may be the cause of threats to the fortunes of an organisation. As explained in more detail in the next chapter, an awareness of the marketing environment may lead to strategic windows of opportunity. The SWOT analysis, in its simplistic way, has the benefit of placing an organisation's strengths and weaknesses in the context of the identified opportunities and threats, so implying the extent to which an organisation is capable of leveraging an opportunity or fending off an apparent threat. The SWOT analysis can be an effective scene-setting tool, but *only* if the guidelines detailed in the Marketing Tools and Techniques box below are followed.

Ansoff matrix
Ansoff's product–market matrix for determining competitive strategies: market penetration, market development, product development or diversification

Marketing Tools and Techniques

Practitioners' Use of SWOT Analysis

The SWOT analysis is a very simplistic tool, yet it appears in most marketing plans and is popular with boards of directors because it conveys so much information: strengths (S) on which to build, weaknesses (W) to rectify, opportunities (O) to consider and threats (T) to address.

The first SWOT depicted (top of page 46) is typical. This was produced by a brainstorming workshop involving 25 sales and marketing personnel. Workshops are often used to generate SWOTs; alternatively, individual managers may spend a few minutes producing them – while killing time at an airport, say. The problems in the example are that:

- the lists were not ranked in order of importance, only listed in the order they were suggested
- many of the bulleted points are vague or ambiguous
- there is no validation or evidence to support these points being included, only the personal judgement of the managers present at the meeting
- the implications are not detailed
- there are far too many non-prioritised points listed to act upon.

45

Strengths	Weaknesses
• Experience & quality of people • Safety/environmental standards • Brand heritage – low price perception • Co-op mode of operation • Teamwork/alignment • New concept • Merchandising • Category management structure • Store locations • Streamlined organisation • Fully integrated company • Ability to change quickly • Dealer Loyalty	• Multiple image • Inconsistent site presentation • Brand equity value • Inflexible logistics • Lack of maintaining business investment • High break-even cost • Lack of flexible resources • Inflexible technology • Inconsistent focus on retailing/lack of selling structure • Staff turnover • Quality of data and analysis • Inadequate benchmarking • Consumer research • Reactive rather than proactive • Communication – quality/mode • Poor succession planning • Cost control • Total overheads too high • Too many non-performing sites
Opportunities	**Threats**

• Dealer buying group
• Customer loyalty promotion
• Optimising distribution e.g. push/pull
• Market growth of forecourt convenience
• Synergies for services with other brands
• Green products
• European purchasing agreements
• Joint venture on payment card
• Detailed economical analysis for sites
• Concessions/cebranding
• Alcohol/fast food/bakeries
• Technology
• Small profitable dealers (brand standards)
• Cost effective store and design
• More and better use of consumer/customer research industry data
• Active selling by sales attendants
• Optimisation of site opening hours
• Promoting underperforming sites/micro marketing
• Margin enhancement through loyalty scheme
• Alliance with shop retailers
• Market attrition
• Linking site to local community
• Co-op portfolio management
• Differentiation through customer service excellence
• Closer supplier relations
• Telesales
	• Industry restructuring
	  – by store categories
	  – by supplier/retailer alliances/JVs
	• Lack of loyalty programme
	• Government transport policy
	• Lack of shop image and investment
	• Majors targeting smaller dealers
	• Cost of environmental legislation
	• Control of costs
	• Continued low margins
	• Failure to capture convenience market growth

By contrast, the following SWOT grid for a major insurance company has a more manageable set of issues, although the points are still ambiguous.

SWOT Grid for an Insurance Business

	STRENGTHS	WEAKNESSES
Internal issues	Brand recognition Expertise in underwriting Network British, leading UK market Wide product range	Share price Press reports → Media targeting Uncertainty re. direction/market segments Poor product differentiation Cost base Wide network
External issues	Profitable markets still far from mature Broker loyalty Business unit focus strategy Technology Joint ventures with 3rd parties, such as major retailers entering fin/servs OPPORTUNITIES	Regulation Solvency Share price & ownership Negative press Losing customers Competitors – many mergers taking place Our markets are desirable to Euro-rivals Changing weather patterns THREATS

More importantly, this business has abided by some of the following essential guidelines.

• Be as focused as possible – no huge lists.
• Use teamwork to generate a range of opinions, then verify with external stakeholders (e.g. channel members, suppliers, customers) and benchmark against any available marketing research or customer satisfaction audit data.
• Concentrate on a customer orientation in allocating priorities: deal first with issues of importance to customers, particularly weaknesses that rivals could exploit.
• Strengths and weaknesses are more revealing when benchmarked against key rivals.
• Use an analysis of the macro marketing environment (see Chapter 3) as input to the opportunities and threats.
• Rank the points listed in order of importance: senior managers assume lists presented to them to be prioritised.
• Have supporting evidence, otherwise exclude the issue from the list.
• Be honest! Bad news, too.

Having produced the top-line SWOT depicted lower left, the insurance company team then debated in detail each point in order to clarify the issues, verify their importance and discuss the implication of each issue to the business. This discussion led to a prioritisation of tasks to action. This phase is crucial if the SWOT is to help direct a business's thinking.

By following these guidelines, this insurance business produced a meaningful, objective SWOT that led to specific action programmes, notably to address the stated weaknesses and steer the board's thinking about possible opportunities to consider.

Source: © Dibb/Simkin.

Note: a more extensive explanation of this technique is offered in either *The Market Segmentation Workbook* (Dibb and Simkin) or *The Marketing Planning Workbook* (Dibb, Simkin and Bradley), both originally published in 1996 by Thomson (London).

Strategic Objectives and Strategic Focus

Having evaluated the overall corporate vision, those responsible for devising the marketing strategy must build on their analysis of opportunities and internal capabilities by analytically assessing the most promising directions for their organisation and marketing activity. Ansoff developed a well-known tool, the market-product matrix, popularly known as the **Ansoff matrix,** to assist in this decision-making, as depicted in Figure 2.4. A business may choose one or more competitive strategies as the basis for its **strategic objectives,**

Strategic objectives
Include intense growth, diversified growth or integrated growth

Figure 2.4
Ansoff's competitive strategies
Source: H.I. Ansoff, The New Corporate Strategy (New York, NY: John Wiley & Sons, 1988), p. 83. Reproduced by permission of the author

	Product	
	Present	New
Market Present	Market penetration	Product development
Market New	Market development	Diversification

Intense growth
Growth that occurs when current products and current markets have the potential for increasing sales

Intense Growth

Market penetration
A strategy of increasing sales of current products in current markets

Market development
A strategy of increasing sales of current products in new markets

Product development
A strategy of increasing sales by improving present products or developing new products for current markets

Diversified Growth

Diversified growth
Growth that occurs when new products are developed to be sold in new markets

Horizontal diversification
A process that occurs when new products not technologically related to current products are introduced into current markets

including intense growth, diversified growth and integrated growth. This matrix can help in determining growth that can be implemented through marketing strategies.

Intense growth can take place when current products and current markets have the potential for increasing sales. There are three main strategies for intense growth – market penetration, market development and product development.

Market Penetration   **Market penetration** is a strategy of increasing sales in current markets with current products. For example, Coca-Cola and PepsiCo try to achieve increased market share through aggressive advertising.

Market Development   **Market development** is a strategy of increasing sales of current products in new markets. For example, a European aircraft manufacturer was able to enter the US market by offering Eastern Airlines financing that Boeing could not match. Evian devised a new use for its mineral water by developing its Brumisateur, an atomiser spray for the skin.

Product Development   **Product development** is a strategy of increasing sales by improving present products or developing new products for current markets. PepsiCo and Coca-Cola both have new container sizes, low-calorie/low-sugar/low-carb versions and vending machine services.

Diversified growth occurs when new products are developed to be sold in new markets. Companies have become increasingly diversified since the 1960s. Diversification offers some advantages over single-business companies, because it allows businesses to spread their risk across a number of markets. More important, it allows them to make better and wider use of their management, technical and financial resources. For example, marketing expertise can be used across businesses, which may also share advertising themes, distribution channels, warehouse facilities or even salesforces.[18] The three forms of diversification are horizontal, concentric and conglomerate.

Horizontal Diversification   **Horizontal diversification** results when new products that are not technologically related to current products are introduced to current markets. Sony, for example, diversified from electronics to movie production through its purchase of Columbia Pictures. The purchase gave Sony a library of 2700 films, including *Ghostbusters 2* and *When Harry Met Sally*, as well as 23,000 television episodes, which it has used to establish its line of video tapes and DVDs.[19]

Concentric Diversification   In **concentric diversification**, the marketing and technology of new products are related to current products, but the new ones are introduced into

47

Concentric diversification
A process that occurs when new products related to current products are introduced into new markets

new markets. For instance, Sony developed business PCs and laptops based on its consumer flatscreen and electronics products, and then successfully used its established position in business computers to tackle the home computing market. Dow Chemical diversified into agricultural chemicals and pharmaceuticals through joint ventures in those industries.

Conglomerate Diversification   Conglomerate diversification occurs when new products are unrelated to current technology, products or markets, and are introduced into markets new to the company. For example, Bass, the British brewer and pubs business, acquired the American Holiday Inn hotel chain. Laura Ashley, the UK clothing and furnishings company, moved into the fragrance market with Laura Ashley No. 1. Samsung diversified into everything from air conditioning and construction equipment to shipbuilding, home entertainment centres and mobile phones.

Integrated Growth

Conglomerate diversification
A process that occurs when new products unrelated to current technology, products or markets are introduced into new markets

Integrated growth
Growth that occurs in three possible directions: forwards, backwards or horizontally

Integrated growth can occur in the same industry that the company is in and in three possible directions: forwards, backwards or horizontally.

1 A company growing through forward integration takes ownership or increased control of its distribution system. For example, a shoe manufacturer might start selling its products through wholly owned retail outlets.
2 In backward integration, a company takes ownership or increased control of its supply systems. A newspaper company that buys a paper mill is integrating backwards.
3 Horizontal integration occurs when a company takes ownership or control of some of its competitors, such as BMW's acquisition of Mini, or Ford's purchases of Land Rover, Jaguar, Volvo and Aston Martin.

In developing strategies, an organisation must consider the competitive positions in the marketplace and formulate marketing strategies and tactics accordingly. Some authors have adopted warfare analogies to describe the strategic options for competing in a market.[20] This chapter later examines the concept of competitive positions.

Target Market Strategy and Brand Positioning

Central to achieving a company's corporate vision is the need to build up a loyal customer base of satisfied customers. Tesco did not overtake Sainsbury's by chance – it developed a clear marketing strategy based on a desire to fully satisfy a carefully targeted set of market segments. Tesco is continuously upgrading its stores, adding new services and product lines, and innovating with channels of distribution through Tesco Metro and Tesco Direct, with the aim of addressing its targeted-segment customer needs. Market segmentation is at the core of robust marketing strategy development. As explained in Chapter 6, this involves identifying customer needs, expectations, perceptions and buying behaviour, so as to group those customers who will be satisfied and marketed to in a similar manner into homogeneous groups or segments. One segment will differ from another in terms of customer profile and buying behaviour, and also with regard to the sales and marketing activity likely to satisfy these customers; but within a segment customers will share similar needs, buying behaviour and expectations. Without a thorough understanding of customers, therefore, it is difficult to produce a marketing strategy. Developing an understanding of customers is explored in chapters 4 and 5.

Taking the time to objectively and sensibly group a market's customers into meaningful market segments is a discipline many organisations are only now discovering, particularly in business-to-business markets. Most of the fast movers, market leaders and successful brands in a marketplace base their marketing strategies on carefully honed market segmentation analyses. It is important to remember that the process of market segmentation involves more than simply grouping customers into segments. Shrewd targeting of certain segments and the development of a clear brand positioning are part of the market segmentation process. **Brand positioning** is the creation of a desirable, distinctive and plausible image for a brand that will have strong appeal for the customers in a target market segment. The basis of Chapter 6's coverage – identifying segments, deciding which to target and developing desirable positionings – is one of the foundations of a marketing strategy.

A **target market strategy** is the choice of which market segment(s) an organisation decides to prioritise and for which to develop marketing programmes. Organisations must identify priority target markets that are worthwhile targeting with bespoke marketing mix programmes: product, price, place (distribution), promotion and people. Even the mighty Ford or General Motors has to decide which segments in the car and van market to pursue, opting not to have models aimed at all buyers in the market. It is important to balance current core target markets with those offering future viability. Once determined, in each target market an organisation must strive to emphasise to those targeted customers the relevance and applicability of its product and marketing mix proposition. This is achieved through all ingredients of the marketing mix, but specifically through developing a distinctive, plausible and memorable brand positioning, such as BMW's 'The Ultimate Driving Machine'. This positioning imagery is communicated to targeted customers primarily through the promotional mix, packaging and design, but product attributes, pricing, choice of distribution and customer service provision must also support the positioning strategy. An upmarket restaurant, for example, requires a suitably lavish ambience, slick service, quality food, appropriate location and a suitable price to match its branding and promotional campaigns. It is important to agree on the target market strategy and required brand positioning before developing the marketing programmes destined to implement this strategy. These marketing mix activities must reflect the marketing analyses and target market strategy requirements rather than being merely a continuation of previous marketing mix activities.

Competitive Advantage

The competition is generally viewed by an organisation as those businesses marketing products similar to, or substitutable for, its products when targeted at the same customers. In order to persuade customers to purchase an organisation's products in preference to those products marketed by its **competitors**, leading strategists argue that it is necessary to develop a **competitive advantage**. Competitive advantage is the achievement of superior performance vis-à-vis rivals, through differentiation, to create distinctive product appeal or brand identity; through offering customer value and achieving the lowest delivered cost; or by focusing on narrowly scoped product categories or market niches so as to be viewed as a leading specialist. The creation of a competitive advantage is a core component of the development of a marketing strategy.

Marketing strategist Michael Porter identified the so-called **generic routes to competitive advantage**, claiming them to result in success for companies competing for position in any particular market. As depicted in Figure 2.5, these three generic strategies are as follows.

1 *Cost leadership*. This involves developing a low cost base, often through economies of scale associated with high market share and economies of experience, to give high contribution. This high financial contribution can then be used to further develop the low cost base. Very tight cost controls are essential to the success of this strategy. Generally, within a single market, only one competitor is secure in adopting this strategy for creating a competitive advantage: the organisation with the lowest cost base.

2 *Differentiation*. Companies adopting a differentiation strategy strive to offer product and marketing programmes that have a distinct advantage or are different to those offered by competitors. Differentiation can be achieved on a number of fronts, including creative and innovative product or brand designs, or novel distribution channel,

Brand positioning
The creation of a desirable, distinctive and plausible image for a brand in the minds of targeted customers

Target market strategy
The choice of for which market segment(s) an organisation decides to develop marketing programmes

Competitors
Organisations viewed as marketing products similar to, or substitutable for, a company's products, when targeted at the same customers

Competitive advantage
The achievement of superior performance vis-à-vis rivals, through differentiation to create distinctive product appeal or brand identity; through providing customer value and achieving the lowest delivered cost; or by focusing on narrowly scoped product categories or market niches so as to be viewed as a leading specialist

Figure 2.5
Porter's generic routes to competitive advantage

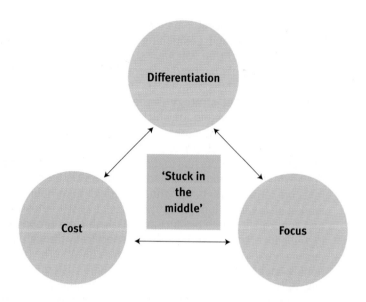

Generic routes to competitive advantage
Cost leadership, differentiation and focus; not mutually exclusive

pricing and customer service policies. This theme is taken further when marketers seek a *differential advantage*, as discussed later in this chapter.

3 *Focus*. Companies must maintain close links with the market so that product and marketing effort are designed with a particular target group in mind. Typically of small size, unable to achieve cost leadership or maintain significant differentiation, such companies succeed by effectively meeting customer needs that may be being missed by larger players in the market and by gaining a reputation for being experts or specialists in their narrowly defined area of activity.

Failure to achieve any of these strategies can result in companies becoming 'stuck in the middle', with no real competitive advantage. It is not usually possible to simultaneously follow all three generic strategies for competitive advantage, but it is common for businesses to gain cost leadership while also differentiating their proposition, and also for organisations to seek both a focused and a differentiated approach. Discounter Aldi adopts a cost leadership and a differentiated approach for developing a competitive advantage, as does no-frills airline easyJet. Sports coupé manufacturer Porsche adopts a focused and differentiated approach to defining a competitive advantage. It is sometimes more difficult to create a focused and cost leadership approach, as niche players rarely have the necessary scale economies, but it is not impossible.

Competitive Positions and Differential Advantage

Competitive set
All competing organisations and brands, irrespective of size and history, including substitutable solutions to customers' needs, as defined by the target market customers

In order to compete effectively, marketers should seek to develop a differential advantage. In order to ensure this will be effective, marketers must understand the nature of the **competitive set** and also identify those rivals with which to do battle. The competitive set includes all competing organisations and brands, irrespective of size and history, including substitutable solutions to customers' needs, as defined by target market customers. Leading marketing strategists David Aaker and Michael Porter both argue that the scoping of the competitive set in many organisations is too limited. Ask most management teams who are their competitors and they will simply name the leading few organisations and brands in the market, ignoring smaller fast-moving rivals, probable new entrants to the market or substitutable solutions to their customers' needs offered by dissimilar organisations. It is often the case that when a company's customers are asked to name the

Figure 2.6
*Steps in analysing
competitors
Source: Veronica
Wong, MBA course
notes, Warwick
Business School, 1996*

competing companies or brands, they list a few names not routinely considered by the company's marketers. The customer's view of his or her options is of paramount importance and marketers should ensure that their interpretation of the competitive set is shared by their target market customers.

The scoping of the competitive arena and the identification of the competitive set are important marketing analysis tasks. Competitors are outside the control of an organisation, so the forces of competition are generally included within the forces of the *marketing environment*, as part of what is termed the 'micro marketing environment'. This concept is described in Chapter 3, which discusses further the forces of the competitive environment.

For the identified competitive set, marketers should assess the objectives and strategies of these rivals, their strengths and weaknesses, and determine how competitors are likely to react to their own marketing strategy and programmes. In effect, this leads to a decision about which competitors to 'fight', which to avoid antagonising and which to treat as unimportant. Wong (after Kotler) suggests that competitor-aware marketers should be able to answer six key questions, as described in Figure 2.6.

Before examining the concept of differential advantage, this chapter looks at the increasingly popular use of warfare analogies in identifying the relative threat posed by the competitors in a market. While *Marketing Essentials* is not intended to be a marketing strategy text, analysis of the competition is a core principle for effective marketing and, as explained in Chapter 1, without a thorough appreciation of the competitive arena an organisation cannot have a marketing orientation.

Competitive Positions

Evidently it is important to understand the nature of competition. This involves more than a cursory examination of like-for-like major rivals. Most organisations consider only similar companies or brands to be their competitors. As shown in Figure 2.7, there are other facets of competition that must be evaluated. What of the smaller players that may one day emerge as dominant in a market or specific segment? Why not pre-empt such an outcome by developing a strategy to destroy them while still only a small rival? What about the new entrant into the marketplace? Could its appearance have been foreseen? What actions are required to minimise its threat? How did Rover and Citroën fend off the entry of Daewoo in the small-car sector? Did they even anticipate Daewoo's entry? Citroën did! What of innovative solutions to customers' problems?

JCB produces construction equipment that digs trenches for pipes and cables. Micro-bore tunnelling moles lay pipes without the need for a trench. Such moles – substitute competition – could be missed by JCB's marketers as a competitive threat without a rigorous analysis of the forces of the competitive environment. Web-comms posed a threat to BT, who then went online in order to remain competitive.

The power of suppliers and of consumers can also vary per company and act as a competitive force, particularly if one organisation encounters greater supply problems or more severe customer bargaining than its rivals face from their suppliers and customers. These

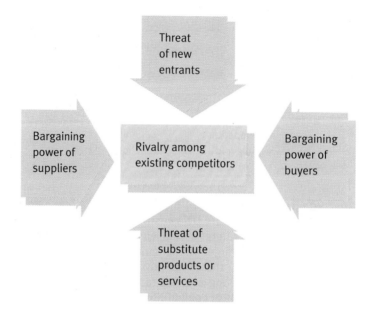

competitor categories are in addition to the like-for-like rivals considered by most organisations to be their competitors.

Michael Porter's view of defining the nature of the competitive arena, as illustrated in Figure 2.7, is particularly useful for scoping the nature of a market place. Porter defined **five competitive forces** that together determine competition in an industry or market:

Five competitive forces
Together these
determine competition
in an industry or market:
rivalry amongst existing
like-for-like players; the
threat of new entrants;
the threat of substitute
solutions; the bargaining
power of buyers; and
the bargaining power of
suppliers

1 rivalry among existing like-for-like players
2 the threat of new entrants
3 the threat of substitute products or services as a solution to customers' problems or needs
4 the bargaining power of buyers
5 the bargaining power of suppliers.

Many marketing directors find this framework ideal for persuading their colleagues to consider competitive threats from more than just like-for-like rivals. Similarly, most marketing dissertations use Porter's framework in order to provide the perspective for describing the competitive pressures prevalent in a particular market.

In addition to realising the importance of examining all categories of competitors, it is necessary to understand what must be known. Most companies can describe their competitors: who, where, with what and at what price. Few organisations genuinely understand their rivals' strategies or endeavour to predict their rivals' reaction to moves they themselves may make. Very few companies attempt to identify those individual competitors it is sensible to avoid in a head-to-head marketing campaign or those most likely to be vulnerable to attack at low risk to the company's resource base. It is prudent to avoid head-to-head conflict with a similarly sized and resourced adversary. It is more desirable to identify the weaknesses of more vulnerable competitors and address these through the proposed marketing mix programmes. No marketing strategy should be formulated without a shrewd analysis of competitors. For some companies, carrying out this kind of analysis has recently been made more complex by the fact that they operate in both the physical and digital marketplace.[21]

Many marketers view their marketplace as a battlefield, opting to compete on only certain fronts, engaging with carefully selected opponents, where there is a perceived differential advantage over the enemy. This warfare analogy has become increasingly popular and hinges on identifying the competitive positions of the various businesses competing in

Competitive positions
Competitors' roles in the marketplace, which influence their marketing strategies and programmes

Market leader
The single player enjoying the largest individual share in the market

Market challengers
Non-market leaders that aggressively try to capture market share from their rivals

Fast movers
Smaller rival companies not yet destined to be major challengers, but growing rapidly on a smaller scale

Market followers
Low-share competitors without the resources, market position, research and development, or the commitment to challenge for extra sales and market share

Market nichers
Companies that specialise by focusing on only a very narrow range of products or on a select band of consumers

Defensive warfare
A policy of striking a balance between waiting for market developments or competitor activity and proactively parrying competitors' actions

a market segment.[22] The categories of **competitive positions** – competitors' roles in the marketplace that influence their marketing strategies and programmes – include the market leader, market challengers, fast movers, market followers and market nichers. These should be identified within each target market segment: a market challenger in one market segment may be a follower or even absent in a second market segment.

In the world of market shares, there has to be one, and only one, **market leader**: the player enjoying individually the largest slice of the market. In some business-to-business markets, a market leader can have a majority of industry sales, particularly when patent protection or technical innovation gives it an advantage over competitors. In most markets, however, the market leader may have only 10 to 20 per cent of the market's sales. The market leader has the highest market share and retains its competitive position by expanding the total market or expanding market share at the expense of its rivals, while protecting or defending current market share by retaining its customer base. In this context, the market leader, although successful, perhaps has the most difficult task: it must find strategies to increase market size and market share, as well as maintaining strategies to defend its current share. The marketing programmes necessary for maintaining ongoing relationships with existing customers are quite different to the marketing programmes used to attract and entice potential customers.

Behind the market leader are competing companies, which are market challengers, fast movers, market followers or market nichers. **Market challengers** are non-market leaders that aggressively attack rivals, including the market leader, to take more market share. In most instances, these players are number two, three and perhaps four in a market, aspiring to market leadership. When Virgin entered the transatlantic market, its intention was to steal BA's market leadership. It is important to remember that to qualify as challengers these companies must be proactive and aggressive in their sales and marketing rather than passively reinforcing the existing hierarchy. **Fast movers** are smaller rival companies not yet destined to be major challengers, but growing rapidly on a smaller scale. A new entrant may have only 2 per cent of the market – but what is to stop it from increasing its share to 8 per cent within two years? A business may only have 4 per cent of the market, but three years ago it only had 1 per cent. What is to prevent it from having 8 per cent or 19 per cent in three years' time? The market leader and key challengers should take steps to prevent such continued growth.

Market followers are low-share competitors without the resources, market position, research and development, or commitment to challenge for extra sales and market share. These companies tend to be the 'me-too, also-rans' in a market, whose raison d'être is to do as before and simply survive. In boom times these players can latch on to the success of their larger rivals, but in recession – or when faced with larger rivals' product innovations – they often struggle to achieve sales. Most markets also contain **market nichers**: companies that specialise by focusing on only a very narrow range of products such as Sock Shop or Saab, or on a select band of consumers, such as Body Shop or Porsche. Nichers survive by finding a safe, small, profitable market segment – often apparently too small to attract the market leaders and challengers. Nichers specialise and can genuinely prepare a marketing mix that exactly matches their target customers' needs. They are vulnerable to market downturns, the entry of rival nichers and the sudden attention of the major players in the marketplace, as happened to Porsche when the North American target market hit a recession and Japanese rivals appeared with cheaper, fast, two-seat sports coupés.

A market leader must defend its position, while simultaneously seeking more market share. Only a market leader should consider **defensive warfare** as a strategic foundation. Strong defence involves striking a balance between waiting for market developments or competitor activity and proactively parrying competitors' actions. As market leader, the company must remember that a false sense of security and passive inactivity lead to disaster: the best defensive strategy is the courage to attack; and strong moves by competitors should always be blocked, never ignored. To defend its market share, a market leader must treat existing customers well and attentively, and never take them for granted. The marketing mix must be updated continually and target customers' needs must regularly be considered. New markets, products and opportunities should always be sought and evaluated. Occasionally, if faced by a strong challenger in a small or declining market, a market leader should consider divesting and concentrating resources in its other markets. Others may have to turn to defensive warfare when attacked by the market leader or challengers, but only the market leader should build a strategy around the desire to defend its current position.

A challenger has to attack for market share, but on what basis? The leader, and perhaps other challengers, will be strong and rich in resources. A challenger's attack must be well thought out and not suicidal in terms of the company's medium-term future. Few observers could accept the logic in Sainsbury's attacking market leader Tesco on the basis of price. Price anyway was not the core facet of Sainsbury's service-led culture, nor was Tesco the weakest of rivals to choose to fight. In **offensive warfare**, the main consideration is the market leader's strength: where are there any chinks in the leader's armour? A challenger seeking market share must identify a weakness in the leader's marketing mix and in other challengers' marketing programmes, and develop a genuine corresponding strength. With such a differential advantage or competitive edge, the challenger's resources may well be sufficient to steal ground successfully from the leader and the other challengers. Any attack, however, should be on a narrow front, where the challenger is perceived by the target customers to have an advantage and where resources can be focused. If no real weakness in the market leader exists, a challenger may attack head-on. Such an attack can be successful only if there are numerous, very weak market followers, if the leader is slow to react and if a price-cutting war does not result. In the last situation, the leader's resource base may fend off the challenger's attack.

Followers are vulnerable, but careful monitoring of market segments, marketing environment forces and competitive trends can help ensure their survival. They must serve exactly only a few market segments, specialising rather than diversifying in terms of products and markets, and making prudent use of what research and development resources are available. Nichers must watch for signs of competitor threats and possible changes in target segment customers' needs, and they may need to consider product development and, ultimately, diversification. Their marketing mixes must be tailored exactly to meet the expectations of their target segment.

All organisations should know, for all their markets and target segments, which companies occupy these competitive positions. They must alter their strategies and marketing programmes accordingly. Organisations should also review their rivals' marketing strategies and marketing programmes: many companies are surprisingly predictable. Response to rivals' pricing policies, frequency of new product launches, entry into new markets and timing of promotional campaigns, for example, can often be accurately anticipated. In this way, thorough **competitor scanning** – the monitoring of competitive positions and competitors' strategies – helps to establish more realistic marketing goals, develop successful strategies and programmes, and pre-empt nasty shocks caused by competitors' actions.[23] The leading marketing strategists agree that it is essential to understand competitors' strategies, their strengths and weaknesses in satisfying customers, and any differential advantages they hold that must be combated.[24] The **competitive positions proforma** has been developed by the authors of *Marketing Essentials*, in conjunction with many organisations, as a way of scoping the competitive set, helping a company in understanding the competitive positions in its target markets and diagnosing the effectiveness of a marketing strategy. This particular tool for practitioners is described in the Marketing Tools and Techniques box on page 55.

Offensive warfare
A policy whereby challengers aggressively seek market share by identifying any weaknesses in the leader's and other challengers' marketing mixes and developing a genuine corresponding strength

Competitor scanning
The monitoring of competitive positions and competitors' strategies

Competitive positions proforma
A tool for scoping the competitive set, helping a company to understand the competitive positions in its target markets and diagnosing the effectiveness of a marketing strategy

Marketing Tools and Techniques

Practitioners' Use of Competitor Intelligence: the Dibb/Simkin Competitive Positions Proforma

The understanding of competition is not generally strong in most organisations. Managers may be able to name their rivals, and these businesses' products, price points and outline promotional activity, but rarely are managers able to suggest rivals' next moves or to identify an individual competitor's strengths or weaknesses. Therefore, managers cannot be taking into account the capabilities and market standing of such rivals when they construct their own target market strategies. The result could be a significant waste, as a company's marketing programme may fail to enable the business to set itself apart from its principal rivals. Worse, the business may be incapable of combating their rivals' marketing strategies.

The ultimate goal in marketing is to produce a differential advantage: something desired by targeted customers and only offered by a single supplier. Failure to analyse rivals means that the creation of a differential advantage is going to occur only by chance, rather than due to knowledge of competitors' strengths and weaknesses.

The strategists also point to the need to address an organisation's own weaknesses. In particular, a management team should be aware of which rivals are best placed to exploit any weaknesses in the organisation or in its marketing mix. Over time, the competitive set will change, as new entrants and substitution solutions to customers' requirements emerge. The relative strengths and weaknesses of competitors will alter, too, often rapidly. The competitive set must be monitored closely and not just occasionally.

Chapter 7 identifies methods for collecting competitor intelligence. Once the competitive set has been defined – through the customer's eyes – and some knowledge has been built up about these brands, a useful tool to deploy is the competitive positions proforma.

This technique is based on warfare analogies and assumes that the analysis is replicated for each individual target market segment. Within each segment, it is necessary to allocate the competitive set – which may include substitutes and possible new entrants – into the following categories.

- *Market Leader.* Only ever one in a segment: the player or brand with the biggest market share. The market leader should (1) expand the total market, (2) expand its own market share, and (3) protect existing market share. The market leader has to defend and attack.
- *Market Challenger*(s). Non-market leaders that want to be the leader! Aggressively attacking for market share gains by investing in new product devel-opment, establishing distribution, promotional activity, field force increases or price incentives.
- *Market Follower*(s). Low-share rivals without resources, market position, R&D or commitment to challenge. The 'me-too' smaller players in a market segment.
- *Market Nicher*(s). Companies that specialise in terms of market/product/customers, by finding a safe, profitable niche or narrowly defined segment.
- *Market Fast Mover*(s). Smaller players with intentions to be much bigger. A rival not yet large enough to be classed as a Challenger, but one worth watching or 'knocking out' before it is too late.

One column of the proforma is completed for each market segment. A company should include itself within the columns. In this way, a management team may assess the business's relative performance across market segments and identify rivals making gains in more than one segment. In this context, the technique is of great value to the Board of a company and not only to marketing managers.

Marketing-oriented businesses repeat this analysis every few months, in order to reveal movements within the columns and to identify fast movers, new entrants or emerging substitute competition. The changing strengths and weaknesses of rivals also become apparent. If a company is not moving up the column – or 'league table' – it is likely that its marketing strategy and/or marketing programme are inappropriately specified. Remedial action should be taken.

The Competitive Positions

For reasons of commercial confidentiality, the identities of the cited retailers have been disguised.

The Dibb/Simkin Competitive Positions Proforma

Position		Grocery Superstores (out-of-town)	Supermarkets (town centres)
Market Leader	ID: Market Share: KCVs: Weaknesses: Differential Adv:	Doing Well plc 28%++ (growing) Range, fresh produce, store amenities, deals Board's focus overseas, Comp Commission Loyalty card scheme	Still Trying plc 24% +/– (static) Locations, fresh produce No compelling wow factor, poor PR —
Challenger 1	ID: Market Share: KCVs: Weaknesses: Differential Adv:	Going For It Ltd 21%+ (growing) Range, non-food mix, clothing, amenities, value Some tired stores, no town centre stores US owner = greater resources, buying power	Doing Well plc 16++ (growing) Brand reputation, e-service, fresh produce Pulled out, now re-establishing —
Challenger 2	ID: Market Share: KCVs: Weaknesses: Differential Adv:	Still Trying plc 19% – (declining) Store ambiance, range, reputation, amenities Poor analysis & PR, limited non-food —	New Kid on the Block (Merger) 9%++ (growing) Many good locations, fresh produce, value Had lost its way, now catching up —
Challenger 3	ID: Market Share: KCVs: Weaknesses: Differential Adv:	New Kid on the Block (Merger) 18%++ (growing) Value, fresh produce In-store amenities, no national coverage —	Still Just About Here plc 9%+ (growing) Value-for-money, brands stocked Poor brand reputation, few strengths —
Follower 'Me Too'	ID: Market Share: KCVs: Weaknesses: Differential Adv:	Still Just About Here plc 5% – (declining) Store ambience No brand strengths, no buying power —	Also Just Surviving Ltd 7% +/– (static) — Mix of merchandise —
Fast Mover	ID: Market Share: KCVs: Weaknesses: Differential Adv:		SavaLot Ltd 6%++ (rapid expansion) Value-for-money, merchandise mix Low brand awareness, poor buying power
Nicher	ID: Market Share: KCVs: Weaknesses: Differential Adv:	HyperLand plc (JV) 3% Range, value, store amenities, one-stop Few outlets, few scale benefits —	Deluxe Deli Ltd 2%+ (growing, SE only) Service, staff attitude, opening hours, locations Poor buying power, limited network, branding Upscale appeal and target marketing

The competitive positions proforma identifies:

- the key players and their relative positions
- current successes and probable reasons

- the KCVs (key customer values or needs) each rival is good at serving – rivals' customer-facing strengths that must be addressed
- any differential advantages (DAs) to fear – these must be combated
- the company's own standing, which should improve over time
- emerging and fast-moving rivals, including substitute solutions to customers' needs
- the evolving competitive set with which to do battle, and how!

The proforma, therefore, is a 'call to action' to a company's marketers. In addition, the technique acts as a diagnostic over time of a business's successes or failures in terms of its marketing strategy and programmes.

Note: The Dibb/Simkin Competitive Positions Proforma is copyright Sally Dibb and Lyndon Simkin. A more extensive explanation of this technique is offered in *The Market Segmentation Workbook* (Dibb and Simkin) and *The Marketing Planning Workbook* (Dibb, Simkin and Bradley), both originally published in 1996 by Thomson (London).

Differential Advantage

Differential advantage
An attribute of a brand, product, service or marketing mix that is desired by the targeted customer and provided by only one supplier

If a marketing mix is developed that matches target market needs and expectations and is superior to those offered by competitors, there is a real – or perceived – differential advantage. A **differential advantage** is an attribute of a brand, product, service or marketing mix that is desired by the targeted customer and provided by only one supplier: it is a unique edge over rivals in satisfying this customer. If successful in developing a differential advantage, an organisation is likely to have its differential advantage copied by rivals. Direct Line innovated in selling car insurance over the telephone, cutting out the broker. This more convenient and cheaper service was very popular with customers, gaining market leadership for Direct Line. Very high profits followed. Rivals caught up, offering their own telephone-based direct selling of car insurance. Nevertheless, Direct Line developed a sizeable and successful customer base, which is still proving difficult for competitors to win back.

Achieving a differential advantage – or competitive edge – requires an organisation to make the most of its opportunities and resources while offering customers a satisfactory mix of tangible and intangible benefits.[25] When striking a balance between customer requirements on the one hand and company resources on the other, competitor activity must also be monitored. For example, there is little sense in promoting speedy distribution to customers if several large competing organisations offer a faster service. An understanding of competitors and customers' perceptions of companies' propositions is an essential part of identifying a differential advantage. Once determined, it is sensible to maximise the use of any differential advantage in the marketing mix, particularly in the promotional mix.

There are many different sources of differential advantage that companies can pursue. It is important to ensure that the promoted differential advantage is:

- unique to the one organisation, otherwise it is not a differential advantage only a strength or capability
- desirable to the targeted customer
- not simply the expected marketing mix taken for granted by the target market
- not simply an internal perception by a team of marketers.

For example, a new range may be superior to its predecessor, but compared to competitors' products may offer few benefits to the customer. The marketers could be guilty of identifying the new range's advantages over the former range, wrongly, as offering a differential advantage.

Low price should also be avoided as a differential advantage at the centre of a marketing programme unless a company genuinely has the scale economies to maintain a low cost base and offer cost leadership. Only one company in any market can occupy this platform, as explained by Porter's generic routes to achieving a competitive advantage. Others are vulnerable to being undercut and losing their apparent differential advantage. Jet's lowest price proposition was undermined by Esso's highly effective Tigerwatch lowest price guarantee. Low price can be utilised as a short-term tactic – to off-load excessive stocks, for example – but should not form a differential advantage unless it can be defended against all challenges.

If there is no observable differential advantage, an organisation must look to its strengths over its rivals. While not unique, these will still form the foundation for its ability to compete effectively. The SWOT analysis assists marketers in identifying their strengths and capabilities. The composite of any differential advantage with any strengths is a company's **basis for competing**, which should form the leading edge of the organisation's marketing strategy. For some companies, such as 3M, innovativeness is the basis for competing, while for others, like Vidal Sassoon hair salons, image plays an important part. The Body Shop concentrates on environmentally friendly cosmetics, whereas for multiplex cinemas the basis for competing is the choice of multiple screens at one location. Some of these ways of gaining an edge are easier to sustain than others. For example, many UK companies that have traditionally focused on low price have found this advantage difficult to maintain in the long term.[26] The airline industry is just one to be plagued by periodic price wars, with many companies turning instead to flexibility and customer service as the basis for competing, while others have adopted a value-based strategy.

Basis for competing
A company's combined strengths as identified in a SWOT analysis and any differential advantage, which should form the leading edge of the company's marketing strategy

Identifying Differential Advantage   There is a straightforward sequence that marketers follow when attempting to identify a differential advantage.

1 Identify the market's segments.
2 Establish what product and service attributes are desired and demanded by customers in each segment.
3 Decide which of these attributes the company in question offers.
4 Determine which attributes the company's competitors offer.
5 Consider what the marketplace perceives the competitors' genuine strengths to be.
6 Identify whether any gaps exist between customer expectations of the product/service on offer and perceptions of the competitors' marketing programmes.
7 Consider whether any gaps identified in step 6 are matched by the company and its own offerings. If the company is able to match one or more of these gaps, the potential exists for a differential advantage to be developed.

8 Question whether any of these potential advantages for the company can be emphasised through sales and marketing programmes.

9 Consider the sustainability of these advantages for the company. How easily and quickly can competitors catch up? Is it possible for the company to defend these advantages?

10 If there are no current advantages for the company, given the gaps identified between competitors' propositions and customer expectations, consider which areas offer potential for developing a future differential advantage.

11 In order to maximise any existing or potential differential advantages, detail the changes the company must make to its research and development, engineering, sales and marketing activities.

It is important to remember that companies frequently examine their relative strengths and weaknesses in relation to their rivals. A strength is not the same as a differential advantage. For example, many rivals may also have strong brand awareness, products that perform well, loyal distributors or high profitability. A differential advantage is something that targeted customers want and value, and that only one supplier is able to provide.

Marketing Objectives

Once an organisation has agreed which marketing opportunities are worth pursuing and on which target markets to focus marketing and sales activities, the organisation must ensure that its marketing strategy specifies its core marketing objectives. These marketing objectives are typically defined in terms of which are the most desirable market segments to target and, for each of these priority market segments, what market share is being sought and thereby what sales volumes or levels are expected to be achieved.

Marketers must specify a raft of performance metrics, including customer satisfaction or brand awareness measures, profitability and financial contribution – or in retailing, sales per square metre of selling space. Marketing objectives may include various product and market developments that marketers expect to achieve. These developments may include new product launches, new territory or market segment entry, the creation of innovative distribution channels or partnerships with marketing channel members. Without specification of these expectations it is difficult to ensure a fit with the organisation's overall corporate strategy. It is impossible, too, to monitor ongoing performance or benchmark the effectiveness of the recommended marketing strategy against competitors' strategies.

Marketing Mix Decisions

As mentioned in Chapter 1, marketers must decide which products or services to offer to selected target markets, the attributes, specifications, performance characteristics and designs of these products, and the levels of customer service required to support them and to encourage customer satisfaction. In addition, prices must be set, payment terms and mechanisms agreed; distribution channels have to be chosen and distribution channel members orchestrated, in order to ensure product availability at places appropriate for the targeted customers. These customers must be made aware of the product through promotional activity – marketing communications – and their interest in the product maintained through promotional campaigns. These product, people, price, place and promotion decisions are what are termed the marketing mix decisions. They occupy the majority of marketers' time and account for most of a marketing department's budget.

Part III explores in detail the ingredients of the marketing mix, and the tactical toolkit utilised by marketers in developing marketing programmes designed to implement their recommended marketing strategy and target market strategy.

These product, people, price, place/distribution and promotion issues should be determined only after the marketing strategy has been agreed. The marketing strategy itself should be developed only after the core marketing analyses have been undertaken addressing market trends, marketing environment forces, customer buying behaviour, competition, opportunities and capabilities. The marketing process outlined in Chapter 1 requires analysis, strategy formulation and then the specification of a marketing mix to facilitate the implementation of the desired target market strategy. Marketing programmes created from the ingredients of the marketing mix are part of the creation of an effective marketing strategy. Without the specification of marketing mixes, marketing strategies will not be effectively operationalised.

Implementation and Performance Monitoring

Marketing programmes depend on a detailed marketing mix specification: product, place/distribution, promotion, price and people issues. In addition, marketing programmes require the specification of budgets for actioning the desired marketing mix recommendations. These budgets must reflect the anticipated sales from the sales forecast and the trends inherent in the targeted market segments. Sales and marketing personnel must know of their responsibilities in implementing the recommended marketing programmes. There may be a requirement on colleagues outside the sales and marketing functions or on senior executives. Schedules must be determined so that it is clear when specific marketing mix activities are expected to occur.

It is essential that the implementation of a marketing strategy be facilitated. This involves specifying by whom, when, how and at what cost the desired marketing mix programmes will be actioned. There may be internal marketing issues to address, such as those connected with the sharing of marketing intelligence and strategies; communication channels within the business; hierarchical support and resources. Finally, marketing must demonstrate its worth. Marketing programmes should be evaluated against predetermined performance measures to ensure their effective implementation and success in terms of the desired marketing objectives detailed within the marketing strategy.

Summary

*M*arketing strategy identifies which opportunities are to be pursued, indicates the specific markets towards which activities are to be targeted and defines the types of competitive advantage that are to be developed and exploited. A marketing strategy aims to target customer segments of most benefit to an organisation in a manner that best utilises the organisation's capabilities, provides a differential advantage over competitors and matches the organisation's corporate goals.

❯❯ A *strategic market plan* is an outline of the methods and resources required to achieve an organisation's goals within specific target markets;
it takes into account all the functional areas of a business unit that must be coordinated. A *strategic business unit (SBU)* is a division, product line or other profit centre within a parent company, and is used to define areas for consideration in a specific strategic market plan. The process of *strategic market planning* yields a marketing strategy that is the framework for a marketing plan. A *marketing plan* includes the framework and entire set of activities to be performed; it is the written document or blueprint for specifying, implementing and controlling an organisation's marketing activities and marketing mixes.

❯❯ Through the process of strategic market planning, an organisation can develop marketing strategies that, when properly implemented and controlled, will contribute to achieving the organisation's overall goals. The marketing mix and associated implementation processes designed to operationalise the marketing strategy are the organisation's *marketing programme*. Most marketing programmes centre around a detailed marketing mix specification and include internal controls and procedures to ensure that they are implemented effectively. Marketing environment forces are important in – and profoundly affect – the strategic market planning process. These forces imply opportunities and threats that influence an organisation's overall goals.

» Central to the marketing strategy is a clear view of the corporate mission and goals. These may well be developed separately to the marketing strategy but the marketing strategy must aim to reflect the overall corporate vision. A company's organisational goals should be derived from its *mission* – that is, the broad, long-term tasks that the organisation wants to achieve. These goals should guide planning efforts and specify the ends, or results, that are sought. *Corporate strategy* determines the means for utilising resources in the areas of production, logistics, finance, research and development, human resources, IT and marketing to reach the organisation's goals.

» There are three major considerations in assessing opportunities and resources:
(1) evaluating marketing opportunities, (2) environmental scanning, and (3) understanding the company's capabilities and assets. A *marketing opportunity* arises when the right combination of circumstances occurs at the correct time, allowing an organisation to take action towards reaching a target market. An opportunity offers a favourable chance for the company to generate sales from identifiable markets. A *strategic window* is a temporary period of optimum fit between the key requirements of a market and the particular capabilities of a company competing in that market. *Market requirements* relate to customers' needs or desired benefits. Market requirements are satisfied by components of the marketing mix that provide buyers with these benefits. *Environmental scanning* is the process of collecting information about the marketing

environment to help marketers identify opportunities and threats, and assist in planning. A company's *capabilities* relate to distinctive competencies that it has developed to do something well and efficiently. A company is likely to enjoy a differential advantage in an area in which its competencies and *marketing assets* out-do those of its potential competition. Marketing assets are a categorisation of an organisation's strengths or capabilities in terms of customer-facing assets; distribution-based assets; and internal, operational or resource assets.

» The *SWOT analysis* is little more than a set of checklists, but it is a popular tool for analysing the capabilities of an organisation in terms of strengths and weaknesses, and for linking identified opportunities and threats to these capabilities. So long as the analysis identifies the most important issues – supported with validation – and managers consider appropriate actions to address the emerging priorities, the SWOT analysis is useful for identifying necessary actions. It is important that any weaknesses that could be leveraged by competitors are rectified, and that managers strive to pre-empt any threats identified.

» Having evaluated the overall corporate vision, those responsible for devising the marketing strategy must build on their analysis of opportunities and internal capabilities by analytically assessing the most promising directions for their business and its marketing activity. *Ansoff's matrix* for determining competitive strategies is a suitable tool, offering four options: market penetration, market development, product development or diversification. *Strategic objectives* that can be implemented through marketing include intense growth, diversified growth and integrated growth. *Intense growth* includes *market penetration*, *market development* or *product development*. *Diversified growth* includes *horizontal*, *concentric* and *conglomerate diversification*. *Integrated growth* includes forwards, backwards and horizontal integration.

» Integral to achieving a company's corporate vision is the need to develop a loyal customer base of satisfied customers. It is essential to continuously improve the company's marketing programmes so as to address evolving target market customer needs and expectations. The market segmentation process of segmentation, targeting and positioning is a core element of a recommended marketing strategy. *Brand positioning* is the creation of a desirable, distinctive and plausible image for a brand that will have strong appeal for the customers in a target market segment. A *target market strategy* is the choice of which market segment(s) an organisation decides to prioritise and for which to develop marketing programmes.

» The *competition* is those organisations viewed as marketing products similar to, or substitutable for, a company's products, when targeted at the same customers. Strategists argue that organisations should work to attain a *competitive advantage*. While not always possible to achieve, success without a competitive advantage is unlikely in most markets. Competitive advantage is the achievement of superior performance vis-à-vis rivals: through differentiation to create distinctive product appeal or brand identity; through providing customer value and achieving the lowest delivered cost; or by focusing on narrowly scoped product categories or market niches so as to be viewed as a leading specialist. The so-called *generic routes to competitive advantage* are cost leadership, differentiation and focus, and are not mutually exclusive: while it is not possible to pursue all three routes to creating a competitive advantage, many businesses successfully pursue two of these routes.

» It is important to understand the nature of competition and to utilise this knowledge in determining a marketing strategy. Aspects of the marketing strategy should be purposely designed to maximise any weaknesses in competitors' activities and pre-empt any impending moves from rivals. As defined by Porter's *five competitive forces*, competitors should not be viewed only as like-for-like rivals: new entrants, substitute products or services, and the bargaining power of suppliers and of buyers can all form competitive

threats or opportunities. The competitive set must be defined by marketers, ensuring it reflects customers' views of direct alternatives and substitute options.

» In developing strategies, an organisation should consider the *competitive positions* in the marketplace. The *market leader* must both defend its position and seek new sales opportunities. Attack may prove the best form of defence. *Market challengers* must aggressively seek market share gains but carefully select the basis on which to attack: a chink in the leader's armour, for example, or a quick response to changing consumer needs. *Fast movers* may be small but they have the potential to win market share from rivals and should be combated. *Market followers* are the 'me-too, also-rans', prone to be squeezed in times of recession or in response to challengers' aggression. *Market nichers* specialise in terms of product and customer segment: they can very successfully tailor their marketing to their customers' needs but are vulnerable to competitors' entry into their target segments. To compete successfully, any organisation needs to consider the principles of *defensive* and *offensive warfare* and to understand its competitors' strategies through *competitor scanning*. The competitive positions proforma is an increasingly popular tool for evaluating competition across a company's segments or markets.

» An organisation should strive for a *differential advantage* or competitive edge in its markets. A differential advantage is an attribute of a brand, product, service or marketing mix that is desirable to targeted customers and provided by only one supplier. Marketers should emphasise the desirable attributes of a company's marketing mix that their target customers consider unmatched by competitors. The combined strengths, as identified in a SWOT analysis, and any differential advantages make up the *basis for competing*, which should form the leading edge of a company's marketing strategy.

» A marketing strategy must specify its core marketing objectives, typically defined in terms of market segments to address, desired market shares, customer satisfaction or brand awareness measures, profitability and financial contribution, plus any planned product and market developments. Without specification of objectives it is difficult to assess the performance of the marketing strategy or to ensure its fit with the overall corporate strategy.

⊗ The ingredients of the marketing mix – product, place/distribution, promotion, price and people issues – should be determined only after a marketing strategy has been specified. The marketing strategy must be decided only after the essential analyses of marketing – market trends, the marketing environment forces, customer buying behaviour, competition, opportunities and capabilities – have been undertaken. Analysis should come first, then strategic thinking and, finally, determination of

implementation programmes, as explained in Chapter 1's examination of the marketing process.

⊗ Marketing programmes depend on detailed marketing mix specifications, but also on the determination of budgets for implementing these marketing mix requirements. These budgets must reflect the sales forecast and trends in the targeted market segments. Sales and marketing personnel should take responsibility for implementing the marketing plan's recommendations, and schedules for marketing mix activity must be established. Implementation of a marketing strategy has to be facilitated, which involves specifying by whom, when, how and at what cost the desired marketing programmes will be implemented. These programmes must be evaluated against predetermined performance measures.

⊙ *Key Links*

The content of this chapter examining marketing strategy must be read after having understood the scope of marketing and the marketing process as outlined in chapter 1. Other links include:

- Chapter 3's explanation of the forces of the macro and micro marketing environment and the importance of environmental scanning.
- Chapter 6's discussion of the market segmentation process, central to developing a target market strategy.

Important Terms

Marketing strategy
Strategic market plan
Strategic business unit (SBU)
Strategic market planning
Marketing plan
Marketing programme
Mission
Corporate strategy
Marketing opportunity
Strategic window
Market requirements
Environmental scanning
Capabilities
Marketing assets
SWOT analysis

Ansoff matrix
Strategic objectives
Intense growth
Market penetration
Market development
Product development
Diversified growth
Horizontal diversification
Concentric diversification
Conglomerate diversification
Integrated growth
Brand positioning
Target market strategy
Competitors
Competitive advantage
Generic routes to competitive advantage
Competitive set
Five competitive forces
Competitive positions
Market leader
Market challengers
Fast movers
Market followers
Market nichers
Defensive warfare
Offensive warfare
Competitor scanning
Competitive positions proforma
Differential advantage
Basis for competing

Discussion and Review Questions

1 Why should an organisation develop a marketing strategy? What is the difference between strategic market planning and the strategy itself?

2 Identify the major components of strategic market planning and explain how they are interrelated.

3 In what ways do marketing environment forces affect strategic market planning? Give some specific examples.

4 What is a mission statement? Why must marketing strategists understand their organisation's corporate strategy?

5 What are some of the issues that must be considered in analysing an organisation's opportunities and resources? How do these issues affect marketing objectives and marketing strategy?

6 Why is marketing opportunity analysis necessary? What are the determinants of marketing opportunity?

7 What are the components of a SWOT analysis?

8 In relation to resource constraints, how can environmental scanning affect a company's long-term strategic market planning? Consider product costs and benefits affected by the environment.

9 What is the difference between market penetration, market development and product development?

10 Why do you think more companies are diversifying? Give some examples of diversified businesses.

11 Target marketing – the market segmentation process – is at the heart of a marketing strategy. Why must this be so?

12 What is competitive advantage?

13 Why should companies attempt to understand the strategies of their competitors? Explain your views.

14 How can a market leader best defend its competitive position?

15 What are the strengths of a market nicher? In what way is a nicher vulnerable?

16 What is meant by the term differential advantage? How does this relate to the concept of competitive advantage?

17 Why must a marketing strategy include detailed marketing objectives?

18 In what ways should implementation of a marketing strategy be facilitated?

Recommended Reading

- Aaker, D., *Strategic Marketing Management* (New York: Wiley, 2004).
- Adcock, D., *Marketing Strategies for Competitive Advantage* (Chichester: Wiley, 2000).
- Baker, M., *Marketing Strategy and Management* (Basingstoke: Palgrave Macmillan, 2007).
- Cravens, D. and Piercy, N., *Strategic Marketing* (London: McGraw-Hill, 2005).
- Littler, D. and Wilson, D., *Marketing Strategy* (Oxford: Butterworth-Heinemann, 1995).
- Porter, M.E., *Competitive Strategy: Techniques for Analysing Industries and Competitors* (New York: Free Press, 1980 and 2004).

🌐 Internet Exercise

Consider a large, well-known company with which you have regular dealings, such as a major retailer, financial institution or hotel group. Or select a supplier whose products you purchase frequently, such as Nestlé, Sony or Vodafone. Log on to the selected organisation's website.

Ignore the investors' pages, corporate information pages, PR releases, and so forth. Look at the site from the perspective of a customer and access only the customer-relevant pages (those to do with products, services, offers, customer services, stockist location, and so on).

1 What customer-relevant information is offered by the website you have chosen?

2 In what ways is the website striving to make the organisation appear 'special' or particularly good?

3 Given the website material, how would you interpret the selected strategy for this organisation? What is its apparent sense of purpose and what seem to be its leading priorities?

⚙ *Applied Mini-Case*

A decade ago, Korean car manufacturer Daewoo entered the European market with wacky advertising, innovative dealer arrangements and value-for-money cars. While based on dated car designs, the company nevertheless made reasonable inroads into the small and medium-sized car sectors. As part of Korea's well-publicised economic woes, conglomerate Daewoo headed for bankruptcy. The car business was acquired by strategic partner General Motors of the USA in 2002. A new corporate identity for Daewoo followed, as well as a relaunch for the brand in 2003.

General Motors, known for Vauxhall and Opel in Europe, owns the Chevrolet marque in the States, which is the company's value-based range and marque. General Motors had to consider how to roll out its Chevrolet marque in Europe. Should it try to sell existing Chevrolet models in Europe, or develop more European-looking models for European consumers? Should Chevrolet establish a new dealer network in Europe, be sold alongside the Vauxhall and Opel ranges in existing GM dealers, or be retailed by third parties or through the Internet? Or should the Daewoo range of cars and dealers in Europe be rebadged as Chevrolet? Perhaps a mix of these options would be preferable? These questions were not easy to answer and General Motor's senior managers agonised for some time to determine their strategy. The best approach is still being considered.

❓ Question

As the senior marketer tasked to assess the market's probable response to these options, what steps would you take?

❀ Case Study

St Andrew's Healthcare: a Charity's Marketing Strategy

St Andrew's Healthcare in Northampton is the market leader in many types of mental health care in the UK. In addition to its large site in Northampton, St Andrew's has created satellite facilities in the south-east of England. As a leading specialist provider, the organisation's patients are referred to its hospitals from throughout the UK and beyond.

As a charity, its focus is not on helping mental health sufferers in the community, or charity shop-style fundraising, or increasing the general public's awareness of mental health issues – other charities and bodies address these important tasks. St Andrew's Healthcare is a fully specified hospital with leading experts, state-of-the-art care pathways and an eminent reputation within the mental health care profession. St Andrew's divisions address everything from adolescent learning difficulties through to major behavioural problems, with patients requiring secure accommodation and lengthy treatment programmes. It has a specialist unit dealing with brain injuries and, through an on-site partner, also offers clinic facilities for patients needing to 'dry out'. Its staff are recognised as being leading-edge thinkers.

The St Andrew's brand reputation is based on the quality of its care, its multiple care pathways and its ability to relate to patients, their families, and to the medical staff or personnel in social services who refer patients to the hospital. St Andrew's has charitable status, but strives to set its fees sufficiently high to permit it to provide the high-quality care that is at the core of its ethos, and to continually reinvest in its facilities and treatment programmes.

Despite its success, its diversity of operations places significant demands on its capital spending: wards and facilities require modernising, newly devised care programmes may require remodelled facilities, the expansion of demand led by reduced state provision of mental health facilities pressurises the organisation's caring professionals to provide expanded facilities. Private-sector commercial businesses have entered the more financially lucrative parts of the market. St Andrew's must defend its position in these segments, as fee income from these activities is required to support the hospital as a whole and to cross-subsidise other segments of the market deemed less financially attractive by new-entrant competitors. In order to defend its market share in these segments, the hospital has to develop marketing strategies and devote resources to marketing programmes designed to maintain the loyalty of referring GPs, medical consultants and social workers. The requirement is growing to tailor marketing messages to a growing mix of audiences. Commercially minded competitors are developing 'glitzy' marketing programmes and St Andrew's has to maintain its visibility to key stakeholders in this quickly evolving marketplace.

While some patients deal directly with the charity, the vast majority are referred from the National Health Service (NHS). St Andrew's has a reputation for being able to deal with difficult patients suffering from complex problems. However, the NHS is increasingly moving towards centralised buying, with numerous NHS Trusts joining forces in order to be able to purchase services – such as those offered by St Andrew's – at lower rates. In addition to the medical staff diagnosing the patients' problems and recommending appropriate courses of treatment, the NHS has risk assessors, financial managers and professional purchasing executives, who all are involved in the decisions concerning which treatment programme to purchase and from which provider. For St Andrew's and other suppliers to the NHS, such formalised purchasing and group decision-making complicate the marketing activity and the engagement programmes the charity runs with its 'customers'. For the patient, to his/her family, to the referring medical staff and the numerous administrators involved, St Andrew's must develop bespoke messages, marketing communications and client-handling programmes. This complex buying centre must be addressed for St Andrew's to operate with full bed occupancy, in order to fulfil its mission to truly help those suffering with mental health problems.

The organisation has responded to these market forces by developing a corporate strategy and a marketing strategy, by allocating resources to producing and implementing marketing programmes, and by recruiting a set of marketing managers to support the various divisions' marketing activities.

Sources: St Andrew's Healthcare, 2004–8; James Watkins, director of marketing and strategy, St Andrew's Healthcare, 2003–8; *Marketing Briefs*, Sally Dibb and Lyndon Simkin (Oxford: Elsevier Butterworth-Heinemann), 2004.

❷ Questions for Discussion

1 For a non-profit organisation such as St Andrew's Healthcare, what aspects of a marketing strategy will be the most important?
2 Why are organisations such as St Andrew's Healthcare turning to marketing and the development of marketing strategies?
3 In what ways would a strategic market plan benefit St Andrew's Healthcare?

Mattel's Barbie
Mattel Takes on the World

Mattel, with $6 billion in annual revenues, is the world leader in the design, manufacture and marketing of children's toys. The company's major toy brands include: Barbie, with more than 120 different Barbie dolls, Fisher-Price, Disney entertainment lines, Hot Wheels and Matchbox cars, Tyco Toys and Polly Pocket, plus many well known games, including Scrabble (International), Outburst and Rebound. The company markets toys and games bearing the names of children's favourites Barney, Bear in The Big Blue House, Blue's Clues, Dora The Explorer, Sesame Street, Winnie The Pooh, Angelina Ballerina, Toy Story, Harry Potter, Rugrats and the Wild ThornBerrys.

In addition, Mattel promotes global sales by tailoring toys for specific international global markets, instead of simply modifying established favourites from company's base in the United States. The company's Headquarters are in El Segundo, California, but Mattel also has offices in 36 countries. In fact, the company markets its products in more than 155 countries throughout the world.

Mattel's marketing prowess and reach have paid off. For example, in a poll conducted by the annual *Power Brands* study, Mattel had strong popularity among consumers: as many as four out of ten people said that if they were shopping for toys, Mattel would be the preferred brand. Retailers also singled out Mattel as the number-one performer, mentioned six out of ten times. This survey proved that both children and adults are enthusiastic about Mattel and its line of products. In 2002, the Mattel and Fisher-Price names topped a survey of consumers who were asked about their brand preferences when buying toys in discount stores or superstores, also mentioning Barbie and Hot Wheels repeatedly. Mattel owned all of the leaders in this US survey's report of top toy brands. Similar surveys in the UK, Benelux and Germany also rate the company's

brands in the 'top ten' for toys. In 2007 Mattel was voted one of the best companies to work for, while an international survey of consumers in 2008 rated the company as one of the best known toy brands in the world.

Customer Orientation at Mattel

Mattel's management philosophy focuses on satisfying the customer's needs and wants. For example, Mattel redesigned Barbie to more naturally reflect a 'normal' athletic woman in an attempt to meet the demands for a more realistic doll. Barbie has also taken on many different professions in order to reach a wider audience. These product modifications and extensions are designed to meet consumer and social demands while still accomplishing company objectives. Some Hot Wheels cars, for example, now display the logos of famous racing teams and major championships around the world, in an attempt to meet the consumer demand for more merchandise related to this popular televised sport.

Mattel's pursuit of interactive multimedia is an attempt to adapt to the shorter span of time that young girls want to spend playing with Barbie and other dolls and more traditional toys. Increasingly children are turning to more interactive toys sooner than was the case in previous years, and Mattel's acquisition of *The Learning Company* was designed to meet this demand. This acquisition, however, did not prove profitable for Mattel, and the company eventually sold the division. This acquisition and disposal demonstrates the company's awareness of evolving customer trends and also a ruthless management of its portfolio against clearly laid down performance measures.

As another indicator of its commitment to customers, Mattel employs marketing research to ensure that its strategy and tactics match customer desires. This is combined with product research and development in an effort to release new products yearly, based on these consumer needs and wants. A recent addition to the Mattel product lines includes the new construction and activity set called Ello, now receiving significant marketing communications support. The product is meant to compete with Lego AG and draws girls to building toys, which traditionally have been marketed almost exclusively to boys. Mattel research teams watched girls play with pipe cleaners, scissors, glue, paper and cardboard. The results indicated that girls wanted to make panels and tell stories about the space created. The idea behind Ello is to build a house or figures using interconnecting plastic shapes, allowing girls to build and create while engaging in social play. Mattel hopes Ello will be a globally recognised brand with a unique name that does not require translation.

2007 was a bad year in the company's enviable history, owing to a series of product safety scares which stemmed from poor manufacturing processes and controls in certain Chinese factories contracted to manufacture some of the company's lines. Although retailers were forced to de-stock a few lines in 2007, following the series of product safety recalls, consumer confidence in Mattel was not for long dented. The company's investment in product development and continuous product improvements, had provided a heritage and reputation that few toy-buying consumers could resist for long. A year later, the company's financial performance had been repaired.

Mattel's Core Products

Barbie

The first Barbie doll sported open-toed shoes, a ponytail, sunglasses, earrings and a zebra-striped bathing suit, with fashions and accessories also available for the doll. While buyers at the annual Toy Fair in New York City took no interest in the Barbie doll, little girls of the time certainly did. The intense demand seen at the retail stores was insufficiently met for several years: Mattel could simply not produce the Barbie dolls fast enough. Barbie is one of Mattel's major product lines, accounting for more than 50 per cent of its total

sales. Around the world, Barbie-related merchandise from Mattel is worth a staggering $3.6 billion at retail prices, making it by far the number one girl's brand globally.

March 1999 marked the 40th anniversary of Barbie. It also heralded a new Barbie campaign, called 'Be Anything', which focused on encouraging girls to become anything, from athletes to computer experts to dreamers. A Barbie doll is barely present in the Be Anything advert, and not one of Barbie's accessories appears. The whole campaign is an attempt to retain the interest of girls for another two years after the usual post-Barbie age of seven and to make Barbie more 'real' with these older girls.

However, by August 2002, Barbie's popularity had slipped and she failed to make the list of the top-five-selling dolls. Mattel reacted by introducing a line of My Scene dolls, which includes a multi-cultural Barbie, aimed at older girls referred to as 'tweens'. The 'tween' market is comprised of girls between ages 8 and 12 who would rather watch MTV than play with dolls. A website at www.myscene.com engages girls in the lives of four friends living in the 'big city' through short 'shows' and music videos. Other efforts targeted at 'tweens' include a crime solving crew called the Mystery Squad and the Barbie Doll as Elle Woods, which is a tribute to the blonde character in the MGM Pictures movie *Legally Blond 2: Red, White and Blonde*. The new lines have given Barbie a fresh lease of life: she stood for election in the last US Presidential elections, supported by a full PR campaign.

Hot Wheels

With millions of boys aged 5–15 collecting Hot Wheels cars, this line of small die-cast vehicles is now involved with almost every racing circuit in the world, including NASCAR (National Association for Stock Car Auto Racing), Formula One (F1), NHRA (National Hot Rod Association), CART (Championship Auto Racing Teams), AMA (American Motorcycle Association), and many other circuits. This immense popularity has created a group of young collectors: the average boy collector owns more than 40 Hot Wheels cars.

Hot Wheels celebrated its 35th Anniversary in 2003, with a massive marketing campaign called the Hot Wheels Highway 35 World Race. Mattel is creating a story-based and character-based package that includes collectible cars, racetracks, comic books, home videos, a video game, a television network special and an online race. The idea is to appeal to the many different age groups of collectors Mattel has acquired in more recent years.

Fisher-Price

Acquired in 1993 as a wholly owned subsidiary, Fisher-Price is the umbrella brand for all of Mattel's infant and pres-school lines. The brand is trusted by parents all over the world and appears on everything from children's software to eyewear and books to bicycles. Some of the more classic products include the Rock-a-Stack and Little People play sets. New favourites include Power Wheels vehicles and Rescue Heroes, a line of fire-fighter action figures. Through licensing agreements, the brand also develops character-based toys such as Sesame Street's Elmo and Big Bird, plus Disney's Winnie the Pooh and Mickey Mouse.

Fisher-Price has built trust with parents by creating products that are educational, safe and useful. In recent years, the brand has earned high regard for innovative car seats and nursery monitors. While not toys, these baby and toddler products are sold to parents already familiar with the company's reputation and often they are retailed in the same stores as Mattel's toys. The company continues to innovate in its core business, too: one project includes collaboration with Microsoft to develop an activity table that teaches children from infants to pre-schoolers with 'smart technology'.

International Sales

Under CEO Robert A. Eckert's leadership, Mattel maintained its strategy of strong expansion overseas with a goal of raising international sales, from 34 per cent in 2002 to 50 per cent of overall sales by 2010. Of the sales outside the North American homeland, close to two-thirds are in Europe and one-third in Latin America, with a small amount in the Asia-Pacific region. International sales have typically increased by 10 per cent each year. The international segment has benefited from Mattel's strategic focus on globalisation of brands, including improved product availability, better alignment of worldwide marketing and sales plans, plus strong product launches.

Worldwide, Mattel's most recognised product continues to be Barbie. In a study conducted by Interbrand and published in *Business Week*, Barbie was the only Mattel brand that made the overall list of the *The 100 Best Global Brands*. However, the traditional Barbie doll has not received a warm welcome in some international markets. The Malaysian Consumers' Association of Penanghas tried to ban Barbie because of her non-Asian appearance and the lack of creativity needed to play with her. Public and media outcry soon rebuffed protests against the ban. Government agencies in other countries, such as Iran, are carrying out similar campaigns against Barbie.

Ethics and Responsibility at Mattel

Like most organisations, Mattel has recognised the different responsibilities it has to various stakeholders, including customers, employees, investors, suppliers and the community. These stakeholders have some claim, or stake, in Mattel's products, markets, and business outcomes. Mattel demonstrates a commitment to economic, legal, ethical and philanthropic responsibilities.

Mattel's core products and business environment can present ethical issues. For example, since the company's products are designed primarily for children, the company must be sensitive about children's rights. In addition, the international environment often complicates business transactions, especially in the areas of employee rights and safety in manufacturing facilities. Different legal systems and cultural expectations about business can create ethical conflict. The use of technology may also present ethical dilemmas, especially with regard to consumer privacy. Mattel has recognised these potential issues and has taken steps to strengthen its commitment to business ethics and social responsibility. Advances in technology have created special issues for Mattel's marketing efforts. Mattel has recognised that because it markets to children, it has the responsibility to communicate with parents about its corporate marketing strategy. The company has taken special steps to inform both children and adults about its philosophy regarding Internet-based marketing tools, such as the Hot Wheels website.

At the Barbie.com website, parents are encouraged to read and follow the suggestions provided by Mattel on Internet safety. This parents' page provides tips for creating rules and regulations for their children's use of the Internet. There is also an example of an Internet Safety Promise for children and parents to complete, forming a type of 'contract' to engage in smart, safe and responsible behaviour when surfing the Internet.

As this case has shown, while the last few years have challenged Mattel's executive leadership and financial standing, the company also made great strides in respect to its ethical and social responsibilities. Today, Mattel faces many market opportunities and threats, including the rate at which children are maturing and abandoning toys, the role of technology in consumer products, purchasing power and consumer needs in global markets. Mattel has much sales growth potential, especially in the international markets. For a company that began with two friends making picture frames, Mattel has demonstrated marketing dexterity and the ability to keep abreast of market developments. The next few years will test the company's resolve and strategy within the highly competitive, yet highly lucrative, toy market, but few toy producers have such a strong portfolio of children's favourite brands.

Questions for Discussion

1 Describe Mattel's target marketing for Barbie and Hot Wheels. How does the company's marketing strategy appeal to these target markets?

2 How has Mattel tried to be a socially responsible company in its world markets?

3 What environmental forces have created challenges for Mattel as it continues expansion moves into global markets? Which have created opportunities?

II Understanding Markets

As explained in chapter 1, a major role for marketers is to help in identifying opportunities to pursue and threats to combat. An assessment of external market drivers and dynamics – known as the forces of the marketing environment – is of fundamental importance not only to marketers but to anyone inside an organisation involved with strategic planning.

Customers should be at the centre of the marketing process. Organisations – whether for-profit or not-for-profit – must target specific groups of customers or stakeholders, understand their needs and endeavour through their marketing activities to satisfy these customer needs.

Lou Linwei/Alamy

Part II of _Marketing Essentials_ examines the concept of the marketing environment before exploring thoroughly the nature of consumer buying behaviour and buying processes, and purchasing behaviour in business markets.

Having developed an understanding of a marketplace and particularly the customers within, marketers must then develop a target market strategy. This should identify which customers they wish to target, what positioning they intend to use and which approach will provide an advantage over competitors. Part II includes, therefore, an explanation of target market strategy selection and the all-important concept of market segmentation.

There are times when managers' existing knowledge of their customers is sufficient for marketing decision-making, or when they are content to trust their intuition. On many occasions, however, marketers may not feel confident with the level of marketing intelligence available and will instigate marketing research in order to fill any gaps in their understanding of customers, competitors or market trends. The nature, uses and types of marketing research are introduced in the final chapter of Part II of _Marketing Essentials_.

Part II explores the essential concepts for developing an understanding of markets and a target market strategy.

Chapter 3, 'The Marketing Environment', examines the many forces at work in a market over which consumers and organisations have little or no control but which tangibly affect the nature of the products and services marketed. These forces of what is termed 'the macro marketing environment' include economic, political, legal, regulatory, societal and technological impacts. Competitive forces – 'the micro marketing environment' – often have a more specific impact on individual organisations. The chapter also examines the concept of environmental scanning, the process many organisations use to address the marketing environment, before discussing the concept of strategic windows of opportunity created by the forces of the marketing environment.

Chapter 4, 'Consumer Buying Behaviour', describes the various types of consumer buying behaviour, the stages of consumer buying decision-making and the different categories of buying decisions. The chapter examines how personal, psychological and social factors influence the consumer buying decision process. Finally, chapter 4 explains why marketers must understand consumer buying behaviour and use their understanding to determine a target market strategy. Having an understanding of customers' buying is fundamental to the marketing concept and to developing a marketing orientation.

Chapter 5, 'Business Markets and Business Buying Behaviour', familiarises readers with the various types of business markets, identifies the major characteristics of business-to-business buyers and transactions, outlines the attributes of business-to-business demand and presents the concept of the buying centre. The chapter emphasises the notion of relationship marketing and exchanges between business buyers and sellers. The focus then shifts to the stages of the business buying process and the factors that influence it. The chapter concludes by examining how to select and analyse business target markets.

Chapter 6, 'Segmenting Markets, Targeting and Positioning', explains the core aspect of developing a marketing strategy: the process of target market strategy selection. The chapter commences by defining the concept of a market and outlining the various types of markets. The focus then shifts to how organisations segment markets, how they make targeting decisions and prioritise target markets, and how they determine a brand or product positioning strategy for each segment selected as a target market. The chapter also highlights how important it is for an organisation to attempt to develop a compelling proposition versus its competitors in the market(s) it has chosen to target, as explained in chapter 2.

Chapter 7, 'Marketing Research', explains the importance of research in marketing decision-making, distinguishes between research and intuition in solving marketing problems, and outlines the basic steps for conducting formal marketing research. The fundamental methods of gathering data for marketing research are examined. The chapter then introduces the wide variety of available marketing research tools and explains their relative pros and cons. The chapter also considers ethical issues regarding marketing research.

By the conclusion of Part II of *Marketing Essentials*, readers should understand the concepts of the marketing environment, buying behaviour in consumer and business-to-business markets, the fundamentals of target market strategy selection, and the nature and use of marketing research.

3
The Marketing Environment

"**All businesses operate within an environment, which directly or indirectly affects the way in which they function, just as we as consumers live within a cultural and social environment which to a greater or lesser degree determines the way in which we behave as individuals.**"

Elaine O'Brien, University of Strathclyde

Objectives

- To understand the concept of the marketing environment and the importance of environmental scanning and analysis

- To explore the broad forces of the macro marketing environment: political forces relevant to marketers, the influence of laws on marketing practices, the impact of government regulations and self-regulatory agencies, societal issues important to marketers, the effects of new technology on society and marketing activities, economic and competitive factors and their impact on organisations and customers' willingness and ability to buy

- To examine the company-specific micro marketing environment forces: the organisation, suppliers, marketing intermediaries, buyers, competitors and other publics

- To understand the role of the marketing environment in marketing opportunity analysis and the importance of strategic windows

Introduction

This chapter explores the external forces that impact on an organisation's trading and ability to satisfy its customers. These forces, over which organisations rarely have any direct control, are termed the *marketing environment* and fall into two categories: the macro and the micro forces of the marketing environment.

The very broad forces are the *macro marketing environment*: the political, legal, regulatory, societal, technological, and economic/competitive forces that impact on all organisations operating in a market and on their ability to carry out their affairs. Authors have increasingly distinguished these broad forces from an additional set of more company-specific external forces termed the *micro marketing environment* forces. These micro marketing environment forces are mostly aspects of the competitive arena.

After defining the marketing environment and considering why it is necessary for marketers to *scan* and analyse these forces, each of these macro and micro forces is discussed. Awareness of these issues and trends may create *strategic windows* of opportunity. Ignorance of such forces jeopardises an organisation's ability to perform well and may leave the organisation more vulnerable to the actions of more aware competitors.

Opener

Regulatory Influence: the EU Single Market

In 1947 the launching of the Marshall Plan presented a blueprint for the economic reconstruction of a Europe devastated by the Second World War. This led in 1948 to the creation of the Organisation for European Economic Co-operation (OEEC), the precursor of today's economic union. In March 1957 the Treaty of Rome was signed to establish the European Economic Community (EEC). By 1973, with the arrival of Denmark, Ireland and the UK, the EEC had grown to nine member states. Greece joined in 1981 and Portugal and Spain in 1986 to create the 'Euro 12'. The momentous signing of the Maastricht Treaty in 1992 established the European Union (EU) and by 1 January 1993 the European single market was at last a reality. The single market is defined by the EU as 'an economic area within which persons, goods, services and capital have unrestricted freedom of movement, which entails not only the elimination of customs barriers, but also of technical, tax and legislative obstacles'. By 2004, membership had swelled to 25 countries, including many eastern European countries, such as the Czech Republic, Estonia, Hungary, Latvia, Lithuania, Poland, Slovakia and Slovenia, plus Mediterranean countries Cyprus, Greece and Malta. Bulgaria and Romania joined in 2007. Applicant countries include and Turkey, Croatia, Serbia, Bosnia, Montenegro, Albania and Macedonia, leaving only Norway and Russia as major countries not seeking membership.

The single market has had a significant impact on the populations of member and non-member trading states, as well as on marketers representing their companies. With the removal of so many bureaucratic barriers on 1 January 1993, professionally qualified personnel could seek employment without retraining in other member states; companies could tender for government contracts throughout the EU; imports and exports became subject to far fewer restrictions, less 'red tape', reduced customs controls and much freer movement within and between EU states. Immigration and travel have become much quicker and simpler than before. Health and safety working regulations have been harmonised, as have air travel regulations and even standards for mobile phone networks and VAT collection. The creation of the euro – the currency to which many member states are now signed up – further simplified cross-border business transactions and travel arrangements.

The EU has many critics, not least due to its Common Agricultural Policy (CAP), which takes more than half of the entire EU budget, is a significant drain on the resources of the richer member states and is currently being renegotiated. There are moans about the often top-heavy bureaucracy of European government in Brussels; and the inevitable formalisation of a great number of working practices when so many countries' rules and regulations are combined to form a single, cohesive approach. The financial conditions that must be met in order to participate in the euro, and the apparent flouting of these conditions by certain 'major league' member states, have added to the criticisms. The inclusion of seemingly 'weaker' eastern European economies has concerned people in the western European economies, which may well cross-subsidise these new member economies. However, there are few marketers who would claim that in the years since the harmonisation of Europe in 1993, doing business across Europe has not been simplified, opening up significant marketing opportunities for many businesses and presenting new competitive threats. The recent expansion of EU membership – doubling the number of consumers inside the single market – is of great interest to marketers. The EU continues to present new challenges and a reason to rethink marketing strategies. There is little doubt that the EU is an external factor in the marketing environment of most businesses and consumers that cannot be ignored.

Sources: EU policy documents, 1990–2007; *Europe in Figures*, Eurostat, Luxembourg, 1995; *Europe on the Move, From Single Market to European Union, Internal Market* – all EU, Brussels, publications; the BBC, 2007. Photo: Courtesy of Alain Dixon.

The EU has a tremendous impact on the decisions and activities of marketers. The regulations and legal directives produced by the EU, plus the financial implications of many of its policies – such as the CAP and the criteria for participating in the euro – are aspects of the macro marketing environment. This chapter discusses both macro and micro forces, commencing with the broader macro issues. It includes a discussion of why and how marketers scan the forces of the marketing environment. The chapter concludes with an examination of how an understanding of these marketing environment forces assists a company in identifying strategic windows and maximising marketing opportunities.

Examining and Responding to the Marketing Environment

Marketing environment
The external forces that directly or indirectly influence an organisation's acquisition of inputs and generation of outputs, comprising six categories of forces: political, legal, regulatory, societal/ Green, technological, and economic/ competitive

The **marketing environment** consists of external forces that directly or indirectly influence an organisation's acquisition of inputs and generation of outputs. Inputs might include personnel, financial resources, raw materials and information. Outputs could be information such as advertisements or packages, goods, services and ideas. As indicated in Chapter 1 and as shown in Figure 1.4, the broad marketing environment consists of six categories of forces: political, legal, regulatory, societal/Green, technological and economic/competitive. Although there are numerous environmental factors, most fall into one of these six categories. These are termed the 'macro forces' of the marketing environment as they affect all organisations operating in a particular market. In addition, many authors have identified a set of issues termed the 'micro forces' of the marketing environment. These micro forces are more situation- and organisation-specific, including the organisation's internal environment, suppliers, marketing intermediaries, buyers, competitors and the organisation's publics.

Whether they fluctuate rapidly or slowly, environmental forces are always dynamic. Changes in the marketing environment can create uncertainty, threats and opportunities for marketers. Although the future is not very predictable, marketers can estimate what will happen, although some fail to do so, thus negatively affecting the performance of their businesses. Astute marketers continually modify their marketing strategies in response to the dynamic environment. Marketing managers who fail to recognise changes in environmental forces leave their companies unprepared to capitalise on marketing opportunities or to cope with threats created by changes in the environment.

Organisations that cannot deal with an unfavourable environment are at risk of going under.[1] For example, during the OPEC-led recession of the mid-1970s many manufacturers cut back on their workforces, causing unemployment rates of over 40 per cent in many suburbs. Many local retailers and small shopkeepers, restaurants, take-aways and garages had anticipated neither the extent of the unemployment nor its effect on their businesses. Dozens of small, local businesses closed down. The 1990 Persian Gulf Crisis caused huge increases in the price of petrol, repeated in 2004 following the start of the latest Gulf War. In the 1990s, the car-buying public became even more concerned about fuel consumption, with a resultant decline in the sales of high-performance sports cars and executive saloons, causing problems for manufacturers such as Porsche and Jaguar. The Gulf Crisis also hit business travel and tourism, affecting the fortunes of many airlines and hotel operators. Civil war in the former Yugoslavia had tragic implications for the peoples of that region and an economic impact on the tour operators who specialised in holidays to the Yugoslav coast. The BSE beef crisis affected farmers, meat producers and supermarkets. Genetically modified (GM) foods caused a more recent storm with implications for food manufacturers and supermarkets. The activities of terrorists have had a significant impact on companies and the general public in many countries, with tourism and airline operators being particularly badly affected. Sub-prime mortgages have led to recent economic troubles. Monitoring the marketing environment is crucial to an organisation's survival and to the long-term achievement of its goals.

Environmental Scanning and Analysis

Environmental scanning
The process of collecting information about the forces in the marketing environment

Environmental analysis
The process of assessing and interpreting the information gathered through environmental scanning

To monitor changes in the marketing environment effectively, marketers must engage in environmental scanning and analysis. **Environmental scanning** is the process of collecting information about the forces in the marketing environment. Scanning involves: observation; keeping 'an ear to the ground'; perusal of secondary sources, such as the web, business, trade, government and general interest publications; and marketing research. However, managers must be careful not to gather so much information that sheer volume makes analysis impossible. **Environmental analysis** is the process of assessing and interpreting the information gathered through environmental scanning. A manager evaluates the information for accuracy, tries to resolve inconsistencies in the data and, if warranted, assigns significance to the findings. Through analysis, a marketing manager seeks to describe current environmental changes and to predict future changes. By evaluating these changes, the manager should be able to determine possible threats and opportunities linked to environmental fluctuations. Understanding the current state of the marketing environment and recognising the threats and opportunities arising from changes within it, help marketing managers assess the performance of current marketing efforts and develop marketing strategies for the future. The Marketing Tools and Techniques box below describes how organisations often conduct an analysis of the marketing environment.

Marketing Tools and Techniques

Practitioners' Assessment of the Macro Marketing Environment

The marketing environment forces are not obviously part of an individual's routine job specification, particularly within the marketing function. However, businesses must monitor these forces through environmental scanning in order to pre-empt possible problems caused by unfavourable market developments, but also in order to leverage any emerging opportunities ahead of competitors. The identification of strategic windows and the chance to take first mover advantage are desires among senior managers and marketers.

The forces of the micro marketing environment and competitive pressures are usually evaluated within a marketing team's analysis of competition (see Chapter 2). Companies must examine the macro forces, too, however. While research indicates that many fail to do so, 'best practice' companies typically adopt one of two approaches to assessing their marketing environments.

1 Individual managers or small work groups are allocated to each of the macro forces: social, economic, legal, regulatory, political, technological. As 'champions' for their allocated topic, such managers collate intelligence from stakeholders, employees and external sources in order to build up a picture of the key trends and developments. These managers either suggest the emerging implications for their business and make recommendations, or they present their findings at a sales and marketing meeting or to senior managers for their debate and consideration. The development of company intranets has significantly assisted the networking so important for the collation of topical and relevant information.

2 An organisation may intermittently stage workshops to which cross-functional and multi-hierarchical personnel are invited. For example, R&D personnel may be aware of technological trends, the company secretary of legal or regulatory issues, the salesforce of economic or social forces, and so on. Typically, each of the macro marketing environment forces is discussed in turn, in a 'brainstorming' exercise. Certain themes or 'hot topics' then emerge to be debated further within the workshop. The company then allocates an individual manager or creates a small taskforce to examine a particular issue in more detail, in order to subsequently develop an action plan based on more information.

Some companies invite external experts, suppliers, partners or even customers to such a workshop. If these external opinions are not sought as part of the workshop, any planned activity by the business resulting from this workshop-based analysis must await some external validation after the workshop.

Such sessions are an excellent way in which a business can harness the expertise across its functions and within its marketing channel in order to prioritise actions that should minimise the impact of a negative external development or maximise an emerging opportunity.

In this type of forum, the senior management team – supported by functional experts and channel partner personnel – brainstormed the key issues from the macro marketing environment for a leading insurance business. The priorities emerged as shown in the list (right).

While some of these forces, such as the weather, were outside the influence of the business, many of them could be addressed. Indeed, while the weather could not be altered, the company did decide to re-examine its exposure to flood plain customers and modified its policy cover accordingly.

Within each of these rather broad-brush summary bullets lay much detail to explore and to discuss. An example of a resulting action was to more closely manage the activities of the field salesforce, harnessing the latest mobile office technology solutions and customer relationship management field systems. As a result, the already low level of client complaints for inappropriate selling approaches virtually disappeared, and the highly ethical stance in controlling the salesforce bolstered the company's brand reputation and thereby its ability to recruit high-calibre personnel. This strategy also reflected the growing litigious culture among consumers and thereby addressed another of the trends identified during the workshop.

It is important to have a good mix of inputs – market information and personnel – to any assessment of the macro forces of the marketing environment, and to solicit the views of stakeholders other than those participating in the session. For example, partners, channel members, market analysts, industry experts or consultants, and even customers, are all useful sources both for marketing intelligence and for checking out suggested action plans.

Having identified the key issues – the macro marketing environment forces – currently of relevance, the business must consider the implications. The 'So what does this mean to us and to our business?' question has to be answered. Is the issue a threat or an opportunity? What resulting actions must be taken? Certain trends and developments may pose a threat, while other forces may be creating an opportunity. Sometimes, the same issue is both an opportunity and a threat. In the above example, had this company failed to implement changes to its field force's working practices, it would not have bolstered its reputation or improved the completion rate of its sales representatives. Worse, rivals may have been able to steal a march and measures designed to minimise the likelihood of client litigation would not now be in place.

© Dibb/Simkin

Note: a more extensive explanation of this technique is offered in either *The Market Segmentation Workbook* (Dibb and Simkin) or *The Marketing Planning Workbook* (Dibb, Simkin and Bradley), both originally published in 1996 by Thomson, London, or in the authors' newer titles *Market Segmentation Success: Making It Happen!* (The Haworth Press, 2008) and *Marketing Planning* (Cengage Learning, 2008).

The Macro Marketing Environment for a Leading Insurance Company

- Stock market (worthless investments, own share price/company value)
- New/more regulations (FSA, Gov, EU, within client sectors, accountancy)
- Over/under capacity in the industry/key sectors
- Many mergers and changes to the competitive set
- Structural changes in the sector and for clients
- Emerging compensation culture amongst clients and brokers
- Customers' expectation of better advice
- Greater role for technology (CRM, online quotes/claims, e-business)
- Distribution channel developments (role of brokers, e-commerce, tele-business, retailer new entrants)
- Recruitment problems/inability to make the sector attractive
- Global warming/changes to weather: greater claims

JCB, the construction equipment producer, allocated to individual managers the task of monitoring aspects of the macro marketing environment: political, legal, regulatory, societal (particularly the Green movement), technological, economic and competitive. A small committee met to prepare short papers and presentations to interested colleagues. When the laws relating to roadworks were amended, making contractors responsible for the safety of their sites and the long-term quality of the re-laid road surface, JCB recognised that many of its customers would have to alter their working practices as a result. So the company produced guides to assist these contractors in responding to the new legislation. In so doing, JCB was able to enhance its image and reputation as a leading player in the industry, and at the same time promote its products.

Responding to Environmental Forces

In responding to environmental forces, marketing managers can take two general approaches: accept environmental forces as uncontrollable or confront and mould them. If environmental forces are viewed as uncontrollable, the organisation remains passive and reactive towards the environment. Instead of trying to influence forces in the environment, its marketing managers tend to adjust current marketing strategies to environmental changes. They approach marketing opportunities discovered through environmental scanning and analysis with caution. On the other hand, marketing managers who believe that environmental forces can be shaped adopt a proactive approach. For example, if a market is blocked by traditional environmental constraints, marketing

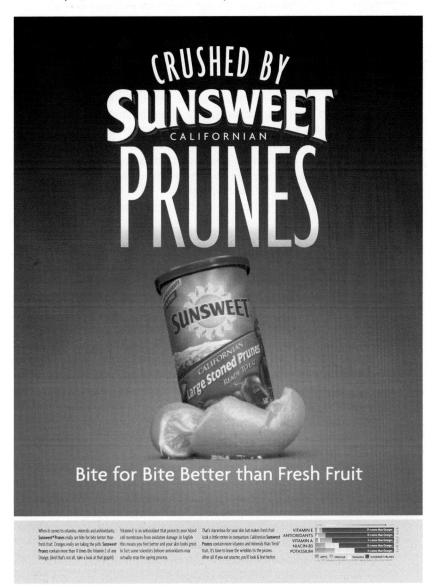

Figure 3.1
The growing social awareness of healthy eating and the problems of obesity have created opportunities for many products, including Sunsweet's prunes Source: Courtesy of Sunsweet

77

managers may apply economic, psychological, political and promotional skills to gain access to it or operate within it. Once they identify what blocks a marketing opportunity, marketers can assess the power of the various parties involved and develop strategies to try to overcome environmental forces.[2]

In trying to influence environmental forces, marketers may seek to either create new marketing opportunities or extract greater benefits relative to costs from existing marketing opportunities. For instance, a company losing sales to competitors with lower-priced products may strive to develop technology that would make its production processes more efficient; greater efficiency would allow it to lower the prices of its own products. Political action is another way of affecting environmental forces. UK retailers, for example, successfully lobbied government to permit longer Sunday trading and legal opening of retail outlets all day. Airlines such as bmi lobbied government ministers to persuade the EU to enact its 'open skies' policy, providing more routes and landing slots for its planes. A proactive approach can be constructive and bring desired results. However, managers must recognise that there are limits on how much an environmental force can be shaped and that these limits vary across environmental forces. Although an organisation may be able to influence the enactment of laws through lobbying, it is unlikely that a single organisation can significantly increase the national birth rate or move the economy from recession to prosperity!

Generalisations are not possible. It cannot be stated that either of these approaches to environmental response is better than the other. For some organisations, the passive, reactive approach is more appropriate, but for other companies, the aggressive approach leads to better performance. What is certain is that ignorance of the forces of the marketing environment leads to problems and creates opportunities for rivals. The selection of a particular approach depends on an organisation's managerial philosophies, objectives, financial resources, customers and human skills, and on the specific composition of the set of environmental forces within which the organisation operates.

The rest of this chapter explores in detail the macro and micro marketing environment forces, and then examines the link between an understanding of these issues and marketing opportunity analysis.

Political Forces

The political, legal and regulatory forces of the marketing environment are closely interrelated. Legislation is enacted, legal decisions are interpreted by the courts, and regulatory agencies are created and operated, for the most part, by people elected or appointed to political offices or by civil servants. Legislation and regulations (or the lack of them) reflect the current political outlook. Consequently, the political force of the marketing environment has the potential to influence marketing decisions and strategies.

Marketers need to maintain good relations with elected political officials for several reasons. When political officials are well disposed towards particular companies or industries, they are less likely to create or enforce laws and regulations unfavourable to these companies. For example, political officials who believe that oil companies are making honest efforts to control pollution are unlikely to create and enforce highly restrictive pollution control laws. In addition, governments are big buyers, and political officials can influence how much a government agency purchases and from whom. The UK government's liking of public–private partnerships for financing capital projects such as schools and hospitals has created significant opportunities for construction companies Carillion and Laing O'Rourke or outsourcing specialists such as Capita and Fujitsu. Finally, political officials can play key roles in helping organisations secure foreign markets.

Many marketers view political forces as beyond their control; they simply try to adjust to conditions that arise from those forces. Some organisations, however, seek to influence political events by helping to elect to political office individuals who regard them positively. Much of this help is in the form of contributions to political parties. A sizeable contribution to a campaign fund may carry with it an implicit understanding that the party, if elected, will perform political favours for the contributing company. There are, though, strict laws governing donations and lobbying in most countries and, increasingly, ethical considerations for donor marketers.

Legal Forces

A number of laws influence marketing decisions and activities. This discussion focuses on procompetitive and consumer protection laws and their interpretation.

Procompetitive Legislation

Procompetitive legislation
Laws enacted to preserve competition and to end various practices deemed unacceptable by society

Office of Fair Trading
UK government office set up to oversee the trading practices of organisations and individuals in the UK

Competition Commission
An independent body in the UK that investigates monopolies to determine whether they operate against the public interest

Procompetitive legislation is enacted to preserve competition and to end various practices deemed unacceptable by society – for example, monopolies and mergers. In the UK, the Department for Business, Enterprise and Regulatory Reform (BERR) and the director general of the **Office of Fair Trading** (OFT) can refer monopolies for investigation by the **Competition Commission**, an independent body whose members are drawn from a variety of backgrounds, including lawyers, economists, industrialists and trades unionists. The legislation defines a monopoly as a situation in which at least a quarter of a particular kind of good or service is supplied by a single person or a group of connected companies, or by two or more people acting in a way that prevents, restricts or distorts competition. Local monopolies can also be referred to the Commission. If the Commission finds that a monopoly operates against the public interest, BERR has power to take action to remedy or prevent the harm that the Commission considers may exist. Alternatively, the director general of the Office of Fair Trading may be asked to negotiate undertakings to remedy the adverse effects identified by the Commission. The government believes that the market is a better judge than itself of the advantages and disadvantages of mergers, so most takeovers and proposed mergers are allowed to be decided by the companies' shareholders. However, when too much power would be placed in the hands of one organisation, company or person, the government will insist on a Competition Commission appraisal. If the Commission believes it is against the public interest for a take-over or merger to proceed, then it will prohibit or limit any agreement between the companies or organisations involved. For example, when Morrisons acquired rival supermarket chain Safeway, the deal was permitted only on the basis that a number of Safeway stores were sold to a third party, ultimately Waitrose. The EU has a commissioner responsible for competition. In recent years, the commissioner has ruled on anti-competitive practices in many industries, from airlines to financial services, forcing companies to alter their trading practices and encouraging competition from a broader base of organisations.

Under the Financial Services Act of 1986, the director general of the Office of Fair Trading is required to consider the implications for competition of rules, regulations, guidance and other arrangements and practices of the regulatory bodies, investment exchanges and clearing houses. The director general must report to BERR whenever a significant or potentially significant effect on competition has been identified. This legislation is for the protection of investors, and the secretary of state may refuse or revoke recognition of the organisation or require it to make alterations to its activities.

Under anti-competitive practices legislation, the director general of the Office of Fair Trading can investigate any business practice, whether in the public or private sector, that may restrict, distort or prevent competition in the production, supply or acquisition of goods or services. The Secretary of State has power to take remedial action. With the introduction of the Restrictive Trade Practices Act 1976, if two or more people who are party to the supply of goods or services accept some limitation on their freedom to make their own decisions about matters such as prices or conditions of sale, the Office of Fair Trading must be notified and such an agreement must be registered. Once an agreement has been registered, the director general is under a general duty to refer it to the Restrictive Practices Court, and the court must declare the restrictions in it contrary to the public interest unless the parties can satisfy the court that the public interest is not an issue. The vast majority of agreements never reach the court because parties elect to give up the restrictions rather than go through such a procedure.

Within the European Union, the objective of the competition policy is to ensure that there is free and fair competition in trade among member states and that the government trade barriers, which the Treaty of Rome seeks to dismantle, are not replaced by private barriers that fragment the Common Market. The EU has powers to investigate and terminate alleged infringements and to impose fines. The Treaty of Rome prohibits agreements or concertive practices that may affect trade among member states, and aims to prevent restriction or distortion of competition within the Common Market.[3] Most countries have similar procompetitive legislation. For example, in the United States the Sherman AntiTrust Act prevents monopolistic situations, the Clayton Antitrust Act specifically prohibits price discrimination, and the Federal Trade Commission Act broadly prohibits unfair methods and empowers the Federal Trade Commission to work with the Department of Justice to enforce the provisions of the Clayton Antitrust Act. The Wheeler–Lea Act essentially makes unfair and deceptive acts or practices unlawful, regardless of whether they incur competition. The Robinson–Patman Act deals with discriminatory price differentials.[4]

Consumer Protection Legislation

The second category of regulatory laws – consumer protection legislation – is not a recent development. However, consumer protection laws mushroomed in the mid-1960s and early 1970s. A number of them deal with consumer safety, while others relate to the sale of various hazardous products such as flammable fabrics and toys that might injure children. In the UK, the Fair Trading Act 1973 provides a mechanism – headed by the director general of the Office of Fair Trading – for the continuous review of consumer affairs, for actions dealing with trading practices that unfairly affect consumers' interests, for action against persistent offenders under existing law and for the negotiation of self-regulatory codes of practice to raise trading standards. Consumers' interests with regard to the purity of food, the description and performance of goods and services, and pricing information are safeguarded by the Food Act 1984, the Medicines Act 1968, the Misrepresentations Act 1967, the Trade Descriptions Act 1968, the Prices Act 1974, the Unfair Contract Terms Act 1977, the Sale of Goods Act 1979 and the Supply of Goods and Services Act 1982. The marking and accuracy of quantities are regulated by the Weights and Measures Act 1985. The Consumer Credit Act 1974 provides comprehensive protection for consumers who enter into credit or hire transactions. The Consumer Protection Act 1987 implements a harmonised European Union code of civil law covering product liability, creates a general criminal offence of supplying unsafe consumer goods, makes it an offence to give any misleading price indication and consolidates the powers provided under safety-related acts. The Financial Services Act 1986 offers greater protection to investors by establishing a new regulatory framework for the industry. Currently, legislation is pending concerning the production, packaging, supply and use of food.

In addition, consumer advice and information are provided to the general public at the local level by the Citizens Advice Bureau, and the Trading Standards or Consumer Protection departments of local authorities, and in some areas by specialist consumer advice centres. The independent, non-statutory National Consumer Council, which receives government finance, ensures that consumers' views are made known to those in government and industry. Nationalised industries and utilities have consumer councils whose members investigate questions of concern to the consumer, and many trade associations in industry and commerce have established codes of practice. In addition, several private organisations work to further consumer interests, the largest of which is the **Consumers' Association**, funded by the subscriptions of its membership of over one million people. The association conducts an extensive programme of comparative testing of goods and investigation of services; its views and test reports are published in its monthly magazine *Which?*, and other publications.

Interpreting Laws

Laws certainly have the potential to influence marketing activities, but the actual effects of the laws are determined by how marketers and the courts interpret them. Laws seem to be quite specific because they contain many complex clauses and sub-clauses. In reality, however, many laws and regulations are stated in vague terms that force marketers to rely on legal advice rather than their own understanding and common sense. Because of this vagueness, some organisations attempt to gauge the limits of certain laws by operating in a legally questionable way to see how far they can go with certain practices before being prosecuted. Other marketers, however, interpret regulations and statutes very conservatively and strictly to avoid violating a vague law. Although court rulings directly affect businesses accused of specific violations, they also have a broader, less direct impact on other businesses. When marketers try to interpret laws in relation to specific marketing practices, they often analyse recent court decisions, both to understand better what the law is intended to do and to gain a clearer sense of how the courts are likely to interpret it in the future.

Regulatory Forces

Interpretation alone does not determine the effectiveness of laws and regulations; the level of enforcement by regulatory agencies is also significant. Some regulatory agencies are created and administered by government units; others are sponsored by non-governmental sources.

Government

In the UK, the Department for Environment, Food and Rural Affairs (DEFRA) develops and controls policies for agriculture, horticulture, fisheries and food; it also has responsibilities for environmental and rural issues and food policies. The Department for Employment and Learning controls the Employment Service, employment policy and legislation, training policy and legislation, health and safety at work, industrial relations, wages councils, equal opportunities, small businesses and tourism, statistics on labour and industrial matters for the UK, the Careers Service, and international representation on employment matters and educational policy. DEFRA controls policies for planning and regional development, local government, new towns, housing, construction, inner-city matters, environmental protection, water, the countryside, sports and recreation, conservation, historic buildings and ancient monuments. The Export Credit Guarantee Department is responsible for the provision of insurance for exporters against the risk of not being paid for goods and services, access to bank finance for exports, and insurance cover for new investment overseas.

The Central Statistical Office prepares and interprets statistics needed for central economic and social policies and management; it coordinates the statistical work of other departments. The Department for Business, Enterprise and Regulatory Reform (BERR) controls industrial and commercial policy, promotion of enterprise and competition in the UK and abroad, and investor and consumer protection. The Department of Transport is responsible for: land, sea and air transport; rail network regulation; domestic and international civil aviation; international transport agreements; shipping and ports industries; navigation issues, HM Coastguard and marine pollution; motorways and trunk roads; road safety; and overseeing local authority transport.

These examples of British government departments are not unusual. Similar administrative bodies exist in most countries. Increasingly in the EU, political, legal and regulatory forces are being harmonised to reflect common standards and enforcement.

Local Authorities

The functions of UK local authorities are far-reaching; some are primary duties, whereas others are purely discretionary. Broadly speaking, functions are divided between county and district councils on the basis that the county council is responsible for matters requiring planning and administration over wide areas or requiring the support of substantial resources, whereas district councils on the whole administer functions of a more local significance. English county councils are generally responsible for strategic planning, transport planning, highways, traffic regulations, local education, consumer protection, refuse disposal, police, the fire service, libraries and personal social services. District councils are responsible for environmental health, housing decisions, most planning applications and refuse collection. They may also provide some museums, art galleries and parks. At both county and district council level, arrangements depend on local agreements.

Most countries in Europe have a similar structure: resource-hungry issues with wide-ranging social and political consequences are controlled centrally. Planning and service provision within the community are viewed as being better controlled at the local level by the actual communities that will experience the advantages or problems resulting from such decision-making. The European Union aims to establish commonly accepted parameters for planning, service provision and regulation, and a framework to assist in inter- and intra-country disputes.

Non-governmental Regulatory Forces

In the absence of governmental regulatory forces and in an attempt to prevent government intervention, some organisations try to regulate themselves. For example, many newspapers have voluntarily banned advertisements for telephone chat services used for undesirable activities, even though such services are technically not illegal. Trade associations in a number of industries have developed self-regulatory programmes. Even though these programmes are not a direct outcome of laws, many were established to stop or stall the development of laws and governmental regulatory groups that would regulate the associations' marketing practices. Sometimes trade associations establish codes of ethics by which their members must abide, or risk censure by other members or even exclusion from the programme. For example, many cigarette manufacturers have agreed, through a code of ethics, not to advertise their products to children and teenagers. The Ofcom Code of Advertising Standards and Practice aims to keep broadcast advertising 'legal, decent, honest and truthful'.[5]

Self-regulatory programmes have several advantages over governmental laws and regulatory agencies. They are usually less expensive to establish and implement, and their guidelines are generally more realistic and operational. In addition, effective industry self-regulatory programmes reduce the need to expand government bureaucracy. However, these programmes also have several limitations. When a trade association creates a set of industry guidelines for its members, non-member organisations do not have to abide by them. In addition, many self-regulatory programmes lack the tools or the authority to enforce guidelines. Finally, guidelines in self-regulatory programmes are often less strict than those established by government agencies.

Deregulation

Governments can drastically alter the environment for businesses. In the UK, the privatisation of the public utilities created new terms and conditions for their suppliers and sub-contractors. The state's sales of Jaguar and Rover in the car industry and of British Airways created commercially lean companies that suddenly had new impetus to become major competitors in their industries. In the European Union, deregulation has created opportunities across borders and also new threats. Car manufacturers were previously able to restrict certain models to specific countries. They placed rigorous controls on their dealers, forbidding them to retail cars produced by rival manufacturers in the same showroom or on the same site. Many of these controls have since been swept aside.

Societal/Green Forces

Societal/Green forces
Individuals and groups, and the issues engaging them, that pressure marketers to provide high living standards and enjoyable lifestyles through socially responsible decisions and activities

Societal/Green forces comprise the structure and dynamics of individuals and groups and the issues that engage them. Society becomes concerned about marketers' activities when those activities have questionable or negative consequences. For example, in recent times, well-publicised incidents of unethical behaviour by marketers and others have perturbed and even angered consumers. When marketers do a good job of satisfying society, praise or positive evaluation rarely follows. Society expects marketers to provide a high standard of living and to protect the general quality of life. This section examines some of society's expectations, the means used to express those expectations, and the problems and opportunities that marketers experience as they try to deal with society's often contradictory wishes.

Living Standards and Quality of Life

Most people want more than just the bare necessities; they want to achieve the highest standard of living possible. For example, there is a desire for homes that offer not only protection from the elements but also comfort and a satisfactory lifestyle. People want many varieties of safe and readily available food that is also easily prepared. Clothing protects bodies, but many consumers want a variety of clothing for adornment and to project a certain image to others. Consumers want vehicles that provide rapid, safe and efficient travel. They want communications systems that give information from around the globe – a desire apparent in the popularity of products such as PDAs, mobile phones, fax machines and the 24-hour news coverage provided by cable and satellite television networks and by the Internet. In addition, there is a demand for sophisticated medical services that prolong life expectancy and improve physical appearance. Education is expected to help consumers acquire and enjoy a higher standard of living.

Society's high material standard of living is often not enough. Many desire a high degree of quality in their lives. People do not want to spend all their waking hours working: they seek leisure time for hobbies, voluntary work, recreation and relaxation. Quality of life is enhanced by leisure time, clean air and water, unlittered beaches, conservation of wildlife and natural resources, and security from radiation and poisonous substances. A number of companies are expressing concerns about quality of life. Consumers, too, are expressing concern over 'Green' issues such as pollution, waste disposal and the so-called greenhouse effect. Society's concerns have created both threats and opportunities for marketers. For example, one of society's biggest environmental problems is lack of space for refuse disposal, especially of plastic materials such as disposable nappies and Styrofoam packaging, which are not biodegradable. In the United States, several cities have passed laws banning the use of all plastic packaging in stores and restaurants, and governments around the world are considering similar legislation. This trend has created problems for McDonald's and other fast-food restaurants, which have now developed packaging alternatives. Other companies, however, see such environmental problems as opportunities. Procter & Gamble, for example, markets cleaners in bottles made of recycled plastic.[6] Environmentally responsible, or Green, marketing is increasingly extensive. For example, the German companies Audi, Volkswagen and BMW are manufacturing 'cleaner' cars that do not pollute the atmosphere as much as traditional ones. BP launched a 'Green' diesel fuel with hardly any noxious emissions. Italian chemical companies are investing billions to reduce toxic wastes from their plants, and British industry is investing equally large sums to scrub acid emissions from power stations and to treat sewage more effectively.[7]

Green movement
The trend arising from society's concern about pollution, waste disposal, manufacturing processes and the greenhouse effect

The **Green movement** is concerned about these environmental issues. Several years ago few consumers were concerned about the well-being of their natural environment – their planet. Resources were not seen as scarce, pollution was barely acknowledged and people had a short-term, perhaps selfish, perspective. Now there is a growing awareness that is affecting everyone: consumers, manufacturers and legislators. Supermarket shelves are rapidly filling with packaging that can be recycled or reused, and products for which manufacturing processes have altered. Children are now taught in the classroom to 're-educate' their parents to take a more responsible view of the earth's environment. The changes are not just in the supermarkets and schools, with ever more households sorting their rubbish into various containers for collection by local authorities striving to recycle growing amounts of trash.

The rising importance and role of the Green aspect of the societal forces must not be underestimated. Changes in the forces of the marketing environment require careful monitoring, and often demand a clear and effective response. Since marketing activities are a vital part of the total business structure, marketers have a responsibility to help provide what members of society want and to minimise what they do not want.

Consumer Movement Forces

Consumer movement
A diverse collection of independent individuals, groups and organisations seeking to protect the rights of consumers

The **consumer movement** is a diverse collection of independent individuals, groups and organisations seeking to protect the rights of consumers. The main issues pursued by the consumer movement fall into three categories: environmental protection, product performance and safety, and information disclosure. The movement's major forces are individual consumer advocates, consumer organisations and other interest groups, consumer education and consumer laws.

Consumer advocates take it upon themselves to protect the rights of consumers. They band together into consumer organisations, either voluntarily or under government sponsorship. Some organisations, such as the Consumers' Association, operate nationally, whereas others are active at local levels. They inform and organise other consumers, raise issues, help businesses develop consumer-oriented programmes and pressure legislators to enact consumer protection laws. Some consumer advocates and organisations encourage consumers to boycott products and businesses to which they have objections. For marketers, it is better to work with such activists than to incur their displeasure.

Educating consumers to make wiser purchasing decisions is perhaps one of the most far-reaching aspects of the consumer movement, which is now impacting on a growing number of organisations (see Figure 3.2). This is a motive of the Fairtrade Organisation, as detailed in the marketing insight box (see page 86). Increasingly, consumer education is becoming a part of school curricula and adult education courses. These courses cover many topics – for instance, what major factors should be considered when buying specific products, such as insurance, housing, cars, appliances and furniture, clothes and food. The courses also cover the provisions of certain consumer protection laws and provide the sources of information that can help individuals become knowledgeable consumers.

Technological Forces

Technology
The application of knowledge and tools to solve problems and perform tasks more efficiently

The word technology brings to mind creations of progress such as cellphones, computers, the web, superconductors, lasers, GM foods, wind farms, cloning and organ transplants. Even though such items are outgrowths of technology, none of them is technology. **Technology** has been defined as the application of knowledge and tools to solve problems and perform tasks more efficiently.[8] Often this knowledge comes from scientific research. The effects of technology are broad in scope and today exert a tremendous influence on everyone's lives. Technology grows out of research performed by businesses, universities and not-for-profit organisations. Much of this research is paid for by governments, which support investigations in a variety of areas, including health, defence, agriculture, energy and pollution. Because much centrally funded research requires the use of specialised

Figure 3.2
*Envirowise's business-
to-business
proposition capitalises
on a growth in concern
for natural resources
and technological
advancements in
manufacturing
processes
Source: Courtesy of
Envirowise*

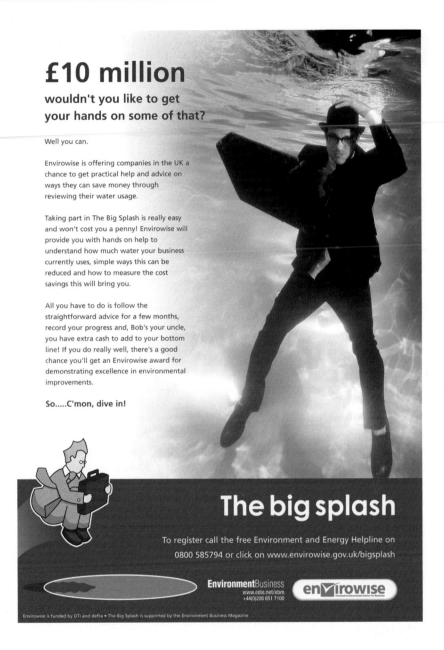

machinery, personnel and facilities, a sizeable proportion of this research is conducted by large commercial organisations or research institutions that already possess the necessary specialised equipment and people.

The rapid technological growth of recent decades is expected to continue. Areas that hold great technological promise include digital electronics, artificial intelligence, superconductors, materials research and biotechnology. Current research is investigating new forms of memory chips and computers that will think for themselves or be more responsive to their specific users' characteristics. Because these and other technological developments will clearly have an impact on buyers' and marketers' decisions, it is important to discuss here the effects of technology on society and marketers, and to consider several factors that influence the adoption and use of technology.

✿ Marketing Insight

Kraft and Nestlé Look to Fairtrade

Fairtrade labelling was created in the Netherlands in the 1980s, with coffee from Mexico being the first recipient of the eco-label. Fairtrade exists to guarantee that the suppliers of products consumed in the developed world, based in the developing regions, benefit from a fair price. By negotiating better deals, improving the negotiating power and marketing expertise of farmers and producers, and seeking a greater proportion of the retail price, the movement helps sustain development and is largely welcomed by the leading development agencies. A core aim is to minimise dramatically fluctuating prices that, when low, force farmers into crippling debt or out of production.

Now there are 18 organisations around the world, including the Fairtrade Foundation, overseeing the labelling of Fairtrade products. Over 360 Fairtrade-certified producer groups in 40 countries have helped many impoverished and vulnerable regions. In order to achieve this, the movement must lobby retailers, the media and consumers to purchase or support Fairtrade products. In the UK there are over 250 Fairtrade retail products, from tea to fruit, roses to footballs, snacks to wines. One key product receiving such high-profile attention is coffee.

Leading coffee houses Costa Coffee, Prêt à Manger and Starbucks have retailed Fairtrade coffees for a while, but now it is the turn of the major manufacturers. Until relatively recently, most Fairtrade products were niche brands produced by marginal manufacturers. Now, even the giants of the global food industry have embraced the movement,

reflecting the growing interest in ethical trading by consumers and major retail chains.

First, Nestlé announced plans for a Fairtrade addition to its Nescafé brand. Before its launch, however, rival Kraft stole a march by introducing a Fairtrade coffee range under its well-known Kenco brand. Kenco Sustainable Development comprises two lines: a filter pack and an espresso bean pack. First available to consumers in restaurants, hotels, coffee shops and vending machines, then through supermarkets. Both Kenco lines carry an eco-label from sustainable agriculture organisation the Rainforest Alliance, which guarantees that the beans are from certified farms. Kraft also reformulated its flagship brands Maxwell House and Kenco Really Smooth so that they contain at least 5 per cent certified beans, but they do not carry the eco-label.

Did growing consumer interest in Fairtrade encourage these manufacturers to launch the new lines? Were moves by socially aware retailers responsible? Had lobbying by organisations such as the Rainforest Alliance or Fairtrade Foundation created the necessary swell of positive public opinion? Were Kraft and Nestlé simply reaping the rewards of their environmental scanning of market trends? In reality, a mix of these drivers combined to create the impetus for these products.

Sources: Kraft, 2004; www.fairtrade.org.uk, 2004; Mark Sweeney, 'Kraft beats Nestlé to launch of fair trade coffee', *Marketing*, 7 July 2004, p. 1.

The Impact of Technology

Marketers must be aware of new developments in technology and their possible effects because technology does affect marketing activities in many different ways. Consumers' technological knowledge influences their desire for goods and services. To provide marketing mixes that satisfy consumers, marketers must be aware of these influences. The various ways in which technology affects marketing activities fall into two broad categories:

1 effects on consumers and society in general
2 influences on what, how, when and where products are marketed.

Effects of Technology on Society   Technology determines how consumers as members of society satisfy their physiological needs. In various ways and to varying degrees, eating and drinking habits, sleeping patterns, sexual activities and healthcare are all influenced both by existing technology and by changes in technology. Technological developments have improved standards of living, thus creating more leisure time; they have also enhanced information, entertainment and education. Nevertheless, technology can detract from the quality of life through undesirable side-effects, such as unemployment, polluted air and water, and other health hazards. Some people believe that further applications of technology can soften or eliminate these undesirable side-effects. Others argue, however, that the best way to improve the quality of our lives is to decrease the use of technology.

Effects of Technology on Marketing   Technology also affects the types of product that marketers can offer. The introduction and general acceptance of cassette tapes and compact discs drove most manufacturers of vinyl long-playing (LP) albums out of business or forced them to invest in new technology. Yet this technology provided new marketing opportunities for recording artists and producers, record companies, retailers and those in related industries. More recently, music downloads from the web have created a new set of opportunities and challenges for marketers in the music industry. The following items are just a few of the many thousands of existing products that were not available to consumers 20 years ago: webcams, digital cameras, cellphones, ultra-light laptop computers, high-resolution televisions, hand-held video cameras and the Internet. All of these are products that have transformed lifestyles and people's access to information.

Computer technology helps make warehouse storage and keeping track of stored products more efficient and, therefore, less expensive. Often, these savings can be passed on to consumers in the form of lower prices. Because of technological changes in communications, marketers can now use a variety of media to reach large masses of people more efficiently. The development and widespread use of fax, e-mail and text messaging, for example, allow marketers to send their advertisements or sales specifications directly to selected groups of customers who want their products. In recent years the Internet has permeated the lives of many, bringing a world of information into the home and allowing consumers to shop for products online. Technological advances in transport enable consumers to travel further and more often to shop at a larger number of stores. Changes in transport have also affected producers' ability to get products to retailers and wholesalers. The ability of present-day manufacturers of relatively lightweight products to reach any of their dealers within hours via express-delivery services would astound their counterparts of 50 years ago.

The Adoption and Use of Technology

Technology assessment
A procedure by which managers try to foresee the effects of new products and processes on their company's operation, on other commercial organisations and on society in general

Through a procedure known as **technology assessment**, some managers try to foresee the effects of new products and processes on their company's operation, on other organisations and on society in general. With the information gained through a technology assessment, management tries to estimate whether the benefits of using a specific kind of technology outweigh the costs to the business and to society at large. The degree to which an organisation is technologically based will also influence how its management responds to technology. Companies whose products and product changes grow out of recent technology strive to gather and use technological information. Although available technology could radically improve their products or other parts of the marketing mix, some companies may put off applying this technology as long as their competitors do not try to use it. The extent to which an organisation can protect inventions stemming from research also influences its use of technology. The extent to which a product is secure from imitation depends on how easily others can copy it without violating its patent. If new products and processes cannot be protected through patents, a company is less likely to market them and make the benefits of its research available to competitors. How a company uses – or does not use – technology is important for its long-term survival. An organisation that makes the wrong decisions may well lose out to the competition. Poor decisions may also affect its profits by requiring expensive corrective action. Poor decisions about technological forces may even drive a company out of business.

Economic and Competitive Forces

The **economic and competitive forces** in the marketing environment influence both marketers' and customers' decisions and activities. This section first examines the effects of general economic conditions, also focusing on buying power, willingness to spend and spending patterns. Then the discussion moves to the broad competitive forces, including types of competitive structure, competitive tools and some methods for monitoring competitive behaviour. The strategic importance of understanding and evaluating the competitive arena has been discussed in Chapter 2.

General Economic Conditions

Economic and competitive forces
Factors in the marketing environment—such as the effects of general economic conditions; buying power; willingness to spend; spending patterns; types of competitive structure, competitive tools and competitive behaviour—that influence both marketers' and consumers' decisions and activities

Business cycle
Fluctuations in the economy that follow the general pattern of prosperity, recession, depression and recovery

Prosperity
A period during which unemployment is low and total income is relatively high

Recession
A period during which unemployment rises and total buying power declines

Depression
A period during which unemployment is extremely high, wages are very low, total disposable income is at a minimum and consumers lack confidence in the economy

The overall state of the economy fluctuates in all countries. Table 3.1 presents some economic measures of performance for Europe. These changes in general economic conditions affect – and are affected by – the forces of supply and demand, buying power, willingness to spend, consumer expenditure levels and the intensity of competitive behaviour. Therefore, current economic conditions and changes in the economy have a broad impact on the success of organisations' marketing strategies.

Fluctuations in the economy follow a general pattern often referred to as the **business cycle**. In the traditional view, the business cycle consists of four stages: prosperity, recession, depression and recovery.

Prosperity During **prosperity**, unemployment is low and total income is relatively high. Assuming a low inflation rate, this combination causes buying power to be high. To the extent that the economic outlook remains prosperous, consumers are generally willing to buy. In the prosperity stage, marketers often expand their marketing mixes (product, place/distribution, promotion, price and people) to take advantage of the increased buying power. They sometimes capture a larger market share by intensifying distribution and promotion efforts.

Recession Unemployment rises during a **recession**, so total buying power declines. The pessimism that accompanies a recession often stifles both consumer and business spending. As buying power decreases, many consumers become more price- and value-conscious; they look for products that are basic and functional. For instance, people ordinarily reduce their consumption of more expensive convenience foods and strive to save money by growing and preparing more of their own food. Individuals buy fewer durable goods and more repair and do-it-yourself products. During a recession, some companies make the mistake of drastically reducing their marketing efforts and thus damage their ability to survive. Obviously, marketers should consider some revision of their marketing activities during a recessionary period. Because consumers are more concerned about the functional value of products, a company must focus its marketing research on determining what product functions buyers want and then make sure that these functions become part of its products. Promotional efforts should emphasise value and utility.

Depression A **depression** is a period in which unemployment is extremely high, wages are very low, total disposable income is at a minimum and consumers lack confidence in the economy. Governments have used both monetary and fiscal policies to off-set the effects of recession and depression. Monetary policies are employed to control the money supply, which in turn affects spending, saving and investment by both individuals and businesses. Through the establishment of fiscal policies, the government is able to influence the amount of saving and expenditure by adjusting the tax structure and by changing the levels of government spending. Some economic experts believe that the effective use of monetary and fiscal policies can completely eliminate depressions from the business cycle.

TABLE 3.1 SOME ECONOMIC MEASURES OF PERFORMANCE FOR EUROPE — DATA ON WESTERN EUROPEAN COUNTRIES†

		Austria	Belgium	Denmark	France	Germany	Ireland	Italy	Netherlands	Norway	Spain	Sweden	Switzerland	United Kingdom
A	Total population, 2006¹	millions	8.27	10.51	5.43	63.39	82.44	4.24	58.46	16.33	4.64	44.40	9.05	7.46	60.59
A	**Population growth at annual rates**														
	Population growth 06/05¹	%	1.1	1.1	0.4	3.8	-0.1	2.5	1.5	0.4	0.7	2.3	0.6	1.0	0.6
	Population growth 06/96¹	%	3.9	3.5	3.2	9.2	1.0	16.6	2.2	5.2	5.9	12.9	2.5	6.0	3.8
A	**Population by sex and age, 2006¹**														
	Male	%	48.6	48.9	49.5	48.6	48.9	49.8	48.5	49.5	49.6	49.4	49.6	49.0	49.0
	Female	%	51.4	51.0	50.5	51.4	51.1	50.2	51.5	50.5	50.4	50.6	50.4	51.0	51.0
	Under 15	%	15.9	17.0	18.8	18.5	14.1	20.4	14.2	18.2	19.6	14.2	17.3	16.0	17.7
	15–64	%	67.6	65.8	66.0	65.3	66.6	68.5	66.3	67.5	65.7	69.0	65.4	68.0	66.3
	65+	%	16.5	17.2	15.2	16.2	19.3	11.1	19.5	14.3	14.7	16.8	17.3	16.0	16.0
A	Births, 2005¹	per 000	9.5	11.3	11.9	13.1	8.3	14.8	9.4	11.5	12.3	10.7	11.2	9.8	12.0
A	Marriages, 2005²	per 000	4.8	4.1	6.7	4.3	4.7	5.0	4.3	4.5	4.8	4.8	4.9	5.4	4.7
A	Inhabitants per sq. km, 2006¹	no.	100	347	128	99	236	61	199	482	15	89	22	188	251
A	Number of households, 2006³	000s	3,475	4,482	2,517	27,490	39,178	1,288	23,600	7,146	2,010	15,976	4,400	3,115	24,800
	Persons per household³	no.	2.4	2.3	2.2	2.3	2.1	3.1	2.5	2.3	2.3	2.7	2.1	2.3	2.4
B	Commonly used unemployment rate, 2006 Proportion of labour force	%	6.8	12.4	4.4	9.0	10.8	4.4	6.8	5.5	3.5	8.5	5.3	3.3	2.9
C	**Civilian employment by main sectors⁴**														
	Agriculture	%	3.0	1.3	3.0	4.1	2.8	8.0	5.0	2.0	4.0	5.3	2.0	4.6	1.4
	Industry	%	27.0	24.5	21.0	24.4	33.4	29.0	32.0	19.0	22.0	30.1	24.0	26.3	18.2
	Services	%	70.0	74.2	76.0	71.5	63.8	64.0	63.0	79.0	74.0	64.6	74.0	69.1	80.4
D	Strikes, 2006⁵ Working days lost per 1,000 employees	no.	—	—	476	699	—	10	549	31	12	783	9	3	158
B	**Gross Domestic Product (local currency, constant 2000 prices⁶)**														
	Total, 2006	billions	233.6	301.9	1,431.9	1,593.3	2,183	170.8	1,255.8	457.3	1,840.1	768.7	2,594.9	464.0	1,209.3
	Per capita	000s	28.3	28.7	263.7	25.1	26.5	40.3	21.5	28.0	396.6	17.3	286.7	62.2	20.0
B	Gross fixed capital formation, 2006 (local currency, constant 2000 prices⁶) Proportion of GDP	%	20.9	20.5	23.5	20.3	19.6	25.4	20.9	20.5	20.4	29.1	18.1	22.1	17.9

Notes: ¹ Where data for the reference period were not available, the most recent were used. All countries use the Euro except for Denmark (DKK), Norway (NOK), Sweden (SEK), Switzerland (CHF) and UK (GBP) ¹ Data for Austria, Germany, Italy, Sweden and Switzerland are for 2005; the population growth for these countries is based on 2004 and 1995 respectively. ² Data for France are 2000 estimates. ³ Data for Switzerland are for 2000. Data for Ireland are for 2002. Data for Austria, Germany, Italy, Norway, Spain and Sweden are for 2005. ⁴ Data for Belgium are for 2003, data for Denmark, Netherlands and Spain are for 2004. Data for Austria are for 2005. Data for the UK are for 2006. Data for Belgium and Germany are unavailable. Data for France are for 2004. ⁵ Data for UK are in 2003 prices. Data for Belgium and Norway are in 2004 prices. Data for Ireland are in 2005 prices.

Sources: A *European Marketing Pocket Book 2007*, WARC; Local sources.
B OECD Main Economic Indicators © OECD, September 2007.
C CIA 'World Fact Book', (www.cia.gov/cia/publications/factbook), 2007.
D 'Strikes and Lockouts — Days not worked', International Labour Office (ILO) 2007.

MEMBER STATES OF THE EUROPEAN UNION

Full Members
Austria, Belgium, Bulgaria, Cyprus, Czech Republic, Denmark, Estonia, Finland, France, Germany, Greece, Hungary, Ireland, Italy, Latvia, Lithuania, Luxembourg, Malta, Netherlands, Poland, Portugal, Romania, Slovenia, Slovak Republic, Spain, Sweden, United Kingdom.

Candidate Countries
Croatia, Former Yugoslav Republic of Macedonia, Turkey.

TABLE 3.1 SOME ECONOMIC MEASURES OF PERFORMANCE FOR EUROPE   DATA ON WESTERN EUROPEAN COUNTRIES (continued)

		Austria	Belgium	Denmark	France	Germany	Ireland	Italy	Netherlands	Norway	Spain	Sweden	Switzerland	United Kingdom
A Consumption per capita per year														
Beer, 2003	litres	110.6	96.2	96.2	35.5	117.5	141.2	30.1	78.7	50.5	78.3	54.2	58.1	101.5
Wine, 2003	litres	29.8	23.0	32.6	48.5	23.6	15.2	47.5	19.6	12.4	30.6	16.6	40.9	20.1
Spirits, 2003	100% alc., litres	1.4	1.4	1.1	2.4	2.0	2.0	0.4	1.5	0.8	2.4	0.9	1.6	1.8
B Chocolate confectionery, 2005	kg	9.4	11.0	7.7	6.8	11.1	3.9	4.3	4.5	8.5	3.1	6.8	10.7	10.2
Sugar confectionery, 2005	kg	3.8	4.2	8.9	3.4	5.9	1.7	2.2	7.5	4.6	2.7	11.7	3.2	5.6
Biscuits & other baked goods, 2005[1]	kg	8.2	5.9	9.1	8.6	7.7	3.4	3.6	14.5	–	6.6	3.5	8.1	15.7
C Media and telecommunications, 2006[2]														
Daily newspapers – weekly reach[3]	%	73.7	56.7	79.7	18.4	73.7	56.9	64.1	72.5	90.9	41.8	93.0	90.7	62.9
Radio – weekly reach[3]	%.	83.6	82.2	95.9	83.3	79.3	86.0	84.8	91.3	97.8	56.3	94.0	90.7	90.4
TV – weekly reach[3]	%	69.2	91.3	93.1	95.9	75.4	91.0	95.4	96.5	90.4	87.9	88.2	92.8	93.8
Household penetration:														
Telephone mainlines	%	75.9	76.6	–	86.0	–	87.8	85.3	–	–	76.1	–	88.4	93.1
Mobile phones	%	87.5	80.4	94.0	79.3	77.9	86.4	88.0	86.3	94.2	80.3	93.0	81.0	84.7
Personal computers	%	64.3	66.4	–	52.9	47.0	63.3	36.3	78.2	69.0	40.8	70.0	77.5	56.9
Internet	%	49.9	55.2	78.8	42.6	43.9	44.7	31.6	71.5	69.0	28.8	70.0	70.9	56.9
C/D Indicators of living standards														
Physicians, 2003[4]	per '000 popn.	3.4	3.9	2.9	3.4	3.4	2.8	4.2	3.1	3.1	3.2	3.3	3.6	2.2
Life expectancy at birth, 2005[5]	years	79.5	79.5	77.9	80.7	79.0	77.7	80.4	79.0	80.1	80.3	80.5	81.3	79.2
Infant mortality, 2005[6]	per '000 live births	4.2	4.4	4.4	3.7	3.9	4.0	4.2	4.9	3.2	4.1	2.4	4.2	4.9
Health expenditure, 2003	% of GDP	7.5	9.4	9.0	10.1	11.1	7.3	8.4	9.8	10.3	7.7	9.4	11.5	8.0
Public spending on education, 2002[7]	% of GDP	5.7	6.3	8.5	5.6	4.8	4.3	4.7	5.1	7.6	4.5	7.7	5.8	5.5
C Vehicles														
Total motor vehicles, 2005[1]	000s	5,647	5,862	4,134	36,039	54,519	2,139	38,224	8,494	2,523	27,657	4,615	5,369	32,897
E The retail grocery trade, 2000														
Grocery store numbers		6,417	9,891	3,026	37,559	64,230	9,118	107,669	4,663	4,564	59,689	4,834	6,223	33,348
Market share by store type:														
Hypermarkets	%	12	14	19	52	25	19	18	5	4	33	18	19	53
Large supermarkets	%	17	46	25	25	17	35	18	39	18	17	38	32	24
Small supermarkets	%	44	29	37	11	39	11	21	19	47	18	29	25	12
Superettes	%	27	8	17	4	14	34	19	9	28	18	13	19	11
Traditionals	%	–	3	1	–	4	–	18	–	2	13	2	5	–
D International tourism, 2004[8]														
Arrivals	% of popn.	223.4	124.2	61.8	118.5	22.3	164.7	63.4	59.1	77.6	120.7	85.2	89.0	45.8
Departures	% of popn.	78.4	134.9	85.3	33.3	90.4	127.6	39.9	101.5	56.5	11.5	154.4	156.9	106.0

Notes: In each category, where data for the reference period were not available, the most recent have been used.

1 Data in italics are for 2004.
2 Data in italics are for 2005.
3 Data for Austria, Germany, Ireland, Italy and Spain are daily reach.
4 Data for Belgium, Denmark, Sweden and Switzerland are for 2002; data for France, Ireland and Italy are for 2004.
5 Data for Belgium and Spain are for 2004; data for France and UK are 2006 estimates.
6 Data for Denmark and Italy are for 2004; data for France are 2006 estimates.
7 Data for the UK are for 2006.
8 All data for Belgium and Germany; arrivals data for Sweden and Switzerland; and departures data for Netherlands and Norway are all for 2003. Departures data for Switzerland are for 2002.

Sources: A   *World Drink Trends 2005*, WARC; Commissie Gedistilleerd/WARC.
B   CAOBISCO.
C   *European Marketing Pocket Book 2007*, WARC; Local sources.
D   *World Development Indicators 2006*, World Bank.
E   Nielsen.

Recovery
The stage of the business cycle in which the economy moves from depression or recession to prosperity

Recovery   **Recovery** is the stage of the business cycle in which the economy moves from depression or recession to prosperity. During this period, the high unemployment rate begins to decline, total disposable income increases and the economic gloom that lessened consumers' willingness to buy subsides. Both the ability and the willingness to buy rise. Marketers face some problems during recovery – for example, the difficulty of ascertaining how quickly prosperity will return and of forecasting the level of prosperity that will be attained. During this stage, marketers should maintain as much flexibility in their marketing strategies as possible to be able to make the required adjustments as the economy moves from recession to prosperity. Fluctuations in economic conditions have a significant impact on marketers' activities and fortunes.

Consumer Demand and Spending Behaviour

Marketers must understand the factors that determine whether, what, where and when people buy. Chapters 4 and 5 look at the behavioural factors underlying these choices, but here the focus is on the economic components: buying power, willingness to purchase and spending patterns.

Buying power
Resources such as goods, services and financial holdings that can be traded in an exchange situation

Buying Power   The strength of a person's **buying power** depends on the size of the resources that enable the individual to purchase, as well as on the state of the economy. The resources that make up buying power are goods, services and financial holdings. Fluctuations of the business cycle affect buying power because they influence price levels and interest rates. For example, during inflationary periods, when prices are rising, buying power decreases because more pounds or euros are required to buy products. The major financial sources of buying power are income, credit and wealth. From an individual's viewpoint, **income** is the amount of money received through wages, rents, investments, pensions and subsidy payments for a given period, such as a month or a year. Normally, this money is allocated among taxes, spending for goods and services, and savings. However, because of the differences in people's educational levels, abilities, occupations and wealth, income is not distributed equally in any country.

Income
The amount of money received through wages, rents, investments, pensions and subsidy payments for a given period

Marketers are most interested in the amount of money that is left after payment of taxes. After-tax income is called **disposable income** and is used for spending or saving. Because disposable income is a ready source of buying power, the total amount available in a country is important to marketers. Several factors affect the size of total disposable income. One, of course, is the total amount of income. Total national income is affected by wage levels, rate of unemployment, interest rates and dividend rates. These factors in turn affect the size of disposable income. Because disposable income is the income left after taxes are paid, the number of taxes and their amount directly affect the size of total disposable income. When taxes rise, disposable income declines; when taxes fall, disposable income increases. Disposable income that is available for spending and saving after an individual has purchased the basic necessities of food, clothing and shelter is called **discretionary income**. People use discretionary income to purchase entertainment, holidays, cars, education, pets and pet supplies, furniture, appliances, and so on. Changes in total discretionary income affect the sales of these products – especially cars, furniture, large appliances and other costly durable goods. The marketers of such products must monitor factors likely to alter their target customers' discretionary income.

Disposable income
After-tax income, which is used for spending or saving

Discretionary income
Disposable income that is available for spending and saving after an individual has purchased the basic necessities of food, clothing and shelter

Credit enables people to spend future income now or in the near future. However, credit increases current buying power at the expense of future buying power. Several factors determine whether consumers use or forgo credit. First, credit must be available to them. Interest rates, too, affect consumers' decisions to use credit, especially for expensive purchases such as homes, appliances and cars. When credit charges are high, consumers are more likely to delay buying expensive items. Use of credit is also affected by credit terms, such as the size of the down payment and the amount and number of monthly payments. Many marketers offer 'interest-free credit' or low interest rates as part of the marketing proposition for their products.

Wealth
The accumulation of past income, natural resources and financial resources

A person can have a high income and very little wealth. It is also possible, but not likely, for a person to have great wealth but not much income. **Wealth** is the accumulation of past income, natural resources and financial resources. It may exist in many forms, including cash, securities, savings accounts, jewellery, antiques and property. Like income, wealth is distributed unevenly. The significance of wealth to marketers is that as people become wealthier they gain buying power in three ways: they can use their wealth to make current purchases, to generate income and to acquire large amounts of credit. Buying power information is available from government sources, trade associations and research agencies. One of the most current and comprehensive sources of buying power data is the Central Statistical Office's *National Income and Expenditure Survey*. The EU's *Eurostat* provides similar data. Income, wealth and credit equip consumers to purchase goods and services. Marketing managers should be aware of current levels and expected changes in buying power in their own markets because buying power directly affects the types and quantities of goods and services that consumers purchase, as explained later in the discussion of spending patterns. Just because consumers have buying power, however, does not necessarily mean that they will buy. Consumers must also be willing to use their buying power. Marketers must encourage them to do so.

Willingness to spend
A disposition towards using buying power, influenced by the ability to buy, expected satisfaction from a product and numerous psychological and social forces

Consumers' Willingness to Spend   People's **willingness to spend** is, to some degree, related to their ability to buy – that is, people are sometimes more willing to buy if they have the buying power. However, a number of other elements also influence willingness to spend. Some elements affect specific products; others influence spending in general. A product's absolute price and its price relative to the price of substitute products influence almost everyone. The amount of satisfaction currently received or expected in the future from a product already owned may also influence consumers' desire to buy other products. Satisfaction depends not only on the quality of the functional performance of the currently owned product, but also on numerous psychological and social forces.

Factors that affect consumers' general willingness to spend are expectations about future employment, income levels, prices, family size and general economic conditions. If people are unsure whether or how long they will be employed, willingness to buy ordinarily declines. Willingness to spend may increase if people are reasonably certain of higher incomes in the future. Expectations of rising prices in the near future may also increase willingness to spend in the present. For a given level of buying power, the larger the family, the greater the willingness to buy. One of the reasons for this relationship is that as the size of a family increases, a larger amount of money must be spent to provide the basic necessities of life to sustain the family members. Finally, perceptions of future economic conditions influence willingness to buy. For example, rising short-term interest rates cool consumers' willingness to spend.

Consumer spending patterns
Information indicating the relative proportions of annual family expenditures or the actual amount of money spent on certain kinds of goods and services

Consumer Spending Patterns   Marketers must be aware of the factors that influence consumers' ability and willingness to spend, but they should also analyse how consumers actually spend their disposable incomes. Marketers obtain this information by studying consumer spending patterns. **Consumer spending patterns** indicate the relative proportions of annual family expenditures or the actual amount of money spent on certain kinds of goods and services. Families are usually categorised by one of several characteristics, including family income, age of the head of household, geographic area and family life cycle. There are two types of spending pattern: comprehensive and product-specific.

Comprehensive spending patterns
The percentages of family income allotted to annual expenditures for general classes of goods and services

The percentages of family income allotted to annual expenditures for general classes of goods and services constitute **comprehensive spending patterns**. Comprehensive spending patterns or the data to develop them are available in government publications and in reports produced by the major marketing research companies and by trade associations. **Product-specific spending patterns** indicate the annual monetary amounts families spend

Product-specific spending patterns
The annual monetary amounts families spend for specific products within a general product class

for specific products within a general product class. Information sources used to construct product-specific spending patterns include government publications, trade publications and consumer surveys. A marketer uses spending patterns to analyse general trends in the ways that families spend their incomes for various kinds of product. Analyses of spending patterns yield information that a marketer can use to gain perspective and background for decision-making. However, spending patterns reflect only general trends and thus should not be used as the sole basis for making specific decisions.

Assessment of Competitive Forces

Competition
Those companies marketing products that are similar to, or can be substituted for, a given business's products in the same geographic area or marketing channel

Monopoly
A market structure that exists when a company turns out a product that has no close substitutes or rivals

Few organisations, if any, operate free of competition. Broadly speaking, all companies compete with each other for consumers' money. From a more practical viewpoint, however, a business generally defines **competition** as those organisations marketing products that are similar to, or can be substituted for, its own products in the same geographic area or marketing channel. For example, a local Tesco or Aldi supermarket manager views all grocery stores in a town as competitors, but almost never thinks of other types of local or out-of-town stores (DIY or electrical, for example) as competitors. This section considers the types of competitive structure and the importance of monitoring competitors.

Types of Competitive Structure The number of organisations that control the supply of a product may affect the strength of competition. When only one or a few companies control supply, competitive factors will exert a different sort of influence on marketing activities than when there are many competitors. Table 3.2 presents four general types of competitive structure: monopoly, oligopoly, monopolistic competition and perfect competition.

A **monopoly** exists when a company turns out a product that has no close substitutes or rivals. Because the organisation has no competitors, it completely controls the supply of

TABLE 3.2 SELECTED CHARACTERISTICS OF COMPETITIVE STRUCTURES

Type of Structure	Number of Competitors	Ease of Entry into Market	Product	Knowledge of Market	Examples
Monopoly	One	Many barriers	Almost no substitutes	Perfect	Non-privatised railways, many government departments
Oligopoly	Few	Some barriers	Homogeneous or differentiated (real or perceived differences)	Imperfect	Airlines, petroleum retailers, some utility providers
Monopolistic competition	Many	Few barriers	Product differentiation with many substitutes	More knowledge than oligopoly; less than monopoly	Jeans, fast food, audio-visual
Perfect competition	Unlimited	No barriers	Homogeneous products	Perfect	The London commodity markets, vegetable farms

93

the product and, as a single seller, can erect barriers to potential competitors. In reality, the monopolies that survive today are some utilities, such as telephone, electricity and some railways (in many countries), and cable companies, which are heavily regulated. These monopolies are tolerated because of the tremendous financial resources needed to develop and operate them; few organisations can obtain the resources to mount any competition against a local electricity producer, for example. An **oligopoly** exists when a few sellers control the supply of a large proportion of a product. In this case, each seller must consider the reactions of other sellers to changes in marketing activities. Products facing oligopolistic competition may be homogeneous, such as aluminium, or differentiated, such as cigarettes and cars. Usually, barriers of some sort make it difficult to enter the market and compete with oligopolies. For example, because of the enormous financial outlay required, few companies or individuals could afford to enter the oil-refining or steel-producing industries. Moreover, some industries demand special technical or marketing skills that block the entry of many potential competitors.

Oligopoly
A market structure that exists when a few sellers control the supply of a large proportion of a product

Monopolistic competition exists when an organisation with many potential competitors attempts to develop a differential marketing strategy to establish its own market share. For example, Levi's has established a differential advantage for its blue jeans through a well-known trademark, design, advertising and a quality image. Although many competing brands of blue jeans are available, this company has carved out its market share through use of a differential marketing strategy. **Perfect competition**, if it existed at all, would entail a large number of sellers, not one of which could significantly influence price or supply. Products would be homogeneous, and there would be full knowledge of the market and easy entry. The closest thing to an example of perfect competition would be an unregulated agricultural market. Few, if any, marketers operate in a structure of perfect competition. Perfect competition is an ideal at one end of the continuum, with monopoly at the other end. Most marketers function in a competitive environment that falls somewhere between these two extremes.

Monopolistic competition
A market structure that exists when a business with many potential competitors attempts to develop a differential marketing strategy to establish its own market share

Perfect competition
A market structure that entails a large number of sellers, not one of which could significantly influence price or supply

Competitive Tools   Another set of factors that influences the level of competition is the number and types of competitive tools used by competitors. To survive, an organisation uses one or several available competitive tools to deal with competitive economic forces. Once a company has analysed its particular competitive environment and decided which factors in that environment it can or must adapt to or influence, it can choose among the variables that it can control to strengthen its competitive position in the overall marketplace. Probably the competitive tool that most organisations grasp is price. Bic, for example, markets disposable pens and lighters that are similar to competing products but less expensive. However, there is one major problem with using price as a competitive tool: competitors will often match or beat the price. This threat is one of the primary reasons for employing non-price competitive tools that are based on the differentiation of market segments, product offering, service, promotion, distribution or enterprise.[9] By focusing on a specific market segment, a marketer sometimes gains a competitive advantage. For instance, Saab cars and Porsche sports coupés are narrowly targeted at specific groups of consumers. Most manufacturers try to gain a competitive edge by incorporating product features that make their brands distinctive to some extent. Companies use distinguishing promotional methods to compete, such as advertising and personal selling. Competing producers sometimes use different distribution channels to prevail over one another. Retailers may compete by placing their outlets in locations that are convenient for a large number of shoppers. Dealers and distributors offer wide ranges, advice and service.

Monitoring Competition Marketers in an organisation need to be aware of the actions of major competitors. They should monitor what competitors are currently doing and assess the changes occurring in the competitive environment, as explained in Chapter 2. **Competitor monitoring** allows organisations to determine what specific strategies competitors are following and how those strategies affect their own. It can also guide marketers as they try to develop competitive advantages and can aid them in adjusting current marketing strategies, as well as in planning new ones. Information may come from direct observation or from sources such as the web, sales people, customers, trade publications, syndicated marketing research services, distributors and marketing studies. An organisation needs information about competitors that will allow its marketing managers to assess the performance of its own marketing efforts. Comparing their company's performance with that of competitors helps marketing managers recognise strengths and weaknesses in their own marketing strategies. Data about market shares, product movement, sales volume and expenditure levels can be useful. However, accurate information on these matters is often difficult to obtain.

Competition exists in most markets and situations. Even charities compete with one another and with manufacturers for consumers' attention and financial commitment. Marketing places an emphasis on meeting consumers' needs and offering satisfaction. To be successful, however, competing organisations need to identify unique marketing mixes; otherwise all rival products and services will merely replicate each other. The search for a competitive edge over competitors is central to effective marketing strategy. As well as monitoring direct competitors, marketers should be aware of new entrants coming into a market with competing propositions, and of the danger of substitute products or services being developed. Marketers' strategic understanding of competition is addressed in Chapter 2.

The Micro Marketing Environment

Many authors, notably Michael Porter,[10] have made a distinction between the very broad forces of the **macro marketing environment** discussed up to now in this chapter – political, legal, regulatory, societal/Green, technological, economic/ competitive – and a set of more company-specific forces often termed the **micro marketing environment** forces. The distinction, put simply, is that the broad macro forces have an impact on every organisation operating in a particular market, from manufacturers to distributors to customers, and such an impact is largely universally felt by such organisations. The micro forces, on the other hand, often have an organisation-specific impact subject to the characteristics and status of the individual business.

The Core Aspects of the Micro Marketing Environment Although categorisations vary among authors, the core aspects of the micro marketing environment worthy of note include the organisation itself, suppliers, marketing intermediaries, buyers, competitors and publics (see Figure 3.3).

The Organisation It is necessary when creating and implementing marketing strategies and marketing mix programmes to consider the reaction, attitudes and abilities of the internal environment: top management, finance, research and development, purchasing, manufacturing, sales and marketing, and logistics. The marketing function's recommendations must be consistent with senior management's corporate goals; be conveyed to other functions within the organisation; and reflect colleagues' views, input, concerns and abilities to implement the desired marketing plan. Marketers must be aware of these organisational factors, monitor them, and modify their actions accordingly to ensure internal take-up of their ideas and plans.

Competitor monitoring
The process by which a company studies the actions of its major competitors in order to determine what specific strategies they are following and how those strategies affect its own; also used by marketers as they try to develop competitive advantages, adjust current marketing strategies and plan new ones

Macro marketing environment
The broader forces affecting all organisations in a market: political, legal, regulatory, societal/Green, technological and economic/competitive

Micro marketing environment
The more company-specific forces reflecting the nature of the business, its suppliers, marketing intermediaries, buyers, all types of competitors—direct, substitute and new entrant—and its publics

Figure 3.3
The forces of the marketing environment: macro and micro

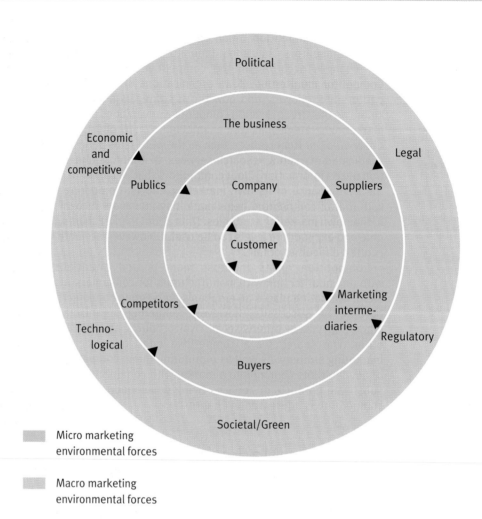

Micro marketing environmental forces

Macro marketing environmental forces

Suppliers   Most organisations source raw materials, components or supplies from third parties. Without the understanding and cooperation of these other organisations, a business would fail to deliver a quality product or service that satisfies its customers' needs. Marketers must be aware of aspects of supply that might affect the way in which their organisation functions in satisfying its customers. These forces could include supplier innovations; deals with rivals; supply shortages, delays or quality concerns; strikes or recruitment difficulties; legal actions or warranty disputes; supply costs and price trends; new entrants into the supply chain; or anything prone to altering the business's receipt of its required supplies.

Marketing Intermediaries   Some businesses sell directly to their targeted customers. Most, though, utilise the skills, network and resources of intermediaries to make their products available to the end-user customer. Intermediaries are discussed later (see Part III) and include resellers such as retailers, wholesalers, agents, brokers, dealers; as well as physical distribution companies responsible for logistical needs; providers of marketing services such as advertising agencies or packaging design consultancies; and financial facilitators of credit lines and export guarantees. Without the smooth cooperation of such intermediaries, an organisation is unlikely to be able to deliver its products as required by its customers. For example, the collapse of a credit company or bank severely reduces the ability of a client business to fund its activities. A striking workforce in a business's preferred road haulage company will lead to the urgent need to negotiate alternative

logistical support with a new haulier, requiring time and perhaps legal intervention given existing contractual arrangements. An advertising agent's new account win might be that of a direct rival to an existing client. The existing client business might sensibly choose to find a different advertising agency, but this move will have a penalty in terms of management time and perhaps the timely execution of a planned advertising campaign.

In each of these examples, shrewd awareness of developments by an organisation's marketers would have reduced the likelihood of any impediment to its own activities and ability to serve its own customers. Failure to pick up on any of these events would have resulted in a loss of business as the marketers and colleagues in other business functions sought alternative lines of credit, haulage agreements or advertising expertise.

Buyers Customers are central to the marketing concept. They are often fickle and have ever changing requirements, needs and perceptions, which marketers must understand, anticipate and satisfy. As Chapters 4 and 5 describe, consumers and business customers should be analysed, and the marketing mix developed by a set of marketers must be designed to satisfy these customers' requirements. Each individual organisation will have a unique set of resources, skills, marketing programmes and products to offer its customers. Therefore, as customers' needs evolve, separate businesses will find that their required response is different. As the consumer has come to demand more customer service from supermarket retailers, Tesco and Sainsbury's have been better placed to upgrade their service-oriented propositions than, say, Somerfield or Iceland. This micro environmental force has had a variable impact on these retailers' strategies.

Competitors Marketers must strive to satisfy their target customers but in a manner that differentiates their product, brand and overall proposition from competing companies' marketing mixes. In order to achieve this, marketers require an in-depth understanding of their competitive arena, as explained in Chapter 2. There are two important considerations in this analysis. First, competition stems not only from like-for-like or direct rivals. There are substitute solutions to monitor and new entrants to anticipate. For example, construction equipment manufacturer JCB competes with a plethora of similar businesses such as Caterpillar or Case. Iseki manufactures none of the same equipment, but it produces a micro-bore tunnelling 'mole' that lays pipes without the need to dig trenches, thus rendering the need for a JCB backhoe loader digger redundant. Such substitute competition can seriously erode an organisation's market position if not observed and combated. New entrant car producer Daewoo made significant sales inroads in the European small and medium car market. Certain car manufacturing rivals had anticipated Daewoo's arrival with pre-emptive product launches and marketing campaigns. Other rivals had no contingency plans and saw their market share seriously eroded.

The second consideration is the organisation's own position: resources, market standing, capabilities, strengths and any competitive edge held over rivals. These characteristics are different for each organisation, so the impact of any competitive activity will vary between businesses. Marketers must be aware of direct, substitute and new entrant competitor activity but should also gauge the likely impact of competition on their own business in the context of a sound understanding of their capabilities and standing as explained in Chapter 2.

Publics The micro marketing environment also includes any group – public – that does or could impact on an organisation's ability to satisfy its target customers and achieve its corporate objectives.[11] These include: financial bodies such as banks, investment houses, financial analysts or shareholders; newspaper, magazine, radio, television, or Internet media that carry features about a business, its products and activities; government bodies that may intervene over operating or consumer issues; consumer and pressure groups; neighbourhood publics such as residents adjacent to a large manufacturing plant; the general public, whose view of an organisation must be assessed and taken into account when developing marketing programmes; and internal publics such as the workforce. Most businesses are increasingly recognising the importance of communicating effectively with these sets of people. The notion of relationship marketing outlined in Chapter 1 is designed to emphasise the need to address more publics than solely customers through marketing programmes and communications. In order to achieve this effectively, however, it is necessary for an organisation to understand these micro marketing environment forces.

The Marketing Environment and Strategic Opportunities

Strategic windows
Major developments or opportunities triggered by changes in the marketing environment

When changes occur in the marketing environment they can trigger major developments. If large enough, such changes are called **strategic windows** or paradigm shifts.[12] If market leaders have failed to spot the underlying development or evolutionary change, rivals may have an opportunity to gain an advantage over established companies and brands by 'stepping through the open window'. The established company must strive to 'close the window' with its own proposition speedily enough to pre-empt competitors' inroads. Failure to monitor the marketing environment and take appropriate action invariably results in an organisation being unable to react to the change quickly enough to keep out competitors.

Opening Strategic Windows

Marketing strategists believe there are six broad causes of strategic windows opening, as described below.[13]

New Technology   Duracell overtook market leader EverReady because it took advantage of new lithium technology before EverReady modified its product range. Direct Line gained leadership in the car insurance market because it turned to direct selling via telephone call centres before any of the major insurance companies recognised this evolving use of technology.

New Markets   Security services and logistics company Securicor was quick to spot the likely take-off of the mobile phone market, taking the majority share in the then leading network provider Cellnet (O2). This awareness of new markets enabled Securicor to firmly establish itself as a multi-faceted communications business.

New Distribution Channels   Telecommunications provider Vodafone was quick to recognise that some customers were reluctant to venture into specialist mobile phone shops, feeling they would be confused by the sales person's fast patter. Vodafone created point-of-sale displays with self-service selection for mainstream retailers such as Woolworths and Halfords. This self-selection appealed to a segment of the market and this innovative channel of distribution – cutting out mobile phone shops and specialists – helped to expand Vodafone's market share.

Market Redefinition   NCR – National Cash Registers – used to dominate the market for providing electronic cash tills in retailers' stores. As retailers discovered the convenience of stock management through barcodes and EPoS systems, they turned to more sophisticated systems. Retail management's desire to monitor and record detailed sales data altered the buyer's requirement for in-store technology. ICL (Fujitsu) and Nixdorf were quick to spot this change and build on their computer industry resources to develop all-in retail systems that incorporated the cash till with much more. This redefinition of the market eroded NCR's once dominant position while giving rivals a marketing opportunity.

New Legislation and Regulation   Laws, regulations and international agreements create strategic windows. The 'open skies' policy of the EU has created route opportunities for smaller airlines once precluded from hubs by state-protected national airlines. Privatisation of the UK rail network enabled Stagecoach and Virgin to diversify their businesses into rail services.

Financial and Political 'Shocks'   Sudden changes in currency prices, interest rates, trade agreements, inflation, unemployment levels, protectionist policies or political leadership can have a major impact on business. A new government might decide to privatise state-owned assets or regulate an industry's activities more tightly. A trade war between states will impact on organisations operating in such markets.

The Importance of Keeping a Lookout for the Strategic Window

Often managers only notice sales dips months after a marketing environment force has created a problem. In the meantime, this has created a window for competitors to enter. While there are many psychological factors that can hinder managerial activity, such as a preference for retrenchment and an aversion to change,[14] a common problem is simply the failure to formally and routinely monitor the forces of the marketing environment through environmental scanning – the process of collecting and analysing information about the forces of the marketing environment. An organisation must determine which aspects of the marketing environment – macro and micro – to monitor and how. Strategists believe a regular and routinised system enables identification of strongly signalled issues, which senior management or a marketing function can then prioritise for more detailed investigation. Clearly, given the vast array of issues examined in this chapter, it is not feasible or desirable for a set of managers to address every conceivably pertinent facet of the trading environment. However, failure to examine the marketing environment is a major problem for many poorly run organisations lacking a marketing orientation.

As described in the Marketing Tools and Techniques box, companies opt for different solutions.[15] Some require line managers to undertake environmental scanning in addition to their other responsibilities. Occasionally, a strategic planner undertakes such monitoring, although this head office position is often too divorced from the organisation's operations to identify which crucial core forces to investigate. A few large companies have created a bespoke marketing environment unit of cross-functional managers responsible for researching, analysing, disseminating and recommending. This ensures scanning occurs but is costly and, again, can be too removed from a company's operations. More frequently, marketing planning identifies core trends and evolving forces to monitor.[16]

Marketing planning is practised in most medium-sized and large companies, and part of the cross-functional, multi-hierarchical team's remit is to report annually on marketing environment forces likely to have implications for the organisation. Some companies have no more than a box in the centre of an open-plan office in which any manager can deposit marketing environment information stemming from press comments, customer feedback, dealer observations, trade show intelligence, analysts' reports or any other inputs. This material is sifted regularly, summarised and circulated, with individual issues followed up as determined necessary by managerial judgement. Other organisations have formalised this approach using e-mail newsletters and intranet boards to personnel and sites within the organisation, often globally, with interactive dialogue aiding the understanding of the environmental forces noted.

PEST analysis
A popular name for an evaluation of the marketing environment, looking at political — including legal and regulatory issues — economic, social and technological developments, and assessing the implications of such issues

No matter how it is orchestrated, it is essential that the marketing environment is monitored thoroughly and regularly.[17] This must translate into managerial recommendations when necessary, with target market strategies and marketing programmes reflecting the issues identified. Such an analysis is often termed a **PEST analysis**, looking at political (P) – including legal and regulatory issues – economic (E), social (S) and technological (T) developments, and assessing the implications of such issues. An understanding of the marketing environment – macro and micro forces – is essential for a rigorous and meaningful assessment of marketing opportunities. Without such an analysis, any recommended marketing strategy is unlikely to take account of newly opening strategic windows. Competitors may be offered the chance to make inroads and the organisation may fail to benefit from potential marketing opportunities.

Summary

The *marketing environment* consists of external forces that directly or indirectly influence an organisation's acquisition of inputs (personnel, financial resources, raw materials, information) and generation of outputs (information, packages, goods, services, ideas). Generally, the forces of the marketing environment are divided into two categories: macro and micro. The macro marketing environment comprises political, legal and regulatory forces, societal forces, including Green concerns for the earth's natural environment, and technological forces. Along with economic forces and trends, these macro, broader, aspects of the marketing environment have an impact on manufacturers and their customers. The forces of the micro marketing environment are more company-specific and include the business's internal environment, suppliers, marketing intermediaries, buyers, competitors and publics.

» To monitor changes in these forces, marketers should practise environmental scanning and analysis. *Environmental scanning* is the process of collecting information about the forces in the marketing environment; *environmental analysis* is the process of assessing and interpreting the information obtained in scanning. This information helps marketing managers predict opportunities and threats associated with environmental fluctuation. Marketing management may assume either a passive, reactive approach or an active, aggressive approach in responding to these environmental fluctuations. The choice depends on an organisation's structure and needs, and on the composition of the environmental forces.

» The political, legal and regulatory forces of the marketing environment are closely interrelated. The current political outlook is reflected in legislation and regulations, or the lack of them.

The political environment may determine what laws and regulations affecting specific marketers are enacted, and how much the government purchases and from which suppliers; it can also be important in helping organisations secure foreign markets.

» Legislation affecting marketing activities can be divided into *procompetitive legislation* – laws designed to preserve competition and to end various practices deemed unacceptable by society – and consumer protection laws. In the UK, the Restrictive Trade Practices Act and the Competition Act sought to prevent monopolies and activities that limit competition; while legislation such as the Financial Services Act, the Sale of Goods Act and the Consumer Credit Act was directed towards more specific practices. Consumer protection laws generally relate to product safety and information disclosure. The actual effects of legislation are determined by how marketers and the courts interpret the laws.

» Regulatory agencies influence most marketing activities. For example, in the UK the *Competition Commission* and the *Office of Fair Trading* usually have the power to enforce specific laws and some discretion in establishing operating rules and drawing up regulations to guide certain types of industry practice. Self-regulation by industry represents another regulatory force; marketers are more in favour of this type of regulation than government action, because they have more opportunity to take part in creating the guidelines. Self-regulation may be less expensive than government regulation, and its guidelines are often more realistic. However, such regulation generally cannot assure compliance as effectively as government agencies.

» *Societal/Green forces* refer to the structure and dynamics of individuals and groups, and the issues that concern them. Many members of society want a high standard of living and a high quality of life, and they expect business to help them achieve these goals. Of growing concern is the well-being of the earth, its resources, climate and peoples. The *Green movement* is increasing general awareness of the natural environment and is altering product design, manufacture, packaging and use. The *consumer movement* is a diverse collection of independent individuals, groups and organisations that attempt to protect the rights of consumers. The major issues taken up by the consumer movement fall into three categories: environmental protection, product performance and safety, and information disclosure. Consumer rights organisations inform and organise other consumers, raise issues, help organisations develop consumer-oriented programmes and pressure legislators to enact consumer protection laws. Some are quite formally organised, such as the *Consumers' Association*.

» *Technology* is the knowledge of how to accomplish tasks and goals. Product development, packaging, promotion, prices and distribution systems are all influenced directly by technology. Several factors determine how much and in what way a particular organisation will make use of technology. These factors include the company's ability to use technology; consumers' ability and willingness to buy technologically improved products; the business's perception of the long-term effects of applying technology; the extent to which the company is technologically based; the degree to which technology is used as a competitive tool; and the extent to which the business can protect technological applications through patents. Many organisations conduct a *technology assessment*.

» The *economic forces* that can strongly influence marketing decisions and activities are general economic conditions, buying power, willingness to spend, spending patterns and *competitive forces*. The overall state of the economy fluctuates in a general pattern known as the *business cycle*. The stages of the business cycle are *prosperity*, *recession*, *depression* and *recovery*.

» Consumers' goods, services and financial holdings make up their *buying power*—their ability to purchase. The financial sources of buying power are *income*, credit and wealth. After-tax income used for spending or saving is called *disposable income*. Disposable income left after an individual has purchased the basic necessities of food, clothing and shelter is called *discretionary income*. It is important to identify levels of *wealth*. Two measures of buying power are: effective buying income (which includes salaries, wages, dividends, interest, profits and rents, less taxes); and the buying power index (a weighted index consisting of population, effective buying income and retail sales data). The factors that affect consumers' *willingness to spend* are product price, the level of satisfaction obtained from currently used products, and expectations about future employment, family size, income, prices and general economic conditions. *Consumer spending patterns* indicate the relative proportions of annual family expenditures, or the actual amount of money spent, on certain kinds of goods and services. *Comprehensive spending patterns* specify the percentages of family income allotted to annual expenditures for general classes of goods and services. *Product-specific spending patterns* indicate the annual amounts families spend for specific products within a general product class.

» *Competition* is a fundamental concern for all marketers. Although all businesses compete for consumers' spending, a company's direct competitors are usually the organisations in its geographic area marketing products that resemble its own or which can be substituted for them. The number of businesses that control the supply of a product may affect the strength of competition. There are four general types of competitive structure: *monopoly*, *oligopoly*, *monopolistic competition* and *perfect competition*. Marketers use *competitor monitoring* to determine what competitors are currently doing and to assess the changes occurring in the competitive environment.

» Increasingly, marketers make a distinction between the broader trading *macro marketing environment* forces – political, legal, regulatory, societal/Green, technological, economic/ competitive – and the more company-specific forces of the *micro marketing environment*. Micro forces include the business in question, its suppliers, marketing intermediaries, buyers, business-specific competition – direct, substitute and new entrant rivals – and the various publics of an organisation: financial bodies, media, government, consumer and pressure groups, neighbours, the general public and the internal workforce.

❯❯ Changes in the marketing environment often create *strategic windows* that, if they are not quickly identified, can enable rivals to gain an edge. There are six key causes of the creation of strategic windows, all aspects of the macro or micro marketing environment: new technology, new markets, new distribution channels, market redefinition, new legislation and regulation, plus financial and political

'shocks'. Often, managers fail to notice sales dips until months after the impact of an aspect of the marketing environment. This may be because they are averse to change and prefer retrenchment, but often it stems from a lack of environmental scanning. Strategists believe a regular and routinised assessment of the marketing environment is essential prior to the formulation of any target market strategies or marketing mix programmes. Practitioners often name such an assessment a *PEST analysis*. Companies adopt different solutions to monitoring the marketing environment, it can be carried out by: line managers, strategic planners, bespoke units or be incorporated as an integral part of the annual marketing planning process. It is essential that the marketing environment – macro and micro forces – is monitored continually in order to maximise marketing opportunities and fend off competitors' actions.

◉ *Key Links*

Marketers must analyse the marketing environment in order to identify opportunities and minimise threats. This chapter should be read in conjunction with:
- Chapter 1, examining marketing opportunity analysis.
- Chapter 2, the overview of marketing strategy development.

Important Terms

Marketing environment
Environmental scanning
Environmental analysis
Procompetitive legislation
Office of Fair Trading
Competition Commission
Consumers' Association
Societal/Green forces
Green movement
Consumer movement
Technology
Technology assessment
Economic and competitive forces
Business cycle
Prosperity
Recession
Depression

Recovery
Buying power
Income
Disposable income
Discretionary income
Wealth
Willingness to spend
Consumer spending patterns
Comprehensive spending patterns
Product-specific spending patterns
Competition
Monopoly
Oligopoly
Monopolistic competition
Perfect competition
Competitor monitoring
Macro marketing environment
Micro marketing environment
Strategic windows
PEST analysis

Discussion and Review Questions

1 Why are environmental scanning and analysis so important?
2 How are political forces related to legal and regulatory forces?
3 Describe marketers' attempts to influence political forces.

4 What types of procompetitive legislation directly affect marketing practices?

5 What is the major objective of most procompetitive laws? Do the laws generally accomplish this objective? Why or why not?

6 What types of problem do marketers experience as they interpret legislation?

7 What are the goals of the Competition Commission? How does the Commission affect marketing activities?

8 Name several non-governmental regulatory forces. Do you believe that self-regulation is more or less effective than governmental regulatory agencies? Why?

9 How is the so-called 'Green movement' altering the shape of business?

10 Describe the consumer movement. Analyse some active consumer forces in your area.

11 What does the term 'technology' mean to you?

12 How does technology affect you as a member of society? Do the benefits of technology outweigh its costs and dangers?

13 Discuss the impact of technology on marketing activities.

14 What factors determine whether an organisation adopts and uses technology?

15 In what ways can each of the business cycle stages affect consumers' reactions to marketing strategies?

16 What is the current business cycle stage? How is this stage affecting businesses in your area?

17 Define income, disposable income and discretionary income. How does each type of income affect consumer buying power?

18 How is consumer buying power affected by wealth and consumer credit?

19 How is buying power measured? Why should it be evaluated?

20 What factors influence a consumer's willingness to spend?

21 What are the principal types of competition?

22 What differentiates the forces of the micro marketing environment from those of the macro marketing environment?

23 Why must marketers monitor changes in supplier and marketing intermediary practices?

24 Why should marketers not only track direct, like-for-like competitors? What other types of competitor are there?

25 Why should marketers be aware of their organisation's publics?

26 How does an assessment of marketing environment forces assist in marketing opportunity analysis?

27 What are the main causes of the opening of strategic windows?

28 How can a business instigate environmental scanning?

Recommended Reading

- Dibb, S. and Simkin, L., *Marketing Planning* (London: Cengage, 2008).
- Drucker, P., *Management in Turbulent Times* (London: Butterworth-Heinemann/Pan, 1994).
- Jain, S.C., *Marketing Planning & Strategy* (Cincinnati, OH: South Western, 1999).
- Palmer, A., Worthington, I., Hartley, B. and Mulholland, M., *The Business and Marketing Environment* (Maidenhead: McGraw-Hill, 1999).
- Peattie, K., *Environmental Marketing Management* (London: Pitman, 1995).
- Porter, M.E., 'How competitive forces shape strategy', *Harvard Business Review*, March–April 1979, pp. 137–45.

🌐 Internet Exercise

Choose the websites of key government departments, EU departments or of leading regulatory bodies and learn more about the ways in which their activities and powers impact on marketers and consumers. For example, log on to the websites for the Competition Commission and the Office of Fair Trading at:
www.competition-commission.org.uk and www.oft.gov.uk

1 What are the implications of these organisations' powers and recommendations for marketers?

2 In what ways do the activities of these bodies impact on consumers?

🌐 Applied Mini-Case

Until recently, excepting the low-sugar variants, few observers would have included the producers of the leading colas as aiding healthy diets or encouraging greater awareness of obesity issues. First, the leading suppliers launched low-carb versions, and now they are proactively striving to educate consumers. Coca-Cola, for example, launched a major initiative to encourage people to exercise more. Coke launched an anti-obesity campaign under the title 'Active Lifestyle', engaging with young people through a variety of media. The initiative aimed to promote the route to a healthy lifestyle through a combination of effective hydration, a balanced diet and physical activity.

Sources: Coca-Cola, 2004; Ben Bold, 'Coca-Cola debuts healthy living initiative in UK', *Marketing*, 1 July 2004, p. 1.

❓ Question

As Coca-Cola's marketing manager, how would an understanding of the marketing environment have led to the Active Lifestyle initiative? How might the company have monitored the forces of its marketing environment?

🌐 Case Study

Social Awareness: BMW Recycling the Consumer

The creation of the European Recovery and Recycling Association (ERRA) is indicative of growing concern for the environment and consumer awareness of this social issue. With members including Cadbury Schweppes, Coca-Cola, Heineken, Nestlé, L'Oréal, and Tetra Pak, the Brussels-based ERRA has developed a recycling scheme that could lead to the regular collection of discarded packaging – containers and bottles from housing estates, factories, schools, offices and shops – and their sorting and reuse. The scheme in many countries is far from becoming reality, requiring the significant commitment of government, local authorities and, of course, consumers. However, ERRA exists, supported by an extensive array of manufacturers and environmental pressure groups. The public's interest in the environment and in safeguarding the planet and its resources for generations to come has led companies to pay real attention to the Green lobby.

BMW, the German deluxe car maker, has been stressing the 'recyclability' of its vehicles in its television and press advertising for its 3 Series range. These cars are produced using more environmentally friendly production processes, with a greater proportion of components suitable for reworking.

BMW's commitment to the future, however, goes further. In Landshut, Germany, it has a recycling factory. Two workers can strip all the reusable parts from a 1970s car in under 45 minutes, including the careful draining of all fluids, at a cost of about £90.

Landshut's role is as a huge scrap merchant, but one that adheres to the strictest code of ethical working practices and the latest understanding of how to dispose of redundant vehicles with the least harm to the environment. BMW executives support the notion of a Europe-wide initiative, requiring an authorised recycler to issue a disposal certificate for every car at the end of its life. Until such a certificate is issued, the last registered owner would continue to be liable to pay road taxes. This initiative would eventually require legislation and the support of governments. Meanwhile, several leading car manufacturers have joined forces, adopting standardised colour coding for all reusable parts.

The investment for BMW is significant, but anticipating eventual EU legislation to enforce recycling, the German manufacturer believes it is thinking strategically and is working towards maintaining its position as a major producer of vehicles. BMW has many partner recycling plants worldwide, with its first UK site in Sussex. Simultaneously, BMW is striving to make more of its cars reclaimable: 50 per cent of the current 3 Series can be stripped down and reused. BMW is clear: 'we feel socially, politically and ecologically responsible for everything we do', leading to the creation of the 'Sustainability. It can be done' forum for addressing manufacturing issues of concern to the wider community.

It is not only companies such as BMW that have responded to increasing social awareness of environmental and Green issues. Bottle banks, which exist in most towns at multiple locations, have been joined by collection containers for waste paper, food and drink cans, and even discarded clothes. The charity Oxfam has provided clothing collection banks in many car parks nationwide. Local councils collect householders' waste paper separately from their refuse for recycling. School children are taught to care for their environment and to encourage their parents to use bottle banks and waste paper collections. Societal pressure has created a new way of thinking that marketers must reflect.

Sources: www.bmwgroup.com/e, 2004; 'The can and bottle story: environment', Coca-Cola & Schweppes Beverages Ltd, 1993; 'Helping to solve the waste management puzzle', ERRA, Brussels, 1991; John Eisenhammer, 'Where cars will go when they die', *Independent on Sunday*, 21 February 1993, pp. 24–5; 'Helping the earth begins at home', Central Office of Information, Department of the Environment, HMSO, 1992; BMW 3 Series promotional material, 1995–2004; Warwickshire County Council, 1999; Oxfam, Kenilworth, 1999, 2004; Warwickshire County Council, 2004–7; The European Recovery and Recycling Association, 2007.

❓ *Questions for Discussion*

1 What has persuaded BMW to launch such initiatives as its recycling plants and the 'Sustainability. It can be done' forum?

2 In what ways are local authorities encouraging recycling?

3 What are the implications of the growing consumer interest in recycling for manufacturers of consumer goods?

4

Consumer Buying Behaviour

"Anticipating consumer behaviour is not an option for marketing managers: it is their job description."

Gordon Foxall, Cardiff Business School, University of Wales

Objectives

- **To understand the different types of consumer buying behaviour**

- **To recognise the stages of the consumer buying decision process and understand how this process relates to different types of buying decisions**

- **To explore how personal factors may affect the consumer buying decision process**

- **To learn about the psychological factors that may affect the consumer buying decision process**

- **To examine the social factors that influence the consumer buying decision process**

- **To understand why it is important for marketers to attempt to understand consumer buying behaviour and the role of this behaviour in marketing strategy**

Buying behaviour
The decision processes and actions of people involved in buying and using products

Consumer buying behaviour
The buying behaviour of ultimate consumers – those who purchase products for personal or household use

Introduction

The decision processes and actions of people involved in buying and using products are termed their **buying behaviour**.[1] **Consumer buying behaviour** is the buying behaviour of ultimate consumers – those who purchase products for personal or household family use. Consumer buying behaviour is not concerned with the purchase of items for business use. The next chapter of *Marketing Essentials* examines business or organizational buying behaviour.

There are important reasons for marketers to analyse consumer buying behaviour. The success of a company's marketing strategy will depend on how buyers react to it. As Chapter 1 indicates, the marketing concept requires companies to develop a marketing mix that meets customers' needs. To find out what satisfies customers, marketers must examine the main influences on what, where, when and how consumers buy. Having a good understanding of these consumer buying behaviour factors enables marketers to satisfy customers better because they are able to develop more suitable marketing strategies. Ultimately, this information helps companies compete more effectively in the marketplace.

Although marketers try to understand and influence consumer buying behaviour, they cannot control it. Some critics credit them with the ability to manipulate buyers, but marketers have neither the power nor the knowledge to do so. Their knowledge of behaviour comes from what psychologists, social psychologists and sociologists know about human behaviour in general.

Opener

Pester Power Hits Parents Everywhere

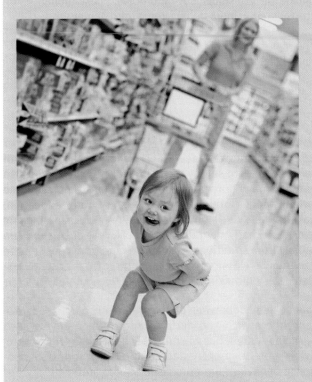

Pressure exerted by children on their parents while shopping has become widely known as 'pester power'. Certain products, such as snacks, training shoes, computer games and leisure activities, are known to be particularly susceptible to this form of persuasion. How often when shopping in the supermarket have you heard a small child plaintively asking their parents to purchase a particular brand of breakfast cereal or snack? In many cases the request may simply reflect the taste preferences of the child. However, research also suggests that these incidents are often triggered by an advertisement the child has seen on the television, or by a promotion the manufacturer is currently running.

Pester power was first mentioned back in 1979. Today it is widely recognised by many parents, even having its own definition: 'The ability children have to nag their parents into purchasing items they would otherwise not buy or performing actions they would otherwise not do' (www.wordspy.com). The fact that children influence the purchase decisions made by their parents is well established.

In fact, this is just one of many influences on the buying decision processes of these individuals. A typical incidence of pester power starts when a child expresses interest in or requests the purchase of a product. This may take place at home, perhaps triggered by the viewing of a television or print advertisement. Perhaps it follows a discussion among classmates at school earlier in the day. In other cases the pestering starts in-store when a favoured brand is spotted on the supermarket shelves or in a shop window. Often a period of negotiation between the child and parent will follow. During this time the views of both parties will be discussed to a greater or lesser extent. This discussion may or may not result in a purchase being made.

Recently, pester power has attracted bad publicity due to increasing problems with childhood obesity. As snack foods are a key target for this kind of pestering, some health experts have criticised the marketing and advertising of unhealthy foodstuffs aimed at children. They point out that, in some countries, advertising aimed at children is banned. It is prohibited now in the UK for certain food and drink products, but not yet for toys and DVDs. As a result of these emerging concerns many marketing practitioners are looking carefully at how their companies' products are marketed to youngsters. For example, Coca-Cola is carrying out its promise to stop advertising to those under the age of 12. As part of this initiative, the company has removed advertising images from vending machines in schools. At this time, a key challenge for marketers is the need to balance the desire to target children using certain kinds of marketing message with not antagonising their parents. Of course, pester power is not limited to foodstuffs. Children are increasingly playing a role in the decisions their families make about larger purchases such as holidays, the family car and even housing. Whatever the result of current initiatives to curtail some of the marketing activities aimed at kids, it seems that their influence in many buying decisions will remain.

Sources: David Murphy, 'Pester-free POP', *Marketing*, 11 March 2004, pp. 27–8; John Roedder, 'Consumer socialization of children: 25 years of research', Journal of Consumer Research, 1999, 26 (3), www.wordspy.com; www.foe.co.uk; James McNeal, *Kids as Customers*, 1992, Lexington Books; BBC news, 2007. Photo: Istockphoto.com

Throughout their lives consumers purchase numerous products of different kinds. In most families, children play an important role in a wide range of these purchase decisions. Given their role it is not surprising that manufacturers and retailers go to such trouble in their marketing efforts to influence these young consumers. However, the views of the kids are just one of many influences that shape the consumer buying process. These influences on what and how consumers buy are considered in more detail later in this chapter.

This chapter begins by examining the types of decision-making in which consumers engage. Chapter 5 then analyses the major stages of the consumer buying decision process and the personal, psychological and social factors that influence it. The chapter concludes by examining why marketers must develop a good understanding of consumer buying behaviour.

Types of Consumer Buying Behaviour

Different consumers have a varied and wide range of needs and wants. The acquisition of products and services helps these consumers to satisfy their current and future needs. To achieve this objective, consumers make many purchasing decisions. For example, people make many decisions daily regarding food, clothing, shelter, medical care, education, recreation or transport. When making these decisions, they engage in decision-making behaviour. The amount of time and effort, both mental and physical, that buyers expend in decision-making varies considerably from situation to situation – and from consumer to consumer. Consumer decisions can thus be classified into one of three broad categories: routine response behaviour, limited decision-making and extensive decision-making.[2]

Routine Response Behaviour

A consumer practises **routine response behaviour** when buying frequently purchased, low-cost, low-risk items that need very little search and decision effort. When buying such items, a consumer may prefer a particular brand, but will probably be familiar with several brands in the product class and view more than one as acceptable. The products a consumer buys through routine response behaviour are purchased almost automatically. For most buyers, the time and effort involved in selecting a bag of sugar or a bar of soap is minimal. If the supermarket has run out of the preferred brand, the buyers will probably choose an alternative brand instead.

Limited Decision-making

Buyers engage in **limited decision-making** when they buy products occasionally and when they need to obtain information about an unfamiliar brand in a familiar product category. This type of decision-making requires a moderate amount of time for information gathering and deliberation. For example, if Nintendo launches a new computer game aimed at teenagers, buyers may seek additional information about the new product, perhaps by asking a friend who has tested the game or seen it reviewed. Similarly, if a well-known brand appears in a new form, the consumer will take extra time.

Extensive Decision-making

The most complex decision-making behaviour, **extensive decision-making**, comes into play when a purchase involves unfamiliar, expensive, high-risk or infrequently bought products – for instance, cars, homes, holidays or personal pensions. The buyer uses many criteria to evaluate alternative brands or choices, and takes time seeking information and comparing alternative brands before making the purchase decision.

Impulse Buying   By contrast, **impulse buying** involves no conscious planning but a powerful, persistent urge to buy something immediately. Self-control failure is one factor that appears to affect whether or not consumers indulge in this kind of buying.[3] As the Marketing Insight box explains, research suggests that consumers are increasingly engaging in impulse buying. For some individuals, impulse buying may be the dominant buying behaviour. Impulse buying,

---

Routine response behaviour
Behaviour that occurs when buying frequently purchased, low-cost, low-risk items that need little search and decision effort

Limited decision-making
Behaviour that occurs when buying products purchased only occasionally, for which a moderate amount of information gathering and deliberation is needed

Impulse buying
Behaviour that involves no conscious planning but results from a powerful, persistent urge to buy something immediately

❂ Marketing Insight

Impulse Shopping on the Increase

How often have you come back from a shopping expedition with more items than you planned to buy? If the answer is 'usually', then you are not alone! Consumers are apparently becoming increasingly impulsive in their shopping behaviour. People are now more likely than ever to buy items on impulse when they go out shopping. The trend is away from the carefully planned shopping trips and routine saving of spare income of the past. Recent research highlights that over the last 20 years consumer attitudes toward impulse buying have shifted. Figures for the purchase of clothing, food, toiletries, computer games, PDAs, MP3 players, mobile phones and home electronics all suggest increasing levels of buying on impulse. However, the extent of impulse shopping in these categories varies, with consumers being much more likely to buy clothing or food on impulse than mobile phones or other electrical goods. This apparently relates to the level of pre-planning involved in different kinds of purchases. Thus shoppers are more likely to impulse buy less complex or routinely purchased products. Ready meals, snacks, cosmetics and magazines are just a few of the typical purchases.

Different consumers vary in their levels of impulse buying. Research suggests that the impulse buying trait is particularly marked among young consumers and those in the 55–64 age range. One of the reasons for the trend might be rising disposable income, as these groups are known to have relatively high levels of spare income once day-to-day expenses have been met. Experts suggest that other influential factors are the ready availability of credit, increasingly well-designed and tempting retail environments, and a greater emphasis on shopping as a leisure activity. The ease with which consumers can acquire store payment cards and the widespread promotion of personal loans mean that even those with restricted incomes can indulge in such

impromptu buying behaviour. Enticing retail design and greater variety on the high street contribute to the notion of shopping as a leisure activity. Many consumers enjoy the opportunity to meet up with friends or family, and spend time perusing the products and brands in their local shopping centres. Some are prepared to travel further afield to larger towns or shopping villages to maximise the leisure experience. Recent research highlights the connection between this kind of enjoyment and the propensity to impulse buy, showing that consumers are more likely to make unplanned purchases when they have enjoyed the shopping experience.

The implications of these trends for marketing practitioners and retailers are far-reaching. If consumers are devoting less attention to advance planning in favour of more impulse buying, the retail environment will become more important than ever in shaping the buying decisions that are made. One outcome might be that balance of marketing spend will shift away from traditional media and towards in-store promotions. For example, recent initiatives to introduce in-store television and radio into supermarkets and department stores typify some of the possible developments in this area. Part of the rationale is that consumers walking into the likes of Tesco, Sainsbury's and Carrefour are already in shopping mode and are therefore likely to be receptive to these kinds of media. Retail experts believe that one of the keys to success will be to design content that dovetails with the shopping experience in which the consumer is engaged. Thus short, snappy commercials will be favoured over longer 30-second formats.

Sources: Caroline Parry, 'Enthusiastic for listless shopping', *Marketing Week*, 4 March 2004, pp. 30–1; Amanda Wilkinson, 'Box on shelf on box on …', *Marketing Week*, 26 February 2004, pp. 24–27; shopping habit surveys, 2007.

however, often provokes emotional conflict. For example, a young woman buying a new outfit for clubbing, may later regret the expense because a friend has purchased the same item. Marketers often capitalise on the tendency towards impulse buying – for example, by placing magazines and confectionery next to supermarket checkout counters.

Variations in Decision-making Behaviour

The purchase of a particular product does not always elicit the same type of decision-making behaviour.[4] In some instances, buyers engage in extensive decision-making the first time they purchase a certain kind of product but find that limited decision-making suffices when they

Extensive decision-making

Behaviour that occurs when a purchase involves unfamiliar, expensive, high-risk or infrequently bought products for which the buyer spends much time seeking information and comparing brands before deciding on the purchase

Consumer buying decision process

A five-stage process that includes problem recognition, information search, evaluation of alternatives, purchase and post-purchase evaluation

buy the product again. If a routinely purchased brand no longer pleases the consumer, either limited or extensive decision processes may be used to switch to a new brand. For example, if the video tapes a family usually buys are too easily damaged, a better-quality brand may be sought in the future.

The Consumer Buying Decision Process

A major part of buying behaviour is the decision process used in making purchases. The **consumer buying decision process**, shown in Figure 4.1, includes five stages:

1 problem recognition
2 information search
3 evaluation of alternatives
4 purchase
5 post-purchase evaluation.

Although a detailed understanding of these stages is needed, a number of general observations are also pertinent. First, the actual act of purchasing is only one stage in the process; the process begins several stages before the purchase itself. Second, not all decision processes lead to a purchase, even though the diagrammatical process implies that they do. A consumer may stop the process at any time. It is also possible that a different sequence of stages will be followed, with buyers revisiting certain stages. Finally, consumer decisions do not always include all five stages. People engaged in extensive decision-making usually go through all stages of this decision process, whereas those engaged in limited decision-making and routine response behaviour may omit certain parts.

Figure 4.1
The consumer buying decision process and possible influences on the process

Stage 1: Problem Recognition

Problem recognition occurs when a buyer becomes aware that there is a difference between a desired state and an actual condition. For example, consider a sales manager who needs to keep a record of appointments. When, at the end of the year, her old diary is finished, she recognises that a difference exists between the desired state (a current diary) and the actual condition (an out-of-date one). She therefore makes the decision to buy a new diary.

Sometimes a person has a problem or need but is unaware of it. Some consumers may be concerned about their weight but may not be aware that low-calorie options exist for favourite products. Marketers use sales staff, advertising, sales promotion and packaging to help trigger such need recognition. For example, travel agents may advertise package holidays immediately after the Christmas and New Year holidays. People who see the advertisements may realise that now is a good time to plan their summer holidays. The speed of consumer problem recognition can be either slow or rapid, depending on the individual concerned and the way in which need recognition was triggered.

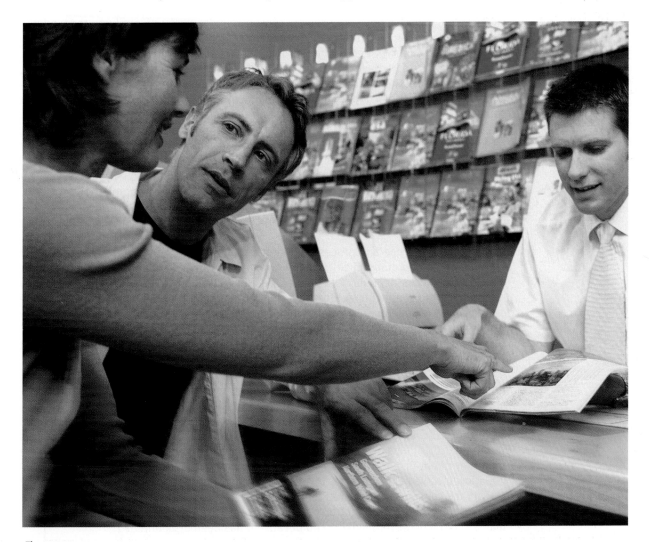

Figure 4.2
Along with the web, travel agents provide a valuable source of information for consumers selecting a holiday
Photo © Royalty-Free/CORBIS

Stage 2: Information Search

After recognising the problem or need, the buyer (if continuing the decision process) searches for information about products that will resolve the problem or satisfy the need. For example, after people have recognised the need to plan their holiday, they may search for information about different tour operators, travel options and possible locations. Information is acquired over time from the consumer's surroundings and, ever more frequently, on the Internet. The impact the information has will depend on how the consumer interprets it.

Internal search
One in which the buyer searches his or her memory for information about products

External search
One that focuses on information not available from the consumer's memory

There are two aspects to information search. In the **internal search**, buyers search their memory for information about products that might solve the problem. If they cannot retrieve enough information from their memory to make a decision, they seek additional information in an **external search**. The external search may involve communicating with friends and colleagues, comparing available brands and prices, or reviewing television or press advertisements, and public sources including the Internet. An individual's personal contacts – friends, relatives, associates – are often viewed as credible sources of information because the consumer trusts and respects them. A consumer study has shown that word-of-mouth communication often impacts more strongly on consumer judgements of products than printed communications. Using marketer-dominated information sources, such as sales staff, advertising, packaging, in-store demonstrations and displays, typically does not require much effort on the consumer's part. Buyers can also obtain information from public sources – for instance, government reports, news stories, the Internet, consumer publications and reports from product testing organisations. Many companies use public relations to try to capitalise on these sources because consumers often perceive them as factual and unbiased. The external search is also characterised by the extensiveness, manner and order in which brands, stores, attributes and sources are considered. For example, a man buying a new suit for work may look at or try on several styles at a number of clothing outlets before reaching a final decision.

Consumer groups are increasingly demanding access to greater quantities of relevant product information. However, research shows that buyers make poorer choices if overloaded with too much information.[5] Improving the quality of information and stressing features important to buyers in the decision process may help buyers make better purchase decisions.

How consumers use and process the information obtained in their search depends on features of the information itself, namely availability, quantity, quality, repetition and format. If all the necessary information for a decision is available in the store, consumers may have no need to conduct an internal information search and the decision process may be easier.[6] However, adequate information may not always be available, and consumers may have to make do with whatever data are to hand. For example, a motorist replacing a broken windscreen following a road accident may not have enough time to review all relevant sources of information because the car is needed again urgently.

Repetition   Repetition, a technique well known to advertisers, increases consumer learning of information. When seeing or hearing an advertisement for the first time, the recipient may not grasp all its important details but learns more as the message is repeated. Nevertheless, even when commercials are initially effective, repetition eventually causes 'wear-out': consumers pay less attention and respond less favourably to the advertisement than they did at first.[7] Consumers are more likely to be receptive to repetition when making a low-involvement purchase. **Involvement** refers to the level of interest, emotion and activity the consumer is prepared to expend on a particular purchase. For example, a consumer who buys a box of light bulbs may have very low interest in the product itself but may elect to buy the particular brand because it has been discounted.

Involvement
The level of interest, emotion and activity the consumer is prepared to expend on a particular purchase

Format   The format in which information is transmitted to the buyer may also determine its effectiveness. Information can be presented verbally, numerically or visually. Consumers often remember pictures better than words, and the combination of pictures and words further enhances learning.[8] Consequently, marketers pay great attention to the visual components of their advertising materials.

A successful information search yields a group of possible brand alternatives. This group of products is sometimes called the buyer's **evoked set**. For example, an evoked set of televisions might be those manufactured by Sony, LG, JVC and Philips.

Evoked set
The group of products that a buyer views as possible alternatives after conducting an information search

Stage 3: Evaluation of Alternatives

Salience
The level of importance a buyer assigns to each criterion for comparing products

When evaluating the products in the evoked set, a buyer establishes criteria for comparing the products. These criteria are the characteristics or features that the buyer wants (or does not want). For example, one buyer may favour a mobile phone with blue-tooth technology, whereas another may require a model with a flap, but be unwilling to pay a premium for blue tooth. The buyer also assigns a certain **salience**, or level of importance, to each criterion; some features carry more weight than others. The salience of criteria varies from buyer to buyer. For example, when choosing a newspaper one buyer may consider the political stance of the editorial to be crucial, while another may place greater importance on the quality and coverage of sports. The criteria and their salience are used by the buyer to rank the brands in the evoked set. This involves comparing the brands with each other as well as with the criteria. If the evaluation stage does not yield a brand that the buyer wishes to buy, further information search may be necessary.

Marketers can influence consumers' evaluation by *framing* the alternatives – that is, by the manner in which the alternative and its attributes are described. Framing can make a characteristic seem more important and can facilitate its recall from memory. For example, by emphasising whitening ingredients in toothpaste, manufacturers can encourage the consumer to consider this particular aspect to be important. Framing affects the decision processes of inexperienced buyers more than those of experienced ones. If the evaluation of alternatives yields one or more brands that the consumer is willing to buy, the consumer is ready to move on to the next stage of the decision process: the purchase.

Stage 4: Purchase

The purchase stage, when the consumer chooses which product or brand to buy, is mainly the outcome of the consumer's evaluation of alternatives, but other factors have an impact, too. The closeness of alternative stores and product availability can both influence which brand is purchased. For example, if the brand the buyer ranked highest is not available locally, an alternative may be selected.

During this stage, the buyer also picks the seller from whom the product will be purchased and finalises the terms of the sale. Other issues such as price, delivery, guarantees, service agreements, installation and credit arrangements are discussed and settled. Finally, provided the consumer does not terminate the buying decision process before then, the purchase is made.

Stage 5: Post-purchase Evaluation

After the purchase has taken place, the buyer begins evaluating the product to check whether its actual performance meets expected levels. Many of the criteria used in evaluating alternatives are revisited during this stage. The outcome will determine whether the consumer is satisfied or dissatisfied, and will influence future behaviour. The level of satisfaction a consumer experiences will determine whether they make a complaint, communicate with other possible buyers or purchase the product again.[9] The extent to which consumers are angered by the outcome of a purchase also influences how they will behave in the future.[10] Figure 4.3 illustrates the types of action that dissatisfied consumers may take. The likelihood that consumers will stop buying a particular product will depend on a range of factors, including how much knowledge they have about alternatives.[11] Some marketing experts believe that increasing consumer assertiveness is a positive move, which illustrates industry's willingness to respond to feedback about products and services.[12] The impact of post-purchase evaluation is illustrated by the feedback loop in Figure 4.1.

Figure 4.3
The nature of customer complaints Source: Neill Denny, 'Why complaining is our new hobby', from Marketing Magazine, 26 November 1998, p. 16. Reprinted with permission

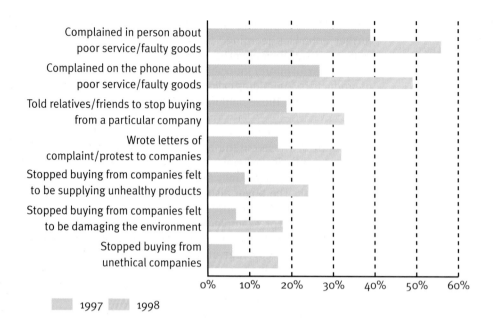

1997 ▨ 1998

Cognitive dissonance
Doubts that occur as the buyer questions whether he or she made the right decision in purchasing the product

The evaluation that follows the purchase of some products, particularly expensive or important items, may result in **cognitive dissonance** – doubts that occur because the buyer questions whether the best purchase decision was made. For example, after buying a new personal computer, an accountant may feel anxious about whether the brand will be reliable or if the warranty is adequate. A buyer who experiences cognitive dissonance may attempt to return the product or may seek positive information about it to justify the choice. For example, motoring journalists often note with amusement that car shows and exhibitions are frequented by consumers who have recently purchased a new car.

As shown in Figure 4.1, three major categories of influence are believed to affect the consumer buying decision process: personal, psychological and social factors. These factors determine which particular instant coffee, shampoo, washing powder, DVD player, holiday, car or house a particular consumer will buy. Understanding these aspects helps marketers gain valuable insights into their customer base and can help ensure that a more suitable marketing mix is developed. The remainder of this chapter focuses on these factors. Although each major factor is discussed separately, it is a combination of their effects that influences the consumer buying decision process.

Personal Factors Influencing the Buying Decision Process

Personal influencing factors
Factors unique to a particular individual

Personal influencing factors are unique to a particular person. Many different personal factors can influence purchasing decisions. In this section, three types are considered: demographic factors, situational factors and level of involvement.

Demographic Factors

Demographic factors are individual characteristics such as age, sex, race, ethnic origin, income, family life cycle and occupation. (These and other characteristics are discussed in Chapter 6 as possible segmentation variables.) Given the potential impact of such features on buying requirements and behaviour, marketing professionals must develop a clear understanding of such characteristics.

Demographic factors have a bearing on who is involved in family decision-making. For example, it is estimated that in the next few years the UK, Germany and Turkey will have

Demographic factors
Individual characteristics such as age, sex, race, ethnic origin, income, family life cycle and occupation

the largest market for children's toys and clothes in the EU, based on the number of children in the population. Children aged 6 to 17 are known to have growing influence in the buying decision process for breakfast cereals, ice cream, soft drinks, holidays and even the family car.[13] This influence is increasingly reflected in the way such products are designed and marketed. For example, holiday brochures now contain pictures and information designed to appeal to children and teenagers. Demographic factors may also shape behaviour during a specific stage of the decision process. For example, during information search, a young person may consult a greater number of information sources than an older, more experienced adult.

Demographic factors also affect the manner in which products in a specific product category are used. While consumers aged 18 to 30 may spend a lot of their disposable income on necessities for establishing their households, such as furniture, appliances and DIY products, those aged 45 to 54 whose children have left home spend more on luxury and leisure items.[14] Brand preferences, store choice and timing of purchases are also affected by demographic factors. Consider, for example, how differences in occupation result in variations in product needs. A car mechanic and a nanny may earn similar incomes, yet spend their earnings entirely differently. While both require work clothes to carry out their jobs, the mechanic will buy heavy-duty boots and overalls, while the nanny opts for a smart, more formal uniform. Their choice of vehicle will also be quite different. While the mechanic selects a basic but robust van, the nanny buys a small four-door hatchback with room for her charges and a pushchair. Thus occupation clearly affects consumer buying behaviour.

Situational Factors

Situational factors
External circumstances or conditions that exist when a consumer is making a purchase decision

Situational factors are the external circumstances or conditions that exist when a consumer is making a purchase decision. These factors can influence the buyer at any stage of the consumer buying decision process and may cause the individual to shorten, lengthen or terminate the process. For example, a school teacher who usually commutes to work by car may be forced to travel by train while her car is being serviced. Similarly, a family holiday may have to be postponed if the children fall ill with chickenpox.

The effects of situational factors can be felt throughout the buying decision process. Uncertainty about employment may sway a consumer against making a purchase. On the other hand, a conviction that the supply of a particular product is sharply limited may impel an individual to buy it. For example, consumers have purchased and hoarded petrol, food products and even toilet tissue when these products were believed to be in short supply. These and other situational factors can change rapidly; their influence on purchase decisions is generally as sudden as it is short-lived.

The amount of time a consumer has available to make a decision strongly influences buying decisions. If there is little time for selecting and purchasing a product, an individual may quickly decide to buy a readily available brand. The time available also affects the way consumers process the information contained in advertisements[15] and the length of the stages within the decision process. For example, if a family is planning to redecorate their house, everyone may get together to collect and review a wide range of information from a variety of sources. They may read home and garden magazines, visit DIY outlets to collect paint charts and wallpaper samples, talk to friends and decorators, look at a number of advertisements and spend time comparing special offers in a number of stores. However, if the family is hit by a house fire that destroys the existing decorations in the house, the extent of the information search, the number of alternatives considered and the amount of comparative shopping may be much more restricted.

Levels of Involvement

Many aspects of consumer buying decisions are affected by the individual's **level of involvement**. This term refers to the level of interest, emotional commitment and time spent searching for a product in a particular situation. The level of involvement determines the extent to which a buyer is motivated to spend time seeking information about a particular product or brand. The extensiveness of the buying decision process therefore varies

Level of involvement
The level of interest, emotional commitment and time spent searching for a product in a particular situation

greatly with the consumer's level of involvement. The sequence of the steps in the process may also be altered. Low-involvement buyers may form an attitude towards a product – perhaps as a result of an advertising campaign – and evaluate its features after purchasing it rather than before.[16] Conversely, high-involvement buyers often spend a great deal of time and effort researching their purchase beforehand. For example, the purchase of a car, such as those from Honda shown in Figure 4.4, is a high involvement decision.

The level of consumer involvement is linked to a number of factors. Consumers tend to be more involved in the purchase of high-priced goods and products that are visible to others, such as clothing, white goods or cars. As levels of perceived risk increase, involvement levels are likely to rise.

Enduring Involvement   Sometimes individuals experience enduring involvement with a product class. Enduring involvement is an ongoing interest in a product class because of

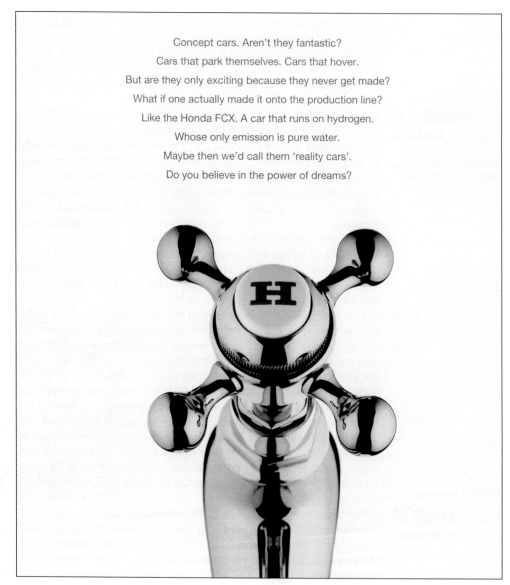

Figure 4.4
The purchase of a car is high involvement, particularly for those utilising unfamiliar and innovative energy solutions
Source: Courtesy of Wieden & Kennedy

personal relevance. For example, people often have enduring involvement with products associated with their leisure activities. These individuals engage in ongoing search and information gathering for these products over extensive periods of time, irrespective of whether or not a purchase is imminent. Football fans often watch the sport on television, attend their local club's games, read the football pages of the newspaper and may even buy their favourite team's football strip.

Situational Involvement   Situational involvement is experienced by buyers as a result of the particular circumstance or environment in which they find themselves. This type of involvement, sometimes also called pre-purchase involvement, is temporary because the conditions that triggered this high involvement may change.[17] A man searching for an engagement ring for his prospective fiancée, for example, will probably experience a high level of involvement in the purchase decision. His information search and evaluation of alternatives may be lengthy. However, once the choice is made, an engagement ring is probably no longer personally relevant.

Low Consumer Involvement   Many purchase decisions do not generate much consumer involvement. When the involvement level is low, as with routine response purchases, the buying is almost automatic, and the information search and evaluation of alternatives are extremely limited. Thus the purchase of floor cleaner is low involvement for many consumers; the product is chosen out of habit and with minimal effort.

Psychological Factors Influencing the Buying Decision Process

Psychological factors operating within individuals partly determine people's general behaviour and thus influence their behaviour as consumers. The primary psychological influences on consumer behaviour are:

- perception
- motives
- learning
- attitudes
- personality.

Even though these psychological factors operate internally, it will become apparent later in this chapter that they are highly affected by social forces external to the individual.

Psychological factors
Factors that influence consumer behaviour, including perception, motives, learning, attitudes and personality

Perception

Perception
The process of selecting, organising and interpreting information inputs to produce meaning

Information inputs
The sensations received through sight, taste, hearing, smell and touch

Are the fish in Figure 4.5 changing into birds or are the birds changing into fish? It could be either depending on how you perceive the birds. People's perception of the same thing varies. Similarly, the same individual at different times may perceive the same item in a number of ways. **Perception** involves a three-step process of selecting, organising and interpreting information inputs to produce meaning. **Information inputs** are the sensations received through sight, taste, hearing, smell and touch. Each time

Figure 4.5
Fish or birds? Do you see the fish changing into birds or the birds changing into fish?
Source: M.C. Escher's "Fish and Birds" © 2004 The M.C. Escher Company – Baarn – Holland. All rights reserved.

117

we see an advertisement, go online, visit shops or use a product, we receive information inputs.

The first step of the perceptual process is the selection of information. Individuals receive numerous pieces of information all the time, yet only a few of these reach awareness. Certain inputs are selected while others are ignored. **Selective exposure** occurs because consumers cannot be conscious of all inputs at the same time, and involves the selection of inputs that are to be exposed to awareness. A student word-processing a report may be unaware that the light is on, that the computer is making a humming sound, that there is background noise in the room or that other students are working at the same table. All of these inputs are being received, but the student will ignore them unless their attention is specifically drawn to them.

An input is more likely to reach awareness if it relates to an anticipated event or relates to current needs. If a violent storm has damaged the roof of a couple's house, they are much more likely to notice a local newspaper advertisement promoting a building and repairs service. Similarly, hungry people are more likely to notice a KFC sign than are those who are not. Finally, an input is more likely to be noticed if its intensity changes significantly. Consumers are much more likely to notice if a furniture store cuts its prices by half than if the same store offers a much smaller reduction.

The selective nature of perception leads to two other conditions: selective distortion and selective retention. **Selective distortion** is the changing or twisting of currently received information. This sometimes happens when someone receives information that is inconsistent with personal feelings or beliefs. For example, an individual who reads some favourable publicity about a company he or she dislikes is likely to distort the information to make it more consistent with personally held views. The publicity may therefore have greater impact on another consumer who views the same brand more positively. **Selective retention** means that an individual remembers information inputs that support personal feelings and beliefs, and forgets inputs that do not. After hearing a sales presentation and leaving the shop, a customer may forget many of the selling points if they contradict pre-existing beliefs.

The information inputs that do reach awareness are not received in an organised form. For them to be meaningful, an individual must enter the second step of the perceptual process – organising and integrating the new information with that already stored in the memory. Although this step is usually carried out quickly, it may take longer when the individual is considering an unfamiliar product area.

Interpretation – the third step in the perceptual process – is the assignment of meaning to what has been organised. All consumers base their interpretation on what is familiar, on knowledge already stored in memory. For this reason, a company that changes a package design or logo faces a major problem. Since people look for the product in the old, familiar package, they may not recognise it in the new one. Unless a package or logo change is accompanied by a promotional programme making people aware of the change, a company may lose sales. Even when such a programme is conducted, positive reaction from the consumer cannot be guaranteed. For example, when British Airways changed its corporate identity and redesigned its aeroplane tail fins to reflect themes from around the world, consumer reaction to the reduction in the company's overt Britishness was mixed. Companies often try to get around this difficulty by making only small changes to their logo or brand identity.

Although marketers cannot control people's perceptions, they often try to influence them. This may be difficult to achieve for a number of reasons. First, a consumer's perceptual process may prevent the information from being received. Second, a buyer may receive the information but perceive it differently from the way that was intended. For example, when an anti-wrinkle face cream manufacturer advertises that '80 per cent of consumers using this product notice a reduction in wrinkles', a customer might infer that 20 per cent of the people who use the product have more wrinkles. Third, buyers who perceive information inputs to be inconsistent with their personally held beliefs tend to forget the information

Selective exposure
The selection of inputs that people expose to their awareness

Selective distortion
The changing or twisting of currently received information

Selective retention
The process of remembering information inputs that support personal feelings and beliefs, and of forgetting those that do not

quickly. Sometimes consumers can be overwhelmed by the large number of information inputs they encounter, making it difficult to interpret the information.[18] For example, a student travelling by bus to college may pass more than 30 different advertising hoardings, but notice only one or two.

In addition to perceptions about packages, products, brands and organisations, individuals also have self-perceptions. These perceptions are known as the **self-concept** or self-image. It seems likely that a person's self-concept affects purchase decisions and consumption behaviour. The results of some studies suggest that buyers purchase products that reflect and enhance their self-concepts. For instance, one man might buy a Boss suit to project a sophisticated and businesslike image, while another might buy an outfit from Gap to enhance acceptability within their peer group.

Motives

Self-concept
A person's perception of himself or herself; self-image

Motive
An internal, energy-giving force that directs a person's activities towards satisfying a need or achieving a goal

Patronage motives
Those motives that influence where a person purchases products on a regular basis

In-depth interview
The collection of data from an individual by interview

Focus group
A semi-structured discussion involving six to twelve people, led by a moderator

Projective techniques
Tests in which subjects are asked to perform specific tasks for particular reasons, while actually being evaluated for other purposes

A **motive** is an internal, energy-giving force that directs an individual's activities towards satisfying a need or achieving a goal. Motivation is the set of mechanisms for controlling movement towards goals.[19] At any time a buyer's actions are affected by a set of motives rather than by just one. These motives are unique to the individual and to the situation. At any point in time some motives in the set will have priority. For example, someone's motives for taking a shower are particularly strong after a trip to the gym. Motivation affects the direction and intensity of behaviour, as individuals must choose which goals to pursue at a particular time.

Motives influencing where a person regularly purchases products are called patronage motives. A buyer may use a particular shop because of **patronage motives** such as price, service, location, honesty, product variety or friendliness of sales staff. Marketers seeking to capitalise on these motives should determine why regular customers patronise a store and then emphasise these characteristics in the store's marketing mix.

Motivation research can be used to analyse the major motives that influence whether consumers buy particular products. However, some of these motives are subconscious and people are therefore unaware of them. As a consequence, marketers cannot always elicit these motives through direct questioning. Most motivation research therefore relies on interviews or projective techniques (see Figure 4.6).

Researchers using interviews to study motives may use individual **in-depth interviews**, focus groups or a combination of the two. In an in-depth interview, the researcher encourages the subject to talk freely about general topics before focusing the discussion on the areas of interest. In a process that may last for several hours, the interviewer can then probe the subject's answers for clarification. In a **focus group**, the moderator – through leadership that appears to be not highly structured – tries to generate discussion about one or several topics in a group of six to twelve people. Through what is said in the discussion, the moderator attempts to discover people's motives relating to some issue such as the use of a product. The researcher usually cannot probe as far in a focus group as in an in-depth interview, and some products may not be suitable for such group discussion. To determine successfully the subconscious motives reflected in the interviews, motivation researchers must have certain qualities: they must be perceived as non-threatening by members of the group, must be able to adopt a demeanour appropriate to the characteristics of those in the group and must be well trained in clinical psychology. The use of sound and video recordings can simplify the process of analysis. Both in-depth and focus-group techniques can yield a variety of information. For example, they may help marketers discover why customers continue to buy and smoke cigarettes despite being aware of the profound health risks.

Projective techniques are tests in which subjects are asked to perform specific tasks for particular reasons, while actually being evaluated for other purposes. Such tests are based on the assumption that subjects will unconsciously 'project' their motives through the tasks they perform. Researchers trained in projective techniques can analyse the results and make predictions about the subject's subconscious motives. Common types

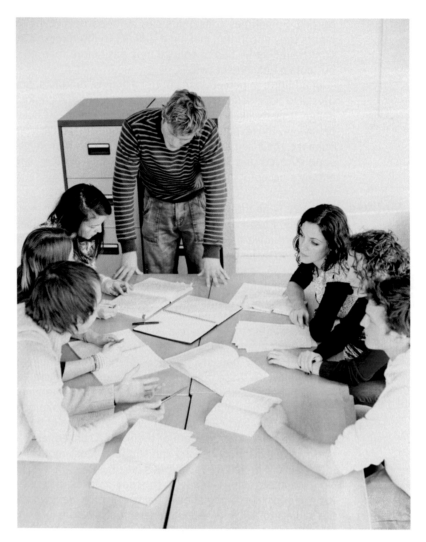

Figure 4.6
Discussing customers' buying decision-making, perceptions and attitudes is an important aspect of the marketer's role. Photo: Istockphoto.com

of projective technique include word association tests, sentence completion tests and bubble drawings. These are illustrated in Figure 4.7. Such tests can be useful to marketers in a number of ways, such as helping to make advertising more effective.[20]

The complexity of motivation research means that marketers wishing to research people's motives should employ the services of professional psychologists with specific skills in the area.[21]

Learning

Learning
Changes in a person's behaviour caused by information and experience

Learning refers to changes in behaviour caused by information and experience. The consequences of behaviour strongly influence the learning process. Thus behaviour resulting in satisfying consequences tends to be repeated. For example, if a consumer buys a hair gel that he believes makes him appear more fashionable, he is more likely to buy the same brand next time. In fact, he may continue to purchase the brand until he is no longer satisfied with it. If the consumer's hair subsequently starts to look out of condition, he may switch allegiance to an alternative brand.

Figure 4.7
Common types of projective technique

Word association tests

Subjects are asked to say what words come into their minds when a particular topic/product is mentioned.

Fresh foods are . . .	Frozen foods are . . .
Natural	Processed
Fresh	Quick
Healthy	Simple
Expensive	Convenient
Good for you	Preservatives
Real	Manufactured

Sentence completion tests

Subjects are asked to complete the sentences.

'People who use recycled toilet tissue . . .'
'People who look for the ingredients on packets before they buy them are . . .'
'People who buy Swatch watches . . .'

Bubble drawings

Subjects are asked to say what the man is thinking.

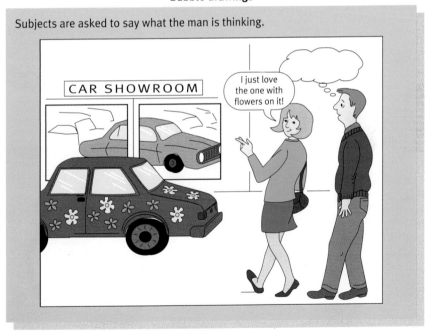

The ability of buyers to process information when making purchasing decisions varies. For example, when purchasing a computer, a well-educated potential buyer who has experience with computers may be able to read, comprehend and synthesise the considerable quantities of information found in the technical brochures for competing brands. On the other hand, a buyer with more limited abilities may be incapable of performing this task and will have to rely instead on information obtained from advertisements or from sales representatives.

Knowledge
Familiarity with the product and expertise – the ability to apply the product

A critical aspect of an individual's ability to process information is knowledge. **Knowledge**, in this context, has two components: familiarity with the product, and expertise or the ability to apply the product.[22] The duration and intensity of the buying decision process depends on the buyer's familiarity with or prior experience in purchasing and using the product. The individual's knowledge influences his or her search for, recall and use of information.[23]

Inexperienced buyers may use different types of information from more experienced shoppers when making purchasing decisions. Inexperienced buyers use price as an indicator of quality more frequently than buyers who are knowledgeable about a particular product category.[24] Thus two potential buyers of a pedigree dog may use quite different types of information in making their purchase decision. The more experienced buyer, wishing to take the animal to dog shows, may seek detailed information about the dog's pedigree; the less experienced buyer, looking for a loyal family pet, may judge the animal by how approachable and friendly it appears.

Consumers who lack expertise are more likely to seek advice from others when making a purchase. More experienced buyers have greater confidence; they also have more knowledge about the product or service, and can tell which features are reliable indicators of product quality. For example, consider two families choosing a long-haul holiday. Members of one family are unused to overseas travel, are unsure of the suitability of locations offered in travel brochures, and do not understand how to investigate flight options or medical and insurance requirements. Members of the other family have holidayed abroad on a regular basis. Although on this occasion they intend to visit a country that is new to them, they are sufficiently conversant with this type of travel to make their purchase without assistance and with confidence.

Figure 4.8
These advertisements for 'posh' crisps evidently play on consumers' aspirations to portray a certain image through the brands and products they select
Source: Courtesy of Kate Plumb, Abbot Mead Vickers. BBDO

Marketers sometimes help customers to learn about and gain experience of their products. Free samples encourage consumer trial and reduce purchase risk. In-store demonstrations help people acquire knowledge of product uses. DIY retailer B&Q has, over several years, run a series of extended television advertisements offering detailed guidance on home improvements and decorating. Each advertisement featured step-by-step instructions towards the completion of a particular project. This helps consumers to learn and can create a more favourable attitude towards the company's products. Consumers also learn when they experience products indirectly through information received from sales people, friends and relatives.

Influencing what consumers learn is difficult to achieve. Marketers encounter problems in attracting and holding consumers' attention, providing the kinds of information that are important for making purchase decisions, and convincing consumers to try the product. These attempts are most likely to be successful when designed to appeal to a well-defined target market. In Figure 4.8, Walkers is striving for attention through strong and evocative images for its 'posh crisps'.

Attitudes

Attitude
An individual's enduring evaluation, feelings and behavioural tendencies towards an object or activity

An **attitude** is an individual's enduring evaluation, feelings and behavioural tendencies towards an object or activity. These objects or activities may be tangible or intangible, living or non-living. Some attitudes relate to things that have a major impact on our lives, while others are less important. For example, we have attitudes towards relationships, culture and politics, just as we do towards rock music, skiing and pizza.

An individual learns attitudes through experience and interaction with others. Just as attitudes are learned, they can also be changed. Nevertheless, an individual's attitudes are generally quite stable and do not change from moment to moment. Likewise, at a particular point in time, some attitudes may be stronger than others. For example, a consumer who recently became the victim of credit card fraud after shopping on the Internet, may have strong views about the need for consumer protection legislation in this area.

An attitude consists of three major components: cognitive, affective and behavioural. The cognitive (or thinking) component is a person's knowledge and information about the object or idea, whereas the affective (or feeling) component comprises feelings and emotions towards the object or idea. The behavioural (or action) component consists of the action tendencies exhibited towards the object or idea. Changes in one of these components may or may not alter the other components. Thus consumers may become more knowledgeable about a specific brand without changing the affective or behavioural components of their attitude towards that brand.

Consumer attitudes towards a company and its products greatly influence the products individuals will buy, and therefore impact on the success or failure of the company's marketing strategy. When consumers are strongly negative towards aspects of a business's marketing practices, they may stop using the business's product, and may urge relatives and friends to do the same. For example, following the execution of human rights activists in Nigeria, some motorists chose to boycott Shell petrol because of allegations about Shell's activities in Nigeria.

Since attitudes can play such an important part in determining consumer behaviour, marketers should measure consumer attitudes towards prices, package designs, company logos and brand names, advertisements, warranties, store design and location, features of existing or proposed products, and social responsibility issues. Marketers can use a range of techniques to gauge these attitudes. One of the simplest ways is to question people directly. A marketing research agency carrying out attitude research for Rayban, for example, might question consumers about their opinions on the latest trends in eye wear. Sometimes marketers evaluate attitudes through attitude scales. An **attitude scale** usually consists of a series of adjectives, phrases or sentences about an object. Subjects are asked to indicate the intensity of their feelings towards the object by reacting to the adjectives, phrases or sentences in a certain way. For example, attitudes towards flexible mortgages might be measured by asking respondents to state the degree to which they agree or disagree with a

Attitude scale
A series of adjectives, phrases or sentences about an object used by a subject to indicate his or her feelings towards that object

number of statements, such as 'When I have spare money I would like the opportunity to pay more than my usual monthly repayment amount.'

If marketers identify particularly negative attitudes towards an aspect of a marketing mix, they may try to make consumer attitudes more favourable. This task is generally long, expensive, difficult and may require extensive promotional efforts. For example, in the UK, Post Office Counters has been advertising to draw customers' attention to the fact that local post offices offer a wide range of services. This publicity is attempting to alter customers' perceptions away from the traditional view that the Post Office exists purely for mailing letters and parcels.

Personality

Personality

All the internal traits and behaviours that make a person unique

Personality includes all the internal traits and behaviours that make a person unique. Each person's unique personality is both inherited and the result of personal experiences. Personalities are typically described as having one or more characteristics, such as compulsiveness, ambitiousness, gregariousness, dogmatism, authoritarianism, introversion, extroversion, aggressiveness and competitiveness. Many marketers believe that a consumer's personality does influence the types and brands of products purchased, and there has been a drive to increase research in this area.[25] For example, the type of make-up or clothing that people buy, as well as the social activities in which they engage, may reflect one or more personality characteristics. Perhaps surprisingly, marketing researchers who have tried to find relationships among such characteristics and buying behaviour have reported inconclusive results. However, some of these researchers see this apparently weak association between personality and buying behaviour as due to unreliable measures rather than because no such relationship exists.[26]

At times, marketers aim advertising campaigns at general types of personality. In doing so, they use positively valued personality characteristics, such as gregariousness, independence or competitiveness. Products promoted in this way include drinks, cars, cigarettes, clothing and computer games. For example, television advertising promoting the alcoholic beverage Lambrini is designed to appeal to young, outgoing consumers.

Social Factors Influencing the Buying Decision Process

Social factors

The forces other people exert on buying behaviour

The forces that other people exert on buying behaviour are called **social factors**. As shown in Figure 4.1, they can be grouped into four major areas:

1 roles and family
2 reference groups
3 social classes
4 culture and sub-cultures.

Roles and Family

Role

A set of actions and activities that a person in a particular position is supposed to perform, based on the expectations of both the individual and surrounding people

All of us occupy positions within our family, social setting, organisations and institutions. Associated with each position is a **role** – a set of actions and activities that a person is supposed to perform, based on their own expectations and those of others around them. Because people occupy numerous positions, they also have many roles. For example, one woman may perform the roles of mother, wife, grandmother, daughter, sister, teacher, part-time youth club organiser and member of the local music society. Thus there are several sets of expectations for each person's behaviour.

An individual's roles influence both general behaviour and buying behaviour. The demands of different roles may be inconsistent and confusing. For example, assume that a man is thinking about buying a boat. While he wants a boat for fishing, his children want one suitable for water skiing. His wife wants him to delay the boat purchase until next year. A colleague at work insists that he should buy a particular brand, known for high performance. Thus an individual's buying behaviour may be partially affected by the opinions of family and friends.

Family roles relate directly to purchase decisions. The male head of household is likely to be involved heavily in the purchase of products such as household insurance and alcohol. Although female roles have changed, women still make buying decisions related to many household items, including healthcare products, washing products, household cleaners and food. Husbands and wives are often jointly involved in buying many durable goods, such as a washing machine or television set. As this chapter's 'Opener' explained, children are increasingly involved in household purchase decisions that were traditionally made only by husbands and wives. Some buying decisions, such as the purchase of a family holiday, are made by the whole family, with different family members playing different roles in the process. When two or more individuals participate in a purchase, their roles may dictate that each is responsible for performing certain tasks: initiating the idea, gathering information, deciding whether to buy the product or selecting the specific brand. The particular tasks performed depend on the types of product being considered.

Marketers need to be aware of how roles affect buying behaviour. To develop a marketing mix that precisely meets the target market's needs, marketers must know not only who does the actual buying but also what other roles influence the purchase.

Reference Groups

Reference group
A group with which an individual identifies so much that he or she takes on many of the values, attitudes or behaviour of group members

A group is referred to as a **reference group** when an individual identifies with it so much that he or she takes on many of the values, attitudes or behaviour of group members. Most people have several reference groups, such as families, friends, work colleagues, and social, religious and professional organisations.

A group can be a negative reference group for an individual. Someone may have been a part of a specific group at one time but later have rejected its values and members, even taking specific action to avoid it.[27] However, in this discussion reference groups mean those that the individual involved views positively.

An individual may use a reference group as a point of comparison and a source of information. Sometimes individuals may change their behaviour to be more in line with other group members. For example, a student may stop visiting a particular nightclub on the advice of a close friend. An individual may seek information from a reference group about the best brand to buy or about other purchase factors, such as where to buy a certain product. The degree to which a reference group will affect a purchase decision depends on an individual's susceptibility to its influence, and the strength of his or her involvement with the group. Young people are often especially susceptible to this kind of influence. In general, the more conspicuous a product, the more likely the brand decision will be influenced by reference groups.

A marketer sometimes tries to use reference group influence in advertisements by suggesting that people in a specific group buy and are highly satisfied with a product. The advertiser is hoping that people will accept the suggested group as a reference group and buy (or react more favourably to) the product as a result. Whether this kind of advertising succeeds depends on three factors:

1 how effectively the advertisement communicates the message
2 the type of product
3 the individual's susceptibility to reference group influence.

Opinion leader
The member of a reference group who provides information about a specific sphere of interest to reference group participants seeking information

In most reference groups, one or more members stand out as opinion leaders. An **opinion leader** provides information about a specific sphere of interest to reference group participants who seek such information. Opinion leaders are viewed by other group members as being well informed about a particular area, and easily accessible. Such individuals often feel a responsibility to remain informed about the sphere of interest, and thus seek out advertisements, manufacturers' brochures, sales people, websites and other sources of information.

Social Classes

Social class
An open group of individuals who have similar social rank

Within all societies, people rank others into higher or lower positions of respect. This ranking results in social classes. A **social class** is an open group of individuals who have similar social rank. A class is referred to as 'open' because people can move into and out of it. The criteria for grouping people into classes vary from one society to another. In the UK, as in other western countries, many factors are taken into account, including occupation, education, income, wealth, race, ethnic group and possessions. In the former Soviet Union, wealth and income are less important in determining social class than education and occupation: although Russian doctors and scientists do not make a great deal of money, they are highly valued in Russian society. A person who is ranking someone does not necessarily apply all of a society's criteria. The number and importance of the factors chosen depend on the characteristics of the individual being ranked and the values of the person who is doing the ranking. For example, one individual may particularly respect status within a church or religious sect, while another may regard it as having little relevance.

To some degree, people within social classes develop and assume common patterns of behaviour. They may have similar attitudes, values, language patterns and possessions. Social class influences many aspects of people's lives. For example, it affects whom they marry, their likelihood of having children and the children's chances of surviving infancy. It influences childhood training, choice of religion, selection of occupation and the way in which people spend their time. Because social class has a bearing on so many aspects of a person's life, it also affects buying decisions. For example, upmarket fashion labels Donna Karan and Versace are popular among upper-class Europeans because they believe these brands symbolise their status, income and aspirations.

Social class affects the type, quality and quantity of products that a person buys and uses. Social class also affects an individual's shopping patterns and the types of store patronised. Advertisements are sometimes based on an appeal to a specific social class. Different countries often collate data about their populations based on social or socio-economic factors. For example, for many years the UK, like some other countries, used a relatively simple classification based on social status and occupation (see Table 4.1). However, in 2001, the UK's Office for National Statistics introduced a modified system known as NS SEC (National Statistics Socio-Economic Status). This approach is still based on occupation, but

Social grade	Social status	Head of household's occupation
TABLE 4.1 SOCIO-ECONOMIC CLASSIFICATION		
A	Upper middle class	Higher managerial, professional or administrative positions; often living in expensive accommodation in the best residential areas
B	Middle class	Middle managerial, professional or administrative jobs; good living standards, usually in good accommodation in reasonable areas
C1	Lower middle class	Junior managerial, professional or administrative, supervisory or clerical jobs; sometimes referred to as 'white collar' workers
C2	Skilled working class	Skilled manual workers, perhaps who have served some kind of apprenticeship to train
D	Manual workers	Semi-skilled and unskilled manual workers
E	Those at lowest levels of subsistence	Old age pensioners, widows, casual workers, the unemployed or those who are dependent on social security or have little in the way of independent means
See www.medialive.ie for more details of socio-economic groups.		

aims to more closely reflect consumers' purchasing power on the basis of their position in the labour market.[28] Table 4.2 describes the new NS SEC social class categories.

Culture and Sub-cultures

Culture
All the things around us that are made by human beings: tangible items, such as food, furniture, buildings, clothing and tools; and intangible concepts, such as education, the legal system, healthcare and religion; plus values and behaviours

Culture consists of everything in our surroundings that is made by human beings. It includes tangible items, such as food, furniture, buildings, clothing and tools, and intangible concepts, such as education, the legal system, healthcare and religion. Culture also includes the values and wide range of behaviours that are acceptable within a specific society. The concepts, values and behaviours that make up a culture are learned and passed on from one generation to the next.

Culture influences buying behaviour, determining what people wear and eat, how they socialise, where they live and travel. Society's interest in the health-giving aspects of food has affected companies' approaches to developing and promoting their products. Recent concern about increasing levels of obesity and its impact on health has caused the food industry to question how it markets high-fat and high-sugar products.[29] Culture also influences how consumers buy and use products, and the satisfaction gained from them. For example, the consumption of packaged goods, and the usage and ownership of durable goods varies across cultures.[30] In many western cultures, shortage of time is a growing problem because of the increasing number of women who work and the current emphasis placed on physical and mental self-development. Many people buy convenience and labour-saving products to cope with this problem.[31]

Because culture partly determines how products are purchased and used, it also affects the development, promotion, distribution and pricing of products. Food marketers have needed to radically overhaul their marketing efforts to reflect day-to-day changes in how consumers live their lives. Some 30 years ago, most families ate at least two meals a day together, and the mother devoted four to six hours a day to preparing those meals. Today, more than

Class	Occupation groups
	TABLE 4.2 NS SEC EIGHT-CLASS SOCIO-ECONOMIC CLASSIFICATION
1	*Higher managerial and professional occupations* (ABs): e.g. business executives, doctors, vets, teachers
2	*Lower managerial and professional occupations* (C1s): e.g. nurses, police sergeants and constables, market researchers, junior managers
3	*Intermediate occupations* (C2s): e.g. secretaries, clerical staff, technicians and telephone engineers
4	*Small employers and own-account workers*: e.g. the self-employed and those employing fewer than 25 people
5	*Lower supervisory and technical occupations*: e.g. supervisors in factories
6	*Semi-routine occupations*: e.g. drivers, assembly-line workers, shop staff
7	*Routine occupations*: e.g. porters, labourers, domestic staff
8	*Never worked or long-term unemployed*

Source: adapted from Angela Donkin, Yuan Huang Lee and Barbara Toson, 'Implications of change in the UK social and occupational classifications in 2001 for vital statistics', *Population Trends*, 107, *National Statistics*, Spring 2002, pp. 23–9.

60 per cent of women aged 25 to 54 are employed outside the home, and average family incomes have risen considerably. These shifts, along with lack of time, have resulted in dramatic increases in per capita consumption of shelf-stable foods like Pot Rice and Pot Noodle, frozen meals and take-away foods.[32] As a result of increasing demands from those wishing to 'eat on the move', petrol stations now stock a variety of prepared sandwiches and snacks.

◊ Marketing Insight

Marketing to Ethnic Consumers

The 2001 census revealed the true multicultural character of the UK population. Approaching 8 per cent of those living in the UK belong to an ethnic minority, an increase of more than 50 per cent over a 10-year period. The commercial implications of these changes are huge, with professional marketers facing increasing pressure to cater more effectively for the needs and buying requirements of these groups. Studies on culture illustrate the diversity of attitudes and behaviour across ethnic groups, showing that these differences are also reflected in product preferences and consumer buying behaviour. Tesco has led the way in creating over 400 'ethnic stores' catering for the diversity of consumers in particular store catchments, Lloyds has launched banking products tailored to the Polish community in the UK, and Tilda has rice varieties targeted at separate ethnic communities. Yet recent research findings suggest that not enough is being done to reflect these characteristics in product design and marketing.

For example, despite a recent rise in Bollywood-style advertisements, such as those for Peugeot and Walkers Crisps, the advertising industry has been accused of tokenism and ethnic stereotyping. Even though an analysis of television advertising reveals 13 per cent of actors used are non-white, a more systematic review shows that the vast majority of these are included in minor roles. According to a report by Mediaedge:cia, a large global player in media communications and part of the WPP Group, current advertising campaigns are still failing to reflect the cultural characteristics of Asian, African-Caribbean and other ethnic minorities.

So what needs to be done to ensure that cultural variety is better reflected in marketing practice? Industry experts suggest that the first challenge is to develop a fuller picture of ethnic diversity by collecting appropriate research data across the different communities. This raises challenges of its own, as agencies must equip themselves to overcome the cultural and religious barriers sometimes associated with such data-collection exercises. For example, some experts highlight the importance of including community leaders in the process; others suggest that researchers from the same ethnic groups as respondents must be used and that appropriate settings for the research must be chosen. Not surprisingly, the number of marketing research agencies specialising in researching ethnic minorities is on the increase and various initiatives have been established to improve the availability and quality of work in this area. For example, the Market Research Society recently established the Ethnic Research Network. This body provides a forum for those with interests in ethnic research, aiming to share knowledge and drive forward best practice in the area.

The potential benefits of such research are readily apparent. When broadcaster Sky researched the viewing behaviour of the UK's South Asian population, it identified the importance this group attaches to Asian TV channels such as Zee TV and StarTV. According to the findings, 96 per cent of respondents from this group regarded these kinds of channel as essential. Yet only 54 per cent had the same view about ITV1. The analysis also revealed the level of Internet access among South Asians to be much higher than the UK norm. The implications for advertisers and marketers seeking to target these individuals are readily apparent. Yet, even here, care is needed. The research also showed striking viewership patterns across the South Asian community, illustrating the danger of developing ethnic stereotypes. In the words of Saber Khan, the research director of Ethnic Focus (the specialist research company conducting the study):

These channels reflect the heterogeneity of the Asian community. Marketers have had the will to reach communities. But what they sometimes need assistance with is to capture the diversity. It's more than just Bollywood or Caribbean – it's capturing the fusion.

Sources: Robert Gray, 'Ethnic insight', *Marketing*, 4 March 2004, pp. 25–6; 'Ethnic marketing: "a double edged sword"', www.redhotcurry.com, 3 March 2003; www.mediaedge.com; www.mrw.org.uk; Tesco plc, 2007; BBC news, 2007; Tilda, 2007.

An increase in ethnic diversity in many societies has important implications for the way in which new products and services are developed and marketed. A key part of this process is ensuring the availability of good-quality data, so that the attitudes and behaviour of minority groups are properly understood. The Marketing Insight box shows how the need to better understand cultural diversity among ethnic minorities and its impact on consumer behaviour is spawning initiatives to drive forward best practice in marketing research.

When marketers sell products overseas, they often see the tremendous impact that culture has on the purchase and use of products. International marketers find that people in other regions of the world have different attitudes, values and needs, which call for different methods of doing business. Some international marketers fail because they do not adjust to cultural differences.

Sub-cultures
Sub-divisions of culture according to geographic regions or human characteristics, such as age or ethnic background

A culture can be divided into **sub-cultures** according to geographic regions or human characteristics, such as age or ethnic background. In any country, there are a number of different sub-cultures. Within these, there are even greater similarities in people's attitudes, values and actions than within the broader culture, resulting in stronger preferences for specific types of clothing, furniture or leisure activity. For example, the wearing of kilts tends to be confined to Scotland rather than England or Wales. Marketers must recognise that, even though their operations are confined to one country, state or city, sub-cultural differences may dictate considerable variations in what products people buy and how they make their purchases. To deal effectively with these differences, marketers may have to alter their product, promotion, distribution systems, price or people to satisfy members of particular sub-cultures.

Understanding Consumer Behaviour

Marketers try to understand consumer buying behaviour so that they can satisfy consumers more effectively. For example, consumer concerns about the exploitation of workers in less developed countries have encouraged supermarkets to stock more ethical products. An appreciation of how and why individuals buy products and services helps marketers design more appropriate and relevant marketing programmes.[33] For example, by understanding the readership habits of prospective digital camera buyers, companies such as Pentax and Nikon are able to make more informed decisions about where to place print advertisements for their products.

At a time when consumer expectations of products and services are rising, it is more important than ever to keep abreast of trends in consumer behaviour. If marketers are to keep consumers satisfied, they must focus carefully on the marketing concept and on being consumer oriented. In particular, they must be equipped with a clear understanding of the process and motivations of consumer buying.

The fact that it may be difficult to analyse consumer behaviour precisely, does not detract from the importance of doing so. Even though research on consumer buying behaviour has not supplied all the knowledge that marketers need, considerable progress has been made in recent years. Advances in technology and changing shopping habits are increasing the opportunities for capturing and managing information about consumers. For example, the increasing use of online banking has been made possible by the development of computer systems that can handle the full range of banking transactions in which consumers wish to engage. The same systems are enabling providers such as First Direct and ing.com to store and analyse a huge variety of information about customers' spending and savings patterns. When analysed, this information provides vital insights into the needs and wants of different customer types. These insights can be used to develop and market new products and services. At a time when an increasingly competitive business environment is making it more difficult to develop an edge over rival organisations, the demands for such information are only likely to grow.

Summary

Buying behaviour comprises the decision processes and actions of people involved in buying and using products. *Consumer buying behaviour* refers to the buying behaviour of ultimate consumers – those who purchase products for personal or household use, not for business purposes. Analysing consumer buying behaviour helps marketers to determine what satisfies customers, so that they can implement the marketing concept and better predict how consumers will respond to different marketing programmes.

» Consumer decisions can be classified into three categories: routine response behaviour, limited decision-making and extensive decision-making. A consumer uses *routine response behaviour* when buying frequently purchased, low-cost, low-risk items that require very little search and decision effort. *Limited decision-making* is used for products purchased occasionally or when a buyer needs to acquire information about an unfamiliar brand in a familiar product category. *Extensive decision-making* is used when purchasing an unfamiliar, expensive, high-risk or infrequently bought product. *Impulse buying* is an unplanned buying behaviour involving a powerful, persistent urge to buy something immediately. The purchase of a certain product does not always elicit the same type of decision-making behaviour. Individuals differ in their response to purchase situations. Even the same individual may make a different decision in other circumstances.

» The *consumer buying decision process* comprises five stages: problem recognition, information search, evaluation of alternatives, purchase and post-purchase evaluation. Decision processes do not always culminate in a purchase, and not all consumer decisions include all five stages. Problem recognition occurs when a buyer becomes aware that there is a difference between a desired state and an actual condition. After recognising the problem, the buyer searches for product information that will help resolve the problem or satisfy the need. *Internal search* involves buyers searching their memory for information about products that might solve the problem. If insufficient information is retrieved in this way, additional information is sought through *external search*. A successful information search will yield a group of brands, called an *evoked set*, that are viewed as possible alternatives. The level of involvement, which is the amount of interest, emotion and activity expended on a purchase, affects the degree of the external search. To evaluate the products in the evoked set, a buyer establishes certain criteria and assigns each a certain *salience* – or level of importance – by which to compare, rate and rank the different products. During purchase, the consumer selects the product or brand on the basis of results from the evaluation stage and on other factors. The buyer also chooses the seller from whom to buy the product. After the purchase, the buyer evaluates the product's actual performance. Shortly after the purchase of an expensive product the post-purchase evaluation may provoke *cognitive dissonance* – dissatisfaction brought on by the consumer's doubts as to whether he or she should have bought the product in the first place. The results of the post-purchase evaluation will affect future buying behaviour.

» Three major categories of influences are believed to affect the consumer buying decision process: personal, psychological and social factors. A *personal factor* is one that is unique to a particular person. Personal factors include demographic factors, situational factors and level of involvement. *Demographic factors* are individual characteristics such as age, sex, race, ethnic origin, income, family life cycle and occupation. *Situational factors* are the external circumstances or conditions that exist when a consumer is making a purchase decision, such as the time available. An individual's *level of involvement* – the level of interest, emotional commitment and time spent searching for a product in a particular situation – also affects the buying decision process. Enduring involvement is an ongoing interest in a product class because of personal relevance. Situational involvement is a temporary interest resulting from the particular circumstance or environment in which buyers find themselves.

» *Psychological factors* partly determine people's general behaviour and thus influence their behaviour as consumers. The primary psychological influences on consumer behaviour are perception, motives, learning, attitudes and personality. *Perception* is the process of selecting, organising and interpreting *information inputs* (the sensations received through sight, taste, hearing, smell and touch) to produce meaning. The first step in the perceptual process is the selection of information. *Selective exposure* is the phenomenon of people selecting the inputs that are to be exposed to their awareness; *selective distortion* is the changing or twisting of currently received information. *Selective retention* involves remembering information inputs that support personal feelings and beliefs, and forgetting those that do not. The second step of the perceptual process requires organising and integrating the new information with that already stored in memory. Interpretation – the third step in the perceptual process – is the assignment of meaning to what has been organised. In addition to perceptions of packages, products, brands and organisations, individuals also have a *self-concept*, or self-image.

» A *motive* is an internal, energy-giving force directing a person's activities towards satisfying a need or achieving a goal. *Patronage motives* influence where a person purchases products on a regular basis. To analyse the major motives that influence consumers to buy or not buy products, marketers conduct motivation research, using *in-depth interviews*, *focus groups* or *projective techniques*. Common types of projective technique include word association tests, bubble drawings and sentence completion tests.

» *Learning* refers to changes in a person's behaviour caused by information and experience. *Knowledge*, in this context, has two components: familiarity with the product, and expertise – the ability to apply the product.

» *Attitude* refers to an individual's enduring evaluation, feelings and behavioural tendencies towards an object or activity. Consumer attitudes towards a company and its products greatly influence the success or failure of its marketing strategy. Marketers measure consumers' attitudes using *attitude scales*.

» *Personality* comprises all the internal traits and behaviours that make a person unique. Though the results of many studies have been inconclusive, some marketers believe that personality does influence the types and brands of products purchased.

» *Social factors* are the forces that other people exert on buying behaviour. They include the influence of roles and family, reference groups, social classes, and culture and sub-cultures. We all occupy positions within groups, organisations and institutions. Each position has a *role* – a set of actions and activities that a person in a particular position is supposed to perform. A group is a *reference group* when an individual identifies with the group so much that he or she takes on many of the values, attitudes or behaviours of group members. In most reference groups, one or more members stand out as *opinion leaders*. A *social class* is an open group of individuals who have similar social rank. *Culture* is everything in our surroundings that is made by human beings. A culture can be divided into *sub-cultures* on the basis of geographic regions or human characteristics, such as age or ethnic background.

» Marketers try to understand consumer buying behaviour so that they can offer consumers greater satisfaction. Improvements in technology and refinements in research methods are increasing opportunities to capture and manage data about consumers and their behaviour. The combination of the pressure of rising consumer expectations, combined with an increasingly competitive business environment, will spur marketers to seek a fuller understanding of consumer decision processes.

⊕ *Key Links*

This chapter, about consumer buying behaviour, should be read in conjunction with Chapter 5, which examines buying behaviour in business markets.

- Without an understanding of customers' buying behaviour, it is difficult for marketers to develop effective marketing programmes, as discussed in Part III.
- An understanding of customer buying behaviour is also essential for two core facets of marketing strategy: developing target market strategies (see Chapter 6); creating powerful brand propositions (see Chapter 14).

Important Terms

Buying behaviour
Consumer buying behaviour
Routine response behaviour
Limited decision-making
Impulse buying
Extensive decision-making
Consumer buying decision process
Internal search
External search
Involvement
Evoked set
Salience
Cognitive dissonance
Personal influencing factors
Demographic factors
Situational factors
Level of involvement
Psychological factors
Perception
Information inputs
Selective exposure
Selective distortion
Selective retention
Self-concept
Motive
Patronage motives
In-depth interview
Focus group
Projective techniques
Learning
Knowledge
Attitude
Attitude scale
Personality
Social factors
Role
Reference group
Opinion leader
Social class
Culture
Sub-cultures

Discussion and Review Questions

1 Name the types of buying behaviour consumers use. List some products that you have bought using each type of behaviour. In what circumstances have you bought a product on impulse?

2 What are the five stages in the consumer buying decision process? Are all these stages used in all consumer purchase decisions?

3 What are the personal factors that affect the consumer buying decision process? How do they affect the process?

4 How does a consumer's level of involvement affect his or her purchase behaviour?

5 What is the function of time in a consumer's buying decision process?

6 What is selective exposure and what effect does it have on consumer buying?

7 How do marketers attempt to shape consumers' learning?

8 Why are marketers concerned about consumer attitudes?

9 Describe reference groups. How do they influence buying behaviour? Name some of your own reference groups.

10 In what ways does social class affect a person's purchase decisions?

11 What is culture? How does it affect a person's buying behaviour?

12 Describe the sub-cultures to which you belong. Identify buying behaviour that is unique to your sub-culture.

13 What is the impact of post-purchase evaluation on future buying decisions?

14 If consumers are dissatisfied with a particular purchase, what actions are open to them? What can marketers do to respond to these actions?

Recommended Reading

- Blackwell, R. D., Engel, J. F. and Miniard, P. W., *Consumer Behaviour* (Cincinnati, OH: South-Western, 2005).
- Foxall, G. R., *Understanding Consumer Choice* (Basingstoke: Palgrave Macmillan, 2005).
- Lamkin, M., Foxall, G., Van Raaij, F. and Heilbrunn, B., *European Perspectives on Consumer Behaviour*, (Harlow: Pearson/FT, 1997).
- Solomon, M., Bamossy, G., Askegaard, S. and Hogg, M. K., *Consumer Behaviour* (Harlow: Pearson/FT, 2007).

Internet Exercise

Some mass-market e-commerce sites, such as Amazon.co.uk, have extended the concept of customisation to their customer base. Amazon has analysed its customer data, then used its understanding of certain users' likes and dislikes to make recommendations to other users. Take a look at this online retailer at:

www.amazon.co.uk or www.amazon.com

1 What might motivate some consumers to read a 'best-selling' list?
2 Is the consumer's level of involvement with online book purchase likely to be high or low?
3 Discuss the consumer buying decision process as it relates to a decision to purchase from Amazon.co.uk.

Applied Mini-Case

InterContinental Hotels Group is the world's largest hotel group, with 3,650 hotels and 540,000 guest rooms in nearly one hundred countries. The company has adopted a multi-segment strategy in order to address a variety of consumer requirements in the lodging industry. Its hotels include the upmarket InterContinental and Crown Plaza brands, boutique chain Hotel Indigo, Holiday Inn, budget brand Holiday Inn Express, as well as suites hotel operations Staybridge and Candlewood. In deriving its brand and target market strategies, InterContinental's marketers have considered a host of customer characteristics, requirements and behaviours, such as duration of stay, hotel location and proximity to other addresses, amenities and services sought or expected, desired luxury, value-for-money, hotel ambiance and feel, hotel usage, size of guest room, purpose of stay, booking/decision-making personnel and organizations, amongst other variables.

Sources: Sally Dibb and Lyndon Simkin, *Market Segmentation Success: Making It Happen!*, 2008, New York: The Haworth Press; www.ichotelsgroup.com; InterContinental Hotels Group marketing materials, 2007.

❓ Question

A large company such as InterContinental Hotels Group is interested in finding out more about the factors that influence people buying hotel weekend breaks. Relating your answer to this example, review the different personal, psychological and social influences that might impact on someone seeking to make this kind of purchase.

Case Study

Binney & Smith Plans for Crayola Crayons

While Nintendo and Playstation games, MTV music videos, satellite TV cartoon channels and web-based interactive gaming, have captured children's attention, Crayola Crayons have maintained a roll in children's play and remained on store shelves. Binney & Smith, a division of Hallmark Cards, fought back with a new marketing strategy and marketing plan for the venerable crayon. The company launched a huge MTV-style campaign, targeted at children rather than parents.

Traditionally Binney & Smith targeted Crayola Crayons at parents, using educational themes. But after recognising that children's purchasing power and influence on family purchases have increased in recent years, the company decided to change the crayon's image as an old fashioned toy to an exciting way for kids and teens to express themselves. To this end, the company developed new advertisements featuring rock music, 'hip' kids and soaring colours for showing during television programmes seen by children. In-store videos provided to toy stores and retailers of children's clothing followed up the theme.

After marketing research indicated that children prefer brighter colours, the company decided to retire blue grey, green blue, lemon yellow, maize, orange red, orange yellow, raw umber and violet blue to the Crayola Hall of Fame and to replace them with the more vivid cerulean, dandelion, fuchsia, jungle green, royal purple, teal blue, vivid tangerine and wild strawberry. This decision was controversial, however. The company was inundated with phone calls, letters and petitions from people who missed the old colours. Protesters marched on the company, carrying placards with slogans like 'We hate the new 8!' and 'They call it a retirement, I call it a burial'. RUMPS, the Raw Umber and Maize Preservation Society, finally got its way. The company issued a commemorative tin containing the 64 crayon box and a special pack of the eight colours dropped one year earlier. Even though children liked the new colours, parents liked the old eight colours. The company issued a statement saying that the old colours were revived partly because the company is in the business of providing what the consumer wants.

Along with new advertisements and colours, the company introduced ColourWorks, a line of erasable crayon sticks and retractable coloured pencils and pens. The company brought out Silver Swirls, crayons that have twirls of silver mixed in with the wax colours. Pictures coloured with Silver Swirls can be buffed to a high sheen with tissue. The new line was not only tested by children but also named by them. The company licensed its brand to Concord Cameras for a range of brightly coloured single use cameras aimed at children under 12. Several software companies have recognised the Crayola brand appeal: Micrografx offers the Crayola Amazing Art Adventure and the Crayola Art Studio – software games that encourage art and design a long way from the traditional wax crayon. IBM brought out Crayola Creation Corner to 'transform ordinary household items into toys, animals, jewellery, spaceships, greeting cards, stationery, party decorations, and all sorts of other inventions'.

A full range of PC interactive software products emerged, still focusing on drawing and creativity, but not based purely on the familiar wax crayon. The latter remains the company's core line, though it now features as part of making kits – Badge Bonanza or Crayola Jewellery – and a whole host of design sets. Clearly, the Crayola brand is still very popular with children, parents and toy stores. More and more children are discovering the Crayola name, encouraged by Binney & Smith's embracing of the Internet. The website www.crayola.com has a wealth to offer, with games, craft ideas and products aimed at three target audiences: parents, educators and 'Crayola kids'. The company has very effectively created an online community around its wax crayon brand.

Despite its new focus on children, Binney & Smith has not forgotten who actually holds the purse strings. The company continues to target parents with advertisements in women's and parents' magazines, while new products or services – such as www.crayola.com – include educational and child development messages aimed at parents. However, the revised marketing strategy and accompanying marketing plan have led more children to reach for Crayola Crayons instead of the Nintendo joystick or LEGO bricks. Sales are up and shelf space in toy stores could not be better, despite stiff competition from a host of rival entertainment products and toys.

Sources: www.crayola.com/kids, 2004; Ellen Neuborne, 'Crayola crayons have old colors back', *USA Today*, 2 October 1991, p. 2B; Ken Riddle, 'Crayola draws brighter lines in the market', *Marketing*, 21 January 1991, p. 4; Beefeater Restaurants, 1993; Toys 'R' Us, Leicester, 1996; Loretta Roach, 'Single use explosion', *Discount Merchandiser*, September 1995, pp. 28–30; Robyn Parets, 'Children's edutainment titles vie for shelf space', *Discount Store News*, 19 June 1995, pp. C6–C9; Binney & Smith UK, 1999; Toys 'R' Us, 1999, 2004, 2007; www.crayola.com, 2007.

❷ Questions for Discussion

1 Why did Binney & Smith have to update its marketing of Crayola and change its strategy?
2 What are Crayola's target audiences? Why did the company need to approach them differently?
3 Why has the company embraced the Internet?

5
Business Markets and Business Buying Behaviour

"**Business marketing is not simply about making sales. It's the task of establishing, developing and managing a portfolio of customer relationships.**"

David Ford, University of Bath

Objectives

- **To become familiar with the various types of business market**

- **To identify the major characteristics of business buyers and transactions**

- **To understand several attributes of business demand**

- **To become familiar with the major components of a buying centre**

- **To understand relationship marketing and exchanges between industrial buyers and sellers**

- **To understand the stages of the business buying decision process and the factors that affect this process**

- **To learn how to select and analyse business target markets**

- **To appreciate some of the nuances of marketing business products**

Introduction

Most readers of this book will have related the material in the previous chapter to their own purchasing experiences as consumers. Many marketers, though, do not address consumers. Instead, their target customers are other businesses or organisations. This chapter addresses the nature of business-to-business marketing, known here as business marketing.

A **business market** is one in which the customer is not a consumer – a private individual or household. In business markets, the target customers are other businesses and organisations that purchase a specific type of product or service for resale, for use in making other products or for use in their daily operations. In older books, this used to be known as **industrial** or **organisational marketing**. More recently, the term **business-to-business marketing** has become popular. Now, this has been abbreviated to 'business marketing'. Whether known as industrial, organisational, business-to-business or simply business marketing, the emphasis is on other businesses and organisations as customers, rather than end-user consumers.

135

Opener

Sara Lee Courtaulds: Consumer Brands but Mainly Business Customers

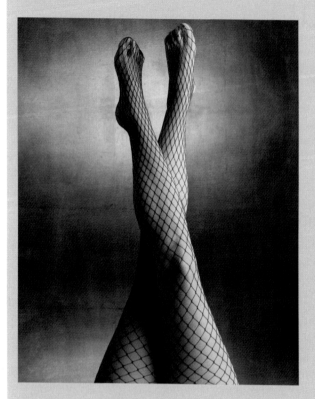

Sara Lee Courtaulds is a large international producer of fabrics to garment makers and ready-made garments to retailers including Marks & Spencer, Victoria's Secret and other leading retailers. With production facilities across the globe, the company has significant design and manufacturing interests in the UK and France. The business is divided into two units: fabrics and garments.

The fabric marketers are constantly innovating in terms of fabrics, designs and seaming techniques. Some of the latest products are fabrics that, when warm, release smells such as citrus odours – very useful in sports and swimwear. Only a few of the fabric brands are known to consumers (Calais-produced Desseilles lace, for example, is world renowned). On the whole, however, the various fabric brands are familiar only to Sara Lee Courtaulds' immediate business customers, the garment makers and retailer merchandisers.

For the garment-producing side of Sara Lee Courtaulds, most of the clothing produced is retailer own-label branded goods, purchased by consumers as St Michael (Marks & Spencer), Bhs or Tesco own-label branded merchandise. In addition, Sara Lee Courtaulds' garment division produces brands that are promoted directly to the consumer under the very familiar lingerie, clothing and household textiles names of Well, Aristoc, Berlei, Gossard, Georges Rech, Zorbit and Christy towels.

Although Berlei and Gossard underwear are advertised in consumer magazines, and Aristoc lingerie appears on billboards, the vast majority of the company's marketing activity is targeted at companies retailing or manufacturing clothing: business marketing.

For Sara Lee Courtaulds' businesses supplying the large retail chains, retail merchandisers expect them to provide all the packaging, design, labelling and photography, but to the retailers' own specifications. Sara Lee Courtaulds must do much more than simply produce a satisfactory product for a customer such as Marks & Spencer (M&S). Subsidiary Meridian, for example, pays for photography, packaging, hangers, ticketing and displays for Bhs and Tesco. The retailers only have to find space for the display stand and manage inventory levels.

For garments, each season for a design eventually included in the ranges sold in M&S or Bhs stores, between 25 and 35 new products are offered by Sara Lee Courtaulds. There is a lead time of three seasons to enable the design, selection, manufacturing and promotion of the new ranges. First, there are fabric searches, then design searches. The garment makers and, separately, the retailer merchandisers travel the world for ideas: fabrics, seaming methods and designs. Retailers give some guidelines to their garment makers. Then the garment makers produce prototypes in the right colours and fabrics in order to pitch their wares to M&S or Bhs. There is a round of selection meetings in which buyers turn down most prototypes and then make the final choice. A supplier is almost assured that if the garment maker supplied three items in this season's M&S range, it will receive three slots in next season's range. The difficulty is in seeking the fourth item, particularly as the overall range will not grow – any additional item will be at the expense of a competitor garment maker. To win an additional inclusion requires innovation in design, method, fabric or price – a new look alone will not suffice.

The fact is that, before a new line in lingerie, nightwear or clothing is even stocked in a retailer's stores – let alone before a member of the public has made any purchase – the fabric and made-up garment have both been marketed to Sara Lee Courtaulds' customers: the retailers. This is business marketing.

Sources: Well; Sara Lee Courtaulds, Courtaulds Textiles; Desseilles Textiles, France and UK.

Photo © Royalty-Free/CORBIS

Business market
The customers are not consumers, private individuals or households: instead the target customers are other businesses and organisations that purchase a specific type of product or service for resale, for use in making other products or for use in their daily operations

Industrial, organisational or **business-to-business marketing**
See *business market*

Sara Lee Courtaulds has some consumer brands such as Gossard or Aristoc, but mainly it markets products to garment manufacturers and retailers – other businesses. This chapter explores what is meant by business marketing, before examining the characteristics of business buying and the nature of demand for business products. The chapter's focus is on the buying centre and the buying decision process as applied to business-to-business marketing. The chapter concludes by examining how marketers select and analyse business markets, and the ways in which marketers in business markets modify their use of the marketing toolkit. For example, in terms of branding, addressing customer needs, determining market segments, understanding competitive forces, undertaking marketing research and in constructing marketing programmes.

Types of Business Market

There are four kinds of business markets: producers, resellers, public sector and governments, plus institutions. The following section describes the characteristics of the customers that make up these markets.

Producer Markets

Producer markets
Buyers of raw materials and semi-finished and finished items used to produce other products or in their own operations

Individuals and business organisations that purchase products to make a profit by using them to produce other products or by using them in their own operations are classified as **producer markets**. Producer markets include buyers of raw materials and semi-finished and finished items used to produce other products. For example, a manufacturer buys raw materials and component parts to use directly in the production of its products. Grocers and supermarkets are producer markets for numerous support products, such as paper and plastic bags, displays, scanners and floorcare products. Hotels are producer markets for food, cleaning equipment, laundry services and furniture. Figure 5.1 targets retailers stocking the manufacturer's range of freezers. Producer markets cover a broad array of industries, ranging from agriculture, forestry, fisheries and mining, to construction, transport, communications and public utilities.

Manufacturers tend to be geographically concentrated. This concentration occurs in Europe too, with heavy industry centred on the Ruhr valley in Germany, and on the Midlands and the north-west in the UK. Sometimes an industrial marketer may be able to serve customers more efficiently as a result. Within certain areas, production in just a few industries may account for a sizeable proportion of total industrial output.

Reseller Markets

Reseller markets
Intermediaries, such as wholesalers and retailers, who buy finished goods and resell them to make a profit

Reseller markets consist of intermediaries, such as wholesalers and retailers, who buy finished goods and resell them to make a profit. These intermediaries are discussed in Chapter 11. Other than making minor alterations, resellers do not change the physical characteristics of the products they handle. With the exception of items that producers sell directly to consumers, all products sold to consumer markets are first sold to reseller markets.

Figure 5.1
This Electrolux advertisement targets retailers stocking the manufacturer's range of freezers
Source: Courtesy of Electrolux Home Products

Wholesalers
Intermediaries who purchase products for resale to retailers, other wholesalers and producers, governments and institutions

Retailers
Intermediaries that purchase products and resell them to final consumers

Wholesalers   **Wholesalers** purchase products for resale to retailers, other wholesalers and producers, governments and institutions. Although some highly technical products are sold directly to end users, many products are sold through wholesalers, who in turn sell products to other companies in the distribution system. Thus wholesalers are very important in helping to get a producer's product to customers. Wholesalers often carry many products, perhaps as many as 250,000 items. From the reseller's point of view, having access to such an array of products from a single source makes it much simpler to buy a variety of items. When inventories are vast, the reordering of products is normally automated and the wholesaler's initial purchase decisions are made by professional buyers and buying committees.

Retailers   **Retailers** purchase products and resell them to final consumers. Some retailers carry a large number of items. Chemists, for example, may stock up to 12,000 items, and some supermarkets may handle in excess of 20,000 different products. In small, family-owned retail stores, the owner frequently makes purchasing decisions. Large department stores or supermarket retailers have one or more employees in each department who are responsible for buying products for that department. As for chain stores, a buyer or buying committee in the central office frequently decides whether a product will be made available for selection by store managers. For many products, however, local store managers make the actual buying decisions for a particular store.

Factors Considered by Resellers   When making purchase decisions, resellers consider several factors. They evaluate the level of demand for a product to determine in what quantity and at what prices it can be resold. They assess the amount of space required to handle a product relative to its potential profit. Sometimes resellers will put a product on trial for a fixed period, allowing them to judge customers' reactions and to make better-informed decisions about shelf space and positions as a result. Retailers, for example, sometimes evaluate products on the basis of sales per square metre of selling area. Since customers often depend on a reseller to have a product when they need it, a reseller typically evaluates a supplier's ability to provide adequate quantities when and where wanted. Resellers also take into account the ease of placing orders, and the availability of technical assistance and training programmes from the producer.

More broadly, when resellers consider buying a product not previously carried, they try to determine whether the product competes with or complements the products the company is currently handling. These types of concern distinguish reseller markets from other markets. Sometimes resellers will start stocking a new line of products in response to specific requests from customers. Marketers dealing with reseller markets must recognise these needs and be able to serve them.

Government and Public Sector Markets

Government markets
Departments that buy goods and services to support their internal operations, and to provide the public with education, water, energy, national defence, road systems and healthcare

Public sector markets
Government and institutional not-for-profit customers and stakeholder groups

National and local governments make up **government markets** and contribute to **public sector markets**. They spend huge amounts annually for a variety of goods and services to support their internal operations and to provide the public with education, utilities, national defence, road systems and healthcare. In Europe, the amount spent by local governments varies from country to country, depending on the level and cost of services provided. As a result of the European single market, the services provided by different governments may eventually become standardised.

The types and quantities of products bought by government markets reflect social demands on various government agencies. As the public's needs for government services change, so do the government markets' demands for products.

Because government agencies spend public funds to buy the products they need to provide services, they are accountable to the public. This accountability is responsible for a relatively complex set of buying procedures. Some organisations, unwilling to deal with so much red tape, do not even try to sell to government buyers, while others have learned to deal efficiently with government procedures. For certain companies, such as BAe, and for certain products, such as defence-related items, the government may be one of only a few customers.

Governments usually make their purchases through bids or negotiated contracts. To make a sale under the bid system, a company must apply and receive approval to be placed on a list of qualified bidders. When a government unit wants to buy, it sends out a detailed description of the products to these qualified bidders. Organisations that wish to sell such products then submit bids. The government unit is usually required to accept the lowest bid. When buying non-standard or highly complex products, a government unit often uses a negotiated contract. Under this procedure, the government unit selects only a few companies, negotiates specifications and terms, and eventually awards the contract to one of the negotiating companies. Most large defence contracts held by such companies as BAe or Raytheon are reached through negotiated contracts.

Although government markets have complicated requirements, they can also be very lucrative. When government departments or healthcare providers modernise obsolete computer systems, for example, successful bidders can make high sales with attractive margins during the life of a contract, which may last for five years or more. Some companies have established separate departments to facilitate marketing to government units, while others specialise entirely in this area. The buying behaviour of governments is complex, though. A business such as Fujitsu sells IT services to banks, retailers, manufacturers and utility companies. Fujitsu is a leading supplier of IT services to central and local government and the health service: it has specialist management teams and sales and marketing specialists who focus purely on these public-sector clients owing to the specialised nature of their buying.

Institutional Markets

Institutional markets
Organisations with charitable, educational, community or other non-business goals

Organisations with charitable, educational, community or other non-business goals constitute **institutional markets**. Members of institutional markets include libraries, museums, universities, charitable organisations, and some churches and hospitals. Some of these are also public-sector bodies, such as libraries and museums. Increasingly, government and institutional markets are being grouped together and referred to as public sector markets. Institutions also purchase large amounts of products annually to provide goods, services and ideas to members, congregations, students and other stakeholder groups. For example, a library must buy new books for its readers; pay rent, fuel and water bills; fund the staffing and cleaning of its buildings; invest in IT facilities; and pay to produce publicity material about its services. Because such institutions often have different goals and fewer resources than other types of organisation, marketers may use special marketing activities to serve these markets. Public sector markets consist of government and institutional not-for-profit customers and stakeholder groups: public sector marketing is a significant growth area within the marketing discipline.

Dimensions of Business Buying

Having clarified the different types of business customer, the next step is to consider the dimensions of business-to-business buying. After first examining several characteristics of business transactions, this section then discusses various attributes of business buyers and some of their primary concerns when making purchase decisions. Next it looks at methods of business buying and the major types of purchase that organisations make. The section concludes with a discussion of how the demand for business products and services differs from the demand for consumer products and services.

Characteristics of Business Transactions

Although the marketing concept is equally applicable to business and consumer markets, there are several fundamental differences between the transactions that occur in each. Business buyers tend to order in much larger quantities than do individual consumers. Suppliers must often sell their products in large quantities to make profits; consequently, they prefer not to sell to customers who place small orders.

Generally, business purchases are negotiated less frequently than consumer sales. Some purchases involve expensive items, such as machinery or office equipment, that are used for a number of years. Other products, such as raw materials and component items, are used continuously in production and may have to be supplied frequently. However, the contract regarding the terms of sale of these items is likely to be a long-term agreement, requiring periodic negotiations.

Negotiations in business sales may take much longer than those for consumer sales. Most consumers do not negotiate on prices paid, whereas many business customers never pay the list price. Purchasing decisions are often made by a committee; orders are frequently large, expensive and complex; and products may be custom built. There is a good chance that several people or departments in the purchasing organisation will be involved.

One department might express a need for a product; a second department might develop its specifications; a third might stipulate the maximum amount to be spent; and a fourth might actually place the order. This approach allows individuals with relevant expertise to be incorporated into the process when required. Sales personnel play an important role in negotiations with customers. The quality of the relationship that develops has been shown to impact on the outcome of such negotiations.

Reciprocity
An arrangement unique to business-to-business marketing in which two organisations agree to buy from each other

One practice unique to business-to-business sales is **reciprocity**, an arrangement in which two organisations agree to buy from each other. In some countries, reciprocal agreements that threaten competition are illegal, and action may be taken to stop anti-competitive reciprocal practices. None the less, a certain amount of reciprocal dealing occurs among small businesses and, to a lesser extent, among larger companies as well. Such companies often find that developing long-term relationships of this kind can be an effective competitive tool.[1] Reciprocity can create a problem because coercive measures may be used to enforce it or because reciprocity influences purchasing agents to deal only with certain suppliers.

Attributes of Business Buyers

Business buyers are usually thought of as being different from consumer buyers in their purchasing behaviour because they are better informed about the products they purchase. The viability of their employer's business and thereby their own careers may well depend on their purchasing decisions, so they must be well informed. To make purchasing decisions that fulfil an organisation's needs, business buyers demand detailed information about a product's functional features and technical specifications.

Business buyers, however, also have personal goals that may influence their buying behaviour. Most buyers seek the psychological satisfaction that comes with promotion and financial rewards. In general, agents are most likely to achieve these personal goals when they consistently exhibit rational buying behaviour and perform their jobs in ways that help their companies achieve their organisational objectives. Suppose, though, that a business buyer develops a close friendship with a certain supplier. If the buyer values the friendship more than organisational promotion or financial rewards, he or she may behave irrationally from the company's point of view. Dealing exclusively with that supplier regardless of better prices, quality or service from competitors may indicate an unhealthy or unethical alliance between the buyer and seller. Companies have different ways of dealing with such problems. Some require more than one person to be involved in buying products, while others periodically review their use of suppliers.

Primary Concerns of Business Buyers

When they make purchasing decisions, business customers take into account a variety of factors. For example, in the business advertisement in Figure 5.2 the range of pack options is emphasised by Winalot. Among their chief considerations are quality, delivery, service and price. Product range, innovation, reliability and logistical support may also be significant considerations. Increasingly, business buyers are concerned with service support levels and ongoing commitment from their selected suppliers. There is a growing view, too, that a supplier's personnel in terms of knowledge, motivation, attitude and passion for assisting the customer, are an integral part of the product proposition being 'consumed' by the business customer (see Chapter 8).

Most business customers try to achieve and maintain a specific level of quality in the products they offer to their target markets. To accomplish this goal, they often buy their products on the basis of a set of expressed characteristics, commonly called specifications. These allow a business buyer to evaluate the quality of the products being considered according to particular features and thus to determine whether or not they meet the organisation's needs.

Meeting specifications is extremely important to business customers. If a product fails to meet specifications and malfunctions for the ultimate consumer, that product's supplier may be dropped and an alternative sought. On the other hand, a business buyer is usually

Figure 5.2

This business-to-business advertisement for pet food Winalot promotes the wide selection of pack options offered to retail stockists
Source: All work created by Star Chamber

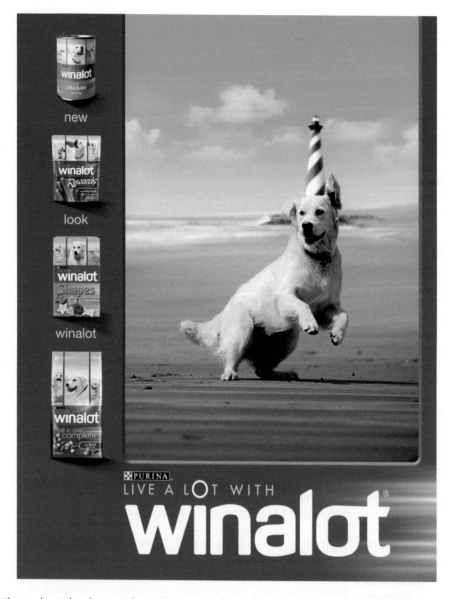

cautious about buying products that exceed specifications, because such products often cost more and thus increase production costs. Suppliers, therefore, need to design their products carefully to come as close as possible to their customers' specifications without incurring any unnecessary extras.

Business buyers also value service. The services offered by suppliers directly and indirectly influence their customers' costs, sales and profits. When tangible goods are the same or quite similar – as with most raw materials – they may have the same specifications and be sold at the same price in the same kind of containers. Under such conditions, the mix of services a business marketer provides to its customers represents its greatest opportunity to gain a competitive advantage. For example, bitumen supplier Nynas has a reputation for technical expertise, technical assistance and flexible logistics. Competitors may be able to offer a similar bitumen product, but few can emulate Nynas's ability to look after customers.

Among the most commonly expected services are market information, inventory maintenance, on-time delivery, flexible ordering and logistical support, technical assistance, warranty back-up, repair services and credit facilities. Specific services vary in importance, however, and the mix of services that companies need is also affected by environmental conditions.

Market Information   Business buyers in general are likely to need technical product information, data regarding demand, information about general economic conditions or supply and delivery information. For example, when technology is changing rapidly, forcing companies to change their production machinery, the demand for consultancy support services and warranty assurances will be especially high.

Inventory Maintenance   It is critical for suppliers to maintain an adequate inventory in order to keep products accessible for when a business buyer needs them and to reduce the buyer's inventory requirements and costs.

On-time Delivery   Reliable, on-time delivery by suppliers also enables business customers to carry less inventory.

Warranty Back-up   Purchasers of machinery are especially concerned about adequate warranties. They are also keen to obtain repair services and replacement parts quickly, because equipment that cannot be used is costly.

Credit Facilities   Suppliers can also give extra value to business buyers by offering credit. Credit helps to improve a business customer's cash flow, reduces the peaks and troughs of capital requirements and thus lowers the company's cost of capital. Although no single supplier can provide every possible service to its customers, a marketing-oriented supplier will try to create a service mix that satisfies the target market.

The Importance of Service Quality   Service quality has become a critical issue because customer expectations of service have broadened. Marketers also need to strive for uniformity of service, simplicity, truthfulness and accuracy; to develop customer service objectives; and to monitor or audit their customer service programmes. Companies can monitor the quality of their service by formally surveying customers or calling on them informally to ask questions about the service they have received. Marketers with a strong customer service programme reap a reward: their customers keep coming back long after the first sale.[2] With customer expectations increasing, it is becoming more difficult for companies to achieve a differential advantage in these areas, and companies must take care to ensure that complaints are handled properly.[3] This reduces the likelihood that dissatisfied customers will give negative feedback to others in the marketplace.[4] One study found that boosting customer retention by 5 per cent could double a small company's profitability.[5]

The Importance of Price   Price matters greatly to a business customer because it influences operating costs and costs of goods sold, and these costs affect the customer's selling price and profit margin. When purchasing major equipment, an industrial buyer views the price as the amount of investment necessary to obtain a certain level of return or savings. Such a purchaser is likely to compare the price of a machine with the value of the benefits that the machine will yield. Caterpillar lost market share to foreign competitors because its prices were too high. A business buyer does not compare alternative products by price alone, though; other factors, such as product quality and supplier services, are also major elements in the purchase decision. For example, one study found that in the buying decision process for mainframe computer software operating systems, intangible attributes, such as the seller's credibility and understanding of the buyer's needs, were very important in the buyer's decision process.[6]

Methods of Business Buying

Although no two business buyers go about their jobs in the same way, most use one or more of the following purchase methods: description, inspection, sampling and negotiation.

Description   When products being purchased are commonly standardised according to certain characteristics – such as size, shape, weight and colour – and graded using such standards, a business buyer may be able to purchase simply by describing or specifying quantity, grade and other attributes. Agricultural produce often falls into this category. In some cases a buyer may specify a particular brand or its equivalent when describing the desired product. Purchases on the basis of description are especially common between a buyer and seller who have established an ongoing relationship built on trust.

Inspection   Certain products, such as large industrial machinery, used vehicles and buildings, have unique characteristics and are likely to vary in condition. For example, a transport depot may need its parking area to be resurfaced. Consequently, buyers and sellers of such products must base their purchase decisions on inspection.

Sampling   In buying based on sampling, a sample of the product is taken from the lot and evaluated. It is assumed that the characteristics of this sample represent the entire lot. This method is appropriate when the product is homogeneous – for instance, grain – and examination of the entire lot is not physically or economically feasible.

Negotiation   Some business purchasing relies on negotiated contracts. In certain instances, a business buyer describes exactly what is needed and then asks sellers to submit bids. The buyer may take the most attractive bids and negotiate with those suppliers. In other cases, the buyer may not be able to identify specifically what is to be purchased but can provide only a general description – as might be the case for a special piece of custom-made equipment. A buyer and seller may negotiate a contract that specifies a base price and contains provisions for the payment of additional costs and fees. These contracts are most likely to be used for one-off projects, such as buildings and capital equipment. For example, the prices that Orbital Sciences Corporation charges its customers for launching and placing satellites in orbit are determined through negotiated contracts.

Types of Business Purchase

Most business purchases are one of three types: new task purchase, modified rebuy purchase or straight rebuy purchase. The type of purchase affects the number of individuals involved and the length of the buying process.

New task purchase
An organisation's initial purchase of an item to be used to perform a new job or to solve a new problem

New Task Purchase   In a **new task purchase**, an organisation makes an initial purchase of an item to be used to perform a new job or to solve a new problem. This may take a long time because it might require the development of product specifications, supplier specifications and procedures for future purchases. To make the initial purchase, the business buyer usually needs a good deal of information and may formally review a set of possible suppliers. A new task purchase is important to the supplier because it may lead to the sale of large quantities of the product over a period of years.

Modified rebuy purchase
A new task purchase that is changed when it is reordered or when the requirements associated with a straight rebuy purchase are modified

Modified Rebuy Purchase   In a **modified rebuy purchase**, a new task purchase is changed the second or third time it is ordered, or the requirements associated with a straight rebuy purchase are modified. For example, an organisation might seek faster delivery, lower prices or a different quality of product specifications. When modified rebuying occurs, regular suppliers may become more competitive to keep the account. Competing suppliers may have the opportunity to obtain the business.

Straight Rebuy Purchase   A **straight rebuy purchase** occurs when a buyer repurchases the same products routinely under approximately the same terms of sale. For example,

Straight rebuy purchase
A routine repurchase of the same products under approximately the same terms of sale

when reordering photocopying paper, a buyer requires little additional information and can usually place the order relatively quickly, often using familiar suppliers that have provided satisfactory service and products in the past. These suppliers try to set up automatic reordering systems to make reordering easy and convenient for business buyers, and may even monitor the organisation's inventory to indicate to the buyer what needs to be ordered.

Demand for Business Products

Products sold to business customers are called business products and, consequently, the demand for these products is called business demand. Unlike consumer demand, business demand – formerly known as industrial demand – is:

- derived
- inelastic
- joint, and
- more fluctuating.

Derived demand
Demand for business products that arises from the demand for consumer products

Derived Demand   As business customers, especially producers, buy products to be used directly or indirectly in the production of goods and services to satisfy consumers' needs, the demand for business products arises from the demand for consumer products; it is, therefore, called **derived demand**. In fact, all business demand can in some way be traced to consumer demand. This occurs at a number of levels, with business sellers being affected in various ways. For instance, consumers today are more concerned with good health and nutrition than ever before, and as a result are purchasing food products containing less cholesterol, saturated fat, sugar and salt. When some consumers stopped buying high-cholesterol cooking fats and margarine, the demand for equipment used in manufacturing these products also dropped. Thus factors influencing consumer buying of various food products have ultimately affected food processors, equipment manufacturers, suppliers of raw materials and even fast-food restaurants, which have had to switch to lower-cholesterol oils for frying. Changes in derived demand result from a chain reaction. When consumer demand for a product changes, a wave is set in motion that affects demand for all of the items involved in the production of that consumer product.

Inelastic demand
Demand that is not significantly affected by a price increase or decrease

Inelastic Demand   The demand for many business products at the industry level is **inelastic demand** – that is, a price increase or decrease will not significantly alter demand for the item. The concept of price elasticity of demand is discussed further in Chapter 12. Because many business products contain a number of parts, price increases that affect only one or two parts of the product may yield only a slightly higher per-unit production cost. Of course, when a sizeable price increase for a component represents a large proportion of the total product's cost, demand may become more elastic, because the component price increase will cause the price at the consumer level to rise sharply. For example, if manufacturers of aircraft engines substantially increase the price of these engines, forcing Boeing in turn to raise the prices of its aircraft, the demand for aircraft may become more elastic as airlines reconsider whether they can afford them. An increase in the price of windscreens, however, is unlikely to affect greatly the price of the aircraft or the demand for them.

The characteristic of inelasticity applies only to industry demand for the business product, not to the demand curve faced by an individual company. For example, suppose that a car component company increases the price of rubber seals sold to car manufacturers, while its competitors retain their lower prices. The car component company would probably experience reduced unit sales because most of its customers would switch to the lower-priced brands. A specific organisation is vulnerable to elastic demand, even though industry demand for a particular product is inelastic.

Joint demand
Demand that occurs when two or more products are used in combination to produce another product

Joint Demand   The demand for certain business products, especially raw materials and components, is subject to joint demand. **Joint demand** occurs when two or more items are used in combination to produce a product. For example, a company that manufactures cork noticeboards for schools and colleges needs supplies of cork and wood to produce the item; these two products are demanded jointly. A shortage of cork will cause a drop in the production of wooden surrounds for noticeboards.

Marketers selling many jointly demanded items must realise that when a customer begins purchasing one of the jointly demanded items, a good opportunity exists for selling related products. Similarly, when customers purchase a number of jointly demanded products, the producer must take care to avoid shortages of any one of them, because such shortages jeopardise sales of all the jointly demanded products. The susceptibility of producers to the shortage of a particular item is illustrated clearly when industrial action at companies producing microchips results in a halt in production at manufacturers of computers and related goods.

Fluctuating Demand   Because the demand for business products fluctuates according to consumer demand, when particular consumer products are in high demand, their producers buy large quantities of raw materials and components to ensure that they can meet long-run production requirements. Such producers may also expand their production capacity, which entails the acquisition of new equipment and machinery, more workers, a greater need for business services, and more raw materials and component parts.

Conversely, a decline in the demand for certain consumer goods significantly reduces the demand for business products used to produce those goods. When consumer demand is low, business customers cut their purchases of raw materials and components, and stop buying equipment and machinery, even for replacement purposes. This trend is especially pronounced during periods of recession.

A marketer of business products may notice changes in demand when its customers change their inventory policies, perhaps because of expectations about future demand. For example, if several dishwasher manufacturers who buy timers from one producer increase their inventory of timers from a two-week to a one-month supply, the timer producer will experience a significant immediate increase in demand.

Sometimes price changes can lead to surprising temporary changes in demand. A price increase for a business item may initially cause business customers to buy more of the item because they expect the price to rise further. Similarly, demand for a business product may be significantly lower following a price cut as buyers wait for further price reductions. Such behaviour is often observed in companies purchasing information technology. Fluctuations in demand can be significant in industries in which price changes occur frequently.

Business Buying Decisions

Business (or business-to-business) buying behaviour
The purchase behaviour of producers, resellers, the public sector, government units and institutions

Business (or business-to-business) buying behaviour refers to the purchase behaviour of producers, resellers, the public sector, government units and institutions. Although several of the same factors that affect consumer buying behaviour (discussed in Chapter 4) also influence business buying behaviour, a number of factors are unique to the latter. This section first analyses the buying centre to learn who participates in making business purchase decisions and then focuses on the stages of the buying decision process and the factors that affect this process.

The Buying Centre   Most business-to-business purchase decisions are made by more than one person. The group of people within an organisation who are involved in making business purchase decisions are usually referred to as the **buying centre**. These individuals include users, influencers, buyers, deciders and gatekeepers, although one person may perform several

Buying centre
The group of people within an organisation who are involved in making business-to-business purchase decisions

of these roles.[7] Participants in the buying process share the goals and risks associated with their decisions. Effective marketers strive to understand the constituents of risk, as perceived by their target customer personnel, so that they may tailor their messages and marketing propositions to reassure members of the buying centre. In this way, marketers hope to gain an advantage over those rivals that fail to understand these customer concerns and issues.

Users are those in the business who actually use the product being acquired. They frequently initiate the purchase process and/or generate the specifications for the purchase. After the purchase, they also evaluate the product's performance relative to the specifications. Although users do not ordinarily have sufficient power to make the final decision to buy, it is important that their views be considered. A user who is unhappy with a piece of equipment may not work efficiently. Influencers are often technical personnel, such as engineers, who help develop the specifications and evaluate alternative products. Technical personnel are especially important influencers when the products being considered involve new, advanced technology. For example, a chemicals manufacturer seeking to install new processing equipment may take advice from a wide range of technical experts.

Buyers are responsible for selecting suppliers and actually negotiating the terms of purchase. They may also become involved in developing specifications. Buyers are sometimes called purchasing agents or purchasing managers and in retailers, merchandisers. Their choices of suppliers and products, especially for new task purchases, are heavily influenced by individuals occupying other roles in the buying centre. For straight rebuy purchases, the buyer plays a major role in the selection of suppliers and in negotiations with them. Deciders actually choose the products and suppliers. Although buyers may be the deciders, it is not unusual for different people to occupy these roles. For routinely purchased items, buyers are commonly the deciders. However, a buyer may not be authorised to make purchases that exceed a certain monetary value, in which case higher-level management personnel are the deciders. Gatekeepers, such as secretaries and technical personnel, control the flow of information to and among others in the buying centre. The flow of information from supplier sales representatives to users and influencers is often controlled by buyers or other personnel in the purchasing department. Unfortunately, relations between members of the buying centre can become strained at times.

🔘 Marketing Tools and Techniques

Practitioners' Use of the Buying Behaviour Theory: the Dibb/Simkin Buying Proforma

Most practitioners do not want to read an 500-page text book about understanding customers, but equally they recognise that in order to fully appreciate a business customer's requirements or consumers' buying behaviour, they must be able to:

- profile the targeted customers/consumers – be them!
- understand the composition of the buying centre
- identify their key customer values (KCVs) – customer/consumer needs and expectations
- determine how the customers/consumers buy – their buying process
- understand the influences at work on this process.

In order to devise effective marketing strategies and programmes, marketers must be able to answer three key questions.

1 What needs must be satisfied and for whom?
2 Where should marketers be active in the customer/consumer buying process?
3 Which influencing factors can they in turn influence?

There are many approaches to addressing such an understanding of business customers or consumers, but one proposed by Dibb and Simkin has been widely adopted across consumer, business and service markets. Two examples are presented here in order to illustrate this approach.

A leading supplier of herbicides, pesticides and seeds segmented the farmers – the customers – in Latin America, identifying 22 market segments (see Chapter 6). As an example, one segment is profiled below, illustrating the types of farmer in this segment, the nature of the buying centre and the very specific, ego-led customer needs. In order to operate successfully in this market segment, a supplier has to satisfy these needs but also tailor marketing campaigns to the characteristics of these farmers and the varied mix of professionals within this buying centre. In developing a better understanding of the buying process, this agrichemicals business realised there were important influencing factors impacting on customer choice that it had previously ignored. Contact was made with organisers of the technical seminars and the trade association in order to gain an advantage over rivals.

In common with most banks and building societies, the bank that conducted this research marketed its products directly to the targeted consumers: first-time house buyers. Marketing research (see Chapter 7) identified the important influencing role played by the parents of these potential customers, and of independent financial advisers, estate agents and the bank's own staff involved in daily routine banking activities with such customers. Different marketing messages and campaigns were produced to appeal to these various target audiences. The real added value came from targeting information about its mortgage products to the parents of young adults aged in their 20s. It was quite straightforward for this bank to trawl through its customer database in order to identify customers with children in such an age range. Market share in this mortgage segment duly quadrupled in less than a year. This bank undertook a similar analysis across all of its segments in both consumer markets – as illustrated below – and in its business markets.

The Dibb/Simkin Buying Proforma:

- forces managers to 'think customer'!
- provides much more than just a description of 'who to sell to'
- identifies exactly what a company must provide/offer
- reveals the influences the company in turn must strive to influence
- provides a framework against which to compare competitors' moves and marketing programmes.

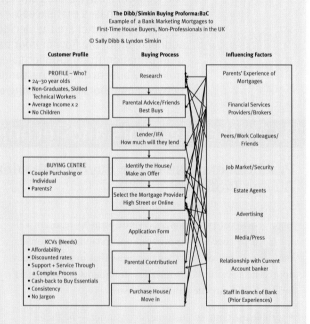

The Dibb/Simkin Buying Proforma is copyright Sally Dibb and Lyndon Simkin. A more extensive explanation of this technique is offered in either *The Market Segmentation Workbook* (Dibb and Simkin) or *The Marketing Planning Workbook* (Dibb, Simkin and Bradley), both originally published in 1996 by Thomson, London; or in the authors' newer titles *Market Segmentation Success:* *Making It Happen!* (The Haworth Press, 2008) and *Marketing Planning* (Cengage Learning, 2008).

The size and characteristics of an organisation's buying centre are affected by the number of its employees and its market position, the volume and types of products being purchased and the company's overall managerial philosophy regarding exactly who should be involved in purchase decisions. A marketer attempting to sell to a business customer needs to know who is in the buying centre, the types of decisions each individual makes and which individuals are the most influential in the decision process. The marketer should also strive to understand the respective needs of these members and how each perceives risk in terms of the proposed purchase: the marketer should then tailor messages to reassure the various members of the buying centre. Then the marketer will be in a position to contact those in the buying centre who have the most influence. Such an approach is detailed in the Marketing Tools and Techniques box on pages 147–148, which also explains how many organisations deploy the buying behaviour concepts presented in this chapter as they build up an understanding of their customers.

Relationship Marketing and Managing Exchange Relationships

Relationship marketing
All of the activities an organisation uses to build, maintain and develop customer relations

The relationship that exists between a supplying organisation and its customers is an important aspect of the buying process that deserves special consideration. In fact, marketing experts have recently become much more interested in marketing relationships in general.[8] The term **relationship marketing** has been used to express this particular development as explained in Chapter 1. Instead of being concerned about individual transactions between suppliers and buyers, the relationship marketing approach emphasises the importance of the whole relationship between the parties. Relationship marketing can, therefore, be regarded as all of the activities an organisation uses to build, maintain and develop ongoing customer relations.[9] The intention is to nurture a mutually beneficial sustainable relationship and to maximise the 'share of wallet' from the customer over a period of time.

Put simply, relationship marketing is concerned with getting and keeping customers by ensuring that an appropriate combination of marketing, customer service and quality is provided.[10] Underlying the relationship marketing concept is the idea that the relationship between a supplying organisation and its buyers is essentially similar to the relationship between two individuals. For example, bitumen company Nynas, featured in the case at the end of this chapter, has achieved market leadership through building ongoing relationships with a diversity of customers 24 hours a day, 365 days a year. Such relationships are conducted over a period of time through a series of meetings, which allow each party to get to know the other, to share information, to adapt to each other, and generally to build trust and cooperation.[11]

As explained in Chapter 1, the concept of relationship marketing is changing the way in which marketers are looking at marketing. However, it is also particularly pertinent to this chapter's discussion of the exchange relationships that develop between buyers and sellers.[12] When a company buys a product or service from another company, both organisations become involved in an exchange process. During the transaction, both buyer and seller will exchange items of value in return for something else. For example, when a software company provides a printer with a desktop publishing package, it will provide the buyer with a package of benefits that include the software disks, detailed users' guide, warranty details, a variety of payment options and the opportunity to attend a training course. In exchange, the printer will agree to pay the price negotiated with the manufacturer. Figure 5.3 shows the range of factors that can be exchanged during the purchase process.

Relationship management
The process of encouraging a match between the seller's competitive advantage and the buyer's requirements over an item's life cycle

It is often in the interests of both parties to develop long-term relationships. If buying and selling companies are used to dealing with each other, they are more likely to be able to adapt to each other's needs and to reach an agreement quickly and easily. Some research suggests that adaptation by suppliers happens more often than adaptation by buyers. However, long-term relationships are often attractive to both companies because they reduce the level of risk – financial and practical – associated with the purchase. The trend towards long-term relationships has resulted in the development of what is called **relationship management**.[13] This process encourages a match between the seller's competitive advantage and the buyer's requirements over the life cycle of the item being purchased.

Figure 5.3
The exchange process in business buying

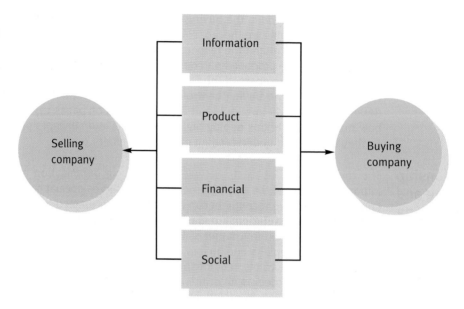

Stages of the Business Buying Decision Process

Like consumers, businesses follow a buying decision process. This process is summarised on the right-hand side of Figure 5.4.

Stage 1   In the first stage, one or more individuals recognise that a problem or need exists. Problem recognition may arise under a variety of circumstances, either from inside or outside the company. For example, a machine might reach the end of its working life and need to be replaced, or changes in fire regulations might dictate the need for a new approach to manufacturing. Often, the problem recognised is simply the need to replenish stocks of raw materials or components. Individuals in the buying centre, such as users, influencers or buyers, may be involved in problem recognition, but this may be stimulated by external sources, such as sales representatives or customers.

Stage 2   The second stage of the process – development of product specifications – requires those involved to assess the problem or need, and to determine what is necessary to resolve or satisfy it. During this stage, users and influencers, such as technical personnel, production managers and engineers, often provide information and advice for developing product specifications. By assessing and describing needs, the organisation should be able to establish product specifications.

Stage 3   Searching for possible products to solve the problem and then locating suitable suppliers is the third stage in the decision process. Search activities may involve surfing the Internet, looking in company files and trade directories, contacting suppliers for information, visiting trade shows, identifying suppliers used by rivals, soliciting proposals from known suppliers, and examining catalogues and trade publications. Suppliers may be viewed as unacceptable because they are too small to supply the quantities needed, or because they do not have the necessary information technology systems to keep appropriate delivery records. In some instances, the product may not be available from any existing supplier and the buyer must then find an innovative company, such as 3M, that can design and build the product. During this search stage, some organisations engage in **value analysis**, which is an evaluation of each component of a potential purchase. Value analysis examines quality, designs, materials, and possibly item reduction or deletion to acquire the product in the most cost-effective way. Usually suppliers are judged against

Value analysis
An evaluation of each component of a potential purchase

Figure 5.4
The business buying
decision process and
factors that may
influence it
Source: adapted from
Frederick E. Webster,
Jr, and Yoram Wind,
Organisational Buying
Behaviour *(Englewood*
Cliffs, NJ: Prentice-Hall,
1972), pp. 33–7
Adapted by
permission

Supplier analysis
A formal and systematic
evaluation of current
and potential suppliers

several criteria and some will be ruled unsuitable. Some organisations practice **supplier analysis**, a formal and systematic appraisal of current and potential suppliers or vendors, focusing on factors such as price, product quality, delivery service, product availability, reliability, reputation, client profile and customer service.

If all goes well, the search stage will result in a list of several alternative products and suppliers.

Stage 4   The fourth stage is evaluating the products on the list to determine which options (if any) meet the product specifications developed in the second stage. The advertisement in Figure 5.5 stresses the particular product quality attributes that may help customers evaluate whether a particular offering meets their requirements. At this point, too, various suppliers

151

Figure 5.5
Dalgety promotes the quality and reliability of its seeds, targeted at the farming community
Source: Courtesy of Dalgety – a division of MASSTOCK ARABLE (UK) LTD

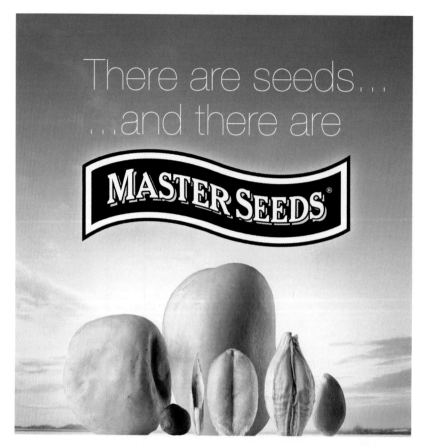

Not all seeds are equal.

When you see the **Master Seeds** brand on a bag it means the seeds inside have passed the highest standards in British agriculture.

Dalgety works hand in hand with the breeders to evaluate varieties for several years ahead of commercialisation, carrying out tests at **Throws Farm** (the Dalgety arable research centre) and other independent trials sites all over the UK.

 Quality is monitored at every stage of processing to ensure you put only the best seeds into the soil as the foundation for profitability across your whole farm.

And when you're ready to drill, we can give you innovative agronomic advice from our **COGS** and **SMARTfarming** research to make certain you get the maximum returns from all your crops.

There are other seeds on the market, but **Master Seeds** are only available from Dalgety and other Masstock Group companies.

Dalgety is a division of Masstock Arable (UK) Ltd

seed.marketing@dalgety.co.uk

are evaluated according to multiple criteria, such as price, service, technical support and ability to deliver.

Stage 5   The results of the deliberations and assessments in the fourth stage are used during the fifth stage to select the most appropriate product and supplier. In some cases the buyer may decide on several suppliers. In others, only one supplier is selected – a situation known as **sole sourcing**. Sole sourcing has traditionally been discouraged except when a product is available from only one company. In recent times sole sourcing has become more popular, partly because such an arrangement means better communications between buyer and supplier, stability and higher profits for the supplier and, often, lower prices for the buyer. The popular manufacturing approach of just-in-time often requires sole sourcing, in order to facilitate the logistical arrangements between buyer and supplier. However, many organisations prefer to purchase goods and services from several suppliers – **multiple sourcing** – to reduce the possibility of disruption caused by

Sole sourcing
A buying process that involves the selection of only one supplier

Multiple sourcing
A business's decision to use several suppliers

strikes, shortages, quality problems, delivery glitches or bankruptcy. The actual product is ordered in this fifth stage and specific details regarding terms, credit arrangements, delivery dates and methods, and technical assistance are worked out.

Stage 6 During the sixth stage, the product's performance is evaluated by comparing it with specifications and customer expectations of the relationship. Sometimes, even though the product meets the specifications, its performance does not adequately solve the problem or satisfy the need recognised in the first stage. In such cases, the product specifications must be adjusted. The supplier's performance is also evaluated during this stage, and if it is found wanting, the buyer seeks corrective action from the supplier or searches for a new supplier. Buyers are increasingly concerned with obtaining high-quality service from suppliers and may formally set performance targets for them. The results of such performance evaluations become feedback for the other stages and influence future purchase decisions. In many business relationships, particularly long-term relationships, suppliers formally audit their customers' satisfaction levels in order to minimise any problems that may eventually lose a customer to a competitor.

Uses of the Business Buying Decision Process This business buying decision process is used in its entirety primarily for new task purchases. Several of the stages, but not necessarily all, are used for modified rebuying and straight rebuying, and fewer individuals are likely to be involved in these decisions. If a buyer–supplier relationship is working well, there may be no consideration of alternative suppliers, for example. Indeed, customers may work with such well-regarded suppliers when specifying their next product or purchasing needs. There is a desire in many business markets, particularly in supplier–manufacturer relationships, to create mutually beneficial ongoing partnerships, with customers and suppliers openly sharing market data, knowledge of product or competitor developments, and future plans.

Influences on Business Buying

Environmental factors
Uncontrollable forces such as politics, competitive and economic factors, legal and regulatory issues, technological changes and socio-cultural issues

Organisational factors
Include the buyer's objectives, purchasing policies and resources, as well as the size and composition of its buying centre

Interpersonal factors
The relationships among the people in the buying centre

Figure 5.4 also lists the four major categories of factors that influence business buying decisions: environmental, organisational, interpersonal and individual.

Environmental Factors Chapter 3 explained that **environmental factors** are uncontrollable forces such as politics, laws, regulations and regulatory agencies, activities of interest groups, changes in the economy, competitors' actions and technological changes. These forces generate a considerable amount of uncertainty for an organisation, which can make individuals in the buying centre apprehensive about certain types of purchase. Changes in one or more environmental forces can create new purchasing opportunities. For example, changes in competition and technology can make buying decisions difficult in the case of products such as computers, a field in which competition is increasingly affected by new cooperative strategies between companies. Compaq Computers, for instance, grew into a billion-dollar company by competing only against IBM and developing cooperative relationships with all other potential competitors, ultimately tying up with HP.[14]

Organisational Factors **Organisational factors** influencing the buying decision process include the buyer's objectives, purchasing policies and resources, as well as the size and composition of its buying centre. An organisation may have certain buying policies to which buying centre participants must conform. For instance, a company's policies may require long-term contracts, perhaps longer than most sellers desire. The nature of an organisation's financial resources may require special credit arrangements. Any of these conditions could affect purchase decision processes.

Interpersonal Factors **Interpersonal factors** are the relationships among the people in the buying centre, where the use of power and the level of conflict significantly influence organisational buying decisions. Certain managers in the buying centre may be better communicators than others and thus more persuasive. Often these interpersonal dynamics are hidden, making them difficult for marketers to appraise. There are also interpersonal factors to consider between supplier and customer personnel. While a customer may be purchasing a particular product, the supplier's personnel involved with placing the order, offering technical assistance or customer service, and in logistical arrangements, become a very important concern for the customer's managers. No matter how good the product may be, if the supplier's personnel are not regarded in a good light by the customer's managers, there is unlikely to be a high level of customer satisfaction. Suppliers must select, train, motivate and reward, control and orient their customer-facing personnel very carefully. The individual factors pertinent to particular managers are, therefore, important.

Individual factors
The personal characteristics of individuals in the buying centre, such as age, education, personality, position in the organisation and income level

Individual Factors   **Individual factors** are the personal characteristics of individuals in the buying centre, such as age, education, personality, position in the organisation and income level. For example, a 60-year-old manager who left school at 16 and has been with the organisation ever since may affect the decisions of the buying centre differently from a 30 year old with a two-year employment history, who left university with a business studies degree and an MBA. How influential these factors will be depends on the buying situation, the type of product being purchased and whether the purchase is new task, modified rebuy or straight rebuy. The negotiating styles of individuals will undoubtedly vary within an organisation and from one organisation to another. To be effective, a marketer needs to know customers well enough to be aware of these individual factors and the effects they may have on purchase decisions.

Selection and Analysis of Business Markets

Marketing research is becoming more important in business markets. Most of the marketing research techniques discussed in Chapter 7 can be applied to **business marketing**. This section focuses on important and unique approaches to selecting and analysing business markets.

Business marketing
Activities directed towards facilitating and expediting exchanges between business markets and business producers

Many business marketers have easy access to a considerable amount of information about potential customers, particularly in industrial or manufacturing markets, for much of this information appears in government and industry publications. However, comparable data about ultimate consumers are not available. Even though marketers may use different procedures to isolate and analyse target markets, most follow a similar pattern:

1 determining who potential customers are and how many there are
2 locating where they are
3 estimating their purchase potential.

Identifying Potential Customers

All marketers must determine who are potential customers. In the Marketing Insight box (see page 155), for example, food giant Unilever has decided to market its new-look ice cream units to convenience stores and forecourt outlets, rather than to the supermarkets.

The Standard Industrial Classification System   Much information about business customers is based on the **Standard Industrial Classification (SIC) system**, which provides information on different industries and products, and was developed to classify selected economic characteristics of industrial, commercial, financial and service organisations. In the UK, this system is administered by the Central Statistical Office. Table 5.1 shows how the SIC system can be used to categorise products.

⚙ Marketing Insight

Unilever Targets Forecourts and Convenience Stores

In the battle for market share in the ice cream market, it has long been the practice of the major manufacturers to make branded freezer units available to retailers. The hope is that prominently branded units will both encourage consumers to purchase ice cream lines but also persuade retailers to maintain stocks of a particular manufacturer's ice cream brands. Until recently, the freezer units were chests with sliding tops: there was no access from the front or sides. There was only limited display potential, as consumers could only see inside through the top by leaning over the units.

In the summer of 2004, Wall's owner Unilever launched eye-catching three-tier units that displayed the contents at three tilted levels. The new units also made the merchandise easier to access. In test market trials, the Maxivision freezer increased forecourt sales by 29 per cent. In addition to being more eye-catching and easier to access, the unit holds much more than its predecessor and reduces running costs by around 15 per cent. However, the improved freezer was more expensive. The older unit cost retailers around £600, whereas the new unit costs over £900. These prices to retail customers include £300 worth of Wall's stock vouchers.

For Unilever's marketers, the challenge had been to increase consumer sales by providing the company's retail customers with a better display and storage solution. The new unit had to encourage more consumer demand, help maximise floor space utilisation and minimise operating costs. The older storage units were cumbersome, often unsightly and, out of season, occupied a disproportionate amount of space relative to winter sales levels. The test market revealed that retailers appreciated the better space utilisation as much as the improved appeal to their shoppers.

Unilever decided not to prioritise the major supermarket chains as sales targets for these freezer units. These retailers tend to have their own freezer units designed to display and store many lines from a variety of manufacturers. Unilever's marketers instead determined that garage forecourts and convenience stores were far better sales prospects. Even within these target categories, the national chains were targeted as priority sales prospects, ahead of the independently owned one-off retailers and small regional chains. The units were made available to all retailers, but promotional activity and the salesforce were tasked to initially focus on convenience stores and forecourt chains.

Most of the brands you as consumers purchase have teams of marketers developing marketing programmes to appeal to consumers, but also marketers whose focus is trade customers. Without these business customers stocking these products, consumers would fail to locate and purchase their favourite brands. For example, Masterfoods – behind Mars and Uncle Ben's – has marketing strategies and associated marketing programmes targeting the intended consumers, but also trade campaigns designed to ensure shelf-space and secure in-store promotional slots.

Sources: *The Grocer*, 8 May 2004, p. 64; One Stop Stores; Unilever Wall's.

Standard Industrial Classification (SIC) system
A system that provides information on different industries and products, and classifies economic characteristics of industrial, commercial, financial and service organisations

The most recent SIC manual contains 10 broad divisions, each denoted by a single digit from 0 to 9. These are sub-divided into classes (each denoted by the addition of a second digit), the classes are divided into groups (three digits) and the groups into activity headings (four more digits). There are 10 divisions, 60 classes, 222 groups and 334 activity headings. For example, Division 4 (see Table 5.1), 'Other manufacturing industries', has 8 classes, 50 groups and 91 activity headings. The numbering system follows that of NACE (Nomenclature Générale des Activités Économiques dans les Communautés Européennes) as far as possible.[15] To categorise manufacturers in more detail, the *Census of Distribution* further sub-divides manufacturers.

Data are available for each SIC category through various government publications and departments. Table 5.2 shows the types of information that can be obtained from government sources. Some data are available by town, county and metropolitan area. Business market data also appear in such non-government sources as Dun & Bradstreet's *Market Identifiers*.

The SIC system is a ready-made tool that allows business marketers to divide industrial organisations into market segments based mainly on the type of product manufactured or

TABLE 5.1 THE STANDARD INDUSTRIAL CLASSIFICATION (SIC) SYSTEM FOR CATEGORISING INDUSTRIAL CONSUMERS	
0	Agriculture, forestry and fishing
1	Energy and water supply industries
2	Extraction of minerals and ores other than fuels; manufacture of metals, mineral products and chemicals
3	Metal goods, engineering and vehicles
4	Other manufacturing industries
5	Construction
6	Distribution, hotels and catering; repairs
7	Transport and communication
8	Banking, finance, insurance, business services and leasing
9	Other services

TABLE 5.2 TYPES OF GOVERNMENT INFORMATION AVAILABLE ABOUT INDUSTRIAL MARKETS (BASED ON SIC CATEGORIES)

Value of industry shipments	Imports as a percentage of apparent consumption
Number of establishments	Compound annual average rate of growth
Number of employees	Major producing areas
Exports as a percentage of shipments	

handled. Although the SIC system is a vehicle for segmentation – identifying groupings of customers (see Chapter 6) – it must be used in conjunction with other types of data to enable a business marketer to determine exactly which customers he or she can reach and how many of them can be targeted. The SIC system is a convenient grouping categorisation, but it does not negate the need to fully explore customer buying behaviour, as depicted in the Marketing Tools and Techniques box on pages 147–148, in order to properly consider target market priorities.

Input–Output Analysis   Input–output analysis works well in conjunction with the SIC system. This type of analysis is based on the assumption that the output or sales of one industry are the input or purchases of other industries. For example, component manufacturers provide products that form an input for manufacturers of white goods such as washing machines, dishwashers and fridges. **Input–output data** tell what types of industries purchase the products of a particular industry.

Input–output data
Information on what types of industries purchase the products of a particular industry

After discovering which industries purchase the major portion of an industry's output, the next step is to find the SIC numbers for those industries. Because organisations are grouped differently in the input–output tables and the SIC system, ascertaining SIC numbers can be difficult. However, the Central Statistical Office does provide some limited conversion tables with the input–output data. These tables can assist business marketers in assigning SIC numbers to the industry categories used in the input–output analysis. Having determined the SIC numbers of the industries that buy the company's output, a business marketer is in a position to ascertain the number of establishments that are potential buyers nationally, by town and by county. Government publications report the number of establishments within SIC classifications, along with other types of data, such as those shown in Table 5.2.

Identifying and Locating Potential Customers   Once business marketers have achieved this level of information, they can identify and locate potential customers using the Internet or business directories such as *Kompass* and *Kelly's*. These sources contain information about a company such as its name, SIC number, address, phone number and annual sales, allowing organisations to develop lists of potential customers by area.

A second approach, which is more expedient but also more expensive, is to use one of the many marketing services businesses. For example, Market Locations and Experian are able to provide lists of organisations that fall into particular SIC groups. Information can include name, location, sales volume, number of employees, types of product handled and names of chief executives. Business marketers can then decide which companies on the list to pursue. This will usually involve an assessment of attractiveness and purchase potential (see Figure 5.6). As described in chapters 6 and 9, there are also many techniques that assist marketers in assessing the relative attractiveness of customers and market segments, such as the directional policy matrix and 'ABC sales: contribution' analysis.

In business marketing, situation-specific variables may be more relevant in segmenting markets than general customer characteristics. Business customers concentrate on benefits

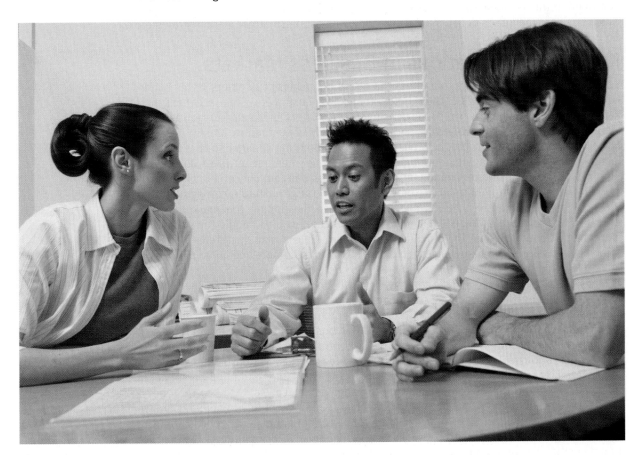

Figure 5.6
Networking, discussing and engaging with prospective business customers is an important part of identifying likely sales leads and honing an appropriate marketing proposition
Photo © Royalty-Free/CORBIS

157

sought; therefore, understanding the end use of the product is more important than the psychology of decisions or socio-economic characteristics. Segmenting by benefits rather than by customer characteristics can provide insight into the structure of the market and opportunities for new customers.[16]

To estimate the purchase potential of business customers or groups of customers, a marketer must find a relationship between the size of potential customers' purchases and a variable available in SIC data, such as the number of employees. For example, a fabric manufacturer might attempt to determine the average number of metres of different materials purchased by a specific type of potential clothing manufacturer relative to the number of people employed. If the marketer has no previous experience in this market segment, it will probably be necessary to survey a random sample of potential customers in order to establish a relationship between purchase sizes and numbers of people employed. Once this relationship has been established, it can be applied to potential customer segments to estimate their purchases. After deriving these estimates, the marketer selects the customers to be included in the target market.

More and more businesses are adopting segmentation schemes that are based on the needs, buying behaviour and characteristics of their customers, rather than on simple trade categories or SIC codes. Such segmentation demands a thorough understanding of the nature of purchasing, the buying decision-making process and influencing factors, as described in this chapter. The next chapter of *Marketing Essentials* explores the ways in which business marketers derive market segments and establish target market strategies.

Marketing's Variations in Business Markets

Business marketers often have to address the needs of business customers within a marketing channel and the needs of their intended business customers. Some business marketers must also serve the needs of consumers. Marketers of consumer goods often manage many products and deal with perhaps thousands of customers. Mostly, although not always, such consumer products pass through a marketing channel so that a manufacturer's marketing managers deal primarily with channel member business customers. So for example, the marketers handling Snickers or Mars bars are concerned with understanding and satisfying their retail customers, such as the large cash-and-carry groups and the supermarkets. However, these marketers are also developing the marketing programmes targeting the end user consumers – Mars' marketers also handle the company's marketing activity aimed at the individual consumer. While a manufacturer's marketers often have to address dual audiences – channel member customers and consumers – it is more likely that their focus will be on the business customer.

Many business marketers handle a relatively small number of clients and the need to tailor marketing propositions to these customers' wishes is arguably more important than in consumer markets. While all marketers must properly understand buying behaviour and purchasers' characteristics, it is absolutely crucial in business marketing for marketers to develop such an understanding. Sales staff play a central role in building this understanding. Their relationships with customers can be leveraged to gain a particularly in-depth appreciation of customers' needs. Not surprisingly, the sales and marketing personnel in many business-to-business companies work together very closely.

There are other nuances, too, that it is worth mentioning. Most advertisements shown on television over the course of an evening are for consumer goods and services: they are eye-catching, emotive and highly persuasive. This style of advertising reflects the emotive brand positionings developed for many consumer goods, such as Nike or Guinness. While business marketers also strive to create strong brands (see Chapter 14) that are distinctive and attractive, much business branding lacks the emotion of consumer branding and suffers from a relative paucity of investment in supportive marketing communications activity and spending. Business branding tends to be more simplistic, focusing on identification and product differentiation. There are, of course, exceptions, with some business-to-business brands such as IBM or JCB being just as powerful as consumer brands.

The role of competition is different, too. It is unlikely that arch-rivals Tesco, Sainsbury's and ASDA would ever cooperate and work together. Similarly, why would KP and Walkers ever unite? Many brands between which a consumer may choose are unlikely ever to cooperate and work in harmony with each other. Indeed, the Competition Commission and EU regulators would probably be unimpressed if they did. In many business situations, though, individual companies pool their expertise and resources in order to win contracts with customers. For example, to offer retailers a viable chip-and-pin payment service, IT services company Fujitsu joined forces with Barclaycard Merchant Services (payment transactions), Box (hardware) and Cybertill (installation and maintenance) as a partnership. However, partners in one market segment may in fact be arch-rivals in another. Fujitsu may compete with KPMG, BT or IBM in one segment, but partner such companies in order to serve the needs of business customers in another. The implication is that the understanding of competitive forces is often more complex and intriguing in many business markets and rivals cannot always be treated as the enemy!

Target market strategies are important to all marketers. In order to develop a target market strategy, marketers must be able to allocate a market's customers into groups or market segments. The consumer marketer may use lifestyles, socio-economic information or consumers' perceived benefits to create market segments or groups of like-minded consumers. The business marketer, however, may fall back on more simple criteria, such as SIC codes or the trade sectors of their customers, in order to determine market segments. This very important aspect of marketing strategy is explored in Chapter 6. Until an understanding of business customers' buying behaviour has been developed, as described in this chapter, it is not possible to produce a market segmentation scheme.

If consumer marketers feel they have an inadequate appreciation of consumers' issues and buying behaviour, it is relatively straightforward to embark on suitable marketing research activities in order to rectify this deficiency. As described in Chapter 7, undertaking observations or surveys of consumers is fairly routine. However, busy executives and decision-makers inside business customers rarely offer to attend focus groups, they discard questionnaires and are not easy to access for interviews. Apart from access problems, business customers may well use any surveying to lobby. For example, they may feedback to the supplier's marketers behind the survey, the apparent importance of a better pricing option or improved customer service systems, rather than objectively and openly engage in the marketing research activity. Consumer products are readily visible on retailers' shelves; their prices, marketing communications campaigns, product features or attributes, and their channels to market are there to be seen by competitors' marketers. In most business markets, it is not easy to gain access to rivals' products or services, and the marketing programmes are not so readily visible.

The marketing mix is the set of tactical ingredients manipulated by marketers in marketing programmes designed to implement a target market strategy. As described in Part III of *Marketing Essentials,* all marketers manipulate the marketing mix in order to reflect the nature of their market, customer buying behaviour, the activities of competitors, organisational capabilities and corporate objectives. Compared with consumer marketers, those tasked with marketing business products have to make certain adjustments to their marketing mix programmes.

The overall implication is that business marketers must modify their use of the marketing toolkit to reflect the nature of their markets and the characteristics of their business customers. The overall marketing process and the toolkit apply irrespective of the marketplace, but it is evident that business marketers, consumer goods marketers and the marketers of services need to make certain modifications. These themes are discussed in more detail in Chapter 10.

Business marketers often have to address the needs of customers within a marketing channel as well as the needs of their intended customers. Some business marketers must also serve the needs of consumers. Many business marketers handle a relatively small number of customers and must tailor marketing propositions to these customers' specific wishes. The sales and marketing personnel in many business-to-business companies work together very closely.

Summary

*B*usiness marketing used to be known as *organisational, industrial* or *business-to-business marketing*. Business markets consist of individuals or groups that purchase a specific kind of product for resale, for direct use in producing other products, or for use in their day-to-day operations. *Producer markets* include those individuals and business organisations that purchase products for the purpose of making a profit by using them either to produce other products or in their own operations. Classified as *reseller markets* are intermediaries, such as *wholesalers* and *retailers*, who buy finished products and resell them for the purpose of making a profit. *Government markets* consist of national and local governments, which spend huge amounts annually on goods and services to support their internal operations and provide citizens with needed services. Many businesses refer to government, local government and institutions collectively as the public sector, and the *public sector market* is a growing area of activity within the marketing discipline. Organisations that seek to achieve charitable, educational, community or other non-business goals constitute *institutional markets*.

❱❱ Business-to-business transactions differ from consumer transactions in several ways. The transactions tend to be larger, and negotiations occur less frequently, though they are often lengthy. Business transactions sometimes involve more than one person or one department in the purchasing organisation. They may also involve *reciprocity*, an arrangement in which two organisations agree to buy from each other, although some countries have strict rules governing such agreements. Business customers are usually viewed as more rational and more likely to seek information about a product's features and technical specifications than are ultimate consumers.

❱❱ When purchasing products, business customers must be particularly concerned about quality, delivery, service and price. Quality is important because it directly affects the quality of the organisational buyer's ultimate product. To achieve an exact standard, organisations often buy their products on the basis of a set of expressed characteristics, called specifications. Reliable and fast delivery is crucial to many organisations, whose production lines must be fed with a continuous supply of component parts and raw materials. Because services can have a direct influence on a company's costs, sales and profits, such matters as market information, on-time delivery and availability of parts can be crucial to a business buyer. Although a business customer does not decide which products to purchase solely by their price, cost is of prime concern because it directly influences a company's profitability. Product range, innovation, reliability and logistical support may also be significant considerations. Increasingly, business buyers are concerned with service support levels and the ongoing commitment from their selected suppliers. There is a view that a supplier's personnel in terms of knowledge, motivation, attitude and passion for assisting the customer, are an integral part of the product proposition being 'consumed' by the business customer.

❱❱ Business buyers use several purchasing methods, including description, inspection, sampling and negotiation. Most business purchases are new task, modified rebuy or straight rebuy. In a *new task purchase*, an organisation makes an initial purchase of an item to be used to perform a new job or to solve a new problem. In a *modified rebuy purchase*, a new task purchase is changed the second or third time it is ordered, or the requirements associated with a straight rebuy purchase are modified. A *straight rebuy purchase* occurs when a buyer repurchases the same products routinely under approximately the same terms of sale.

» Business demand differs from consumer demand along several dimensions. *Derived demand* is the demand for business products that arises from the demand for consumer products. At the industry level, *inelastic demand* is a demand that is not significantly affected by a price increase or decrease. If the price of an industrial item changes, demand for the product will not change proportionally. Some business products are subject to *joint demand*, which occurs when two or more items are used in combination to make a product. Finally, because business demand ultimately derives from consumer demand, the demand for business products can fluctuate widely.

» *Business (or business-to-business) buying behaviour* refers to the purchase behaviour of producers, resellers, government units and institutions. Business purchase decisions are made through a *buying centre* – the group of people who are involved in making organisational purchase decisions. Users are those in the organisation that actually use the product. Influencers help develop the specifications and evaluate alternative products for possible use. Buyers are responsible for selecting the suppliers and negotiating the terms of the purchases. Deciders choose the products and suppliers. Gatekeepers control the flow of information to and among people who occupy the other roles in the buying centre.

» When a company buys a product or service from another company, both organisations enter into a process during which items of value are exchanged in return for something else. This exchange process may lead to a long-term relationship between buyer and seller. *Relationship marketing* is the term used

to explain the special attention being given to this area and is defined as the activities an organisation uses to build, maintain and develop customer relations. The trend toward long-term relationships has resulted in *relationship management*, increased *value analysis* and the more systematic evaluation of suppliers in *supplier analysis*.

» The stages of the business buying decision process are (1) problem recognition, (2) development of product specifications to solve the problem, (3) search for products and suppliers, (4) evaluation of products relative to specifications, (5) selection and ordering of the most appropriate product, and (6) evaluation of the product's and the supplier's performance. The evaluation of product and suppliers will directly affect future purchasing decisions. *Sole sourcing*, the process of selecting only one supplier, is becoming more popular, particularly where manufacturers are practising just-in-time production. Many organisations still opt to practise *multiple sourcing*.

» Four categories of factors influence business buying decisions: environmental, organisational, interpersonal and individual. *Environmental factors* include politics, laws and regulations, economic conditions, competitive forces and technological changes. *Organisational factors* include the buyer's objectives, purchasing policies and resources, as well as the size and composition of its buying centre. *Interpersonal factors* refer to the relationships among the people in the buying centre, and relationships between supplier and customer personnel. *Individual factors* refer to the personal characteristics of individuals in the buying centre, such as age, education, personality, position in the organisation, and income.

» *Business marketing* is a set of activities directed at facilitating and expediting exchanges involving business products and customers in business markets.

» Business marketers have a considerable amount of information available to them for use in planning their marketing strategies and for identifying sales potential. Much of this information is based on the *Standard Industrial Classification (SIC) system*, which classifies businesses into major industry divisions, classes, groups and activities. The SIC system provides business marketers with information needed to identify market segments. It can best be used for this purpose in conjunction with other information, such as *input–output data*. After identifying target industries, the marketer can locate potential customers by using the Internet or directories, or by employing a marketing services business. The marketer must then estimate the potential purchases of business customers by finding a relationship between a potential customer's purchases and a variable available (information which is available in published sources).

❯❯ Business-to-business branding tends to be more simplistic than is the case with consumer brands, focusing on identification and product differentiation. In many business situations,

individual companies pool their expertise and resources in order to win contracts with customers. However, partners in one market segment may in fact be arch-rivals in another. The implication is that the understanding of competitive forces is often more complex and intriguing in business markets and rivals cannot always be treated as 'the enemy'.

❯❯ Although SIC codes and industry trade categories are often used by business marketers, increasingly the approaches deployed by consumer marketers in creating market segments are being deployed in business markets. The next chapter explores market segmentation and target marketing in more detail. Undertaking marketing research in business markets is quite different from researching consumers. Compared with consumer markets, those tasked with marketing business products have to reflect certain market nuances when developing their marketing mix programmes.

◉ *Key Links*

This chapter must be read in conjunction with Chapter 4, which details the buying behaviour of consumers.

- A popular examination question is to compare and contrast the buying behaviour models in consumer and business markets.
- In strategic marketing, a key use of an understanding of customer behaviour is the construction of market segments, as discussed in Chapter 6.
- The marketing mix should reflect the nuances of the market in question, as described in Chapters 8 to 14.

Important Terms

Business market
Industrial, organisational or business-to-business market
Producer markets
Reseller markets
Wholesalers
Retailers
Government markets
Public sector markets
Institutional markets
Reciprocity
New task purchase
Modified rebuy purchase
Straight rebuy purchase

Derived demand
Inelastic demand
Joint demand
Business (or business-to-business) buying behaviour
Buying centre
Relationship marketing
Relationship management
Value analysis
Supplier analysis
Sole sourcing
Multiple sourcing
Environmental factors
Organisational factors
Interpersonal factors
Individual factors
Business marketing
Standard Industrial Classification (SIC) system
Input–output data

Discussion and Review Questions

1 Identify, describe and give examples of four major types of business market.
2 Why are business buyers generally considered more rational in regard to their purchasing behaviour than ultimate consumers?
3 What are the primary concerns of business customers?
4 List several characteristics that differentiate business transactions from consumer ones.

5 What are the commonly used methods of business buying?

6 Why do buyers involved in a straight rebuy purchase require less information than those making a new task purchase?

7 How does industrial/business demand differ from consumer demand?

8 What are the major components of a buying centre?

9 What elements may be exchanged by a buyer and seller when a purchase transaction takes place?

10 Why has relationship management attracted so much interest in business markets?

11 Identify the stages of the business buying decision process. How is this decision process used when making straight rebuys?

12 What impact does the evaluation of a particular purchase have on future buying decisions?

13 How do environmental, organisational, interpersonal and individual factors affect business purchases?

14 What function does the SIC system help business marketers perform?

15 List some sources that a business marketer can use to determine the names and addresses of potential customers.

16 In what ways do business marketers have to reflect the nuances of business markets when deploying the marketing toolkit?

Recommended Reading

- Chisnall, P., *Strategic Business Marketing* (Harlow: Pearson, 1995).
- Ford, D., *Understanding Business Markets and Purchasing* (London: Thomson Learning, 2001).
- Ford, D., Gadde, L.-E., Hakansson, H. and Snehota, I., *Managing Business Relationships* (Chichester: Wiley, 2003).
- Hutt, M.D. and Speh, T.W., *Business Marketing Management: Strategic View of Industrial and Organisational Markets* (Cincinnati, OH: South Western, 2006).
- Naude, P., Michel, D., Salle, R. and Valla, J.-P., *Business to Business Marketing* (Basingstoke: Palgrave Macmillan, 2003).
- Webster, F.E., *Industrial Marketing Strategy* (New York: Wiley, 1995).

🌐 Internet Exercise

Log onto Sony's website. Ignore the sections aimed at consumers. Instead, go to *Business Products*. This section details Sony's business-to-business products, services and upcoming events such as trade shows. There are sections offering solutions to Healthcare, Retail and Manufacturing target markets and for specific product categories such as CCTV or semiconductors. Visit Sony's website at: www.sony.com

1 In what ways do Sony's web pages for *Business Products* reflect the requirements of business customers?

2 How have the messages been tailored to reflect the buying behaviour of Sony's business customers?

🌀 *Applied Mini-Case*

St Andrew's Healthcare in Northampton is the market leader in mental health hospital care in the UK. Its divisions address everything from adolescent learning difficulties through to major behavioural problems with patients requiring secure accommodation and lengthy treatment programmes. St Andrew's – a charity – has a specialist unit dealing with brain injuries and, through an on-site partner, also offers clinic facilities for patients needing to 'dry out'. Its staff are recognised as being leading-edge thinkers. St Andrew's brand reputation is based on the quality of its care, its multiple care pathways and its ability to relate to patients, their families and to the medical staff or personnel in social services who refer patients to the hospital.

While some patients deal directly with St Andrew's Healthcare, the vast majority of patients are referred from the National Health Service (NHS). St Andrew's has a reputation for being able to deal with difficult patients suffering from complex problems. However, the NHS is increasingly moving towards centralised buying, with numerous Trusts joining forces in order to be able to purchase services – such as those offered by St Andrew's – at lower rates. In addition to the medical staff who diagnose the patients' problems and recommend appropriate courses of treatment, the NHS has risk assessors, financial managers and professional purchasing executives, who are all involved in the decision concerning which treatment programme to purchase from which provider. For St Andrew's and other suppliers to the NHS, such formalised purchasing and group decision-making complicate the marketing activity and the engagement programmes the charity runs with its customers. For the patient, for his/her family, for the referring medical staff and the numerous administrators involved, St Andrew's must develop bespoke messages, marketing communications and client-handling programmes. This complex buying centre must be addressed in order for St Andrew's to operate with full bed occupancy, and to fulfil its mission to truly help those suffering with mental health problems.

Sources: St Andrew's Healthcare, 2004–8; James Watkins, director of marketing and strategy, St Andrew's Healthcare, 2003–8; Sally Dibb and Lyndon Simkin, *Marketing Briefs*, Oxford: Butterworth-Heinemann, 2004.

❷ *Question*

As the marketing director of such an organisation, what aspects of customer buying behaviour would you identify as priorities to understand?

❀ *Case Study*

Nynas: in the Black and Leading

For most people, oil is evident as a fuel for cars, heating and the generation of electricity, or as the basis for the plastics industry. What about the black surfaces of pavements, roads, driveways, car parks and school playgrounds? Bitumen is an oil-based product most of us take for granted, but it is a major part of the revenue for companies such as Shell, BP, Esso, Total, Colas or Lanfina. The leading bitumen player in the UK, Scandinavia and much of western Europe is Stockholm-based Nynas. In the UK, this relatively small player in the petrochemicals industry has overall market leadership in the bitumen market and is renowned for its innovative product development with polymer formulations.

Bitumen is one of the most ubiquitous materials made by industry, underfoot almost everywhere as a core ingredient of the macadams and asphalts in roads and pavements. There are numerous specialist applications too, such as the backing for carpet tiles, roofing felts, sealants for mighty dams and waterproofing for bridge decks. Inevitably this results in a diverse customer base for an organisation such as Nynas. In a market with competitors as large as Esso or Shell, Nynas's leadership has not occurred by accident. Nynas has established its enviable position by astutely utilising the resources required to develop innovative products, customer service schemes and flexible delivery capabilities in order to ensure customer satisfaction. At the heart of its business strategy is a desire to innovate, listen to customers and develop services that genuinely enable customers to be served properly.

Nynas believes it has several important edges over its rivals, as described below.

Customer Dialogue

As a major producer with significant R&D technical support, Nynas's laboratories can determine a product formulation for most bitumen-based applications. Whether the customer is a local authority requiring a cost-effective thin surfacing for a housing estate's ageing pavements; a contractor such as Tarmac requiring 24-hour supply of high-quality, state-of-the-art bitumen for the construction of a new motorway; or a builder buying polymer-enhanced mastic asphalts to act as a waterproofing membrane for regency mews properties, Nynas can develop a quality bitumen-based product.

Consistent Quality and Innovative Product Development

Refineries in Belgium, Sweden and the UK, supported by a network of terminals and research laboratories across Europe, enable Nynas to continually improve its products and their performance. Customers do not want to have to resurface major roads or busy shopping centre pavements on a frequent basis. Specialist applications such as waterproofing dams or houses are time consuming, costly and inconvenient remedial activities that clients do not want to repeat in a hurry. Nynas has access to high-grade Venezuelan bitumen, not readily available to its major competitors, which gives it added flexibility in producing high-quality bitumen grades for specific applications. Whether it is for a routine commodity bulk job such as a school playground surface or an unusual requirement for waterproofing a royal building, Nynas has developed a reputation as being a leading supplier.

Logistical Support

Users of bitumen often require deliveries at very short notice, in specific quantities and to guaranteed quality levels. These deliveries may be anywhere at any time. A contractor repairing a busy commuter route out of daylight hours needs on-time delivery of ready-to-use bitumen products. Repairs to a remote bridge still require guaranteed on-time delivery. Nynas's depots operate around the clock despatching computer monitored deliveries by tanker to clients as and when the customer has specified. Twenty-four hours a day, 365 days a year, Nynas prides itself on its high levels of responsiveness and reliability of delivery.

Nynas's composition of customers is varied. A major new road-building scheme will involve formal tendering and guarantees with penalties for inferior product or missed deliveries. The buying process of such customers will be highly formal, involving numerous managers, and functions as diverse as purchasing, technical support, construction, finance and logistical support. On both sides – customer and Nynas – cross-functional teams of scientists, engineers, managers and the field force will spend many months agreeing on the product requirements, contractual obligations, delivery requirements and

application techniques. For other customers, the purchase is perhaps more of a routine rebuy, with only limited interaction and discussion between Nynas and the customer. On other occasions, the Nynas helpline may receive a midnight telephone call from a highways agency surveyor who has just discovered cracks in the surface of a major road and requires immediate assistance in both identifying the cause of the problem and rectifying the situation before commuters awake the next morning.

For a rather bland-looking substance such as bitumen, the market is diverse and challenging. Nynas has established its successful position in the European market for bitumen-based products by practising the best principles of marketing. The company strives to understand its customers' needs and to offer reliable products supported with effective customer service, round the clock. Product innovation is at the forefront of the company's strategy and, coupled with constantly improving ways of offering peace of mind to customers, provides an edge over rivals. Shrewd marketing analysis constantly monitors product changes, customers' expectations, competitors' activities and those aspects of the marketing environment – notably technological and regulatory forces – that will impact on the business's fortunes. Resources are allocated to match this thorough assessment of market opportunities and marketing requirements.

Sources: Siobhan McKelvey and Willie Hunter, Nynas UK; *Network* magazine; the Nynas Annual Review.

❓ *Questions for Discussion*

1 Who are Nynas's customers?
2 What types of business markets – as classified in this chapter – purchase the products made by Nynas?
3 Would most purchases of Nynas's products be new task, modified rebuy or straight rebuy?

6

Segmenting Markets, Targeting and Positioning

"**The essence of successful segmentation lies not in fragmentation but in building an excellent understanding of the marketplace.**"

Sally Dibb, Warwick Business School

Objectives

- **To understand the definition of a market**
- **To recognise different types of market**
- **To learn how companies segment markets**
- **To understand targeting decisions**
- **To discover how marketers prioritise target markets**
- **To learn about strategies for positioning**

Introduction

As explained in Chapter 2, marketing strategy revolves around the choice of which opportunities should be pursued and the specification of an appropriate target market strategy. Market segmentation is a fundamental part of marketing strategy, assisting organisations to deal with the fact that not all consumers or business customers share identical needs, buying behaviour or product requirements. Limited resources generally result in organisations being unable to serve all of the needs in the market, and marketers must make trade-off choices based on the relative merits of different market segments in determining which groups to prioritise. The consumers or business customers in those market segments deemed to be priorities for a company must be communicated with in a manner that emphasises their importance to the company: this is the positioning task. The market segmentation process, therefore, has a number of stages: segmenting, targeting and positioning. Many marketers believe these aspects of marketing are the most important decisions made by marketers.[1]

Opener

Targeting Students and the Over-50s

Marketing magazine targets marketing practitioners such as brand managers, marketing managers, marketing directors and those working in agencies supplying advertising or marketing research to the marketing community. Recently, a flyer inserted in the weekly magazine promoted a conference that specifically aimed to address the marketing of products and services to students.

The accompanying text explained that students in the UK spend more than £13 billion per annum. With over two million UK students, more and more brands are targeting marketing programmes at these consumers. Such consumers are very aware of current forms of communication, possibly more so than the older marketers attempting to entice them with marketing communications. Texting, e-mail, the Internet, posters, stunts aimed at students, sponsoring student events and advertising on campus radio stations are important forms of communicating with students, often requiring a separate campaign from many brands' more mainstream marketing communications. It is not only marketing communications that must be modified. Peer group influences are important among students, buying processes are very specific in nature and purchasing is driven by a mix of value for money, brand image and utility drivers.

Another *Marketing*-sponsored conference was entitled 'Older Richer Wiser? Challenge your perceptions of the over-50s market'. This conference targeted clients and agency personnel currently targeting, or who should be targeting, the over-50s age group. The text explained:

Fifty somethings lived through the sixties, seventies, eighties and nineties. They know more about music; more about money and business; more about freedom and creativity. They understand what is good value. They have more money than any other sector of the population.

They have 80% of the country's personal wealth and account for 40% of consumer spending. They've seen it all, heard it all and experienced a lot of it. And now you've got to find a way to catch their hearts, imaginations and wallets.

Speakers examined how to advertise to a 'disenfranchised generation'; how to harness the Internet, cinema and other marketing communications; the importance of creating propositions directly relevant to these consumers; and the role of understanding their buying behaviour. Keynote speakers represented Saga FM, Help the Aged, health and fitness clubs, the travel industry, pensions and investments.

Marketing magazine is itself targeted at a narrowly defined market segment: marketing professionals. The two conferences were designed to help marketers address students and the over-50s, with the belief that these two demographic groups exhibit different buying behaviour and have needs that are different to those of the rest of the population. Such sub-division of the overall population into homogeneous groups of consumers for marketing purposes is the aim of market segmentation.

Sources: *Marketing* magazine, 2004/5; *Marketing to Students*, *Marketing* and Campus Vision, London, 29 June 2004; 'Older Richer Wiser?', *Marketing*, 7 July 2004. Photo: Istockphoto.com

This chapter begins by considering the nature of markets, first defining the term and then describing the different types. The market segmentation concept is then explained and the rationale for its use explored. Not only conferences aimed at attracting students or the over-50s apply the concept of market segmentation. Management consultancies, manufacturers, healthcare providers, leisure operators and universities all practise market segmentation. The segmenting, targeting and positioning stages of the segmentation process are explored in turn. The explanation of segmenting focuses on the variables used to segment consumer and business markets. An understanding of customer needs and buying behaviour, as described in Chapters 4 and 5, is essential for developing market segments. The review of targeting considers the strategies used to select and prioritise target markets. Approaches for developing a positioning are examined. The chapter concludes by emphasising the importance of assessing the sales potential in the market segments deemed to be the focus of the organisation's target market strategy.

What are Markets?

The word 'market' has various meanings. It used to refer primarily to the place where goods were bought and sold. It can also refer to a large geographic area. In some cases, the word is used to describe the relationship between the demand and supply of a specific product. For instance, 'What is the state of the market for copper?' Sometimes, 'market' is used to mean the act of selling something. The dictionary defines 'market' as an occasion on which goods are publicly exposed for sale, a place in which goods are exposed for sale, or to offer for sale. In marketing terms, a market is defined in terms of customers, their need for a product, and their ability to purchase or consume.

Market
An aggregate of people who, as individuals or within organisations, have a need for certain products and the ability, willingness and authority to purchase such products

In this book a **market** is defined as a group of people who, as consumers or as part of organisations, need and have the ability, willingness and authority to purchase products in a product class. In general use, the term 'market' sometimes refers to the total population, or mass market, that buys products. However, the definition used here is more specific, referring to individuals seeking products in a specific product category. For example, students are part of the market for textbooks, as well as being markets for calculators, laptops, pens and pencils, paper, food, music and other products. Obviously, there are many different markets in any economy. In this section, the requirements for markets are considered in conjunction with these different types.

Requirements for a Market

For a group of people to be a market, the members of the group must meet the following four requirements.

1 They must need or want a particular product or service.
2 They must have the ability to purchase the product or service. Ability to purchase is related to buying power, which consists of resources such as money, goods and services that can be traded in an exchange situation.
3 They must be willing to use their buying power.
4 They must have the authority to buy the specific products or services.

Consumer market
Purchasers or individuals in their households who personally consume or benefit from the purchased products and do not buy products primarily to make a profit

Individuals sometimes have the desire, the buying power and the willingness to purchase certain products but may not be authorised to do so. For example, secondary school students may want, have the money for and be willing to buy alcoholic drinks, but a brewer does not consider them a market until they are legally old enough to buy alcohol. An aggregate of people that lacks any one of the four requirements thus does not constitute a market.

Types of Market

Markets can be divided into two categories: consumer markets and business markets. A **consumer market** consists of purchasers and/or individuals in their households who personally consume or benefit from the purchased products and who do not buy products primarily to make a profit. Each of us belongs to numerous consumer markets for such products as housing, cars, appliances, furniture, clothing, food, financial services and leisure activities. Consumer markets are discussed in more detail in Chapter 4 of *Marketing Essentials*.

Business market
Individuals or groups that purchase a specific kind of product to resell, use directly in producing other products or use in general daily operations

A **business market** – also referred to as an *organisational* or *business-to-business market* – consists of individuals or groups that purchase a specific kind of product for one of three purposes: resale, direct use in producing other products or use in general daily operations. The four categories of business market – producer, reseller, government and institutional – are discussed in Chapter 5.

What is Market Segmentation?

Chapter 1 explained that at the heart of marketing strategy are the decisions about which opportunities to pursue and which markets to target. Segmentation is a popular approach to identifying target markets. As will be explained later in this chapter, organisations sometimes decide to target the total market, using an **undifferentiated (or total market) approach**. However, it is much more usual for a differentiated approach using market segmentation to be followed.

Defining Market Segmentation

Heterogeneous markets
Markets in which all customers have different requirements

Market segmentation
The process of grouping customers in markets with some heterogeneity into smaller, more similar or homogeneous segments. The identification of target customer groups in which customers are aggregated into groups with similar requirements and buying characteristics

Market segment
A group of individuals, groups or organisations sharing one or more similar characteristics that cause them to have relatively similar product needs and buying characteristics

Undifferentiated (or total market) approach
An approach which assumes that all customers have similar needs and wants, and can be served with a single marketing mix

The varying characteristics, needs, wants and interests of customers mean that there are few markets where a single product or service is satisfactory for all. The extensive array of goods on supermarket shelves reflects basic differences in customers' requirements. The trend, it seems, is away from a mass-marketing approach. Even markets that were traditionally undifferentiated have undergone change, with an ever increasing number of products on offer. For instance, the market for food seasoning used to be dominated by salt. Now, low-sodium substitutes are being offered as alternatives for the increasingly health-conscious consumer.

Markets in which all customers have different requirements are termed **heterogeneous markets**. For example, the market for wrist watches is quite diverse. Swatch designs relatively low-priced watches for the fashion-conscious customer; Rotary markets much more conservative and expensive designs for an older customer group. In completely heterogeneous markets the only way to satisfy everyone is by offering tailor-made or bespoke products. This situation is more prevalent in business-to-business markets, where, for example, plant machinery is designed for a specific task and situation. However, while it may not be feasible to offer every customer a tailor-made product, it is often possible to aggregate customers into groups with similar product needs and wants.

Market segmentation is the process by which customers in markets with some heterogeneity can be grouped into smaller, more similar or homogeneous segments. A **market segment** is therefore a group of individuals, groups or organisations sharing one or more similar characteristics that cause them to have relatively similar product needs and buying characteristics. Market segmentation involves identifying such groups, so that marketers are better able to develop product or service benefits that are appropriate for them (see Figure 6.1). They do this by designing products and brands to appeal to particular target segments and to be supported by an appropriate promotional campaign, relevant customer service, and suitable pricing and place/distribution strategies. For example, clothing sold through Top Shop or New Look is manufactured for youthful female consumers; this is reflected in both the product styling and the promotional campaign.

Once market segments have been identified, marketers decide which, if any, they intend to enter. A marketing programme covering all elements of the marketing mix can then be designed to suit the particular requirements of the segments targeted. German-owned BMW previously concentrated on selling premium-priced luxury vehicles aimed at the luxury and executive segments of the car market. In order to appeal to a younger age group, during the 1990s BMW introduced the Compact version of its popular 3 Series. This had the desired effect of attracting buyers who previously could not afford this aspirational marque. Now BMW has gone further, with the launch of the 1 Series, aiming to further broaden the appeal of its brand – to young professionals. The 4x4 X3 and X5 appeal to other customers.

Figure 6.1
Market segmentation approach

Reasons for Using Market Segmentation

Companies have turned to market segmentation with good reason.[2] Whitbread, Diner's Club and Bird's Eye Walls have all demonstrated that success can follow the effective implementation of market segmentation strategies. For example, the variety of offerings in the market for frozen, ready-to-eat meals illustrates the spread of customer needs: healthy options, quick snacks, gourmet selections. Careful segmentation, and the customer understanding underlying it, can make it easier for companies to identify and exploit different market opportunities. For example, segmentation can help minor players in the market achieve a foothold in a particular niche, perhaps by identifying an opportunity not directly exploited by market leaders. Figure 6.2 relates to construction equipment manufacturer Caterpillar's entry into footwear and clothing.

Segmentation is seen to offer businesses a number of advantages that make it easier to develop and capitalise on opportunities available to them. These advantages can be considered at the customer level, in relation to the competition or in terms of the effectiveness of resource allocation and strategic planning.[3]

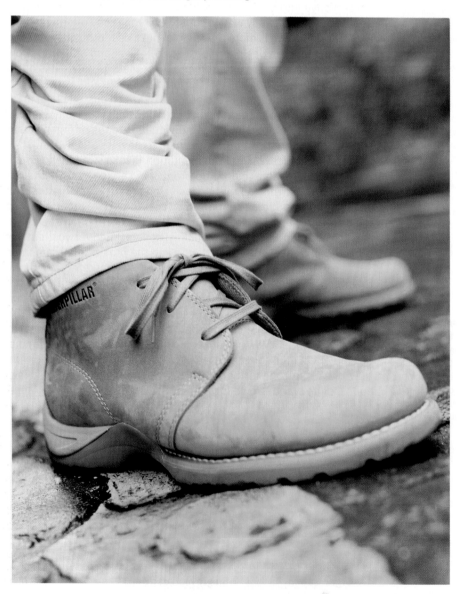

Figure 6.2
Appreciation for Caterpillar Inc. products goes far beyond the people who work with the machines and engines daily. Licencing the image and lifestyle of Caterpillar, the company has been able to successfully transfer its image into licenced merchandise including rugged footwear and clothing ranges for specific target market segments
Source: Courtesy of Caterpillar Inc.

Customer Analysis Segmenting markets facilitates a better understanding of customers' needs, wants and other characteristics. The sharper focus that segmentation offers, allows those personal, situational and behavioural factors that characterise customers in a particular segment to be considered. In short, questions about how, why and what customers buy can be addressed. By being closely in touch with segments, marketers can respond quickly to even slight changes in what target customers want. For example, by monitoring the trends towards healthier eating and lifestyles, McDonald's was able to respond by introducing a wider range of salads and healthy eating options – including grilled chicken, fruit and yoghurt – on to its menus.

Competitor Analysis Most markets are characterised by intense competition. Within this environment, companies need to understand the nature of the competition they face. Who are their main competitors? At which segments are they targeting their products? Answering these questions allows marketers to make decisions about the most appropriate segments to target and the kind of competitive advantage to seek. For example, before opening a new café outlet, Costa needs to build a picture of the existing café, restaurant and other outlets offering a comparable service in the location. The company must also appraise the extent to which the needs of the consumers it aims to target are already served by what is currently available. Companies that do not understand their competitive environment risk encountering competition they had not envisaged or putting resources into unattractive areas of the market.

Effective Resource Allocation All companies have limited resources. To target the whole of the market is usually unrealistic. The effectiveness of personnel and material resources can be greatly improved when they are more narrowly focused on a particular segment of customers. With limited resources, Saab and Porsche target only a few market segments compared with Ford or Toyota. Segmentation enables Saab and Porsche to identify homogeneous groups of customers at whom the Saab 95 or Porsche 911 models can be targeted. This maximises these companies' use of resources and marketing mix activities.

Strategic Marketing Planning Companies operating in a number of segments are unlikely to follow the same strategic plans in them all. Dividing up markets allows marketers to develop plans that give special consideration to the particular needs and requirements of customers in different segments. The timescale covered by the strategic plan can also be structured accordingly, because some segments change more rapidly than others. The market for recorded music is a typical example. While tastes in classical music remain fairly steady, tastes in pop music change very rapidly. Companies like EMI and Sony clearly need to consider this factor when developing corporate plans.

Segmenting, Targeting and Positioning

There are three stages to carrying out market segmentation: segmentation, targeting and positioning. Figure 6.3 gives an overview of these stages.

Segmenting the Market There are many ways in which customers can be grouped and markets segmented. In different markets, the variables that are appropriate change. The key is to understand which are the most suitable for distinguishing between different product requirements. Understanding as much as possible about the customers in the segments is also important, as marketers who 'know' their targets are more likely to design an appropriate marketing mix for them. For example, the Post Office has reintroduced savings stamps after an absence of 40 years to help people who struggle to balance their finances. They are aimed at people who have regular outgoings such as household bills; in particular, they are targeted at the five million people in the UK who do not have any kind of bank account.

Targeting Strategy

Once segments have been identified, decisions about which and how many customer groups to target can be made. There are several options:

- adopt an undifferentiated approach, focusing on the total market
- concentrate on a single segment with one product and marketing programme
- offer one product and marketing programme to a number of segments
- target a different product and marketing programme at each of a number of segments.

These options are explored in more detail later in this chapter. The choices companies make should take resource implications into consideration.

Positioning the Product

Companies must decide precisely how and where within the targeted segments to aim a product or products, brand or brands. The needs and wants of targeted customers must be translated into a tangible mix of product/service, personnel, price, promotion and place/distribution. The consumers' view of the product and where it is positioned relative to the competition is particularly critical. After all, the paying public does not always perceive a product or brand in the way the manufacturer would like. For example, to the dismay of those who developed it, the Sinclair C5 electric trike was perceived as an object of ridicule. Apple's move into Sony's MP3 territory with iPod was based on a very shrewd targeting and positioning strategy.

Each of the three market segmentation stages will now be considered.

Segmentation variables or bases
The dimensions or characteristics of individuals, groups or businesses that are used for dividing a total market into segments

Segmentation Variables

Segmentation variables or **bases** are the dimensions or characteristics of individuals, groups or businesses that are used for dividing a total market into segments.[4] There is rarely one best way to segment a market. Companies must make choices about the most appropriate variables to use but they must consider the needs and buying behaviour of their intended customers, as discussed in Chapters 4 and 5. In consumer markets, background characteristics

Segmentation
- Consider variables for segmenting market.
- Look at profile of emerging segments.
- Validate segments emerging.

Targeting
- Decide on targeting strategy.
- Decide which and how many segments should be targeted.

Positioning
- Understand consumer perceptions.
- Position products in the mind of the consumer by communicating the desired positioning.
- Design appropriate marketing mix.

Figure 6.3
Basic elements of segmentation

like age, sex and occupation are widely used. In business-to-business markets, customer size, location and product use are often the focus.

The choice of segmentation variables is based on several factors. The variables chosen should relate to customers' needs for, uses of or behaviour towards the product or service. The selected bases should be usable and easy to measure. Laptop computer manufacturers might segment the market on the basis of income and age, but not on the basis of religion, because one person's usage of computer equipment does not differ from those of people of other religions. Furthermore, if individuals or businesses in a total market are to be classified accurately, the segmentation variable must be measurable. For example, segmenting a market on the basis of intelligence or moral standards would be quite difficult because these attributes are hard to measure accurately.

Creativity is also a factor; sometimes organisations benefit from moving away from a traditionally popular segmentation approach. For example, first direct led the way in telephone banking, by responding to the fact that some customers' needs were not being met by existing banking operations. By developing a better understanding of the demographics, lifestyle and needs of these customers, the bank was able to develop a new kind of service. Later in this chapter there is a more detailed review of segmentation effectiveness, which focuses on some of these issues.

Selecting Appropriate Variables

Selecting appropriate variables for market segmentation is an important marketing management decision, because the variable is the primary factor in defining the target market.[5] In some cases, segmentation is based on more than one variable. Decisions about the number of segmentation variables used are partly based on a company's resources and capabilities. The type of product and degree of variation in customers' needs also dictate the number and size of segments targeted.

In general, as developments in information technology make it easier to capture and manage customer information, the move is towards more complex segmentation schemes. Many organisations now have databases providing a wider range of segmentation variables than was previously possible.[6] One outcome is that there is, increasingly, a tendency to use multivariable segmentation rather than single-variable segmentation.[7] Indeed, technological advance means that it is now technically feasible to capture information about and respond to the needs and wants of smaller and smaller segments.[8] Taken to its extreme, this means that instead of dealing at the mass-market or segment level, it is even possible to develop relationships with *individual* customers. This principle has been variously referred to as 'customer-centric marketing'[9] or 'one-to-one marketing'.[10] **One-to-one marketing** involves developing long-term relationships with individual customers in order to understand and satisfy their needs.[11] However, despite the attention these new ideas have attracted, it is widely recognised that one-to-one segmentation involves a substantial injection of resources, raising concerns about whether the returns are sufficiently high to justify the required investment.

One-to-one marketing
Involves developing long-term relationships with individual customers in order to understand and satisfy their needs

Single variable segmentation
Segmentation achieved by using only one variable, the simplest type of segmentation to perform

Single Variable Segmentation   **Single variable segmentation**, which is the simplest to perform, is achieved by using only one variable – for example, country. However, the sales of one product in different countries will differ and the numbers of relevant consumers in each country will vary. A single characteristic gives marketers only moderate precision in designing a marketing mix to satisfy individuals in a specific segment.

Multivariable segmentation
Segmentation using more than one characteristic to divide a total market

Multivariable Segmentation   To achieve **multivariable segmentation**, more than one characteristic is used to divide a total market (see Figure 6.4). Notice in the figure that the market is segmented by three variables: annual income, population density and volume usage. The people in the highlighted segment earn more than £40,000, are urban dwellers and heavy users. Multivariable segmentation provides more information about the individuals in each

Figure 6.4
Multivariable segmentation

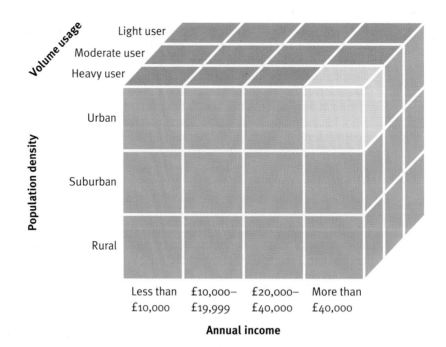

segment, which may enable a company to develop a marketing mix that will satisfy customers in a given segment more precisely.

The major disadvantage of multivariable segmentation is that the more variables used, the greater the number of segments likely to be identified. This proliferation reduces the sales potential of many of the segments. It may also be more complicated to resource and manage the proliferation of segments that result. A marketing manager must therefore consider whether additional variables will actually help improve the company's marketing mix. Where many variables are deployed, it may be prudent to utilise multivariate statistical techniques – such as cluster analysis[12] – to assist in the grouping of customers into market segments.

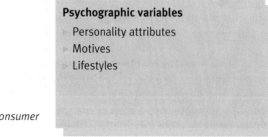

Demographic variables

Age	Occupation
Gender	Family size
Race	Family life cycle
Ethnicity	Religion
Income	Social class
Education	

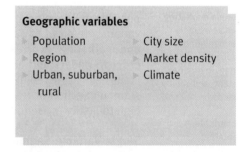

Geographic variables

Population	City size
Region	Market density
Urban, suburban, rural	Climate

Psychographic variables

- Personality attributes
- Motives
- Lifestyles

Behaviouristic variables

- Volume usage
- End use
- Benefit expectations
- Brand loyalty
- Price sensitivity

Figure 6.5
Segmentation variables for consumer markets

Variables for Segmenting Consumer Markets

Companies developing their strategy for segmentation can choose one or several variables or bases from a wide range of choices. As Figure 6.5 shows, segmentation variables can be grouped into four categories: demographic, geographic, psychographic and behaviouristic.

Demographic Variables　Demographers study aggregate population characteristics such as the distribution of age and gender, fertility rates, migration patterns and mortality rates. Demographic characteristics that marketers commonly use in segmenting markets include age, gender, race, ethnicity, income, education, occupation, family size, family life cycle, religion and social class. Marketers rely on these demographic characteristics because they are often closely linked to customers' needs and purchasing behaviour, and can readily be measured. Manufacturers of tea bags, such as PG and Twinings, offer their products in packages of different sizes to satisfy the needs of consumers ranging from singles to large families.

Financial institutions such as banks and building societies attempt to interest children in their products by offering free gifts such as book vouchers. Meanwhile, retired customers

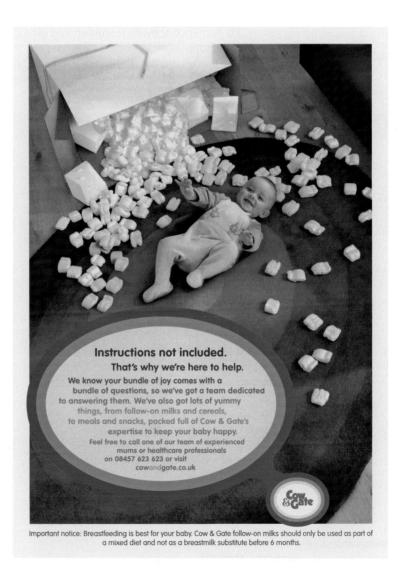

Figure 6.6
Cow and Gate targets new parents with its baby foods.
Source: Image courtesy of The Advertising Archives

175

are targeted with products designed for a leisure-oriented lifestyle. The emphasis is on tailoring the service package to suit particular needs.

Age is a commonly used segmentation variable. Population statistics help marketers to understand and keep track of changing age profiles (see Table 6.1 and Figure 6.7). As the population of western Europe continues to increase, the numbers in the 0- to 19-year-old age band is falling, while the number of those over 60 continues to rise. This has ramifications for marketers, who must increasingly cater for an ageing population. Given the relative affluence of this particular group, many companies (particularly those in leisure and service industries) have benefited from this demographic change. Marketers are also recognising the purchasing influence of children and are targeting their marketing efforts at them. Numerous products are aimed specifically at children: toys, clothing, food, drinks, video games and entertainment. In addition, children profoundly influence certain purchasing decisions made by their parents.[13] For example, in households with only one parent or in which both parents work, children often take on additional responsibilities such as cooking, cleaning and food shopping, and thus influence the products and brands that are purchased.

Gender is another demographic variable commonly used to segment markets, including the markets for clothing, alcoholic drinks, books, magazines, non-prescription drugs and even cigarettes. EU statistics show that women and girls outnumber men and boys by just over 1 per cent in the population.

The confectionery market did not traditionally segment its market on the basis of gender. Chocolate manufacturers, including Cadbury's, tried to change this by developing assortments

TABLE 6.1 POPULATION STATISTICS, EUROPE

POPULATION FORECASTS (in thousands)

	2005	2010	2015	2020	2025	2030	2040	2050
Austria	8,183	8,231	8,279	8,323	8,368	–	–	8,206
Belgium	10,426	10,530	10,625	10,724	10,818	10,894	10,965	10,953
Denmark	–	5,421	–	5,431	–	5,428	5,358	5,261
Finland	–	5,268	–	5,317	–	5,291	–	–
France	–	61,061	61,975	62,734	–	63,927	–	64,032
Germany	–	81,422	80,909	80,152	–	77,672	74,155	69,940
Greece	10,627	10,653	10,626	10,555	–	–	–	–
Ireland[1]	3,938	4,014	4,040	4,039	4,009	3,955	–	–
Italy[2]	58,409	58,587	–	57,936	–	56,807	54,778	51,890
Luxembourg	399	403	406	410	–	–	–	–
Netherlands[1]	–	16,938	–	17,545	–	17,947	–	–
Norway	–	4,692	–	–	–	5,085	–	5,220
Poland	38,634	38,788	39,005	39,003	38,657	38,025	–	–
Portugal	10,562	10,626	10,587	10,489	10,356	–	–	–
Slovenia	1,988[1]	2,012[2]	2,020[1]	2,019	–	–	–	–
Sweden	9,013[1]	9,308[1]	–	9,765	–	10,130	–	–
Switzerland	7,274	7,332	–	7,389	–	–	–	–
Turkey	70,225	–	–	–	–	–	–	–
Ukraine	–	50,040	–	49,936	–	49,831	–	–
UK	–	61,956	–	64,105	–	65,568	65,822	–

Notes: [1] Add 1 year to date(s) shown.   [2] Add 2 years to date(s) shown.
Sources: National statistical offices.

Percentage change

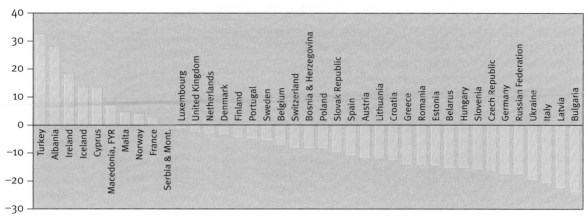

Sources: National statistical offices

Figure 6.7
Forecasted total population change 2000–2020
Source: The European Marketing Pocket Book, *published by the World Advertising Research Center, Henley-on-Thames, 2004*

aimed primarily at men. In general, despite the care taken in each product's design, packaging and promotion, these were not successful. However, efforts by manufacturers of skincare products to develop lines specifically aimed at men have been more successful.

The way in which marketers treat ethnicity varies in different parts of the world. For instance, in the USA, where a quarter of the population is made up of ethnic minorities, ethnicity is widely used as a means of segmenting markets for goods and services of all kinds. The US Hispanic population, comprising people of Mexican, Cuban, Puerto Rican, and Central and South American heritage, is growing five times faster than the general population. Consequently, it is being targeted by more and more companies, including Campbell Soup Co., Nabisco and Procter & Gamble. However, targeting Hispanic customers is not an easy task. For example, although marketers have long believed that Hispanic consumers are exceptionally brand loyal and prefer Spanish-language media, research does not support these assumptions. Not only do advertisers disagree about the merits of using Spanish-language media, they also question whether it is appropriate to advertise to Mexicans, Puerto Ricans and Cubans using a common Spanish language.[14] In other areas the proportion of ethnic minorities is much lower than in the USA, affecting the level of marketing attention they receive. In the UK, the percentage of the population from ethnic minorities increased from 3.9 per cent in 1980 to 7.4 per cent in 2001: it is now estimated at 11 per cent. As Case 6 explains, marketers are now looking for new ways to connect with the needs of these particular groups.

Product and service needs also vary according to marital status, and the number and age of children. These factors are collectively taken into consideration by the 'family life cycle' concept. Some of the more obvious markets in which the impact of different life cycles is seen are tourism, housing and financial services. The family life cycle has been broken down in several different ways. Table 6.2 illustrates one such scheme.

The scheme presented in Table 6.2 assumes that individuals at different life cycle stages have varying product needs. Marketers can respond to this by targeting such groups with marketing mixes designed to capitalise on these differences. For example, parents whose children have grown up and left home ('empty nesters') tend to have more disposable income than those with young children, and tend to spend more on the home, holidays and new cars.

177

TABLE 6.2 THE WELLS AND GUBAR LIFE CYCLE STAGES

Bachelor stage (young single people not living with parents)
Newly married couples without children
Full nest I (youngest child under 6)
Full nest II (youngest child 6 or over)
Full nest III (older married couple with dependent children)
Empty nest I (no children living at home, family head working)
Empty nest II (family head retired)
Solitary survivor (working)
Solitary survivor (retired)

Source: Copyright © ESOMAR® 2000. Permission for using this material has been granted by ESOMAR®, Amsterdam, the Netherlands (www.esomar.ni).

Banks and financial institutions in particular are getting better at gearing their marketing efforts to life cycle changes. Critics of the life cycle concept point out that it can be difficult to decide to which categories families belong. Some households, such as single-parent families and older married couples who have never had children, do not appear to fit in at all.

Obviously, this discussion of demographic variables is not exhaustive. However, the variables described above probably represent the most widely used demographics. Other examples of the use of demographics include segmenting the cosmetic and haircare markets on the basis of race and directing certain types of food and clothing towards people of specific religious sects.

Socio-economic variables include income, occupation, education and social class. Some marketing academics and practitioners include certain of these variables under the 'demographics' label. Income can be a very useful way of dividing markets because it strongly influences people's product needs. It affects their ability to buy (as discussed in Chapter 2) and their aspirations for a certain style of living. Obvious products in this category include housing, furniture, clothing, cars, food, certain kinds of sporting goods, and leisure activities.

The occupations of the members of the household are known to have an impact on the types of products and services that are purchased. The type of housing individuals and families own or rent is strongly linked to this variable. It is obvious, for example, that sales of products for refurbishment and decoration, such as paints, fabrics and wallpapers, will occur predominantly among those professions that have owner-occupier status. Occupation is also known to affect the types of sporting and leisure activities people prefer. For example, professionals may be active with walking, swimming, cycling and jogging, but not so involved with darts or football. Intermediate managers enjoy walking, swimming and keep fit/yoga. Unskilled manual workers are not particularly active in sports and physical activities.[15]

Other socio-economic variables that may be used to segment markets include education level and social class.

Geographic Variables The needs of consumers in different geographic locations may be affected by their local climate, terrain, natural resources and population density. Markets may be divided into regions because one or more geographic variables may cause customers' needs to differ from one region to another. A company that sells products throughout the EU will, for example, need to take the different languages spoken into account when labelling its goods.

City size can be an important segmentation variable. For example, one franchised restaurant organisation will not locate in cities of fewer than 100,000 people because experience shows that a smaller population base could make the operation unprofitable. The same company may add a second, or even a third, restaurant once the city reaches a certain size. Other businesses, however, seek out opportunities in smaller towns. The major petroleum retailers, such as Esso and Shell, have traffic density thresholds, below which they perceive a local market as unviable. It is, therefore, quite common – particularly in villages and small towns in rural areas – for petroleum retailing to be dominated by independent garage owners and the smaller petroleum companies.

Market density refers to the number of potential customers within a unit of land area, such as a square kilometre. Although market density is generally related to population density, the correlation is not exact. For example, in two different geographic markets of approximately equal size and population, the market density for office supplies might be much higher in the first than in the second if the first contains a significantly greater proportion of business customers. Market density may be a useful segmentation variable because low-density markets often require different sales, advertising and distribution activities from high-density markets.

In Europe, climate can be used as a geographic segmentation variable. Companies entering new markets in Europe increasingly need to consider the impact of climate on their customer base. For example, washing machines sold in Italy do not require such fast spin speeds as those sold in Germany because the Italian climate is much sunnier. Other markets affected by climate include air conditioning and heating equipment, clothing, gardening equipment, recreational products and building materials.

Marketers are increasingly using geodemographic segmentation. **Geodemographic segmentation** clusters people according to postcode areas. For example, ACORN (A Classification Of Residential Neighbourhoods) uses information taken from census data and allows people to be grouped according to a number of factors, including geography, socio-economics, culture and lifestyle. All 1.9 million UK postcodes have been described using over 125 demographic statistics and 287 lifestyle variables. The underlying concept is that customers living in different residential neighbourhoods have different profiles in respect of these variables. Their product needs in terms of styling and features, therefore, also vary. Consumers can be classified under ACORN on the basis of the postcode of their home address and then allocated to one of the groups in Table 6.3. These categories further sub-divide to give a total of 17 groups and 56 neighbourhood types. For example, *Wealthy Achievers* includes several groups, such as *Wealthy Executives, Affluent Greys* and *Flourishing Families*. The *Wealthy*

Market density
The number of potential customers within a unit of land area

Geodemographic segmentation
Clustering people according to postcode areas and census data

TABLE 6.3 THE ACORN CATEGORISATION OF UK CONSUMERS		
Category	**Group**	**Type**
Wealthy Achievers	Wealthy Executives	01 Affluent mature professionals, large houses 02 Affluent working families with mortgages 03 Villages with wealthy commuters 04 Well-off managers, larger houses
	Affluent Greys	05 Older affluent professionals 06 Farming communities 07 Old people, detached houses 08 Mature couples, smaller detached houses
	Flourishing Families	09 Larger families, prosperous suburbs 10 Well-off working families with mortgages 11 Well-off managers, detached houses 12 Large families & houses in rural areas *(Continued...)*

179

TABLE 6.3 THE ACORN CATEGORISATION OF UK CONSUMERS (CONTINUED)

Category	Group	Type
Urban Prosperity	Prosperous Professionals	13 Well-off professionals, larger houses and converted flats 14 Older professionals in detached houses and apartments
	Educated Urbanites	15 Affluent urban professionals, flats 16 Prosperous young professionals, flats 17 Young educated workers, flats 18 Multi-ethnic young, converted flats 19 Suburban privately renting professionals
	Aspiring Singles	20 Student flats and cosmopolitan sharers 21 Singles & sharers, multi-ethnic areas 22 Low-income singles, small rented flats 23 Student terraces
Comfortably Off	Starting Out	24 Young couples, flats and terraces 25 White collar singles/sharers, terraces
	Secure Families	26 Younger white-collar couples with mortgages 27 Middle income, home-owning areas 28 Working families with mortgages 29 Mature families in suburban semis 30 Established home-owning workers 31 Home-owning Asian family areas
	Settled Suburbia	32 Retired home owners 33 Middle income, older couples 34 Lower income people, semis
	Prudent Pensioners	35 Elderly singles, purpose-built flats 36 Older people, flats
Moderate Means	Asian Communities	37 Crowded Asian terraces 38 Low-income Asian families
	Post-industrial Families	39 Skilled older family terraces 40 Young family workers
	Blue-collar Roots	41 Skilled workers, semis and terraces 42 Home-owning, terraces 43 Older rented terraces
Hard-pressed	Struggling Families	44 Low-income larger families, semis 45 Older people, low income, small semis 46 Low income, routine jobs, unemployment 47 Low-rise terraced estates of poorly-off workers 48 Low incomes, high unemployment, single parents 49 Large families, many children, poorly educated
	Burdened Singles	50 Council flats, single elderly people 51 Council terraces, unemployment, many singles 52 Council flats, single parents, unemployment *(Continued...)*

Category	Group	Type
Hard-pressed (continued)	High-rise Hardship	53 Old people in high rise flats 54 Singles & single parents, high rise estates
	Inner-city Adversity	55 Multi-ethnic purpose-built estates 56 Multi-ethnic, crowded flats

TABLE 6.3 THE ACORN CATEGORISATION OF UK CONSUMERS (CONTINUED)

Source: CACI, November, 2007.

☯ Marketing Insight

Profiling and Targeting Customers with ACORN

Along with Experian's Mosaic system, ACORN from CACI is a leading geodemographic tool used by marketing practitioners to identify and understand the UK population and the demand for products and services. Clients of CACI use this information to improve their understanding of customers and target markets, and to determine where to locate operations. The geodemographic and lifestyle data provided by ACORN's detailed analysis of the official census statistics, supplemented with financial, purchasing and behaviour information, are an invaluable input to the market segmentation analyses of many consumer marketers.

As CACI explains, informed decisions can be made on where direct marketing and advertising campaigns will be most effective; where branches should be opened or closed; or where sites are located, including retail outlets, leisure facilities and public services.

ACORN categorises all 1.9 million UK postcodes, which have been described using over 125 demographic statistics within England, Scotland, Wales and Northern Ireland, and 287 lifestyle variables, making it a most powerful discriminator, which offers a clearer understanding of clients and prospects. The basic principle is that people in similar areas – postcode zones – have the same needs and lifestyles.

With the 2001 government census of the entire population fully analysed, CACI had to update its ACORN profiles, as detailed in Table 6.3. The associated analysis revealed some interesting shifts since the last full census. Consumer habits and behaviour have changed over the past decade, and the new ACORN takes into account these key shifts.

Here are some examples.

- As the wealth of the nation increases and borrowing becomes easier, car ownership has risen and more people commute by car.
- More consumers are asset-rich, with a growth of 20 per cent of home owners having paid off their mortgages.
- Conversely, there is much less unemployment.
- New building has increased, with more detached and semi-detached properties. There are now different types of people living in traditional housing.
- The workplace is now more flexible, illustrated by an increase in people working from home.
- The population is becoming more educated and the number of students has nearly doubled.
- Family structure is changing, with significant growth in the number of single parents. Despite an increase in the number of grown-up children remaining in the family home, there are more 'empty nester' consumers than ever before as older couples become free of the financial responsibility of schoolchildren.
- There is a significant growth of the very elderly: the population is becoming older.

Such changes present both opportunities and threats for the marketers of a large selection of products and services.

CACI claims the new ACORN is more accurate for targeting than previous versions, across all sectors – for example, finance, automotive, e-commerce, holidays, food shopping and brown goods. As detailed on CACI's website, just some of the consumer profiling and targeting information available includes:

- mortgages
- winter snow holidays
- time left on mortgage
- weekend breaks
- company medical insurance
- classical music/opera
- private pension
- weekly food spend
- car insurance
- eating out
- child savings plan
- family income
- guaranteed income bonds
- house price
- National Savings
- 'new player' credit cards
- stocks and shares
- own a DVD player
- unit trusts
- have cable TV/phone

- buy new car
- have satellite TV
- buy car over £20,000
- own a laptop computer
- can choose company car
- use PC for finance
- car kept in garage
- use PC for education
- European holidays
- use e-mail
- USA holidays.

Marketers may purchase reports about specific products or concerning ACORN's consumer classifications. A popular application is to capture the postcodes of customers of a company, so as to analyse the ACORN profile of these customers. Armed with such a profile, the client company's marketers are able to locate similar consumers to target with their marketing communications.

Source: CACI, 2004 and 2007.

Executives group then sub-divides into several types, such as *Affluent Working Families with Mortgages*, *Villages with Wealthy Commuters*, or *Well-off Managers in Larger Houses*. The Marketing Insight box above describes ACORN in more detail.

Psychographic Variables   Marketers sometimes use psychographic variables such as personality characteristics, motives and lifestyles to segment markets. A psychographic dimension can be used by itself or combined with other types of segmentation variable.

Personality characteristics are useful when a product is similar to many competing products and when consumers' needs are not significantly affected by other segmentation variables. However, segmenting a market according to personality characteristics can be problematic. Although marketing practitioners have long believed that consumer choice and product use should vary with personality and lifestyle, marketing research has shown only weak relationships. However, the weakness of such relationships may be due to the difficulty of accurately measuring personality traits, because most existing personality tests were developed for clinical use, not for segmentation purposes. As the reliability of more recent measurement instruments increases, a greater association between personality and consumer behaviour has been demonstrated.[16] For example, it has been shown that personality sometimes influences the clothes, make-up and hairstyles that individuals adopt.

When motives are used to segment a market, it is divided on the basis of consumers' reasons for making a purchase. Product durability, value for money, concern for the environment, convenience and status are all motives affecting the types of product purchased and the choice of stores in which they are bought. For example, one consumer may be motivated to purchase recycled kitchen paper out of concern for the environment. Another may travel to a large supermarket in order to buy the most absorbent, high-quality brand of kitchen towel.

Individuals are grouped by lifestyle segmentation according to how they live and spend their time, the importance of items in their surroundings (their homes or their jobs, for example), their beliefs about themselves and broad issues, and some socio-economic characteristics, such as income and education.[17] Lifestyle analysis provides a broad view of buyers because it encompasses numerous characteristics related to people's activities, interests and opinions (see Table 6.4). It can be thought of as going beyond a simple understanding of personality.

The use of lifestyle as a segmentation variable is problematic, because it is so difficult to measure accurately compared with other types of segmentation variable. In addition, the relationships between psychographic variables and consumers' needs are sometimes obscure and unproven, and the segments that result from psychographic segmentation may not be reachable.[18] For example, a marketer may determine that highly compulsive individuals want a certain type of clothing. However, no specific stores or particular media – such as television or radio programmes, newspapers or magazines – appeal precisely to this group and this group alone. Psychographic variables can sometimes offer a more useful way of understanding segments that have been defined using other base variables.

One of the more popular programmes studying lifestyles is conducted by the Stanford Research Institute's Value and Lifestyle Programme (VALS). This programme surveys consumers to select groups with identifiable values and lifestyles. Initially, VALS identified three broad consumer groups: Outer-directed, Inner-directed, and Need-driven consumers. The current VALS classification categorises consumers into eight basic lifestyle groups: Innovators, Thinkers, Achievers, Experiencers, Believers, Strivers, Makers and Survivors. The VALS studies have been used to create products as well as to segment markets.

Behaviouristic Variables   Marketers can also segment markets on the basis of an aspect of consumers' behaviour towards the product. This might relate to the way the particular product is used or purchased, or perhaps to the benefits consumers require from it.

Purchase behaviour can be a useful way of distinguishing between groups of customers, giving marketers insight into the most appropriate marketing mix. For example, brand-loyal customers may require a different kind of treatment from those who switch between brands. On-pack sales promotions are often geared towards building loyalty in brand switchers.

The occasion on which customers buy a particular product may impact upon product choice because in different sets of circumstances different product selection criteria may be applied. For instance, a customer who replaces a car tyre in an emergency will probably be less concerned about price than one who is routinely maintaining his or her car.

Benefit segmentation is the division of a market according to the benefits consumers want from the product.[19] Although most types of market segmentation are based on the

Benefit segmentation
The division of a market according to the benefits consumers want from the product

TABLE 6.4 CHARACTERISTICS RELATED TO ACTIVITIES, INTERESTS AND OPINIONS

Activities	Interests	Opinions
Work	Family	Themselves
Hobbies	Home	Social issues
Social events	Job	Politics
Holidays	Community	Business
Entertainment	Recreation	Economics
Club membership	Fashion	Education
Community	Food	Products
Shopping	Media	Future
Sports	Achievements	Culture

Source: Reprinted, adapted from Joseph Plummer, 'The concept and application of life style segmentation', *Journal of Marketing*, January 1974, p. 34. Reprinted by permission of the American Marketing Association.

assumption that there is a relationship between the variable and customers' needs, benefit segmentation is different in that the benefits the customers seek are their product needs. By determining the benefits desired, marketers may be able to divide people into groups seeking certain sets of benefits.

The effectiveness of benefit segmentation depends on several conditions. First, the benefits people seek must be identifiable. Second, using these benefits, marketers must be able to divide people into recognisable segments. Finally, one or more of the resulting segments must be accessible to the companies' marketing efforts.

Product usage is another method marketers sometimes use to segment their customers. Individuals can be divided into users and non-users of a particular product. Users can then be classified further as heavy, moderate or light. To satisfy a specific user group, marketers sometimes create a distinctive product, set special prices or initiate special promotion and distribution activities. Thus airlines such as British Airways and KLM offer frequent-flier programmes to reward their regular customers with free trips and discounts for car hire and hotel accommodation. Light users or non-users of products often receive little attention from companies. There is a tendency sometimes to dismiss these groups when developing a marketing programme. For example, research in the holiday industry tends to focus on feedback from current customers, often forgetting to question why non-users failed to buy.

How customers apply the product may also determine segmentation. To satisfy customers who use a product in a certain way, some feature – say, packaging, size, texture or colour – may have to be designed with special care to make the product easier to use, more convenient or more environmentally friendly. For instance, Lever Brothers and Procter & Gamble are focusing more and more on the development of refill packs of detergents and other household products, to cater for increasing consumer concerns about the environment.

The varying attitude of customers towards products constitutes another set of variables that can be used to segment markets. Clothing retailers like River Island and Benetton are particularly conscious of this. While one customer seeks outfits that are practical and comfortable, another is concerned with achieving a highly fashionable image.

As this brief discussion shows, consumer markets can be divided according to numerous characteristics. Ultimately, the choices marketers make will depend on a host of market and company factors.

Variables for Segmenting Business Markets

Like consumer markets, business (organisational) markets are often segmented. Here the marketer's aim is to satisfy the needs of businesses for products. Marketers may segment business markets according to company demographics, operating variables, purchasing approach, situational factors or the personal characteristics of buyers.

Marketers attempting to segment business markets may face various problems.[20] The particular characteristics of the market or the distribution structure in place may restrict the types of segment bases that can be used. For example, many European car manufacturers are dependent upon the fleet car market. This market tends to be structured on the basis of car engine and vehicle size, with companies providing their more senior managers with more powerful, larger and expensive vehicles. It is likely that customers would resist a move away from this accepted structure by the car manufacturers, who are therefore not in a position to use possibly contradictory segmentation approaches. Various segmentation approaches have been developed to try to make it easier for companies to deal with these kinds of constraints.[21]

Whatever the approach adopted, just as in consumer markets, some segment bases are easier to measure and apply than others.[22] For example, it is much more straightforward to segment on the basis of company size, which is a measurable and visible characteristic, than on the basis of buying centre structure (see Chapter 5), which may be much more difficult to appraise. Table 6.5 provides an overview of the variables for segmenting business markets, and illustrates the relative ease with which they can be measured. Variables at the base of the table are easier to measure and more objective than those at the top.

TABLE 6.5 VARIABLES FOR SEGMENTING BUSINESS MARKETS

Personal Characteristics of Buyers

Just as in consumer markets, the demographics, personality and lifestyle of those individuals in the buying centre impact upon purchasing decisions, practices, attitudes towards risk and loyalty to suppliers.

Situational Factors

The urgency of purchase, size of order or product application can play an important role in the choices that are made.

Purchasing Approach

Buying centre structure (centralised/decentralised), buying policies (sealed bidding, service contracts, leasing), nature of existing relationships (focus on new or existing customers), balance of power among decision-makers and buying criteria (quality, delivery, service, price, product range, innovation) may shape an organisation's purchase decisions.

Operating Variables

The technologies applied by an organisation, the manner in which products are used or customer capabilities can fundamentally affect purchase choice.

Demographics

Company age, location, industry (SIC code) and size are likely to alter product requirements.

Company Demographics Variables relating to the type of business or industry, geographic location, company age and size are probably the most widely used segmentation variables in business markets.

A company sometimes segments a market by the types of business within that market, perhaps on the basis of industry area or SIC code (see Chapter 5). Different types of organisation often require different product features, distribution systems, price structures and selling strategies. Given these variables, a company may either concentrate on a single segment with one marketing mix (concentration strategy) or focus on several groups with multiple mixes (multi-segment strategy). A paint manufacturer could segment customers into several groups, such as paint wholesalers, do-it-yourself retail outlets, vehicle manufacturers, decorators and housing developers.

The demand for some consumer products can vary considerably by geographic area because of differences in climate, terrain, customer preference or similar factors. Demand for business-to-business products also varies according to geographic location. For example, the producers of certain types of timber divide their markets geographically because their customers' needs vary regionally. Geographic segmentation may be especially appropriate for reaching industries that are concentrated in certain locations, for example, textiles in West Yorkshire, information technology (IT) along the M4 corridor in England or financial services in London. Examples of such concentration in Europe include heavy industry around Lille or in the Ruhr Valley, and banking in Zurich.

Operating Variables Customer requirements can be affected in a range of ways by different operating variables such as the technology applied by the buying organisation or the product types used. Certain products, especially raw materials such as steel, petrol, plastics and timber, are used in numerous ways. Sometimes the technology used by a company will play an important role. How a company uses products affects the types and amounts it purchases, as well as the method of making the purchase.[23] For example, computers are used for engineering purposes, basic scientific research, business operations such as word processing and book-keeping, as well as Internet access and games in the home. A computer manufacturer may segment the computer market by types of use because organisations' needs for computer hardware and software depend on the purpose for which the products are purchased.

Purchasing Approach   Although it may be difficult for a company to appraise the buying approach of its customers, this is none the less sometimes an appropriate way for business markets to be segmented. The characteristics of the buying centre, including its structure (where the balance of buying power lies), and the nature of any buying policies can all affect the product requirements of customers. For example, suppliers of building materials must organise their sales efforts to satisfy a wide array of customer types who organise their buying activities in vastly different ways. While dealing with large buyers, such as Carillion or Tarmac, will require an understanding of a relatively complex buying structure, small local builders may be perfectly satisfied with a much simpler supply arrangement.

Situational Factors   Sometimes it is appropriate to segment a business market on the basis of situational factors such as the urgency or size of an order. How urgently the order is required may have an impact on the importance a customer attaches to particular product features. For example, if a robot on a car production line has broken down, bringing the entire production process to a standstill, the price of replacement parts to fix it may be less important than their availability. However, if the same part is being replaced as part of a routine service, price may be the most important factor. The size and frequency of different orders can be effective segmentation variables because they have ramifications concerning the way the customer relationship is handled. For example, a university that regularly orders vast amounts of stationery would expect a different level of service to that of a small business that only infrequently buys small quantities of paper and envelopes.

Personal Characteristics   Although individuals involved in business buying may not have as much control over the products and services selected as when they are making purchases for personal or family use, their individual characteristics still play a role in the preferences they demonstrate. For this reason it is sometimes appropriate to segment business markets on the basis of the characteristics of individuals within the buying centre. For example, the demographics, personality and lifestyle of managers tasked with buying a selection of new office furniture will influence the preferred designs. If power in the buying centre rests with one senior manager who strongly dislikes modern designs, say, this will influence the final selection of products.

Segmentation Effectiveness

As Table 6.6 illustrates, segmentation analysis invariably involves several stages. Marketers must be aware that whatever the approach followed and whichever base variables are used, haphazard implementation can lead to ineffective market segmentation, missed opportunities and inappropriate investment. To avoid such difficulties marketers should take note of the following criteria. The first is that there must be real differences in the needs of consumers for the product or service. There is no value in segmenting a homogeneous market. Equally, dissimilar consumers in terms of their needs and purchasing behaviour must not be grouped together in the same market segment. In addition, the segments revealed must be:

- *measurable* – easy to identify and measure; some basis must be found for effectively separating individuals into groups or segments with relatively homogeneous product or service needs
- *substantial* – large enough to be sufficiently profitable to justify developing and maintaining a specific marketing mix
- *accessible* – easy to reach with the marketing mix developed – for example, the promotional effort should target the relevant consumers

> **TABLE 6.6 STAGES IN SEGMENTATION ANALYSIS**
>
> **Objectives**
> Marketers must know the purpose of the exercise and have clear objectives.
>
> **Data**
> Required information must be specified and collected. This may encompass a qualitative phase to develop a robust view of consumer attitudes, motives, behaviour and perceptions, and a quantitative phase involving larger samples and statistical analysis of questionnaire responses (see Chapter 7).
>
> **Analysis**
> Various statistical packages, such as SPSS, can be used. Factor analysis, conjoint analysis and cluster analysis are commonly used techniques for analysing the collected data. Multidimensional scaling (MDS) is widely used in product positioning studies. Such techniques should not be applied by those without the necessary statistical skills, if inappropriate solutions are to be avoided.[24]
>
> **Interpretation**
> Marketers must interpret the proposed solutions to ensure any adopted segmentation scheme is statistically valid (complies with the relevant statistical significance tests) and managerially or intuitively valid, and that it presents market segments that are effective. Ultimately, the analysis should comply with statistical validity tests. Any recommendations must also be sensible in the view of managers.[25]
>
> **Recommendation**
> The final proposed solution must first be presented internally to senior and line managers expected to approve the segments, and then actioned for the external audience of distributors and customers.
>
> **Sources**[26, 27, 28]

- *stable* – the question of segment stability over time is not often addressed; if companies are to make strategic decisions on the basis of revealed segments, they need to be reasonably certain that those segments will be around long enough for action to be taken
- *useful* – the selected segments must be meaningful to the managers tasked with operationalising them and be likely to enable the company to better satisfy its target market.

Using market segmentation also requires a good deal of common sense. It is often difficult for companies to implement totally new segmentation schemes because they would be at odds with the existing marketing structures and ways of doing things. In such cases companies sometimes choose to make minor changes to what is already in place.

Profiling Market Segments

Whatever the variable, or combination of variables, used to group customers, a more comprehensive understanding of the characteristics of individuals is likely to be required. For example, a company that segments the market for energy drinks on the basis of age, focusing on customers in their late teens, would do well to understand as much as possible about its particular target group in other respects. What reference groups influence them? Where do they live? Where and when do they socialise? What social background are they from? What motivates them? The more comprehensive the image developed, the better the opportunity to develop an effective marketing mix with maximum appeal.

Profiling
The task of building up a fuller picture of the target segments

Descriptors
Variables used to profile or build a fuller picture of target segments

Profiling is the task of building up a fuller picture of target segments, and the variables being used in the description are termed **descriptors**. The types of descriptors available to marketers are broadly the same as the variables used to segment markets in the first place – that is, demographics, socio-economics, and so on. This is sometimes a cause of confusion for students, who struggle to remember whether they are dealing with base or descriptor variables. It helps to note that while base variables should discriminate between customer needs, descriptors are simply used to enrich the picture, to help summarise what else can be gleaned about the customers in a particular segment. This gives added inspiration to the creative team developing the product and promotional material, and helps to fine-tune decisions on price and distribution. Overall, profiling segments in this way ensures that the impact of the marketing mix on the customer is maximised. If segments are not properly profiled, it is unlikely sales personnel, advertising agency staff or senior managers will fully comprehend the proposed segmentation scheme. Therefore its effective implementation may be jeopardised.

Targeting Strategies

Targeting

The decision about which market segment(s) an organisation decides to prioritise for its sales and marketing efforts

Targeting involves marketers in decisions about which market segment(s) an organisation should prioritise for its sales and marketing efforts. As Figure 6.8 shows the three basic targeting strategies are: undifferentiated, concentrated and differentiated. The decision made on the targeting strategy to follow must be based on a clear understanding of company capabilities and resources, the nature of the competition and the characteristics of the product markets in question.

Undifferentiated Strategy

An organisation sometimes defines an entire market for a particular product as its target market. When a company designs a single marketing mix and directs it at the entire market for a particular product, it is using an undifferentiated targeting strategy. This is a strategy in which an organisation defines an entire market for a particular product as its target market, designs a single marketing mix, and directs it at that market. The strategy assumes that all customers in the target market for a specific kind of product have similar needs, and thus the organisation can satisfy most customers with a single marketing mix. This mix consists of one type of product with little or no variation, one price, one promotional programme aimed at everybody, and one distribution system to reach most customers in the total market. Products marketed successfully through the undifferentiated strategy include staple food items, such as sugar and salt, and certain kinds of farm produce.

The undifferentiated targeting strategy is effective under two conditions. First, a large proportion of customers in a total market must have similar needs for the product, a situation termed a 'homogeneous market'. A marketer using a single marketing mix for a total market of customers with a variety of needs would find that the marketing mix satisfies very few people. A 'universal car' meant to satisfy everyone would satisfy very few customers' needs for cars because it would not provide the specific attributes a particular person wants. Second, the organisation must be able to develop and maintain a single marketing mix that satisfies customers' needs. The company must be able to identify a set of needs common to most customers in a total market and have the resources and managerial skills to reach a sizeable portion of that market.

Concentration strategy

A process by which an organisation directs its marketing effort towards a single market segment through one marketing mix

Although customers may have similar needs for a few products, for most products their needs are quite different. In such instances, a company should use a concentrated or a differentiated strategy.

Concentrated Strategy

When an organisation directs its marketing efforts towards a single market segment by creating and maintaining one marketing mix, it is employing a **concentration strategy**. The fashion house Chanel targets the exclusive fashion segment, directing its marketing effort towards high-income customers who want to own the most chic apparel. Cross Pen Company aims its products at the upmarket gift segment of the pen market and does not compete with Bic, which focuses on the inexpensive, disposable pen segment.

188

Figure 6.8
Targeting Strategies. The letters in each target market represent potential customers. Customers with the same letters have similar characteristics and similar product needs

Figure 6.9
*The contents of this store retailing sports goods have been selected for a narrowly defined group of shoppers in a concentration strategy
Photo: Courtesy of Karen Beaulah*

The chief advantage of the concentration strategy is that it allows a company to specialise. The company can analyse the characteristics and needs of a distinct customer group and then focus all its energies on satisfying that group's needs.

A company may be able to generate a large sales volume by reaching a single segment. In some cases, concentrating on a single segment permits a company with limited resources to compete with much larger organisations, which may have overlooked some smaller segments.

Concentrating on one segment also means that a company puts 'all its eggs in one basket' – clearly a disadvantage. If a company's sales depend on a single segment and the segment's demand for the product declines, the company's financial strength declines as well. When the North American sports coupé market declined in the late 1980s, Porsche found itself in severe trouble as it had no exposure to other parts of the car market. Moreover, when a company penetrates one segment and becomes well entrenched, its popularity may keep it from moving into other segments. For example, it is hard to imagine that Rolex would start producing low-cost watches, or that Swatch might compete at the high end of the luxury watch segment.

Differentiated Strategy

Differentiated strategy
A strategy by which an organisation directs its marketing efforts towards two or more market segments by developing a marketing mix for each

With a **differentiated strategy** (see Figure 6.8), an organisation directs its marketing efforts at two or more market segments by developing a marketing mix for each segment selected. Sometimes this is a natural progression from the successful application of a concentration strategy in one market segment. For example, Jockey underwear has traditionally been aimed at one segment: men. However, the company has expanded its efforts and now markets underwear for women and children as well. The marketing mixes used for a differentiated strategy may vary as to product/service differences, place/distribution methods, promotion methods and prices. The majority of users of Gatwick Airport near London are packaged holiday travellers. A significant minority, however, are business users.

An organisation can usually increase its sales in the aggregate market through a differentiated strategy because its marketing mixes are aimed at more people. For example, Gap, which established its retail clothes reputation by targeting people under 25, now targets several age groups, from infants to people over 60. A company with excess production capacity may find a differentiated strategy advantageous because the sale of products to additional segments may absorb this excess capacity. On the other hand, a differentiated strategy often demands a greater number of production processes, materials and people. Thus production costs may be higher than with a concentration strategy.

Factors Affecting Choice of Targeting Strategy

Irrespective of the type of targeting strategy an organisation chooses to adopt, when faced with the decision about whether or not to enter a new segment, it must consider a number of issues. These issues include:

1 the nature of the needs and wants of end users
2 the size, structure and future potential of the segment
3 the availability of company resources
4 the intensity of the competition
5 the size of the company's existing market share, and
6 the possibility of any production/marketing scale economies.

Figure 6.10 sums up the core factors affecting the choice of targeting strategy. A company may recognise that a fit between its products or capabilities and target customer needs is

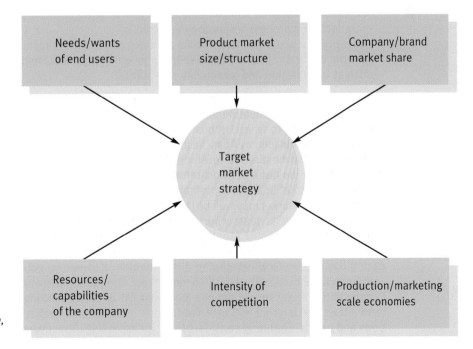

Figure 6.10
Factors affecting choice of target market strategy
Source: data from D. Cravens, Strategic Marketing *(Homewood, Ill.: Irwin, 1982)*

191

stronger and more 'marketable' in one market segment than in another. In some cases a decision may be made to expand into a new area, market or territory where the fit between customer needs and the product and marketing proposition is poor, with the intention of rectifying such shortcomings. Certain markets' size or value makes them attractive, as does a company's existing or potential sizeable market share. There may be economies of scale available in targeting a particular market segment alongside related ones, so that certain aspects of the production, sales and marketing activity may be shared. Of course, if truly homogeneous market segments have been identified, then each segment will require certain unique aspects of sales and marketing activity. If two segments really can be treated identically in terms of tactical marketing mix programmes, then they are probably one segment. Highly intensive and well-established competition may to some companies be something of a 'turn-off', whereas others may take such competitor activity to be indicative of extensive market growth and business opportunity. Finally, even a company the size of Ford or GM does not have the time, people or financial resources to develop a marketing mix for every single segment in the vehicle market. Available resources play a significant role in management's target market decisions.

There are many factors considered by companies determining which markets to target and which target market strategy to deploy. Figure 6.10 is nevertheless a useful summary of the core factors. Marketing planning expert Malcolm McDonald suggests[29] a variety of issues to consider when determining which and how many target market segments to prioritise. These include market, competition, financial and economic, technological, socio-political and regulatory factors – the forces of the marketing environment (see Chapter 3) and core market trends, as outlined below.

- *Market factors* – size (money, units or both); growth rate per annum; diversity of the market; sensitivity to price, service features and external factors; cyclicality; seasonality; bargaining power of upstream and downstream suppliers.
- *Competition* – types of competitor; degree of concentration; changes in type and mix; entries and exits; changes in market share; substitution by new technology; degrees and types of integration.
- *Financial and economic* – contribution margins; leveraging factors such as economies of scale and experience; barriers to entry or exit; capacity utilisation.
- *Technology* – maturity and volatility; complexity; differentiation; patents and copyrights; manufacturing process technology required.
- *Socio-political and regulatory* – social attitudes and trends; influence with pressure groups, government and regulatory bodies; laws, government and EU regulations; human factors such as unionisation and community acceptance.

A survey[30] of marketing practices in the largest UK companies revealed an interesting set of variables utilised in determining target market attractiveness (see Table 6.7). This study revealed the extent to which UK businesses are overly restricted by the City's short-termism, and the emphasis placed by financial journalists and pundits on performance only in terms of profitability in the most recent few months. US, German and South-east Asian financial markets tend not to be quite so short-termist in their thinking.[31] Outside the UK, organisations worry about market share and profitability, not just for today and tomorrow, but for a few years to come. A market may well be targeted because of its future potential, not just because of current sales. It is reassuring to see customer satisfaction, sustainable differential/competitive advantage and likely product differentiation well up the list of factors considered in the UK, as Chapter 1 explained the importance in marketing of satisfying customers, outpacing competitors and developing differentiation. It is not so good to see the marketing environment and issues relating to non-direct competitor activity so low down the list. Organisations really should adopt a balanced list of criteria, mixing short-term and longer-term issues and internal and external factors – market characteristics, financial considerations and trends. Chapter 9 considers tools for assessing attractiveness.

TABLE 6.7 MARKET ATTRACTIVENESS FACTORS ADOPTED BY UK COMPANIES

Companies' Market Attractiveness Criteria

First Tier:
- Profitability

Second Tier:
- Market growth
- Market size
- Likely customer satisfaction
- Sales volume

Third Tier:
- Likelihood of a sustainable differential advantage over rivals
- Ease of access for the business
- Opportunities in the industry
- Product differentiation
- Competitive rivalry

- Market share
- Relative strength/key functions
- Customers' price sensitivity
- Customer image of company

Fourth Tier:
- Technological factors
- Fit with business strategy
- Stability of market
- Environmental factors
- Threat of substitutes
- Barriers to entry
- Negotiating power of buyers
- Ease of profiling customers
- Supplier power

Source: Reprinted with permission from S. Dibb and L. Simkin, 'Marketing planning: still barriers to overcome', European Marketing Academy Conference Proceedings, Warwick Business School, University of Warwick, UK.

Positioning

Figure 6.3 illustrated the link between market segmentation, targeting and positioning. Having identified the segments in a market and decided on which segment (or segments) to target, a company must position its product, service or idea. A product's positioning has been described as the place occupied in a particular market, as perceived by the customer segment at which that product is targeted.[32] Another definition suggests that the positioning of a product is

> the sum of those attributes normally ascribed to it by the consumers – its standing, its quality, the type of people who use it, its strengths, its weaknesses, any other unusual or memorable characteristics it may possess, its price and the value it represents.[33]

Positioning
The process of creating an image for a product in the minds of target customers

Positioning starts with a product, a piece of merchandise, a service, a company, an institution or even a person. **Positioning** is not what is done to the product, it is what is created in the minds of the target customers. The product is positioned in the minds of these customers and is given an image.[34] There may be a few cosmetic changes to the product, to its name, price, packaging, styling or channel of distribution, but these are to facilitate the successful promotion of the image desired by the target customers. Target customers must perceive the product to have a distinct image and positioning vis-à-vis its competitors. Product differentiation is widely viewed as the key to successful marketing; the product must stand out and have a clearly defined positioning.

Determining a Positioning

Positioning is based on customers' perceptions and is therefore only partly within the control of marketers. Positionings are essentially selected by customers, based on variables and within parameters that are important to them. Price may be the key in grocery shopping, service level in selecting a bank, quality and reliability in buying computer hardware, value for money in choosing which theme park to visit. In-depth marketing research (commonly using depth interviews or focus group discussions) is required if customer motivations and expectations in a particular market are to be fully understood. Management's intuition is not always sufficient. For example, research revealed that consumers often have to decide between replacement living room or dining room furniture and a family package holiday abroad. Managers at most leading furniture retailers perceived other furniture retailers to be their competitors, when in reality they were competing for a consumer's disposable income against other product areas. In the budget-conscious sector of the furniture buying market, retailers believed only price to be important. In-depth research proved that value for money, a concept that includes product quality and durability in addition to price, was perceived to be the main purchase consideration.

Consumers generally assign positionings to a company or a product that is the market leader – and probably has the highest profile – and the limited number of competitors they can recollect are oriented to this market leader. For example, in the market for tomato ketchup, perceptions of brands are oriented towards market leader Heinz. Occasionally the brand consumers regard as the market leader may not be the genuine market leader in terms of market share, but simply the one most visible at that time, possibly because of heavy promotional exposure. Customers respond to the attributes of a product and to its promotional imagery, but the product's positioning as perceived by its target customers is affected by the reputation and image of the company, coupled with its other products, and by the activities of its competitors. For example, bad publicity, such as that experienced by British Airways following allegations of dirty tricks against Virgin Atlantic, can negatively affect a brand's positioning. The opening of Terminal 5 at Heathrow damaged BA's image.

In-depth marketing research leads to an understanding of how consumers perceive different brands and companies, which marketing variables they believe to be most important and by what magnitude. **Perceptual mapping** is a tool commonly adopted by marketers and marketing researchers to visually depict such consumer perceptions and prioritising of brands and their perceived attributes. Figure 6.11 illustrates a hypothetical example in which consumers thought product range width and price – the two axes – were the key characteristics of the market. A cross marks the ideal positioning, with high product range width and above average price (typical of high-quality shopping goods such as cameras or

Perceptual mapping
A tool used by marketers and marketing researchers to visually depict consumer perceptions and prioritising of brands and their perceived attributes

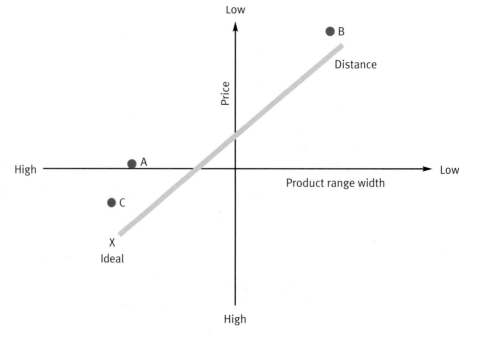

Figure 6.11
Positioning map of hypothetical consumer preferences
Source: D. Knee and D. Walters, Strategy in Retailing *(Herts, UK: Philip Allan, 1985), p. 27. Reproduced by permission of Philip Allan, a division of Hodder Education*

hi-fi systems). Brands (or companies) A and C are perceived as being relatively close to the ideal – their pricing policy does not fully match the image required – but brand (or company) B is viewed as being too cheap, with inadequate product range width.

Steps in Determining a Positioning Plan

Although customers' perceptions play an important role in positioning, the role of marketers is also crucial. A simple step-by-step approach can be used for establishing a clear positioning plan for a product. This process commences with the identification of target market priorities, as outlined below.

1 Define the segments in a particular market.
2 Decide which segment(s) to target.
3 Understand what the target consumers expect and believe to be the most important considerations when deciding on the purchase.
4 Develop a product or products catering specifically for these needs and expectations.
5 Evaluate the positioning and images, as perceived by the target customers, of competing products in the selected market segment or segments.
6 Select an image that sets the product or products apart from the competing products, thus ensuring that the chosen image matches the aspirations of the target customers. The selected positioning and imagery must be credible: consumers would not believe Kia or Skoda if they promoted their cars in the same manner as Porsche or Aston Martin.
7 Inform target consumers about the product. Although this is primarily a promotional task, it is also vital that the product is made readily available at the right price, through the development of the full marketing mix.

The Marketing Tools and Techniques box below illustrates how Ford developed the positioning of the Focus to broaden its appeal to female drivers.

⊚ Marketing Tools and Techniques

Practitioners' Use of Brand Positioning Theory

There are essential stages in developing a brand positioning, assuming target segments have already been decided.

1 Identify the positionings of the competitive set.
2 Determine the desired positioning for the brand in question.
3 Develop a set of actions in order to achieve the desired positioning – it will not happen by itself!
4 Decide on an appropriate brand positioning statement to communicate the positioning.
5 Produce a marketing communications plan to promote the brand positioning to the target audience: the target market segment and key stakeholders inside the business and within the marketing channel.

Ford benchmarks itself against many competitors, but particularly VW. The Ford Focus is either market leader in its category or a leading challenger in most countries. In order to build on this success, the company had to attract greater numbers of customers, but also to stretch the brand so that not only middle-aged males purchased the Focus. A few years ago, the company wanted to attract more female purchasers, to emulate VW's Golf customer profile. This resulted from production of a perceptual map of the competing brands, featuring the age and sex of the drivers.

'Life's Better When You Take Control' was one of several working brand positioning statements developed, aimed to appeal to younger, aspirational female car buyers.

The action plan included:

- no TV campaign targeted at independent, confident females; the company could not confuse the marketplace and risk alienating the existing customer base
- special edition models of the Focus; research identified the required product features and colours

- direct mail dialogue campaign, with 48-hour test drive on offer
- brand liaison with relevant magazines, such as *Elle*; led to the Ford Focus Elle special edition
- targeted interactive promotional campaign, such as at Handbag.com or TotallyJewish.com
- interactive micro sites, such as public relations at the *Elle* Style Awards and associated branding, including key rings.

Subscribers to *Elle* magazine received bespoke brochures, linking Ford, *Elle* magazine and the Ford Focus Elle special edition:

Ford Focus Elle
The place to be seen this season

In colours such as Ebony, Moondust Silver and Chic, this model offered a 1.6i three-door Zetec, with alloy wheels, chrome tailpipe, remote-control CD/radio, air conditioning, ABS, side airbags and leather trim. The brochures featured a fashion shoot and the Focus Elle car, with captions such as:

Pink sheer 'Butterfly' dress, Rodeo Drive
Two-tone V-neck contoured vest, Milan
Ford Focus, the perfect accessory

Visitors to *Elle*'s website were greeted with information about the Focus Elle, plus a pop-up link directly into Ford's website. If they wanted further information or to arrange a test drive, the Ford system dealt with such requests, not *Elle*'s.

This strategy proved to be highly effective for Ford. Every two months, a new special edition was offered, in limited numbers to maintain exclusivity. All editions sold out quickly. This success for Ford resulted from researching the target market's requirements, thinking carefully about the required brand positioning, and being smart in terms of executing the associated promotional activity.

At the heart of this marketing activity was the use of the brand positioning perceptual map, the development of a brand positioning statement deemed relevant by the target audience – aspirational young female drivers – and the specification of a detailed action plan. Note, though, that without the clearly thought through action plan, the desired brand positioning would never have been achieved. Marketers must plan their brand positioning strategy but then manage its implementation and roll-out.

© Dibb/Simkin

Sources: Ford; *Elle* magazine; 'Ford Focus Elle – the place to be seen this season' (brochure), Ford GB, August 2002; automotive sources.

Note: the information above, and the interpretation placed upon it, is not the official Ford view and is based on a variety of industry sources. A more extensive explanation of these brand positioning techniques is offered in either *The Market Segmentation Workbook* (Dibb and Simkin) or *The Marketing Planning Workbook* (Dibb, Simkin and Bradley), both originally published in 1996 by Thomson, London, or in the authors' newer titles *Market Segmentation Success: Making It Happen!* (The Haworth Press, 2008) and *Marketing Planning* (Cengage Learning, 2008).

There are various options when determining a positioning:

1 The approach most plausible in terms of the consumer and the most defensible against competitors' marketing ploys is to identify product attributes or features that are superior, desirable and matched by few or no rivals. This is at the heart of the positioning deployed by Bang & Olufsen, BMW and Bosch.
2 The next best option is to identify key benefits encountered as a result of consumption, as illustrated by Anadin's painkiller advertising or Andrew's Salts saving the day from *that* hangover.

If a product has no such distinctions or is lagging behind major rivals, there are other approaches, such as:

3 emphasising specific usage occasions, such as Campbell's soups as a cooking ingredient
4 depicting user groups, as with the Pepsi Generation
5 deliberately adopting a head-to-head positioning against a rival – 'Avis is No. 2, but we try harder' ran for over two decades.

Or, if all else fails:

6 dissociating from direct rivals in order to develop a clear image and differentiation – Dr Pepper and 7 Up both try to persuade the marketplace they are fizzy and refreshing drinks, but not sickly brown colas.

Positioning statement
A plausible, memorable image-enhancing written summation of a product's or brand's desired stature

The final stage in developing a positioning in many instances is the determination of a suitable **positioning statement**, a plausible, memorable image-enhancing written summation of a product's or brand's desired stature. This should strike a chord with the targeted consumers; reflect the nature of the product, its branding and attributes; plus demonstrate to targeted consumers the company's understanding of customer needs – similar to a strapline in advertising. Everest double glazing's positioning statement is decades old, yet instantly recognisable: 'Fit the best, fit Everest'. 'The ultimate driving machine' can only be BMW; 'Because I'm worth it' is L'Oréal; and 'We try harder' is still used by car rental company Avis, as mentioned above. Ultimately, a product or brand positioning must be memorable, plausible and relevant to the target market's perceptions. The intention is to develop a distinctive image for the product or service and, through a well-honed positioning statement, to establish a platform for its effective communication.

Evaluating Markets and Forecasting Sales

Whatever segmentation choices organisations make, measuring the sales potential of the chosen target market or markets is crucial. Moreover, a marketing manager must determine the portion or share of the selected market that the company can capture relative to its objectives, resources and managerial skills, as well as to those of its competitors. Developing and maintaining a marketing mix consumes a considerable amount of a company's resources. Thus the target market or markets selected must have enough sales potential to justify the costs of developing and maintaining one or more marketing mixes.

The potential for sales can be measured along several dimensions, including product, geographic area, time and level of competition.[35] With respect to product, potential sales can be estimated for a specific product item (for example, Diet Coke) or an entire product line (for example, Coca-Cola, Coca-Cola Classic, Diet Coke, Diet Caffeine-Free Coke and Cherry Coca-Cola are one product line). A manager must also determine the geographic area to be included in the estimate. In relation to time, sales potential estimates can be: short range, one year or under; medium range, one to five years; or long range, longer than five years. The competitive level specifies whether sales are being estimated for a single company or for an entire industry. Marketers measure sales potential both for the entire market and for their own companies, and then develop a sales forecast. A target market strategy is incomplete without an appraisal of the likely sales potential and expected levels of sales within the prioritised target market segments.

Summary

Amarket is defined as a group of people who, as consumers or as part of organisations, need and have the ability, willingness and authority to purchase products in a product class. A *consumer market* consists of purchasers and/or those in their households who intend to consume or benefit from the purchased products and who do not buy products for the main purpose of making a profit. A *business market* consists of people and groups who purchase a product for resale, direct use in producing other products or for general day-to-day operations. Because products are classified according to use, the same product may be classified as both a consumer product and an industrial product.

❯❯ At the heart of marketing strategy are the decisions about which opportunities to pursue and which market segments to target. The varying characteristics, needs, wants and interests of customers mean that there are few markets where a single product or service is satisfactory for all.

» Markets made up of individuals with different needs are called *heterogeneous markets*. The *market segmentation* approach divides the total market into smaller groups of customers who have similar product needs and buying characteristics. A *market segment* is a group of individuals, groups or organisations sharing one or more similar characteristics that cause them to have relatively similar product needs.

» Segmentation and the customer understanding underlying it can make it easier for companies to identify and exploit different market opportunities. The approach offers businesses a number of advantages at the customer level, in relation to the competition or in terms of the effectiveness of resource allocation and strategic planning.

» There are three stages to carrying out market segmentation: segmentation, targeting and positioning. Segmentation uses one or more base variables to group similar customers into segments. *Targeting* involves decisions about which and how many customer groups to target. *Positioning* involves deciding precisely how and where within the targeted segments to aim a product or products, brand or brands.

» Marketers must decide how many segmentation variables to use. *Single variable segmentation* involves only one variable, but in *multivariable segmentation*, more than one characteristic is used to divide a total market. The latter is often more meaningful. *One-to-one marketing* involves developing long-term relationships with individual customers in order to understand and satisfy their needs. Although technological advances are making it easier for companies to achieve this goal, this approach involves considerable investment.

» *Segmentation variables or bases* are the dimensions or characteristics of individuals, groups or businesses that are used for dividing a total market into segments. The segmentation variable should be related to customers' needs for, uses of or behaviour towards the product. Consumer segmentation variables can be grouped into four categories: demographics (age, gender, race, ethnicity, income, education, occupation, family size, family life cycle, religion and social class), geographic (population, *market density*, climate), psychographic (personality traits, motives, lifestyles) and behaviouristic (volume usage, end use, expected benefits, brand loyalty, price sensitivity). *Geodemographic segmentation*, which combines geographic and demographic factors, involves clustering people according to postcode areas. Variables for segmenting business markets include demographic factors, operating variables, purchasing approach, situational factors and the personal characteristics of buyers. *Benefit segmentation* is the division of a market according to the benefits consumers want from the product.

» Certain conditions must exist for market segmentation to be effective. First, consumers' needs for the product should be heterogeneous. Second, the segments of the market should be measurable so that the segments can be compared with respect to estimated sales potential, costs and profits. Third, at least one segment must be substantial enough to have the profit potential to justify developing and maintaining a special marketing mix for that segment. Fourth, the company must be able to access the chosen segment with a particular marketing mix. Fifth, the segment should be reasonably stable over time. Sixth, the resulting segmentation scheme must be managerially useful. Customers with dissimilar needs and buying behaviour must not be grouped together in the same market segment.

» *Profiling* segments using *descriptor* variables can help the marketer build up a fuller picture and design a marketing mix (or mixes) that more precisely matches the needs of people in a selected market segment (or segments).

» *Targeting* is the task of prioritising which market segment(s) to address. When a company designs a single marketing mix and directs it at the entire market for a particular product, it is using an *undifferentiated (or total market) approach* as its targeting strategy. Although customers may have similar needs for a few products, for most products their needs are very different. In such instances, a company should use a concentrated or a differentiated strategy. In the *concentration strategy*, an organisation directs its marketing efforts towards a single market segment through one marketing mix. In the *differentiated strategy*, an organisation develops different marketing mixes for two or more market segments. The decisions about which segment or segments to enter are linked to considerations about company resources, expertise and the nature of customers and competitors.

» Having decided which segment or segments to target, the marketer must position the product in order to create a clearly defined image in the minds of its target consumers. The product's positioning must be perceived by its consumers to be different from the positionings of competing products.

Perceptual maps assist marketers in graphically depicting the relative positionings of the products in a particular market. Although a product's attributes and styling, along with its pricing, service levels and channel of distribution, contribute to how consumers perceive the product, a marketer uses mainly promotion to establish a product's positioning. The final stage in developing a positioning is the *positioning statement*, a plausible and memorable written summation of a product's or brand's desired stature.

» Measuring the sales potential of the chosen target market or markets is crucial, as a target market strategy is incomplete without an appraisal of the likely sales potential and expected levels of sales within the prioritised target market segments. This can be measured along several dimensions, including product, geographic area, time and level of competition, as well as at segment level.

❂ *Key Links*

This chapter has explained a core aspect of marketing strategy: target market selection. It should be read in conjunction with:

- Chapter 2's overview of marketing strategy
- The requirement to understand consumers and business customers, as described in Chapters 4 and 5
- Chapter 14's explanation of effective branding
- The analytical tools – notably the directional policy matrix – used for choosing priority target markets, as presented in Chapter 9

Important Terms

Market
Business market
Consumer market
Undifferentiated or total market approach
Heterogeneous markets
Market segmentation
Market segment
Segmentation variables or bases
One-to-one marketing
Single variable segmentation
Multivariable segmentation
Market density
Geodemographic segmentation
Benefit segmentation

Profiling
Descriptors
Targeting
Concentration strategy
Differentiated strategy
Positioning
Perceptual mapping
Positioning statement

Discussion and Review Questions

1 What is a market? What are the requirements for a market?
2 In the area where you live, is there a group of people with unsatisfied product needs who represent a market? Could this market be reached by an organisation? Why or why not?
3 Identify and describe the two major types of market. Give examples of each.
4 What is the total market approach? Under what conditions is it most useful? Describe a current situation in which a company is using a total market approach. Is the business successful? Why or why not?
5 What is the market segmentation approach? Describe the basic conditions required for effective segmentation. Identify several companies that use the segmentation approach.

6 List the differences between concentration and differentiated strategies. Describe the advantages and disadvantages of each strategy.

7 Identify and describe four major categories of base variables that can be used to segment consumer markets. Give examples of product markets that are segmented by variables in each category.

8 What dimensions are used to segment business markets?

9 How do marketers decide whether to use single variable or multivariable segmentation? Give examples of product markets that are divided using multivariable segmentation.

10 Choose a product and discuss how it could best be positioned in the market. Determine a suitable positioning statement.

11 What are the essential stages in developing a positioning?

12 Why must marketers evaluate the sales potential of possible priority target market segments?

Recommended Reading

- Dibb, S. and Simkin, L., *Market Segmentation Success: Making It Happen!* (New York: The Haworth Press, 2008).
- Dibb, S. and Simkin, L., 'Market segmentation: diagnosing and overcoming the segmentation barriers', *Industrial Marketing Management*, 30, 2001, pp. 609–25.
- Dibb, S. and Simkin, L., *The Market Segmentation Workbook* (London: Thomson, 1996).
- Dibb, S. and Wensley, R., 'Segmentation analysis for industrial marketing: problems of integrating customer requirements into operations strategy', *European Journal of Marketing*, 36 (1/2), 2002, pp. 231–51.
- Hooley, G., Saunders, J., Piercy, N.F. and Nicoulaud, B., *Marketing Strategy and Competitive Positioning* (Harlow: Pearson/FT, 2004).
- Hutt, M.D. and Speh, T.W., *Business Marketing Management: A Strategic View of Industrial and Organizational Markets* (Cincinnati, OH: South Western, 2006).
- Keller, K.L., *Building, Measuring and Managing Brand Equity* (Englewood Cliffs, NJ: Pearson, 2007).
- McDonald, M. and Dunbar, I., *Market Segmentation* (London: Palgrave Macmillan, 2004).
- McDonald, M. and Dunbar, I., *Market Segmentation: how to do it, how to profit from it* (Oxford: Elsevier Butterworth-Heinemann, 2004).
- Ries, A. and Trout, J., *Positioning: The Battle for Your Mind* (New York: McGraw-Hill, 2001).
- Stone, M. and Foss, B., *Successful Customer Relationship Marketing: New Thinking, New Strategies, New Tools for Getting Closer to Your Customers* (London: Kogan Page, 2001).
- Webber, H., *Divide and Conquer: Target your Customer through Market Segmentation* (Hoboken, NJ: Wiley, 1998).
- Weinstein, A., *Handbook of Market Segmentation: Strategic Targeting for Business and Technology Firms* (New York: The Haworth Press, 2004).

🌐 Internet Exercise

Voyage is an Internet company that offers a variety of travel and adventure products. Learn more about its goods, services and travel advice through its website at: www.voyageconcepts.co.uk

1 Based on the information provided at the website, what are some of Voyage's basic products?

2 What market segments does Voyage appear to be targeting with its website?

3 What segmentation variables is the company using to segment these markets?

🎲 *Applied Mini-Case*

Banking is not generally perceived as innovative or creative. HSBC's telephone and online bank *first direct* broke the mould when it was launched in the 1980s, and it still strives to be different, as explained on its website:

What it's all about

We've put some thought into banking. We think current accounts are for spending, rather than saving. Which is why we'd rather give you a current account that helps you manage your money on an every day basis. So instead of offering you credit interest, we're giving you more interest on your savings and a package of services which we think offer you better value.

We're here for you 24 hours a day, seven days a week, 365 days a year. You'll get straight through to a real person every time you call. And they'll be ready to help. *First direct* isn't like other banks.

We know you'll prefer banking with us – and if for some reason you don't, we'll help you move to another bank and give you £100.

24 7 365

We're here for you 24 hours a day, 7 days a week, 365 days a year. In fact, ever since we started, more than 18 years ago, we've never closed. So when we say you can give us a call anytime, we really mean it.

Real people, real conversations

You'll always speak to a real person when you call us. No automated routing systems, no punching in numbers on your keypad, no waiting at the tone to say 'yes' or 'no'. Just a friendly voice every time you call.

Sources: *first direct*, November, 2007; http://www.firstdirect.com/1st-account/in-detail.shtml, November, 2007.

❓ *Question*

What is the brand positioning proposition at the heart of *first direct's* marketing strategy? To what extent does this differentiate *first direct* from the other principal banking groups?

🌐 *Case Study*

Ethnic Marketing's Challenge to Mainstream Marketers

Mediaedge:cia is a global media communications specialist, part of the WPP group, with billings of over US$15 billion in 80 countries. The company produced a report in 2003 in conjunction with the UK's Channel 4 television, News International and the Broadcasting Standards Commission, examining how mainstream marketers could better reach the larger ethnic groups – notably Asians and African-Caribbeans – through gaining a deeper insight into the cultural differences that impact on their acceptance of marketing communications.

An important finding from the study was that many advertisers fail to connect with ethnic audiences through perceived stereotyping and tokenism. Too many mainstream brand managers have created an ethnic market segment to sit alongside their core mainstream target markets. Such 'we have an interest in ethnic markets' tokenism fails to reflect that, as in the so-called 'mainstream market', the ethnic market is in fact sub-divided into many groups. This sub-division represents generation, age, language, location, country of origin, and acculturation (the process by which minority groups adapt to the culture of the majority or the mainstream market).

The use of ethnic actors, settings and experiences in advertising is seen as desirable, but not if the advertisement simply draws attention to perhaps false stereotyping, and ultimately fails to strike a chord with either the intended ethnic target audience or the mainstream market also addressed by a particular brand.

The research revealed some interesting challenges for marketers, as described below.

- Asians were typically more up-front in their response to advertising, seeking an instant answer to the questions 'What is being offered?' and 'What is the relevance to me?'

- The impact of mainstream culture varied, too. The family home provides a 'cultural earthing point', either rejecting mainstream culture or deliberately embracing aspects of it, and amalgamating such practices and values with the ethnic group's own culture. Clearly, marketers must understand the extent to which a group of consumers has embraced mainstream values and buying characteristics.

- Some households are a hybrid of media behaviour, viewing mainstream and traditional ethnic broadcast media, while others have either turned their backs on their heritage or have refused to allow mainstream media to enter their households.
- Children tend to be more influenced by mainstream culture and marketing programmes than their parents.
- More so than in many mainstream households, a great deal of consumer decision-making is made at a family level, and there are interesting dynamics between male and female family members.

These variations in attitudes, behaviour and perceptions of mainstream values have important implications for marketers seeking to attract these consumers, make them aware of their products and influence their buying behaviour.

At a time when 'ethnic marketing' is seen as increasingly important by a large number of mainstream brands and retailers, the Mediaedge:cia study also identified a significant gap in the understanding of minority ethnic groups by these marketers and their advertising agency colleagues. Tesco and Lloyds Bank are just two leading brands to have already turned to ethnic marketing. There is no doubt that ethnic marketing will be embraced by ever more mainstream brands, but in so doing, their marketers must properly understand the buying behaviour and decision-making of these important consumers.

Sources: *Ethnic Marketing: 'A Double Edged Sword?'*, Mediaedge:cia, London, March 2003; www.redhotcurry.com/news/ethnic_marketing.htm, March 2004. Lloyds Bank, 2007; Tesco Stores, 2007.

❷ Questions for Discussion

1 Why are mainstream marketers increasingly interested in targeting ethnic markets?
2 Are certain mainstream brands or products more likely to be marketed along these lines? If so, which and why?
3 For a product as ubiquitous as Coca-Cola, does the notion of ethnic marketing present any benefits or potential? Why or why not?

7
Marketing Research

" **The researcher's challenge is not just generating data, but in creating a vision from that data.** "

Dave Birks, University of Bath

Objectives

- To understand the importance of marketing research in marketing decision-making

- To distinguish between research and intuition in solving marketing problems

- To learn the five basic steps of the marketing research process

- To understand the fundamental methods of gathering data for marketing research

- To gain a sense of the relative advantages and disadvantages of marketing research tools

- To understand how tools such as databases, decision support systems and the Internet facilitate marketing research

- To identify key ethical considerations in marketing research

Marketing research
The process of gathering, interpreting and reporting information to help marketers solve specific marketing problems or take advantage of marketing opportunities

Introduction

As the preceding chapters have explained, effective marketing is contingent upon marketers having a clear understanding of customers, competitors, market trends and aspects of the marketing environment. **Marketing research** is the systematic design, collection, interpretation and reporting of information to help marketers solve particular problems or take advantage of marketing opportunities. As the word 'research' implies, it is the process of gathering information not currently available to decision-makers. The purpose of marketing research is to inform an organisation about customers' needs and desires, marketing opportunities for particular goods and services, and changing attitudes and purchase patterns. Detecting shifts in buyers' behaviour and attitudes helps companies stay in touch with the ever-changing marketplace, which often necessitates marketing research.

Opener

P&G and Reactivity

Imagine waking up in the morning, stumbling to the bathroom wash basin, putting Crest toothpaste on your toothbrush and looking up to see the fuzzy reflection of a video camera in the mirror. Maybe you think that you might have signed up for a reality TV show? No, it's just the Procter & Gamble (P&G) research crew you allowed into your home to observe how you perform your daily activities. Although marketing research has traditionally focused on problems that consumers generally recognise, P&G researchers hope this direct observation approach will help them identify and address problems that consumers do not even know they have.

Globally, around one-third of consumers buys products made by US-based P&G. With sales growth of just a few per cent each year, the company hopes to boost its revenues by capitalising on growth opportunities in its overseas markets. To achieve this goal, much of P&G's marketing research effort is now targeted in international markets such as the UK, Italy, Germany and China.

Compared with other research methods, direct observation of consumers provides several benefits. Video clips can be placed on a secure website for viewing by 150 P&G employees. A bigger audience gives the company greater potential for valuable feedback. More problems can be identified and solutions found to address those issues. Direct observation can also generate information that participants might normally forget or choose not to disclose when being interviewed or surveyed. For example, many people say they brush their teeth twice a day because they believe this is the correct and expected response. But the reality is that many people do not brush twice daily. Direct observation of consumers can uncover such information. Another advantage of this approach is that it contributes to the insights gained through the coordinated and integrated research studies it conducts annually or to its existing database of 50,000 studies. Finally, P&G gets global perspectives on the wants and needs of its target market.

This new form of research also has some drawbacks, however – especially in terms of concerns about privacy. Although participants in these studies willingly allow themselves to be videotaped, the company must be careful about what it records, inform any unsuspecting visitors about the recording, and guarantee the videos will only be viewed internally for research purposes. Another issue is reactivity, which occurs when participants modify normal behaviours because they know they are being watched. For example, a participant might increase his or her daily intake of vegetables during the observation period to appear more in line with social norms or expectations. Another drawback is that it is not practical to pore through hours of videotape for just a few clues about human behaviour. Although the information gained may be interesting, not all of it will be relevant. Finally, such research does not guarantee than any product innovation or improved marketing programme will result.

Photo: istockphoto.com

he marketing research conducted by P&G illustrates that to implement marketing concepts, marketers need information about the characteristics, needs and desires of target market customers. When used effectively, such information facilitates the relationship with the customers, by helping organisations focus their efforts on meeting, and even anticipating, the needs of their customers.

This chapter of *Marketing Essentials* begins by defining marketing research and examining its importance. It then analyses the five basic steps of the marketing research process, including various methods of collecting data. This is followed by a review of how technology aids in collecting, organising and interpreting marketing research data. Finally, the ethical aspects of marketing research are considered.

The Importance of Marketing Research

Building an understanding of customers, competitors, market trends and the marketing environment requires that marketers have access to information and marketing intelligence.[1] Sometimes the available information will be judged inadequate to tackle a specific decision or marketing task, in which case marketing research may provide the additional insights required. Such research is generally conducted on a project-by-project basis, with research methods being adapted to the context and problems being studied.

The Market Research Society defines marketing research in the following way:

> The collection and analysis of data from a sample of individuals or organisations relating to their characteristics, behaviour, attitudes, opinions or possessions. It includes all forms of marketing and social research such as consumer and industrial surveys, psychological investigations, observational and panel studies.[2]

The purpose of marketing research is to provide information about customers' needs and desires, marketing opportunities for particular goods and services, and the changing attitudes and purchase patterns of customers. Marketing planning requires marketing research to facilitate the process of assessing opportunities and threats. Marketing research can help a company better understand market opportunities, ascertain the potential for success of new products, and determine the feasibility of a particular marketing strategy. Pizza Hut, for example, conducted research to learn more about its most profitable group of customers: school and college students. The research involved asking a carefully chosen group of 350 students to refrain from eating pizza products for 30 days and record their cravings for pizza and feelings about 'going without' during the study period. One objective was to help better understand the effects of 'pizza deprivation', food cravings and food desires among this attractive market, which may lead to modifications in its marketing strategy.[3]

Marketing intelligence
The composite of all data and ideas available within an organisation, which assists in decision-making

Quantitative research
Research aimed at producing data that can be statistically analysed and whose results can be expressed numerically

Qualitative research
Research that deals with information too difficult or expensive to quantify, such as subjective opinions and value judgements, typically unearthed during interviews or discussion groups

All organisations have some marketing intelligence. **Marketing intelligence** is the composite of all data and ideas available within an organisation – for example, a company or a marketing department that assists in decision-making. Often the available information is deemed inadequate, which may lead to the commissioning of marketing research. There are, broadly, two types of marketing research: quantitative and qualitative.[4] In **quantitative research**, techniques and sample sizes lead to the collection of data that can be statistically analysed and whose results can be expressed numerically. These data tend to come from large surveys, sales data or market forecasts (see Figure 7.1). **Qualitative research** deals with information that is too difficult or expensive to quantify: subjective opinions and value judgements that are not amenable to statistical analysis and quantification,[5] typically unearthed during in-depth interviews or discussion groups.

While some organisations continue to handle their own information needs, others buy in help from outside agencies that specialise in market research. The global marketing and

Figure 7.1
Questionnaires are an integral part of marketing research, often but not exclusively for quantitative studies
Photo: Courtesy of Karen Beaulah

opinion research industry is huge, accounting for over £10 billion (more than €15 billion) and employing more than 650,000 people. With ten countries accounting for more than 80 per cent of the turnover globally, it is also highly competitive and increasingly dominated by international research agencies.[6] Recent growth in the industry highlights marketing research's status as a management tool. Some experts suggest that this is also because the marketing research agencies have worked hard to quantify the effects of their work on business performance.[7]

The Marketing Insight box on page 207 describes the kinds of activities undertaken by VNU, the world's largest marketing research company.

All kinds of organisations use marketing research to help them develop marketing programmes that match the needs of customers or to find out more about their stakeholders' views. The CEO of a large marketing research business recently generalised the categories in which his company received requests for research help. For quantitative studies, these included customer satisfaction surveys, advertising tracking analyses, evaluations of new or modified products, brand awareness studies and customer attitude surveys. For qualitative research, the main categories were customer attitude and satisfaction studies, followed by concept testing (new products or new brand identities). After these came the testing of advertisements, packaging concepts and promotional offers.

As managers recognise the benefits of marketing research, they assign it a much greater role in decision-making. For example, Japanese managers, who put much more faith in

✪ Marketing Insight

The World's Largest Marketing Research Company

Publishing company VNU Inc., founded in the Netherlands in 1964, became the largest marketing research business after acquiring ACNielsen and Nielsen Media in 2001. Originally called Verenigde Nederlandse Uitgeversbedrijven (United Dutch Publishers), the company now serves clients in more than 100 countries, answering questions such as 'What is happening in the marketplace?', 'Why is it happening?', 'What will happen next?' and 'What is the best way to grow my business?' In 2006, VNU was acquired and taken private by a consortium of six private equity firms and in 2007, VNU changed its name to *The Nielsen Company*.

Through ACNielsen, the corporation provides retail measurement information on competitive sales volume, market share, distribution, pricing, merchandising and promotional activities to manufacturers and retailers of fast-moving consumer goods. Its consumer panel services provide marketers with insights based on actual consumer purchase information for more than 155,000 households in 22 countries. To provide customised research services in more than 60 countries, ACNielsen conducts hundreds of thousands of customer surveys, interviews and focus groups every year in order to offer its clients greater understanding of consumer attitudes and purchase behaviour. The company's modelling and analytical services integrate and analyse information from a variety of sources to improve marketing decisions on pricing, promotion, product, and media use and placement.

Although most marketing businesses rely on outside sources such as ACNielsen to gain insight into key marketing questions, it is crucial that marketing managers know what questions to ask and are able to recognise effective marketing research and information system development. It is important that companies acquire the data that provide the insights necessary to develop effective marketing strategies. The marketing research conducted by ACNielsen enables marketers to implement the marketing concept by helping them acquire information about the characteristics, needs and desires of target market customers. When used effectively, such information facilitates relationship marketing by helping marketers focus their efforts on meeting, and even anticipating, the needs of their customers.

Sources: 'VNU Inc.', *Marketing News*, 9 June 2003, pp. H6–H8; 'Insights into today's global customers', VNU, www.vnu.com/vnu/page.jsp?id=104 (accessed 20 December 2003); 'A leading information and media company', VNU, www.vnu.com/vnu/page.jsp?id=84 (accessed 20 December 2003); VNU corporation, 2006; http://www2.acnielsen.com/company/history.shtml (accessed 27 November 2007).

Intuition
The personal knowledge and past experience on which marketing managers may base decisions

Scientific decision-making
An orderly and logical approach to gathering information

information they get directly from wholesalers and retailers, are beginning to grasp the importance of consumer surveys and scientific methods of marketing research as they seek ways to diversify their companies.[8]

The increase in marketing research activities represents a transition from intuitive to scientific problem-solving. In relying on **intuition**, marketing managers base decisions on personal knowledge and past experience. However, in **scientific decision-making**, managers take an orderly and logical approach to gathering information. They seek facts on a systematic basis, and they apply methods other than trial and error or generalisation from experience. This does not mean that intuition has no value in marketing decision-making; successful decisions blend both research and intuition. Consider an extreme example. A marketing research study conducted for Xerox Corporation in the late 1950s indicated a very limited market for an automatic photocopier. Xerox management judged that the researchers had drawn the wrong conclusions from the study, and they decided to launch the product anyway. That product, the Xerox 914 copier, was an instant success. An immediate backlog of orders developed, and the rest is history. Although the Xerox example is certainly an extreme one, by and large a proper blend of research and intuition offers the best formula for a correct decision. Table 7.1 distinguishes between the roles of research and intuition in decision-making.

TABLE 7.1 DISTINCTIONS BETWEEN RESEARCH AND INTUITION IN MARKETING DECISION-MAKING

	Research	Intuition
Nature	Formal planning, predicting based on a scientific approach	Preference based on personal feelings or 'gut instinct'
Methods	Logic, systematic methods, statistical inference	Experience and demonstration
Contributions	General hypotheses for making predictions, classifying relevant variables, carrying out systematic description and classification	Minor problems solved quickly through consideration of experience, practical consequences
Situation	High risk decision-making involving high costs, investment, strategic change or long-term effects	Low-risk problem solving and decision-making

Despite the obvious value of formal research, marketing decisions are often made without it. Certainly, minor, low-risk problems that must be dealt with at once can and should be handled on the basis of personal judgement and common sense. If good decisions can be made with the help of currently available information, costly formal research may be superfluous. However, as the financial, social or ethical risks increase or the possible courses of action multiply, full-scale research as a prerequisite for marketing decision-making becomes both desirable and rewarding.

Marketing research improves a marketer's ability to make decisions. Marketers should treat information in the same manner as other resources utilised by the company, and they must weigh the costs of obtaining information against the benefits derived. Information is worthwhile if it results in marketing activities that better satisfy the needs of the company's target markets, leads to increased sales and profits, or helps the company achieve some other goal.

The Marketing Research Process

To maintain the control needed for obtaining accurate information, marketers approach marketing research in logical steps, as follows (see Figure 7.2):

1 locating and defining problems or research issues
2 designing the research
3 collecting data
4 analysing and interpreting research findings
5 reporting research findings.

These five steps should be viewed as an overall approach to conducting research rather than a rigid set of rules to be followed in each project. In planning research projects, marketers must think about each of the steps and how they can best be adjusted for each particular problem.

Figure 7.2
The five steps of the marketing research process

Step 1: Locating and Defining Problems or Research Issues

Problem definition
The process of uncovering the nature and boundaries of a situation or question

The first step in launching a research study is **problem definition**, which focuses on uncovering the nature and boundaries of a situation or question related to marketing strategy or implementation. The first sign of a problem is usually a departure from some normal function, such as failures to attain objectives. If a company's objective is a 12 per cent return on investment and the current return is 6 per cent, this discrepancy should be analysed to help guide future marketing strategies. Decreasing sales, increasing expenses or decreasing profits also signal problems. Conversely, when an organisation experiences a dramatic rise in sales, or some other positive event, it may conduct marketing research to discover the reasons and maximise the opportunities stemming from them.

To pin down the specific boundaries of a problem or an issue through research, marketers must define the nature and scope of the problem in a way that requires probing beneath

Figure 7.3
Many marketing research agencies, data analysis houses and marketing services businesses support marketers
Source: Courtesy of jra research

Whatever your research brief, you can rely on jra for dazzling results everytime. Tried and tested by 100's of top UK brands.

Call Paul Summers on
0115 9551133
or email paul@jraresearch.com

Victoria Court
Kent Street
Nottingham NG1 3LZ
Tel: 01159551133
Fax: 01159537077
www.jraresearch.com

the superficial symptoms. The interaction between the marketing manager and the marketing researcher should yield a clear definition of the problem. Researchers and decision-makers should remain in the problem definition stage until they have determined precisely what they want from the research and how they will use it. Deciding how to refine a broad, indefinite problem into a clearly defined and researchable statement is a prerequisite for the next step in planning the research: the design phase.

Step 2: Designing the Research

Research design
An overall plan for obtaining the information needed to address a research problem or issue

Once the problem or issue has been defined, the next step is **research design**, an overall plan for obtaining the information needed to address it. This step requires detailed research objectives or hypotheses to be formulated, and the most appropriate type of research to be designed to ensure that the results are reliable and valid.

Developing Research Objectives and Hypotheses

Research objective
The desired outcome from the marketing research project being undertaken

Hypothesis
An informed guess or assumption about a certain problem or set of circumstances

A clear statement of research objectives plays an important part in guiding a research project. A **research objective** is the desired outcome from the marketing research project being undertaken. Sometimes researchers develop hypotheses that may be drawn both from previous research and expected research findings. A **hypothesis** is an informed guess or assumption about a certain problem or set of circumstances. It is based on all the insight and knowledge available about the problem from previous research studies and other sources. As information is gathered, a researcher can test the hypothesis. For example, a food manufacturer such as Kellogg's might propose the hypothesis that children today have more influence than those of previous generations on their families' buying decisions with regard to breakfast cereals and other grocery products. A marketing researcher would then gather data, perhaps through surveys of children and their parents, and draw conclusions as to whether or not the hypothesis was correct.

Supermarkets worried about shoplifting would be interested in the findings of research showing that 40 per cent of supermarket managers surveyed reported cigarettes and alcohol as their most frequently shoplifted items. If a supermarket manager had hypothesised that other products, such as confectionery, were more susceptible to shoplifting, the research would lead this individual to reject that hypothesis. Sometimes several hypotheses are developed during the actual study; the hypotheses that are accepted or rejected become the study's chief conclusions.

Types of Research

Exploratory research
Deliberately flexible data gathering used to discover the general nature of a problem and the factors that relate to it

The research objectives and any hypotheses being tested determine the approach to be used for gathering data. When marketers need more information about a problem or want to make a tentative hypothesis more specific, they may conduct **exploratory research**. Exploratory studies discover the general nature of a problem and the factors that relate to it. The design is deliberately flexible.[9] For instance, this kind of research may involve reviewing the information in the company's own records or examining publicly available data. Questioning knowledgeable people inside and outside the organisation may also yield new insights into the problem. Information available on the Internet about industry trends or demographics may also be an excellent source for exploratory research. For example, information on the buying power of different ethnic groups is readily available through this source.

Descriptive research
Data collection that focuses on providing an accurate description of the variables in a situation

If marketers need to understand the characteristics of certain phenomena to solve a particular problem, **descriptive research** can aid them. Descriptive studies focus on providing an accurate description of the variables in a situation. Such studies may range from general surveys of consumers' education, occupation or age to specifics on how many pairs of sports shoes individuals purchase each year. For example, if Nike and Reebok wanted to target more young women, they might ask 15–34-year-old females how often they work out, how often they buy sports footwear and whether they wear them for casual use.

Descriptive studies generally demand much prior knowledge and assume that the problem is clearly defined. The marketers' major task is to choose adequate methods of collecting and measuring data.

Hypotheses about causal relationships call for a more complex approach than a descriptive study. In **causal research**, it is assumed that a particular variable X causes a variable Y. Marketers must plan the research so that the data collected prove or disprove that X causes Y. To do so, marketers must try to hold constant all variables except X and Y. For example, to find out whether new carpeting, curtains and ceiling fans increase the leasing rate in a block of flats, marketers need to keep all variables constant except the new furnishings and the leasing rate. Table 7.2 compares the features of these types of research study.

Causal research
Data collection that assumes that a particular variable X causes a variable Y

Research Reliability and Validity

Reliability
The quality of producing almost identical results in successive repeated trials

Validity
A condition that exists when an instrument measures what it is supposed to measure

In designing research, marketing researchers must ensure that their research techniques are both reliable and valid. A research technique has **reliability** if it produces almost identical results in successive repeated trials. But a reliable technique is not necessarily valid. To have **validity**, the method must measure what it is supposed to measure, not something else. A valid research method provides data that can be used to test the hypothesis being investigated. For example, although a group of customers may express the same level of satisfaction based on a rating scale, the individuals may not exhibit the same repurchase behaviour because of different personal characteristics. This result might cause the researcher to question the validity of the satisfaction scale if the purpose of rating satisfaction was to estimate repurchase behaviour.[10]

Step 3: Collecting Data

The next step in the marketing research process is collecting data to satisfy research objectives and to help prove (or disprove) research hypotheses. The research design must specify what types of data to collect and how they will be collected.

Types of Data

Primary data
Information gathered by observing phenomena or surveying respondents

Secondary data
Information compiled inside or outside the organisation for some purpose other than the current investigation

Marketing researchers have two types of data at their disposal. **Primary data** are observed and recorded or collected directly from respondents. This type of data must be gathered by observing phenomena or surveying respondents. **Secondary data** are compiled inside or outside the organisation for some purpose other than the current investigation. Secondary data include general reports supplied to an enterprise by various data services. Such reports might concern market share, retail inventory levels and consumer buying

TABLE 7.2 COMPARISON OF DATA-GATHERING APPROACHES

Project Component	Exploratory Studies	Descriptive or Causal Studies
Purpose	Provide general insights	Confirm insights, Verify hypotheses
Data sources	Ill-defined	Well defined
Collection form	Open-ended	Structured
Sample	Small	Large
Collection procedure	Flexible	Rigid
Data analysis	Informal	Formal
Recommendations	Tentative	Conclusive

Source: A. Parasuraman, *Marketing Research*, p. 122, © 1986. Reprinted by permission.

behaviour. Figure 7.4 illustrates how primary and secondary sources differ. Secondary data are generally already available in private or public reports, or have been collected and stored by the organisation itself. Because secondary data are already available – 'second hand' – to save time and money they should be examined prior to the collection of any primary data. Clearly, primary data collection is bespoke and therefore both time-consuming and costly. For relatively straightforward problems, secondary data may prove adequate. More complex or risky situations may require specific primary data collection. Figure 7.5 reveals how Wegener promotes its data analysis services.

Sources of Secondary Data

Marketers often begin the marketing research process by gathering secondary data. They may use available reports and other information from both internal and external sources to study a marketing problem.

Internal sources of secondary data can contribute tremendously to research. An organisation's own databases may contain information about past marketing activities, such as sales records and research reports, that can be used to test hypotheses and pinpoint problems. From sales reports, for example, a company may be able to determine not only which product sold best at certain times of the year, but also which colours and sizes were preferred. Such information may have been gathered for management or financial purposes.[11] Table 7.3 reveals some commonly available internal company information that may be useful for marketing research purposes.

An organisation's accounting records and feedback available from any service function are excellent sources of data that are often overlooked. This is partly because the volumes

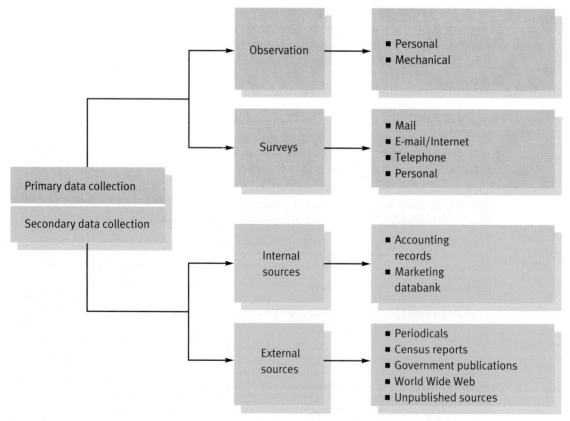

Figure 7.4
Approaches to collecting data

Figure 7.5
A business-to-business advertisement for Wegener's data collection, data analysis and data modelling services
Source: Courtesy of Wegener DM

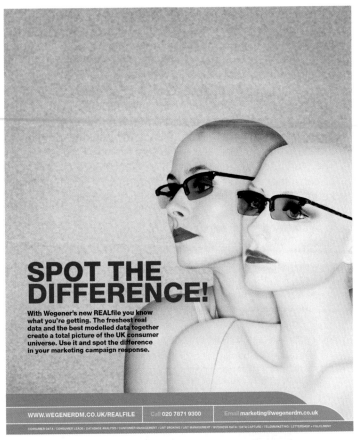

SPOT THE DIFFERENCE!

With Wegener's new REALfile you know what you're getting. The freshest real data and the best modelled data together create a total picture of the UK consumer universe. Use it and spot the difference in your marketing campaign response.

WWW.WEGENERDM.CO.UK/REALFILE   Call 020 7871 9300   Email marketing@wegenerdm.co.uk

CONSUMER DATA / CONSUMER LEADS / DATABASE ANALYSIS / CUSTOMER MANAGEMENT / LIST BROKING / LIST MANAGEMENT / BUSINESS DATA / DATA CAPTURE / TELEMARKETING / LETTERSHOP / FULFILMENT

weɡeneʀ DM

TABLE 7.3 INTERNAL SOURCES OF SECONDARY DATA	
Sales data taken from periodic sales reports	The frequency with which this information is updated will vary for different organisations and industry sectors. However, the increasing use of technology to monitor sales is leading to improvements in the quality and availabiliy of such data.
Customer feedback gathered by the salesforce or services functions	In addition to sales information, the salesforce is in a position to provide other data on customer views and preferences. The service functions of many organisations also have access to a range of customer feedback. Organisations with systems in place for capturing and managing these data are more likely to be able to take advantage of such insights.
Accounting information	This can include detailed data on sales, expenses and profit levels in different product categories.
Competitive information collected by the salesforce	Through contact with customers and by attending sales-related events, such as trade shows, the salesforce is often in a position to accumulate information about competitors, their product portfolios and strategies.

of data that these departments collect may not automatically flow to the marketing area. As a result, detailed information about costs, sales, customer accounts or profits by product category may not be part of the marketing information system (MIS) (see page 225). This situation occurs particularly in organisations that do not store marketing information on a systematic basis.

External sources of secondary data include periodicals, census reports, government publications, the Internet and unpublished sources. Periodicals such as *Investors' Chronicle*, *Marketing*, *Campaign*, *Marketing Week*, *Wall Street Journal* and *Fortune* print general information that is helpful for defining problems and developing hypotheses. Business Monitor contains sales data for major industries. Mintel publishes sector reports. The World Advertising Research Center's *Marketing Pocket Books* are an excellent source of consumer, market, media and product information for national and international marketing. Table 7.4 summarises the major external sources of secondary data, excluding syndicated services.

Syndicated data services periodically collect general information, which they sell to clients. BARB, for example, supplies television stations and media buyers with estimates of

Syndicated data services
Organisations that collect general information and sell it to clients

TABLE 7.4 GUIDE TO EXTERNAL SOURCES OF SECONDARY DATA	
Trade Journals	Virtually every industry or type of business has a trade journal. These journals give a feel for the industry – its size, degree of competition, range of companies involved and problems. To find trade journals in the field of interest, check *The Source Book*, a reference book that lists periodicals by subject.
Trade Associations	Almost every industry, product category and profession has its own association. Depending on the strength of each group, they often conduct research, publish journals, conduct training sessions and hold conferences. A telephone call or a letter to the association may yield information not available in published sources.
International Sources	Periodical indices, such as *Anbar*, are particularly useful for overseas product or company information. More general sources include the *United Nations Statistical Yearbook* and the *International Labour Organisation's Yearbook of Labour Statistics*.
Commercial Sources	Market survey/report organisations produce many sector reports and analyses of companies or brands, for example, *Verdict, Mintel, Kompass, The Times 1000, Key British Enterprises*.
Governments	Governments, through their various departments and agencies, collect, analyse and publish statistics on practically everything. Government documents also have their own set of indices. A useful index for government generated information in the UK is the government's weekly *British Business*.
Books in Print (BIP)	*BIP* is a several volume reference book found in most libraries. All books issued by publishers and currently in print are listed by subject, title and author.
Periodical Indices	Library reference sections contain indices on virtually every discipline. *ABI Inform (Pro-Quest)*, for example, indexes each article in all major periodicals.
Computerised Literature Retrieval Databases	Literature retrieval databases are periodical indices stored on computer disks. Books and dissertations are also included. Key words (such as the name of a subject) are used to search a database and generate references. Examples include *Textline, Harvest* and *Pro-Quest*.
WWW pages	Many companies have established 'home pages' on the Internet's World Wide Web for disseminating information on their products and activities.

the number of viewers at specific times. SAMI furnishes monthly information that describes market shares for specific types of manufacturer. ACNielsen provides retail tracking and other data. This information includes total sales in a product category, sales of clients' own brands and sales of important competing brands.

Another type of secondary data, which is available for a fee, is demographic analysis. Companies, such as CACI or Experian (formerly CCN), that specialise in demographic databanks have special knowledge and sophisticated computer systems to work with the very complex census databanks. These were explored in Chapter 6. As a result, they are able to respond to specialised requests. Such information may be valuable in tracking demographic changes that have implications for consumer behaviour and the targeting of products.[12]

Primary Data Collection Methods

The collection of primary data is a more lengthy, expensive and complex process than the collection of secondary data. To gather primary data, researchers use sampling procedures, survey methods, observation and experimentation. These efforts can be handled in-house by the company's own research personnel or contracted out to private research businesses such as Taylor Nelson Sofres, Millward Brown UK or Research International.

Population
All elements, units or individuals that are of interest to researchers for a specific study

Sample
A limited number of units chosen to represent the characteristics of a total population

Sampling
The selection of representative units from a total population

Probability sampling
Every element in the population has a known chance of being selected for study

Random sampling
A sampling method in which all the units in a population have an equal chance of appearing in the sample

Stratified sampling
A sampling method in which the population of interest is divided according to a common characteristic or attribute; a probability sampling is then conducted within each group

Sampling   Because the time and resources available for research are limited, it is almost impossible to investigate all the members of a target market or other population. A **population**, or 'universe', comprises all elements, units or individuals that are of interest to researchers for a specific study. A **sample** is a limited number of units chosen to represent the characteristics of a total population. For example, if a Gallup poll is designed to predict the results of an election, all the registered voters in the country would constitute the population. A representative national sample of several thousand registered voters would be selected in the Gallup poll to project the probable voting outcome. The projection would be based on the assumption that no major political events would occur before the election. The objective of **sampling** in marketing research, therefore, is to select representative units from a total population. Sampling procedures allow marketers to predict buyer behaviour fairly accurately on the basis of responses from the representative portion of the population of interest. Most types of marketing research employ sampling techniques.

There are two basic types of sampling: probability sampling and non-probability sampling. With **probability sampling**, every element in the population being studied has a known chance of being selected for study. Random sampling is basic probability sampling. When marketers employ **random sampling**, all the units in a population have an equal chance of appearing in the sample. The various events that can occur have an equal or known chance of taking place. For example, a specific playing card in a pack has a 1/52 probability of being drawn at any one time. Sample units are ordinarily chosen by selecting from a table of random numbers which have been statistically generated so that each digit, from zero to nine, will have an equal probability of occurring in each position in the sequence. The sequentially numbered elements of a population are sampled randomly by selecting the units whose numbers appear in the table of random numbers.

Another kind of probability sampling is **stratified sampling**, in which the population of interest is divided into groups according to a common characteristic or attribute, and a probability sampling is then conducted within each group. Employing a stratified sample may reduce some of the error that could occur as a result of using a simple random sample. By ensuring that each major group or segment of the population receives its proportionate share of sample units, investigators avoid including too many or too few sample units from each stratum. Usually, samples are stratified when researchers believe that there may be variations among different types of respondent. For example, many political opinion surveys are stratified by sex, race and age.

215

Area sampling
A sampling method that involves selecting a probability sample of geographic areas and selecting units or individuals within the selected areas for the sample

Area sampling, a variation of stratified sampling, involves two stages:

1 selecting a probability sample of geographic areas, such as streets, census tracts or census enumeration districts

2 selecting units or individuals within the selected geographic areas for the sample.

To select the units or individuals within the geographic areas, researchers may choose every nth house or unit, or they may adopt random selection procedures to pick out a given number of units or individuals from a total listing within the selected geographic areas. Area sampling may be used when a complete list of the population is not available.

Quota sampling
A sampling method in which the final choice of respondents is left to the interviewers, who base their choices on two or three variables (such as age, sex and education)

In **quota sampling**, researchers divide the population into groups and then arbitrarily choose participants from each group. A study of consumers who wear glasses, for example, may be conducted by interviewing any person who wears glasses. In quota sampling, there are some controls—usually limited to two or three variables such as age, sex and education – over the selection of respondents. The controls attempt to ensure that representative categories of respondents are interviewed. Because quota samples are not probability samples, not everyone has an equal chance of being selected and sampling error therefore cannot be measured statistically. Quota samples are used most often in exploratory studies, in which hypotheses are being developed. Often a small quota sample will not be projected to the total population, although the findings may provide valuable insights into a problem. A probability sample used to study people allergic to cats would be highly inefficient.

Survey methods
Interviews by mail, telephone, web and personal interviews

Survey Methods   Marketing researchers often employ sampling to collect primary data through mail, telephone, online or personal interview surveys. Selection of a **survey method** depends on the nature of the problem, the data needed to satisfy the research objectives and any hypotheses, and the resources, such as funding and personnel, that are available to the researcher. Table 7.5 illustrates the current breakdown of research budgets across the different techniques in Great Britain.

Gathering information through surveys is increasingly difficult because respondent rates are declining. Many people believe that responding to surveys takes too long and have become fatigued by the frequency with which they are asked to become involved in such studies. The unethical use of 'sugging' ('selling under the guise of marketing research', i.e. sales techniques disguised as market surveys) has also contributed to decreased respondent cooperation, while Internet surveys have been affected by concerns about spam (junk e-mails).

Mail surveys
Questionnaires sent by mail to respondents, who are encouraged to complete and return them

In a **mail survey**, questionnaires are sent by mail to respondents, who are encouraged to complete and return them. Mail surveys are used most often when the individuals chosen for questioning are spread over a wide area and funds for the survey are limited. A mail survey is the least expensive survey method as long as the response rate is high enough to produce reliable results. The main disadvantages of mail surveys are the possibility of a low response rate or of misleading results, if respondents are significantly different from the population being sampled.

Researchers can boost response rates in mail surveys by offering respondents an incentive to return the questionnaire. Incentives and follow-ups have consistently been found to increase response rates. On the other hand, promises of anonymity, special appeals for cooperation and questionnaire length have no apparent impact on the response rate. Other techniques for increasing the response rate, such as advance notification, personalisation of survey materials, type of postage, corporate or university sponsorship, or foot-in-the-door techniques, have had mixed results, varying according to the population surveyed.[13] Although such techniques may help increase the response rates, they can introduce

TABLE 7.5 BREAKDOWN OF RESEARCH BUDGETS ACROSS THE DIFFERENT TECHNIQUES IN THE UK

Expenditure on Market Research

Estimated value of commercially available research in the UK:

	2002	2003	2004	2005	2006
£m	1,189	1,222	1,288	1,321	1,353
Yr-on-yr % change	2.6	2.8	5.4	2.5	2.4

Total revenue by client sector, 2006

	% of total		% of total
Media	8.1	Other consumer goods & services	5.0
Transport, travel & tourism	4.0	Government & public services	15.6
Non-OTC pharmaceutical	9.7	IT/telecomes & consumer technology	8.9
Vehicle manufacturers	4.5	Retailing (incl. mail order)	3.7
Food & beverages	10.7	Financial services	7.9
Other FMCG	16.4	Business goods & services	5.6

Quantitative revenue by data collection method, 2006

	%[2]		%[3]
Face-to-face[1]	31.6	Non-internet access panel	1.1
Telephone	22.7	Other web/internet[2]	7.6
Continuous panel (internet based)	0.6	Postal/other paper self completion[2]	7.8
Continuous panel (non-internet)	13.7	Mystery customer/observation	3.3
Internet based access panel	8.3	Other quantative data collection method	3.3

Notes: [1]Including self completion recruitment. [2]No interviewer involvement. [3]Percentages are of quantative revenue only, which accounts for 80% of total revenue.
Sources: MRS *Annual Survey of UK Market Research Industry*, published with permission from MRS (The Market Research Society); *The Marketing Pocket Book*, published by the World Advertising Research Center, Henley-on-Thames, 2008.

Mail panels
Groups of consumers selected to represent a market or market segment, who agree to be interviewed regularly by mail

Consumer purchase diaries
A marketing research tool in which consumers record their purchases

sample composition bias, or non-response bias, which results when those responding to a survey differ in some important respect from those not responding to the survey. In other words, response-enhancing techniques may alienate some people in the sample and appeal to others, making the results non-representative of the population of interest. Organisations devote relatively little funding to mail surveys.

Premiums or incentives encouraging respondents to return questionnaires have been effective in developing panels of respondents who are interviewed by mail on a regular basis. **Mail panels** of consumers selected to represent a market or market segment are especially useful for evaluating new products, providing general information about consumers and providing records of consumers' purchases. Many companies use consumer mail panels; others use **consumer purchase diaries**. These surveys are similar to mail panels, but consumers keep track of purchases only. Consumer mail panels and consumer purchase diaries are much more widely used than mail surveys, but they do have shortcomings. Research indicates that the people who take the time to fill out a consumer purchase diary have a higher income and are better educated than the general population. If researchers include less well-educated consumers in the panel, they must risk poorer response rates.[14]

Telephone surveys
Surveys in which respondents' answers to a questionnaire are recorded by interviewers on the phone

Telephone surveys, where respondents' answers to a questionnaire are recorded by interviewers on the phone, are widely used by businesses. A telephone survey has some advantages over a mail survey. The rate of response is higher because it takes less effort to answer the telephone and talk than to fill out a questionnaire and return it. If there are enough interviewers, telephone surveys can be conducted very quickly. Thus they can be used by political candidates or organisations seeking an immediate reaction to an event. In addition, this survey technique permits interviewers to develop a rapport with respondents and ask some probing questions.

Telephone interviews also have drawbacks, especially as a large proportion of the population is becoming increasingly unwilling to become involved. Furthermore, these interviews are limited to oral communication; visual aids or observation cannot be included. Interpreters of results must make adjustments for subjects who are not at home or who do not have telephones. Many households are excluded from the telephone directory. Others use answering machines, voicemail or caller ID to screen or block calls. Researchers seeking business respondents can also face non-response problems, particularly as secretaries frequently 'gatekeep' calls, preventing researchers from talking to their targets.

Telephone surveys, like mail and personal interview surveys, are sometimes used to develop panels of respondents who can be interviewed repeatedly to measure changes in attitudes or behaviour. Reliance on such panels is increasing.

Computer-assisted telephone interviewing
A survey method that integrates questionnaire, data collection and tabulations, and provides data to aid decision-makers in the shortest time possible

Computer-assisted telephone interviewing integrates questionnaire, data collection and tabulations, and provides data to aid decision-makers in the shortest time possible. Questionnaire responses are entered on a terminal keyboard, or the interviewer can use a light-pen (a pen-shaped torch) to record a response on a light-sensitive screen. On the most advanced devices, the interviewer merely points to the appropriate response on a touch-sensitive screen with his or her finger. Open-ended responses can be typed on the keyboard or recorded with paper and pencil. This kind of interviewing saves time and facilitates monitoring the progress of interviews. Because data are available as soon as they are entered into the system, interim results can be retrieved quickly. With some systems, a laptop computer may be taken to off-site locations for use in data analysis. Some researchers believe that computer-assisted telephone interviewing is less expensive than conventional paper and pencil methods.[15]

Online survey
Questionnaires that are sent to an individual's e-mail account or that are available over the Internet or via a website

Online surveys have evolved as an alternative to telephone surveys. In an **online survey** questionnaires can be transmitted to respondents who have agreed to be contacted and have provided their e-mail addresses. Because e-mail is semi-interactive, recipients can ask for clarification of specific questions or pose questions of their own. The fact that the data are instantly available in electronic format also eases the process of data entry. The potential advantages of e-mail surveys are quick response and lower costs than traditional mail and telephone surveys. However, these advantages cannot yet be fully realised because of limited access to some respondents. In general, though, the opportunities for using e-mail and the Internet to collect data are increasing significantly, especially as companies are pooling their e-contact lists and some are selling their e-lists to third parties. There has also been a growth in surveying by SMS via people's mobile phones.

Personal interview survey
Face-to-face situation in which the researcher meets the consumer and questions him or her about a specific topic

In a **personal interview survey**, participants respond to questions face to face.[16] Various audio-visual aids – pictures, products, diagrams or pre-recorded advertising copy – can be incorporated into a personal interview. Rapport gained through direct interaction usually permits more in-depth interviewing, including probes, follow-up questions or psychological tests. In addition, because personal interviews can be longer, they can yield more information. Finally, respondents can be selected more carefully, and reasons for non-response can be explored. A **depth interview** is a lengthy, one-to-one structured interview examining a consumer's views about a product in detail.

The object of a **focus group interview** is to observe group interaction when members are exposed to an idea or concept. Focus groups are frequently held in viewing facilities, as illustrated in Figure 7.6. Often these interviews are conducted informally, without a structured questionnaire, in small groups of 8 to 12 people. Consumer attitudes, behaviour, lifestyles, needs and desires can be explored in a flexible and creative manner through this widely used technique (see Chapter 4). Questions are open-ended and stimulate consumers to answer in their own words. Researchers can ask probing questions to clarify something they do not fully understand, or something unexpected and interesting that may help to explain consumer behaviour.

When Cadbury's used information obtained from focus groups to change its advertising and to test product concepts, the new advertisements and product launches pushed up sales.[17] The Case Study at the end of this chapter describes focus group research. Focus group interviews usually start with a general discussion, which will be led by a researcher or moderator. The conversation is then narrowed during the course of the session, enabling the moderator to home in on a specific brand, product or advertisement – hence the term 'focus' group.

Figure 7.6
Primary data collection. Viewing facilities are often used for experiments or for conducting focus group interviews
Photo: Courtesy of West Midlands Viewing Facility

Depth interview
A lengthy, one-to-one structured interview, examining in detail a consumer's views about a product

Focus group interview
A survey method that aims to observe group interaction when members are exposed to an idea or concept

Quali-depth interviews
25- to 30-minute intercept interviews that incorporate some of the in-depth advantages of focus group interviews with the speed and flexibility of shopping mall/pavement intercept interviews

Quali-depth interviews are 25- to 30-minute intercept interviews that incorporate some of the in-depth advantages of focus group interviews with the speed and flexibility of shopping mall/pavement intercept interviews (see below). Typically, intercepted consumers are taken to a nearby hall or café and asked more probing and searching questions than is possible in a three- to four-minute shopping mall/pavement intercept interview. They can also be shown a greater variety of stimulus material. This is a useful approach for sensitive issues that people might not wish to discuss in a group – gambling and drugs, for example.

Another research technique is the **in-home interview**. Because it may be desirable to eliminate group influence, the in-home interview offers a clear advantage when thoroughness of self-disclosure is important. In an in-depth interview of 45 to 90 minutes, respondents can be probed to reveal their real motivations, feelings, behaviours and aspirations. In-depth interviews permit the discovery of emotional 'hot buttons' that provide psychological insights.[18] Door-to-door interviews last only a few minutes and are similar to pavement intercepts.

The nature of personal interviews has changed. In the past, most personal interviews, which were based on random sampling or pre-arranged appointments, were conducted in the respondent's home. Today, most personal interviews are conducted in shopping centres or malls, or on pavements. **Shopping mall/pavement intercept interviews** involve interviewing a percentage of people who pass by certain 'intercept' points in a shopping centre or pavement. Like any face-to-face interviewing method, shopping mall/pavement intercept interviewing has many advantages. The interviewer is in a position to recognise and react to respondents' non-verbal indications of confusion. Respondents can be shown product prototypes, videotapes of advertisements and the like, and reactions can be

In-home interview
45- to 90-minute interview in which the researcher visits the respondent in his or her home

Shopping mall/ pavement intercept interviews
Personal interviewing of a percentage of individuals who pass by certain 'intercept' points in a shopping centre or on a pavement

On-site computer interviewing
A survey method that requires respondents to complete a self-administered questionnaire displayed on a computer monitor

Questionnaire
Base document for research purposes, providing the questions and structure for an interview or self-completion, and providing space for respondents' answers

sought. The environment lets the researcher deal with complex situations. For example, in taste tests, researchers know that all the respondents are reacting to the same product, which can be prepared and monitored from the shopping centre's test kitchen or some other facility. In addition, lower cost, greater control and the ability to conduct tests requiring bulky equipment make shopping mall/pavement intercept interviews popular.

Research indicates that given a comparable sample of respondents, shopping mall/pavement intercept interviewing is a suitable substitute for telephone interviewing.[19] In addition, there seem to be no significant differences in the completeness of consumer responses between telephone interviewing and shopping mall/pavement intercept interviewing. In fact, for questions dealing with socially desirable behaviour, shopping mall/pavement intercept respondents appear to be more honest about their past behaviour.[20]

In **on-site computer interviewing**, a variation of the shopping mall/pavement intercept interview, respondents complete a self-administered questionnaire displayed on a computer monitor. A computer software package can be used to conduct such interviews in shopping centres. After a brief lesson on how to operate the software, respondents can go through the survey at their own pace. Questionnaires can be adapted so that respondents see only those items that may provide useful information about their attitudes.[21]

Questionnaire Construction   A carefully constructed questionnaire is essential to the success of any survey. A **questionnaire** is a base document for research purposes that provides the questions and the structure for an interview or self-completion, and has provision for respondents' answers.[22] Questions must be designed to elicit information that meets the study's data requirements. These questions must be clear, easy to understand and directed towards a specific objective. Researchers need to define the objective before trying to develop a questionnaire because the objective determines the substance of the questions and the amount of detail. A common mistake in constructing questionnaires is to ask questions that interest the researchers but do not yield information useful in deciding whether to accept or reject a hypothesis. Finally, the most important rule in composing questions is to maintain impartiality.

The questions are usually of four kinds:

1 open-ended
2 dichotomous
3 multiple choice
4 Likert scale

Here are some examples.

1. OPEN-ENDED QUESTION
   What is your general opinion of broadband Internet access for your computer?

   _____

   _____

   _____

2. DICHOTOMOUS QUESTION
   Do you presently have broadband access at home, work, school or college?
   Yes _____   Provider's identity _____
   No _____

3. MULTIPLE-CHOICE QUESTION
   What age group are you in?
   Under 20   _____
   20–29   _____
   30–39   _____

40–49 ——
50–59 ——
60 and over ——

4. LIKERT SCALE QUESTION
To what extent do you expect to use the Internet for buying travel products (flights, hotel accommodation) in the future?

Not at   A great
all | | | | | | deal
        1   2   3   4   5

The design of questionnaires is extremely important because it affects the validity and use-fulness of the results. Testing a questionnaire on a few respondents before conducting a full survey helps to eliminate such difficulties. There are also certain guidelines that should be followed when undertaking questionnaire design. The questions must relate to the research objectives. The layout of the questionnaire must not be off-putting to respondents or to the researchers conducting the work. This is particularly pertinent given that technological advances mean that carefully laid-out questionnaires can be read (scanned) and analysed by computers. This can save researchers a great deal of time. Question type is also an important factor. Open-ended questions can be the most revealing, but are time-consuming – and there-fore off-putting – for respondents, as well as difficult to analyse. Dichotomous questions are straightforward but not very revealing. Multiple-choice questions are popular, but care must be exercised in the choice of categories. Likert scale questions are very popular and can enable batches or strings of questions to be listed together in a space-saving style that can be time-saving for the respondent. They allow respondents to express degrees of a positive or negative response, rather than give an absolute yes or no. There is also the option to give a 'neutral' ('3') answer. Most questionnaires include a mix of question styles.

Sometimes respondent fatigue can affect the quality of questionnaire responses. This may result in answers being rushed, or the questionnaire being abandoned altogether. For exam-ple, sometimes when faced with a long list of Likert scale questions, respondents move through the questions ticking the same point in the scale, rather than taking time to reflect on their answers. The wording of questions is also critical. Researchers must ensure that personal questions, such as those about income or educational attainment, are worded in as inoffensive a manner as possible. These types of question are often placed towards the end of the questionnaire, because it is believed that they are more likely to be answered once the respondent has invested time in the research instrument.

Observation methods
Methods by which researchers record respondents' overt behaviour and take note of physical conditions and events

Observation Methods   In using **observation methods**, researchers record respondents' overt behaviour, taking note of physical conditions and events. Direct contact with respon-dents is avoided; instead, their actions are examined and noted systematically. For exam-ple, researchers might use observation methods to answer the question, 'How long does the average McDonald's restaurant customer have to wait in line before being served?'. As the 'Opener' box at the beginning of this chapter demonstrates, observation may include the use of ethnographic techniques, such as watching customers interact with a product in a real-world environment. Ethnography is increasingly being used by many marketing research agencies to gain greater insights into consumer lifestyles. Indeed, in a recent survey of the marketing research industry, 27 per cent of respondents giving an opinion about the most exciting developments mentioned ethnographic research.[23]

Observation may also be combined with interviews. For example, during a personal inter-view, the condition of a respondent's home or other possessions may be observed and recorded, and demographic information such as ethnic origin, approximate age and sex can be confirmed. Observation is not confined to consumers; shops and service establishments can also be observed, through 'mystery shopper' research, as the Marketing Tools and Techniques box below explains.

Marketing Tools and Techniques

'Mystery Shopper' Research Programmes: Pros and Cons

Retailers and providers of services depend increasingly not only on the products they sell or deliver but also on the ability, attitude and quality of their personnel and the internal environment of their branch outlets. The regional directors and head office managers who check such standards all too often enter through the staff door at the rear of the branch, focusing primarily on operations and not on customer concerns. The branch's customers enter from the front, having first seen the exterior of the branch. They deal with all levels of personnel, not just the manager or manageress to whom the visiting director talks. These customers are not wrapped up in the company's products and operations; they seek help and advice. They expect courtesy and professionalism.

Customers buy a company's products; quite often the company's management never does, instead requesting items direct from storage at staff discount rates without ever visiting shops or showrooms. Car manufacturers give their senior management vehicles and offer all employees highly attractive deals. The result is that few senior managers ever visit a showroom or dealer – even their servicing is taken care of – so they never see the 'sharp end', their dealers, as customers do.

One car producer instigated a programme of 'mystery shopper' surveys. This programme involved visits by bogus potential car buyers to dealers to rate the upkeep and appearance of showrooms, technical knowledge and attitude of personnel, quality of displays, negotiating criteria and adherence to company policies. Dealers did not know who the bogus buyers were, or when they were to visit. Service reception staff were similarly targeted. A favourite ploy by the researchers was to book a car service by telephone and then phone again to cancel, judging the receptionist's response to the lost business. As a result of these frequent – always anonymous – visits, the car producer was able to improve the standards of its dealers, the attitude of its personnel and ultimately the quality of its service and customer satisfaction.

This form of marketing research – 'mystery shopper' – is one of the fastest-growing areas in the industry. The largest research company in the UK, BEM, has 3000 mystery shoppers on its books, many working part-time, and its annual sales exceed £5 million – £3.5 million from mystery shopper surveys. BEM's employees are trained to evaluate how customers are greeted, how the store looks and whether shop assistants understand the products on sale. They are expected to blend in inconspicuously while assessing branches; they are not loud customers visibly asking awkward questions. For many businesses, mystery shopper researchers are evaluating standards and service quality, and supplying management with measures of performance and benchmarks against which improvements can be made.

The European Society for Opinion and Marketing Research (ESOMAR) is attempting to clamp down on the use of mystery shopper research, arguing that it is laudable for organisations to wish to improve the appearance of their facilities and the capabilities of their personnel, but not by tricking employees into handling awkward customers in an off-hand or aggressive manner. ESOMAR is concerned that the staff member does not have the up-front opportunity to withdraw from the interview – something respondents can do in other forms of research surveys – and that the process of dealing with the mystery shopper takes up valuable staff time, which may put pressure on the member of staff when dealing with the next customer.

Another concern is that in most forms of ethical marketing research, the respondent is guaranteed anonymity, but if mystery shopper research is deployed to check up on staff or to develop 'league tables' of branch performance, it is difficult for the research findings not to identify the personnel in question. ESOMAR's recommendations are that mystery shopper research must not waste informants' time and should permit anonymity, or that staff should be told beforehand of the impending research and the ultimate uses for the findings. A study intended to form a supervisory procedure for checking individuals' performance is not permitted under ESOMAR's code: the purpose of any mystery shopper research should be solely to boost consumer demand.

Sources: *Marketing Guides: Market Research*, 13 June 1996; Customer Concern and BEM promotional literature; Rover Cars; Peter Jackson, *Adsearch*, 1999; ESOMAR, Amsterdam, 1998; the Market Research Society, 2004.

Data gathered through observation can sometimes be biased if the respondent is aware of the observation process. An observer can be placed in a natural market environment, such as a grocery store, without biasing or influencing shoppers' actions. However, if the presence of a human observer is likely to bias the outcome or if human sensory abilities are inadequate, mechanical means may be used to record behaviour. **Mechanical observation devices** include cameras, recorders, counting machines and other equipment that records physiological changes in individuals. For instance, a special camera can be used to record the eye movements of respondents looking at an advertisement, and to detect the sequence of reading and the parts of the advertisement that receive greatest attention. Electronic scanners in supermarkets can provide accurate data on sales and consumers' purchase patterns, and marketing researchers may buy such data from the supermarket.

Observation is straightforward and avoids a central problem of survey methods: motivating respondents to state their true feelings or opinions. However, observation tends to be descriptive. When it is the only method of data collection, it may not provide insights into causal relationships. Another drawback is that analyses based on observation are subject to the biases of the observer or the limitations of the mechanical device.

Experimentation **Experimentation** can be used to determine which variable or variables caused an event to occur. It involves keeping certain variables constant so that the effects of the experimental variables can be measured. For instance, if an online fashion vendor wishes to examine the effect of a price reduction on sales, all other marketing variables should be held constant except the change in price.

In experimentation, an **independent variable** (a variable not influenced by or dependent on other variables) is manipulated and the resulting changes measured in a **dependent variable** (a variable contingent on, or restricted to, one value or a set of values assumed by the independent variable). Figure 7.7 illustrates the relationship between these variables. For example, when Houghton Mifflin Company introduces a new edition of its *American Heritage Dictionary*, it may want to estimate the number of dictionaries that could be sold at various levels of advertising expenditure and price. The dependent variable would be sales, the independent variables would be advertising expenditure and price. Researchers would design the experiment to control other independent variables that might influence sales, such as distribution and variations of the product.

Experiments may be conducted in the laboratory or in the field; each research setting has advantages and disadvantages. In **laboratory settings**, participants or respondents are invited to a central location to react or respond to experimental stimuli. In such an isolated setting it is possible to control independent variables that might influence the outcome of an experiment. The features of laboratory settings might include a taste kitchen, video equipment, slide projectors, tape recorders, Internet hook-ups, one-way mirrors, central telephone banks and interview rooms. In an experiment to determine the influence of price (independent

Mechanical observation devices
Cameras, recorders, counting machines and other equipment that records physiological changes in individuals

Experimentation
Data collection that involves maintaining certain variables as constant so that the effects of the experimental variables can be measured

Independent variable
A variable not influenced by or dependent on other variables in experiments

Dependent variable
A variable that is contingent on, or restricted to, one value or a set of values assumed by the independent variable

Laboratory settings
Central locations at which participants or respondents are invited to react or respond to experimental stimuli

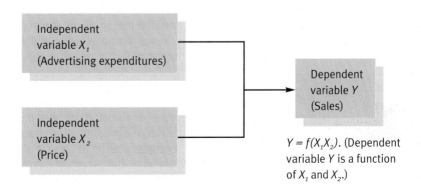

Figure 7.7 Relationship between independent and dependent variables

Independent variable X_1 (Advertising expenditures)

Independent variable X_2 (Price)

Dependent variable Y (Sales)

$Y = f(X_1 X_2)$. (Dependent variable Y is a function of X_1 and X_2.)

variable) on sales of a new canned soup (dependent variable), respondents would be invited to a laboratory – a room with table, chairs and sample soups – before the soup was available in stores. The soup would be placed on a table with competitors' soups. Analysts would then question respondents about their reactions to the soup at various prices. One problem with a laboratory setting is its isolation from the real world, making it difficult, or impossible, to duplicate all the conditions that affect choices in the marketplace.

Field settings
'Real world' environments in which experiments take place

Home placements
Experiments in which a product is used in a home setting

Diary tests
Experiments in which households log their weekly purchases and consumption patterns

The experimental approach can also be used in **field settings**, which are 'real world' environments. A taste test of regional cheeses conducted in a supermarket is one example of an experiment in a field setting. Field settings can allow a more direct test of marketing decisions than laboratory settings. However, these experiments also have their drawbacks. It may be difficult to encourage respondents to cooperate with the experiment, or the findings may be influenced or biased by unexpected events, such as the weather or major economic news. Sometimes the experiment itself can cause bias. For example, in **home placements** (when a product is used in the home in a real setting) or **diary tests** (when households log their weekly purchases and consumption patterns), people may become artificially involved with the product. They might sniff items they would not normally sniff, or ask for their children's opinions about a food item when, normally, they would just give their children the meal and expect them to eat it.[24]

Step 4: Analysing and Interpreting Research Findings

After collecting data to test their hypotheses, marketers analyse and interpret the research findings. Interpretation is easier if marketers plan their data analysis methods carefully and early in the research process. All too often, when data collection has been completed, it is discovered that different wording of questions or ordering of the sections in a questionnaire could have simplified the analysis. Marketers should also allow for continual evaluation of the data during the entire collection period. They can then gain valuable insight into areas that ought to be probed during the formal interpretation.

The first step in drawing conclusions from most research is displaying the data in table format. If marketers intend to apply the results to individual categories of the things or people being studied, cross-tabulation may be quite useful, especially in tabulating joint occurrences. For example, a cross-tabulation of data using the two variables 'gender' and 'purchase rates of car tyres' would show differences in how men and women purchase this product.

Statistical interpretation
An analysis of data that focuses on what is typical or what deviates from the average

After the data are tabulated, they must be analysed. **Statistical interpretation** focuses on what is typical or what deviates from the average. It indicates how widely responses vary and how they are distributed in relation to the variable being measured. This interpretation is another facet of marketing research that relies on marketers' judgement or intuition. Moreover, when they interpret statistics, marketers must take into account estimates of expected error or deviation from the true values of the population. The analysis of data helps researchers to achieve their research objectives and may lead to the hypothesis being studied being accepted or rejected.[25]

Data require careful interpretation by the marketer. If the results of a study are valid, the decision-maker should take action; however, if it is discovered that a question has been worded incorrectly, the results should be ignored. For example, if a study by an electricity company reveals that 50 per cent of its customers believe that meter readers are 'friendly', is that finding good, bad or indifferent? Two important benchmarks help interpret the result: how the 50 per cent figure compares with that for competitors and how it compares with a previous time period. The point is that managers must understand the research results and relate them to a context that permits effective decision-making.[26]

Step 5: Reporting Research Findings

The final step in the marketing research process is reporting the research findings. Before preparing the report, the marketer must take a clear, objective look at the findings to see how well the gathered facts answer the research question, or support or negate the hypotheses posed in the beginning. In most cases, it is extremely doubtful that the study can provide everything needed to answer the research question. Thus the report must highlight the deficiencies and the reasons for them, perhaps suggesting areas that require further investigation.

The report presenting the results is usually a formal, written document. Researchers must allow time for the writing task when they plan and schedule the project. Since the report is a means of communicating with the decision-makers who will use the research findings, researchers need to determine beforehand how much detail and supporting data to include. They should keep in mind that corporate executives prefer reports that are short, clear and simply expressed. Often researchers will give their summary and recommendations first, especially if decision-makers do not have time to study how the results were obtained. Such summary findings tend to be presented via an audio-visual presentation. A technical report allows its users to analyse data and interpret recommendations because it describes the research methods/procedures and the most important data gathered. Thus researchers must recognise the needs and expectations of the report user and adapt to them.

When marketing decision-makers have a firm grasp of research methods and procedures, they are better able to integrate reported findings and personal experience. If marketers can spot limitations in research from reading a report, their personal experience assumes additional importance in the decision-making process. Marketers who cannot understand basic statistical assumptions and data gathering procedures may misuse research findings. Consequently, report writers should be aware of the backgrounds and research abilities of those who will rely on the report in making decisions. Clear explanations presented in plain language make it easier for decision-makers to apply the findings and less likely that a report will be misused or ignored. Talking to potential research users before writing a report can help researchers supply information that will improve decision-making.

Care must be taken when writing the report to avoid bias and distortion. Marketing researchers want to find out about behaviour and opinions, and they need accurate data for making decisions. Reliable marketing research and marketing information systems provide a clearer understanding of dynamics in the marketplace and are more likely to be used by managers in decision-making.

Using Technology to Improve Marketing Information Gathering and Analysis

Marketing Information Systems

Marketing information system (MIS)
The framework for the day-to-day management and structuring of information gathered from sources both inside and outside an organisation

A **marketing information system (MIS)** is a framework for the day-to-day management and structuring of information gathered regularly from sources both inside and outside an organisation. As such, an MIS provides a continuous flow of information about prices, advertising expenditure, sales, competition and distribution expenses.[27] Kraft General Foods, for example, operates one of the largest marketing information systems in the food industry, maintaining, using and sharing information with others to increase the value of what the company offers customers. Kraft seeks to develop a dialogue with customers by providing Freefone numbers. It receives hundreds of thousands of calls annually from customers asking questions and providing product feedback.

The main focus of the marketing information system is on data storage and retrieval. Regular reports of sales by product or market category, data on inventory levels and records of sales people's activities are all examples of information that is useful in making marketing decisions. In the MIS, the means of gathering data receive less attention than do the procedures for expediting the flow of information. Figure 7.8 illustrates the chief components of an MIS. The inputs into a marketing information system include the information sources inside and outside the organisation assumed to be useful for future decision-making.

An effective marketing information system starts by determining the objective of the information – that is, by identifying decision needs that require certain information. The business can then specify an information system for continuous monitoring to provide regular, pertinent information on both the external and internal environment. FedEx, for example, has developed interactive marketing systems to provide instantaneous communication between the company and its customers. Through the telephone and the Internet, customers can track packages and receive immediate feedback concerning delivery. The company's website provides valuable information about customer usage, and it allows customers to express directly what they think about company services. The evolving telecommunications and computer technology is allowing marketing information systems to cultivate one-to-one relationships with customers.

Databases

Most marketing information systems include internal databases. A database is a collection of information arranged for easy access and retrieval. Databases allow marketers to tap into an abundance of information useful in making marketing decisions: internal sales reports, newspaper articles, company press releases, government economic reports, bibliographies and more, often accessed through a computer system. Information technology has made it possible to develop databases to guide strategic planning and help improve customer services. Wal-Mart, for example, maintains one of the largest company databases, with data on sales and inventory levels, as well as data mined from customer receipts in its stores. These data help Wal-Mart pinpoint purchasing patterns, which helps the company manage inventory levels and determine effective product placement. Many commercial websites require consumers to register and provide personal information in order to access the site or make a purchase. Frequent-flier programmes permit airlines to ask loyal customers to participate in surveys about their needs and desires, allowing the airlines to track their best customers' flight patterns by time of day, week, month and year. Supermarkets, such as Tesco and Sainsbury's, gain a substantial amount of data through checkout scanners tied to loyalty cards.

Marketing researchers can also use commercial databases developed by information research organisations to obtain useful information for marketing decisions. Many of these commercial databases are accessible online for a fee. In most commercial databases, the user typically does a computer search by key word, topic or company, and the database service generates abstracts, articles or reports that can be printed out. Accessing multiple reports or a complete article may cost extra. Information provided by a single company – for example, on household demographics, purchases, television viewing behaviour, and responses to promotions such as coupons or loyalty schemes, is called **single-source data**.[28]

Single-source data
Information provided by a single marketing research company

Inputs	Processing	Outputs
External and internal information sources	Classifying Storing Indexing Retrieving	Information for marketing decision-making

Feedback: Adjusting information intake

Figure 7.8
An organisation's marketing information system

For example, CACI provides demographic and lifestyle information on people living in different UK neighbourhoods.

Marketing Decision Support Systems

Marketing decision support system (MDSS) Customised computer software that aids marketing managers in decision-making

A **marketing decision support system (MDSS)** is customised computer software that aids marketing managers in decision-making by helping them anticipate the effects of certain decisions. Some decision support systems have a broader range and offer greater computational and modelling capabilities than spreadsheets; they let managers explore a greater number of alternatives. For example, a decision support system can determine how sales and profits might be affected by higher or lower interest rates or how sales forecasts, advertising expenditures, production levels and the like might affect overall profits. For this reason, decision support system software is often a major component of a company's marketing information system. For example, both Oracle and Ford Motor Company use a software product called NeuroServer that acts as a customer interface to solve problems and answer questions for customers. Based on customised parameters, it allows marketers to acquire specific information on customers, which then goes into the decision support system.[29] Some decision support systems incorporate artificial intelligence and other advanced computer technologies.

The Internet and Online Information Services

The Internet has evolved as a powerful communication medium, linking customers and companies around the world via computer networks with e-mail, forums, web pages and more. Growth of the Internet, and especially the World Wide Web, has launched an entire industry that is working to make market information easily accessible both to marketing organisations and customers.

Companies can also mine their own websites for useful information. Amazon, for example, has built a relationship with its customers by tracking the types of books and music they purchase. Each time a customer logs on to its website, Amazon can offer recommendations based on the customer's previous purchases. Such a marketing system helps the company track the changing desires and buying habits of its most valued customers.

Marketing researchers can also subscribe to online services such as Google and MSN. These services typically offer their subscribers such specialised services as databases, news services and forums, as well as access to the Internet itself. Marketers can subscribe to 'mailing lists' that periodically deliver electronic newsletters to their computer screens and they can participate in on-screen discussions with thousands of network users. This enhanced communication with a business's customers, suppliers and employees provides a high-speed link that boosts the capabilities of the business's marketing information system.

While most web pages are open to anyone with Internet access, big organisations like Cisco Systems also maintain internal web pages, called 'intranets', that allow employees to access such internal data as customer profiles and product inventory – information once hidden in databases only technicians could unlock. Such sensitive company information can be protected from outside users of the World Wide Web by special security software called firewalls. Marketers who get into the habit of accessing their companies' internal web pages often move on to seek information externally as well, via the rest of the World Wide Web.

The Importance of Ethical Marketing Research

Marketing managers and other professionals are relying more and more on marketing research, marketing information systems and new technologies to make better decisions. It is therefore essential that professional standards are established by which to judge the reliability of such research. Such standards are necessary because of the ethical and legal issues that develop in gathering marketing research data. In addition, the relationships between research suppliers, such as marketing research agencies, and the marketing managers who make strategy decisions require ethical behaviour. Without such clear standards, ethical conflict can lead to mistrust and questionable research results.[30] Attempts to stamp out shoddy practices and establish generally accepted procedures for conducting research are important developments in marketing research. Other issues of great concern relate to researchers' honesty, manipulation of research techniques, data manipulation, invasion of privacy, and failure to disclose the purpose or sponsorship of a study in some situations. Too often, respondents are unfairly manipulated and research clients are not told about flaws in data. For example, one dubious practice that damages the image of marketing research is 'sugging', as mentioned earlier in the chapter. More recently, direct marketers have disguised their selling mailings with questionnaires, adding to respondents' confusion and dislike of honest marketing research.[31]Organisations like ESOMAR and the Market Research Society have developed codes of conduct and guidelines to promote ethical marketing research.[32] To be effective, such guidelines must instruct those who participate in marketing research on how to avoid misconduct. Table 7.6, which illustrates part of the ICC/ESOMAR International Code of Marketing and Social Research Practice, details the information to which any research client is entitled.

Marketing research is essential in planning and developing marketing strategies. Information about target markets provides vital input in planning the marketing mix and in controlling marketing activities. It is no secret that companies can use information technology as a key to gaining an advantage over the competition.[33] In short, the marketing concept – the marketing philosophy of customer orientation – can be implemented better when adequate information about customers, competition and trends is available.

TABLE 7.6 INFORMATION ABOUT MARKETING RESEARCH PROJECTS TO WHICH RESEARCH CLIENTS ARE ENTITLED

1 Background
For whom the study was conducted
The purpose of the study
Names of subcontractors and consultants performing any substantial part of the work

2 Sample
(a) A description of the intended and actual universe covered
(b) The size, nature and geographical distribution of the sample (both planned and achieved); and, where relevant, the extent to which any of the data collected were obtained from only part of the sample
(c) Details of the sampling method and any weighting methods used
(d) When technically relevant, a statement of response rates and a discussion of any possible bias due to non-response

3 Data collection
(a) A description of the method by which the information was collected
(b) A description of the field staff, briefing and field quality control methods used
(c) The method of recruiting respondents, and the general nature of any incentives offered to secure their cooperation
(d) When the fieldwork was carried out
(e) In the case of 'desk research', a clear statement of the sources of the information and their likely reliability

4 Presentation of results
(a) The relevant factual findings obtained
(b) Bases of percentages (both weighted and unweighted)
(c) General indicators of the probable statistical margins of error to be attached to the main findings, and of the levels of statistical significance of differences between key figures
(d) The questionnaire and other relevant documents and materials used (or, in the case of a shared project, that portion relating to the matter reported on)

Source: Rule 25, http://www.esomar.org/print.php?a=2&p=75 © Copyright 2004 by ESOMAR® – The World Association of Research Professionals. This article first appeared in ICC/ESOMAR International Code of Marketing and Social Research Practice, published by ESOMAR.

Summary

Effective marketing is contingent on marketers having information about the characteristics, needs and wants of their target markets. Marketing research and information systems that furnish practical, unbiased information help companies avoid the assumptions and misunderstandings that could lead to poor marketing performance.

» *Marketing research* is the systematic design, collection, interpretation and reporting of information to help marketers solve specific marketing problems or take advantage of marketing opportunities. Marketing research projects are adapted to the context and problems under study.

» All organisations have some *marketing intelligence*, which is the composite of all data and ideas available within the organisation. Often the information is inadequate, leading to the commissioning of marketing research.

» *Quantitative marketing research* leads to findings that can be quantified and statistically analysed. *Qualitative research* examines subjective opinions and value judgements.

» The increase in marketing research activities represents a transition from intuitive to scientific problem-solving. Intuitive decisions are made on the basis of personal knowledge and past experience. *Scientific decision-making* is an orderly, logical and systematic approach to gathering information. Minor, non-recurring low-risk problems can be handled successfully by *intuition*. As the amount of risk and alternative solutions increases, the use of research becomes more desirable and rewarding.

» The five basic steps of planning marketing research are: (1) locating and defining problems or research issues; (2) designing the research; (3) collecting data; (4) analysing and interpreting research findings; (5) reporting research findings.

» The first step towards finding a solution or launching a research study means uncovering the nature and boundaries of a negative, or positive, situation or question. Researchers and decision-makers should remain in the *problem definition* stage until they have determined precisely what they want from the research and how they will use it.

» Careful *research design* is of vital importance as a clear statement of research objectives guides a research project. Sometimes hypotheses – or informed guesses or assumptions about a certain problem or set of circumstances – are formulated. The *research objectives* and any *hypotheses* determine the approach for gathering data: *exploratory research*, *descriptive research* or *causal research*. Researchers need to be concerned about issues of reliability and validity: techniques are *reliable* if they produce almost identical results in successive repeated trials; they have *validity* if they measure what they are supposed to measure and not something else.

» Collecting data is the third step of the research process. *Secondary data* are compiled inside or outside the organisation for some purpose other than the current investigation. Secondary data may be collected from an organisation's databank and other internal sources; from periodicals, census reports, government publications, the World Wide Web and unpublished sources; and from *syndicated data services*, which collect general information and sell it to clients. Secondary data 'pre-exists' and should be examined prior to the collection of any primary data.

» To gather *primary data*, researchers use sampling procedures, survey methods, observation and experimentation. *Sampling* involves selecting a limited number of representative units, or a *sample*, from a total *population*. There are two basic types of sampling: probability and non-probability. In *probability sampling*, every element of the population has a known chance of being selected. In *random sampling*, all the units in a population have an equal chance of appearing in the sample. In *stratified sampling*, the population of interest is divided into groups according to a common characteristic or attribute, and then a probability sampling is conducted within each group. *Area sampling* involves selecting a probability sample of geographic areas such as streets, census tracts or census enumeration districts, and selecting units or individuals within the selected geographic areas for the sample. *Quota sampling* differs from other forms of sampling in that it is judgemental (or non-probability).

» *Survey methods* include *mail surveys* and *mail panels*, e-mail and Internet surveys (*online surveys*), *consumer purchase diaries, telephone surveys, computer assisted telephone interviewing* and *personal interview surveys*, such as *depth interviews, shopping mall/pavement intercept interviews, on-site computer interviewing, focus group interviews, quali-depth interviews* and *in-home interviews*. *Questionnaires* are instruments used to obtain information from respondents and to record observations; they should be unbiased and objective. *Observation methods* including ethnographic techniques that involve researchers recording respondents' overt behaviour and taking note of physical conditions and events. Observation may be facilitated by *mechanical observation devices*.

» *Experimentation* involves maintaining as constants those factors that are related to or may affect the variables under investigation, so that the effects of the experimental variables can be measured. Marketing experimentation is a set of rules and procedures according to which the task of data gathering is organised so as to expedite analysis and interpretation. In experimentation, an *independent variable* is manipulated and the resulting changes are measured in a *dependent variable*.

» Experiments may take place in *laboratory settings*, which provide maximum control over influential factors, or in *field settings*, which are preferred when marketers want experimentation to take place in 'real world' environments, such as with *home placements* and *diary tests*.

» To apply research findings to decision-making, marketers must tabulate, analyse and interpret their findings properly. *Statistical interpretation* is analysis of data that focuses on what is typical or what deviates from the average. After interpreting their research findings, researchers must prepare a report of the findings that the decision-makers can use and understand. Information provided by a single firm is called *single-source data*.

» The *marketing information system (MIS)* is a framework for the day-to-day managing and structuring of information regularly gathered from sources both inside and outside an organisation. The inputs into a marketing information system include the information sources inside and outside the organisation considered useful for future decision-making. They may include internal databases. Processing information involves classifying it and developing categories for meaningful storage and retrieval. Marketing decision-makers then determine which information – the output – is useful for making marketing decisions. Feedback enables those who are responsible for gathering internal and external data to adjust the information inputs systematically.

» A *marketing decision support system (MDSS)* is customised computer software that aids marketing managers in decision-making. Some decision support systems have a broader range and offer greater computational and modelling capabilities than spreadsheets, allowing managers to explore a greater number of alternatives.

» Growth of the Internet, and especially the World Wide Web, has launched an entire industry that is working to make market information easily accessible to both organisations and customers. Companies can also mine their own websites for useful information, subscribe to online services, and join 'mailing lists' that periodically deliver electronic newsletters to their computer screens so that they can participate in on-screen discussions with thousands of network users.

>> Marketing managers and other professionals are relying more and more on marketing research, marketing information systems and new technologies to make better decisions. Professional standards are needed to judge the reliability of such research. These enable ethical and legal issues associated with data gathering to be handled.

⊛ Key Links

This chapter has concentrated on the marketing research tools available to capture information about markets and customers. It should be read in conjunction with:

- Chapter 2's examination of the nature of opportunity analysis and the importance of analysing competitors
- Chapters 4 and 5, reviewing the required insights into buying behaviour
- Chapter 6's discussion of how to create market segments from an understanding of customers, and how best to develop a brand positioning strategy.

Important Terms

Marketing research
Marketing intelligence
Quantitative research
Qualitative research
Intuition
Scientific decision-making
Problem definition
Research design
Research objective
Hypothesis
Exploratory research
Descriptive research
Causal research
Reliability
Validity
Primary data
Secondary data
Syndicated data services
Population
Sample
Sampling
Probability sampling
Random sampling
Stratified sampling
Area sampling
Quota sampling
Survey methods
Mail surveys
Mail panels
Consumer purchase diaries
Telephone surveys
Computer-assisted telephone interviewing
Online survey
Personal interview survey
Depth interview
Focus group interview
Quali-depth interviews
In-home interview
Shopping mall/pavement intercept interviews
On-site computer interviewing
Questionnaire
Observation methods
Mechanical observation devices
Experimentation
Independent variable
Dependent variable
Laboratory settings
Field settings
Home placements
Diary tests
Statistical interpretation
Marketing information system (MIS)
Single-source data
Marketing decision support system (MDSS)

Discussion and Review Questions

1 What is the marketing information system (MIS) of a small organisation likely to include?
2 What is the difference between marketing research and marketing information systems? In what ways do marketing research and the MIS overlap?
3 What are the differences between quantitative and qualitative marketing research?
4 How do the benefits of decisions guided by marketing research compare with those of intuitive decision-making? How do marketing decision-makers know when it will be worthwhile to conduct research?
5 Give specific examples of situations in which intuitive decision-making would probably be more appropriate than marketing research.
6 What are the differences between exploratory, descriptive and causal research?
7 What are the major limitations of using secondary data to solve marketing problems?
8 List some of the problems of conducting a laboratory experiment on respondents' reactions to the taste of different brands of beer. How would these problems differ from those of a field study of beer taste preferences?

231

9 In what situation would it be best to use random sampling? Quota sampling? Stratified or area sampling?

10 Suggest some ways to encourage respondents to cooperate in mail surveys.

11 What are the benefits of the focus group technique?

12 Give some examples of marketing problems that could be solved through information gained from observation.

13 Why is questionnaire design important? Why should questionnaires be tested?

14 What is 'sugging'? Why is it damaging to the marketing research industry?

Recommended Reading

- Birn, R., *The Effective Use of Market Research* (London: Kogan Page, 1999).
- Chisnall, P.M., *Marketing Research* (Maidenhead: McGraw-Hill, 2004).
- McQuarrie, E.F., *The Market Research Toolbox: A Concise Guide for Beginners* (London: Sage, 2005).
- Malhotra, N.K. and Birks, D.F., *Marketing Research: An Applied Approach* (Harlow: FT Prentice Hall, 2002).
- Tull, D.S. and Hawkins, D.I., *Marketing Research* (New York: Macmillan, 1993).

 Internet Exercise

The World Association of Opinion and Marketing Research Professionals (ESOMAR, founded as the European Society for Opinion and Marketing Research in 1948) is a non-profit association for marketing research professionals. ESOMAR promotes the use of opinion and marketing research to improve marketing decisions in companies worldwide and works to protect personal privacy in the research process. Visit the association's website at:
www.esomar.nl/

1 How can ESOMAR help marketing professionals conduct research to guide marketing strategy?

2 How can ESOMAR help marketers protect the privacy of research subjects when conducting marketing research in other countries?

3 ESOMAR introduced the first professional code of conduct for marketing research professionals in 1948. The association continues to update this document to address new technology and other changes in the marketing environment. According to ESOMAR's code, what are the specific professional responsibilities of marketing researchers?

🌐 *Applied Mini-Case*

Advances in information technology, especially in terms of data storage and processing capacity, have made available an ever-growing quantity of data about customer buying behaviour. To extract from this mound of data potentially useful information to guide marketing decisions, marketers are developing methods of mining data. Data mining refers to the discovery of patterns hidden in databases that have the potential to contribute to marketers' understanding of customers and their needs. Data mining employs computer technology to extract data from internal and external sources; translate and format the data; analyse, substantiate, and assign meaning to data; organise databases; and build and implement decisions support systems to make data mining results accessible to decision-makers.

❓ *Question*

Adopt the role of a retail analyst who is helping a large retail group to organise its databases. You have been asked to help guide the process by providing a list of the kind of information that is helpful to a company when making decisions about marketing strategy.

⊕ *Case Study*

Focus Group Interviewing: In-depth Views from Group Discussions

Focus group interviews, which are generally informal group discussions about marketing ideas or concepts conducted by a marketer or marketing research company, are used by most major organisations in developing marketing or business plans. In the 1980s, focus group interviewing became one of the most widely practised types of marketing research, expanding from the packaged goods industry into financial services and industrial applications.

However, the function of focus group interviewing is expected to change. Traditionally, companies have relied on focus group interviews to define the input going into quantitative studies, but a new trend is to conduct focus group interviews after tabulating research results, to provide insight into why the results were achieved. The trend is also towards higher costs (the average today is £1,600 for 90 minutes and £2,200 for an extended, video-recorded group lasting two and a half hours).

Other changes pertain to moderator guides and their reports. The moderator guides will be expected to involve clients in the development process. Their reports will concentrate on providing conclusions that interpret the findings and on making recommendations for action by the client. The reports will also contain fewer actual quotations from individual focus group participants. The post-focus group debriefing techniques are also being altered. The shift is towards disciplined debriefing that asks participants their reactions to the group session. Such debriefing can provide the link between concept development and application, and can serve as a rough check on validity and reliability.

Another new development in focus group interviewing is the use of electronics to offer three-way capabilities. Computerised decision-making software can supplement research findings and consolidate opinions from three different audiences. For example, in healthcare research in a hospital setting, the three audiences would be former patients, medics and employees. The advantages of using electronics include easier scheduling of participating groups and more interaction among the three audiences.

A major UK service retailer was faced with declining sales and two new competitors. In order to re-establish itself as the dominant force in its market, it decided to undertake some in-depth qualitative marketing research using focus groups. The retailer's new competitors were opening stores at the rate of six per month, and the company realised it had to act quickly to defend its position. However, it had conducted no consumer research for many years and was uncertain why its customers preferred its stores, how competitors were perceived and what types of people constituted its customer profile. Before modifying its marketing mix and launching an advertising campaign to combat its new competitors, the company had to gain a better understanding of its target market. For approximately £14,000 (1989), using a specialist consumer qualitative agency, in just three weeks the company managed to get a good 'feel' for its standing in its core trading area, as perceived by customers. The table shows that the information resulted from a fairly 'standard' programme of focus groups.

Each group had eight consumers, four of whom were shoppers in the retailer's stores and four of whom shopped in competitors' stores. Each group

Group Composition	Social Class	Location
1 Male 25–39, white-collar commuters[†]	A, B	Eastcheap
2 Male 40–55, white-collar commuters	A, B	Hitchin
3 Female 25–44, executives/PAs	A, B, C1	Bristol
4 Female 25–44, semi-skilled	C2	Woking
5 Female 35–40 'housewives'	A, B	Leamington
6 Female 25–34, 'housewives'	C1, C2	Sheffield
7 Male 18–29, young earners[†]	C1, C2	Ealing
8 Female 18–29, young earners	C1, C2	Telford

[†]Held in branches after hours

session lasted three hours, and a free merchandise voucher and buffet meal were provided for participants. The same moderator ran all eight groups to maintain consistency. Each session was tape recorded, the tapes being transcribed later into a report and presentation to the retailer's board of directors. Two sessions were video recorded, and several were 'secretly viewed' by the company's marketing executives.

Sources: Lynne Cunningham, 'Electronic focus groups offer 3-way capability', *Marketing News*, 8 January 1990, pp. 22, 39; Thomas L. Greenbaum, 'Focus group spurt predicted for the '90s', *Marketing News*, 8 January 1990, pp. 21, 22; Nino DeNicola, 'Debriefing sessions: the missing link in focus groups', *Marketing News*, 8 January 1990, pp. 20, 22; Peter Jackson, *Adsearch*, Richmond, 1989 and 2007.

❷ Questions for Discussion

1 What are the strengths and benefits of focus group marketing research?
2 This retailer chose to commission a programme of focus groups. Given the aims of the company's research, what other research tools might the company have used? Explain your selection.

Birmingham Women's Hospital
Giving Birth – the Consumer's Choice!

The provision of maternity services is an area of health care which most people encounter at some point in their adult life. Despite being a significant life event, until relatively recently most women in the UK having a baby had very little control over the health care side of the maternity experience. The type of care on offer was largely outside a patient's control and usually determined more by locality than by patient choice. The characteristics of antenatal care, the maternity unit where delivery took place and even the position adopted during labour, were all likely to be predetermined by others.

In recent years, much has changed. The Government's *Changing Childbirth report* compiled in 1992 indicated that women should be offered choice in their maternity provision. Regulatory changes, allowing General Practitioners (doctors) more flexibility in where they are allowed to refer their patients, have helped foster a greater sense of choice. Recent Government initiatives to increase patient control over these decisions have underlined this change. Social changes have led to people becoming more proactive in making decisions about issues affecting their lives. As consumers, for example, they are more likely than ever to change their bank account, shop around for insurance or buy products over the Internet. In such an environment, it is no surprise that women are increasingly likely to exert control over maternity decisions. This tendency has been supported by advances in technology which have made information about maternity services much more readily available.

Today's expectant mother and her partner now have far more control over the antenatal and birthing process than previously. There is greater flexibility in the style of antenatal care on offer. Perhaps the most significant issue is that women can now choose the hospital unit at which they deliver their baby. This is important because it is the characteristics of the unit, more than any other factor, which impact upon the maternity care received:

> What happens to you during labour will probably depend less on what you say you want to happen than on where you choose to have your baby. The simple fact is that between two similar hospitals, you could be twice as likely to be delivered by caesarean section in one than in the other. Your postcode will often determine whether you are more likely to be induced, be assisted by forceps, or be elected for caesarean section. Your chances of benefiting from the latest antenatal scans and tests, as well as being offered a full range of pain relief also depend on which hospital you go to.
>
> dr foster Good Birth Guide, *(2002), Vermilion, London, p. 10.*

It is now common practice for medical staff to encourage women to write their own birth plans. This document describes the patient's preferences for all aspects of delivery, from pain relief to monitoring and intervention. The patient's desire to exercise some form of control over this important life event is consistent with changes in how people live. Women have grown accustomed to exercising control over other aspects of their lives and careers: this expectation has been extended to the antenatal and birth experience. From the patient's viewpoint, the provision of maternity care is just like any other service.

How busy a maternity unit becomes is now partly affected by the preferences of expectant mothers. A greater level of hospital responsiveness is, therefore, needed to ensure that the needs and wants of these patients are met. Hospitals and their staff must be more aware of 'consumer' expectations, demands and information requirements. One implication is that many hospital units have been forced to devote far greater attention to the ways in which they are branded and perceived in the maternity 'marketplace', requiring improved marketing communications and more tailoring of information.

Ensuring that the services provided are acceptable to patients is a complex task. While the provision of good quality patient care is paramount, the service on offer extends beyond the purely medical. In addition to the medical provision, units have to provide appropriate facilities with a mix of amenities to cater for patients and their visitors. The hospital environment should be amenable to the well-being of its users. Appropriate processes must be in place to control the smooth flow of patients through the unit. The mix of medical and support staff has to be carefully managed to ensure that units can cater for the peaks and troughs associated with demand for maternity services.

The Role of Information

The decision process involved in making choices about antenatal and delivery care is driven by the availability of information. Women making these decisions acquire this information from a variety of informal and formal sources. Some will rely on previous experiences of childbirth, either their own or those of their friends and acquaintances. Others will discuss the options with their family doctor or midwife. Some will consult the increasing array of pregnancy and birth related publications or tune-in to a relevant television programme or radio broadcast. Overall, an increasingly diverse array of sources is available. Pregnancy books, parenting magazines, specialist websites, midwife groups and organisations dealing with birth issues, all provide advice on how this can be achieved. Google *Birmingham Women's Hospital* and review the mix of information sources offered in seconds, from the hospital's own web pages, to NHS and Government sources, plus the views of many specialist information providers focusing on medical issues. Comparable statistics and patient comments are freely available.

The *dr foster Good Birth Guide* is freely available on the Internet or at low cost through major bookstores. This independent guide, which is one of a range available covering health services in the UK, has been compiled under the supervision of an Ethics Committee of leading medical professionals.

The *Good Birth Guide* contains information on all the UK's maternity units, so that comparisons can be made regarding the numbers of home births, rates of caesareans and levels of intervention during delivery. The guide also includes descriptive information capturing the characteristics of each unit.

The BirthChoiceUK website (http://www.birthchoiceuk.com) was set up to help parents make informed choices about their maternity care. The website objectives are:

> For women throughout the United Kingdom there are several options for birth. This may mean choosing a particular place to give birth, such as at home, in a small maternity unit or in one of a number of hospitals. Or it could involve choosing the type of maternity care, such as care shared between a GP and a midwife, or being cared for by a team of community midwives attached to a hospital, or by an independent midwife. This website aims to bring together information to enable prospective parents to make these choices. This website does not favour one place of birth over any other, nor one type of maternity care over any other. Instead, it encourages readers to ask questions of themselves and their health care providers to help them make choices which will result in the birth experiences they wish for.

http://www.birthchoiceuk.com/AboutWebsite.htm

The BirthChoiceUK website encourages prospective parents to visit their chosen unit and there are tips on the kinds of questions to ask about facilities and services. Guidance is given on the booking-in process. The website also provides additional features designed to support those seeking further information. Further reading is offered on a variety of issues and a range of maternity-related research findings is explored. An extensive reference list of publications supporting the information provided is also available. Finally, the website provides web links, among others, to:

- NCT Pregnancy and Babycare: The National Childbirth Trust offers advice on pregnancy, birth and parenthood.
- AIMS (Association for Improvements in Maternity Services): details on maternity choices.
- *dr foster*: statistics and information on maternity units.

- Independent Midwives' Association: register enabling patients to contact a local independent midwife.
- Association of Radical Midwives: information about birth choices.
- Home Birth Reference Site: guidance for those considering a home birth.
- MIDIRS (Midwives' Information and Resource Service): provides a series of Informed Choice Leaflet for patients and healthcare professions and the Informed Choice database.
- The VBAC (Vaginal Birth After Caesarean): information on the birth options for mothers who have previously delivered by caesarean section.
- Sheila Kitzinger: author who campaigns for women's rights in childbirth.

Birmingham Women's Hospital

Birmingham Women's Health Care NHS Trust, which manages Birmingham Women's Hospital, was established in 1993. The unit provides care exclusively for women and is a teaching hospital linked to Birmingham University's Medical School. As a regional referral unit, the hospital provides maternity services for the local community in Birmingham and for more complex cases from the West Midlands as a whole. The Trust operates antenatal clinics, offers pre-pregnancy counselling and specialises in care for patients following miscarriage or bereavement. There is also an assisted conception unit, which provides fertility treatment. In addition, the Trust runs a foetal medicine unit which offers specialist care in relation to various foetal and maternal conditions, has a 43 cot Neonatal Intensive Care Unit to treat sick and premature babies, and provides care in the areas of genetics and gynaecology.

The hospital is also home to the regional Human Milk Bank, offering a service for collecting and pasteurising donor breast milk. The donated milk is circulated to neonatal units in the Midlands and further afield for premature and sick babies whose mothers are unable to breast feed. The managing Trust also hosts the Cancer Intelligence Unit, the West Midlands Public Health Observatory and the NHS National Genetics Education and Development Centre.

With an income annually around £70 million, the hospital looks after 50,000 patients each year and carries out over 3,000 operations. The abilities of its 1,500 staff, the hospital's practices, its reputation and success rates, in 2008 enabled the hospital to achieve Foundation status, placing the unit among the elite of UK hospitals. While this has resulted in a re-naming of the Trust to Birmingham Women's NHS Foundation Trust, the hospital remains branded as Birmingham Women's Hospital. The mission is simple, 'to be a place that women and families choose first, and where people want to work'.

Birmingham Women's Hospital Basic Features

Number of beds	142
Births per midwife per year	33
Births per bed per day	1.20
Home births	1%
Obstetrician available 24 hours	Yes
Paediatrician available 24 hours	Yes
Epidural pain relief 24 hours	Yes

Source: *dr foster Good Birth Guide,* (2002/8), Vermilion, London

Birmingham Women's Hospital is a large unit, responsible for the delivery of around 7,000 babies each year. Not all women who deliver their babies at the hospital attend the unit for their antenatal care. Some patients are completely or predominantly looked after by their local midwife and family doctor, while others may have some or all of their antenatal care at the unit. The delivery statistics for Birmingham Women's Hospital are, to a degree, influenced by the number of complex cases referred to the unit from elsewhere. The delivery suite itself is able to cater for all kinds of births, ranging from different forms of normal delivery including water births, through to caesarean section and instrumental delivery – the use of forceps and venthouse. A full range of pain relief options is generally available and women have the opportunity to visit and look around the unit prior to their expected due date. The patient's wishes are genuinely regarded as a key priority when determining the characteristics of care.

There is a strong focus on the provision of information for patients and visitors. Information leaflets on a wide range of topics are freely available on stands in the public areas of the hospital. There are many noticeboards and e-displays providing information on areas such as blood donation and NHS Direct (the telephone helpline which members of the public can call with queries about their health). There is also a feature on the hospital's Assisted Conception Unit, together with leaflets seeking sperm donors. The provision of information in different languages helps cater for the diverse ethnic catchments. For example, the 'Your Guide to the NHS' leaflet is available in many different Asian languages. Some leaflets are specific to maternity patients, who receive a *welcome* pack at their booking-in visit. This pack contains information about the antenatal period, a free pregnancy magazine and various product samples and coupons deemed appropriate for expectant mothers. A second pack containing further leaflets, product information and samples targeted at new mothers and their babies is offered to patients who deliver at the hospital. A typical pack might include leaflets on breastfeeding and the dangers of cot death, together with samples of nappy cream, detergent or fabric conditioner. There is also an option to receive a further two packs during baby's first year.

The information theme is a particular focus in the hospital's innovative health shop. This area, which is located close to the main entrance, provides a wealth of information leaflets and posters about health-related issues and voluntary groups. The 'shop' is open to patients, the public and staff seeking information on a wide range of topics.

Providing the Care Desired by Patients

As the emphasis on choice in maternity services increases, there is more pressure on hospitals to be responsive. Women are increasingly likely to review and compare a number of alternative care providers. Although quality of care will almost certainly remain the paramount consideration, many other aspects of the antenatal and delivery experience are likely to influence the decisions which are made. The implications for units such as Birmingham Women's Hospital are clear. In particular, the need to understand and respond to the expectations of patients and other stakeholders is greater than ever. The hospital has also to devote more resources to creating a brand reputation and managing its multi-channel communications to prospective parents, through an increasing array of marketing communications channels and information sources.

Questions for Discussion

1 Given the nature of the 'buying process' for maternity care, what is the role of marketing communications?
2 What are the key pieces of information required by prospective parents? How best can these be communicated to this target audience?
3 What is the role of the Internet in patients' search for information? How must Birmingham Women's Hospital respond to the role of the web?

Part II Strategic Case 2

Reebok
Reebok Races into the Urban Market

Reebok's UK founder produced some of the first ever running shoes with spikes, as athletes in the late 1890s wanted to run even faster. In 1924, J.W. Forster and Sons was making by hand the running shoes used in the 1924 Summer Games, as depicted in the movie *Chariots of Fire*. In 1958, two of the founder's grandsons started a sister company called Reebok, named after the African gazelle. By 1979, three running shoe styles were introduced to the USA: at $60 per pair, they were the most expensive on the market. In 1982, Reebok caught the market unawares with the launch of Freestyle, the first ever athletic shoe designed specifically for women. By the 1980s Reebok was a publicly quoted company active in more than 170 countries. Continual product innovation and customer research gave the company leadership in most of its key target markets.

Step Reebok followed in 1989, a totally revolutionary workout programme that led to millions of users across the globe. By 1992 the company was broadening its ranges to include footwear and clothing products linked to many sports. These moves were supported with major sponsorship deals of leading sports starts, teams and sporting events. Venus Williams is one of the latest Reebok stars. Recently, Reebok has again transformed the way in which people train, with the creation of *Core Training*, based on a board that tilts, twists, torques and recoils with the body's movements. In 2002, Reebok launched the *Rbk* brand for street-inspired clothing and footwear, aimed at young men and women who expect the style of their gear to reflect the attitude of their lives – cool, edgy, authentic and aspirational.

Reebok wanted to give front-runner Nike a run for its money in the race for market share in athletic footwear, clothing and equipment. Reebok, still based in Massachusetts, gained speed from the 1980s into the early 1990s by marketing special aerobics shoes for women, before Nike pulled ahead with new clothing and equipment endorsed by high-profile athletes such as Michael Jordan and Tiger Woods. Nike remained the market leader, completely outdistancing all competitors to dominate the industry with 35% share of the market. In contrast, Reebok's market share by 2005 was about half that of Nike's and Reebok's $3.5 billion in annual sales about a third that of Nike's. Reebok sought to close the distance by changing its selection of target markets. In the process, Reebok aimed to change consumers' perceptions of and attitudes toward its brand and its products, with the objective of boosting both sales and profits.

Breaking Tradition with Hip-Hop

Traditionally, manufacturers of athletic shoes have captured market attention by signing successful or up and coming sports stars to promote their shoes. Reebok still likes to link its brand to popular sports and individual champions. The fierce rivalry with Nike continues on the playing field: Reebok has lucrative contracts to make branded hats for the US National Basketball Association and to supply the National Football League with uniforms and equipment, while Nike has an exclusive contract to provide performance wear to all 30 Major League Baseball teams. Many other sports around the world are similarly supported by Reebok and Nike, including stadia, teams and individual players.

Looking beyond sports, Reebok's marketers investigated the urban market, where fashion, rather than performance, is the deciding factor in buying decisions. Urban teens tend to be extremely style-conscious, buying as many as ten pairs of athletic shoes a year so they can be seen in the very latest thing. In the States, many are also fans of hip-hop music and buy clothing designed by hip-hop celebrities such as Jay-Z, Sean 'P. Diddy' Combs and Russell Simmons. Reebok's marketing research confirmed this market's considerable buying power and the influence of hip-hop artists. To effectively reach this market, Reebok needed a new brand, new products and new promotional efforts: the Reebok brand did not have a suitably desirable image with this youth market in any of the company's principle countries of operation. First, the company took the focus off its mainstream Reebok brand by creating *Rbk* as a new brand specifically for the urban market. Next, it partnered with hip-hop artists such as Jay-Z and 50 Cent to develop special footwear collections, backed by targeted promotional efforts emphasizing style with attitude.

New Street Credibility

Reebok found it was tapping into a significant market opportunity. Soon after it introduced soft leather, flat soled *S. Carter* shoes – after Jay-Z's original name, Shawn Carter – the line sold out. Demand for the $100 shoes quickly peaked, leading to eager buyers bidding up to $250 for one pair on the eBay auction website. Within eight months, the company had shipped 500,000 pairs to retailers around the USA and was preparing to launch a second *S. Carter* shoe.

On the back of this success, Reebok introduced *G-Unit* footwear, named after a hit song by the rapper 50 Cent, who says that "Reebok's *Rbk Collection* is the real thing when it comes to connecting with the street and hip-hop culture". Hip-hop's Eve was also asked to design a shoe. "She is one of the first artists in the campaign who has male and female appeal, urban and suburban", observed Reebok's director of global advertising; "she is as much a fashion icon as a music icon". The company also found a way to bring sports and hip-hop together by launching the *13 Collection* line of shoes by basketball star Allen Iverson. Iverson promoted the line by appearing in a series of fast-paced adverts filmed in rap video style. Although he was shown playing basketball for a second or two, the adverts focused more on his off-court style than his on-court technique.

Despite the added credibility that such celebrities brought to the *Rbk* brand, the strategy entailed some risks. Fads in street fashion and music can come and go at a dizzying pace, which means a shoe that is 'red hot' on one day may be 'ice cold' on the next. Reebok could also suffer from negative repercussions if one of its celebrities runs into trouble. Still, the company's chief marketing executive is committed to the strategy. "With athletes, they wear the shoes for the length of a basketball season", he comments. "With hip-hop, the publicity is intense but short, just like movies". The advantage, in his view, is that, "you'll know very quickly whether you hit or miss".

Reebok's New *Vector*

Nike has one of the most recognized trademarks in the world and now Reebok has *Vector*, a streamlined trademark designed to communicate the brand's attributes in a fast and fun way. The idea is to make the *Vector* synonymous with Reebok, just as the *sSwoosh* is synonymous with Nike. "Our research suggests that consumers react better to logos than words, and it's a very effective marketing tool", stresses Reebok's head of marketing.

In addition, the company is giving its brand a touch of glamour with 'showcase stores' in major cities. In New York City, for example, Reebok opened a new men's store right next to its women's store. Both feature footwear, clothing and accessories, and both share the building with the Reebok Sport Club/NY. The displays are as stylish as the products, showing a mix of cashmere sweaters, jackets, wristwatches and sunglasses along with shoes. "We want people to say, 'I didn't know Reebok made that'", notes Reebok's director of retailing. Former CEO Paul Fireman observed, "The ultimate thing we are striving for is not brand recognition, but how people perceive us". Reebok wants to reflect in its brand positioning and communications the aspirations, desires and preferences of its consumers, in a more 'personally relevant' manner than Nike.

Targeting Urban Markets in China

In pursuit of growth, Reebok is also targeting promising global markets, with China high on the company's list of priorities. Interest in sports is skyrocketing in China, thanks in part to Chinese basketball star Yao Ming's move to the NBA. According to the company's research, 93% of Chinese males aged 13–25, a prime market for athletic shoes, watch NBA broadcasts on a regular basis. Reebok's Asia Pacific general manager cites one projection showing 50% annual growth in footwear sales, stating that, "it's hard to say what the [actual sales] numbers are going to be, but they are going to be huge". China's successes at the Olympics in Athens merely fuelled market growth, and hosting the 2008 Games cemented Chinese consumers' interest in athletics.

To make the most of the Chinese opportunity, Reebok set up "Yao's House" basketball courts around central Shanghai. Each featured the Reebok trademark and a giant *Sports Illustrated* cover showing the basketball star. By giving teens and young adults a place to hone their slam-dunks, Reebok hoped to shape their attitudes toward its products. "The trends [in China] are made in the urban areas and on street basketball courts, just like in the United States", says one Reebok executive. Reebok is not the only athletic shoe manufacturer entering this market. Nike sponsors a basketball court in Beijing, New Balance is building awareness of its shoes, and Pony is selling sneakers in Beijing, Shanghai and Guandong.

Adidas and Reebok

In early 2006 German rival Adidas, head quartered in Herzogenaurach, acquired Reebok to jointly grapple with Nike. With renewed resources, Reebok launched *Run Easy*, to inspire consumers to fulfil their potential and celebrate their individuality. The message highlighted the camaraderie, joy and fun of running – *Run Easy* – rather than the 'blood, sweat and tears' of running. The subsequent *There are Two People in Everyone* campaign celebrated the balance between sport and life: leading sports personalities declared that there was more to their lives than 'just' sport. Reebok's mission states that it aims to reflect the brand's unlimited creative potential, and this is executed strongly through its brand positioning. Reebok is far more than a passive clone of Nike and the enlarged Adidas corporation – bringing together the numbers two and three in the global sportswear market – is now a significant threat to Nike.

- Reebok's Vision: *Fulfilling Potential*.
- Reebok's Mission: *Always Challenge and Lead Through Creativity*.
- Reebok's Positioning: *Celebrate Individuality in Sport and Life*.
- Reebok's Purpose: *To Empower Global Youth to Fulfil Their Potential*.

Questions for Discussion

1 What segmentation variables is Reebok using for its products? Why are these variables appropriate?
2 Which of the three targeting strategies is Reebok applying? Explain.
3 What influences on the consumer buying decision process appear to have the most impact on Reebok's customers' purchase decisions?
4 In terms of segmentation and buying behaviour, explain the meaning of this statement by a Reebok executive, "The trends are made in the urban areas and on street basketball courts, just like in the United States".

III Developing Marketing Programmes

In Chapter 1, marketing was said to involve marketing opportunity analysis, target market selection and the development of a marketing mix for each target market. The marketing mix is the set of marketing programme activities deployed by marketing managers in order to implement an organisation's agreed target market strategy. The marketing mix centres on the '5Ps' of product, people, place (distribution), promotion and pricing decisions.

The marketing mix must endeavour to match the identified needs of targeted business customers or consumers in order to satisfy these customers' requirements. It must also communicate the desired brand or product positioning and emphasise any differential advantage held by an organisation and its products or services over its rivals. As explained in chapters 1 and 2, marketers should first analyse the forces of the marketing environment, customer buying behaviour, competitors' strategies and their own organisational capabilities before developing their marketing strategies. The marketing mix for a specific target market should only be specified once the marketing strategy has been formulated and agreed by senior management.

Part III of _Marketing Essentials_ examines the product and people ingredients of the marketing mix, the

integral issues of branding and customer service, as well as the important concepts of the product life cycle and the management of product portfolios. Also explored are marketing communications (promotion), marketing channel selection (place) and pricing strategies.

Chapter 8, 'Product Decisions', introduces the concepts of how marketers define and classify products; examines the differences between product item, product line and product mix; discusses the various levels of a product, and explores the important concept of the product life cycle. The chapter then

©iStockphoto.com/photomorphic

discusses organisational structures available to manage products, and concludes by examining the importance of the levels of a product in determining a competitive edge over rivals' products.

Chapter 9, 'Developing Products and Managing Product Portfolios', outlines the organisational alternatives for managing products, explains how an organisation develops a product idea into a commercial product, and analyses the role of product development in the marketing mix. The chapter includes a discussion of how products should be managed during the various stages of a product's life cycle. It discusses how existing products can be modified and how product deletion can sometimes benefit a marketing mix. The chapter concludes with a look at some of the related analytical tools associated with the planning of a product portfolio: the BCG product portfolio analysis, the market attractiveness-business position model or directional policy matrix (DPM), and the ABC sales: contribution analysis.

Chapter 10, 'The Marketing of Services', explores how services differ from tangible goods and considers the implications for marketers. The chapter begins by explaining the nature and characteristics of services, classifying services and the development of marketing strategies for services. It goes on to discuss the significant problems encountered in developing a differential advantage for a service and also addresses the crucial concept of service quality. The chapter then explores the concept of marketing in non-business situations, the development of marketing strategies in non-business organisations and methods for controlling non-business marketing activities.

Chapter 11, 'Marketing Channels', explains the marketing channel concept, the functions and different types of marketing channels. The chapter considers channel integration and the levels of market coverage, and then examines the selection of distribution channels, including the increasingly popular option of direct marketing. Behavioural aspects of channels, particularly the concepts of co-operation and relationship building, conflict and leadership, are then explored. The chapter concludes by examining legal issues in channel management.

Chapter 12, 'Pricing Concepts', explains the characteristics and role of price in marketing, outlines the differences between price and non-price competition, examines different pricing objectives and explores key factors that affect marketers' pricing decisions. The chapter then discusses perceived value for money, before turning to the complex aspect of pricing in business-to-business markets. Having examined the concept of economic value to the customer, the chapter concludes with an overview of the major stages in the process used to establish prices.

Chapter 13, 'An Overview of Marketing Communications', discusses the role of promotion in the marketing mix, the process of communication *per se*, the nature of marketing communications and the way in which the concept of the product adoption process relates to promotional activity. The chapter goes on to explain the aims of promotion and the elements of the promotional mix. The chapter concludes by examining the factors that influence the selection of promotional mix ingredients. Throughout the chapter, the notion of *integrated marketing communications* (IMC) is discussed.

Chapter 14, 'Branding', recognises the fundamental importance of brands and brand equity in marketing, and looks at different types of brands, their benefits, selection, naming, protection and licensing. In most organisations, marketers are the champions of the brand: the chapter presents the key concepts for creating strong and effective brands. The chapter goes on to discuss the functions of packaging, design considerations and the role of packaging in marketing strategy. Finally, it explores the functions of labelling and the associated legal issues.

By the conclusion of Part III of *Marketing Essentials*, readers should understand the core decisions that must be made in determining a marketing mix, including products; people and service delivery issues; the management of product life cycles and portfolios of products; marketing services; the selection of marketing channels; pricing; marketing communications; branding, and packaging.

8

Product Decisions

> "Developing great new products is not just about great ideas. It's about transforming them into products and services that customers want, that competitors have difficulty in copying and that exploit the strengths of the company."

Susan Hart, University of Strathclyde

Objectives

- To learn how marketers define products

- To define product levels

- To understand how to classify products

- To become familiar with the concepts of product item, product line and product mix

- To understand the concept of product life cycle

- To understand the types of organisational structure used to manage products

- To grasp the importance of the levels of a product in determining a competitive edge

Introduction

The product is defined as everything that is received in an exchange, whether favourable or unfavourable. It is a complexity of tangible and intangible attributes, including functional, social and psychological utilities or benefits.[1] A product can be a physical good, a service, an idea, or any combination of these three. This definition also covers supporting services that go with goods, such as installation, guarantees, product information and promises of repair or maintenance.

The product is a key element of the marketing mix and is central to a company's marketing proposition. Without the 'right' product it is unlikely that marketers will be able to satisfy their customers and persuade them to become repeat buyers. As will be explored in this chapter, there is much more to the product component of the marketing mix than the actual tangible product or the service supplied to a customer.

A successful product will not remain so indefinitely. Marketers must judge when to modify their products, launch new ones and delete existing – perhaps once highly successful – products.

Opener

Smelly Fabrics!

Ambrosia, Apple, Bouquet, Coffee, Cola, Eau de Cologne, Fiji, Forest, Lavender, Lemon, Lime, Orange, Peppermint, Pineapple, Pizza, Rose, Strawberry, Tropical Paradise, Vanilla, Wild Flowers, Floral Bouquet, Jasmine and Banana.

What is the connection between these exotic-sounding names? Foods? Paint colours? Brand names? No, the connection is that they are all odours! Courtaulds Textiles, part of Sara Lee, has developed an innovative range of Fragrance Fabrics. The 'micro-encapsulated' scent is 'glued' to the fabric via an acrylic polymer and applied in solution to the fabric during its final production process (known as the 'stenter run'). When the fabric is rubbed, the scent 'capsules' are broken, releasing the fragrance. Staggeringly, after over 30 washes at 40°C, the fragrance is still evident.

The Japanese producers of the micro-capsules have carried out extensive skin-sensitivity tests at the Japanese Laboratory for Cutaneous (Skin) Health. Courtaulds Jersey Underwear Ltd has found ways of 'sticking' the fragrance to 150g cotton single jersey and to 150g cotton/Lycra fabrics. The following are the core fragrances in demand.

- *Lemon* – a refreshing scent, with characteristic uplifting properties, associated with cleansing and the ability to revive the skin.
- *Orange* – a slightly sweet scent, known for its calming qualities.

- *Rose* – the 'queen' of essential oils, associated with beauty, femininity and purity, as well as a relaxed state of mind.
- *Vanilla* – commonly linked with taste, a distinctive smell that is obtained from the pods of a beautiful tropical orchid.
- *Lavender* – a beautiful scent with endearing qualities, encourages restful sleep and has balancing properties; widely used in perfumery and with an oil base to ease muscular aches and pains.
- *Apple and strawberry* – fresh and fruity fragrances that are the essence of a sunny summer.
- *Forest and wild flowers* – mirroring the scents of woodland, two fragrances that combine tranquillity and freshness.

So why the excitement? Well, in fabric development, innovations tend to be based around texture and durability – for example, the stretchy Lycra phenomenon. New product development has rarely been so innovative in this market, and for Sara Lee Courtaulds the result has been a competitive edge over rivals. The main target market is currently users of sportswear: using this new technology, such clothing emits a pleasant odour when the wearer gets hot and sweaty on the squash court or in the gym. However, it's not only overheated sports enthusiasts for whom this new product technology has appeal – it can also be used in the creation of 'intelligent' fabrics, which can detect, for example, when a women is menstruating, and will then release soothing lavender or rose fragrances.

It is likely that, in the next few years, many clothing applications will make use of these micro-encapsulated scents. The task for fabric manufacturers' marketers will be to promote these attributes to the garment makers, whose marketers will need to entice retailers to stock these new lines and consumers to trial these fragrant products.

Sources: *Fragrance Fabrics* and *Essential Oils and Their 'Well Being' Qualities*, Courtaulds Jersey Underwear; Courtaulds Textiles, Nottingham.
Photo: Courtesy of Karen Beaulah

Products such as the Fragrance Fabrics devised by SaraLee Courtaulds, are among a company's most crucial and visible contacts with buyers. If a company's products do not meet its customers' desires and needs, the company will have to adjust its offering in order to survive. Developing a successful **product** requires knowledge of fundamental marketing and product concepts. Courtaulds' range of Fragrance Fabrics will need to appeal both to garment makers and consumers if it is to achieve long-term success. This chapter starts by introducing and defining the concepts that help clarify what a product is, and looks at how buyers view products. The next section examines the concepts of product mix and product line as an introduction to product planning. The chapter then explores the stages of the product life cycle. Each life-cycle stage generally requires a specific marketing strategy, operates within a certain competitive environment and has its own sales and profit pattern. The final section discusses the elements that make up a product.

What is a Product?

A **good** is a tangible physical entity, such as a bottle of Pantene shampoo, a loaf of Hovis bread or a Muse CD. A **service**, by contrast, is intangible; it is the result of the application of human and mechanical efforts to people or objects. Examples of services include hairdressing, tennis tuition and medical treatment. (Chapter 10 provides a detailed discussion of services marketing.) **Ideas** are concepts, philosophies, images or issues. They provide the psychological stimulus to solve problems. For example, Oxfam provides famine relief and attempts to improve the long-term prospects of people in hunger-stricken countries.

When buyers purchase a product, they are really buying the benefits and satisfaction they think the product will provide. A pair of Predator football boots, for example, is purchased for status and image, not just to protect the feet. Services, in particular, are bought on the basis of promises of satisfaction. Promises, with the images and appearances of symbols, help consumers make judgements about tangible and intangible products.[2] Symbols and cues are often used to make intangible products more tangible to the consumer. MasterCard, for example, uses globes to symbolise the company's financial power and worldwide coverage.

Classifying Products

Products fall into one of two general categories. **Consumer products** are purchased to satisfy personal and family needs. **Industrial** or **business products** are bought for use in a company's operations or to make other products. The same item can be both a consumer product and an industrial product. For example, when consumers purchase light bulbs for their homes, they are classified as consumer products. However, when a large company purchases light bulbs to provide lighting in a factory or office the same goods are considered industrial products. Thus the buyer's intent, or the ultimate use of the product, determines whether an item is classified as a consumer or an industrial/business-to-business product. It is common for more people to be involved in buying an industrial product than in a consumer purchase. Chapters 4 and 5 explain the differences in buying and decision-making for consumer and business-to-business products.

It is important to know about product classifications because different classes of product are aimed at particular target markets, and classification affects distribution, promotion and pricing decisions. Furthermore, the types of marketing activity and effort needed – in short, the entire marketing mix – differ according to how a product is classified. This section examines the characteristics of consumer and industrial products and explores the marketing activities associated with some of them.

Product
Everything, both favourable and unfavourable, tangible and intangible, received in an exchange of an idea, service or good

Good
A tangible physical entity

Service
The application of human and mechanical efforts to people or objects in order to provide intangible benefits to customers

Ideas
Concepts, philosophies, images or issues that provide the psychological stimulus to solve problems or adjust to the environment

Consumer products
Items purchased to satisfy personal or family needs

Industrial or **business products**
Items bought for use in a company's operations or to make other products

Consumer Products

The most widely accepted approach to classifying consumer products relies on the common characteristics of consumer buying behaviour. It divides products into four categories: convenience, shopping, speciality and unsought products. However, not all buyers behave in the same way when purchasing a specific type of product. Thus a single product can fit into more than one category. To minimise this problem, marketers think in terms of how buyers *generally* behave when purchasing a specific item. In addition, they recognise that the 'correct' classification can be determined only by considering a particular company's intended target market.

Convenience Products   Relatively inexpensive, frequently purchased and rapidly consumed items on which buyers exert only minimal purchasing effort are called **convenience products**. They range from chocolate, magazines and chewing gum to petrol and soft drinks. The buyer spends little time planning the purchase or comparing available brands or sellers. Even a buyer who prefers a specific brand will readily choose a substitute if the preferred brand is not conveniently available.

Convenience products
Inexpensive, frequently purchased and rapidly consumed items that demand only minimal purchasing effort

Classifying a product as a convenience product has several implications for a company's marketing strategy. A convenience product is normally marketed through many retail outlets. Because sellers experience high inventory turnover, the per unit gross margins can be relatively low. Producers of convenience products such as PG Tips tea and Domestos bleach expect little promotional effort at the retail level and so must provide their own through advertising, sales promotion and the item's packaging. The package may have an especially important role to play, because many convenience items are available only on a self-service basis at the retail level. The use of on-pack sales promotion and point-of-sale displays are ways to maximise the impact of the package.

Shopping Products   Items that are chosen more carefully than convenience products are called **shopping products**. They are purchased infrequently and are expected to last a long time. Buyers are willing to expend effort in planning and purchasing these items. They allocate time for comparing stores and brands with respect to prices, credit, product features, qualities, services and perhaps guarantees. Appliances, furniture, bicycles, stereos, jewellery and cameras are examples of shopping products. Even though shopping products are more expensive than convenience products, few buyers of shopping products are particularly brand loyal. If they were, they would be unwilling to shop and compare brands.

Shopping products
Items chosen more carefully than convenience products; consumers will expend effort in planning and purchasing these items

Marketers seeking to market shopping products effectively must consider that they require fewer retail outlets than convenience products. Because they are purchased less frequently, inventory (stock) turnover is lower and middlemen (retailers) expect to receive higher gross margins. Although large sums of money may be required to advertise shopping products, an even larger proportion of resources is likely to be used for personal selling. Indeed, the quality of the service may be a factor in the consumer's choice of outlet. Thus a couple that buys a new dishwasher might expect sales personnel in the chosen retail outlet to explain the advantages and features of competing brands. In many cases, the producer and the middlemen also expect some cooperation from one another with respect to providing parts and repair services, and performing promotional activities.

Speciality products
Items that possess one or more unique characteristic; consumers of speciality products plan their purchases and will expend considerable effort to obtain them

Speciality Products   Products that possess one or more unique characteristic and which a significant group of buyers is willing to expend considerable effort to obtain are called **speciality products**. Buyers plan the purchase of a speciality product carefully; they know exactly what they want and will not accept a substitute. An example of a speciality product is a painting by L.S. Lowry or a Cartier watch. When searching for speciality products, buyers do

Figure 8.1
*Confectionary brands
are convenience
products
Source: Neil Holmes
Freelance Digital/
Alamy*

not compare alternatives; they are concerned primarily with finding an outlet that has a pre-selected product available.

The marketing of a speciality product is very distinctive. The exclusivity of the product is accentuated by the fact that speciality products are often distributed through a limited number of retail outlets. Some companies go to considerable lengths to control this aspect of their distribution. Like shopping goods, speciality products are purchased infrequently, causing lower inventory turnover and thus requiring relatively high gross margins.

Unsought products
Items that are
purchased when a
sudden problem arises
or when aggressive
selling is used to obtain
a sale that would not
otherwise take place

Unsought Products   Products that are purchased when a sudden problem arises or when aggressive selling obtains a sale that otherwise would not take place are called **unsought products**. The consumer does not usually expect to buy these products regularly. Emergency windscreen replacement services and headstones are examples of unsought products. Life insurance is an example of an unsought product that often needs aggressive personal selling.

**Business or
Industrial
Products**

Business products are usually purchased on the basis of a company's goals and objectives. The functional aspects of these products are usually more important than the psychological rewards sometimes associated with consumer products. Business products can be classified into seven categories according to their characteristics and intended uses:

1 raw materials
2 major equipment
3 accessory equipment
4 component parts

5 process materials
6 consumable supplies
7 industrial/business services.[3]

Raw materials
The basic materials that become part of physical products

Raw Materials   The basic materials that become part of physical products are **raw materials**. These include minerals, chemicals, agricultural products, and materials from forests and oceans. They are usually bought and sold in relatively large quantities according to grades and specifications.

Major equipment
Large tools and machines used for production purposes

Major Equipment   Large tools and machines used for production purposes, such as cranes and spray painting machinery, are types of **major equipment**. Major equipment is often expensive, may be used in a production process for a considerable length of time and is often custom-made to perform specific functions. For example, Alsthom manufactures purpose-built large gears and turbines. Other items are more standardised, performing similar tasks for many types of company. Because major equipment is so expensive, purchase decisions are often long and complex, and may be made by senior management. Marketers of major equipment are frequently called upon to provide a variety of services, including installation, training, repair, maintenance assistance and financing. This may lead to long-term relationships being developed between suppliers of major equipment and their customers.

Accessory equipment
Tools and equipment used in production or office activities that do not become part of the final physical product

Accessory Equipment   Equipment that does not become a part of the final physical product, but is used in production or office activities is referred to as **accessory equipment**. Examples include telephone systems, stationery supplies, fractional horsepower motors, and tools. Compared with major equipment, accessory items are usually much cheaper, are purchased routinely with less negotiation and are treated as expenditure items rather than capital items because they are not expected to last long. More outlets are required for distributing accessory equipment than for major equipment, but sellers do not have to provide the multitude of services expected of major equipment marketers.

Component parts
Parts that become a part of the physical product and are either finished items ready for assembly or products that need little processing before assembly

Component Parts   Parts that become part of the physical product and are either finished items ready for assembly or products that need little processing before assembly are called **component parts**. Although they become part of a larger product, component parts can often be easily identified and distinguished. Tyres, spark plugs, gears, lighting units, screws and wires are all component parts of a delivery van. Buyers purchase such items according to their own specifications or industry standards. They expect the parts to be of specified quality and delivered on time so that production is not slowed or stopped. Producers that are primarily assemblers, such as most washing machine or lawnmower manufacturers, depend heavily on suppliers of component parts.

Process materials
Materials used directly in the production of other products, but not readily identifiable

Process Materials   Materials that are used directly in the production of other products are called process materials. Unlike component parts, however, **process materials** are not readily identifiable. For example, Reichhold Chemicals markets a treated fibre product: a phenolicresin, sheet-moulding compound used in the production of flight deck instrument panels and aircraft cabin interiors. Although the material is not identifiable in the finished aircraft, it retards burning, smoke and formation of toxic gas when subjected to fire or high temperatures.

Consumable supplies
Supplies that facilitate production and operations but do not become part of the finished product

Consumable Supplies   Supplies that facilitate production and operations but do not become part of the finished product are referred to as **consumable supplies**. Paper, print cartridges, pencils, oils, cleaning agents and paints are in this category. They are purchased by many

MRO items
Consumable supplies in the subcategories of maintenance, repair and operating (or overhaul) supplies

Industrial/business services
The intangible products that many organisations use in their operations, including financial, legal, marketing research, computer programming and operation, caretaking and printing services

Core product
The level of a product that provides the perceived or real core benefit or service

Actual product
A composite of the features and capabilities offered in a product, quality and durability, design and product styling, packaging and brand name

Augmented product
Support aspects of a product, including customer service, warranty, delivery and credit, personnel, installation and after-sales support

different types of business. Consumable supplies are purchased routinely and sold through numerous outlets. To ensure that supplies are available when needed, buyers often deal with more than one seller. Consumable supplies can be divided into three subcategories – maintenance, repair and operating (or overhaul) supplies – and are sometimes called **MRO items**.

Industrial/Business Services   **Industrial/Business Services** are the intangible products that many organisations use in their operations. They include financial, legal, marketing research, computer programming and operation, caretaking and printing services for business. Some companies decide to provide their own services internally, while others outsource them. This decision depends largely on the costs associated with each alternative and the frequency with which the services are needed.

The Three Levels of Product

The product may appear obvious – a carton of fresh orange juice or a designer handbag – but generally the purchaser is buying much more than a drink or a means of carrying personal items. To be motivated to make the purchase, the product must have a perceived or real core benefit or service. This level of product, termed the **core product**, is illustrated in Figure 8.2. The **actual product** is a composite of several factors: the features and capabilities offered, quality and durability, design and product styling, packaging and, often of great importance, the brand name.

In order to make the purchase, the consumer often needs the assistance of sales personnel; there may be delivery and payment credit requirements and, for bulky or very technical products, advice regarding installation. The level of warranty back-up and after-sales support, particularly for innovative, highly technical or high value goods, will be of concern to most consumers. Increasingly, the overall level of customer service constitutes part of the purchase criteria, and in many markets it is deemed integral to the product on offer. These 'support' issues form what is termed the **augmented product** (see Figure 8.2).

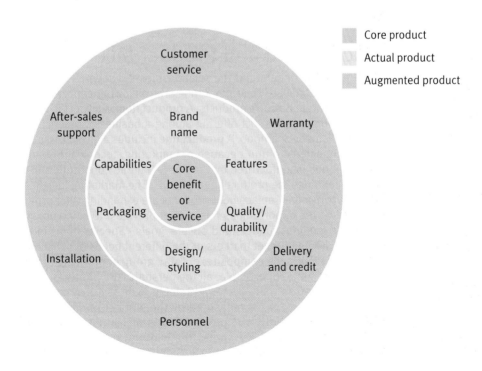

Figure 8.2
The three levels of product: core, actual and augmented

When a £30,000 BMW 3 Series executive car is purchased, the vehicle's performance specification and design may have encouraged the sale. Speed of delivery and credit payment terms may have been essential to the conclusion of the deal. The brand's image, particularly in the case of a car costing £30,000, will also have influenced the sale. Once behind the wheel of the BMW, its new owner will expect reliability and efficient, friendly, convenient service in the course of maintenance being required. The purchase might have been lost at the outset had the salesperson mishandled the initial enquiry. Repeat servicing business and the subsequent sale of another new car may be ruled out if the owner encounters incompetent, unhelpful service engineers. The core benefit may have been a car to facilitate journeys to work, transport for the family or the acquisition of a recognised status symbol. Customer satisfaction will depend on the product's actual performance and also on service aspects of the augmented product. This example is not unusual. For most consumer or business products and services, the consumer is influenced by the three levels of the product: core, actual and augmented. Marketers need to take this into consideration when developing product offers. Careful consideration of all levels of the product can provide the basis for a competitive edge. Several years ago BP launched an environmentally friendly diesel fuel with 90 per cent reduced emissions. This coincided with increasing environmental awareness among customers and provided a benefit at the augmented product level. Soon all rivals were offering similar clean diesels. This illustrates how organisations must increasingly strive to consider all product levels when developing their offerings.[4]

Many marketers now recognise the important role that personnel play in product exchanges. People are responsible for the design, production, marketing, sale and distribution of products. As will be explained in Chapter 10, personnel are especially important in the sale and delivery of services. Thus, a financial services adviser must have considerable expertise in the sector to give good advice. Similarly, a good-quality haircut can only be delivered by a skilled hairdresser. As consumers, people make decisions and ultimately adopt products for use and consumption. When deciding which products to adopt and use, people now pay considerable attention to the skills, attitudes and motivations of personnel involved in the marketing channel. As explained in Chapter 1, personnel also constitute an essential ingredient of the marketing mix for consumer and business goods.

Product Line and Product Mix

Product item
A specific version of a product that can be designated as a distinct offering among a business's products

Product line
A group of closely related product items that are considered a unit because of marketing, technical or end-use considerations

Product mix
The composite group of products that a company makes available to customers

Depth (of product mix)
The number of different products offered in each product line

Width (of product mix)
The number of product lines a company offers

Marketers must understand the relationships between all their organisation's products if they are to coordinate their marketing. The following concepts describe the relationships between an organisation's products. A **product item** is a specific version of a product that can be designated as a distinct offering among a business's products – for example, Procter & Gamble's Pantene shampoo. A **product line** includes a group of closely related product items that are considered a unit because of marketing, technical or end-use considerations. All the shampoos manufactured by Procter & Gamble constitute one of its product lines. Figure 8.3 illustrates the product line for Hovis. The Marketing Insight box explains how manufacturers of nicotine replacement products are expanding their product line to allow them to capitalise on the opportunities this market provides. To come up with the optimum product line, marketers must understand buyers' goals.[5] Specific items in a product line reflect the desires of different target markets or the different needs of consumers.

A **product mix** is the composite, or total, group of products that a company makes available to customers. For example, all the personal care products, laundry detergent products and other products that Procter & Gamble manufactures constitute its product mix. The **depth** of a product mix is measured by the number of different products offered in each product line. The **width** of a product mix is measured by the number of product lines a company offers. Figure 8.4 shows the width of the product mix and the depth of each product line for selected Procter & Gamble products in the USA. Procter & Gamble is

Marketing Insight

A New Generation of Nicotine Replacement Products

Nicotine replacement therapy (NRT) fights nicotine dependence and relieves the symptoms of withdrawal in smokers who are trying to give up. Leading brands include Nicotinell, NiQuitin CQ and Nicorette. Novartis, the company behind Nicotinell nicotine replacement gum and patches, also launched food products designed to help smokers quit the habit. Many consumers are already familiar with the Nicotinell brand. As smoking becomes increasingly socially unacceptable, the company now believes that there are a variety of new product development opportunities for its brand. Novartis launched a nicotine replacement lozenge that, when sucked, provides a continual, low-level boost of nicotine for relatively light smokers. Other initiatives include the possible development of nicotine-enhanced food and a detoxification programme for ex-smokers. Supportive counselling services are viewed as a key part of the therapy, and most of the leading players have examined how to offer such services alongside their patches, gums, pills and lozenges.

It is not difficult to understand the attractions of the nicotine replacement therapy market and to appreciate why Novartis is seeking to extend its product offerings. As millions seek to leave their smoking habit behind, the market for nicotine replacement products is growing rapidly. Indications also show that 1 in 20 of those attempting to 'kick the habit' will use some form of nicotine replacement therapy. Not surprisingly, Novartis is not alone in seeking to develop its product range. Since NRT products were first launched in the UK more than a decade ago, several companies have dominated the market: Novartis, with its Nicotinell patch and gum; Pharmacia & Upjohn (P&U), with its Nicorette gum, inhalator and patches; and Boots, with its own-label patches and gum. Recent developments include Boots' inhalator and competing brand Nicorette's launch of its micro-tab, a kind of nicotine pill that, when placed under the tongue, takes half an hour to dissolve.

Perhaps the most aggressive challenge to the market has come from pharmaceutical giant SmithKline Beecham (SKB), which spent £12 million on the UK launch of NiQuitin CQ (CQ stands for 'committed quitters'). SKB claimed this to have been the largest ever over-the-counter launch in the UK. Clearly the company expected the brand, already the best-seller in the USA, to claim a large slice of the UK market. Company representatives suggested that this was achieved by the unique 'personalised literature

pack' included with the NiQuitin CQ product. This pack includes a questionnaire for smokers to fill in, detailing the circumstances in which they are most vulnerable to lighting up. Advice is then offered that is tailored to match the answers provided in the questionnaire. According to Elaine MacFarlane, SKB's director of consumer healthcare communications, this represented a unique approach in the NRT market. She explains, 'When these products first launched, they were positioned as a magic bullet – "take this and you won't want to smoke". Now with all the noise from the political, health and economic perspectives, you know it doesn't make sense to smoke any more, and we felt the time was right for a more mature consideration of people's motivation'.

In such a volatile market, future trends are difficult to predict. When NRT products were first launched in the UK in 1993, they were met with considerable consumer excitement. However, following an initial growth in sales, consumer confidence in the capabilities of the products declined. Today, with the products widely available in supermarkets as well as pharmacies, and governments throughout the EU considering bans on smoking in public places and other anti-smoking measures, the key players are looking for innovative ways to ensure that their products play a major role in the continued fight against smoking. New product development is likely to be just part of the solution, with manufacturers also seeking a fresh and more realistic promotional stance. For Novartis, with its original slogan 'Helps you stop smoking', this involves repositioning the brand to stress its role in harm reduction and Nicotinell's role in supporting the quitter's willpower and resolve to stop smoking, while making the product desirable. The new advertising strapline requires little explanation, accompanying images of a leather-clad attractive female biker: *Lose the Smoke. Keep The Fire!* With smokers over 30 years old as the key target, and the biggest increase in new smokers among those in their early teens and twenties, the market potential is considerable. Time will tell whether Novartis and the other players continue to meet the challenge.

Sources: Novartis Consumer Healthcare, 2004–7; Neil Denny, 'Smokers may be offered nicotine food to help quit', *Marketing*, 28 January 1999, p. 1; Sue Beenstock, 'Queuing up to quit', *Marketing*, 28 January 1999, p. 1; www.Nicotinell.com, June 2004 and November, 2007; www.mypharmacy.co.uk/medicines/topics/n/nicotine_replacement_therapy, June 2004; Boots, November, 2007; http://www.nicotinell.co.uk/football/ 26 November, 2007.

Figure 8.3
This advertisement for leading bread brand Hovis makes clear that the Hovis line includes more than the familiar Hovis brown loaf Source: All work created by Star Chamber

known for using distinctive technology, branding, packaging and consumer advertising to promote individual items in its detergent product line. Tide, Bold and Cheer – all Procter & Gamble detergents – share similar distribution channels and manufacturing facilities. Yet due to variations in product formula and attributes, each is promoted as distinct, adding depth to the product line.

Product life cycle
The four major stages through which products move: introduction, growth, maturity and decline

Product Life Cycles

Just as biological cycles progress through growth and decline, so too do **product life cycles**. A new product is introduced into the marketplace; it grows; it matures; and when it loses appeal and sales decline, it is terminated.[6] As explained in Chapter 9, different marketing

	Laundry detergents	Toothpastes	Bar soaps	Deodorants	Shampoos	Tissue/towel
Product line depth	Ivory Snow 1930	Gleem 1952	Ivory 1879	Old Spice 1948	Head & Shoulders 1961	Charmin 1928
	Dreft 1933	Crest 1955	Camay 1926	Secret 1956	Pantene Pro 1965	Puffs 1960
	Tide 1946		Zest 1952	Sure 1972	Vidal Sassoon 1974	Bounty 1965
	Cheer 1950		Safeguard 1963		Pert Plus 1979	Royale 1996
	Bold 1965		Olay 1993		Ivory 1983	
	Gain 1966					
	Era 1972					

Product mix width

Figure 8.4
The concepts of width of product mix and depth of product line applied to selected Procter & Gamble products
Source: information provided and reprinted by permission of the Procter & Gamble Company, Public Affairs Division, 1 Procter & Gamble Plaza, Cincinnati, OH 45202-3315

strategies are appropriate at different stages in the product life cycle. Thus packaging, branding and labelling techniques can be used to help create or modify products that have reached different points in their life.

As Figure 8.5 shows, a product life cycle has four major stages:

1 introduction
2 growth
3 maturity
4 decline.

When a product moves through its cycle, the strategies relating to competition, promotion, place/distribution, pricing and market information must be evaluated periodically and possibly changed. Astute marketing managers use the life-cycle concept to make sure that the introduction, alteration and termination of a product are timed and executed properly. By understanding the typical life-cycle pattern, marketers are better able to maintain profitable products and drop unprofitable ones.

Introduction

Introduction stage
A product's first appearance in the marketplace, before any sales or profits have been made

The **introduction stage** of the life cycle begins at a product's first appearance in the marketplace, when sales are zero and profits are negative. Profits are below zero because a new product incurs development costs, initial revenues are low, and at the same time a company must generally incur the significant expenses incurred during promotion and distribution. As time passes, sales should move upwards from zero and profits should build up from the negative position (see Figure 8.5).[7]

Because of cost, very few product introductions represent major inventions. Developing and introducing a new product can mean an outlay of many millions of pounds. The failure rate for new products is quite high, ranging from 60 to 90 per cent depending on the industry and on how product failure is defined. For example, in the food and drinks industry, 80 per cent of all new products fail. Typically, however, product introductions involve a new deodorant, a new type of vacuum cleaner or a new leisure concept rather than a major product innovation. In general, the more marketing-oriented the company, the more likely it will be to launch innovative products that are new to the market.[8]

New product ideas are more likely to be successful when senior management is involved in product development and launch. In addition, research shows that a clear, stable vision, flexibility and improvisation, information exchange and collaboration are also key ingredients in new product success.[9]

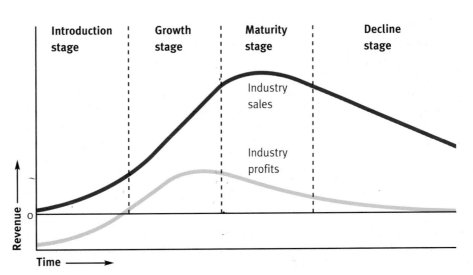

Figure 8.5
The four stages of the product life cycle

Potential buyers must be made aware of the new product's features, uses and advantages. Two difficulties may arise at this point. Only a few sellers may have the resources, technological knowledge and marketing know-how to launch the product successfully; and the initial product price may have to be high in order to recoup expensive marketing research or development costs. Given these difficulties, it is not surprising that many products never get beyond the introduction stage; indeed many are never launched commercially at all.

Growth

Growth stage
The stage at which a product's sales rise rapidly and profits reach a peak, before levelling off into maturity

During the **growth stage**, sales rise rapidly, and profits reach a peak and then start to decline (see Figure 8.5). The growth stage is critical to a product's survival because competitive reactions to its success during this period will affect the product's life expectancy. For example, Mars successfully launched Ice Cream Mars, the first ice-cream version of an established confectionery product. Today the product competes with more than a dozen other brands. Some of the competing brands failed quickly and others followed. Profits decline late in the growth stage as more competitors enter the market, driving prices down and creating the need for heavy promotional expenses. At this point a typical marketing strategy encourages strong brand loyalty, perhaps using sales promotion, and competes with aggressive emulators of the product. During the growth stage, a company tries to strengthen its market share and develop a competitive position by emphasising the product's benefits.

Aggressive promotional pricing, including price cuts, is typical during the growth stage. The Internet industry is now well into its growth stage, and many competitors have entered the market. Companies like AOL must battle hard to maintain their existing positions in this competitive arena.

Maturity

Maturity stage
The stage during which a product's sales curve peaks and starts to decline, and profits continue to decline

During the **maturity stage**, the sales curve peaks and starts to decline, and profits continue to decline (see Figure 8.5). This stage is characterised by severe competition, with many brands in the market. Competitors emphasise improvements and differences in their versions of the product. Inevitably, during the maturity stage, some weaker competitors are squeezed out or switch their attention to other products. For example, some brands of DVD player are perishing now that the product is reaching the maturity stage.

During the maturity stage, the producers who remain in the market must make fresh promotional and distribution efforts. These efforts must focus on dealers as much as on consumers to ensure that brand visibility is maintained at the point of sale. Advertising and dealer-oriented promotions are typical during this stage of the product life cycle. The promoters must also take into account the fact that, as the product reaches maturity, buyers' knowledge of it attains a high level. Consumers of the product are no longer inexperienced generalists, but rather experienced specialists.

Decline

Decline stage
The last stage of a product's life cycle, during which sales fall rapidly

During the **decline stage**, sales fall rapidly (see Figure 8.5). New technology or a new social trend may cause product sales to take a sharp downturn. For example, iPods have reduced CD sales and green concerns have damaged the sales volumes of certain models of vehicles. When this happens, the marketer must consider pruning items from the product line to eliminate those not earning a profit. Sony surprised the market by announcing it would be pulling out of selling PDAs. The decision came because Sony believed that technology changes are signalling a move away from handheld organisers towards multifunctional mobile phones.[10] At this time, too, the marketer may cut promotion efforts, eliminate marginal distributors and, finally, plan to phase out the product.

Because most businesses have a product mix consisting of multiple products, a company's destiny is rarely tied to one product. A composite of life-cycle patterns is formed when various products in the mix are at different stages in the cycle. As one product is declining, other products are in the introduction, growth or maturity stage. Marketers must deal with the dual problems of prolonging the life of existing products and introducing new products to meet sales goals. More details of this kind of portfolio management activity are given in

Chapter 9, which also explores the development of new products and considers how they can be managed in their various life-cycle stages.

Why Some Products Fail and Others Succeed

Thousand of new products are introduced each year and many of them fail. Some estimates put the product failure rate as high as 60 to 90 per cent. Failure and success rates vary in different industries and from company to company. Figures suggest that consumer products are more likely to fail than those directed at business markets. Being one of the first brands launched in a product category is no guarantee of success. One study found that in 50 product categories, only half of the pioneers survived.[11]

Products fail for many reasons. One of the most common is the company's failure to match product offerings to customer needs. When products do not offer value and lack the feature customers want, they fail in the marketplace. Ineffective or inconsistent branding has also been blamed for product failures. Other reasons often given for new product failure include technical or design problems, poor timing, overestimation of market size, ineffective promotion and inefficient distribution. The problems leading to the downfall of Coca-Cola's UK launch of bottled water Dasani were widely debated in the press. Technical difficulties led to bromide contamination at the company's plant. At a time when consumers were already concerned about the purity of tap water, the withdrawal of the product was inevitable.[12] For Cadbury Trebor Bassett's 24-7 chewing gum, failure was blamed on distribution problems and lack of in-store support.[13]

Degrees of Product Failure

It is important to distinguish between degrees of product failure. Absolute failure occurs when a company loses money on a new product because it is unable to recover development, production and marketing costs. Such a product is usually deleted from the product mix. Relative product failure occurs when a product returns a profit but does not meet a company's profit or market share objectives. If a relative product failure is repositioned or improved, it may become a successful member of the product line. Some products experience relative product failure after years of success. Drinks business Diageo recently stepped in to stem declining sales of Guinness stout. Part of this effort involved reformulating the canned version of the drink, to make its taste closer to that of draught Guinness. The cans were also redesigned to appeal to a younger segment of drinkers. As the Marketing Insight explains, Guinness has been looking at various ways to reinvigorate its brand.

The Ingredients for Success

Despite this gloomy picture of product failure, some new products are very successful. Perhaps the most important ingredient for success is the product's ability to provide a significant and perceivable benefit to a sizeable number of customers. New products with an observable advantage over similar available products – such as more features, ease of operation or improved technology – have a greater chance of success.

Tangible and Intangible Product Characteristics

When developing products, marketers make many decisions. Some of these involve the tangible, or physical, characteristics of the product; others focus on less tangible support services that are very much a part of the total product.

Physical Characteristics and Product Quality

The question of how much **quality** to build into the product is crucial for marketers. In the core product, quality constitutes the product's ability to achieve the basic functional requirements expected of it. A major dimension of quality is durability. Higher quality often demands better materials and more expensive processing, which increases production costs and, ultimately, the product's price. How much the target market is prepared to pay

⚙ Marketing Insight

Old Brands Battle the Effects of Ageing

Guinness and Kit-Kat have something in common. They are both very well-established brands that have attracted considerable customer support over the lengthy relationship they have enjoyed with different generations of consumers. Yet these well-loved brands are also facing crisis. Diageo's Guinness in the middle of the decade suffered a UK sales decline of 3 per cent. In Ireland, the brand's domestic market, the sales fall reached 7 per cent during the same period. Meanwhile Nestlé's Kit-Kat was also struggling, with UK sales declining by 5.4 per cent in just 12 months.

So what were the reasons for this malaise? According to the former executive chairman of The Henley Centre, 'The trouble with most mature brands is that they are being marketed to a population that is changing rapidly.' Over-extension of the Kit-Kat brand may have diluted the consumer franchise for Kit-Kat, while a move away from the familiar advertising strapline, *Have a Break . . .* also alienated some consumers who failed to latch on to newer campaigns. The challenge for both brands is to continue to communicate strongly with their loyal customer base, while doing more to reflect the needs of potential new customers.

For Guinness, there is a positive side to figures for the brand: the stout's global fortunes appear to be on the ascendant, with a 3 per cent increase in volume. So what went wrong in the UK and Ireland? Some believe that the brand's marketing may be partly to blame for the decline. During its 75 years of advertising, Guinness developed a reputation for innovative campaigns, many of which achieved iconic status. This started in 1929, with the now famous 'Guinness is good for you' strapline. Soon afterwards, in 1935, the toucan was featured for the first time on advertising posters. Initially the plan had been to use a pelican. The idea was to run a 'Guinness-a-day' theme (building on the 'Guinness is

good for you' concept). The plan was to feature an image of a pelican with seven pints positioned along its beak. In the event, a toucan was substituted and an appropriate verse was written to accompany the advertising:

> 'If he can say as you can
> Guinness is good for you
> How grand to be a toucan
> Just think what toucan do'

The toucan was finally retired in 1982. Other high-profile campaigns, such as the 'Pure Genius' advertising followed. However, recent advertising executions, including the 'moth' advertisement, which featured young people leaving a car in a dark forest to follow a cloud of moths towards the light coming from a Guinness bar, were criticised as uninspiring. Other industry experts suggest that the Guinness brand has been diluted by confusing innovations. Product extension Guinness Extra Cold, which some argued flew in the face of the warmth associated with traditional Guinness, was pinpointed as one culprit. Now Diageo wants to battle the effects of the mature stage of Guinness's life cycle, by focusing on its heritage as a status brand, and is backing up this strategy with a range of new advertising initiatives. The latest advertising, 'Hands' waiting in anticipation, has been well received and recent performance has improved. Maintaining consumer interest in long-standing products, no matter how successful they have been previously, is no easy matter. Both Nestlé with Kit-Kat and Diageo with Guinness are perpetually introducing new product varieties, innovative packaging and up-rated advertising concepts so as to avoid maturity creeping into the decline stage.

Sources: 'Guinness in facelift as volume dips', *Marketing Week*, 20 May 2004, p. 8; Sonoo Singh, 'Struggling to keep up', *Marketing Week*, 20 May 2004, pp. 24–7; www.thetoucan.co.uk, 26 November, 2007; http://landingpage.guinness.com, 26 November, 2007.

Quality
The core product's ability to achieve the basic functional requirements expected of it

will affect the level of quality specified. The concepts of quality and value are related. A consumer may be happy to pay a premium for a hard-wearing paint, because they perceive it as better value than competing offerings. In general, a company should set consistent quality levels for all products with a similar brand. The quality of competing brands is also an important consideration. As explained in Chapter 7, marketing research plays an important role in determining the optimum physical features – such as quality – of a product.

Supportive Product-related Services

All products possess intangible features. When prospective customers are unable to experience the product in advance, they are making decisions based on promises of satisfaction.[14] A woman buying lingerie over the Internet hopes that when the garments she ordered arrive, they will meet her expectations of quality, look and fit. Should she be disappointed, she will expect to be able to return the items. Arrangements for product returns are just one of many product-related services. Others include product guarantees, credit and repair facilities. Although these product features may be less tangible than the product itself, they are often a strong influence on the choices that customers make. Can you imagine buying a watch with no guarantee, or a television that cannot be repaired?

The type of guarantee a company provides can be critical for buyers, especially when expensive, technically complex goods such as appliances are involved. A **guarantee** specifies what the producer or supplier will do if the product malfunctions. Some photographic processors offer free processing on prints not ready within 24 hours. Guarantors are legally required to state more simply and specifically the terms and conditions under which the company will take action. For example, changes in EU law now require electrical items to carry a two-year guarantee. Marketers are now using guarantees more aggressively as tools to give their brands a competitive advantage.

Guarantee
An agreement specifying what the producer or supplier will do if the product malfunctions

An effective guarantee should be unconditional, easy to understand and communicate, meaningful, easy to invoke, and quick and easy to act on. The customer should be able to return a product and get a replacement, a refund or a credit for the returned item. Such guarantees are beneficial because they generate feedback from customers and help build customer loyalty and sales.[15] Although it is more difficult to provide guarantees for services than for goods, some service marketers do guarantee customer satisfaction. For example, some opticians offering a one hour turnaround for new lenses or frames do not charge customers who have to wait longer than this time.

Establishing a system to provide replacement parts and repair services is an essential support service for complex and expensive consumer or business products. For example, builders expect construction machinery manufacturers like Caterpillar to be able to provide replacement parts quickly and without fuss. Sometimes these services are provided directly to buyers, in other cases regional service centres or middlemen are used.

Finally, a company must sometimes provide credit services to customers. Even though credit services place a financial burden on a business, they can be beneficial. For instance, a company may acquire and maintain a stable market share. Many major oil companies, for example, have competed effectively against petrol discounters by providing credit services. For marketers of relatively expensive items, such as cars or soft furnishings, offering credit services enables a larger number of people to buy the product, thus enlarging the market for the item.

Summary

A *product* is everything, both favourable and unfavourable, that is received in an exchange. It is a complex set of tangible and intangible attributes, including functional, social and psychological utilities or benefits. A product can be a *good*, a *service*, an *idea* or any combination of these three. Consumers buy the benefits and satisfaction they think the product will provide.

❯❯ Products can be classified on the basis of the buyer's intentions. *Consumer products* are purchased to satisfy personal and family needs. *Industrial* or *business products* are purchased for use in a company's operations or to make other products. The same product may be classified as both a consumer product and a business product. Consumer products can be subdivided into *convenience*, *shopping*, *speciality* and *unsought products*. Business products can be divided into *raw materials*, *major equipment*, *accessory equipment*, component parts, *process materials*, *consumable supplies (MRO items)* and *business services.*

» It is important to remember that a product has three levels: core, actual and augmented. The purchaser buys a core benefit or service (the *core product*) in addition to the product's brand name, features, capabilities, quality, packaging and design (the *actual product*). Increasingly, aspects of the *augmented product* are important considerations for purchasers of consumer goods, services and business goods. Warranties, delivery and credit, personnel, installation, after-sales support and customer service are integral to the actual product's appeal and perceived benefits. The role of personnel in particular is of fundamental concern to marketers; people and customer service now form a central part of the marketing mix.

» A *product item* is a specific version of a product that can be designated as a distinct offering among a business's products. A *product line* is a group of closely related product items that are a unit because of marketing, technical or end-use considerations. A company's total group of products is called the *product mix*. The *depth* of a product mix is measured by the number of different products offered in each product line. The *width* of the product mix is measured by the number of product lines a company offers.

» The *product life cycle* describes how product items in an industry move through four major stages: (1) *introduction stage*, (2) *growth stage*, (3) *maturity stage* and (4) *decline stage*. The life-cycle concept is used to make sure that the introduction, alteration and termination of a product are timed and executed properly. The sales curve is at zero on introduction, rises at an increasing rate during growth, peaks at maturity and then declines. Profits peak towards the end of the growth stage of the product life cycle. The life expectancy of a product is based on buyers' wants, the availability

of competing products and other environmental conditions. Most businesses have a composite of life-cycle patterns for various products. It is important to manage existing products and develop new ones to keep the overall sales performance at the desired level.

» Thousands of new products are introduced each year and many of them fail. Some estimates put the product failure rate as high as 60 to 90 per cent. Failure and success rates vary in different industries and from company to company. Products fail for many reasons: because of a failure to match product offerings to customer needs, ineffective or inconsistent branding, technical or design problems, poor timing, over-estimation of market size, ineffective promotion and inefficient distribution.

» It is important to distinguish between degrees of product failure. Absolute failure occurs when a company loses money on a new product because it is unable to recover development, production and marketing costs. Relative product failure occurs when a product returns a profit but does not meet a company's profit or market share objectives.

» Despite this gloomy picture of new product failure, some new products are very successful. Perhaps the most important ingredient for success is the product's ability to provide a significant and perceivable benefit to a sizeable number of customers.

» When creating products, marketers must take into account other product-related considerations, such as physical characteristics and less tangible support services. Specific physical product characteristics that require attention are the level of quality and product features, such as textures, colours and sizes. Support services that may be viewed as part of the total product include guarantees, repairs/replacements and credit.

⊙ *Key Links*

This chapter has given an overview of the product element of the marketing mix.

- It must be read in conjunction with Chapter 9, which examines how marketers manage portfolios of products.
- For those involved in marketing services, there are additional considerations, as discussed in Chapter 10.

Important Terms

Product
Good
Service
Ideas
Consumer products
Industrial or business products
Convenience products
Shopping products
Speciality products
Unsought products
Raw materials
Major equipment
Accessory equipment
Component parts
Process materials
Consumable supplies
MRO items
Industrial/business services
Core product
Actual product
Augmented product
Product item
Product line
Product mix
Depth
Width
Product life cycle
Introduction stage
Growth stage
Maturity stage
Decline stage
Quality
Guarantee

Discussion and Review Questions

1 List the tangible and intangible attributes of a spiral notebook. Compare the benefits of the spiral notebook with those of an intangible product such as life insurance.

2 A product has been referred to as a 'psychological bundle of satisfaction'. Is this a good definition of a product?

3 Is a roll of carpet in a shop a consumer product or a business product? Defend your answer.

4 How do convenience products and shopping products differ? What are the distinguishing characteristics of each type of product?

5 Would a music system that sells for £500 be a convenience, shopping or speciality product?

6 In the category of business products, how do component parts differ from process materials?

7 How does a company's product mix relate to its development of a product line? When should a company add depth to its product lines rather than width to its product mix?

8 How do industry profits change as a product moves through the four stages of its life cycle?

9 What is the relationship between the concepts of product mix and product life cycle?

10 What factors must marketers consider when deciding what quality level to build in to a product? What support services can be offered to back up product quality?

11 What are aspects of the augmented product for a new car?

12 Why is the augmented product increasingly important when determining a differential advantage?

Recommended Reading

- Baker, M. and Hart, S., *Product Strategy and Management* (Harlow: Pearson/FT, 2007).
- Lehmann, D. and Winer, R., *Product Management* (Boston, Mass.: McGraw-Hill, 2004).
- Rifkin, G., 'Product development: the myth of short life cycles', *Harvard Business Review*, vol. 72, no. 4, 1994, p. 11.
- Trott, P., *Innovation Management and New Product Development* (Harlow: Pearson/FT, 2004).
- Wind, Y.J., *Product Policy: Concepts, Methods and Strategy* (Reading, Mass.: Addison-Wesley, 1982).

Internet Exercise

Goodyear Tyres

In addition to providing information about the company's products, Goodyear's website helps customers find the exact products they want and will even direct them to the nearest Goodyear retailer. Visit the Goodyear site at:
www.goodyear.com

1 How does Goodyear use its website to communicate information about the quality of its tyres?
2 How does Goodyear's website demonstrate product design and features?
3 Based on what you learned at the website, describe what Goodyear has done to position its tyres.

◈ Applied Mini-Case

The Volkswagen Golf has hit 30! VW celebrated the launch of the fifth generation of the model, which seems to have defied middle age and maintained its status as a trendy brand. An advertising campaign accompanying the launch charted the development of the Golf through its three decades of life. The creative work highlighted the changing design and features of the car over time. This illustrates VW's decision to continually upgrade the Golf, rather than replace it with a different model.

Sources: Samuel Solley, 'VW plays on Golf's heritage with evolutionary approach', *Marketing*, 25 March 2004, p. 9; VW 2004–2006.

❓ Question

Several years from now you have secured a job as brand manager for the Golf. Assume that VW is about to make a decision about whether to launch a new generation of the Golf or replace it with a new model with a new name. Prepare a report arguing in support of one of these options. You should explore the arguments for and against each option.

◈ Case Study

Heineken's Portfolio of Brands

Heineken is Europe's largest brewer, having recently acquired part of the UK's Scottish & Newcastle. While around half of its sales are European, worldwide Heineken is second only to US-based Anheuser-Busch. Heineken beer is recognised around the globe. With a presence in more than 170 countries and more than 80 per cent of sales originating outside the domestic Dutch market, Heineken has been described as the most international beer brand. However, there is more to the company than the single Heineken brand. While some rivals have tackled the global market with a strategy of focusing only on international premium beer brands, Heineken has adopted a tiered approach, with strong international premium brands such as Amstel and Heineken; dominant national brands rarely seen outside their respective countries; plus a raft of speciality beers – over 170 beer brands.

Despite its activities in the USA, Latin America, Africa, South-east Asia and Asia, Heineken recognises the significance of its strength in Europe – a particularly important market, which accounts for over 40 per cent of world beer sales. Here, despite the mass appeal of the Heineken brand, to stay ahead of the competition the company has to adjust its product mix to suit the needs of different countries, fitting in with local cultures and tastes. In general, Heineken achieves this goal by offering a portfolio of three core brands in each European country:

1 a local brand, aimed at the standard and largest market segment. In Italy this is Dreher, in France '33' and in Spain Aguila Pilsener
2 a brand targeted at the 'upper' end of the market; sometimes this is a locally produced brand, such as the Spanish Aguila Master, in other cases a newer Heineken brand, Amstel, is preferred
3 the Heineken brand itself, aimed at the premium market segment; the beer offered may be manufactured locally or it may be exported from the Netherlands; either way, the Dutch head office works hard to maintain product quality and brand image.

Former Chairman Thony Ruys believes that it is the proven combination of the Heineken brand with local mainstream brands that creates the successful level of distribution in the market and adequate economies of scale in production. Heineken has a share in over 60 brewing companies around the globe to help facilitate this strategy. The company also keeps up with trends, including Murphy's, iced beers and non-alcoholic brews such as Buckler.

Branding policy in the UK differs slightly from that implemented in other parts of Europe. The standard Heineken brand in the UK is a lower-strength version of the beer offered in Europe. The lower-strength lager first became popular in pubs across the UK in the 1960s. With the increasing sophistication of the UK beer drinker, the company introduced the Heineken Export Strength brand – more closely related to the 'standard' Heineken offered throughout Europe.

Currently, significant growth is evident in the company's sales in Italy, Poland, Spain, France and the Far East. Sales of Heineken in the premium segment are rising at around 6 per cent per annum,

while Amstel's sales are rising at close to 2 per cent per annum. Sales of Amstel Light are more sluggish. No brewer has secured strong market positions in as many countries, Heineken is proud to state, and no individual beer brand is as successful in as many countries as the Heineken brand. Heineken is market leader in Austria, Romania, Hungary, Poland, Slovakia, Bulgaria and Macedonia, illustrating the company's identification some time ago of the growing commercial opportunities in eastern Europe. The new additions to the EU, and Russia, are currently priority targets. Outside Europe, the focus for growth is on the east coast of North America, North Africa, China, Vietnam, Chile and Argentina.

Sources: www.Heineken.com, 2004–2007; Caroline Farquhar, Warwick MBA, 1991–92; 'The Netherlands trade review – the beverage market', Economic Intelligence Unit, *Marketing in Europe*, no. 347, October 1991, p. 36; Heineken annual report and accounts, 1991, 1994 and 1996; David Benardy, 'Heineken Euro '96 plot', *Marketing Week*, 23 February 1996, p. 7; Nina Munk, 'Make mine Hoegaarden', *Forbes*, 18 December 1995, pp. 124–6; Havis Dawson, 'Brand brewing', *Beverage World*, October 1995, pp. 50–60; 'Heineken stresses sponsorship in marketing non-alcoholic beer', *Crossborder Monitor*, 11 January 1995, p. 9; Thony Ruys, Heineken, 2003; http://www.heinekeninternational.com/aboutheineken.aspx, 26 November, 2007; BBC News, 2002.

❷ *Questions for Discussion*

1 Why was the UK's version of Heineken lager weaker than its counterpart in the rest of Europe? What problems has this product variation caused Heineken?
2 Why does Heineken opt for a mix of internationally known brands marketed alongside local beers?
3 In what ways is Heineken continuously updating its product portfolio and its marketing mix?

9
Developing Products and Managing Product Portfolios

"**In the globally competitive world, product and brand management represents the most important resource responsibility in the portfolio of the marketing manager's job.**"

Michael J. Thomas, University of Strathclyde

Objectives

- To become aware of organisational alternatives for managing products

- To understand how organisations develop a product idea into a commercial product

- To understand the importance and role of product development in the marketing mix

- To acquire knowledge of the management of products during the various stages of a product's life cycle

- To become aware of how existing products can be modified

- To learn how product deletion can be used to improve product mixes

- To examine tools for the strategic planning of product or market portfolios

Introduction

Companies have to create new ideas for products and turn some of these into marketable product or service propositions. Such a process is far from easy, with more new product launches failing than succeeding.

As additional products are included in a company's portfolio, it becomes increasingly difficult to identify on which of them investment and sales/marketing resources should be focused. A range of tools, known as product portfolio techniques, exists to assist marketers in such decision-making.

A related and important concept is that of product life cycle management: the logic being that products are launched and – if successful – they grow, then mature, before going into decline. Marketers must be aware of the relative standings of their respective products and brands.

Opener

Virgin Money: is Innovation Enough?

Richard Branson's Virgin brand is known to consumers across a range of products and services, from airlines to entertainment to mobile phones. In 1995, Virgin launched its financial services arm with Virgin Direct. At a time when major retailers such as Marks & Spencer and Tesco were entering many sectors of financial services, from banking to insurance, the entry of Virgin Direct made many of the traditional businesses in the financial services sector very anxious. Branson's reputation among consumers for 'taking on faceless corporations' gave Virgin Direct a head start.

Virgin Direct, replicating the activities of Virgin in other sectors, intended to be seen as an innovator that always strives to offer a value-for-money proposition that strongly benefits the consumer. Virgin launched a tracker fund that tracked shares across the entire stock market rather than across only a limited selection. This innovation was subsequently copied by many rivals. Then Virgin lobbied the government to launch stakeholder pensions. Although successful, it is widely accepted that the eventual appearance of stakeholder pensions has been far from a success story for the industry. Virgin also led the way with off-set mortgages, with the Virgin One account. Virgin found this complex proposition difficult to market to consumers, without face-to-face contact via branches. In 2001, the One Account was handed over to Royal Bank of Scotland, which did have a suitable branch network and has been able to sell this mortgage product to consumers.

Despite such teething problems, Virgin Money – as the company is now known – is profitable and thanks largely to its tie-up with card provider MBNA, has a growing credit card business, too. The philosophy is simple: Virgin Money intends to introduce more interesting propositions, rather than simply churning out new products. The company has a focus on being customer-led, rather than product-led. The Virgin-branded financial services products are always innovative and place an emphasis on addressing consumer needs and consumer concerns about the sprawling global financial services corporations. Value for money, simplicity, ease of setting up and the Virgin brand have proved irresistible propositions for thousands of consumers who perceive Virgin and Branson to represent a desirable alternative to large, faceless corporations. As a result of this approach, Virgin Money has won countless industry awards in recent years, notably for its credit card operation, car insurance, pet insurance and pensions.

Sources: Virgin Money; David Benady, 'Virgin Money pushes for its renaissance', *Marketing Week*, 6 May 2004, pp. 20–1; virginmoney.com, January, 2008.

To compete effectively and achieve their goals, companies must develop products that reflect consumer needs and preferences, while seeking to be different from competitors. This is certainly the approach adopted by Virgin Money. A company often has to modify existing products, introduce new products or eliminate products that were successful perhaps only a few years ago. Sometimes, product alterations are required to keep pace with changing consumer demographics and new technologies. Whatever the reasons for altering products, the product mix must be managed and kept fresh, reflecting customer expectations, changing market trends and competitors' products. It may be appropriate to expand a company's product mix to take advantage of excess marketing and production capacity.

The product portfolio approach tries to create specific marketing strategies to achieve a balanced mix of products that will maximise a company's longer-term profits. This chapter begins by considering how businesses are organised to develop and manage products. Next, several ways to improve a company's product mix, including new product development from idea generation to commercialisation, are reviewed. The chapter then considers issues and decisions associated with managing a product through the growth, maturity and declining stages of its life cycle. Different types of product modification are also examined. The deletion of weak products from the product mix, often one of the hardest decisions for a marketer, is examined. The chapter concludes with a look at some of the related analytical tools associated with the planning of product portfolio: the BCG product portfolio analysis, the market attractiveness–business position model or directional policy matrix (DPM), and the ABC sales: contribution analysis.

Organising to Manage Products

A company must often manage a complex set of products, markets or both. Often, too, it finds that the traditional functional form of organisation – in which managers specialise in business functions such as advertising, sales and distribution – does not fit its needs. Consequently, management must find an organisational approach that accomplishes the tasks necessary to develop and manage products. Alternatives to functional organisation include the product or brand manager approach, the marketing manager approach, and the venture or project team approach.

Product manager
The person responsible for a product, a product line or several distinct products that make up an interrelated group within a multiproduct organisation

Brand manager
The person responsible for a single brand

The Product or Brand Manager Approach   A **product manager** is responsible for a product, a product line or several distinct products that make up an interrelated group within a multiproduct organisation. A **brand manager**, on the other hand, is responsible for a single brand – for example, Lipton's Yellow Label tea or Virgin Cola. A product or brand manager operates cross-functionally to coordinate the activities, information and strategies involved in marketing an assigned product. Product managers and brand managers plan marketing activities to achieve objectives by coordinating a mix of place/distribution, promotion – especially sales promotion and advertising – and price. They must consider packaging and branding decisions, and work closely with research and development, engineering and production departments. The product manager or brand manager approach is used by many large, multiproduct companies in the consumer goods sector. Increasingly it is a popular approach adopted by marketers responsible for services brands and business-to-business markets.

Marketing manager
The person responsible for managing the marketing activities that serve a particular group or class of customers

The Marketing Manager Approach   A **marketing manager** is responsible for managing the marketing activities that serve a particular group or class of customers. This organisational approach is particularly effective when a company engages in different types of marketing activity to provide products to diverse customer groups. For example, a company may have one marketing manager for business markets and another for consumer markets. These broad market categories may be broken down into more limited market responsibilities.

IT services company Fujitsu has identified core target market sectors, such as government customers, retail, financial services, utilities, and so forth – there is a separate marketing manager responsible for each sector, all reporting to the central marketing director. Each Fujitsu marketing manager handles the implementation of marketing programmes bespoke to his or her clients, but is also tasked with developing new products or services relevant to their category of clients.

Venture or **project team**
The group that creates entirely new products, perhaps aimed at new markets, and is responsible for all aspects of the products' development

The Venture or Project Team Approach   A **venture** or **project team** is designed to create entirely new products that may be aimed at new markets. Unlike a product or marketing manager, a venture team is responsible for all aspects of a product's development: research and development, production and engineering, finance and accounting, and marketing. Venture teams work outside established divisions to create inventive approaches to new products and markets. As a result of this flexibility, new products can be developed to take advantage of opportunities in highly segmented markets. Fujitsu has a separate team of marketers and new product development specialists working outside any specific client sectors, who are also striving to develop the next generation of attractive IT services but are not focused on a particular client sector, which is the role of the marketing managers.

The members of a venture team come from different functional areas of an organisation. Companies are increasingly using such cross-functional teams for product development in an effort to boost product quality. Quality may be positively related to information integration within the team, customers' influence on the product development process, and a quality orientation within the business.[1] When the commercial potential of a new product has been demonstrated, the members may return to their functional areas, or they may join a new or existing division to manage the product. The new product may be turned over to an existing division, a marketing manager or a product manager. Innovative organisational forms such as venture teams are especially important for well-established companies operating in mature markets. These companies must take a dual approach to marketing organisation. They must accommodate the management of mature products and also encourage the development of new ones.[2]

New Product Development

Developing and introducing new products is frequently expensive and risky. The development of Gillette's Sensor razor took over eight years and resulted in a £150 million investment.[3] Thousands of new consumer products are introduced annually, and anywhere from 60 to 90 per cent of them fail. Lack of research, technical problems in design or production, and errors in timing the product's introduction are all causes of failure. Although developing new products is risky, so is failing to introduce new products. For example, the makers of Timex watches gained a large share of the watch market through effective marketing strategies during the 1960s and early 1970s. By 1983, Timex's market share had slipped considerably, in part because the company had failed to introduce new products. Timex has since regained market share by introducing a number of new products, but in the meantime competitors such as Swatch established their brands and stole significant market share from Timex.

The term 'new product' can have more than one meaning. It may refer to a genuinely new product – such as digital cameras – offering innovative benefits. But products that are merely different and distinctly better are also often viewed as new, such as lighter-weight wireless laptops. The following items, listed in no particular order, are product innovations of the last 30 or 40 years: Post-it notes, birth-control pills, personal computers, felt-tip pens, anti-ulcer drugs, Viagra, VCRs, DVDs, deep-fat fryers, compact disc players, mobile phones, e-mail, soft contact lenses and telephone banking. Thus, a new product can be an innovative variation of an existing product, as in the example shown in Figure 9.1.

A radically new product involves a complex development process, including an extensive business analysis to determine the possibility of success.[4] It can also be a product that a

267

Figure 9.1
Building on the popularity of crisps and cheesy snacks, Quaker launched rice and corn-based Snack-a-Jacks, promoting the product's low fat content
Source: All work created by Star Chamber

New product development
The process a product goes through before introduction, involving seven phases: idea generation, screening ideas, concept testing, business analysis, product development, test marketing and commercialisation

given company has not marketed previously, although similar products may be available from other companies. The first company to introduce a video cassette recorder was clearly launching a new product, yet if Boeing introduced its own brand of video cassette recorder, this would also be viewed as a new product for Boeing, because it has not previously marketed such products. Managers in companies trying something new are often highly excited by sales prospects, yet the targeted consumers have probably been able to purchase similar products from a variety of other suppliers for some time; so, to be successful, the new entrant must have a visible and desirable competitive edge.

Before a product is introduced, it goes through the seven phases of **new product development** shown in Figure 9.2:

1   idea generation
2   screening ideas
3   concept testing
4   business analysis
5   product development
6   test marketing
7   commercialisation.

A product may be dropped, and many are, at any of these stages of development. This section examines the process through which products are developed from the inception of an idea to a product offered for sale. Table 9.1 shows how companies can improve their new product success rate.

Figure 9.2
Phases of new product development

TABLE 9.1 HOW TO IMPROVE NEW PRODUCT SUCCESS

1	Talk with consumers; don't introduce a product just because you have the technology to make it.
2	Set realistic sales goals. Unrealistic goals can result in potentially successful products being terminated.
3	Make all parts of the company (research, manufacturing, marketing and distribution) work together for customer orientation.
4	At each stage of development, the product should have consumer acceptance, the ability to be manufactured at an acceptable cost and sales support.
5	Test market a product long enough to get an accurate assessment. Some products fail because consumers buy them early as a novelty only.
6	Carefully evaluate all product failures to provide information for future product introductions.
7	Monitor competitor developments – a new product must not merely replicate a rival.
8	Keep internal colleagues up-to-date and explain new developments to them.

Source: Christopher P. Power, Kathleen Kerwin, Ronald Grover, Keith Alexander and Robert D. Hof, 'Flops: too many new products fail. Here's why – and how to do better', from *Business Week*, 16 August 1993, pp. 78–9.

Idea generation
The process by which companies and other organisations seek product ideas that will help them achieve their objectives

Idea Generation   Idea generation involves companies and other organisations seeking product ideas that will help them achieve their objectives. This task is difficult because only a few ideas are good enough to be commercially successful. Although some organisations get their ideas almost by chance, companies trying to manage their product mixes effectively usually develop systematic approaches for generating new product ideas. Indeed, there is a relationship between the amount of market information gathered and the number of ideas generated by work groups in organisations.[5] At the heart of innovation is a purposeful, focused effort to identify new ways to serve a market. Unexpected occurrences, incongruities, new needs, industry and market changes, and demographic changes may all indicate new opportunities.[6] The forces of the marketing environment (see Chapter 3) often create new opportunities – as well as threats to combat.

New product ideas can come from several sources. They may come from internal sources: marketing managers, researchers, sales personnel, engineers or other organisational personnel. Brainstorming and incentives or rewards for good ideas are typical intra-organisation devices for stimulating the development of ideas. The company 3M is well known for encouraging the generation of new ideas. The idea for 3M's Post-it adhesive-backed yellow notes came from an employee. As a church choir member, he used slips of paper for marking songs in his hymn book. Because the pieces of paper fell out, he suggested developing an adhesive-backed note. Hewlett-Packard keeps its labs open to engineers 24 hours a day to help generate ideas; it also encourages its researchers to devote 10 per cent of company time to exploring their own ideas for new products.[7] Company suggestion boxes for employees' ideas provide many of the stimuli for BMW's automotive innovations.

New product ideas may also arise from sources outside the company – for example, customers, competitors, advertising agencies, management consultants and private research organisations. Johnson & Johnson, for example, acquired the technology for its new, clear orthodontic braces through a joint venture with Saphikon, the developer of the technology behind the braces. Developing new product alliances with other businesses has also been found to enhance the acquisition and use of information helpful for creating new product ideas.[8] Sometimes ideas come from potential buyers of a product. Asking weekend fishermen what they wanted in a sonar fish finder led Techsonic to develop its LCR (liquid crystal recorder) fish finder. The practice of asking customers what they want from its products has helped Techsonic maintain its leadership in the industry.[9] For example, Chapter 3 outlined how companies such as Fujitsu discuss with clients their marketing environment drivers so that they can develop new products and services that reflect these client issues. In some markets, it is particularly important for new ideas to stem from customers. For example, many defence programmes take ten years to instigate, and the big defence equipment manufacturers are led by the stated buying plans and budgets of government defence departments.

Screening ideas

The process by which a company assesses whether product ideas match its organisational objectives and resources

Screening Ideas   **Screening ideas** involves first assessing whether they match organisational objectives and resources, and then choosing the best ideas for further review. Next, the company's overall ability to produce and market the product is analysed. Other aspects of an idea that should be weighed are the nature and wants of buyers, and possible marketing environment changes. More new product ideas are rejected during the idea-screening phase than during any other phase.

Sometimes a checklist of new product requirements is used to ensure that the screening process is as systematic as possible. If a critical factor on the checklist remains unclear, the type of formal marketing research described in Chapter 7 may be needed. To screen ideas properly, it may be necessary to test product concepts; a product concept and its benefits can be described or shown to consumers. Several product concepts may be tested to discover which might appeal most to a particular target market.

Concept testing

Seeking potential buyers' responses to a product idea

Concept Testing   **Concept testing** is a phase in which a small sample of potential buyers is presented with a product idea, often in focus groups, through a written or oral description – and perhaps a few drawings – to determine their attitudes and initial buying intentions regarding the product. For a single product idea, an organisation can test one or several concepts of the same product. Concept testing is a low-cost procedure that lets a company determine customers' initial reactions to a product idea before it invests considerable resources in research and development. The results of concept testing can be used by product development personnel to better understand which product attributes and benefits are most important to potential customers.

Business analysis

A company's evaluation of a product idea to determine its potential contribution to the company's sales, costs and profits

Business Analysis   During the **business analysis** phase, the product idea is evaluated to determine its potential contribution to the company's sales, costs and profits. In the course of a business analysis, evaluators ask a variety of questions.

- Does the product fit in with the company's existing product mix? Does the company have the right expertise to develop the new product?
- Is demand strong enough to justify entering the market and will the demand endure?
- What types of environmental and competitive changes can be expected, and how will these changes affect the product's future sales, costs and profits?
- Are the organisation's research, development, engineering and production capabilities adequate?
- If new facilities must be constructed, how quickly can they be built and how much will they cost?
- Is the necessary financing for development and commercialisation on hand or obtainable at terms consistent with a favourable return on investment?
- Will the new product or idea benefit the company's existing portfolio of products?
- Is there any danger that existing products or services will be cannibalised?

In the business analysis stage, companies seek market information. The results of consumer surveys, along with secondary data, supply the specifics needed for estimating potential sales, costs and profits. At this point, a research budget should explore the financial objectives and related considerations for the new product.

Product development
The phase in which the organisation determines if it is technically and financially feasible to produce a new product

Product Development   **Product development** is the phase in which the organisation determines if it is technically feasible to produce the product and if it can be produced at costs low enough to make the final price reasonable. To test its acceptability, the idea or concept is converted into a prototype, or working model. Concept cars are used in the development of new vehicles. The prototype should reveal tangible and intangible attributes associated with the product in consumers' minds. The product's design, mechanical features and intangible aspects must be linked to wants in the marketplace. This includes the service aspects of the product, which are a vital component of many products. Failure to determine how consumers feel about the product and how they would use it may lead to the product's failure. For example, the Sinclair C5 electric buggy was developed as a serious on-road, single-seater car for city or country use. However, drivers felt unsafe in the buggy, and campus students ended up using the remaining stocks as on-pavement runabouts.

The development phase of a new product is frequently lengthy and expensive; thus a relatively small number of product ideas are put into development. If the product appears sufficiently successful during this phase to merit testing, then during the latter part of the development phase marketers begin to make decisions regarding branding, packaging, labelling, pricing and promotion for use in the test marketing phase.[10]

Test marketing
The limited introduction of a product in geographic areas chosen to represent the intended market

Test Marketing   The limited introduction of a product in geographic areas chosen to represent the intended market is called **test marketing**. Its aim is to determine the reactions of probable buyers. For example, after McDonald's developed fried chicken products for its fast-food menu, it test marketed the idea in certain McDonald's restaurants to find out how those customers felt about eating chicken at McDonald's. The company followed a similar strategy for test marketing its range of salads and pizza. Test marketing is not an extension of the development phase – it is a sample launching of the entire marketing mix, and should be conducted only after the product has gone through development and after initial plans regarding the other marketing mix variables have been made.

Companies of all sizes use test marketing to reduce the risk of product failure. The dangers of introducing an untested product include undercutting already profitable products and, should the new product fail, loss of credibility with distributors and customers. When Lever Brothers launched Wisk – previously only a washing powder – in liquid form in 1986, the company had misjudged consumer usage. Many blocked washing machines later, P&G offered liquid Ariel with Arielettes, containers to be placed inside the machines together with the clothes. Costly reformulations overcame such problems.

Test marketing provides several benefits. It lets marketers expose a product to a natural marketing environment to gauge its sales performance. While the product is being marketed in a limited area, the company can seek to identify weaknesses in the product or in other parts of the marketing mix. Corrections can be made more cheaply than if the product had already been introduced nationwide. Test marketing also allows marketers to experiment with variations in advertising, price and packaging in different test areas and to measure the extent of brand awareness, brand switching and repeat purchases that result from alterations in the marketing mix.

The accuracy of test marketing results often hinges on where the tests are conducted. The selection of appropriate test areas is very important. The validity of test marketing results depends heavily on selecting test sites that provide an accurate representation of the intended target market. The criteria used for choosing test cities or television regions depend on the product's characteristics, the target market's characteristics, and the company's objectives and resources.

Test marketing can be risky because it is expensive and a company's competitors may try to interfere. This is common in the confectionery market. A competitor may invalidate test results in an attempt to 'jam' the test programme by increasing advertising or promotions, lowering prices or offering special incentives – all to combat the recognition and purchase of a new brand. Sometimes, too, competitors copy the product in the testing stage and rush to introduce a similar product. It is therefore desirable to move quickly and commercialise as soon as possible after testing. When the product introduction is delayed to the point where the public begins to doubt its existence, such products may become known as 'vapourware', particularly in the computer software industry.[11]

To avoid these risks, companies may use alternative methods to gauge consumer preferences. One such method is simulated test marketing. Typically, consumers at shopping centres are asked to view an advertisement for a new product and are given a free sample to take home. These consumers are subsequently interviewed over the phone and asked to rate the product. The major advantages of simulated test marketing are lower costs, tighter security and, consequently, a reduction in the flow of information to competitors, and the elimination of jamming. Scanner-based test marketing is another, more sophisticated version of the traditional test marketing method. Some marketing research companies, such as ACNielsen, offer test marketing services to help provide independent assessment of products.

Commercialisation

The process of refining and settling plans for full-scale manufacturing and marketing

Commercialisation   During the **commercialisation** phase, plans for full-scale manufacturing and marketing must be refined and settled, and budgets for the project must be prepared. Early in the commercialisation phase, marketing management analyses the results of test marketing to find out what changes in the marketing mix are needed before the product is introduced. For example, the results of test marketing may tell the marketers to change one or more of the product's physical attributes, modify the distribution plans to include more retail outlets, alter promotional efforts or change the product's price. During this phase, the company also has to gear up for production and may therefore face sizeable capital expenditure and personnel costs.

The product enters the market during the commercialisation phase. One study indicates that only 8 per cent of new product projects started by major companies reach this stage.[12] When introducing a product, marketers often spend enormous sums of money on advertising, personal selling and other types of promotion. These expenses, together with capital outlays, can make commercialisation extremely costly; such expenditures may not be recovered for several years. For example, when Ford introduced its new Focus model, the company spent millions of pounds on advertising to communicate the new car's attributes. Commercialisation is easier when customers accept the product rapidly, which they are more likely to do if marketers can make them aware of its benefits.

Line Extensions

Line extension

A product that is closely related to existing products in the line, but meets different customer needs

A **line extension** is the development of a product that is closely related to one or more products in the existing product line but is designed specifically to meet the somewhat different needs of customers. For example, Fairy Liquid washing-up detergent was used as a springboard for various detergent-based Fairy products including washing powder for automatic washing machines. Many of the so-called new products introduced each year by organisations are in fact line extensions. Line extensions are more common than new products because they are a less expensive, lower-risk alternative for increasing sales. A line extension may focus on a different market segment or may be an attempt to increase sales within the same market segment by more precisely satisfying the needs of people in that segment. For example, Nestlé launched an extra-strong variant of its Polo mints, Supermints, aimed at lovers of strong peppermints. However, one side-effect of employing a line extension is that it may result in a more negative evaluation of the core product.[13] It has been suggested that the success of line extensions is partly affected by consumer perceptions of how well the extension fits with the core brand.[14]

Product Adoption Process

The following stages of the **product adoption process** are generally recognised as those that buyers go through in accepting a product, from gaining awareness of it to buying the product.

1 *Awareness* – the buyer becomes aware of the product.
2 *Interest* – the buyer seeks information and is generally receptive to learning about the product.
3 *Evaluation* – the buyer considers the product's benefits and determines whether to try it.
4 *Trial* – the buyer examines, tests or tries the product to determine its usefulness relative to his or her needs.
5 *Adoption* – the buyer purchases the product and can be expected to use it when the need for this general type of product arises again.[15]

In the first stage, when individuals become aware that the product exists, they have little information about the product and are not concerned about obtaining more. Consumers enter the interest stage when they are motivated to attain information about the product's features, uses, advantages, disadvantages, price or location. During the evaluation stage, individuals consider whether the product will satisfy certain criteria that are crucial for meeting their specific needs. In the trial stage, they use or experience the product for the first time, possibly by purchasing a small quantity, by taking advantage of a free sample or demonstration, or by borrowing the product from someone. Supermarkets, for instance, frequently offer special promotions to encourage consumers to taste products. During this stage, potential adopters determine the usefulness of the product under the specific conditions for which they need it.

Individuals move into the adoption stage by choosing the specific product when they need a product of that general type. However, the fact that a person enters the adoption process does not mean that she or he will eventually adopt the new product. Rejection may occur at any stage, including adoption. Both product adoption and product rejection can be temporary or permanent. Just because a consumer or business customer adopts a particular product once, does not guarantee future loyalty to the product or brand. Marketers must work hard to achieve a customer's ongoing loyalty.

This adoption process model has several implications for the commercialisation phase. First, the company must promote the product to create widespread awareness of its existence and its benefits. Samples or simulated trials should be arranged to help buyers make initial purchase decisions. Marketers should also emphasise quality control and provide solid guarantees to reinforce buyer opinion during the evaluation stage. Finally, production and physical distribution must be linked to patterns of adoption and repeat purchase. The product adoption process is also discussed in Chapter 13, as marketing communications are not only important for achieving awareness, but also for informing and persuading customers right through the product adoption process. When launching a new product, companies must realise that buyers differ in the speed with which they adopt a product. Identifying buyers who are most open to new products can help expedite this process.

Consumers do not always pass through all the stages of the product adoption process as formally as this overview may have implied. A minor upgrade to a familiar brand may not cause consumers much concern, whereas an innovative product launched by an unknown supplier will give rise to much more extensive consumer decision-making. Business customers making routine rebuys or consumers making routine response purchases – see Chapters 4 and 5 – already have awareness of a particular product and are interested in it. Previously, they have tried and adopted the product, so their limited decision-making does not require them to pass through this product adoption process in this manner. On the whole, though, marketers would do well to remember the importance of all five stages in this important concept. Consumers and business-to-business customers must be aware of, have interest in, and be prepared to evaluate and try out a product or service if they are to adopt it: that is, to buy and consume it. The marketing task does not end with first-time adoption, however. The ongoing requirement for marketers is to ensure customer loyalty and repeat purchase.

Products are not usually launched nationwide overnight but are introduced through a process called a roll-out. In a roll-out, a product is introduced in stages, starting in a set of geographic areas and gradually expanding into adjacent areas. Thus, Cadbury's Wispa bar appeared initially in the north-east of England. It may take several years to market a product nationally. Sometimes the test cities are used as initial marketing areas, and the introduction becomes a natural extension of test marketing. Gradual product introduction reduces the risks of introducing a new product. If the product fails, the company will experience smaller losses. Furthermore, it may take some time for a company to develop a suitable distribution network. Also, the number of units needed to satisfy the national demand for a successful product can be enormous, and a company cannot usually produce the required quantities in a short time.

Despite the good reasons for introducing a product gradually, marketers realise that this approach creates some competitive problems. A gradual introduction allows competitors to observe what a company is doing and to monitor results, just as the company's own marketers are doing. If competitors see that the newly introduced product is successful, they may enter the same target market quickly with similar products. Avoiding competition is critical when a company introduces a brand into a market in which it already has one or more brands. Marketers usually want to avoid cannibalising sales of their existing brands, unless the new brand generates substantially larger profits. When Coca-Cola reintroduced Tab, it attempted to position the cola so as to minimise the adverse effects on Diet Coke sales. Similarly, when KP introduces a new snack brand, it must take care to ensure that sales of other KP brands do not suffer.

If a product has been planned properly, its attributes and brand image will give it the distinctive appeal needed. Style, shape, construction, quality of work and colour help create the image and the appeal. Of course buyers are more likely to purchase the product if they can easily identify the benefits. When the new product does not offer some preferred attributes, there is room for another new product or for repositioning of an existing product.[16] Methods of positioning are discussed in the final part of Chapter 6.

Product Life Cycle Management

Most new products start off slowly and seldom generate enough sales to produce profits immediately. As buyers learn about the new product, marketers should be looking out for any weaknesses and be ready to make corrections quickly, in order to prevent the product's early demise. Computer software companies expect to modify 'bugs' when launching new software products. Consumers must be informed quickly and efficiently of any difficulties if damage to the brand image is to be avoided. Marketing strategy should be designed to attract the segment that is most interested in, and has the fewest objections to, the product. If any of these factors need adjustment, this action, too, must be taken quickly to sustain demand. As the sales curve moves upwards and the break-even point is reached, the growth stage begins. See Figure 8.5 in Chapter 8 for an explanation of the product life cycle concept, which assumes a path from introduction to growth, into maturity and then decline.

Marketing Strategy in the Growth Stage

As sales increase, management must support the momentum by adjusting the marketing strategy. The goal is to establish the product's positioning and to fortify it by encouraging brand loyalty. As profits increase, the company must brace itself for the entrance of aggressive competitors, who may make specialised appeals to selected market segments.

During the growth stage, product offerings may have to be expanded. To achieve greater penetration of an overall market, segmentation may have to be used more intensely. That would require developing product variations to satisfy the needs of customers in several different market segments. Marketers should analyse the product positioning regarding competing products, and correct weak or omitted attributes. Further quality, functional or style modifications may be required.

Gaps in the marketing channels should be filled during the growth period. Once a product has won acceptance, new distribution outlets may be easier to obtain. Sometimes marketers tend to move from **exclusive distribution** or **selective distribution** to a more **intensive distribution** of dealers to achieve greater market penetration. Marketers must also make sure that the physical distribution system is running efficiently and delivering supplies to distributors before their inventories are exhausted. Because competition increases during the growth period, good service and an effective mechanism for handling complaints are important.

Advertising expenditure may be lowered slightly from the high level of the introductory stage but still needs to be quite substantial. As sales increase, promotion costs should drop as a percentage of total sales. A falling ratio between promotion expenditure and sales should contribute significantly to increased profits. The advertising messages should aim to stress brand benefits and emphasise the product's positioning. Coupons and samples may be used to increase market share.

After recovering development costs, an organisation may be able to lower prices. As sales volume increases, efficiencies in production can result in lower costs. These savings may be passed on to buyers. If demand remains strong and there are few competitive threats, prices tend to remain stable. If price cuts are feasible, they can improve price competition and discourage new competitors from entering the market. For example, when compact disc players were introduced in the early 1980s, they carried an £800 price tag. Primarily because of the price, the product was positioned as a 'toy for audiophiles' – a very small market segment. To generate mass-market demand, compact disc player manufacturers dropped their prices to around £150, and the cost of discs also dropped. The price was at a point where the margin was low but the turnover was high. However, with most homes having a CD player, sales volumes inevitably diminished. A similar pattern has emerged in the sale of mobile phones and home PCs, as unit prices have plummeted. Widescreen home entertainment systems are now following this pattern, as margins reduce but volumes increase. CD player sales are being replaced for manufacturers such as Sony with the growth in MP3 players, or cellphones and laptops which play music. In other words, sales of other products compensate for declining sales of CD players, which is why the management of product portfolios – examined later in this Chapter – is so important.

Marketing Strategy for Mature Products

As many products are in the maturity stage of their life cycles, marketers must always be ready to improve the product and marketing mix. During maturity, the competitive situation stabilises and some of the weaker competitors drop out. It has been suggested that as a product matures, its customers become more experienced and their requirements more diverse, so that market segmentation opportunities increase. As customers' needs change, new marketing strategies for mature products may be called for.[17] For example, in the wake of competition from Eurotunnel, car ferry operators now stress excellent on-board shopping, catering facilities and spacious accommodation in their advertising. Marketers may also need to modify the product. Symptoms of a mature product include price cutting, increased competitive action and shifting from a product orientation to a non-product orientation (price, promotion and place/distribution adaptation); in addition, market growth slows.[18]

Product modification means changing one or more characteristics of a company's product. This strategy is most likely to be used in the maturity stage of the product life cycle to give a company's existing brand a competitive edge. Even well-established brands such as Sellotape must be modified from time to time, with innovative dispensers or versions with 'Happy Birthday' or suchlike printed along the tape. Altering a product mix in this way entails less risk than developing a new product because the product is already established in the market. For example, publishers may launch new editions of popular reference books updated with the latest information.

If certain conditions are met, product modification can improve a company's product mix. First, the product must be modifiable. Second, existing customers must be able to

Exclusive distribution
Market coverage in which only one outlet is used in a geographic area

Selective distribution
Market coverage in which only some available outlets in an area are chosen to distribute a product

Intensive distribution
Market coverage in which all available outlets are used for distributing a product

Product modification
The alteration of one or more characteristics of a company's product

275

perceive that a modification has been made, assuming that the modified item is still aimed at them. Third, the modification should make the product more consistent with customers' desires so that it provides greater satisfaction. If these conditions are not met, it is unlikely that the product modification, however innovative, will be successful. The Marketing Insight describes several successful modifications to personal banking that have been developed due to emerging technology. Product modifications fall into three major categories: quality, functional and style modifications.

Quality modifications
Changes that affect a product's dependability and durability

Quality Modifications   Changes concerning a product's dependability and durability are called **quality modifications**. Usually, they are executed by altering the materials or the production process. Reducing a product's quality may allow a company to lower its price and direct the item at a larger target market.

Marketing Insight

E-banking, Telebanking, Text and TV Banking: What Next?

Marketers must constantly look at ways to keep their products 'fresh' and up to date, modifying existing products as appropriate or bringing out new ones. Personal banking has gone through many phases. Many readers will remember the days when high-street banks were open only until mid-afternoon Monday to Friday, and there were no ATMs for easy cash withdrawals. Queuing at ageing tills in austere branches was the primary means of operating current bank accounts. Direct debits and standing orders helped, but the real revolution came in the late 1970s with the growth of ATMs – cash dispensers – and then in the early 1990s as most leading banks extended their opening hours and range of services aimed at private customers. Technology has emerged as a driving force for change via other banking services in addition to ATMs. HSBC's First Direct broke ranks by launching as a telephone-only, 365-days-a-year, 24-hour full-service personal banking provider. The rapid take-off of First Direct encouraged its traditional high-street competitors to offer their own 24-hour telephone banking services – such as Barclays' BarclayCall – based on heavy investment in call centres.

Internet banking is changing the way in which many customers interact with their banks. Barclays initially launched a limited service owing to security fears. The company held back on a full-service launch until its systems could offer greater security to users and until customer concerns about hackers were allayed. The Royal Bank of Scotland, Lloyds TSB and Nationwide led the way in launching Internet banking to their customers. It is not only the major high-street banking giants that have turned to technology. The

Prudential also turned to e-banking with its Egg brand of e-commerce financial services; 65,000 people enquired about this intriguing product departure in the first five days after its launch, more than double the number anticipated by the Prudential. Now many customers prefer e-banking.

Another departure from the traditional high-street bank branch is the launch of TV banking. NatWest joined with Microsoft to provide an interactive banking service on Microsoft's WebTV network. The service included information about mortgages, travel insurance, currency rates, plus standard current account banking, based on NatWest's PC banking package already established online. NatWest has its own OnLine division, which has focused on high-security access for its PC-based customers using only a direct dial service rather than any Internet server or third-party host. This is in response to customer fears about hackers being able to access their financial dealings via Internet links. Telephones, Internet-hooked home PCs, even TVs with set-top boxes are all emerging as means by which personal bankers can avoid traipsing into their local branch in order to execute financial transactions and manage their accounts. First Direct offers mobile phone users texting access to their banking details. As more people use their web browsers on their mobile phones, there is an increase in accessing bank accounts via mobiles on the go: a far cry from the queues in fuddy-duddy branches. No doubt other technological solutions will emerge. To banking customers, such product developments are revolutionising their banking habits.

Sources: NatWest, First Direct and Barclays websites, 2000–08.

By contrast, increasing the quality of a product may give a company an advantage over competing brands. During the last 25 years, marketers have been forced by increased global competition, technological change and more demanding customers to improve product integrity.[19] Higher quality may enable a company to charge a higher price by creating customer loyalty and by lowering customer sensitivity to price. However, higher quality may require the use of more expensive components, less standardised production processes, and other manufacturing and management techniques that force a company to charge higher prices.[20] At the beginning of the 1990s, concern for quality increased significantly, with many companies, such as Tesco, Volvo and Caterpillar, finding ways both to increase quality and reduce costs.

Functional Modifications   Changes that affect a product's versatility, effectiveness, convenience or safety are called **functional modifications**; they usually require the product to be redesigned. Typical product categories that have undergone considerable functional modifications include home computers, audio equipment and cleaning products. Functional modifications can make a product useful to more people, thus enlarging its market, or improve the product's competitive position by providing benefits that competing items do not offer. Functional modifications can also help a company achieve and maintain a progressive image. For example, washing machine manufacturers such as Whirlpool or AEG have developed appliances that use less heat and water. In Figure 9.3, well-known detergent brand Surf has opted to promote stain removal and freshness. At times, too, functional modifications are made to reduce the possibility of product liability claims.

Style Modifications   **Style modifications** change the sensory appeal of a product by altering its taste, texture, sound, smell or visual characteristics. Such modifications can be important, because when making a purchase decision, a buyer is swayed by how a product looks, smells, tastes, feels or sounds.

Although style modifications can be used by a company to differentiate its product from competing brands, their major drawback is that their value is highly subjective. A company may strive to improve the product's style, but customers may actually find the modified product less appealing. Some companies try to minimise these problems by altering product style in subtle ways. For example, Mattel's Barbie doll has gradually changed over the years to reflect changing fashions.

During the maturity stage of the cycle, marketers actively encourage dealers to support the product, perhaps by offering promotional assistance or help in lowering their inventory costs. In general, marketers go to great lengths to serve dealers and to provide incentives for selling the manufacturer's brand, partly because own-label or retailer brands are a threat at this time. Own-label brands are both an opportunity and a threat to manufacturers, who

Functional modifications
Changes that affect a product's versatility, effectiveness, convenience or safety

Style modifications
Changes that alter a product's sensory appeal – taste, texture, sound, smell or visual characteristics

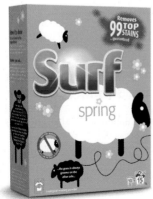

Figure 9.3
Surf's functional modification focused on stain removal and laundry freshness
Source: All work created by Star Chamber

may be able to sell their products through recognised own-label or retailer brand names as well as their own. However, own-label or retailer brands frequently undermine manufacturers' brands.

Maintaining market share during the maturity stage requires moderate and sometimes heavy advertising expenditure. Advertising messages focus on differentiating a brand from numerous competitors, and sales promotion efforts are aimed at both consumers and resellers.

A greater mixture of pricing strategies is used during the maturity stage. In some cases, strong price competition occurs and price wars may break out. Sometimes marketers develop price flexibility to differentiate offerings in product lines. Mark-downs and price incentives are more common, but prices may rise if distribution and production costs increase. Marketers of mature products also often alter packaging and even positioning strategies. For example, in the USA, Heinz repackaged and repositioned its vinegar as an all-natural cleaning product.

Marketing Strategy for Declining Product

As a product's sales curve turns downwards, industry profits continue to fall. A business can justify maintaining a product as long as it contributes to profits or enhances the overall effectiveness of a product mix. In this stage of the product life cycle, marketers must determine whether to eliminate the product or seek to reposition it in an attempt to extend its life. Usually, a declining product has lost its distinctiveness because similar competing products have been introduced. Competition engenders increased substitution and brand switching as buyers become insensitive to minor product differences. For these reasons, marketers do little to change a product's style, design or other attributes during its decline. New technology, product substitutes or environmental considerations may also indicate that the time has come to delete a product. For example, the ill-fated Betamax video cassette technology was quickly pushed out by the VHS format, which in turn is threatened by DVDs.

During a product's decline, outlets with strong sales volumes are maintained and unprofitable outlets are weeded out. An entire marketing channel may be eliminated if it does not contribute adequately to profits. Sometimes a new marketing channel, such as a factory outlet, will be used to liquidate remaining inventory of an obsolete product. Advertising expenditure is at a minimum. Advertising or special offers may slow the rate of decline. Sales promotions, such as coupons and premiums, may temporarily regain buyers' attention. As the product continues to decline, the sales staff shifts its emphasis to more profitable products. The strategy pursued depends heavily on the nature of the portfolio. Sony can downgrade the role of CD players and switch its focus to downloadable music players. However, CD and DVD retailer HMV faces a tough challenge, as consumers move to downloads from purchasing software and increasingly have no need to visit an HMV store.

To have a product return a profit may be more important to a company than to maintain a certain market share. To squeeze out all possible remaining profits, marketers may maintain the price despite declining sales and competitive pressures. Prices may even be increased as costs rise if a loyal core market still wants the product, such as those consumers preferring turntables to CD players. In other situations, the price may be cut to reduce existing inventory so that the product can be deleted. Severe price reductions may be required if a new product is making an existing product obsolete.

Deleting Products

Product deletion
The process of eliminating a product that no longer satisfies a sufficient number of customers

Product deletion is the process of eliminating a product that no longer satisfies a sufficient number of customers. Products cannot usually contribute to an organisation's goals indefinitely, and a declining product reduces a company's profitability, draining resources that could be used to modify other products or develop new ones. A marginal product may require shorter production runs, which can increase per unit production costs. Finally, when a dying product completely loses favour with customers, the negative feelings may transfer to some of the company's other products.

Most companies find it difficult to delete a product. It was probably a hard decision for IPC to drop magazine Options and admit that it was a failure. A decision to drop a product may be opposed by management and other employees who feel that the product is necessary in the product mix, or by sales people who still have some loyal customers. Considerable resources and effort are sometimes spent in trying to improve the product's marketing mix enough to increase sales and thus avoid having to delete it.

Some companies delete products only after they have become heavy financial burdens. Robert Maxwell's London newspaper the *Daily News* closed after only a few weeks, having lost £25 million. A better approach is to institute some form of systematic review to evaluate each product and monitor its impact on the overall effectiveness of the company's product mix. Such a review should analyse a product's contribution to the company's sales for a given period and should include estimates of future sales, costs and profits associated with the product. It should also gauge the value of making changes in the marketing strategy to improve the product's performance. A systematic review allows a company to improve product performance and to ascertain when to delete products. Although many companies do systematically review their product mixes, one research study found that few companies have formal, written policies concerning the process of deleting products. The study also found that most companies base their decisions to delete weak products on poor sales and profit potential, low compatibility with the company's business strategies, unfavourable market outlook and historical declines in profitability.[21]

Basically, there are three ways to delete a product, either:

Phase out
An approach that lets the product decline without a change in marketing strategy

1 phase it out
2 run it out
3 drop it immediately (see Figure 9.4).

Run out
A policy that exploits any strengths left in the product

A **phase out** approach lets the product decline without a change in the marketing strategy. No attempt is made to give the product new life. A **run out** policy exploits any strengths left in the product. Intensifying marketing efforts in core markets or eliminating some marketing expenditures, such as advertising, may cause a sudden profit increase. This approach is commonly taken for technologically obsolete products, such as older models of camcorders or computers, and is often accompanied by a price reduction. Some car manufacturers use a run out approach to dispose of certain models just before a new launch. The third option, an **immediate drop** of an unprofitable product, is the best strategy when losses are too great to prolong the product's life.

Immediate drop
An option that drops an unprofitable product immediately

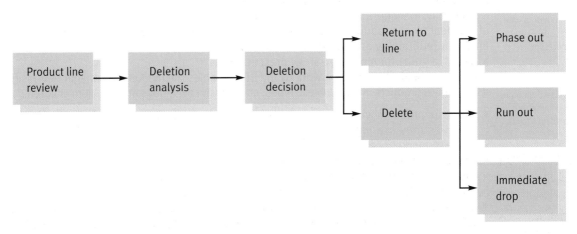

Figure 9.4
Product deletion process
Source: Martin L. Bell, Marketing: Concepts and Strategies, *3rd edn, p. 267; copyright © 1979, Houghton Mifflin Company. Reproduced by permission of Mrs Martin L. Bell*

Tools for Managing Product Portfolios

A number of tools have been developed to aid marketing managers in their planning efforts. Based on ideas used in the management of financial portfolios, several models that classify an organisation's product portfolio have been proposed. These models allow strategic business units (SBUs) or products to be classified and visually displayed both according to the attractiveness of various markets and a business's relative market share within those markets. Four of these tools are the Boston Consulting Group (BCG) product portfolio analysis, the market attractiveness – business position model, the Profit Impact on Marketing Strategy (PIMS) and the ABC sales: contribution analysis. In addition, the product life cycle concept explored in Chapter 8 is an important tool often utilised in determining future strategies for brands and products. This assessment – based on the notion of the introduction, growth, maturity and decline stages in the life of a product or market – is useful in recommending marketing strategy. As described above, the options are quite different for marketers facing growth or mature stages, and markedly so for the introduction versus the decline stages. The Boston Consulting Group matrix, described next, builds on this suggestion.

The Boston Consulting Group (BCG) Product Portfolio Analysis

Product portfolio analysis
A strategic planning tool that takes a product's market growth rate and its relative market share into consideration in determining a marketing strategy

Stars
Products with a dominant share of the market and good prospects for growth

Cash cows
Products with a dominant share of the market but low prospects for growth

Dogs
Products that have a subordinate share of the market and low prospects for growth

Problem children
Products that have a small share of a growing market, generally requiring a large amount of cash to build share

Just as financial investors have different investments with varying risks and rates of return, businesses have a portfolio of products characterised by different market growth rates and relative market shares. **Product portfolio analysis**, the Boston Consulting Group approach, is based on the philosophy that a product's market growth rate and its relative market share are important considerations in determining its marketing strategy. All the company's products should be integrated into a single, overall matrix and evaluated to determine appropriate strategies for individual SBUs and the overall portfolio strategies. However, a balanced product portfolio matrix is the end result of a number of actions, not just the analysis alone. Portfolio models can be created on the basis of present and projected market growth rates and proposed market share strategies. These strategies include four options:

1 build share
2 maintain share
3 harvest share
4 divest business.

Managers can use these models to determine and classify each product's expected future cash contributions and future cash requirements.

Generally, managers who use a portfolio model must examine the competitive position of a product – or product line – and the opportunities for improving that product's contribution to profitability and cash flow.[22] The BCG analytical approach is more of a diagnostic tool than a guide for making strategy prescriptions.

Figure 9.5, which is based on work by the BCG, enables the marketing manager to classify a company's products into four basic types: stars, cash cows, dogs and problem children.[23]

- **Stars** are products with a dominant share of the market and good prospects for growth. However, they use more cash than they generate to finance growth, add capacity and increase market share.
- **Cash cows** have a dominant share of the market but low prospects for growth. Typically, they generate more cash than is required to maintain market share. Cash cows generate much needed funds to support the stars and problem children.
- **Dogs** have a subordinate share of the market and low prospects for growth. These are struggling products. They are frequently found in mature markets and often should be phased out or withdrawn immediately.
- **Problem children**, sometimes called 'question marks', have a small share of a growing market and generally require a large amount of cash to build share. The question is, are they capable of becoming star products or are they destined to be dogs?

Figure 9.5
Illustrative growth-share matrix developed by the Boston Consulting Group
Source: Perspectives, 66, 'The product portfolio'. Reprinted by permission from the Boston Consulting Group, Inc., Boston, MA. Copyright © 1970

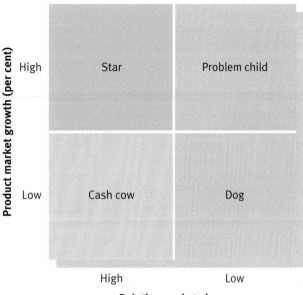

The product portfolio growth-share matrix in Figure 9.5 can be expanded to show a company's whole portfolio by providing for each product:

- its cash sales volume, illustrated by the size of a circle on the matrix
- its market share *relative* to competition, represented by the horizontal position of the product on the matrix
- the growth rate of the market, indicated by the position of the product in the vertical direction.

It should be noted that relative market share is a company's own market share relative to the biggest competitor's. Figure 9.6 suggests marketing strategies appropriate for cash cows, stars, dogs and problem children. By following these guiding philosophies, an organisation can make strategic decisions based on the diagnosis of the BCG product portfolio growth-share matrix.

The long-term health of an organisation depends on having some products that generate cash and provide acceptable profits, plus others that use cash to support growth. Among the indicators of overall health are the size and vulnerability of the cash cows, the prospects for the stars, if any, and the number of problem children and dogs. Particular attention must be paid to those products with large cash appetites. Unless the company has an abundant cash flow, it cannot afford to sponsor many such products at one time. If resources, including debt capacity, are spread too thinly, the company will end up with too many marginal products and will be unable to finance promising new product entries or acquisitions in the future.

Although a popular tool in the 1980s, the BCG growth-share matrix is not commonly deployed these days. Many marketers believe that market attractiveness equates to more than simply the growth rate of a market and a product's – or brand's – respective market share. As marketers have sought more complex approaches, utilising many variables, the market attractiveness – business position model has grown in popularity.

Market attractiveness – business position model
A two-dimensional matrix that helps determine which SBUs have an opportunity to grow and which should be divested

Market Attractiveness– Business Position Model

The **market attractiveness–business position model**, illustrated in Figure 9.7, is another two-dimensional matrix, often known as the directional policy matrix or DPM. However, rather than using single measures to define the vertical and horizontal dimensions of the matrix, the model employs multiple measurements and observations. It is an increasingly popular tool, particularly in businesses producing detailed annual marketing plans. The

	Stars	**Problem children**
High	Characteristics ■ Market leaders ■ Fast growing ■ Substantial profits ■ Require large investment to finance growth Strategies ■ Protect existing share ■ Re-invest earnings in the form of price reductions, product improvements, providing better market coverage, production efficiency and so on ■ Obtain a large share of the new users	Characteristics ■ Rapid growth areas ■ Poor profit margins ■ Enormous demand for cash Strategies ■ Invest heavily to get a disproportionate share of new sales ■ Buy existing market shares by acquiring competitors ■ Divestment (see Dogs) ■ Harvesting (see Dogs) ■ Abandonment (see Dogs) ■ Focus on a definable niche where dominance can be achieved
Low	**Cash cows** Characteristics ■ Profitable products ■ Generate more cash than needed to maintain market share Strategies ■ Maintain market dominance ■ Invest in process improvements and technological leadership ■ Maintain price leadership ■ Use excess cash to suppport research and growth elsewhere in the company	**Dogs** Characteristics ■ Greatest number of products fall in this category ■ Operate at a cost disadvantage ■ Few opportunities for growth at a reasonable cost ■ Markets are not growing; therefore, little new business Strategies ■ Focus on a specialised segment of the market that can be dominated and protected from competitive inroads ■ Harvesting—cut back all support costs to a minimum level; support cash flow over the product's remaining life ■ Divestment—sale of a growing concern ■ Abandonment—deletion from the product line

Product market growth (per cent) (vertical axis label)

High   Low

Relative market share

Figure 9.6

Characteristics and strategies for the four basic product types in the growth-share matrix
Source: concepts in this figure adapted from George S. Day, 'Diagnosing the product portfolio', Journal of Marketing, April 1977, pp. 30–1. Reprinted by permission of the American Marketing Association

vertical dimension – market attractiveness – includes all the strengths and resources that relate to the market. For example, seasonality, economies of scale, competitive intensity, industry sales, and the overall cost and feasibility of entering the market. The horizontal axis – business position – is a composite of factors – for example, sales, relative market share, research and development, price competitiveness, product quality and market knowledge. These are only examples, because each set of marketers will select variables as they relate

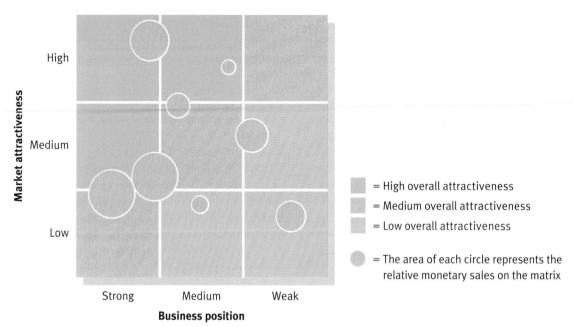

Figure 9.7
Market attractiveness – business position model
Source: adapted from Derek F. Abell and John S. Hammond, Strategic Market Planning: Problems and Analytical Approaches *(Englewood Cliffs, NJ: Prentice-Hall, 1979), p. 213. Used by permission*

to the product and particular market. Each company deploying this tool selects its own criteria, but uses these same ones over time to analyse changes. A slight variation of this matrix is called General Electric's Strategic Business Planning Grid because General Electric is credited with extending the product portfolio planning tool to examine market attractiveness and business strength.

The best situation for a company is to have a strong business position in an attractive market. The upper-left area in Figure 9.7 represents the opportunity for an invest/grow strategy, but the matrix does not indicate how to implement this strategy. The purpose of the model is to serve as a diagnostic tool to highlight SBUs that have an opportunity to grow or that should be divested or approached selectively.[24] SBUs that occupy the invest/grow position can lose their position through faulty marketing strategies.

Decisions on allocating resources to SBUs of medium overall attractiveness should be arrived at on a basis relative to other SBUs that are either more or less attractive. The lower-right area of the matrix is a low-growth harvest/divest area. Harvesting is a gradual withdrawal of marketing resources on the assumption that sales will decline at a slow rate but profits will still be significant at a lower sales volume. Harvesting and divesting – even abandonment, or deletion from the product line – may be appropriate strategies for SBUs characterised by low overall attractiveness.

Marketers proficient in this technique often use the agreed variables and weightings to evaluate market segments in order to determine investment priorities: certain segments will be more attractive than others, while the organisation's strengths will vary between segments (see Chapter 6).

Directional policy matrix (DPM)
A more commonly used name for the market attractiveness – business position model

The Marketing Tools and Techniques box on page 284 offers a step-by-step example of one company's use of the **directional policy matrix (DPM)**, in this instance examining the relative performance of different market segments. The same approach could be deployed to examine SBUs' products, rather than market segments.

Marketing Tools and Techniques

Practitioners' Use of the Directional Policy Matrix (DPM)

Most organisations have more than one product and operate in several markets. This results in the need to prioritise in which markets to focus resources, particularly in terms of sales and marketing activities. Often the 'who shouts the loudest' approach to management meetings wins, or else historical successes with specific clients, products or markets colour the judgement of decision-makers irrespective of current business performance. One effective approach to ensuring that objectivity has an input into such prioritisation is the directional policy matrix (DPM) or GE grid.

Along with the PEST analysis described in Chapter 3, the directional policy matrix is a pivotal tool in strategic business planning. The DPM is useful to marketers as a means for identifying the relative merits of apparently attractive opportunities. Suggested worthwhile opportunities may be benchmarked against a company's existing activities to judge the value of supporting the new ideas. The tool can be used to evaluate the relative merits of individual products or product groups.

The DPM is useful, too, in selecting between market segments (see Chapter 6). The market attractiveness criteria identified for the DPM can easily be utilised to assess the relative merits of market segments.

So, how is a DPM produced? Occasionally, a strategic planner or marketing director may produce such an analysis, but often the variables to be used in order to construct the DPM are selected and weighted by a team of senior decision-makers, often the board of directors, supplemented by marketing managers and analysts who understand the trends and dynamics of individual markets. The steps are as follows.

1 Identify a set of opportunity or market attractiveness criteria. These should be a mix of short-term variables (e.g. sales volumes and current profitability) and longer-term variables (e.g. market growth prospects or ability to sustain a differential advantage). In addition, some variables should be internal-facing (e.g. profitability) and some variables must be market-facing (e.g. customer satisfaction or intensity of competition). The aim is to have a balanced set of criteria.
2 Allocate 100 points across the selected variables in order to weight them in terms of their relative importance.

If a team of managers is involved, each should 'vote' with 100 points, then the whole team's votes should be aggregated.

3 Identify business strength variables and – as with market attractiveness – allocate 100 points between these business strength variables for their weighting.
4 Then the main task. Score each major product group, market segment or marketing opportunity (given the specific context of the analysis). To score, a simple three-category scoring system is usually adequate: $n \times 1 =$ strong/good; $n \times 0.5 =$ 'so-so'/average; $n \times 0 =$ low/weak/poor (where $n =$ the selected variable). When scoring, business strength variables are usually taken as being relative to the dominant player(s) in the market, while market attractiveness scoring is usually one market segment versus 'the others' in the company's portfolio.
5 Weight $\times$ score $=$ total to be plotted. Each product group, segment or opportunity is, therefore, allocated a value between 0 and 100 for market attractiveness and for business strength, so its position may be plotted on the DPM grid. The Y axis represents market attractiveness (0–100), while the X axis represents business strength (0–100).

In the real B2B example depicted on page 285, the company identified 11 market attractiveness criteria and 10 business strength criteria. Each market segment was in turn judged against all 21 variables, warranting 1, 0.5 or 0. For example, market segment 'A' scored 0.5 for 'long-term prospects with the client' ($14 \times 0.5 = 7$) and 0.5 for 'current presence in the client' ($8 \times 0.5 = 4$), and so forth. However, segment 'B' scored 1 for the first variable ($14 \times 1 = 14$). The result is depicted in the DPM chart on page 285.

Having assessed each of its many market segments, this company plotted them on a DPM. In addition, the management team predicted where the segments would head over the following three years. The circle size represents the proportionate income to the company from each market segment.

Further details may be found in the authors' titles *Market Segmentation Success: Making It Happen!* (The Haworth Press, 2008) and *Marketing Planning* (Cengage Learning, 2008).

Marketing Attractiveness	weighting	Business Strengths	weighting
Long-term prospects with the client	14	Clarity and cohesion of message	19
Profitability	14	Thought leadership	16
Strategic fit	12	Easy to do business with/flexibility	15
Size of the opportunity	12	Right people/right support/right milieu	14
(Right) relationship	9	Perceived quality of delivery	12
Ability to deliver the necessary solution	9	Understanding of the market sector	10
How well the opportunity can be defined/realised	8	Referenceability	7
Current presence in the client	8	Price competitive	3.6
Nature of competition	6	Winning business/closure mindset	5
Risk	5	Breadth and depth	2.4
Whether the task can be replicated or referenced	3		

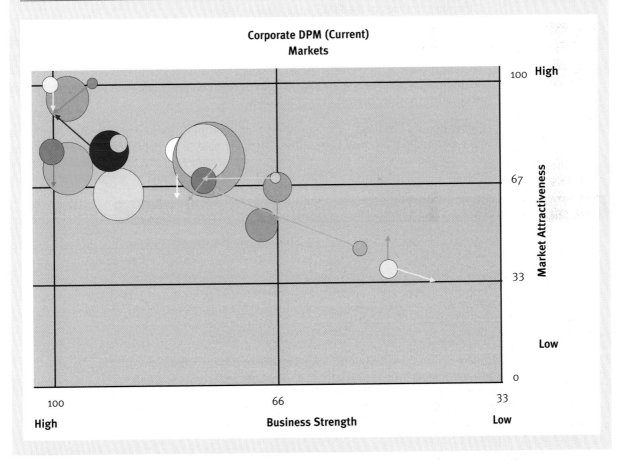

Corporate DPM (Current)
Markets

Profit Impact on Marketing Strategy (PIMS)

The US Strategic Planning Institute (SPI) developed a databank of information on 3000 strategic business units of 200 different organisations during the period 1970 to 1983 for the **Profit Impact on Marketing Strategy (PIMS)** research programme.[25] The sample is somewhat biased because it is composed primarily of large, profitable manufacturing companies marketing mature products; service organisations and distribution companies are

Profit Impact on Marketing Strategy (PIMS)

A research programme that compiled a databank of information on 3000 strategic business units of 200 different businesses in order to assist in analysing marketing performance and formulating marketing strategies

under-represented. However, 19 per cent of the sample is composed of international organisations.[26] The member organisations of the Institute provided confidential information on successes, failures and marginal products. The data have been analysed to provide members with information about how similar organisations performed under a given set of circumstances and about the factors that contributed to success or failure in given market conditions.

The unit of observation in PIMS is the SBU. Table 9.2 shows the types of information provided on each business in the PIMS database. The PIMS database includes both diagnostic and prescriptive information to assist in analysing marketing performance and formulating marketing strategies. The analysis focuses on options, problems, resources and opportunities. The PIMS project has identified more than 30 factors that affect the performance of businesses. These factors can be grouped into three sets of variables:

1 those relating to the structure of the marketplace in which the company competes
2 those that describe the company's competitive position within that market
3 those that relate to the strategy chosen by the company.[27]

These factors may interact, as well as directly affect performance and profitability. Some of the main findings of the PIMS project are as follows.

Strong Market Position   Market position refers to the relative market share that a company holds in relation to its competition. Companies that have a large share of a market tend to be the most profitable. However, it should be noted that market share does not necessarily create profitability. Business strategies, such as the marketing of high-quality products, and the provision of good service result in profitability.

Higher-quality Products   Organisations that offer products of higher quality tend to be more profitable than their competitors. They are able to demand higher prices for those products. Moreover, high-quality offerings instil customer loyalty, foster repeat purchases, insulate companies from price wars and help build market share, as in the case of premium

---

TABLE 9.2 TYPES OF INFORMATION PROVIDED ON EACH BUSINESS IN THE PIMS DATABASE

Characteristics of the Business Environment
Long run growth rate of the market
Short run growth rate of the market
Rate of inflation of selling price levels
Number and size of customers
Purchase frequency and magnitude

Competitive Position of the Business
Share of the served market
Share relative to largest competitors
Product quality relative to competitors
Prices relative to competitors
Pay scales relative to competitors
Marketing efforts relative to competitors
Pattern of market segmentation
Rate of new product introductions

Structure of the Production Process
Capital intensity (degree of automation, etc.)
Degree of vertical integration
Capacity utilisation
Productivity of capital equipment
Productivity of people
Inventory levels

Discretionary Budget Allocations
Research and development budgets
Advertising and promotion budgets
Salesforce expenditures

Strategic Moves
Patterns of change in the controllable elements above

Operating Results
Profitability results
Cash flow results
Growth results

Source: Reproduced by permission of the Strategic Planning Institute [PIMS programme], Cambridge, Mass.

rewarding customers and products that in reality are no longer performing in terms of sales, contribution or both. Often, managers still believe the historical rhetoric rather than recognise that the situation has moved on; new priorities must benefit from the available resources and marketing effort. The ABC analysis generally unearths a few such instances and identifies the rump of unrewarding accounts or customers that are not worth pursuing.

The approaches presented here provide an overview of the most popular analytical methods used in strategic market planning. This chapter has focused on the management of product portfolios, but as has been explained, techniques such as the directional policy matrix (DPM) and the ABC sales: contribution analysis are extremely helpful in evaluating the relative merits of market segments or even individual customer accounts.

The Boston Consulting Group's portfolio analysis, the market attractiveness – business position model, the Profit Impact on Marketing Strategy research programme, the ABC sales: contribution analysis and the product life cycle concept are used not only to diagnose problem areas or to recognise opportunities but also to facilitate the allocation of resources among business units. They are not intended to serve as formulae for success or prescriptive guides, which lay out specific strategic action plans.[28] These approaches are supplements to, not substitutes for, the marketing manager's own judgement. The real test of each approach, or any integrated approach, is how well it helps management diagnose the company's strengths and weaknesses and prescribe strategic actions for maintaining or improving performance. The emphasis should be on making sound decisions with the aid of these analytical tools.[29]

Summary

To maximise the effectiveness of a product mix, a company usually has to alter its mix through the modification of existing products, deletion of a product or new product development. Developing and managing products is critical to a company's survival and growth. The various approaches available for organising product management share common activities, functions and decisions necessary to guide a product through its life cycle. A *product manager* is responsible for a product, a product line or several distinct products that make up an interrelated group within a multiproduct organisation. A *brand manager* is responsible for a single brand. *Marketing managers* are responsible for managing the marketing activities that serve a particular group or class of customers. A *venture or project team* is sometimes used to create and develop entirely new products that may be aimed at new markets.

>> A new product may be an innovation that has never been sold by any organisation; or it can be a product that a given company has not marketed previously, although similar products have been available from other organisations. Before a product is introduced, it goes through the seven phases of *new product development*. (1) In the *idea generation* phase, new product ideas may come from internal or external sources. (2) In the process of *screening ideas*, those with the greatest potential are selected for further review. (3) *Concept testing* presents a small number of potential buyers with the concept idea in order to ascertain early approval indicators. (4) During the *business analysis* stage, the product idea is evaluated to determine its potential contribution to the company's sales, costs and profits. (5) *Product development* is the phase in which the organisation determines if it is technically feasible to produce the product and if it can be produced at costs low enough for the final price to be reasonable. (6) *Test marketing* is a limited introduction of a product in geographic areas chosen to represent the intended market. (7) The decision to enter the *commercialisation* phase means that full-scale production of the product begins and a complete marketing strategy is developed.

» Not all 'new' products are genuinely new! Many product introductions are in fact a *line extension* – the development of a product that is closely related to products in the existing product line, but designed to meet different customer needs. The *product adoption process* that buyers go through in accepting a product includes awareness, interest, evaluation, trial and adoption.

» As a product moves through its life cycle, marketing strategies will require continual adaptation. In the growth stage, it is important to develop brand loyalty and a market position. Marketers may move from an *exclusive distribution* or *selective distribution* to a more *intensive distribution* of dealers. In the maturity stage, a product may be modified or new market segments may be developed to rejuvenate its sales.

» *Product modification* involves changing one or more characteristics of a company's product. This approach to altering a product mix can be effective when the product is modifiable, when customers can perceive the change and when customers want the modification. *Quality modifications* are changes that relate to a product's dependability and durability. Changes that affect a product's versatility, effectiveness, convenience or safety are called *functional modifications*. *Style modifications* change the sensory appeal of a product.

» A product that is declining may be maintained as long as it makes a contribution to profits or enhances the product mix. Marketers must determine whether to eliminate the declining product or to reposition it to extend its life.

» *Product deletion* is the process of eliminating a product that is unprofitable, consumes too many resources and no longer satisfies a sufficient number of customers. *Phase out*, *run out* and *immediate drop* are three ways to delete a product. A product mix should be systematically reviewed to determine when to delete products.

» A number of tools have been developed to aid marketing managers in their portfolio planning efforts; these include the Boston Consulting Group (BCG) *product portfolio analysis*, the market attractiveness–business position model, the Profit Impact on Marketing Strategy (PIMS) and the ABC sales: contribution analysis. The product life cycle concept is also important in determining marketing strategies. The BCG approach is based on the philosophy that a product's market growth rate and its relative market share are key factors influencing marketing strategy. All the company's products are integrated into a single, overall matrix – including *stars*, *cash cows*, *dogs* and *problem children* – and are evaluated to determine appropriate strategies for individual SBUs and the overall portfolio strategies.

» The *market attractiveness – business position model* is a two-dimensional matrix, often known as the *directional policy matrix (DPM)*. The market attractiveness dimension includes variables that relate to the attractiveness of the market or product opportunity, such as seasonality, economies of scale, competitive intensity, industry sales and the cost of competing. The business position axis measures variables that relate to a business's strengths and capabilities, such as sales levels, relative market share, research and development expertise, and other factors that support building market share for a product. Each set of marketers will select variables pertinent to the respective company and industry.

» The *Profit Impact on Marketing Strategy (PIMS)* research programme of the US Strategic Planning Institute developed a databank of confidential information on the successes, failures and marginal products of more than 3000 strategic business units of 200 different businesses. The unit of observation in PIMS is an SBU. The results of PIMS include both diagnostic and prescriptive information to assist in analysing marketing performance and formulating marketing strategies. The analysis focuses on options, problems, resources and opportunities.

» The *ABC sales: contribution analysis* examines the financial worth to a company of its products, product groups or customers. The analysis highlights areas in which to avoid or limit further investment and sales and marketing activity. It also reveals specific targets for financial contribution improvement or sales volume improvement.

❯❯ Tools for portfolio planning are used only to diagnose problem areas or recognise opportunities. They are supplements to, not substitutes for, the marketing manager's own judgement. The real test of each approach, or any integrated approach, is how well it helps management diagnose the company's strengths and weaknesses, and prescribe strategic actions for maintaining or improving performance.

❯❯ The portfolio planning approaches presented here provide an overview of the most popular analytical methods used in strategic market planning. This chapter has focused on the management of product portfolios, but techniques such as the market attractiveness–business position model – more commonly now known as the directional policy matrix (DPM) – and the ABC sales: contribution analysis are extremely helpful in evaluating the relative merits of market segments or even individual customer accounts.

⊙ *Key Links*

- This chapter has examined the development of products and the first part should be read in conjunction with Chapter 8, on product decisions.
- The management of products should be considered in harmony with the material presented in Chapter 14, on branding.
- The product portfolio techniques explained in this chapter, particularly the directional policy matrix and ABC sales: contribution analysis, are often deployed by marketers making trade-off decisions between emerging opportunities or various market segments. These techniques are useful when reading about targeting in Chapter 6's discussion of market segmentation.

Important Terms

Product manager
Brand manager
Marketing manager
Venture or project team
New product development
Idea generation
Screening ideas
Concept testing
Business analysis
Product development
Test marketing
Commercialisation
Line extension
Product adoption process
Exclusive distribution
Selective distribution
Intensive distribution
Product modification

Quality modifications
Functional modifications
Style modifications
Product deletion
Phase out
Run out
Immediate drop
Product portfolio analysis
Stars
Cash cows
Dogs
Problem children
Market attractiveness–business position model
Directional policy matrix (DPM)
Profit Impact on Marketing Strategy (PIMS)
ABC sales: contribution analysis

Discussion and Review Questions

1 What organisational alternatives are available to a company with two product lines, each consisting of four product items?
2 When is it more appropriate to use a product manager than a marketing manager?
3 What type of company might use a venture team to develop new products? What are the advantages and disadvantages of such a team?
4 Do small companies that manufacture one or two products need to be concerned about developing and managing products? Why or why not?
5 Why is product development a cross-functional activity within an organisation? That is, why must finance, engineering, manufacturing and other functional areas be involved?
6 Develop a list of information sources for new product ideas for the car industry.

7 What are the advantages and disadvantages of test marketing?

8 Compare and contrast three ways of modifying a product.

9 What are the stages of the product adoption process, and how do they affect the commercialisation phase?

10 Detail the key stages of the product life cycle.

11 How can a company prolong the life of a mature product? What actions should be taken to try to stem the product's decline?

12 Give several reasons why a company might be unable to eliminate an unprofitable product.

13 In what ways do the stages of the product life cycle impact on a company's management of its product portfolio?

14 What are the major considerations in developing the BCG product portfolio matrix? Define and explain the four basic types of product suggested by the Boston Consulting Group.

15 When should marketers consider using PIMS for strategic market planning?

16 What are the advantages of the directional policy matrix (DPM) over the BCG product portfolio matrix?

17 What are the diagnostic capabilities of the ABC sales: contribution analysis?

Recommended Reading

• Baker, M. and Hart, S., *Product Strategy and Management* (Harlow: Pearson/FT, 2007).

• Day, G.S., *Analysis for Strategic Marketing Decisions* (St Paul, Minnesota: West, 1986).

• Doyle, P. and Stern, P., *Marketing Management and Strategy* (Harlow: Pearson/FT, 2006).

• Lehmann, D. and Winer, R., *Product Management* (Boston, Mass: McGraw-Hill, 2004).

• Trott, P., *Innovation Management and New Product Development* (Harlow: Pearson/FT, 2004).

• Wind, Y.J., *Product Policy: Concepts, Methods and Strategy* (Reading, MA: Addison-Wesley, 1982).

🌐 Internet Exercise

The success of BMW's Mini has been phenomenal. Despite a limited range of cars, each one on the road appears unique, and research reveals that Mini owners feel they have the power to tailor their car to suit their specific tastes and driving styles. BMW and Mini have incorporated this individualisation, of what in reality is far from a bespoke one-to-one product, in their product development process and in their commercialisation of this product. Take a look at either: www.mini.co.uk or www.mini.com and in particular the section detailing accessories.

1 What product features and characteristics are portrayed on the Mini website?

2 To what extent does Mini's commercialisation enable customers to individualise or personalise their cars?

🌐 *Applied Mini-Case*

People visit cinemas to watch a film for many reasons: to catch the latest release, because friends are going, to be entertained, to go on a date, to occupy the children, to escape from the children, to be with people, to have an emotional experience, to kill time, to have a rest, or 'just because it's somewhere to go'. The choice of which film to see may often be the first decision, but these days, with the growth of multiplexes and record cinema attendances, the choice may be which multiplex: Odeon, Cineworld, Gaiety or National Amusements' Showcase? For rival operators, the 'augmented' product is becoming increasingly important as they seek to develop a competitive edge and to encourage customer loyalty. For example, Showcase strongly emphasises many once secondary or minor features in an attempt to add to the appeal of its cinemas:

- state-of-the-art film projection
- acres of free, illuminated car parking
- best seats in town – exclusive rocking loungers
- bargain matinees daily
- freshly popped popcorn
- cinema hire and special group rates
- on main coach/bus routes

- Dolby stereo-equipped auditoria
- air conditioning
- excellent facilities for the disabled
- late-night shows every Friday and Saturday
- efficient, courteous service
- gift certificates always available
- art gallery with prints for sale.

For many companies, not only Showcase, the augmented product is an increasingly important element in the marketing strategy and the search for customer satisfaction. The new product development process increasingly includes the required customer service attributes desired by targeted customers to accompany the purchased product.

Source: National Amusements/Showcase Cinema, Coventry; http://www.showcasecinemas.co.uk, January, 2008.

❓ Question

As a marketing manager, to what extent does inclusion of the augmented product simplify or complicate the new product development process?

⬡ Case Study

Sellotape or Mustard? Increasing Market Penetration

Just as JCB is a generic term for backhoe diggers in the construction industry, Hoover for vacuum cleaners, Post-it for those useful sticky stationery tags, and Bic for disposable pens, for many decades Sellotape has been the term applied to sticky transparent tape. It is even cited in the Oxford Dictionary. Over the years, however, many other brands and suppliers have entered the market and eaten away Sellotape's once dominant market share. So where next for Sellotape?

At the end of 1995, following nearly two years of research and planning, Sellotape enjoyed a £2 million relaunch. This represented the 'most significant change in the brand's 60 year history', according to Neil Ashley, executive director of the company, renamed the Sellotape Company. The name Sellotape has been the company's core marketing asset for many decades, with nine out of ten consumers familiar with the brand. However, the company has for some time sold a wider range of products than its sticky tape association implies. Michael Peters of the branding specialist Identica, responsible for the Sellotape rethink, was more fervent in his view: 'while it is a very famous trademark, it's a grey one'. Qualitative marketing research revealed that, although well known, hardly any consumer asked for Sellotape by name. Worse, they readily accepted other brands because they could see no obvious product or brand features that gave Sellotape a competitive edge or differentiation over rival products.

The relaunch aimed to address the inherent weakness in becoming a generic name for a product by re-establishing a new brand identity alongside existing core brand values. Rival products not using cellulose are cheaper, so alongside its traditional tape, the Sellotape Company now offers a range of tape made from other source materials. Elephant Tape, for example, is a heavy-duty fabric tape that is targeted at the do-it-yourself (DIY) market.

Under the sub-brand Sellotape Office, a range of products aimed at office use has been launched. Ranges have also been targeted at the children's market and the home security market. The view that there are, in effect, three distinct markets – retail, DIY and office – has led to the development of novel product applications and totally separate ranges.

The key problem to overcome has been 'the Colman's mustard dilemma'. Colman's, the market leader, had tremendously high brand awareness, and consumers perceived its mustards to be of high quality. Unfortunately, these consumers usually bought only one type of mustard, English; and that one jar lasted for years! Colman's had to increase usage. It achieved this by both:

1 demonstrating in advertisements and cookery supplements that mustard could be used in a variety of ways, particularly as an additional ingredient in many sauces, just like a herb or spice

2 bringing out a range of different mustards, each with unique strengths, flavours and applications – French, Italian and American mustards, along with the traditional English.

Consumers were encouraged to have several jars in their cupboards and to consume greater quantities.

For Sellotape, research showed that most customers bought only one roll of sticky tape each year, often around Christmas. The launch of ranges designed for different target audiences – retail, DIY and office – and for various applications – children's activities and home security uses – emulated the brand extension principles so well deployed by Colman's.

Sellotape's strong brand awareness and identity meant that the company did not need to advertise heavily. Instead, the Sellotape Company relied on direct marketing and point-of-sale promotion to create awareness of its new sub-brands and their applications. A core task for the company has been to break down the traditional views of the product and its customers held by employees, and to establish additional channels of distribution through toy shops and garden centres to reflect the extended and additional product ranges. It is away from the once core stationery retailers that the Sellotape

Company expects to see the strongest growth, particularly in the DIY sector. There, pan-European sales are rising by around 8 per cent each year and now amount to over £70 million.

If the Sellotape Company can, like Colman's, encourage its customers to buy two products annually instead of just one and to look for its branded products by name, the heritage of the brand and the reorganisation of the company will have reaped significant rewards.

Sources: 'Sellotape acts to avoid getting stuck in a rut', *Independent on Sunday*, 26 November, 1995, IB8; the Sellotape Company, 1996; B&Q, 1996; Sainsbury's Homebase, 1996, 2004. With grateful thanks to Meg Carter; http://sellotape.henkel-online. co.uk/home.php, January, 2008.

❷ *Questions for Discussion*

1 At what stages in their product life cycle are the different Sellotape products, and what are the management implications?

2 Why was it necessary for the Sellotape Company to relaunch its Sellotape range?

3 How might new lines help Sellotape develop its competitive position in this market?

10
The Marketing of Services

"**Delivering services is people's business: only great customers and great employees can guarantee great service quality.**"

Hans Kasper, Rijksuniversiteit Limburg, Maastricht

Objectives

- To understand the nature and characteristics of services

- To classify services

- To understand the development of marketing strategies for services

- To understand the problems involved in developing a differential advantage in services

- To examine the crucial concept of service quality

- To explore the concept of marketing in non-profit situations

- To understand the development of marketing strategies in non-profit organisations

- To describe methods for controlling non-profit marketing activities

Service
An intangible product involving a deed, a performance or an effort that cannot physically be possessed

Introduction

As discussed in Chapter 8, all products – goods, services and ideas – possess a certain amount of intangibility. A **service** is an intangible product involving a deed, a performance or an effort that cannot physically be possessed.[1] This chapter presents concepts that apply specifically to the marketing of services. Services marketing involves marketing in non-profit organisations such as education, healthcare, charities and government, as well as for-profit making areas such as entertainment, tourism, finance, personal services and professional services.

Opener

Keeping TV Sets and Wallets Tuned to Nickelodeon

The cable television network Nickelodeon – Nick for short – has to satisfy a number of tough audiences. Toddlers want fun, engaging programmes such as *Blue's Clues* and *Dora the Explorer*. School-age viewers enjoy slightly wacky cartoons such as *SpongeBob SquarePants*. Younger teens tune in for programmes like *All That* while older teens watch the celebrity specials. And parents want to be sure that Nick's programmes entertain without violence or sex when a child is holding the remote control. Nick delivers for all these audiences, with ratings that top the list of basic cable networks and annual revenues exceeding US$1 billion. Nick airs a range of different channels, such as Nickelodeon, Nicktoonstv, Nick Replay and, for toddlers, the award-winning Nick Jr.

Every programme presents new opportunities to give viewers a good experience and encourage them to tune in again and again. Nick is known for its in-depth marketing research, and its careful control of animation and production. Because no one can predict precisely which characters and shows will resonate with viewers, the network has had both tremendous successes and big disappointments. Management was surprised by the immediate and immense popularity of *SpongeBob SquarePants*. *SpongeBob* first aired as a weekend series then, as the audience grew, it became a regular part of the Saturday-morning schedule and the prime-time weekday schedule. However, children did not take to either the *Animorphs* series or the *Noah Knows Best* series. One Nick executive says these programmes were 'too talky and a little too old'.

With millions of children tuning in every week, Nick has been able to profit from selling advertising time and from licensing its brand for an ever wider mix of goods and services. Retail sales of its branded products total US$3 billion annually. Seeing the problems that Warner Brothers and Walt Disney have had in operating their own retail chains, Nick instead licensed its brand for sale in department stores.

One of its newest licensing ventures involves themed resorts called the Nickelodeon Family Suites by Holiday Inn. In addition to waterslides, pools and games rooms, the hotels are decorated with Nick-character furnishings, offer breakfast with Nick characters and stage live shows starring Nick characters. This deal has presented entirely different service challenges to those of Nick's television business. Still, Nick believes that viewers who enjoy Nick characters will look forward to staying at a Nick-themed hotel – and they are working with Holiday Inn to open more resorts soon. Can the resorts deliver the kind of service that is consistent with the Nick brand? Stay tuned.

Sources: based on information from Karyn Strauss, 'Move over Disney', *Hotels*, January 2004, p. 13; 'He lives in a pineapple under the sea', *Hotel & Motel Management*, 3 November 2003, p. 126; Joe Flint, 'Testing limits of licensing', *Wall Street Journal*, 9 October 2003, p. B1; Diane Brady and Gerry Khermouch, 'How to tickle a child', *Business Week*, 7 July 2003, pp. 48–50; http://www.ichotelsgroup.com/h/d/fs/1/en/home, January, 2008; http://www.nickhotel.com, January, 2008.

The entertainment and leisure products offered by Nickelodeon are services rather than tangible goods: they are experiential. This chapter presents concepts that apply specifically to products that are services. The organisations that market service products include: for-profit businesses, such as those offering financial, personal and professional services; and non-profit organisations, such as educational institutions, religious groups, charities and governments.

The chapter begins by considering the contribution of service industries to the economy. It then addresses the unique characteristics of services and the problems they present to marketers: these traits often form the basis for examination questions and they explain why marketers of services have to manipulate an extended marketing mix, devote extensive resources to branding and often struggle to create a differential advantage over rivals. Next, the chapter presents various classification schemes that can help services marketers develop marketing strategies. Then a variety of marketing mix considerations are discussed, along with the associated problems of creating and sustaining a differential advantage. The important concept of service quality is then explored. Finally, the chapter defines non-profit marketing and examines the development of non-profit marketing strategies and the control of non-profit marketing activities.

The Nature and Importance of Services

Few products can be classified as a pure good or a pure service. Consider, for example, the purchase of a laptop computer. When consumers buy a laptop, they take ownership of a physical item which they might use at work and at home, but the maintenance contract linked with the purchase is a service. Similarly, a helpline facility offering software support is providing a service. Most products, such as computers and other brown goods, contain both tangible and intangible components. An airline provides a service, yet offers tangible items such as lounges and comfortable seats; hotels require tangible items such as pools, beds, bar tables, yet fundamentally provide a service. One component, however, will dominate, and it is this dominant component that leads to the classification of goods, services and ideas.

Figure 10.1 illustrates the tangibility concept by placing a variety of 'products' on a continuum of tangibility and intangibility. Tangible dominant products are typically classified as goods, and intangible dominant products are typically considered services. A restaurant meal or taxi cab may be tangible and physical, but the restaurant or taxi operator is providing a service: refreshment or transportation. Thus, as defined in Chapter 8, services are intangible dominant products that involve the application of human and mechanical efforts to people or objects.

Growth of Services

In Europe, as in the United States, the importance of services in the economy is increasing, with nearly two-thirds of the EU workforce employed in the sector. Service industries encompass trade, communications, transport, leisure, food and accommodation, financial and medical services, education, government and technical services. There are services intended for consumers – **consumer services** – and those designed to satisfy businesses – **business services**.

Economic prosperity has been a major catalyst for consumer services growth, leading to an increase in financial services, travel, entertainment and personal care. Lifestyle changes

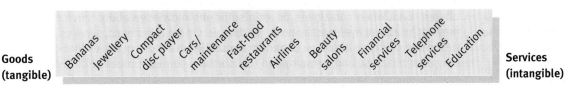

Goods (tangible) Bananas Jewellery Compact disc player Cars/maintenance Fast-food restaurants Airlines Beauty salons Financial services Telephone services Education Services (intangible)

Figure 10.1
A continuum of product tangibility and intangibility

Consumer services
Services such as
education, healthcare,
leisure, catering,
tourism, financial,
entertainment, home
maintenance and other
services to help
consumers

Business services
Services such as repairs
and maintenance,
consulting and
professional advice,
installation, equipment
leasing, marketing
research, advertising,
temporary office
personnel and
caretaking services

have also encouraged expansion of the service sector. Smaller families result in more free time and relatively higher disposable income. Consumers are keener than ever to 'buy in' outside services. With the number of women in the workforce more than doubling in the last 50 years, consumers want to avoid tasks such as meal preparation, house cleaning, home maintenance and preparation of tax returns. Furthermore, Europeans have become more fitness and recreation oriented and, with greater leisure time, the demand for fitness and recreational facilities has escalated. In terms of demographics, the population is growing older, and this change has promoted tremendous expansion of healthcare services. Finally, the number and complexity of goods needing servicing have spurred demand for repair services.

Not only have consumer services grown in the economy, business services have prospered as well. Business or industrial services include repairs and maintenance, consulting and professional advice, installation, equipment leasing, marketing research, advertising, temporary office personnel and caretaking services. Expenditures for business and industrial services have risen even faster than expenditures for consumer services. This growth has been attributed to the increasingly complex, specialised and competitive business environment.[2]

There are three key reasons behind the growth of business-to-business services.

1 Specialisation – the delegation of non-care tasks, such as advertising, executive recruitment and car fleet management.
2 Technology – the increase in sophistication leading to the 'buying in' of expert knowledge and skills, such as IT computing consultants.
3 Flexibility – the need in many organisations to avoid fixed overhead costs; for example, marketing research, maintenance and cleaning are frequently brought in only on an ad hoc basis.

Characteristics of Services

Intangibility
An inherent quality of
services that are
performed and
therefore cannot be
tasted, touched, seen,
smelled or possessed

Search qualities
Tangible attributes of a
service that can be
viewed prior to
purchase

Experience qualities
Attributes that can be
assessed only after
purchase and
consumption, including
satisfaction and courtesy

Credence qualities
Attributes that cannot
be assessed even after
purchase and
consumption

The marketing of services is distinct from goods marketing.[3] To understand the nature of services marketing, it is necessary to appreciate the particular characteristics of services. Services have four key basic characteristics:

1 intangibility
2 inseparability of production and consumption
3 perishability
4 heterogeneity.[4]

Table 10.1 summarises these characteristics and the resulting marketing challenges.

Intangibility   The characteristic of **intangibility** stems from the fact that services are performances. They cannot be seen, touched, tasted or smelled, nor can they be possessed. Intangibility also relates to the difficulty that consumers may have in understanding service offerings.[5] Services have a few tangible attributes, called **search qualities**, that can be viewed prior to purchase, such as the décor in a restaurant or the array of tools in a car mechanic's shop. Business-to-business design specialists JKR offer clients a packaging design service, and use existing clients' executions to entice new clients (see Figure 10.2). When consumers cannot examine a service product in advance, they may not understand exactly what is being offered. Even when consumers do gain sufficient knowledge about service offerings, they may not be able to evaluate the possible choices. On the other hand, services are rich in experience and credence qualities. **Experience qualities** are those qualities that can be assessed only after purchase and consumption (satisfaction, courtesy, pleasure). Leisure centres and holidays are examples of services that are high in experience qualities. **Credence qualities** are those qualities that cannot be assessed even after purchase and consumption.[6] An appendix operation, car repairs, consulting and legal representation are examples of services

TABLE 10.1 SERVICE MARKETING CHALLENGES	
Service characteristics	**Resulting marketing challenges**
Intangibility	Difficult for customer to evaluate Customer does not take physical possession Difficult to advertise and display Difficult to set and justify prices Service process is not usually protectable by patents
Inseparability of production and consumption	Service provider cannot mass-produce services Customer must participate in production Other consumers affect service outcomes Services are difficult to distribute
Perishability	Services cannot be stored Very difficult to balance supply and demand Unused capacity is lost forever Demand may be very time-sensitive
Heterogeneity	Service quality is difficult to control Difficult to standardise service delivery
Client-based relationships	Success depends on satisfying and keeping customers over the long term Generating repeat business is challenging Relationship marketing becomes critical
Customer contact	Service providers are critical to delivery Requires high levels of service employee training and motivation Changing a high-contact service into a low-contact service to achieve lower costs without reducing customer satisfaction

Sources: K. Douglas Hoffman and John E.G. Bateson, *Essentials of Services Marketing* (Fort Worth, TX: Dryden Press, 1997), pp. 25–38; Valarie A. Zeithaml, A. Parasuraman and Leonard L. Berry, *Delivering Quality Service: Balancing Customer Perceptions and Expectations* (New York: Free Press, 1990); Leonard L. Berry and A. Parasuraman, *Marketing Services: Competing through Quality* (New York Free Press, 1991), p. 5.

high in credence qualities. How many consumers are knowledgeable enough to assess the quality of an appendectomy, even after the surgery has been performed?

A Renault car can be test-driven before being purchased. It can be viewed in the dealer's showroom and on the streets. It can, to an extent, be consumed prior to purchase. The same is not true of a beauty treatment or an opera seat. The beauty treatment and the opera may fail to live up to expectations, but by the time this disappointment is recognised it is too late – the service has been partially consumed and paid for.

Inseparability
In relation to production and consumption, a characteristic of services that means they are produced at the same time as they are consumed

Inseparability   Related to intangibility, therefore, is **inseparability** of production and consumption. Services are normally produced at the same time as they are consumed. A medical examination is an example of simultaneous production and consumption. In fact, the doctor cannot possibly perform the service without the patient's presence, and the consumer is actually involved in the production process. With other services, such as taking tennis lessons, consumers are simultaneously involved in production. Because of high consumer involvement in most services, standardisation and control are difficult to maintain. The Marketing Insight box on page 301 illustrates how Dutch banking giant ABN AMRO addresses this difficulty.

Figure 10.2

Many services are targeted at business customers. Here packaging design experts jkr attempt to entice new clients for its services
Source: Courtesy of jones knowles ritchie

Perishability
A characteristic of services whereby unused capacity on one occasion cannot be stockpiled or inventoried for future occasions

Perishability   As production and consumption are simultaneous, services are also characterised by **perishability**. The consumer of a service generally has to be present and directly involved in the consumption of the service at the time of its production. This means that unused capacity in one time period cannot be stockpiled or inventoried for future time periods. This is a problem that airline operators face every day. Each operator engages in an ongoing struggle to maintain seat occupancy levels. Empty seats mean lost business. Many operators offer 'last-minute' cut-price deals to reduce the numbers of empty seats. In many cases it is not possible to change the flight on which the seat is booked and monies paid are generally not refunded in the event of cancellation. This example illustrates how service perishability presents problems very different from the supply and demand problems encountered in the marketing of goods.[7] While an empty airline seat on a flight is a sale lost for ever, cans of soup remaining on the supermarket shelf at the close of business will be available for sale the following day.

Heterogeneity
Variability in the quality of service because services are provided by people, and people perform inconsistently

Heterogeneity   As most services are labour intensive, they are susceptible to **heterogeneity**. For the service to be provided and consumed, the client generally meets and deals directly with the service provider's personnel. Direct contact and interaction are distinguishing features of services. However, the people delivering services do not always perform consistently. There may be variation from one service to another within the same organisation or variation in the service that a single individual provides from day to day and from customer to customer. A good branch manager is crucial for a restaurant chain such

◊ Marketing Insight

Dutch Bankers Build Relationships – ABN AMRO Leads through Services

The 1991 merger between Algemene Bank Nederland and Amsterdam-Rotterdam Bank to create Dutch-based ABN AMRO Bank produced the dominant financial institution in the Netherlands, the 11th-ranked bank in Europe and 23rd in the world, based on tier 1 capital. With branches throughout the Netherlands and Benelux, and over 3000 branches in more than 60 other countries, ABN AMRO deals daily with thousands of customers face to face or through telecommunications. Now acquired by the RBS/Santander-led consortium, ABN AMRO has 110,000 full-time equivalent staff and assets of €650 billion.

The company's policy is to buy relatively small banking operations around the globe and integrate them fully within its existing business. It does not seek mega-mergers with other large international banks. ABN AMRO North America agreed to buy Chicago Corp, which merged with ABN AMRO Securities, Inc., resulting in the addition of 20,000 staff outside the Netherlands and a significant New York-based operation destined for rapid growth. Hoare Govett has already been so integrated, creating the 17th largest insurance broker in the world. Nordic Alfred Berg is now also part of the network. Significant alliances have been established in South-east Asia, with China now seen to be an important market. The strategy is recognised as successful well beyond the banking fraternity; ABN has received many prestigious awards for the competitive success of its global operation.

To facilitate this growth, the bank is one of the world's leading spenders on information systems, maintaining that today's technology helps it to offer an efficient and reliable service to its most valuable asset – its customer base. Customers are kept to the fore through the company's policy of relationship management, a core strategy since 1980. The bank targets only a small number of clients, who are subsequently handled by a large team of relationship managers.

Many consumers find banks' history and formal procedures intimidating, and view them as powerful institutions with which they can enjoy little personal interaction. ABN AMRO has tackled this perception head on recognising that, as fundamentally a service provider dealing with people, its success depends on the attitude and ability of its own personnel. In this respect, ABN AMRO realises it must behave as a service provider and adopt the practices of services marketing.

The company states that it is an ambitious institution, committed to continuous improvement. 'Our success depends on excellent performance and a solid reputation. Transparency and dialogue are of crucial importance in all our relationships if we are to maintain our reputation as a respectable and reliable institution. We strive to provide excellent service.' The bank publicises its corporate values as: integrity, teamwork, respect and professionalism, and says, 'We are determined to deliver outstanding quality so that our relationships with our clients will be long-lasting and close'.

ABN AMRO places significant emphasis on its employees, who are integral to its products, marketing and the services it provides. The bank's internal marketing focuses on training and motivating its staff worldwide to deliver a consistent, friendly, proficient and superior service to ABN AMRO's many customers. ABN AMRO acknowledges that it is only as good as its personnel – those people who, to many customers, epitomise the bank's products and services. The company's human resources and marketing executives highlight these employees' skills in handling customer contact and delivering the bank's services.

Sources: ABN AMRO, 2004; 'European 100', *Information Week*, 11 December 1995, pp. 32–41; Yvette Kantrow, 'ABN AMRO/Chicago Corp will expand "significantly" in NY', *Investment Dealers' Digest*, 2 October 1995, pp. 8–9; 'Jan Kalff, chairman, ABN AMRO', *Euromoney*, September 1995, p. 64; John Anderson et al., 'The 1995 industry all stars', *Independent Energy*, September 1995, pp. 24–30; Matthew Ball, 'ABN AMRO aims for 380 of the best', *Corporate Finance*, July 1995, p. 40; 'Berg sale raises broking stakes', *Euroweek*, June 1995, p. 45; Caroline Farquhar; ABN AMRO annual report and accounts; Barclays de Zoete Wedd Securities; Credit Suisse First Boston; Financial Times Analysis; 'Banking industry report', Salomon Brothers, April 1992; ABN AMRO Utrecht, 1999; www.abnamro.com, June 2004; www.abnamro.com, January, 2008.

as Pizza Express or a coffee shop like Starbucks. Poor customer reaction and branch performance can often be traced back to a poor branch manager.[8] Waiting times in either outlet can vary greatly, often due to teamwork, speed and efficiency variations between branches.

This may result in varying levels of customer satisfaction – for example, between one Starbucks and another. Thus standardisation and quality are extremely difficult to control. However, it is also true that the characteristics of services themselves may make it possible for marketers to customise their offerings to consumers. In such cases, services marketers often face a dilemma: how to provide efficient, standardised service at an acceptable level of quality, while simultaneously treating each customer as a unique person.

Client-based relationships
Interactions that result in satisfied customers who use a service repeatedly over time

Client-based Relationships   The success of many services depends on creating and maintaining **client-based relationships**, interactions with customers that result in satisfied customers who use a service repeatedly over time.[9] In fact, some service providers, such as solicitors, accountants and financial advisers, call their customers 'clients' and often develop and maintain close, long-term relationships with them. Customers are generally more satisfied in relational exchanges than they are with exchanges based on single transactions. Indeed, research suggests that customer loyalty and re-patronage behaviour can be encouraged through this approach.[10] The building of such relationships has also been shown to be important in non-profit contexts.[11] It seems that services businesses are successful only to the degree to which they can maintain a group of clients who use their services on an ongoing basis. For example, a dentist may serve a family for many years. If the family members are confident in the dentist and think he or she offers a good service, they are likely to recommend the dentist to friends. If this positive word-of-mouth communication continues, the dentist may acquire a large number of clients through this route. To ensure that client-based relationships are created and maintained, a service provider must take action to build trust, demonstrate customer commitment, and satisfy customers so well that they become very loyal to the provider and unlikely to switch to competitors.

Customer contact
The level of interaction between the provider and customer needed to deliver the service

Customer Contact   Not all services require a high degree of **customer contact**, but many do. Customer contact refers to the level of interaction between the service provider and the customer that is necessary to deliver the service. High-contact services include healthcare, real estate, and hair and beauty services. Examples of low-contact services are car repairs and dry cleaning. As the following section explains, the level of customer contact is sometimes used as the basis for classifying services.

Classification of Services

Services are a very diverse group of products, and an organisation may provide more than one kind. Examples of services include car hire, maintenance services, healthcare, hairdressing, health centres, childcare, domestic services, legal advice, banking, insurance, air travel, education, entertainment, catering, business consulting, dry cleaning and accounting. Nevertheless, services can be meaningfully analysed using a **five-category classification** scheme:

Five-category classification
A method of analysing services according to five criteria: type of market, degree of labour intensiveness, degree of customer contact, skill of the service provider and goal of the service provider

1 type of market
2 degree of labour intensiveness
3 degree of customer contact
4 skill of the service provider, and
5 goal of the service provider.

Table 10.2 summarises this scheme.

Type of Market   Services can be viewed in terms of the market or type of customer they serve – consumer or business.[12] The implications of this distinction are very similar to those for all products and do not require detailed discussion here. Figure 10.2 illustrates different kinds of marketing services which brand design company jkr offers to its clients.

TABLE 10.2 CLASSIFICATION OF SERVICES	
Category	**Examples**
Type of market	
Consumer	Childcare, legal advice, entertainment
Business	Consulting, caretaking services, installation
Degree of labour intensiveness	
Labour based	Education, haircuts, dentistry
Equipment based	Telecommunications, fitness centres, public transport
Degree of customer contact	
High	Healthcare, hotels, air travel
Low	Home deliveries, postal service
Skill of the service provider	
Professional	Legal advice, healthcare, accountancy
Non-professional	Domestic services, dry cleaning, public transport
Goal of the service provider	
Profit	Financial services, insurance, tourism
Non-profit	Some healthcare, education, government

Degree of Labour Intensiveness   A second way to classify services is by degree of labour intensiveness. Many services – such as domestic cleaning, education and medical care – rely heavily on human labour. Other services – such as telecommunications, fitness centres and public transport – are more equipment intensive.

Labour-based (that is, people-based) services are more susceptible to heterogeneity than most equipment-based services. Marketers of people-based services must recognise that the service providers are often viewed as the service itself. Therefore, strategies relating to selecting, training, motivating and controlling employees are crucial to the success of most service businesses. A bad attitude from Ryanair's ground staff would colour the customer's view not just of the employee concerned but also of the company and all of its service products. A customer who has flown quite happily with Ryanair for many years may, so prompted, consider taking his or her custom to a rival company.

Degree of Customer Contact   The third way in which services can be classified is by degree of customer contact. High-contact services include healthcare, hotels, property agents and restaurants; low contact services include home deliveries, theatres, dry cleaning and spectator sports.[13] High contact services generally involve actions that are directed towards individuals. Because these services are directed at people, the consumer must be present during production. Sometimes – for example, in the case of a car valeting service – it is possible for the service provider to go to the consumer. However, high-contact services typically require that the consumer goes to the production facility. Consequently, the physical appearance and ambience of the facility may be a major component of the consumer's overall evaluation of the service. The enjoyment of a visit to a health spa stems not just from the quality of the beauty treatments, or the suitability of the dietary or fitness programmes on offer, but also from the décor and furnishings, general ambience, and the abilities and attitude of the staff. Because the consumer must be present during production of a high-contact service, the process of production may be just as important as its final outcome. For example, open-plan banks, quick queue systems

303

and ATM facilities aim to improve the transaction process and make the service more enjoyable for the consumer.

Low-contact service, in contrast, commonly involves actions directed at things. Although consumers may not need to be present during service delivery, their presence may be required to initiate or terminate the service. The Post Office maintains a network of branches, sorting offices and vehicles. The process of sending a parcel from Edinburgh to Cardiff or Lille is lengthy. Yet consumers only need to be present to initiate the service. The appearance of the production facilities and the interpersonal skills of actual service providers are thus not as critical in low-contact services as they are in high-contact services.[14]

Skill of the Service Provider   Skill of the service provider is a fourth way to classify services. Professional services tend to be more complex and more highly regulated than non-professional services. In the case of legal advice, for example, the final product is situation specific. As a result, consumers often do not know what the actual service will involve or how much it will cost until the service is completed.

Goal of the Service Provider   Finally, services can be classified according to whether they are profit or non-profit. The second half of this chapter examines non-profit (not-for-profit) marketing, such as that present in the public sector and charities. Most non-profit organisations provide services rather than goods.

Developing Marketing Strategies for Services

Strategic Considerations   In developing marketing strategies, the marketer must first understand what benefits the customer wants, how the company's service offer and brand are perceived relative to the competition and what services consumers buy.[15] In other words, the marketer must develop the right service for the right people at the right price, in the right place with the right positioning and image. The marketer must then communicate with consumers so that they are aware of the need-satisfying services available to them. The key aspects of effective target marketing – as explained in Chapter 6 – and of managing the implementation of the determined marketing strategy apply strongly to the marketing of services.[16]

One of the unique challenges service marketers face is matching supply and demand. Price can be used to help smooth out demand for a service. There are also other ways in which marketers can alter the marketing mix to deal with the problem of fluctuating demand. Through price incentives, advertising and other promotional efforts, marketers can remind consumers of busy times and encourage them to come for service during slack periods. Additionally, the product itself can be altered to cope with fluctuating demand. Restaurants, for example, may change their menus, vary their lighting and décor, open or close the bar, and change the entertainment on offer. A historical tourist destination may stage theatrical events and firework displays to attract customers out of season. Finally, distribution can be modified to reflect changes in demand. For example, some libraries have mobile units that travel to different locations during slack periods.[17]

The strategies that services marketers implement are contingent upon a good understanding of the pattern and determinants of demand. Does the level of demand follow a cycle? What are the causes of this cycle? Are the changes random?[18] An attempt to use price decreases to shift demand for public transport to off-peak periods would achieve only limited success because of the cause of the cyclical demand for public transport. Employees have little control over their working hours and are therefore unable to take advantage of pricing incentives.

Table 10.3 summarises a range of marketing and non-marketing strategies that service businesses may use to deal with fluctuating demand. Non-marketing strategies essentially involve internal, employee-related actions.[19] They may be the only choices available when

TABLE 10.3 STRATEGIES FOR COPING WITH FLUCTUATIONS IN DEMAND FOR SERVICES	
Marketing strategies	**Non-marketing strategies**
Use different pricing	Hire extra staff/lay off employees
Alter product	Work employees overtime/part time
Change place/distribution	Cross-train employees
Use promotional efforts	Use employees to perform non-vital tasks during slack times
Modify customer service levels	Subcontract work/seek subcontract work
Alter branding and positioning	Slow the pace of work
	Turn away business

fluctuations in demand are random. For example, a strike or natural disaster may cause fluctuations in consumer demand for public transport.

Creating a Differential Advantage in Services

Differential advantage
Something desired by the customer that only one company – not its rivals – can offer

The aim of marketing is to satisfy customers, achieving product or brand differentiation with an advantage over competitors' products. This **differential advantage**, sometimes termed a 'competitive edge', is determined by customers' perceptions. A differential advantage is something desired by the customer that only one company can offer, as explained in Chapter 2 of *Marketing Essentials*. If the targeted customers do not perceive an advantage, in marketing terms the product offers no benefit over rival products.

For any product, achieving and sustaining a differential advantage is difficult, but for services the challenge is even greater. The intangibility of the service product and the central role of people in its delivery are the prime causes of this difficulty, but, as Table 10.4 shows, there are others, such as difficulties ensuring consistent service quality and the fact that the interface with the customer may be difficult to control.

The difficulty encountered in creating a differential advantage in services makes it even more important that marketing activities are carried out in a systematic and appropriate manner. Thus services marketers must ensure that the needs of targeted markets are well understood in order to bring service products and the marketing mix into line with customers' exact requirements. There must be a clear appreciation of competitors' service offerings and marketing programmes, and regular efforts are needed to research customers' satisfaction levels. Branding, supported with well-constructed promotional campaigns, is even more central to the reinforcement and communication of any differential advantage for services.

TABLE 10.4 DIFFICULTIES IN CREATING A DIFFERENTIAL ADVANTAGE IN SERVICES
Intangibility minimises product differentiation
No – or little – patent protection exists
Few barriers to entry enable competitors to set up and copy successful initiatives
The interface with customers is difficult to control
Growth is hard to achieve, particularly since key personnel can only be spread so far
Service quality is irregular
It is difficult to improve productivity and lower the cost to the consumer
Innovation leads to imitation
Restrictive regulations abound, particularly in the professions

The Extended Marketing Mix for Services

The standard marketing mix comprises the '4Ps':

- product
- promotion
- price
- place/distribution.

The discussion about the classification of services has emphasised the importance of three additional elements:

- process
- physical evidence (ambience)
- people.

Collectively, these seven elements, which are sometimes called the '7Ps', form what is termed the **extended marketing mix for services** (see Figure 10.3). It is essential for services marketers to recognise the importance of these additional '3Ps'.

Extended marketing mix for services
In addition to the standard '4Ps' marketing mix – product, promotion, price and place/distribution – there are 3Ps: process, physical evidence (ambience) and people

Service Quality

The delivery of high-quality services is one of the most important and difficult tasks that any service organisation faces. Because of their unique characteristics, services are very difficult to evaluate. Hence customers must look closely at service quality when comparing services. **Service quality** is defined as customers' perception of how well a service meets or exceeds their expectations.[20] Service quality is judged by customers, not the organisation. This distinction is critical because it forces services marketers to examine their quality from the customer's viewpoint. For example, a dental surgery may view service quality as having friendly and knowledgeable employees. However, the customers may be more concerned with waiting time, cleanliness and the effectiveness of patient pain relief. Thus it is important for service organisations to determine what customers expect and then develop service products that meet or exceed those expectations.

Service quality
Customers' perception of how well a service meets or exceeds their expectations

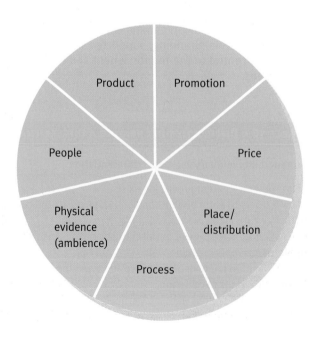

Figure 10.3
The extended marketing mix for services

Customer Evaluation of Service Quality

The biggest obstacle for customers in evaluating service quality is the intangible nature of the service. How can customers evaluate something they cannot see, feel, taste, smell or hear? The evaluation of a good is much easier because all goods possess 'search qualities' in the form of tangible attributes, such as colour, style, size, feel or fit, that can be evaluated prior to purchase. Trying on a new coat and taking a car for a test drive are examples of how customers evaluate search qualities. Services, on the other hand, have very few search qualities; instead, they abound in experience and credence qualities. Experience qualities, such as taste, satisfaction or pleasure, are attributes that can be assessed only during the purchase and consumption of a service. Restaurants and holidays are examples of services high in experience qualities. Credence qualities are attributes that customers may be unable to evaluate even after the purchase and consumption of the service. Examples of services high in credence qualities are surgical operations, vehicle repairs, consulting, and legal representation. Most consumers lack the knowledge or skills to evaluate the quality of these types of service. Consequently they must place a great deal of faith in the integrity and competence of the service provider.

Despite the difficulties in evaluating quality, service quality may be the only way customers can choose one service over another. For this reason, service marketers live or die by understanding how consumers judge service quality. This is one reason behind many retail banks now returning staff to their branches and refocusing on their branches as a key part of their customer relationship building, as described in the Marketing Insight box on page 308. Table 10.5 defines five dimensions consumers use when evaluating service quality:

1 tangibles
2 reliability
3 responsiveness
4 assurance
5 empathy.

Note that all of these dimensions have links to employee performance. Of the five, reliability is the most important in determining customer evaluations of service quality.[21]

Services marketers pay a great deal of attention to the tangibles dimension of service quality. Tangible attributes, or search qualities, such as the appearance of facilities and employees, are often the only aspects of a service that can be viewed before purchases and consumption. Therefore, services marketers must ensure that these tangible elements are consistent with the overall image of the service product.

Except for the tangibles dimension, the criteria that customers use to judge service quality are intangible. For instance, how does a customer judge reliability? Since dimensions such as reliability cannot be examined with the senses, consumers must rely on other ways of judging service criteria. One of the most important factors in customer judgements of service quality is **service expectations**. These are influenced by past experiences with the service, word-of-mouth communication from other customers and the service company's own advertising. For example, customers are usually eager to try a new restaurant, especially when friends recommend it. These same customers may also have seen advertisements placed by the restaurant. As a result, these customers have an idea of what to expect when they visit the restaurant for the first time. When they finally dine at the restaurant, the quality they experience will change the expectations they have for their next visit and affect their own comments to friends. That is why providing consistently high service quality is important. If the quality of a restaurant, or any services marketer, begins to deteriorate, customers will alter their own expectations and word-of-mouth communication to others accordingly.

Service expectations
A factor used in judging service quality involving impressions from past experiences, word-of-mouth communication and the company's advertising

Delivering Exceptional Service Quality

Providing high-quality service on a consistent basis is very difficult. All consumers have experienced examples of poor service: long queues at retail checkouts, trains and buses that are late, or rude cinema employees. Obviously, it is impossible for a service organisation to ensure

⚙ Marketing Insight

Banks Remember Customer Service

A trend for close to 20 years has been for banks to close rural branches and reduce the number of town-centre branches. Many Victorian banks, with their large chambers, grand facades and prime locations, have been turned into bars or restaurants. TV viewers in the UK will have seen a well-known retail bank advertising the last of its branches being turned into wine bars: instead it was decided that branches were to be kept open. A separate advertisement revealed that customers would once again be able to talk directly to staff in their local branch, rather than only to anonymous personnel in a far-flung faceless call centre. So, why the about-turn in these policies?

For some time pundits had forecast the demise of the bank branch, as first telephone banking and then the Internet enabled customers to conduct their transactions and make enquiries via telecommunications. The era of the call centre permitted banks to make further cost savings by directing apparently local calls to regional call centres rather than into branches. This also reduced the number of personnel in branches and often removed mortgage, investment and insurance specialists altogether. In effect, for many customers, this had the impact of further reducing or downgrading the appeal of visiting branches. Mergers and acquisitions in the banking sector have also encouraged a reduction in branch numbers, as newly merged chains close and relocate branches in order to reduce duplication and operating costs. From 1999 to 2003, over 1,700 UK bank branches closed.

There is little doubt that telephone and e-banking have become increasingly popular. Despite their detractors, call centres have reduced operating costs. Mergers are continuing and banks' boards also routinely seek to reduce operating costs. Nevertheless, there recently has been talk of an end to the culling of bank branches. This is because marketing research reveals that not all customers wish to deal with call centres or to conduct their business via a PC or laptop. Many customers find face-to-face contact reassuring, and only the bank branch environment provides this direct interaction.

The role of the branch may be rejuvenated even further, however. Leading consultants Booz Allen Hamilton produced a report pointedly entitled Implementing the Customer-centric Bank – the Rebirth of the Forgotten Branch. The report concluded that 90 per cent of customer relationships are made – and lost – in branches. Even customers utilising e-banking often need to visit branches, and the vast majority of customers still believe that complex enquiries or topics perceived as risky by the consumer are better handled face to face, inside a bank branch. Unfortunately, the removal of specialist staff from many branches and the downgrading of the majority of branches to simple transaction-processing points, have led to a growing level of customer dissatisfaction with bank branches.

Now, in a strategy shift, the leading high-street banking brands are acknowledging that they must reinvest in their bank branches: more and better trained staff, improved IT enabling speedy processing of enquiries and creating more opportunities for the cross-selling of products, plus enhanced interior designs. As part of this shift in emphasis, different staff – with a greater customer orientation – are required. NatWest announced that it planned to invest in 1000 additional members of branch staff. Barclays, Abbey and the other leading brands quickly followed suit. As Alliance & Leicester head Richard Pym stated, 'We want staff who can relate to customers, understand their needs and get something into a computer accurately. That's someone with interpersonal skills, not banking skills.' In order to achieve this, Abbey instigated an additional 60,000 training days for its customer-facing personnel.

While efficiency and reducing operating costs are still important to the boards of these companies, there is an acceptance that customers expect improved service and that many prefer the bank branch as the setting for interactions with, it is hoped, more customer-oriented personnel.

Sources: NatWest 2003–7; Barclays, 2004–8; 'Back to the branch', *Marketing*, 26 May 2004, pp. 30–2; Fujitsu Services, 2003–8; Box Technologies, 2007.

exceptional service quality 100 per cent of the time. However, there are many steps that can be taken to increase the likelihood of providing high-quality service. First, though, the service company must understand the four **service quality factors**. As shown in Table 10.5, they are:

TABLE 10.5 DIMENSIONS OF SERVICE QUALITY

Dimension	Evaluation criteria	Examples
Tangibles Physical evidence of the service	Appearance of physical facilities Appearance of service personnel Tools or equipment used to provide the service	A clean and professional-looking doctor's office A clean and neatly dressed repair person The appearance of food in a restaurant The equipment used in a medical examination
Reliability Consistency and dependability in performing the service	Accuracy of billing or recordkeeping Performing services when promised	An accurate bank statement A confirmed hotel reservation An airline flight departing and arriving on time
Responsiveness Willingness or readiness of employees to provide the service	Returning customer phone calls Providing prompt service Handling urgent requests	A server refilling a customer's cup of tea without being asked An ambulance arriving within three minutes
Assurance Knowledge/competence of employees and ability to convey trust and confidence	Knowledge and skills of employees Company name and reputation Personal characteristics of employees	A highly trained financial adviser A known and respected service provider A doctor's bedside manner
Empathy Caring and individual attention provided by employees	Listening to customer needs Caring about customers' interests Providing personalised attention attention	A store employee listening to and trying to understand a customer's complaint A nurse counselling a heart patient

Sources: Adapted from Leonard L. Berry and A. Parasuraman, *Marketing Services: Competing through Quality* (New York: Free Press, 1991); Valarie A. Zeithaml, A. Parasuraman and Leonard L. Berry, *Delivering Quality Service: Balancing Customer Perceptions and Expectations* (New York: Free Press, 1990); A. Parasuraman, Leonard L. Berry and Valarie A. Zeithaml, 'An empirical examination of relationships in an extended service quality model', *Marketing Science Institute Working Paper Series*, report no. 90–112 (Cambridge, MA: Marketing Science Institute, 1990), p. 29.

Service quality factors
Factors that increase the likelihood of providing high-quality service: understanding customer expectations, service quality specifications, employee performance, managing service expectations

1 analysis of customer expectations
2 service quality specifications
3 employee performance
4 managing service expectations.[22]

Analysis of Customer Expectations Providers need to understand customer expectations when designing a service to meet or exceed those expectations. Only then can they deliver good service. Customers usually have two levels of expectations: desired and acceptable. The desired level of expectations is what the customer really wants. If this level of expectations is provided, the customer would be very satisfied. The acceptable level is viewed as a reasonable level of performance that the customer considers as being adequate. The difference between these two levels of expectations is called the **customer's zone of tolerance**.[23]

Service marketers sometimes use marketing research, such as surveys and focus groups, as a means of discovering customer needs and expectations. Other services

Customer's zone of tolerance
The difference between the customer's desired level of expectations and the customer's acceptable level of expectations

companies, such as hotel chains, seek customer feedback using comment cards. Another approach is to ask employees. Because customer-contact employees interact daily with customers, they often know what customers want from the company. Service managers should interact regularly with their employees to ensure that they remain in touch with this useful source of information.

Service Quality Specifications   Once an organisation understands its customers' needs, it must establish goals to help ensure good service delivery. These goals, or service specifications, are typically set in terms of employee or machine performance. For example, a bank may require its employees to conform to a dress code. The same bank may insist that all incoming phone calls are answered by the third ring. Specifications like these can be very important in providing quality service as long as they are linked to customer needs.

Service managers who are visibly committed to service quality become role models for all employees in the organisation.[24] Such commitment motivates personnel at all levels in the organisation, from customer-contact employees through to senior managers, to comply with service specifications.

Employee Performance   Once an organisation sets service quality standards and managers are committed to them, the organisation must find ways to ensure that customer contact employees perform their jobs well. Contact employees in many service industries – bank tellers, flight cabin crew, waiters, sales assistants – are often the least trained and lowest-paid members of the organisation. Yet these individuals represent the most important link to the customer, and thus their performance is critical to customer perceptions of service quality.[25] Well-managed recruitment and training are essential if employees are to understand properly how to do their jobs. Providing information about customers, service specifications and the organisation itself during the training promotes this understanding.[26]

The use of evaluation and remuneration systems plays a part in employee performance. Many service employees are evaluated and rewarded on the basis of output measures such as sales volume for car salespeople, or lack of errors during work for data-input clerks. Such systems may overlook certain key aspects of job performance: friendliness, teamwork, effort and customer satisfaction. As the importance of customer relationship building comes more to the fore, companies are increasingly considering that customer-oriented measures of performance may be a better basis for evaluation and reward. For example, Dun & Bradstreet has tied employee commissions to customer satisfaction surveys rather than sales volume.[27] This type of system stimulates employees to take care of customer needs rather than focus solely on sales or profits.

Managing Service Expectations   Because expectations are so significant in customer evaluations of service quality, service companies recognise that they must set realistic expectations about the service they can provide. These expectations can be set through advertising and good internal communication. In their advertisements, service companies make promises about the kind of service they will deliver. In fact, a service company is forced to make promises since the intangibility of services prevents it from showing them in the advertisement. However, the advertiser should not promise more than it can deliver; doing otherwise may mean disappointed customers.

To deliver on promises made, a company needs to have good internal communication among its departments – especially management, advertising and operations. Assume, for example, that a supermarket's advertising guarantees that shoppers will not have to queue at the checkout for more than 10 minutes. In order to meet this promise, the retailer will need to ensure that its operations and staff levels can support such a guarantee. Failure to do so may result in customers' service expectations not being met, with a consequent loss of credibility for the company.

Word-of-mouth communication from other customers also shapes customer expectations. However, service companies cannot manage this 'advertising' directly. The best way to ensure positive word-of-mouth communication is to provide exceptional service quality. It has been estimated that customers tell four times as many people about bad service as they do about good service. Consequently, services marketers must provide four good service experiences for every bad experience just to break even.

Non-profit Marketing

Marketing was broadly defined earlier as a set of individual and organisational activities aimed at facilitating and expediting satisfying exchanges in a dynamic environment through the creation, distribution, promotion and pricing of goods, services and ideas. Most of the concepts and approaches to managing marketing activities discussed above also apply to non-profit situations such as the public sector and charities. Of special relevance is the material offered in the first half of this chapter, because many non-profit organisations provide services. As a discipline, marketing is becoming increasingly important in the non-profit sector. The Case Study at the end of this chapter focuses on the changing role of marketing in charities.

Non-profit marketing
Activities conducted by individuals and organisations to achieve some goal other than the ordinary business goals of profit, market share or return on investment

Cause-related marketing
The linking of an organisation's products to a particular social cause on a short-term or ongoing basis

Negotiation
Mutual discussion or communication of terms and methods in an exchange situation

Persuasion
The act of prevailing upon someone by argument to facilitate an exchange

Non-profit marketing includes marketing activities conducted by individuals and organisations to achieve some goal other than the ordinary business goals of profit, market share or return on investment. However, although a non-profit organisation has primary goals that are non-economic, it may be required to become involved in 'profit making' in order to achieve those goals.[28] Thus a charity, such as the Red Cross, must raise funds to support its charitable work. Non-profit marketing can be divided into two categories: non-profit organisation marketing and social marketing. Non-profit organisation marketing is the application of marketing concepts and techniques to organisations such as hospitals and colleges. Social marketing is the development of programmes designed to influence the acceptability of social ideas, such as getting people to recycle more newspapers, plastics and aluminium, or promoting the regeneration of a deprived inner-city area.[29] **Cause-related marketing** is the linking of an organisation's products to a particular social cause, Body Shop-style, on an ongoing or short term basis.

As discussed in Chapter 1, an exchange situation exists when individuals, groups or organisations possess something that they are willing to give up in an exchange. In non-profit marketing, the objects of the exchange may not be specified in financial terms. Usually, such exchanges are facilitated through **negotiation** – mutual discussion or communication of terms and methods – and **persuasion** – convincing and prevailing upon by argument. Often, negotiation and persuasion are conducted without reference to, or awareness of, marketing's role in transactions. The discussion here concerns the non-profit performance of marketing activities, whether exchange takes place or not.

The rest of this chapter first examines the concept of non-profit marketing to determine how it differs from marketing activities in commercial organisations. Next it explores the overall objectives of non-profit organisations, their marketing objectives and the development of their marketing strategies. The discussion closes by illustrating how a marketing audit can control marketing activities and promote marketing awareness in a non-profit organisation.

Why is Non-profit Marketing Different?

Traditionally and mistakenly, people have not thought of non-profit exchange activities as marketing; but consider the following example. Warwick Business School used to promote its degree courses solely through the University of Warwick's prospectuses. In the early 1980s, its main programmes received small advertising budgets. As courses were improved, the wider use of advertising increased awareness of the school and its programmes. The school is not commercially driven in the context of seeking profits for stakeholders: any income from fees, training and consultancy is reinvested into its degree programmes and facilities. A new corporate identity was developed by Coley Porter Bell of

London, and each degree programme, led by the MBA, developed its own full marketing mix and more extensive promotional strategy – all in line with the school's new mission statement. Even when, in the 1990s, the corporate identity was updated, the school continued to ensure a good fit between the marketing mixes for its different programmes and its overall strategy. As the school moved into the twenty-first century, it became a budget holder within the university and managed its own budgets. This move facilitated the appointment of a marketing director, public relations manager and external affairs manager. These personnel developed target market strategies, updated the school's marketing programmes, and monitored the performance of these marketing activities, just as marketers in a for-profit company would do. Many university departments and state-maintained schools are now engaging in developing a marketing strategy and associated marketing programmes.

Many non-profit organisations strive for effective marketing activities. Charitable organisations and supporters of social causes are major non-profit marketers. Political parties, unions, religious groups and student organisations also perform marketing activities, yet they are not considered businesses. Whereas the chief beneficiary of a business enterprise is whoever owns or holds shares in it, the main beneficiaries of a non-profit organisation are its clients, its members or the public at large.

Non-profit organisations have a greater opportunity for creativity than most business organisations, but trustees or board members of these organisations may find it harder to evaluate the performance of doctors, lecturers or social workers than it is for sales managers to evaluate the performance of salespeople in a for-profit organisation.

Another way in which non-profit marketing differs from for-profit marketing is that non-profit organisations are sometimes quite controversial. Amnesty International, the RSPCA and Greenpeace spend lavishly on lobbying efforts to persuade government and even the courts to support their interests, in part because acceptance of their aims is not always guaranteed. Although marketing aims to provide a body of knowledge to further an organisation's goals, it does not attempt to judge their appropriateness. It is for individuals to decide whether they approve of an organisation's goal orientation. Most marketers would agree that profit and consumer satisfaction are appropriate goals for business enterprises, but there may be considerable disagreement about the goals of a controversial non-profit organisation.

Non-profit Marketing Objectives

The basic aim of non-profit organisations is to obtain a desired response from a target market. The response could be a change in values, a financial contribution, the donation of services or some other type of exchange. Non-profit marketing objectives are shaped by the nature of the exchange and the goals of the organisation. BBC-sponsored Children in Need and Comic Relief telethons have raised millions of pounds. Telethons have three specific marketing objectives:

1 to raise funds to support programmes
2 to plead a case on behalf of disadvantaged groups
3 to inform the public about the organisation's programmes and services.

Tactically, telethons have received support by choosing good causes; generating extensive grass-roots support; portraying disadvantaged people in a positive and dignified way; developing national, regional and local support; and providing quality entertainment.[30] Figure 10.4 illustrates how the exchanges and the purpose of the organisation can influence marketing objectives. These objectives are used as examples and may or may not apply to specific organisations.

Non-profit marketing objectives should state the rationale for an organisation's existence. An organisation that defines its marketing objective merely in terms of providing a product can be left without a purpose if the product becomes obsolete. However, serving

Figure 10.4
Examples of marketing objectives for different types of exchange
Source: Philip Kotler, Marketing for Non-profit Organisations, 2nd edn, © 1982, p. 38. Adapted by permission of Prentice-Hall, Inc., Englewood Cliffs, NJ

Police's marketing objective: To serve the public by enforcing laws and to gain public support and cooperation

Police → Protection and security → Citizen
Police ← Taxes, cooperation and support ← Citizen

Church's marketing objective: To inform the public about the church's doctrine and convince people to become members

Church → Religious values and services → Member
Church ← Contributions, service and acceptance of values ← Member

Charity's marketing objective: To serve the needs and wants of clients and the donor public

Charity → Satisfaction from solving social problems or promoting a cause → Donor
Charity ← Financial contributions, time and support ← Donor

and adapting to the perceived needs and wants of a target public or market, enhances an organisation's chances of surviving and achieving its goals.

Developing Non-profit Marketing Strategies

Non-profit organisations must also develop marketing strategies by defining and analysing a target market, and creating and maintaining a marketing mix that appeals to that market.

Target public
A collective of individuals who have an interest in or concern about an organisation, a product or a social cause

Client publics
In non-profit organisations, direct consumers of a product

General publics
In non-profit organisations, indirect consumers of a product

Target Markets   The concept of target markets needs to be revised slightly to apply to non-profit organisations. Whereas a business is supposed to have target groups that are potential purchasers of its product, a non-profit organisation may attempt to serve many diverse groups. A **target public** is broadly defined as a collective of individuals who have an interest in or concern about an organisation, a product or a social cause. The terms target market and target public are difficult to distinguish for many non-profit organisations. The target public for campaigns promoting healthy eating is adults and teenagers of all ages. However, the target market for many of the advertisements may be individuals currently suffering from a weight problem. When an organisation is concerned about changing values or obtaining a response from the public, it views the public as a market.[31]

In non-profit organisations, direct consumers of a product are called **client publics** and indirect consumers are called **general publics**.[32] For example, the client public for a university is its student body, and its general public includes parents, graduates, employers and the university senate. The client public usually receives most of the attention when an organisation develops a marketing strategy. The techniques and approaches to segmenting and defining target markets discussed in Chapter 6 also apply to non-profit target markets.

Developing a Marketing Mix   A marketing mix strategy limits choices and directs marketing activities towards achieving organisational goals. The strategy should outline or develop a blueprint for making decisions about product, place/distribution, promotion, price and personnel. These decision variables should be blended to serve the target market as specified in the marketing strategy.

When considering the product variable, it is important to recognise that non-profit organisations deal more often with ideas and services than with goods. This means it is crucial for organisations to have clearly defined exactly what they are providing. For example, what products do the Women's Institute or a work's social club provide? They offer a forum for social gatherings, courses, outings and a sense of cooperation. Their products are more difficult to define than the average business product. As indicated in the first part of this chapter, the intangibility of services means that the marketing of ideas and concepts is more abstract than the marketing of tangibles, and it requires considerable effort to present benefits.

Because most non-profit products are ideas and services, distribution decisions relate to how these ideas and services will be made available to clients. If the product is an idea, selecting the right media (the promotional strategy) to communicate the idea will facilitate distribution. The availability of services is closely related to product decisions. By nature, services consist of assistance, convenience and availability. Availability is part of the total service. For example, making a product such as health services available on the high street calls for knowledge of such retailing concepts as site location analysis and logistics management.

Developing a channel of distribution to coordinate and facilitate the flow of non-profit products to clients is a necessary task, but in a non-profit setting the traditional concept of the marketing channel may need to be reviewed. The independent wholesalers available to a business enterprise do not exist in most non-profit situations. Instead, a very short channel – non-profit organisation to client – is prevalent, because production and consumption of ideas and services are often simultaneous. For example, local government departments often deal directly with householders. Charities generally pitch their fundraising activities directly to their target customers/householders/donors.

Making promotional decisions may be the first sign that non-profit organisations are performing marketing activities. Non-profit organisations use advertising and publicity to communicate with clients and the public. As the Case Study at the end of this chapter explains, direct mail remains the primary means of fundraising for services such as those provided by Christian Aid and UNICEF. In addition to direct mail, organisations such as these use press advertising, public relations and sponsorship. Many non-profit organisations now have websites to promote their causes. Face-to-face selling is also used by non-profit organisations, although it may be called something else. Churches and charities rely on personal selling when they send volunteers to recruit new members or request donations. The armed forces use personal selling when recruiting officers and when attempting to persuade men and women to enlist. Special events to obtain funds, communicate ideas or provide services are sales promotion activities. Contests, entertainment and prizes offered to attract donations resemble the sales promotion activities of business enterprises. Amnesty International, for example, has held worldwide concert tours, featuring artists such as Sting and Phil Collins, to raise funds and increase public awareness of political prisoners around the world.

The number of advertising agencies that are donating their time for public service announcements (PSAs) or public information films is increasing, and the quality of print PSAs is improving. Not-for-profit groups are becoming more interested in the impact of advertising on their organisations, and they realise that second-rate PSAs can cause a credibility loss.[33] For example, each year the UK government's 'Don't drink and drive' campaign, usually timed to coincide with the Christmas and New Year period, is a high-spending, hard-hitting programme of advertisements designed to attract as much attention as possible.

Although product and promotion techniques may require only slight modification when applied to non-profit organisations, the pricing structure is generally quite different and the decision-making more complex. The different pricing concepts that the non-profit organisation faces include pricing in user and donor markets. There are two types of monetary pricing: fixed and variable. Membership fees, such as the amount paid to become a member of an amateur operatic society, represent a fixed approach to pricing, whereas fundraising activities that lead to donations that help with the society's running costs represent a variable pricing structure.[34]

The broadest definition of price (valuation) must be used when considering non-profit products or services. Financial price, an exact monetary value, may or may not be charged for a non-profit product. Economists recognise the giving up of alternatives as a cost. **Opportunity cost** is the value of the benefit that is given up by selecting one alternative rather than another. This traditional economic view of price means that if a non-profit organisation can persuade someone to donate time to a cause, or to change his or her behaviour, the alternatives given up are a cost to – or a price paid by – the individual. Volunteers who answer phones for a university counselling service or suicide hotline, for example, give up the time they could have spent studying or doing other things, as well as the income they might have earned from working in a business organisation.

For other non-profit organisations, financial price is an important part of the marketing mix. Non-profit organisations today are raising money by increasing the prices of their services or starting to charge for services if they have not done so before. For example, many museums and art galleries, which traditionally allowed free entry to their exhibits, are now charging nominal entrance fees. Organisations like these often use marketing research to determine for what kinds of product people will pay.[35] The pricing strategies of non-profit organisations often stress public and client welfare over equalisation of costs and revenues. If additional funds are needed to cover costs, then donations, contributions or grants may be solicited.

The additional elements of the marketing mix for services are also important in non-profit marketing. The physical environment quite often poses problems: subscribers and donors want an organisation with the appearance of businesslike efficiency without any extravagance. It is important that funds do not appear to have been wasted on luxuries. The process for transactions is increasingly important: regular donors are offered direct debits, automatic payment methods, and regular information packs or leaflets detailing the recipient organisation's activities, expenditures and plans. People, too, are important: capable administrators, sympathetic helpers, trustworthy fundraisers – they, too, must project a caring yet efficient image to the client and general publics.

Opportunity cost
The value of the benefit that is given up by selecting one alternative instead of another

Controlling Non-profit Marketing Activities

To control marketing activities in non-profit organisations, managers use information obtained in the marketing audit to make sure that goals are achieved. Table 10.6 lists several summary statistics that are useful for both planning and control. Control is designed to check that the activities outlined in the marketing strategy have taken place and to take corrective action where any deviations are found. The purpose of control is not only to point out errors but to revise organisational goals and marketing objectives as necessary. One way to measure the impact of an advertisement is to audit the number of requests for information or applications, such as those received by Amnesty International, the Army or the WWF. Hits on an organisation's website via leading search engines are also counted (see Figure 10.5).

Many potential contributors decide which charities to support based on the amount of money actually used for charitable purposes. Charities are more aggressively examining their own performance and effectiveness. For example, compared with other charities, the Salvation Army contributes the majority of every pound (£) it receives to the needy; its employees are largely volunteers, who work for almost nothing. Charities are making internal changes to increase their effectiveness, and many are hiring professional managers and fundraisers to help

---

TABLE 10.6 EXAMPLES OF DATA USEFUL IN CONTROLLING NON-BUSINESS MARKETING ACTIVITIES

1 Product mix offerings
  A Types of product or services
  B Number of organisations offering the product or service

2 Financial resources
  A Types of funding used
    1 Local government grants
    2 Government grants
    3 Foundations
    4 Public appeals
    5 Fees/charges
  B Number using each type of funding
  C Number using combinations of funding sources

3 Size
  A Budget (cash flows)
  B Number of employees

    1 By organisation
    2 Total industry wide
  C Number of volunteers
    1 By organisation
    2 Total industry wide
  D Number of customers/users serviced
    1 By type of service
    2 By organisation
    3 Total industry wide

4 Facilities
  A Number and type
    1 By organisation
    2 Total industry wide
  B Location
    1 By address
    2 By postcode

Source: Adapted from Philip D. Cooper and George E. McIlvain, 'Factors influencing marketing's ability to assist non-profit organizations', John H. Summey and Ronald D. Taylor, eds, *Evolving Marketing Thought* for 1980, *Proceedings of the Southern Marketing Association* (19–22 November 1980), p. 315. Used by permission.

---

with strategic planning in developing short-term and long-range goals, marketing strategies and promotional plans.

To control non-profit marketing activities, managers must make a proper inventory of activities performed, and be prepared to adjust or correct deviations from standards. Knowing where and how to look for deviations and knowing what types of deviation to expect are especially important in non-profit situations. Because non-profit marketing activities may not be perceived as marketing, managers must define clearly what activity is being examined and how it should function.

It may be difficult to control non-profit marketing activities, because it is often hard to determine whether goals are being achieved. A support group for victims of childhood abuse that wants to inform community members of its services may not be able to find out whether it is communicating with those people who need assistance. Surveying to discover the percentage of the population that is aware of the assistance the group offers can show whether the awareness objective has been achieved, but it fails to indicate what percentage of victims of abuse has been assisted. The detection and correction of deviations from standards are certainly major purposes of control, but standards must support the organisation's overall goals. Managers can refine goals by examining the results that are being achieved and analysing the ramifications of those results.

Techniques for controlling overall marketing performance must be compatible with the nature of an organisation's operations. Obviously, it is necessary to control the marketing budget in most non-profit organisations, but budgetary control is not tied to standards of profit and loss; responsible management of funds is the objective. Central control responsibility can facilitate orderly, efficient administration and planning. For example, most universities evaluate graduating students' progress to control and improve the quality of education provided. The audit phase typically relies on questionnaires sent to students and eventual employers. The employer completes a questionnaire to indicate the former student's progress; the graduate completes a questionnaire to indicate what additional

Figure 10.5
Many non-business organisations judge the effectiveness of their marketing in terms of hits on their websites and requests for information
Source: Courtesy of Google

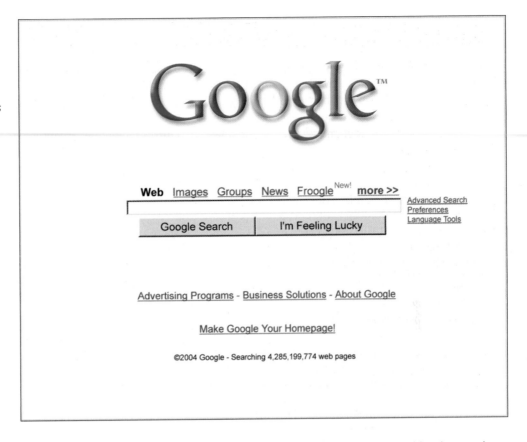

concepts or skills were needed to perform duties. In addition, a number of faculty members may interview certain employers and former students to obtain information for control purposes. Results of the audit are used to develop corrective action if university standards have not been met. Corrective action could include an evaluation of the deficiency and a revision of the curriculum. More information about marketing controls and the marketing audit may be found in the authors' *Marketing: Concepts and Strategies* (Boston: Houghton Mifflin, 2006).

Summary

Services are intangible, dominant products that cannot physically be possessed, the result of applying human or mechanical efforts to people or objects. The importance of services in the economy is increasing. There are *consumer services* and *business services*.

❯❯ Services have a number of distinguishing characteristics: *intangibility*, *inseparability* of production and consumption, *perishability*,

heterogeneity, *client-based relationships* and *customer contact*. Intangibility places greater importance on *search*, *experience* and *credence qualities*. Services can be viewed in terms of a *five-category classification*: type of market, degree of labour intensiveness, degree of customer contact, skill of the service provider and goal of the service provider.

❯❯ Fluctuating demand is a major problem for most service organisations. Marketing strategies and the marketing mix as well as non-marketing strategies and primarily internal, employee-based actions can be used to deal with the problem. Before attempting to undertake any such strategies, however, services marketers must understand the patterns and determinants of demand. The intangibility of the service product, together with the importance of the people component of the extended marketing mix for services, leads to significant difficulties in creating and sustaining a *differential advantage*.

» The basic marketing mix is augmented for services through the addition of people, physical evidence (ambience) and the process of transaction in order to produce the '7Ps' or the *extended marketing mix for services*.

» *Service quality* is the perception of how well a service meets or exceeds customers' *service expectations*. The intangibility of services makes service quality very difficult for customers to evaluate. When competing services are very similar, service quality may be the only way for customers to distinguish between them. It is crucial for marketers to comprehend the four *service quality factors*: (1) understanding customer expectations, (2) service quality specifications, (3) employee performance, and (4) managing service expectations. To achieve customer satisfaction, a service must fall within the *customer's zone of tolerance*.

» *Non-profit marketing* includes marketing activities conducted by individuals and organisations to achieve goals other than normal business goals. The chief beneficiary of a business enterprise is whoever owns or holds shares in the business, but the beneficiary of a non-profit enterprise should be its clients, its members or its public at large. The goals of a non-profit organisation reflect its unique philosophy or mission. Some non-profit organisations have very controversial goals, but many organisations exist to further generally accepted social causes.

» The marketing objective of non-profit organisations is to obtain a desired response from a target market, often through *negotiation* or *persuasion*. Developing a non-profit marketing strategy consists of defining and analysing a target market, and creating and maintaining a marketing mix. *Target*, *client* and *general publics* must all be identified. In non-profit marketing, the product is usually an idea or service. Distribution is involved not so much with the movement of goods as with the communication of ideas and the delivery of services, which results in a very short marketing channel. Promotion is very important in non-profit marketing; personal selling, sales promotion, advertising and publicity are all used to communicate ideas and inform people about services. Price is more difficult to define in non-profit marketing because of *opportunity costs* and the difficulty of quantifying the values exchanged.

» It is important to control marketing strategies in non-profit situations. Control is designed to identify what activities have occurred in conformity with marketing strategy and to take corrective action where deviations are found. The standards against which performance is measured must support the non-profit organisation's overall goals.

⊙ *Key Links*

This chapter about marketing services should be read in conjunction with:
- Chapter 8, the overview of the product ingredient of the marketing mix.
- Chapter 6, which examines the creation of target market strategy.

Important Terms

Service
Consumer services
Business services
Intangibility
Search qualities
Experience qualities
Credence qualities
Inseparability

Perishability
Heterogeneity
Client-based relationships
Customer contact
Five-category classification
Differential advantage
Extended marketing mix for services
Service quality
Service expectations
Service quality factors
Customer's zone of tolerance
Non-profit marketing
Cause-related marketing
Negotiation
Persuasion
Target public
Client publics
General publics
Opportunity cost

Discussion and Review Questions

1 Identify and discuss the distinguishing characteristics of services. What problems do these characteristics present to marketers?

2 What is the significance of 'tangibles' in service industries?

3 Use the five-category classification scheme to analyse a car valeting service, and discuss the implications for marketing mix development.

4 How do search, experience and credence qualities affect the way consumers view and evaluate services?

5 What additional elements must be included in the marketing mix for services? Why?

6 Why is it difficult to create and maintain a differential advantage in many service organisations?

7 Analyse the demand for the hire of sunbeds and discuss ways to cope with fluctuating demand.

8 What is the most important dimension in determining customer evaluation of service quality?

9 Compare and contrast the controversial aspects of non-profit versus business marketing.

10 Relate the concepts of product, place/distribution, promotion and price to a marketing strategy aimed at preventing drug abuse.

11 What are the differences between clients, publics and consumers? What is the difference between a target public and a target market?

12 Discuss the development of a marketing strategy for a university. What marketing decisions should be made in developing this strategy?

Recommended Reading

- Berry, L., *On Great Service* (New York: Free Press, 1995).
- Edvardsson, B., Thomasson, B. and Ovretveit, J., *Quality of Service, Making It Really Work* (London: McGraw-Hill, 1994).
- Gilmore, A., *Services Marketing and Management* (London: Sage, 2003).
- Grönroos, C., *Service Management and Marketing* (Chichester: Wiley, 2007).
- Kasper, H., van Helsdingen, P. and de Vries Jr, W., *Services Marketing Management: An International Perspective* (Chichester: Wiley, 1999).
- Lovelock, C.H. and Wirtz, J., *Services Marketing* (Englewood Cliffs, NJ: Prentice-Hall, 2004).
- Palmer, A., *Principles of Services Marketing* (Maidenhead: McGraw-Hill, 2007).

🗨 Internet Exercise

As Internet usage rises, the number of people using this method to communicate with friends, family and colleagues is also increasing. The founders of the Friends Reunited website spotted an opportunity to provide a service that helped people to get back in touch with friends and acquaintances. Take a look at this online organisation at:
www.friendsreunited.com

1 Classify Friends Reunited's product in terms of its position on the service continuum.

2 How does Friends Reunited enhance customer service and foster its relationship with customers through its Internet marketing efforts?

3 Discuss the degree to which experience and credence qualities exist in the services offered by Friends Reunited.

Applied Mini-Case

Express carriers such as TNT, UPS and Federal Express do much more than provide a swift delivery service for letters and packages. As the sector has become more competitive, the expectations of clients have also risen. Inventory handling, assistance with customs clearance, barcoded tracking that can be monitored over the Internet, and the provision of a responsive customer services function, are just some of the extra services that are now expected as part of the product offering. Some clients even require their carriers to play a role in the packing process in their pursuit of a delivery solution that eases the movement of packages from the point of dispatch to the point of receipt.

Sources: 'Value-added takes on a new meaning', *Purchasing, no.* 120, 15 February 1996, pp. 68 – 9; Sally Dibb and Lyndon Simkin, *Marketing Briefs*, 2004, Oxford: Butterworth Heinemann.

Question

Assume the role of a management consultant who has been retained by one of the express carriers to undertake an analysis of service quality. Prepare a report that outlines the key dimensions of service quality.

Case Study

Increasing Professionalism in Charity Marketing

Marketing is not an activity that consumers automatically associate with charities. Instead they link advertising and sales promotion with big brands such as Coca-Cola, McDonald's and Virgin. In reality, while commercial organisations such as these seek high returns and profits, charities must find ways to increase their revenues to fund their good causes. In recent years, the fundraising activities of charities have become characterised by an increasing professionalism, often involving the appointment of marketing managers, strategists and public relations executives. This has resulted in a greater variety of fundraising methods than ever before, including the use of viral campaigns, creative affinity tie-ups, e-marketing and Internet-based approaches. For example, the Multiple Sclerosis Trust and the Multiple Sclerosis Society backed a joint fundraising initiative with shoe retailers. Known as MyShoes, the innovative scheme involved a partnership with footwear retailers, who donated a fixed amount to the MS charities for every pair of shoes they sold. MyShoes provided participating retailers with point-of-sales material that educated shoppers about MS (there are 85,000 MS sufferers in the UK). Such innovative fundraising is critical in a climate in which all forms of charity participation are thriving but the public's preferences for methods of collecting are changing.

Recent research shows that nearly 90 per cent of UK adults have participated in charitable activities in the past 12 months. Most are involved in giving money, but a third of these have taken part in a special charity activity or event. Others have been involved in organising events or have worked for a charity. Face-to-face fundraising remains the most popular way to give, with 67 per cent of all those donating using this approach. There has, however, been a trend away from traditional tin-rattling and towards the use of 'chugging' or face-to-face recruitment, designed to encourage would-be donors to agree to regular direct debit or covenant arrangements. More than ever, charities are recognising that fundraising activities should be targeted particularly at those in the population who are prepared to become committed donors. In some cases this means attracting a new generation of people prepared to donate regularly. A recent NOP survey suggested that just 15 per cent of fundraising revenue is accrued from long-term donors, with human rights charities the biggest winners, and good causes supporting the young or elderly gaining least from this means.

Even though many consumers dislike the use of direct marketing methods such as direct mail and telephone calls to solicit funds, the second most important channel for donations is by post. This approach has proved particularly popular with human rights and wildlife causes. However, relatively few supporters of children's charities and those supporting the elderly choose this method. Indeed, it seems that traditional personal approaches to collecting funds, such as the use of collecting tins in shopping malls and high streets, are declining in effectiveness. Instead, the public's imagination has been captured by a host of media-based activities. For example, specially organised events, and television appeals and programmes have been shown to be particularly effective ways of attracting funds. The use of high-profile individuals in such appeals, such as royalty, television personalities, and well-known actors or sports stars, is particularly popular. In a recent survey, 80 per cent of consumers questioned also supported the use of commercial and promotional schemes, such as the sale of products through gift shops and catalogues. A similar percentage stated that they like to buy products that involve the manufacturer making a contribution to charity.

Evidence of increasing professionalism in fundraising is readily apparent across the charity sector. Cancer Research has recently overhauled its marketing strategy to focus afresh on fundraising. This follows a period when the charity concentrated on brand building, following its creation out of the merger of Imperial Cancer Research and the Cancer Research Campaign. With plans for a £10m (€15m) spend on advertising and direct marketing, the organisation has engaged two advertising agencies to develop activities in these areas. This comes after the charity's recent highly successful 'All Clear' television advertising campaign.

The promise of the Internet as a medium for generating donations has frequently been suggested, but is yet to develop fully. Relatively few charities have evolved effective means of raising funds online. So far, human rights charities have been among the more successful but, even for this group, online donations represent only 2.9 per cent of the total. However, fundraising using the Internet could soon increase, with a range of innovative campaigns being created. For example, the World Society for the Protection of Animals (WSPA) has developed a joint initiative with Orange, to offer consumers a range of animal ringtones for their mobile phones. Consumers can purchase the ringtones, including everything from an African elephant to a coyote or a Siberian tiger, from the Orange website, and 10 per cent of the royalties for downloading the tones will be donated to the charity. Meanwhile, children's charity Barnardo's has signalled its intention to increase its emphasis on the Internet as a means of recruiting and communicating with its younger donors. In the age of television, the Internet and the mobile phone, it seems that charities such as these must be ready, willing and able to use the full range of media-based approaches available.

Sources: Emily Rogers, 'MS charity initiative to roll out brand identity', *Marketing*, 1 April 2004, p. 10; Ben Bold, 'Cancer Research £10m work goes to Ogilvy Group', *Marketing*, 8 April 2004, p. 3; Caroline Parry, 'Factfile: it's a matter of give and take', *Marketing Week*, 19 February 2004, pp. 36–7; Mark Sweney, 'Barnardo's focuses fundraising on web', *Marketing*, 1 April 2004, p. 8; 'Charities unite in donor appeal', *Marketing*, 14 January 1999, p. 4; 'Spotlight: charity', *Marketing Week*, 17 December 1998, pp. 28–9; Tony Lees, NOP Research Group; www.wspa.org.uk.

❓ *Questions for Discussion*

1 Why are charities such as Barnardo's and Cancer Research UK turning more to the marketing tactics deployed by consumer goods companies?

2 To what kinds of donor must charities appeal? How might collection methods vary for these different groups?

3 How might the marketing strategy vary according to whether a charity is targeting consumers or corporate donors?

11
Marketing Channels

"**Effective management of manufacturer–dealer relationships is formidably problematic but strategically imperative.**"

David Shipley, Trinity College, University of Dublin

Objectives

- To understand the marketing channel concept and the nature of marketing channels

- To discuss the functions of marketing channels

- To examine different types of channel

- To examine channel integration and levels of market coverage

- To consider the selection of distribution channels and the emergence of direct marketing

- To explore the behavioural aspects of channels, especially the concepts of cooperation, relationship building, conflict and leadership

- To examine legal issues in channel management

Introduction

Distribution involves activities that make products available to customers when and where they want to purchase them. It is sometimes referred to as the 'place' element in the marketing mix of the 5Ps: product, place/distribution, promotion, price and people. Choosing which channels of distribution to use is a major decision in the development of marketing strategies. High customer service levels may require heavy investment in distribution and the shrewd identification of channel members with which to work. There has to be a compromise between adequate responsiveness to customers' needs and expectations in a cost-effective manner for the company.

This chapter focuses on the description and analysis of marketing channels, first discussing the nature of channels and their functions, and then explaining the main types of channel and their structures. These sections are followed by a review of several forms of channel integration. Consideration is given to how marketers determine the appropriate intensity of market coverage for a product and to the factors that are considered when selecting suitable channels of distribution. After examining behavioural patterns within marketing channels, and the relationships that develop between channel members, the chapter concludes by looking at several legal issues affecting channel management.

Opener

BA's Focus on E-booking

Not too many years ago, the bulk of BA flights were booked either via travel agents or over the telephone by passengers. BA introduced e-tickets, rather than sending out traditional books of travel coupon tickets, and passengers could print off their own documentation. Soon, even such behaviour was passé, as a simple booking reference sufficed and paperless travel had arrived. Passengers either insert their credit card into a ticket dispenser at the airport or tell a customer service agent their allocated booking reference code in order for the agent to allocate a seat and boarding pass. No paper is necessary.

In late 2003, BA made a radical decision. Its 24-hour telephone booking service ceased: night-time tele-booking or changes to travel itineraries became a thing of the past, too. Although partly driven by a cost-saving strategy, the reduction in call centres also reflected the growth in the airline's e-booking service. 'If you choose to complete your booking by phone, you will incur a £15 off-line service fee per passenger', greeted customers dialling 0870 8507850 intending to book seats by phone, as BA steered customers towards its web-based operation. While passengers wishing to book at night could no longer speak over the telephone to a BA customer service agent, they could go online 24 hours a day in order to make or change a booking.

The BA website reflects this shift in emphasis, suggesting special offers, linking to customer support and providing web users with corporate information, while also providing links to:

- *Flights and More*
- *Manage My Booking*
- *Information*
- *Executive Club*

The primary focus on the home page, though, is on a *Get Flights* menu-driven system providing speedy access to BA's network and timetable. *Get Flights* enables users to check for routes, suitable times, prices and seat availability in seconds, or to place a confirmed booking in under a minute.

The company launched a set of related mobile services in 2004, with timetables for PCs, pocket PCs, palmtops or as pdf downloads, and a booking/ timetable service on 'Vodafone Live!'. Regular users find the e-channel to market both faster and more convenient than call centres or accessing BA via a travel agent. BA still uses advertising, brochures and direct mail, plus travel agencies and telephone call centres to interface with its customers, but the airline has fully embraced e-commerce as a channel to market. At its new Heathrow hub, the mammoth terminal 5, e-booking and check-in are now the norm and generations of customers are being re-educated to appreciate the benefits of e-ticketing.

Sources: www.BA.com, May 2004; BA, BAA, January, 2008; www.ba.com, January, 2008.

s in the example of BA's move to focus on e-commerce, changes in the manner in which products are distributed have a major impact on customers. For example, moves by food retailers to sell petrol from sites adjacent to their supermarkets have affected the UK petrol market in a number of important ways. Reducing petrol prices and increasing promotional activity are damaging margins to a point where profitability is severely threatened. In the long term this may force small suppliers out of business, thus reducing consumer choice. Internet retailing is a new channel that, for some products and services, increasingly cuts out the need for wholesalers and retail stores. It is forecast that, soon, the bulk of music sales and banking transactions will be via e-commerce. Such direct marketing negates the need for high-street shops and bank branches, and changes the nature of the proposition being marketed. This chapter focuses on the nature of marketing channels and their functions, types of channel and their structures. The factors relevant in selecting a channel of distribution are discussed, along with the nature of relationships within the marketing channel.

The Nature of Marketing Channels and Supply Chain Management

Channel of distribution (or marketing channel)
A group of individuals and organisations that direct the flow of products from producers to customers

A **channel of distribution** (sometimes called a **marketing channel**) is a group of individuals and organisations that direct the flow of products from producers to customers. Providing customer satisfaction should be the driving force behind all marketing channel activities. Buyers' needs and behaviour are, therefore, important concerns of channel members. Channels of distribution make products available at the right time, in the right place and in the right quantity by providing such product-enhancing functions as transport and storage.[1]

The basic premise is simple. A manufacturer of a particular product could sell directly to the intended ultimate consumers, or the manufacturer could utilise the services of wholesalers, retailers or other channel members, rather than bear the hassle and costs of dealing with many end-user consumers directly. Alternatively, the manufacturer could opt to use a mix of routes to convey its products to the ultimate consumers: some direct selling, links with wholesalers and retailers, and possibly alliances with the selling activities of other manufacturers. There has, though, to be a balance between optimising customer satisfaction and making an adequate return on investment. These are the challenges of channel management for marketers.

Marketing intermediary
A middleman who links producers to other middlemen or to those who ultimately use the products

Most, but not all, channels of distribution have marketing intermediaries, although there is currently a growth in direct marketing, with some suppliers interacting with consumers without the use of intermediaries. A **marketing intermediary**, or middleman, links producers to other middlemen or to those who ultimately use the products. Marketing intermediaries perform the activities described in Table 11.1. There are two major types of intermediary: merchants and functional middlemen – agents and brokers. **Merchants** take title to products and resell them, whereas **functional middlemen** do not take title to products. Both types facilitate the movement of goods and services from producers to consumers.

Merchants
Intermediaries who take title to products and resell them

Both retailers and wholesalers are intermediaries. Retailers purchase products for the purpose of reselling them to users. Merchant wholesalers resell products to other wholesalers and to retailers. Functional wholesalers, such as agents and brokers, expedite exchanges among producers and resellers, and are compensated by fees or commissions. For purposes of discussion in this chapter, all wholesalers are considered merchant middlemen unless otherwise specified.

Functional middlemen
Intermediaries who do not take title to products

Channel members share certain significant characteristics. Each member has different responsibilities within the overall structure of the distribution system, but mutual profit and success can be attained only if channel members cooperate in delivering products to the market. The area of relationship management has recently received a great deal of

TABLE 11.1 MARKETING CHANNEL ACTIVITIES PERFORMED BY INTERMEDIARIES	
Category of Marketing Activities	**Possible Activities Required**
Marketing information	Analyse information such as sales data; perform or commission marketing research studies
Marketing management	Establish objectives; plan activities; manage and co-ordinate financing, personnel and risk taking; evaluate and control channel activities
Facilitating exchange	Choose and stock product assortments that match the needs of buyers
Promotion	Set promotional objectives; co-ordinate advertising, personal selling, sales promotion, publicity, sponsorship, direct mail and packaging
Price	Establish pricing policies and terms of sales
Physical distribution	Manage transport, warehousing, materials handling, inventory control and communication
Customer service	Provide channels for advice, technical support, after sales back-up and warranty provision
Relationships	Facilitate communication, products and parts, financial support and credit, inventory levels, after market needs, on-time delivery and customer service to maintain relationships with other marketing intermediaries and between suppliers and their targeted customers

attention in marketing circles. This is increasingly important in delivering adequate customer service to target market customers. A supplier desires an ongoing and lucrative relationship with its customers: it recognises the importance of the various channel members in maintaining this relationship and strives for mutually beneficial relationships with its channel intermediaries.

Although distribution decisions need not precede other marketing decisions, they do exercise a powerful influence on the rest of the marketing mix. Channel decisions are critical because they determine a product's market presence and buyers' accessibility to the product. They also affect customers' overall satisfaction with the product or service provider.[2] At a time when organisations increasingly offer their products through multiple channels, the challenge of maintaining quality of delivery irrespective of the channel used, is very much to the fore. The strategic significance of channel decisions is further heightened by the fact that they often entail long-term commitments. For example, it is much easier for a company to change prices or packaging than to change existing distribution systems.

It may be necessary for companies to use different distribution paths in different countries, for different target market segments or for the various products in its portfolio. The links in any channel, however, are the merchants – including producers – and agents who oversee the movement of products through that channel. Marketing channels are commonly classified into channels for consumer products/services or channels for industrial, business-to-business products/services.

Increasingly, an important function of the marketing channel is the joint effort of all channel members to create a supply chain: a total distribution system that serves customers and creates a competitive advantage. **Supply chain management** refers to long-term partnerships among marketing channel members that reduce inefficiencies, costs and redundancies in the marketing channel and develop innovative approaches to satisfying targeted customers. The goal is still to provide customers with the product or service demanded, in line

Supply chain management
Long-term partnerships among marketing channel members that reduce inefficiencies, costs and redundancies in the marketing channel and develop innovative approaches to satisfying targeted customers

with their expectations, but in a more coordinated way that builds on the combined strengths of the members of the distribution channel. Key tasks in supply chain management include: planning and coordination of marketing channel partnerships; sourcing necessary resources, goods and services to support the supply chain; facilitating delivery; and relationship building in order to nurture ongoing customer relationships.

Functions of Marketing Channels

Marketing channels serve many functions. Although some of these functions may be performed by a single channel member, most are accomplished through both the independent and joint efforts of channel members. These functions include creating utility, facilitating exchange efficiencies, alleviating discrepancies, standardising transactions and providing customer service.

Creating Utility

Marketing channels create four types of utility: time, place, possession and form.

1 Time utility is having products available when the customer wants them.
2 Place utility is created by making products available in locations where customers wish to purchase them.
3 Possession utility is created by giving the customer access to the product to use or to store for future use. Possession utility can occur through ownership or through arrangements such as lease or rental agreements that give the customer the right to use the product.
4 Channel members sometimes create form utility by assembling, preparing or otherwise refining the product to suit individual customer needs.

Facilitating Exchange Efficiencies

Marketing intermediaries can reduce the costs of exchanges by performing certain services or functions efficiently. Even if producers and buyers are located in the same city, there are costs associated with exchanges. As Figure 11.1 shows, when four buyers seek products from four producers, sixteen transactions are possible. If one intermediary serves both producers and buyers, the number of transactions can be reduced to eight. Intermediaries are specialists in facilitating exchanges. They provide valuable assistance because of their access to, and control over, important resources used in the proper functioning of marketing channels.

Nevertheless, the press, consumers, public officials and other marketers freely criticise intermediaries, especially wholesalers – retail wholesalers, dealers, distributors. In a US survey of the general public, 74 per cent believed that 'wholesalers frequently make high profits, which significantly increase prices that consumers pay'.[3] Critics accuse wholesalers of being inefficient and parasitic. Consumers often wish to make the distribution channel as short as possible, assuming that the fewer the intermediaries, the lower the price. For example, Virgin's financial services operation aims to offer competitive prices by cutting out brokers. Because suggestions to eliminate them come from both ends of the marketing channel, wholesalers must be careful to perform only those marketing activities that are truly desired. To survive, they must be more efficient and more customer focused than alternative marketing institutions.

Critics who suggest that eliminating wholesalers would lower consumer prices do not recognise that doing so would not remove the need for services that wholesalers provide. Although wholesalers can be eliminated, in many markets the functions they perform cannot. Other channel members would have to perform those functions, and customers would still have to fund them. In addition, all producers would have to deal directly with retailers or consumers, so that every producer would have to keep voluminous records and hire enough personnel to deal with a multitude of customers. Customers might end up paying a great deal more for products because prices would reflect the costs of less efficient channel members.

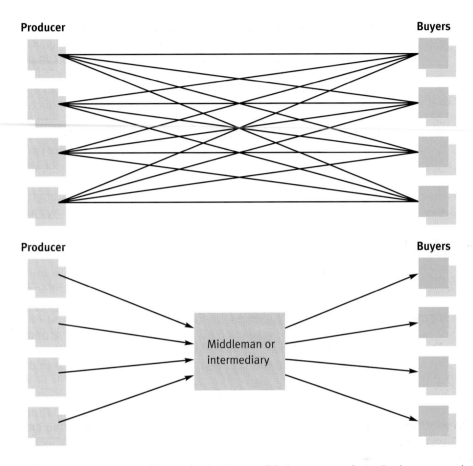

Figure 11.1
Efficiency in exchanges provided by an intermediary

Direct customer–supplier marketing is possible in some markets. For instance, telesales-led Direct Line has a successful direct relationship with its insurance- and mortgage-buying customers. JCB, on the other hand, would find it difficult to sell directly and depends on its dealers for parts and maintenance provision to its construction equipment customers. Heinz, Kellogg's, Sony, Ford and BA all utilise channel members – retailers, dealers or travel agents – in order to sell their products and services. These companies may well use direct mail and the web to contact their existing or potential customers, but channel members play an important role in some of their marketing programmes.

To illustrate wholesalers' efficient services, assume that all wholesalers have been eliminated. Because there are more than 1.5 million retailers, a widely purchased consumer product – say, toilet paper – would require an extraordinary number of sales contacts, possibly more than a million, to maintain the current level of product exposure. For example, Scott would have to deliver its paper products, establish warehouses all over Europe and maintain fleets of trucks. Selling and distribution costs for Scott's products would rocket. Instead of a few contacts with food brokers, large retail businesses and merchant wholesalers, such manufacturers would face thousands of expensive contacts with, and shipments to, smaller retailers. Such an operation would be highly inefficient, and costs would be passed on to consumers. Wholesalers are often more efficient and less expensive.

Alleviating Discrepancies

The functions performed within marketing channels help to overcome two major distribution problems: discrepancies in quantity and discrepancies in assortment. With respect to discrepancies in quantity, consider a company that manufactures jeans. The company specialises in the goods it can produce most efficiently: denim clothing. To make jeans most economically, the producer turns out 100,000 pairs of jeans each day. Few people, however, want to buy 100,000 pairs of jeans – they just want a few pairs. Retail customers may want a few hundred pairs. Thus the quantity of jeans the company can produce efficiently is more than the average customer wants. This is called 'discrepancy in quantity'.

An **assortment** is a combination of products put together to provide customer benefits. Consumers create and hold an assortment. The set of products made available to customers is a company's assortment. Most consumers want a broad assortment of products. Besides jeans, they want to buy shoes, food, cars, hi-fi systems, soft drinks and many other products. Yet the jeans manufacturer has a narrow assortment because it only makes jeans and a few other denim clothes. A discrepancy in assortment exists because consumers want a broad assortment, but an individual manufacturer produces a narrow assortment.

Quantity and assortment discrepancies are resolved through the sorting activities of channel members. **Sorting activities** are functions that allow channel members to divide roles and to separate tasks; they include sorting out, accumulation, allocation and assorting of products (see Figure 11.2).[4]

Assortment
A combination of products put together to provide customer benefits

Sorting activities
Functions that let channel members divide roles and separate tasks

Sorting Out   **Sorting out**, the first step in developing an assortment, is separating conglomerates of heterogeneous products into relatively uniform, homogeneous groups based on product characteristics such as size, shape, weight or colour. Sorting out is especially common in the marketing of agricultural products and other raw materials, which vary widely in size, grade and quality, and would be largely unusable in an undifferentiated mass. A grape crop, for example, must be sorted into grapes suitable for making wine, those best for turning into grape juice and those to be sold by food retailers.

Sorting out
Separating products into uniform, homogeneous groups

Accumulation   **Accumulation** is the development of a bank, or inventory, of homogeneous products with similar production or demand requirements. Farmers who grow relatively small quantities of grapes, for example, transport their sorted grapes to central collection points, where they are accumulated in large lots for movement into the next level of the channel. Accumulation lets producers continually use up stocks and replenish them, thus minimising losses from interruptions in the supply of materials.

Accumulation
The development of a bank of homogeneous products with similar production or demand requirements

Allocation   **Allocation** is the breaking down of large homogeneous inventories into smaller lots. This process, which addresses discrepancies in quantity, enables wholesalers to buy efficiently in lorry loads or railway car loads, and apportion products by cases to other members. A food wholesaler, for instance, serves as a depot, allocating products according to market demand. The wholesaler may divide a single lorry load of Del Monte canned tomatoes among several retail food stores.

Allocation
The breaking down of large homogeneous inventories into smaller lots

Assorting   **Assorting** is the process of combining products into collections or assortments that buyers want to have available in one place. Assorting eliminates discrepancies in assortment by grouping products in ways that satisfy buyers. Assorting is especially

Assorting
The grouping of products that buyers want to have available in one place

Figure 11.2
Sorting activities conducted by channel members

Sorting out	Accumulation	Allocation	Assorting
Classifying heterogeneous products into homogeneous groups	Developing a bank or stock of homogeneous products to provide aggregate inventory	Breaking down homogeneous stocks (inventories) into smaller units	Combining products into collections or assortments that buyers want

⊘ Marketing Insight

Tesco's Multi-channel Approach to Market Leadership

The Internet is changing the way in which consumers shop. In the past, those seeking to replenish their kitchen cupboards, fridges and freezers would usually visit their local supermarket or hypermarket. Now, these same consumers can visit the Internet and order their groceries for direct delivery to their homes. The concept is seen to be particularly attractive to professional, high-earning, ABC1 men and women who work long hours and have limited leisure time. Tesco.com is one service that allows customers to buy their groceries direct over the Internet. Consumers can access the Tesco website at Tesco.com and select their purchase items. Their orders are then compiled by a team of in-store sales assistants for delivery to consumers' homes at a time of their choosing.

Initially, the Tesco.com concept was trialled in 11 stores in two major UK cities. The company's preliminary research showed that around 200,000 consumers were using the service offered by these 11 stores and that this was increasing by 10,000 every week. Before long, the obvious popularity of Internet shopping prompted Tesco to roll out Tesco.com to other parts of the UK. By the end of the first year, the company offered the service from 100 Tesco stores. Careful consideration has been given to the marketing of the Internet shopping service. The sight of the Tesco.com logo displayed by the company's delivery vans has become familiar to those living in the areas where the service is offered. In addition, the retailer is using a combination of local poster and in-store advertising, direct mail and an Internet campaign to promote the Tesco.com operation.

It seems as if the home shopping concept is enjoying a new wave of popularity among consumers. Major competitors ASDA and Sainsbury's have also launched Internet shopping facilities, while Somerfield is engaged in a national roll-out of its home shopping operation. Frozen food retailer Iceland already enjoyed considerable success with its service. Increasing familiarity with shopping on the Internet looks set to increase the demand for services like Tesco.com. How substantial a part of Tesco's business the service will become remains to be seen. However, Tesco management clearly understands that retaining its market-leading position means being ready to respond to changing shopping needs. Even so, industry experts are warning that the new shopping trend could be harmful for supermarket giants, providing considerable opportunities for their smaller rivals. For such smaller businesses, the Internet could offer important additional sales. For example, Waitrose is offering e-sales in territories not serviced by its limited network of supermarkets through a joint venture with Ocado. By contrast, for the likes of Tesco and Sainsbury's, the danger is that existing sales will be cannibalised. Furthermore, a substantial shift in grocery shopping from the supermarkets to the Internet could damage scale advantages and affect profitability. For Tesco, online retailing is supporting its portfolio of stores. In 2004 Tesco.com became the first fully profitable grocery online operation in the world (with profits of £12 million), making Tesco the largest e-retailer of groceries worldwide. In the UK, Tesco.com now warrants over 4.5 million visitors each year with a reach of 14.5 per cent. Only eBay and Amazon get more visitors.

Sources: 'Tesco to roll out Internet shopping service', *Marketing Week*, 15 April 1999, p. 6; Alexandra Jardine, 'Tesco Direct rolls out to 100 outlets', *Marketing*, 15 April 1999, p. 1; Alan Mitchell, 'Home shopping boom a threat to market leaders', *Marketing Week*, 1 April 1999, pp. 26–7; Gordon Ellis-Brown, 'Inspiring new users is key to home shopping survival', *Marketing Week*, 25 March 1999, p. 14; Ben Rosier, 'Web TV ties with Tesco for interactive TV tests', *Marketing*, 1 April 1999, p. 15; Michael Kavanagh, 'Tangled in the net', *Marketing Week*, 28 January 1999, pp. 53–5; Lisa Campbell, 'Tesco in Excite tie-up', *Marketing*, 18 February 1999, p. 12; www.tesco.co.uk. Photo: Courtesy of Tesco Direct; www.Tesco.com, January, 2008; 'Top Internet Sites by Category', *The Marketing Pocket Book 2008*, The Advertising Association/WARC, Henley, p. 237.

important to retailers, for they strive to create assortments matching the demands of consumers who patronise their stores. Although no single customer is likely to buy one of everything in the store, retailers must anticipate the probability of purchase and provide a satisfactory range of product choices. For example, the same food wholesaler that supplies supermarkets with Del Monte tomato products may also buy canned goods from competing food processors so that the grocery store can choose from a wide assortment of canned fruit and vegetables. The Marketing Insight box on page 329 outlines Tesco's multi-channel strategy and the importance of assorting.

Standardising Transactions

Marketing channels help to standardise the transactions associated with numerous products. In many purchase situations, the price is not negotiable; it is predetermined. Although there may be some variation in units of measurement, package sizes, delivery schedules and location of the exchange, marketing channel members tend to limit customers' options with respect to these types of issue. When a customer goes to a supermarket to purchase a loaf of bread, it is unlikely that the individual will be able to buy half a loaf of bread, buy a loaf sliced lengthwise, negotiate the price, obtain a written warranty or return an unused portion of the loaf. Many of the details associated with the purchase of a loaf of bread are standardised.

Providing Customer Service

Channel members participate in providing customer service. Retailers of durable goods are expected to provide in-store advice and demonstrations, technical know-how, delivery, installation, repair services, parts, and perhaps instruction or training. Channel members above the retailers are responsible for supporting retailers' efforts to provide end-user service and satisfaction, even though they may not come into direct contact with ultimate customers. To gain and maintain a differential advantage, channel members make decisions and take actions to provide excellent customer service and support.

In mature markets with relatively little product differentiation between rival brands – such as packaged holidays, audio/hi-fi systems, conference venues or replacement car exhausts/tyres – and in newly emerging markets with innovative products and inexperienced consumers, it is often the customer service provided through the distribution channel that provides marketers with an edge over their competitors. In many markets – from cars and financial services to grocery retailing and PCs – it is the service provided by channel members that maintains an ongoing, mutually satisfactory relationship between supplier and consumer, and that may be responsible for maintaining brand loyalty.

Types of Channel

Because marketing channels appropriate for one product may be less suitable for others, many different distribution paths have been developed. The various marketing channels can be classified generally as channels for consumer products and services, or channels for industrial, business-to-business products and services.

Channels for Consumer Products or Services

Figure 11.3 illustrates several channels used in the distribution of consumer products or services. Besides the channels listed, a manufacturer may use sales branches or sales offices.

Channel A   Channel A describes the direct movement of goods from producer to consumers. Customers who pick their own fruit from commercial orchards or buy cosmetics from door-to-door sales people are acquiring products through a direct channel. A producer who sells goods directly from the factory to end users and ultimate consumers is using a direct marketing channel (for example, Direct Line's teleselling of car insurance). Although this channel is the simplest, it is not necessarily the cheapest or the most efficient

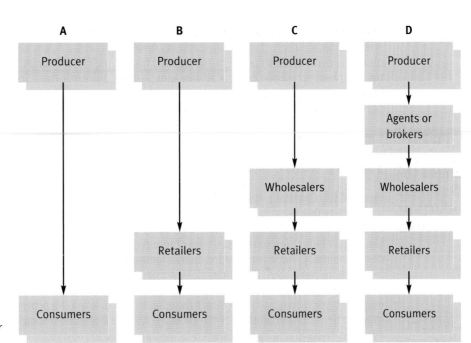

A
Producer

Consumers

B
Producer

Retailers

Consumers

C
Producer

Wholesalers

Retailers

Consumers

D
Producer

Agents or brokers

Wholesalers

Retailers

Consumers

Figure 11.3
Typical marketing channels for consumer products

E-commerce
The use of the Internet for marketing communications, selling and purchasing

method of distribution. **E-commerce** – the use of the Internet for marketing communications, selling and purchasing – has in recent years led to a growth in direct marketing for a variety of products, notably travel tickets, books, videos and CDs, financial services and merchandise retailed by the traditional mail-order catalogue operators. Channel A, the direct approach, is no longer the preserve of farm shops and factory outlets.

Channel B   Channel B, which moves goods from producer to retailers and then to consumers, is often used by large retailers that can buy in quantity from a manufacturer. Such retailers as Marks & Spencer, Sainsbury's, Aldi and Carrefour, for example, sell clothing, food and many other items they have purchased directly from the producers. Cars are also commonly sold through this type of marketing channel.

Channel C   A long-standing distribution channel, especially for consumer products, channel C takes goods from producer to wholesalers, then to retailers and finally to consumers. This option is very practical for a producer who sells to hundreds of thousands of consumers through thousands of retailers. A single producer finds it hard to do business directly with thousands of retailers. For example, consider the number of retailers that stock Coca-Cola. It would be extremely difficult, if not impossible, for Coca-Cola to deal directly with all the retailers that sell its brand of soft drink. Manufacturers of tobacco products, confectionery, some home appliances, hardware and many convenience goods sell their products to wholesalers, who then sell to retailers, who in turn do business with individual consumers.

Channel D   Channel D – through which goods pass from producer to agents to wholesalers to retailers, and only then to consumers – is frequently used for products intended for mass distribution, such as processed food. For example, to place its biscuit line in specific retail outlets, a food processor may hire an agent (or a food broker) to sell the biscuits to wholesalers. The wholesalers then sell the biscuits to supermarkets, vending machine operators and other retail outlets.

Benefits of a Long Channel   Contrary to popular opinion, a long channel may be the most efficient distribution channel for certain consumer goods. When several channel intermediaries are available to perform specialised functions, costs may be lower than if one channel member is responsible for all the functions in all territories. Some manufacturers opt for all or most of these four channels in order to cater for the needs and buying processes of the different customers that make up their various targeted market segments.

Channels for Industrial or Business-to-Business Products or Services

Figure 11.4 shows four of the most common channels for industrial or business products and services. Like their consumer products counterparts, manufacturers of industrial or business products sometimes work with more than one level of wholesalers.

Channel E   Channel E illustrates the direct channel for industrial or business products. In contrast with consumer goods, many business products – especially expensive equipment, such as steam generators, aircraft and mainframe computers – are sold directly to the buyers. For example, Airbus Industries sells aircraft direct to airlines such as British Airways and Air France. The direct channel is most feasible for many manufacturers of business goods because they have fewer customers, and those customers may be clustered geographically, as explained in Chapter 5. Buyers of complex industrial products can also receive technical assistance from the manufacturer more easily in a direct channel. In some cases the provision of such information may continue for the lifetime of the product. As with consumer markets, e-commerce and the desire to develop one-to-one direct relationships have led to a growth in the use of channel E.

Industrial distributor
An independent business that takes title to industrial products and carries inventories

Channel F   If a particular line of business products is aimed at a larger number of customers, the manufacturer may use a marketing channel that includes **industrial distributors**, merchants who take title to products and carry inventory (channel F). Construction products made by Case or JCB, for example, are sold through industrial or business-to-business distributors as are building materials, operating supplies and air-conditioning equipment. Industrial distributors are carrying an increasing percentage of business products. Due to mergers and acquisitions, they have become larger and more powerful.[5] Industrial distributors can be most effectively used when a product has broad market appeal, is easily stocked and serviced, is sold in small quantities and is needed rapidly to avoid high losses.[6]

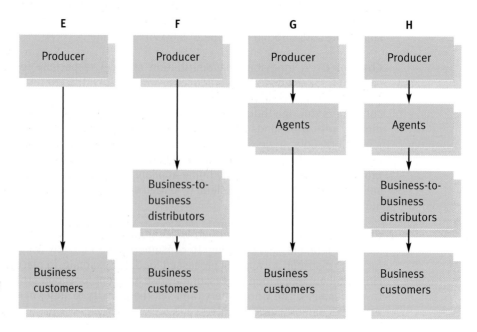

Figure 11.4
Typical marketing channels for industrial or business-to-business products

Channel G   Channel G – from producer to agents to industrial or business buyers – may be chosen when a manufacturer without a marketing department needs market information, when a company is too small to field its own salesforce or when a company wants to introduce a new product or to enter a new market without using its own sales people. Thus a large soya bean producer might sell its product to animal food processors through an agent.

Channel H   Channel H is a variation of channel G: goods move from producer to agents to industrial distributors and then to business customers. A manufacturer without a salesforce may rely on this channel if its business customers purchase products in small quantities or if they must be resupplied frequently and therefore need access to decentralised inventories. Japanese manufacturers of electronic components, for example, work through export agents who sell to industrial distributors serving small producers or dealers overseas.

Multiple Marketing Channels

When aiming at diverse target markets, it may be appropriate for a manufacturer to use several marketing channels simultaneously, with each channel involving a different group of intermediaries. For example, a manufacturer turns to multiple channels when the same product is directed to both consumers and business customers. When Procter & Gamble sells cleaning products for household use, the products are sold to supermarkets through grocery wholesalers or, in some cases, directly to the larger retailers, whereas the cleaning products going to restaurants or institutions follow a different distribution channel. In some instances, a producer may prefer **dual distribution**: the use of two or more marketing channels for distributing the same products. Villeroy & Boch is a respected supplier of fine china and glassware to households across the world. The company also has ranges for the catering industry, sold and promoted through a separate marketing channel.

A **strategic channel alliance** exists when the products of one organisation are distributed through the marketing channels of another. The products are often similar with respect to target markets or product uses, but they are not direct competitors. For example, a brand of bottled water might be distributed through a marketing channel for soft drinks, or a US cereal producer could form a strategic channel alliance with a European food processor. Alliances can provide benefits both for the organisation that owns the marketing channel and for the company whose brand is being distributed through the channel. An example of this is the 'chip and pin' system, which is replacing signatures on credit card slips. Barclaycard Merchant Services provides the banking/payment service, while IT company Fujitsu supplies the technology. In a joint venture, each company markets the same service to its respective clients – in retailing, catering and entertainment establishments.

Dual distribution
A channel practice whereby a producer distributes the same products through two or more different channels

Strategic channel alliance
Arrangement for distributing the products of one organisation through the marketing channels of another

Channel Integration

Channel functions may be transferred among intermediaries, to producers and even to customers. This section examines how channel members can either combine and control most activities or pass them on to another channel member. Remember, though, that the channel member cannot eliminate functions; unless buyers themselves perform the functions, they must pay for the labour and resources needed for the functions to be performed. The statement that, 'you can eliminate middlemen but you can't eliminate their functions', is an accepted principle of marketing.

Many marketing channels are determined by consensus. Producers and intermediaries coordinate their efforts for mutual benefit. Some marketing channels, however, are organised and controlled by a single leader, which can be a producer, a wholesaler or a retailer, depending on the industry. The channel leader may establish channel policies and coordinate the development of the marketing mix. Marks & Spencer and IKEA, for example, are channel leaders for several of the many products they sell, exerting significant pressure on suppliers to adhere to their production, delivery and pricing standards. The various links or stages of the channel may be combined under the management of a channel leader, either horizontally or vertically. Integration may stabilise supply, reduce costs and increase coordination of channel members.

Vertical Channel Integration

Vertical channel integration

The combination of two or more stages of the channel under one management

Combining two or more stages of the channel under one management is **vertical channel integration**. One member of a marketing channel may purchase the operations of another member or simply perform the functions of the other member, eliminating the need for that intermediary as a separate entity. For example, changes in the regulations controlling the UK electricity industry have led to an increase in vertical channel integration, as some companies controlling the generation and distribution of electricity have merged. Total vertical integration encompasses all functions from production to ultimate buyer; it is exemplified by oil companies that own oil wells, pipelines, refineries, terminals and service station forecourts.

Whereas members of conventional channel systems work independently and seldom cooperate, participants in vertical channel integration coordinate their efforts to reach a desired target market.[7] This more progressive approach to distribution enables channel members to regard other members as extensions of their own operations. Vertically integrated channels are often more effective against competition because they result in increased bargaining power, the ability to inhibit competitors, and the sharing of information and responsibilities.[8] At one end of an integrated channel, for example, a manufacturer might provide advertising and training assistance, and the retailer at the other end would buy the manufacturer's products in quantity and actively promote them.

In the past, integration has been successfully institutionalised in marketing channels called vertical marketing systems. A **vertical marketing system (VMS)** is a marketing channel in which a single channel member coordinates or manages channel activities to achieve efficient, low-cost distribution aimed at satisfying target market customers. Because the efforts of individual channel members are combined in a VMS, marketing activities can be coordinated for maximum effectiveness and economy, without duplication of services. Vertical marketing systems are also competitive, accounting for a growing share of retail sales in consumer goods. Most vertical marketing systems today take one of three forms: corporate, administered or contractual.

Vertical marketing system (VMS)

Marketing channel in which a single channel member coordinates or manages channel activities to achieve efficient, low-cost distribution aimed at satisfying target market customers

The Corporate VMS   The corporate VMS combines all stages of the marketing channel, from producers to consumers, under a single ownership. Supermarket chains that own food-processing plants, and large retailers that purchase wholesaling and production facilities, are examples of corporate VMSs. Figure 11.5 contrasts a conventional marketing channel with a VMS, which consolidates marketing functions and roles.

The Administered VMS   In an administered VMS, channel members are independent, but a high level of inter-organisational management is achieved by informal coordination. Members of an administered VMS may agree, for example, to adopt uniform accounting and ordering procedures, and to cooperate in promotional activities. Although individual channel members maintain their autonomy, as in conventional marketing channels, one channel member – such as the producer or a large retailer – dominates the administered VMS, so that distribution decisions take into account the system as a whole. Because of its size and power as a retailer, Marks & Spencer exercises a strong influence over the independent manufacturers in its marketing channels, as do Kellogg's (cereals) and BMW (cars).

The Contractual VMS   Under a contractual VMS, the most popular type of vertical marketing system, inter-organisational relationships are formalised through contracts. Channel members are linked by legal agreements that spell out each member's rights and obligations. For instance, franchise organisations such as McDonald's and KFC are contractual VMSs. Other

A conventional marketing channel

Members	Functions
Producer	Design Make Brand Price Promote Sell
Wholesaler	Buy Stock Promote Display Sell Deliver Service Finance
Retailer	Buy Stock Promote Display Sell Deliver Service Finance
Consumer	

A vertical marketing channel

Members	Functions
Producer Wholesaler Retailer	Design Make Brand Price Promote Buy Stock Display Sell Deliver Service Finance
Consumer	

Figure 11.5
Comparison of a conventional marketing channel and a vertical marketing system
Source: Adapted from Strategic Marketing, *by D.J. Kollat et al. Copyright © 1972. Reprinted by permission*

contractual VMSs include wholesaler-sponsored groups such as SPAR, Mace or IGA (Independent Grocers' Alliance) stores, in which independent retailers band together under the contractual leadership of a wholesaler.

Horizontal Channel Integration

Horizontal channel integration
The combination of institutions at the same level of channel operation under one management

Combining institutions at the same level of channel operation under one management constitutes **horizontal channel integration**. An organisation may integrate horizontally by merging with other organisations at the same level in a marketing channel. For example, the owner of a bistro chain may buy another bistro or a bar chain and then rebrand it in the same way as the existing business and merge the two chains' supply channels. Horizontal integration may enable an organisation to generate sufficient sales revenue to integrate vertically as well.

Although horizontal integration permits efficiencies and economies of scale in purchasing, marketing research, advertising and specialised personnel, it is not always the most effective method of improving distribution. The increase in size may result in decreased flexibility, difficulties in coordination, and the need for additional marketing research and large-scale planning. Unless distribution functions for the various units can be performed more efficiently under unified management than under the previously separate managements, horizontal integration will not reduce costs or improve the competitive position of the integrating company.

Different Levels of Market Coverage

The kind of coverage that is appropriate for different products is determined by the characteristics and behaviour patterns of buyers. Chapter 8 divided consumer products into three broad categories – convenience products, shopping products and speciality products – according to how the purchase is made. In considering products to buy, consumers take into account replacement rate, product adjustment (services), duration of consumption, time required to find the product and similar factors.[9] Three major levels of market coverage are intensive, selective and exclusive distribution.

Intensive Distribution

Intensive distribution
The use of all available outlets for distributing a product

In **intensive distribution**, all available outlets are used for distributing a product. Intensive distribution is appropriate for convenience products such as bread, chewing gum, beer and newspapers. To consumers, availability means a store located nearby and minimal time necessary to search for the product at the store. Sales may have a direct relationship to availability. The successful sale of bread and milk at service stations or of petrol at convenience grocery stores has shown that the availability of these products is more important than the nature of the outlet. Convenience products have a high replacement rate and require almost no service. To meet these demands, intensive distribution is necessary, and multiple channels may be used to sell through all possible outlets.

Producers of packaged consumer items rely on intensive distribution. In fact, intensive distribution is one of Anchor's key strengths: Anchor and other Arla Foods UK products, including butters, cream, cheese and milk, are expected to be readily and intensively available by consumers.

Selective Distribution

Selective distribution
The use of only some available outlets in an area to distribute a product

In **selective distribution**, only some available outlets in an area are chosen to distribute a product. Selective distribution is appropriate for shopping products. Durable goods such as electrical appliances and exclusive fragrances usually fall into this category. Such products are more expensive than convenience goods. Consumers are willing to spend more time searching: visiting several retail outlets to compare prices, designs, styles and other features.

Selective distribution is desirable when a special effort – such as customer service from a channel member – is important. Shopping products require differentiation at the point of purchase. To motivate retailers to provide adequate pre-sale service, selective distribution and company-owned stores are often used. Many business products are sold on a selective basis to maintain a certain degree of control over the distribution process. For example, agricultural herbicides are distributed on a selective basis because dealers must offer services to buyers, such as instructions about how to apply the herbicides safely, or offer the option of having the dealer apply the herbicide.

Exclusive Distribution

Exclusive distribution
The use of only one outlet in a relatively large geographic area to distribute a product

In **exclusive distribution**, only one outlet is used in a relatively large geographic area. Exclusive distribution is suitable for speciality products that are purchased rather infrequently, consumed over a long period of time, or require service or information to fit them to buyers' needs. Exclusive distribution is not appropriate for convenience products and many shopping products. It is often used as an incentive to sellers when only a limited market is available for products. For example, cars such as the Rolls-Royce are sold on an exclusive basis. Royal Copenhagen's premium china is retailed through carefully selected, exclusive retail outlets. A producer who uses exclusive distribution generally expects a dealer to be very cooperative with respect to carrying a complete inventory, sending personnel for sales and service training, participating in promotional programmes and providing excellent customer service. Exclusive distribution gives a company tighter image control because the types of distributors and retailers that distribute the product are monitored closely.[10]

Figure 11.6
Anchor butter and other dairy lines are intensively distributed
Source: Courtesy of Staniforth/Arla Foods

Choosing Distribution Channels

Choosing the most appropriate distribution channels for a product can be a complex affair. The Marketing Insight box on page 338 outlines the channel strategy developed by Games Workshop. Producers must choose specific intermediaries carefully, evaluating their sales and profit levels, performance records, other products carried, clientele, availability, and so forth. In addition, producers must examine other factors that influence distribution channel selection, including organisational objectives and resources, market characteristics, buying behaviour, product attributes and environmental forces. In some markets, such as the distribution of insurance products, these factors may indicate that multiple channels should be used.[11]

Organisational Objectives and Resources

Producers must consider carefully their objectives and the cost of achieving them in the marketplace. A company's objectives may be broad – such as higher profits, increased market share and greater responsiveness to customers – or narrow, such as replacing an intermediary that has left the channel. The organisation may possess sufficient financial and marketing clout to control its distribution channels – for example, by engaging in direct marketing or by operating its own fleet of lorries. On the other hand, an organisation may have no interest in performing distribution services or may be forced by lack of resources and experience to depend on middlemen.

337

○ Marketing Insight

Games Workshop: the Best Model Soldiers in the World!

As its name suggests, Games Workshop manufactures and sells games, but these are no ordinary games and this is no ordinary business. Games Workshop is 'the largest and most successful tabletop fantasy and futuristic battle-games company in the world'. With a turnover of over £112 million, this fast-growing company employs more than 2000 people and has over 350 retail outlets in Australia, Canada, France, Germany, Hong Kong, Spain, the USA and the UK, with the growing Italian market still being serviced from the UK. 70 per cent of sales now come from outside the UK. The fantasy games produced by Games Workshop take place in one of two settings:

1 a fantasy world filled with Dwarves, Elves, rat-like Scaven, green Orcs and Goblins
2 the future of a war-torn universe in the forty-first millennium – a setting occupied by the enigmatic Eldar, genetically enhanced Space Marines and an alien race called the Tyranids, who are all battling for survival.

Games Workshop enthusiasts can buy from a range of boxed games, containing the rule book, charts and templates, dice and miniature figures needed to begin their fantasy battle. The basics can then be added to from the extensive range of Games Workshop troops, special squads and war machines. As enthusiasts develop their armies and paint them in colours of their choice, they begin to build their own personalised version of their game of choice. The success of Peter Jackson's The Lord of the Rings films has added a new dimension, as Games Workshop holds a global licence for a game based on this award-winning trilogy.

For those unfamiliar with the fantasy game concept, the uncharted territory of the retail outlets can itself feel like alien territory. Wall space is stacked high with numerous games, figures, paints, magazines, books and T-shirts. In the centre is a gaming table, which is usually covered with the remains of an ongoing battle. At other times, the shops are full of teenagers and children, conducting a closely fought Warhammer contest. On some days the outlets resemble a crèche for big kids, with staff carefully orchestrating activities. The battles organised in-store are an important part of the weekly itinerary. The featured game varies on different days, so that enthusiasts of Warhammer, Warhammer 40,000, Necromunda and the other Games Workshop products can all get their turn. These games induct newcomers into the gaming experience, while for 'old hands' they showcase new product launches.

The shop staff, always Games Workshop enthusiasts, are vital to the success of the retail outlets. They must be able to maintain an enthusiasm for the brand, keeping up to date with all of the latest new product launches. The ability to handle customers of all ages and backgrounds – from the young teenagers who regularly hang out at the stores to the uninitiated visiting the outlets for the first time – is also essential. Nonplussed parents clutching 'Christmas lists' or birthday present suggestions experience a friendly welcome from staff, who will happily search among the reams of Games Workshop packaging to retrieve some bizarrely named item.

As well as its network of retail stores, Games Workshop has agencies – typically specialist modelling and hobbyist shops – distributing its figures and games, while even the likes of Toys 'Я' Us has been known to stock the popular gaming sets. In total, more than 3500 independent shops retail the company's ranges. In addition, there is a mail-order operation that can be accessed through the retail stores as well as directly by telephone or the Internet. The online operation has grown significantly recently. This £35 million mail-order operation has 40 staff and a database of 250,000 contacts. The aim is to provide a fast and efficient service, despatching all orders within 24 hours. This facility handles up to a thousand calls daily and can deal with enquiries in a range of languages. While the stores are an integral feature of the Games Workshop 'experience', the company has been quick to recognise the value of adopting a mix of distribution channels to support its rapid expansion plans: online sales and mail order contribute significantly to the company's sales. The company believes its destiny is in its own hands, saying, 'Games Workshop remains a vertically integrated company, retaining control over every aspect of design, manufacture, distribution, and retail of our models and rulebooks'.

Sources: Jervis Johnson and Chris Prentice of Games Workshop; Games Workshop website, www.games-workshop.co.uk; James Dibb-Simkin; Sally Dibb and Lyndon Simkin, *The Marketing Casebook*, 2nd edn (London: ITBP, 2001); www.games-workshop.com/aboutus.htm, May, 2004; http://investor.games-workshop.com/about_us.aspx, January, 2008.

Companies must also consider how effective their past distribution relationships and methods have been, and question their appropriateness with regard to current objectives. One organisation might decide to maintain its basic channel structure but add members for increased coverage in new territories. Another company might alter its distribution channel so as to provide same-day delivery on all orders.

Market Characteristics

Beyond the basic division between consumer markets and business markets, several market variables influence the design of distribution channels. Geography is one factor; in most cases, the greater the distance between the producer and its markets, the less expensive is distribution through intermediaries rather than through direct sales. Market density must also be considered; when customers tend to be clustered in several locations, the producer may be able to eliminate middlemen.

Figure 11.7 shows department store John Lewis's home delivery operation. Transport, storage, communication and negotiation are specific functions performed more efficiently in high-density markets. Market size – measured by the number of potential customers in a consumer or business market – is yet another variable. Direct sales may be effective if a producer has relatively few buyers for a product, but for larger markets the services of middlemen may be required.[12] E-commerce is encouraging many suppliers to deal directly with customers, even when they are geographically spread or diverse in nature. There is no doubt that the growing popularity of direct marketing and web-based marketing is forcing marketers to reappraise their market characteristics and deployment of channel intermediaries. This results in direct customer–supplier relationships in those channels where

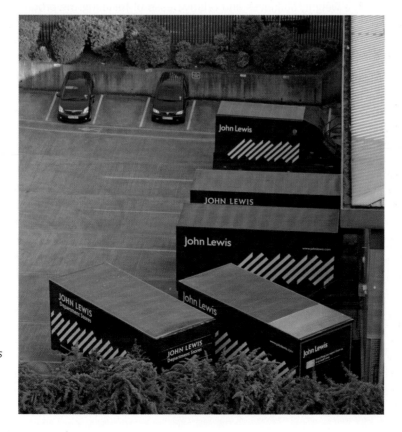

Figure 11.7
Department store retailer John Lewis now operates a successful online catalogue operation, requiring a fleet of home delivery vehicles for this quickly growing marketing channel. Source: AndySmyStock/Alamy

wholesaler/retailer channel members once dominated, such as CDs, books, holidays, clothing and financial services.

Buying Behaviour

Buying behaviour is a crucial consideration in selecting distribution channels. To be able to match intermediaries with customers, the producer must have specific, current information about customers who are buying the product, and how, when and where they are buying it.[13] A manufacturer may find direct selling economically feasible for large-volume sales but inappropriate for small orders.

The producer must also understand how buyer specifications vary according to whether buyers perceive products as convenience, shopping or speciality items (see Chapter 8). Customers for magazines, for example, are likely to buy the product frequently – even impulsively – from a variety of outlets. Buyers of home computers, however, carefully evaluate product features, dealers, prices and after-sales services.

Buyers may be reached most effectively when producers are creative in opening up new distribution channels. In the UK, effective distribution, the essential tool in the highly competitive soft drinks sector, is forcing brand leaders Coca-Cola and Schweppes Beverages to find creative ways of extending distribution. Schweppes launched a company, Vendleader, to increase penetration of sales through vending machines.

Product Attributes

Another variable in the selection of distribution channels is the product itself. Because producers of complex industrial products must often provide technical services to buyers both before and after the sale, these products are usually shipped directly to buyers. Perishable or highly fashionable consumer products with short shelf lives are also marketed through short channels. In other cases, distribution patterns are influenced by the product's value; the lower the price per unit, the longer the distribution chain. Additional factors to consider are the weight, bulkiness and relative ease of handling the products. Producers may find wholesalers and retailers reluctant to carry items that create storage or display problems.[14] For example, manufacturers of breakfast cereals, such as Kellogg's, must use packaging that retailers find easy to handle and display.

Environmental Forces

Finally, producers making decisions about distribution channels must consider the broader forces in the total marketing environment – that is, the political, legal, regulatory, societal/Green, technological, economic and competitive forces. Technology, for example, has made possible electronic scanners, computerised inventory systems such as EPOS (electronic point-of-sale) and electronic shopping devices, all of which are altering present distribution systems and making it harder for technologically unsophisticated companies to remain competitive. Internet access has led to a growth in home shopping and direct marketing. Changing family patterns and the emergence of important minority consumer groups are driving producers to seek new distribution methods for reaching market segments. Interest rates, inflation and other economic variables affect members of distribution channels at every level. Environmental forces are numerous and complex, and must be taken into consideration if distribution efforts are to be appropriate, efficient and effective (see Chapter 3). For example, EU regulation changes have impacted on the retailing of cars, resulting in a power shift away from the car manufacturers to the independently owned showrooms, which can now source vehicles from a variety of manufacturers to sell at a single location.

Behaviour of Channel Members

The marketing channel is a social system with its own conventions and behaviour patterns. Each channel member performs a different role in the system and agrees – implicitly or explicitly – to accept certain rights, responsibilities, rewards and sanctions for non-conformity.

Channel members have certain expectations of other channel members. Retailers, for instance, expect wholesalers and manufacturers to maintain adequate inventories and to deliver goods on time. For their part, wholesalers expect retailers to honour payment agreements and to keep them informed of inventory needs. This section discusses several issues related to channel member behaviour, including cooperation and relationship building, conflict and leadership. Marketers need to understand these behavioural issues in order to make effective channel decisions, and to maintain relationships with facilitating channel members and loyal customers.

Channel Cooperation and Relationship Building

Channel cooperation is vital if each member is to gain something from other members.[15] Without cooperation, neither overall channel goals nor member goals can be realised. Policies must be developed that support all essential channel members, otherwise failure of one link in the chain could destroy the channel.

There are several ways to improve channel cooperation. A marketing channel should consider itself a unified system, competing with other systems. This way, individual members will be less likely to take actions that would create disadvantages for other members. Similarly, channel members should agree to direct their efforts towards a common target market so that channel roles can be structured for maximum marketing effectiveness, which in turn can help members achieve their individual objectives.

Heineken, for example, was having difficulty with its 450 distributors; at one point, the time between order and delivery stretched to 12 weeks. A cooperative system of supply chain management, with Internet-based communications, decreased the lead time from order to delivery to four weeks, and Heineken's sales increased 24 per cent.[16] It is crucial to define precisely the tasks that each member of the channel is to perform. This definition provides a basis for reviewing the intermediaries' performance and helps reduce conflicts because each channel member knows exactly what is expected. It is often in the interests of channel members to build long-term relationships. These relationships can improve channel cooperation and help individual channel members adapt better to the needs of the others.[17]

Channel Conflict

Although all channel members work towards the same general goal – distributing goods and services profitably and efficiently – members may sometimes disagree about the best methods for attaining this goal.[18] Each channel member wants to maximise its own profits while maintaining as much autonomy as possible.[19] However, if this self-interest leads to misunderstanding about role expectations, the end result is frustration and conflict for the whole channel. For individual organisations to function together in a single social system, each channel member must communicate clearly and understand role expectations, especially as channel conflict often arises when a channel member does not conduct itself in the manner expected by the other channel members. Communication difficulties are a particular form of channel conflict and can lead to frustration, misunderstandings and poorly coordinated strategies.

The increased use of multiple channels of distribution, driven partly by new technology, has increased the potential for conflict between manufacturers and intermediaries. For example, Hewlett-Packard makes products available directly to consumers through its website (www.hewlett.packard.com), thereby directly competing with existing distributors and retailers.[20] SonyStyle sells Sony products online directly to consumers, competing with the large number of independent stores and major retail chains stocking Sony's products.

Channel conflicts also arise when dealers over-emphasise competing products or diversify into product lines traditionally handled by other, more specialised intermediaries. In some cases, conflict develops because producers strive to increase efficiency by circumventing intermediaries, as is happening in marketing channels for microcomputer software and video games. Many software-only stores are establishing direct relationships with software producers, bypassing wholesale distributors altogether. Some dishonest retailers also pirate software and make unauthorised copies, thus cheating other channel members of their due compensation. Consequently, suspicion and mistrust may heighten tensions in software marketing channels.

Although there is no single method for resolving conflict, an atmosphere of cooperation can be re-established if two conditions are met. First, the role of each channel member must be specified. To minimise misunderstanding, all members must be able to expect unambiguous, agreed-on levels of performance from one another. Second, channel members must institute certain measures of channel coordination, a task that requires leadership and the benevolent exercise of control.[21] To prevent channel conflict, producers or other channel members may provide competing resellers with different brands, allocate markets among resellers, define direct sales policies to clarify potential conflict over large accounts, negotiate territorial issues between regional distributors and provide recognition to certain resellers for the importance of their role in distributing to others. Hallmark, for example, distributes its Ambassador greetings card line in discount stores and its name brand Hallmark line in upmarket department and specialist card stores, thus limiting the amount of competition among retailers carrying its products.[22]

Channel Leadership

The effectiveness of marketing channels hinges on channel leadership, which may be assumed by producers, retailers or wholesalers. To become a leader, a channel member must want to influence and direct overall channel performance. Furthermore, to attain desired objectives, the leader must possess **channel power**, which is the ability to influence another channel member's goal achievement. As Figure 11.8 shows, the channel leader derives power from seven sources, two of them economic and five non-economic.

The five non-economic sources of power – reward, expert, referent, legitimate and coercive – are crucial for establishing leadership.

Channel power
The ability to influence another channel member's goal achievement

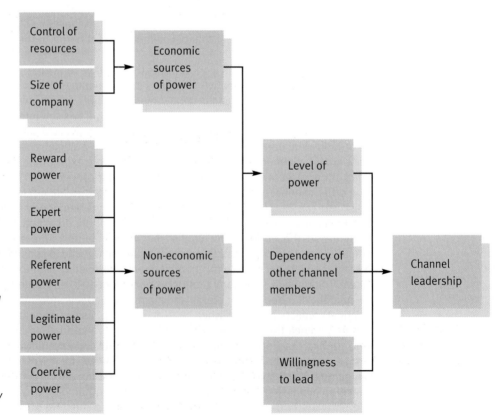

Figure 11.8
Determinants of channel leadership
Source: R.D. Michman and S.D. Sibley, Marketing Channels and Strategies, *2nd edn (Worthington, Ohio: Publishing Horizons, Inc., 1980), p. 413. Reproduced by permission*

1 A channel leader gains *reward* power by providing financial benefits.
2 *Expert* power exists when other channel members believe that the leader provides special expertise required for the channel to function properly.
3 *Referent* power emerges when other members identify strongly with and emulate the leader.
4 *Legitimate* power is based on a superior–subordinate relationship.
5 *Coercive* power is a function of the leader's ability to punish other channel members.[23]

In many countries, producers assume the leadership role in marketing channels. A manufacturer – whose large-scale production efficiency demands increasing sales volume – may exercise power by giving channel members financing, business advice, ordering assistance, advertising and support materials.[24] For example, BMW and Mercedes-Benz control their dealers totally, specifying showroom design and layout, discount levels and quotas of models. Coercion, though, causes dealer dissatisfaction that is stronger than any impact from rewards, so the use of coercive power can be a major cause of channel conflict.[25]

Retailers can also function as channel leaders, and with the domination of national chains and own-label merchandise they are increasingly doing so. For example, Sainsbury's challenged Coca-Cola with its own-label cola, whose packaging bore a strong resemblance to that of the market leader. Small retailers, too, may share in the leadership role when they command particular consumer respect and patronage in local or regional markets. Among large retailers, Carrefour, IKEA, Marks & Spencer and Tesco base their channel leadership on wide public exposure to their products. These retailers control many brands and sometimes replace uncooperative producers. IKEA exercises power by dictating manufacturing techniques, lead times, quality levels and product specifications.

Wholesalers assume channel leadership roles as well, although they were more powerful decades ago, when most manufacturers and retailers were small, under-financed and widely scattered. Today, wholesaler leaders may form voluntary chains with several retailers, which they supply with bulk buying or management services or which market their own brands. In return, the retailers shift most of their purchasing to the wholesaler leader. In Scandinavia, buying groups act as wholesalers, with bulk ordering price advantages, expert advertising and purchasing. Other wholesaler leaders, such as Intersport or SPAR, may also help retailers with store layouts, accounting and inventory control.

Legal Issues in Channel Management

The multitude of laws governing channel management are based on the general principle that the public is best served when competition and free trade are protected. Under the authority of such national legislation as the UK's Competition Commission, Fair Trading Act, Prices Act, Trades Descriptions Act and Consumer Protection Act, or EU Competition Laws and dictates, the courts and regulatory agencies determine under what circumstances channel management practices violate this underlying principle and must be restricted, and when these practices may be permitted. Although channel managers are not expected to be legal experts, they should be aware that attempts to control distribution functions may have legal repercussions. The following practices are among those frequently subject to legal restraint.

Restricted sales territories
System by which a manufacturer tries to prohibit intermediaries from selling its products outside designated sales territories

Restricted Sales Territories

To tighten its control over the distribution of its products, a manufacturer may try to prohibit intermediaries from selling its products outside designated sales territories, creating **restricted sales territories**. The intermediaries themselves often favour this practice, because it lets them avoid competition for the producer's brands within their own territories. Many companies have long followed the policy of restricting sales in this fashion. In recent years, the courts have adopted conflicting positions with regard to restricted sales

Exclusive dealing
System by which a manufacturer forbids an intermediary to carry the products of competing manufacturers

territories. Although they have deemed restricted sales territories a restraint of trade among intermediaries handling the same brands – except for small or newly established companies – the courts have also held that exclusive territories can actually promote competition among dealers handling different brands. At present, the producer's intent in establishing restricted territories and the overall effect of doing so on the market must be evaluated for each individual case.

Tying Contract

Tying contract
Arrangement whereby a supplier (usually a manufacturer or franchiser) furnishes a product to a channel member with the stipulation that the channel member must purchase other products as well

When a supplier – usually a manufacturer or franchiser – furnishes a product to a channel member with the stipulation that the channel member must purchase other products as well, a **tying contract** exists.[26] Suppliers, for instance, may institute tying arrangements to move weaker products along with more popular items. To use another example, a franchiser may tie the purchase of equipment and supplies to the sale of franchises, justifying the policy as necessary for quality control and protection of the franchiser's reputation. A related practice is full-line forcing. In this situation, a supplier requires that channel members purchase the supplier's entire line to obtain any of the products. Manufacturers sometimes use full-line forcing to ensure that intermediaries accept new products and that a suitable range of products is available to customers. The courts accept tying contracts when the supplier alone can provide products of a certain quality, when the intermediary is free to carry competing products as well, and when a company has just entered the market. Most other tying contracts are considered illegal.

Exclusive Dealing

When a manufacturer forbids an intermediary to carry the products of competing manufacturers, the arrangement is called **exclusive dealing**. A manufacturer receives considerable market protection in an exclusive dealing arrangement and may cut off shipments to an intermediary that violates such an agreement. An exclusive dealing contract is generally legally permitted if dealers and customers in a given market have access to similar products or if the exclusive dealing contract strengthens an otherwise weak competitor.

Refusal to Deal

Refusal to deal
Situation in which suppliers will not do business with wholesalers or dealers simply because these wholesalers or dealers have resisted policies that are anti-competitive or in restraint of trade

Producers have the right to choose the channel members with whom they will do business and the right not to choose others. Within existing distribution channels, however, suppliers may not refuse to deal with wholesalers or dealers just because these wholesalers or dealers have resisted policies that are anti-competitive or in restraint of trade. Suppliers are further prohibited from organising some channel members in **refusal to deal** actions against other members who choose not to comply with illegal policies.[27] Recently several supermarket chains, such as ASDA and Tesco, have sought designer clothing from manufacturers such as Levi's. Following the manufacturers' refusal to supply those retailers – as they expected them to discount their lines – the retailers instead acquired the branded leisure wear on the 'grey market', often in eastern Europe or South-east Asia. Several court cases have ensued, with the manufacturers arguing their case for being entitled to select which types of retailer to supply.

Summary

Distribution refers to activities that make products available to customers when and where they want to purchase them. A *channel of distribution* (or *marketing channel*) is a group of individuals and organisations that direct the flow of products from producers to customers.

In most channels of distribution, producers and customers are linked by *marketing intermediaries* or middlemen, called *merchants* if they take title to products and *functional middlemen* if they do not take title. Channel structure reflects the division of responsibilities among members. Ongoing relationships with customers are seen as increasingly important via relationship marketing. Effective distribution channels and the deployment of channel intermediaries are central to the development of mutually satisfactory ongoing relationships between intermediaries, and between producers and their customers.

⊗ *Supply chain management* is the creation of long-term partnerships among marketing channel members that reduce inefficiencies, costs and redundancies in the marketing channel and develop innovative approaches to satisfying targeted customers. The goal is still to provide customers with the product or service demanded, in line with their expectations, but in a more coordinated way that builds on the combined strengths of the members of the distribution channel. Key tasks in supply chain management include planning, sourcing, facilitating delivery and relationship building to nurture ongoing customer relationships.

⊗ Marketing channels serve many functions that may be performed by a single channel member but are mostly accomplished through both the independent and joint efforts of channel members. These functions include creating utility, facilitating exchange efficiencies, alleviating discrepancies, standardising transactions and providing customer service. Although intermediaries can be eliminated, their functions are vital and cannot be dropped; these activities must be performed by someone in the marketing channel or passed on to customers. Because intermediaries serve both producers and buyers, they reduce the total number of transactions that would otherwise be needed to move products from producer to ultimate users. Intermediaries' specialised functions also help keep down costs.

⊗ An *assortment* is a combination of products assembled to provide customer benefits. Intermediaries perform *sorting activities* essential to the development of product assortments. Sorting activities allow channel members to divide roles and separate tasks. Through the basic tasks of *sorting out*, *accumulation*, *allocation* and *assorting* products for buyers, intermediaries resolve discrepancies in quantity and assortment. The number and characteristics of intermediaries

are determined by the assortments and the expertise needed to perform distribution activities.

⊗ Direct marketing, aided by *e-commerce*, has recently encouraged many marketers to cut out channel intermediaries (see below) in both consumer and business-to-business transactions.

⊗ Channels of distribution are broadly classified as channels for consumer products or channels for business products. Within these two broad categories, different marketing channels are used for different products. Although some consumer goods move directly from producer to consumers, consumer product channels that include wholesalers and retailers are usually more economical and efficient. Business goods move directly from producer to end users more frequently than do consumer goods. Channels for business products may also include agents, *industrial distributors* or both. Most producers use *dual distribution* or multiple channels so that the distribution system can be adjusted for various target markets. Sometimes *strategic channel alliances* are used so that the products of one organisation can be distributed through the marketing channels of another.

⊗ Integration of marketing channels brings various activities under the management of one channel member. *Vertical channel integration* combines two or more stages of the channel under one management. In the *vertical marketing system (VMS)* a single channel member coordinates or manages channel activity for the mutual benefit of all channel members. Vertical marketing systems may be corporate, administered or contractual. *Horizontal channel integration* combines institutions at the same level of channel operation under a single management.

⊗ A marketing channel is managed so that products receive appropriate market coverage. In *intensive distribution*, producers distribute a product using all available outlets. In *selective distribution*, outlets are screened to use those most qualified for exposing a product properly. *Exclusive distribution* usually uses one outlet to distribute a product in a large geographic area when there is a limited market for the product.

❯❯ When selecting distribution channels for products, manufacturers evaluate potential channel members carefully. Producers consider the organisation's objectives and available resources; the location, density and size of a market; buying behaviour in the target market; product attributes; and external forces in the marketing environment. Technology, notably e-commerce, has recently played a major role in certain markets in the selection of distribution channels.

❯❯ A marketing channel is a social system in which individuals and organisations are linked by a common goal: the profitable and efficient distribution of goods and services. The positions or roles of channel members are associated with rights, responsibilities and rewards, as well as sanctions for non-conformity. Channels function most efficiently when members cooperate; when they deviate from their roles, channel conflict can arise. Effective marketing channels are usually a result of channel leadership and of relationship building between channel members.

❯❯ Channel leaders can facilitate or hinder other channel members' goal achievement, deriving this *channel power* from seven sources, two of them economic and five non-economic. Producers are in an excellent position to structure channel policy and to use technical expertise and consumer acceptance to influence other channel members. Retailers gain channel control through consumer confidence, wide product mixes and intimate knowledge of consumers. Wholesalers and buying groups become channel leaders when they have expertise that other channel members value and when they can coordinate functions to match supply with demand.

❯❯ Channel management is governed by a variety of legal issues. These are based on the principle that the public is best served when competition and free trade are protected. Various practices may be subject to legal restraint. To tighten their distribution control, manufacturers may try to operate *restricted sales territories*, where intermediaries are barred from selling products outside designated areas. A *tying contract* occurs when a supplier stipulates that another channel member must purchase other products in addition to the one originally supplied. *Exclusive dealing* occurs when a manufacturer forbids an intermediary to carry the products of competing manufacturers. *Refusal to deal* means that a producer will not do business with a wholesaler or dealer that has resisted policies that are anti-competitive or in restraint of trade.

◈ *Key Links*

The choice of marketing channel is critical to the success of a marketing strategy, as explored in this chapter, and channel selection is very much a part of the marketing remit. This chapter should be read in conjunction with:

- Chapter 2, the overview of marketing strategy.
- Chapter 8, the explanation of the product element of the marketing mix.

Important Terms

Channel of distribution (or marketing channel)
Marketing intermediary
Merchants
Functional middlemen
Supply chain management
Assortment
Sorting activities
Sorting out
Accumulation
Allocation
Assorting
E-commerce
Industrial distributor
Dual distribution
Strategic channel alliance
Vertical channel integration
Vertical marketing system (VMS)

Horizontal channel integration
Intensive distribution
Selective distribution
Exclusive distribution
Channel power
Restricted sales territories
Exclusive dealing
Tying contract
Refusal to deal

Discussion and Review Questions

1 Compare and contrast the four major types of marketing channel for consumer products. Through which type of channel is each of the following products most likely to be distributed: (a) new cars, (b) cheese biscuits, (c) cut-your-own Christmas trees, (d) new textbooks, (e) sofas, (f) soft drinks?

2 'Shorter channels are usually a more direct means of distribution and therefore are more efficient.' Comment on this statement.

3 Describe an industrial distributor. What types of product are marketed through industrial distributors?

4 Under what conditions is a producer most likely to use more than one marketing channel?

5 Why do consumers often blame intermediaries for distribution inefficiencies? List several reasons.

6 How do the major functions that intermediaries perform help resolve discrepancies in assortment and in quantity?

7 How does the number of intermediaries in the channel relate to the assortments retailers need?

8 Can one channel member perform all channel functions?

9 Identify and explain the major factors that influence decision-makers' selection of marketing channels.

10 Name and describe companies that use (a) vertical integration and (b) horizontal integration in their marketing channels.

11 Explain the major characteristics of each of the three types of vertical marketing system (VMS).

12 Explain the differences among intensive, selective and exclusive methods of distribution.

13 What impact has the growing popularity of e-commerce had on marketing channels?

14 'Channel cooperation requires that members support the overall channel goals to achieve individual goals.' Comment on this statement.

15 How do power bases within the channel influence the selection of the channel leader?

Recommended Reading

- Christopher, M., *Marketing Logistics* (Oxford: Butterworth-Heinemann, 2003).
- Christopher, M., *Logistics and Supply Chain Management* (Harlow: Pearson/FT, 2004).
- Friedman, L. and Furey, T., *The Channel Advantage* (Oxford: Butterworth-Heinemann, 1999).
- Gattorna, J., ed., *Strategic Supply Chain Alignment: Best Practices in Supply Chain Management* (Aldershot: Gower, 1998).
- Hines, T., *Supply Chain Strategies* (Oxford: Butterworth-Heinemann, 2004).
- Lambert, D.M. and Stock, J.R., *Strategic Logistics Management* (Homewood, Ill.: Richard D. Irwin, 1993).
- Rosenbloom, B., *Marketing Channels: A Management View* (Cincinnati, OH: South Western, 2003).
- Waters, D., *Global Logistics and Distribution Planning: Strategies for Management* (London: Kogan Page, 2003).

🌐 Internet Exercise

The fortunes of many manufacturers depend on their dealer network, particularly producers of construction equipment. Take a look at two such companies' websites, and examine what they say about their dealer network and parts/service support: www.caterpillar.com and www.jcb.com

1 In the context of these websites, how important to these businesses is the chosen route to market: the dealer network?

2 In terms of delivering customer service, what is the role in the marketing channel of these dealerships?

⊛ Applied Mini-Case

Most recorded music used to be purchased by consumers from music stores or mail-order catalogues. First the Internet enabled e-selling from retailers' catalogues, but now it has permitted the instant downloading of a fan's favourite tracks. Not only are bands cutting out traditional distribution channels by offering new material directly to their fans via the web, but mainstream labels are also side-tracking the music store as a response to this growing trend.

It is not only artists and record labels that have embraced the Internet. Non-music brands wishing to appeal to youthful target markets have also sought to do so by making music available online to their customers. For example, Sony – wanting to sell more MPV players, Walkmans and hi-fi systems – has its Connect music download system; Coke launched mycokemusic.com; Starbucks has developed an in-store music service called Hear Music to let coffee drinkers download tracks; and T-Mobile has created a mobile phone-based music download service designed to appeal to its younger mobile phone users.

Source: Rachel Barnes, 'Retailers take on digital music', *Marketing*, 25 March 2004, Sony.com, August 2007.

❓ Question

How can music store operators such as HMV and Virgin Megastores, strive to maintain a strong customer base in the face of such substitute competition from e-downloads and even non-music stores providing music downloads?

⊛ Case Study

First Direct's Innovative Banking Channels

First Direct is a refreshingly different bank.
We like to keep things simple and easy. We put the customer first.

- our services are designed around your day-to-day needs, not ours, so you can talk to a real person 24 hours a day, 365 days a year
- you can call us any time, anywhere, to check a balance, arrange a bill payment or talk about extending your credit limit ...
- and when you don't want to talk, you can view, analyse and manage your money online
- you can even receive information by text message.

Enjoy a little magical support.
www.firstdirect.com/banking/banking.shtml, May 2004

Most consumers have a bank cheque account from which cash is drawn, bills are paid and cheques written, and into which salaries, pensions or grant cheques are paid. For many consumers, the bank is a high-street or shopping-centre office – imposing, formal and often intimidating. Whether it's NatWest, Barclays or Lloyds TSB in the UK, or ABN AMRO or Rabobank in the Netherlands, each high-street bank is fairly alike, with similar products and services, personnel, branch layouts, locations and opening hours. Differentiation has been difficult to achieve and generally impossible to maintain over any length of time as competitors have copied rivals' moves. Promotional strategy and brand image have been the focus for most banking organisations, supported with more minor tactical changes in, for example, opening hours or service charges. For the majority of bank account holders, however, the branch – with its restricted openings, formal ambience and congested town-centre location – is the only point of contact for the bulk of transactions.

First Direct, owned by HSBC but managed separately, broke the mould in 1989. Launched with a then massive £6 million promotional campaign, First Direct bypassed the traditional marketing channel. First Direct has no branches and no branch overhead and operating costs. It provides free banking, unlike its high-street competitors with their systems of bank charges combined with interest paid on positive balances. First Direct is a telephone and online banking service that offers full banking, mortgage, loan, investment/saving, insurance, foreign currency and credit card services, plus ATM 'hole in the wall' cash cards through HSBC's international service-till network.

HSBC has established a purpose-built administrative centre for First Direct in Leeds, UK, guaranteeing immediate, personal response to calls 24 hours a day. All normal banking transactions can be completed over the telephone.

Initial reactions were positive, with many non-HSBC account holders switching to the innovative new style of banking. The more traditional consumer – who equates the marbled halls of the Victorian branches with heritage, security and traditional values – has been less easily converted. For the targeted, more financially aware and independent income earner, First Direct is proving very popular. Research shows that First Direct is the most recommended bank with the most satisfied customers.

First Direct's services and products are not new, but the chosen marketing channels are innovative: no branches, only telephone call centres, online banking and texting. Customers no longer have to reach inaccessible, parked-up, town-centre branches with queues and restricted opening hours. First Direct has introduced a service, alien to some more traditional tastes perhaps, that is more readily available and with fewer costs. Hundreds of thousands of consumers have welcomed the launch of this new option, but millions have preferred to bank the traditional way. For HSBC, this is fine: its HSBC proposition caters for those consumers preferring the more traditional banking format, while First Direct caters for the new breed of telephone, online and texting customers.

Sources: 'Midland fails to bank on a third successive win', *Marketing*, 19 July 1990, p. 7; Mat Toor, 'Taxis fare well with First Direct', *Marketing*, 19 April 1990, p. 1; 'Banking industry report', Salomon Brothers, 1992; First Direct advertising, 1993; First Direct fact file, 1993; Beverly Crany, 'Reading your MIND', *Marketing*, 22 February 1996, pp. 33–4; HSBC, 1999; Fujitsu, 2003; HSBC, 2004; www.firstdirect.com, 2004–2008.

❓ *Questions for Discussion*

1 Why is innovation in marketing channels generally difficult to achieve?
2 Why was First Direct different from its rivals? What gave it differentiation when it first launched?
3 Why might some potential customers of First Direct have reservations about the innovative nature of the service?

12
Pricing Concepts

"The task of setting a price is one of the most important decisions in determining the marketing mix."

Peter Leeflang, Rijksuniversiteit Groningen

Price
The value placed on what is exchanged

Financial price
The basis of market exchanges; the quantified value of what is exchanged

Objectives

- **To understand the characteristics and role of price**

- **To be aware of the differences between price and non-price competition**

- **To explore key factors that affect pricing decisions**

- **To examine different pricing objectives**

- **To understand perceived value for money and how it affects consumers' decisions**

- **To consider issues unique to the pricing of products for business markets**

- **To analyse the concept of economic value to the customer**

- **To appreciate the stages for setting prices**

Introduction

To a buyer, **price** is the value placed on what is exchanged.[1] Something of value – usually buying power – is exchanged for satisfaction or utility. In most marketing situations, the price is very evident, and buyer and seller are aware of the amount of value each must give up to complete the exchange.[2] As described in Chapter 3, buying power depends on a buyer's income, credit and wealth. Because buyers have limited resources they must weigh up the usefulness of a product or the satisfaction derived from it against its cost to decide whether the exchange is worthwhile. **Financial price** is most usually the basis of market exchanges. This can be used to quantify almost anything of value that is exchanged, including ideas, services, rights and goods. Thus the financial value of a Paris penthouse might be 1.5 million euros. Yet price does not always have to have a financial basis. Barter, the trading of products, is the oldest form of exchange.

Price impacts strongly on how organisations fare competitively, so marketers need to give careful consideration to pricing issues. Price is critical to the marketing mix because it affects directly how much revenue is generated. As it can be changed very quickly, price is more flexible than other marketing mix elements. Organisations must avoid seeing price purely in terms of setting monetary price points. Because of the psychological impact of price on customers, price also has a symbolic value. It is therefore desirable to take a broader view of pricing, which takes into account issues such as target customers' perceptions of value for money and requirements for easy payment terms. There are essential stages for establishing prices, as outlined at the conclusion of this chapter.

Opener

Shoe Buying: What's Afoot?

Some people are just fanatical about shoes. Women are apparently particularly vulnerable to this passion. The launch of glossy magazine *Shoo*, featuring the latest in shoe designs and accessories, was testament to the depth of feeling footwear attracts. Some believe that this attraction can be traced back to the days when, as little girls, these women were fascinated with donning their mother's best stilettos and turning out the intriguing contents of their handbags. Of course, the current obsession with shoes is not new. Marie-Antoinette was said to have owned around 500 pairs of footwear, while the shoe collection of Imelda Marcos (reportedly numbering more than 1000 pairs) remains legendary.

Today's interest in footwear follows a resurgence in interest during the 1990s, with the best shoe designers achieving similar levels of acclaim to clothes designers. Pop stars and style icons have helped bring the need for perfectly attired toes to the attention of the current shoe-buying public. In the hit TV comedy series *Sex And The City*, the hugely popular character Carrie was almost as famous for her shoes as for her relationships. For those with particularly large shoe collections, the trend is to adhere photographs of the contents of each shoe box to the front of the container so that the required pair can be accessed readily. Among the most aspirational of brands are Manolo Blahnik, Jimmy Choo and Christian Louboutin. With prices ranging from several hundred pounds upwards, designer shoe brands are not a passion that everyone can afford.

Yet while some shoe aficionados are prepared to commit their savings and join waiting lists to acquire the latest prestigious offerings from the best designers, other women happily shop for more modest footwear in their local shopping centres. Some prefer to buy good quality but much cheaper high street brands. For example, styles by manufacturers like Clarkes, K Shoes and Seibel start from below £50 (€75). Other buyers spend time and effort tracking down even lower prices. As those frequenting markets around Europe can testify, bargain prices of less than £10 (€15) can readily be found. So why is it that some women are prepared to commit up to a month's pay for a pair of designer shoes that they may wear on only a handful of occasions? What is it that drives these individuals to fill every available space in their homes with the latest designs? Why, at the other extreme, are other shoes buyers apparently just as happy to adopt more price-conscious solutions to their footwear needs? And, why are many men completely disinterested in shoe buying?

Sources: Robina Dam, 'Head over heels', *Hildon Magazine*, Autumn/Winter 2003, pp. 20–3; John Roedder, Selfridges, London, January 2008. Photo: Istockphoto.com

All shoe companies, irrespective of whether their products are costly or cheap, use price, along with other elements, to distinguish their products from competitive brands. For these companies, as for most organisations, pricing is a crucial element in the marketing mix. However, as this chapter's 'Opener' clearly illustrates, a variety of factors impact upon pricing decisions. For example, perceptions about price vary for different shoe buying consumers. This and other factors affecting pricing are considered later in this chapter.

This chapter begins by explaining what is meant by price and considers its importance to marketing practitioners. It then explores pricing objectives and the various factors affecting pricing decisions. The notion of perceived value for money is considered next. The chapter then examines pricing in business markets and the concept of economic value to the customer, and concludes by over-viewing the essential stages for organisations when establishing prices.

The Characteristics and Role of Price

Terms Used to Describe Price

Price is expressed differently in different exchanges. For instance, insurance companies charge a *premium* to holidaymakers requiring protection against the cost of illness or injury. A police officer who stops a motorist for speeding writes a ticket that requires a *fine* to be paid. In London, a congestion *charge* is levied on motorists travelling in central areas. An accountant charges a *fee*, and a *fare* is charged for travelling by plane, railway or taxi. A *toll* is sometimes charged for the use of motorway bridges. *Rent* is paid for the use of equipment or for a flat. An estate agent receives a *commission* on the sale of a property. A *deposit* is made to reserve merchandise. A *tip* helps pay waitresses or waiters for their services. *Interest* is charged for loans, and *taxes* are paid for government services. The value of many products is called *price*.

Although price may be expressed in a variety of ways, it is important to remember that the purpose of this concept is to quantify and express the value of the items in a marketing exchange.

The Importance of Price to Marketers

As pointed out in Chapter 9, developing a product may be a lengthy process. It takes time to plan promotion and to communicate benefits. Distribution usually requires a long-term commitment to dealers who will handle the product. Often price and customer service levels are the only aspects a marketer can change quickly to respond to changes in demand or to the actions of competitors. However, as customers may be alienated by significant price changes, this does not mean that price is flexible in all situations.

Price is also a key element in the marketing mix because it relates directly to the generation of total revenue.[3] The following equation is an important one for the entire organisation:

Profits = total revenues − total costs
or
Profits = (price × quantities sold) − total costs

Prices can have a dramatic impact on a company's profits. Price affects the profit equation in several ways. It directly influences the equation because it is a major component. It has an indirect impact because it can be a major determinant of the quantities sold. Even more indirectly, price influences total costs through its impact on quantities sold.[4]

Table 12.1 illustrates clearly the link between price and a company's profitability. As the table shows, for an organisation with a 40 per cent contribution margin and a 10 per cent net profit, even a relatively small change in the prices set can have a major impact on profit levels. Thus a 10 per cent reduction in price would cause profits to fall to zero, while a 10 per cent rise would double the level of profitability. It is also important to consider that a 10 per cent increase or decrease in volume would have a rather smaller impact on profits. Marketers need to be fully aware of these stark relationships when setting prices. In particular, this example

TABLE 12.1 THE IMPORTANCE OF PRICE CHANGE TO PROFITABILITY

Income statement: Alpha Products

	£ million	
Turnover		200
Discounts and allowances	30	
Materials	30	
Direct labour	40	
Other variable costs	20	–
Profit contribution		80
Marketing and advertising	10	
Research and development	10	
Fixed costs	40	–
Net profit		20

Sensitivity analysis: Effect of 10% changes in price and costs on varying assumptions about volume losses.

	Change in profits £m (+%)		
	Volume loss		
Change in	**0%**	**−10%**	**−15%**
Price (+10%)	20 (100)	10 (50)[1]	5 (25)
Total overhead (−10%)	6 (30)	−2 (−10)[2]	−6 (−30)
R & D (−10%)	1 (5)	−7 (−35)	−11 (−55)
Marketing and advertising (−10%)	1 (5)	−7 (−35)	−11 (−55)
Fixed costs (−10%)	4 (20)	−7 (−35)	−11 (−55)
Volume (+10%)	8 (40)	– –	– –

Notes: [1]For example, if prices are increased by 10% and volume falls as a result by 10%, then profits rise by £10m (or +50%).

[2]If total overhead costs are cut by 10% (£6m) and volume falls as a result by 10%, then profits fall by £2m (−10%).

Source: P. Doyle, *Marketing Management and Strategy*. Copyright © 1998 Prentice-Hall Europe.

illustrates the difficulty faced by organisations attempting to build a differential advantage based on low prices.

Because price has a psychological impact on customers, marketers can use it symbolically. By raising a price, they can emphasise the quality of a product and try to increase the status associated with its ownership. The declining fortunes of Chevas Royal Scotch whisky were reversed following a substantial price rise. Lowering a price can also have a dramatic impact on demand, attracting bargain-hunting customers who are prepared to spend extra time and effort to save a small amount.

Price and Non-price Competition

A product offering can compete on either a price or a non-price basis. The choice will affect not only pricing decisions and activities but also those associated with other marketing mix decision variables.

Price Competition

Price competition
A policy whereby a marketer emphasises price as an issue, and matches or beats the prices of competitors

When **price competition** is used, a marketer emphasises price as an issue, and matches or beats competitors' prices (see Figure 12.1). Budget airline easyJet engages in price competition and stresses its low prices in its advertisements. To compete effectively on a price basis, a company should be the low-cost producer of the product. If all companies producing goods in an industry charge the same, the company with the lowest costs is the most profitable. Companies that stress low price as a key element in the marketing mix tend to produce standardised products. For example, suppliers of fuel oils use price competition. Sellers using this approach may be prepared and able to change prices frequently, particularly in response to competitors altering their prices. In many parts of the world, the postal service and UPS or DHL engage in direct price competition in their pricing of overnight express-delivery services.

Price competition gives a marketer flexibility. Prices can be altered to account for changes in the company's costs or in demand for the product, or when competitors cut prices. However, a major drawback of price competition is that competitors may also have the flexibility to adjust their prices to match or beat another company's price cuts. If so, a

Figure 12.1
Retailers' prominent use of 'sales' is a well known example of price competition
Photo: Courtesy of Karen Beaulah

355

price war may result. Furthermore, if a user of price competition is forced to raise prices, competing companies may decide not to do the same. As the 1990s drew to a close, the supermarket giants were locked into a spiral of price competition. Sainsbury's was promoting low prices across hundreds of popular product lines in an attempt to claw back market share from Tesco. Tesco's response was to launch a low-price promotion of its own.[5] **EDLP**[6] (everyday low pricing) is a form of price competition, funded by reducing promotions budgets so that retail prices can be cut while retailers' margins remain static. Companies like Procter & Gamble have attempted to strengthen consumer loyalty by cutting the prices of key brands permanently. The first two categories to benefit were the core markets of washing-up liquids, such as Fairy Liquid, and disposable nappies, such as Pampers.

EDLP
Everyday low pricing; budget savings passed on by the manufacturer to the consumer through reduced prices

Non-price Competition

Non-price competition
A policy in which a seller elects not to focus on price but to emphasise other factors instead

In **non-price competition**, a seller elects not to focus on price but instead emphasises distinctive product features, service, product quality, promotion, packaging or other factors to distinguish the product from competing brands, for example Figure 12.2. As the Marketing Insight box shows below, price is not always the key factor for customers in deciding what to buy. Organisations that use non-price competition aim to increase unit sales in other ways. For example, Dom Perignon champagne stresses the heritage and quality of its champagnes, rather than competitive price. A company can use non-price competition to build customer loyalty towards its brand. If customers prefer a brand or store because of non-price issues,

♻ Marketing Insight

Do Low Prices Build e-loyalty?

Throughout the Internet's short history, many e-businesses have come to believe that online customers are interested only in paying the lowest possible prices. Now this myth has been exploded by research showing that companies can more effectively strengthen e-loyalty and counteract price sensitivity by building trust and enhancing the customer's shopping experience.

When the consulting business Bain & Company studied e-loyalty, it found that online shoppers are generally more interested in convenience than in price, and tend to be loyal to sites that fulfil the promise of simplifying the buying process. Therefore, e-businesses need to build trust among new customers by projecting an image of reliability and responsiveness. In return, as customers learn to trust a site, they become willing to provide more personal information, make repeat purchases and voluntarily refer new customers. Industrial supply company Granger, for example, provides a convenient search tool and knowledgeable phone representatives to help business customers find just the right products among the one million items available on its website. Customers spend less time searching for what they want, and they can check out quickly – benefits they value more than paying a rock-bottom price for a particular product.

In another study, McKinsey & Company, a consulting company, found that few online shoppers take the time to compare prices on every product they want to buy. In fact, 89 per cent of book buyers and 84 per cent of toy buyers actually buy at the first site they visit rather than clicking from site to site seeking the lowest price. As long as they perceive a site's prices to be within a reasonable range, customers will go ahead and make the purchase. What consumers consider a reasonable price range varies from product to product. McKinsey found that although e-businesses could raise prices up to 17 per cent on brand-name beauty products without losing customers, buyers balked at a price increase of less than 1 per cent on certain financial services.

To avoid a backlash, e-businesses – as for any selling organisation – need to conduct ongoing research to analyse each segment's price sensitivity and to test customer reactions carefully before implementing price changes. With the right pricing, and the right mix of trust and convenience, companies can attract new customers and strengthen e-loyalty year after year to build sales and profits, as in the case of online grocery businesses Ocado or Tesco.com, Amazon or eBay.

Sources: W. Pride and O.C. Ferrell, *Marketing: Concepts and Strategies*, 2003, Boston: Houghton Mifflin; 'Top Internet Sites by Category', *The Marketing Pocket Book 2008*, Henley: The Advertising Association/WARC, p. 237.

they may not easily be lured away by competing offers. Indeed, such customers might become confused or irritated if price cuts are offered. Buyers of Chanel clothing, perfume or accessories enjoy the exclusivity associated with the high price. The implication is that price is not the most durable factor in terms of maintaining customer loyalty. However, when price is the primary reason that customers buy a particular brand, the competition can attract such customers through price cuts.

Non-price competition is workable under the right conditions. A company must be able to distinguish its brand through unique product features, higher quality, customer service, promotion, packaging and the like (see Figure 12.2). The brand's distinguishing features should be difficult, if not impossible, for a competitor to copy. Buyers must not only be able to perceive these distinguishing characteristics but must also view them as desirable. Finally, the organisation must promote the distinguishing characteristics of the brand extensively in order to establish its superiority and to set it apart from competitors in the minds of buyers.

Figure 12.2
Although priced to be competitive with rival brands, Comfort Vaporesse promotes functional product benefits
Source: COMFORT and VAPORESSE are registered trade marks of Unilever

Many European companies put less emphasis on price than do their American counterparts. They look for a competitive edge by concentrating on promotion, research and development, marketing research and marketing channel considerations. In a study of pricing strategy, many companies stated specifically that they emphasise research and development and technological superiority; competition based on price was seldom a major marketing consideration.[7]

A marketer attempting to compete on a non-price basis must still consider competitors' prices. The organisation must be aware of competitors' prices and will probably price its brand near, or slightly above, competing brands. As an example, Sony sells television sets in a highly competitive market and charges higher prices than other manufacturers for them. Sony can achieve these because its emphasis on high product quality distinguishes it from its competitors and allows it to set higher prices.

Factors Affecting Pricing Decisions

Pricing decisions are affected by many factors. Often, there is considerable uncertainty about reactions to price on the part of buyers, channel members, competitors and others. Price is also an important consideration in marketing planning, market analysis and sales forecasting. It is a major issue when assessing a brand's positioning relative to competing brands. Most factors that affect pricing decisions can be grouped into one of the nine categories shown in Figure 12.3. This section explores how each of these nine groups of factors enters into price decision-making.

Organisational and Marketing Objectives

Marketers should set prices that are consistent with the organisation's goals and mission. For example, cosmetic brands such as Chanel and Helena Rubenstein are positioned at the exclusive end of the market, and have high price tags to match. Marketers in these organisations know that discounting prices on these brands would not be in line with the overall organisational goal.

Decision-makers should also make pricing decisions that are compatible with the organisation's marketing objectives. Say, for instance, that one of a producer's marketing objectives

Figure 12.3
Factors that affect pricing decisions

is a 12 per cent increase in unit sales by the end of the next year. Assuming that buyers are price sensitive, increasing the price or setting a price above the average market price would not be in line with the company's sales objective. A case in point: GM (Vauxhall) has introduced high-performance, well-specified model variants to the top of each of its model ranges – for example, the £25,000 Vectra VXR V6 and the £21,000 Astra Nurburgring Edition. Such prices ensure that these particular models have only limited appeal. GM's stated objective, however, is to be market leader in terms of sales volume. The company, therefore, is careful to price the great majority of its cars in line with the price expectations of the bulk of the car buying public and fleet operators – far below these £25,000 Vectra and £21,000 Astra levels.

Pricing Objectives

Pricing objectives
Overall goals that describe what a company wants to achieve through its pricing efforts

Pricing objectives are overall goals that describe what a company wants to achieve through its pricing efforts. The type of pricing objective a marketer uses will have considerable bearing on the determination of prices.[8] Marketers often use multiple pricing objectives, including those that emphasise survival, profit, return on investment, market share, cash flow, status quo or product quality (see Table 12.2). Thus a market share pricing objective usually causes a company to price a product below competing brands of similar quality to attract competitors' customers to the company's brand. This type of pricing can lead to lower profits, but may be used temporarily in the hope of gaining market share. By contrast, a cash flow pricing objective may involve setting a relatively high price, which can place the product at a competitive disadvantage. Paradoxically, a cash flow pricing objective sometimes results in a low price sustained in the long term. However, this type of objective is more likely to be addressed by using temporary price reductions, such as sales, refunds and special discounts.

Because pricing objectives influence decisions in most functional areas – including finance, accounting and production – the objectives must be consistent with the company's overall mission and purpose (see Chapter 2). Banking is an area where pricing is a major concern. As competition has intensified, bank executives have realised that their products must be priced to meet both short-term profit goals and long-term strategic objectives. Changes in the pricing objectives that companies use can occur for various reasons. For example, the objective of return on investment may be used less as managers and marketers in diversified companies stress the creation of shareholder value. When shareholder value is used as a performance objective, strategies – including those involving price – are evaluated according to their impact on the value investors perceive in the company.[9]

Costs

Obviously, costs must be an issue when establishing price. An organisation may temporarily sell products below cost to match the competition, to generate cash flow or even to increase market share; but in the long run it cannot survive by adopting this approach. A marketer should be careful to analyse all costs so that they can be included in the total costing for a product.

Marketers must also take into account the costs that a particular product shares with other products in the product line, particularly the costs of research and development, production and distribution. Services are especially subject to cost sharing. For example, the costs of a bank building are spread over the costs of all services the bank offers.[10] Most marketers view a product's cost as a minimum, or floor, below which the product cannot be priced.

Other Marketing Mix Variables

All marketing mix variables are closely interrelated. Pricing decisions can influence decisions and activities associated with product, place/distribution, promotion and customer service variables. A product's price frequently affects the demand for the item. A high price, for instance, may result in low unit sales, which in turn may lead to higher production costs per unit. Conversely, lower per-unit production costs may result from a low price. For many products, buyers associate better product quality with a high price and poorer product quality with a low price. This perceived price–quality relationship influences customers'

TABLE 12.2 DIFFERENT TYPES OF PRICING OBJECTIVE

Survival

A fundamental pricing objective is survival. Most organisations will tolerate difficulties such as short-run losses and internal upheaval if they are necessary for survival. Because price is a flexible and convenient variable to adjust, it is sometimes used to increase sales volume to levels that match the company's expenses.

Profit

Although organisations often claim they aim to maximise profits, in practice this objective is difficult to measure. As a result, profit objectives tend to be set at satisfactory levels. Specific profit objectives may be stated in terms of actual monetary amounts or in terms of percentage change relative to previous profits.

Return on investment

Pricing to attain a specified rate of return on the company's investment is a profit-related pricing objective. Most pricing objectives based on return on investment (ROI) are achieved by trial and error, because not all cost and revenue data needed to project the return on investment are available when prices are set.

Market share

Many companies establish pricing objectives to maintain or increase a product's market share in relation to total industry sales. For example, car companies such as Volkswagen have been known to cut prices on existing models when introducing new ones, to boost share of the car market. Maintaining or increasing market share need not depend on growth in industry sales. A company can increase its market share even though sales for the total industry are decreasing. On the other hand, if the overall market is growing, an organisation's sales volume may actually increase as its market share decreases.

Cash flow

Some companies set prices to recover cash as fast as possible, especially when a short product life cycle is anticipated or the capital spent to develop products needs to be recovered quickly. However, the use of cash flow and recovery as an objective over-simplifies the value of price in contributing to profits. A disadvantage of this pricing objective could be high prices, which might allow competitors with lower prices to gain a large share of the market.

Status quo

In some cases, an organisation may be in a favourable position and may simply wish to maintain the status quo. Such objectives can focus on maintaining a certain market share, meeting (but not beating) competitors' prices, achieving price stability or maintaining a favourable public image. Such an approach can reduce a company's risks by helping to stabilise demand for its products. The use of status quo pricing objectives sometimes leads to a climate of non-price competition in an industry.

Product quality

A company might have the objective of product quality leadership in the industry. For example, the construction equipment manufacturer JCB aims to be ranked as one of the leading companies in its industry in terms of product quality and customer satisfaction.[11] This normally dictates a relatively high price to cover the high product quality and/or the high cost of research and development.

overall image of products or brands. Thus consumers may be prepared to pay a high price for designer sunglasses because they believe they are a high-status item.

Pricing decisions influence the number of competing brands in a product category. When a company introduces a product, sets a relatively high price and achieves high unit sales, competitors may be attracted to this product category. If a company fixes a low price, the low profit margin may be unattractive to potential competition.

The price of a product is linked to several dimensions of its distribution. Premium-priced products are often marketed through selective or exclusive distribution; lower-priced products in the same product category may be sold through intensive distribution. For example, Montblanc pens are distributed through selective distribution and Bic pens through intensive distribution. The way in which a product is stored and transported may also be associated with its price. As Figure 12.4 shows, when deciding about a product's price, a producer must consider the profit margins of marketing channel members such as wholesalers and retailers. This way, channel members can be adequately compensated for the functions they perform.

The way a product is promoted can be affected by its price. Bargain prices are often included in advertisements, whereas premium prices are less likely to be mentioned. However, the exclusivity associated with a premium price is sometimes included in advertisements for upmarket items, such as luxury holidays or exclusive jewellery. Higher-priced

Figure 12.4
Wholesaler and retailer considerations when developing price

products are more likely to require personal selling efforts than lower-priced ones. Indeed, there may be an expectation that a high price is accompanied by enhanced levels of customer service. A customer may purchase an inexpensive watch in a self-service environment but hesitate to buy an expensive watch in the same store, even if it is available there.

The price structure can affect a salesperson's relationship with customers. A complex pricing structure takes longer to explain to customers, is more likely to confuse the buyer and may cause misunderstandings that result in long-term customer dissatisfaction. For example, the pricing structure used by many hotels is complex and can confuse potential guests.

Channel Member Expectations

When making price decisions, a producer must consider what distribution channel members (such as wholesalers, retailers and dealers) expect. A channel member certainly expects to receive a profit for the functions performed. The amount of profit expected depends on the amount of time and resources expended, and on an assessment of what would be gained by handling a competing product instead.

Channel members often expect producers to provide discounts for large orders and quick payment. (Discounts are discussed later in this chapter.) At times, resellers expect producers to provide support activities, such as sales training, repair advisory services, cooperative advertising, sales promotions and perhaps a programme for returning unsold merchandise to the producer. These support activities clearly incur costs, so a producer must consider these costs when determining prices.

Buyers' Perceptions

When making pricing decisions, marketers should be concerned with two vital questions.

1 How will customers interpret prices and respond to them? Interpretation in this context refers to what the price means or what it communicates to customers. Does the price mean 'high quality' or 'low quality', or 'great deal', 'fair price' or 'rip-off'?

2 How will customers respond to the price? Customer response refers to whether the price will move customers closer to the purchase of the product and the degree to which the price enhances their satisfaction with the purchase experience and with the product after purchase.

Customers' interpretation of and response to a price are to some degree determined by their assessment of what they receive compared with what they give up to make the purchase. In evaluating what they receive, customers will consider product attributes, benefits, advantages, disadvantages, the probability of using the product, and possibly the status associated with the product. In assessing the cost of the product, customers will consider its price, the amount of time and effort required to obtain the product, and perhaps the resources required to maintain or use the product after purchase.

At times, customers interpret a higher price as higher product quality. They are especially likely to make this price–quality association when they cannot judge the quality of the product themselves. This is not always the case: whether price is equated with quality depends on the types of customer and product involved. Obviously, marketers relying on customers making a price–quality association who are providing moderate or low-quality products at high prices, will be unable to build long-term customer relationships.

Internal reference price
A price developed in the buyer's mind through experience with the product

External reference price
A comparison price provided by others

When interpreting and responding to prices, how do customers determine if the price is too high, too low or about right? In general, they compare prices with internal or external reference prices. An **internal reference price** is a price developed in the buyer's mind through experience with the product. It is a belief that a product should cost approximately a certain amount. As consumers, previous experiences provide internal reference prices for a number of products. For example, most consumers have a reasonable idea of how much to pay for a can of soft drink, a loaf of bread or a litre of milk. When there is less experience, consumers rely more heavily on external reference prices.[12] An **external reference price** is a comparison price provided by others, such as retailers or manufacturers.[13]

Customers' perceptions of prices are also influenced by their expectations about future price increases, by what they paid for the product recently, and by what they would like to pay for the product. Other factors affecting customers' perception of whether the price is right include time or financial constraints, the costs associated with searching for lower-priced products, and expectations that products will go on sale.

Buyers' perceptions of a product relative to competing products may allow an organisation to set a price that differs significantly from rivals' prices. If the product is deemed superior to most of the competition, a premium price may be feasible. However, even products with superior quality can be over-priced. Strong brand loyalty sometimes provides the opportunity to charge a premium price. On the other hand, if buyers view a product less than favourably – though not extremely negatively – a lower price may generate sales.

In the context of price, buyers can be characterised according to their degree of value consciousness, price consciousness, and prestige sensitivity. Marketers who understand these characteristics are better able to set pricing objectives and policies. **Value-conscious consumers** are concerned about both the price and the quality of a product. **Price-conscious consumers** strive to pay low prices. **Prestige sensitive consumers** focus on purchasing products that signify prominence and status. For example, the Porsche Cayenne, one of the highest-priced sports utility vehicles ever marketed, created record sales and profits for Porsche. Only 18 per cent of Cayenne buyers had previously owned a Porsche; many of the rest were attracted to the vehicle by the prestige associated with the Porsche name. On the other hand, some consumers vary in their degree of value, price and prestige consciousness. In some segments, consumers are increasingly 'trading up' to more status-conscious products: this occurs with cars, electrical appliances, restaurants and even pet food. This trend has benefited companies such as Starbucks and BMW, which can charge premium prices for high quality, prestige products.

Competition

A marketer needs to know competitors' prices so that a company can adjust its own prices accordingly.[14] This does not mean that a company will necessarily match competitors' prices; it may set its price above or below theirs. It is also important for marketers to assess how competitors will respond to price adjustments. Will they change their prices (some may not) and, if so, will they raise or lower them? For example, when motor insurance providers stress their keen pricing, competitors often do the same.

Chapter 3 describes several types of competitive market structure that impact upon price setting. When a company operates as a monopoly and is unregulated, it can set whatever prices the market will bear. However, the company may avoid adopting the highest possible pricing for fear of inviting government regulation or because it wants to penetrate a market by using a lower price. If the monopoly is regulated, it normally has less pricing flexibility; the regulatory body lets it set prices that generate a reasonable, but not excessive, return. A government-owned monopoly may price products below cost to make them accessible to people who could not otherwise afford them. However, government-owned monopolies sometimes charge higher prices to control demand.

In an oligopoly, only a few sellers operate, and there are high barriers to competitive entry. An organisation in such an industry – for example, telecommunications, drugs or steel – can raise its price, hoping that its competitors will do the same. Very little can be gained through price cuts because other companies are likely to follow suit when an organisation cuts its price to gain a competitive edge.

A market structure characterised by monopolistic competition means numerous sellers with differentiated product offerings. The products are differentiated by physical characteristics, features, quality and brand image. The distinguishing characteristics of its product may allow a company to set a different price from its competitors. However, organisations engaged in a monopolistic competitive market structure are likely to practise non-price competition, as discussed earlier in this chapter.

Value-conscious consumers
Those concerned about price and quality of a product

Price-conscious consumers
Those striving to pay low prices

Prestige sensitive consumers
Individuals drawn to products that signify prominence and status

Perceived value for money
The benefit consumers perceive to be inherent in a product or service, weighed against the price demanded

Trade or **functional discount**
A reduction off the list price given by a producer to an intermediary for performing certain functions

Quantity discounts
Reductions off the list price that reflect the economies of purchasing in large quantities

Cumulative discounts
Quantity discounts aggregated over a stated period of time

Non-cumulative discounts
One-off quantity discounts

Under conditions of perfect competition, there are many sellers. Buyers view all sellers' products as the same. All companies sell their products at the going market price and so there is no flexibility in setting prices.

Legal and Regulatory Issues

At times, government action sways marketers' pricing decisions. To curb inflation, the government may invoke price controls, 'freeze' prices at certain levels or determine the rates at which prices can be increased. Following the privatisation of public utilities, the UK government set up regulatory bodies such as Ofwat for water and Oftel (now OFCOM) for telecommunications, which stressed minimum and maximum charges.

Many regulations and laws affect pricing decisions and activities. Not only must marketers refrain from fixing prices, they must also develop independent pricing policies and set prices in ways that do not involve collusion. Over the years, legislation has been established to safeguard consumers and businesses from pricing sharp practices. In the UK, the Competition Commission prevents the creation of monopolistic situations. The consumer is protected by the Trade Descriptions Act, the Fair Trading Act, the Consumer Protection Act and many others. All countries have similar legislation, and the European Union legislates to protect consumers within the community.

Perceived Value

Most discussions about pricing revolve around the actual monetary value – the price – to be charged for the good or service. However, the **perceived value for money** to consumers is also vital. This is the benefit consumers see as inherent in a product or service, weighed against the price demanded. Sometimes, particularly in consumer markets, these benefits are real and measurable, in other cases they are more psychological. For instance, interest-free credit, maintenance contracts and extended warranties are all features that may affect a consumer's perception of value for money. Consumers will not pay more than they value the benefit inherent in a product or service. Consumers balance the price demanded, typically in monetary terms, against the anticipated level of use and satisfaction to be gained from buying and using the specific product. This assessment is influenced by the consumers' previous experience of the brand and similar products, the perceived quality of the product in question, its brand image, purpose, anticipated usage, overall appeal and the nature of competing offers. These emotive issues are often difficult to quantify, but through qualitative marketing research, most organisations are able to assess their target market's views of value.

Pricing for Business Markets

As explored in Chapter 5, business markets consist of individuals and organisations that purchase products for resale, for use in their own operations or for producing other products. Establishing prices for this category of business-to-business buyer sometimes differs from setting prices for consumers. Differences in the size of purchases, geographic factors and transport considerations require sellers to adjust prices. This section discusses several issues unique to the pricing of industrial products and business markets including discounts, geographic pricing, transfer pricing and price discrimination. The section concludes by considering the concept of economic value to the customer (EVC).

Price Discounting

Producers commonly provide intermediaries with discounts from list prices. Although there are many types of discount, they usually fall into one of five categories (see Table 12.3):

Cash discount
A simple price reduction given to a buyer for prompt payment or payment in cash

1 trade
2 quantity
3 cash discounts
4 seasonal discounts
5 allowances.

TABLE 12.3 DISCOUNTS USED FOR BUSINESS MARKETS

Type	Reason for use	Practical examples
Trade (functional)	To attract and keep resellers by compensating them for certain functions, such as transportation, warehousing, selling and providing credit	A university bookstore pays about a third less for a new textbook than the retail price paid by a student
Quantity	To encourage customers to buy large quantities and, in the case of cumulative discounts, to encourage customer loyalty	Large chains of tyre and exhaust outlets purchase parts at lower prices than individually owned outlets
Cash	To reduce expenses associated with accounts receivable by encouraging prompt payment	Companies operating in business markets often offer a discount for prompt payment
Seasonal	To allow resources to be used more efficiently by stimulating sales during off-peak periods	Hotels in large cities offer companies discounted accommodation for sales and other conferences during off-peak periods
Allowance	For trade-in allowances, the buyer is assisted in making the purchase by getting money back on used equipment; for promotional allowances, dealers are able to participate in advertising and sales support programmes	Companies such as Nabisco or Masterproofs pay promotional allowances to supermarkets for setting up and maintaining end-of-aisle displays to push their products

Seasonal discount
A price reduction given to buyers who purchase goods or services out of season

Allowance
A concession in price to achieve a desired goal

Geographic pricing
Pricing that involves reductions for transport costs or other costs associated with the physical distance between the buyer and the seller

FOB factory price
The price of the merchandise at the factory before it is loaded on to the carrier vehicle, which must be paid by the buyer

Trade Discounts   A reduction off the list price given by a producer to an intermediary for performing certain functions is called a **trade** or **functional discount**. The functions for which intermediaries are compensated may include selling, transporting, storing, final processing and perhaps providing credit services. The level of discount can vary considerably from one industry to another.

Quantity Discounts   Reductions from the list price that reflect the economies of purchasing in large quantities are called **quantity discounts**. Cost savings usually occur in four areas. Fewer but larger orders reduce per-unit selling costs; fixed costs, such as invoicing, remain the same or go down; raw materials costs are lower, because quantity discounts may be available; longer production runs mean no increases in holding costs.[15] In addition, a large purchase may shift some of the storage, finance and risk-taking functions to the buyer.

Quantity discounts can be either cumulative or non-cumulative. **Cumulative discounts** are aggregated over a stated period of time. Purchases of £10,000 (€15,000) in a three-month period, for example, might entitle the buyer to a 5 per cent, or £500 (€750), rebate. Such discounts are supposed to reflect economies in selling and encourage the buyer to purchase from one seller. **Non-cumulative discounts** are one-off reductions in prices based on the number of units purchased, the monetary value of the order or the product mix purchased.

Cash Discounts   A **cash discount**, or simple price reduction, is given for prompt payment or payment in cash. A policy to encourage prompt payment is a popular practice in setting prices. For example, '2/10 net 30' means that a 2 per cent discount will be allowed if the account is paid within 10 days. However, if the buyer does not pay within the 10-day period, the entire balance is due within 30 days without a discount. If the account is not paid within 30 days, interest may be charged.

FOB destination price
A price quotation indicating that the producer absorbs the costs of shipping the merchandise

Uniform geographic pricing
Pricing in which the same price is charged to all customers regardless of geographic location

Seasonal Discounts   A price reduction given to buyers who purchase goods or services out of season is a **seasonal discount**. These discounts let the seller maintain steadier production during the year. For example, hotels in holiday resorts offer seasonal discounts at times of year when the weather is poor.

Allowances   Another type of reduction from the list price is an **allowance** – a concession in price to achieve a desired goal. Trade-in allowances are price reductions granted for handing in a used item when purchasing a new one. This type of allowance is popular in the aircraft industry. Another example is promotional allowances, which are price reductions granted to dealers for participating in advertising and sales support programmes intended to increase sales of a particular item.

Geographic Pricing

Zone prices
Regional prices that take advantage of a uniform pricing system

Base point pricing
A geographic pricing policy that includes the price at the factory, plus freight charges from the base point nearest the buyer

Freight absorption pricing
A pricing policy in which the seller absorbs all or part of the actual freight costs

Geographic pricing involves reductions for transport costs or other costs associated with the physical distance between the buyer and the seller. Prices may be quoted as being FOB (free-on-board) factory or destination. An **FOB factory price** indicates the price of the merchandise at the factory before it is loaded on to the carrier vehicle; it thus excludes transport costs. The buyer must pay for shipping. An **FOB destination price** means the producer absorbs the costs of shipping the merchandise to customers.

To avoid the problems involved in charging different prices to each customer, **uniform geographic** pricing, sometimes called postage stamp pricing, may be used. The same price is charged to all customers regardless of geographic location, and the price is based on average shipping costs for all customers. Petrol, paper products and office equipment are often priced on a uniform basis.

Zone prices are regional prices that take advantage of a uniform pricing system; prices are adjusted for major geographic zones as the transport costs increase. For example, the prices of a manufacturer located in the northern French town of Lille may be higher for buyers in the south of France than for buyers in Paris.

Base point pricing is a geographic pricing policy that includes the price at the factory, plus freight charges from the base point nearest the buyer. This policy, which is now rarely used, can result in all buyers paying freight charges from one location, regardless of where the product was manufactured!

When the seller absorbs all or part of the actual freight costs, **freight absorption pricing** is being used. The seller might choose this method because it wishes to do business with a particular customer or to get more business; more business will cause the average cost to fall and counter-balance the extra freight cost. This strategy is used to improve market penetration and to retain a hold in an increasingly competitive market.

Transfer Pricing

Transfer pricing
The type of pricing used when one unit in a company sells a product to another unit within the same company

When one unit in a company sells a product to another unit within the same company, **transfer pricing** occurs. The price is determined by one of the following methods.

- *Actual full cost* – calculated by dividing all fixed and variable expenses for a period into the number of units produced.
- *Standard full cost* – calculated on what it would cost to produce the goods at full plant capacity.
- *Cost plus investment* – calculated as full cost, plus the cost of a portion of the selling unit's assets used for internal needs.
- *Market based cost* – calculated at the market price less a small discount to reflect the lack of sales effort and other expenses.

The choice of transfer pricing method depends on the company's management strategy and the nature of the units' interaction. The company might initially choose to determine price by the actual full cost method but later move to an alternative method.[16]

Price Discrimination

Price discrimination
A policy in which different prices are charged in order to give a particular group of buyers a competitive edge

A policy of **price discrimination** results in different prices being charged to give a group of buyers a competitive edge. Some forms of price discrimination are illegal. In the USA, price differentials are legal only when customers are not in competition with one another. The EU is also keen to stamp out price discrimination.

Price differentiation is a form of market segmentation that companies use to provide a marketing mix that satisfies different segments. Because different market segments perceive the value of a particular product differently, depending on the product's importance and value to the business buyer, marketers may charge different prices to different market segments. Price discrimination can also be used to modify demand patterns, support sales of other products, dispose of obsolete goods or excessive inventories, fill excess production capacity and respond to competitors' activities in particular markets.[17]

Various conditions must be satisfied for price discrimination to be feasible. It must be possible to segment the market and the costs associated with doing so must not exceed the additional revenue generated. The practice should not break the law or breed customer discontent. Finally, the segment that is charged the higher price should not be vulnerable to competitor attack.

Economic Value to the Customer

Economic value to the customer (EVC)
The underlying principle that a premium price can be charged while still offering the customer better value than the competition

The relationship between price and profitability was considered briefly at the start of this chapter. It is already clear that the ability to charge a higher price can have a major impact on profitability. It is also apparent that in order to achieve higher prices, organisations must be able to offer the customer some kind of differential advantage. In business markets, this advantage must usually be measurable in economic terms because organisations are driven by the need to reduce costs and increase revenue. Thus a manufacturer of switch gears may be prepared to change to a more expensive supplier of fork-lift trucks if the products supplied have lower running costs. The concept of economic value to the customer encapsulates this notion and is a useful aid to determining prices in business markets. The underlying principle of **economic value to the customer (EVC)** is that a premium price can be charged while still offering the customer better value than the competition.

There are various reasons why a costly product may provide good economic value to the customer, including lower set-up or running costs, the provision of superior servicing or other after-sales support, or a better warranty deal. It is even possible that the life of the product may be longer or that its productivity may be greater than that of lower-priced alternatives. Whatever the reason behind the value on offer, if EVC is to be demonstrated, the initial high price of the product must be justified by an overall lower lifetime cost. The Marketing Tools and Techniques box below provides a worked example of how EVC works in practice.

⊛ Marketing Tools and Techniques

Business-to-business Pricing using EVC Analysis

Analysing economic value to the customer (EVC) is a useful aid to setting prices for business-to-business organisations. This example concerns the pricing of panel presses, which are supplied to the car parts business. The analysis focuses on the market leader and two other competitors.

The analysis begins by considering a reference product against which the costs of competing products are compared.

In this case, the market leader is used as the reference product. In this example, a car parts company buying the panel press from the market leader would expect to pay the following costs. The purchase price of the press is £60,000. Start-up costs such as installation charges, staff training and lost production during installation are £20,000, and post-purchase costs including operating costs such as labour, servicing/maintenance and power are £130,000.

This means that, over its life cycle, the panel press will cost the car parts company a total of £210,000.

Companies competing with the market leader present the customer with a different profile of costs. Company A has, by incorporating a number of new design features, managed to cut the start-up costs for a comparable panel press to £10,000 and reduced post-purchase costs to £105,000. This means that the total costs for the press are £35,000 less than those for the market leader. The result is that Company A's press offers the customer an EVC of £210,000 less £115,000, which equals £95,000. Assuming that Company A charged a purchase price of £95,000 for the panel press, the customer would face total life cycle costs that were equivalent to the market-leading product. If,

however, Company A decided to offer the panel press at a purchase price of only £80,000, the lower life cycle costs of the product would give the customer a considerable financial incentive to buy.

Consider the position of a second competitor, Company B, with similar start-up and post-purchase costs to the market leader. This company has, through certain technological advances, increased the rate at which the press can be operated, potentially increasing productivity and therefore revenue for the customer. As a result, the press has the potential to offer an additional £50,000 profit contribution over the presses of the market leader and Company A. The EVC associated with this is £110,000, because this is the highest price the customer may be expected to pay.

Stages for Establishing Prices

When going through the stages for establishing prices, marketers must be able to grasp target customers' evaluation of price and perceived value for money, as well as understand market trends and competitors' pricing moves.[18] The 'economics' of pricing – demand curves and price elasticity, plus the relationship in the market in question between demand, costs and profits – must also be addressed. The marketer must ultimately choose from a variety of pricing approaches and specific pricing strategies. Figure 12.5 outlines the eight stages for establishing prices. These stages are explained far more extensively in the authors' sister title *Marketing: Concepts and Strategies* (Boston: Houghton Mifflin, 2006).

The first stage, selecting pricing objectives, is critical because pricing objectives are the foundation on which the decisions of subsequent stages are based. Organisations may use numerous short and long term pricing objectives. The second stage in establishing prices is an assessment of the target market's evaluation of price and its ability to buy. This

Figure 12.5
Stages for establishing prices

shows how much emphasis to place on price and may help determine how far above the competition prices can be set. Understanding customers' buying power and the importance of a product to them in comparison with other products helps the target market's evaluation of price to be accurately assessed. In the third stage, an organisation must determine the demand for its product. The classic demand curve is a graph of the quantity of products expected to be sold at various prices, if other factors are held constant. It illustrates that, as price falls, the quantity demanded usually increases. However, for prestige products, there is a direct positive relationship between price and quantity demanded: up to a certain point demand increases as price increases. Next, price elasticity of demand – the percentage change in quantity demanded relative to a given percentage change in price – must be determined. If demand is elastic, a change in price causes an opposite change in total revenue. Inelastic demand results in a change in the same direction in total revenue when a product's price is changed.

Analysis of demand, cost and profit relationships – the fourth stage of the process – can be accomplished through marginal analysis or break even analysis. Marginal analysis is the examination of what happens to a company's costs and revenues when production (or sales volume) is changed by one unit. Marginal analysis combines the demand curve with a company's costs to develop an optimum price for maximum profit. The optimum price is the point at which marginal cost equals marginal revenue. Marginal analysis offers little help in pricing new products before costs and revenues are established. Break even analysis involves determining the number of units necessary to break even. The point at which the costs of producing a product equal the revenue made from selling the product is the break even point. To use break even analysis effectively, a marketer should determine the break even point for each of several alternative prices, so that the effects on total revenue, total cost and the break even point for each price can be considered. However, this approach assumes that the quantity demanded is basically fixed and that the major task is to set prices to recover costs.

A marketer needs to be aware of the prices charged for competing brands – the fifth stage. This allows a company to keep its prices the same as competitors' prices when non-price competition is used. If a company uses price as a competitive tool, it can price its brand or product below competing brands or products.

The sixth stage is the selection of a basis for pricing. The three major dimensions on which prices can be based are cost, demand and competition. In using **cost based pricing**, a company determines price by adding a monetary amount or percentage to the cost of the product. Two common cost based pricing approaches are known as cost plus pricing and mark-up pricing. **Demand based pricing** is based on the level of demand for a product and requires marketers to estimate the amounts of a product that buyers will demand at different prices, particularly if the company wishes to use **price differentiation** for a specific product. Demand based pricing results in a high price when demand for a product is strong and a low price when demand is weak. In the case of **competition based pricing**, costs and revenues are secondary to competitors' prices. Competition based pricing and cost approaches may be combined to arrive at price levels necessary to generate a profit. The increasingly popular **marketing oriented pricing** involves a company taking account of a wide range of factors including marketing strategy, competition, value to the customer, price-quality relationships, explicability, costs, product line pricing, negotiating margins, political factors and the effect on distributors/retailers.

A **pricing strategy** – stage seven – is an approach designed to achieve pricing and marketing objectives. The most common pricing strategies are differential pricing, new-product pricing, product-line pricing, psychological pricing, professional pricing, and promotional pricing. Using differential pricing involves charging different prices for the same quality or quantity of product. Negotiated pricing, secondary market discounting, periodic discounting and random discounting are forms of differentail pricing. Establishing

Cost based pricing
A pricing approach whereby a monetary amount or percentage is added to the cost of a product

Demand based pricing
A pricing approach based on the level of demand for a product, resulting in a high price when demand is strong and a low price when demand is weak

Price differentiation
A pricing strategy involving charging different prices to different buyers for the same quality and quantity of product

Competition based pricing
A pricing approach whereby an organisation considers costs and revenue to be secondary to competitors' prices

Marketing oriented pricing
A pricing approach whereby a company takes into account a wide range of factors including marketing strategy, competition, value to the customer, price – quality relationships, explicability, costs, product line pricing, negotiating margins, political factors and effect on distributors/retailers

Pricing strategy
An approach to influencing and determining pricing decisions

Price skimming
A pricing strategy whereby a company charges the highest possible price that buyers who most desire the product will pay

Penetration pricing
A pricing strategy of setting a price below the prices of competing brands in order to penetrate a market and produce a larger unit sales volume

Psychological pricing
A pricing strategy designed to encourage purchases that are based on emotional rather than rational responses

Promotional pricing
Pricing related to the short-term promotion of a particular product

the final price through bargaining between seller and customer is negotiated pricing. Secondary market pricing involves setting one price for the primary target market and a different price for another market. Marketers employ a strategy of periodic discounting when they temporarily lower their prices on a systematic basis. Random discounting occurs on an unsystematic basis. Two strategies used in new product pricing are price skimming and penetration pricing. With **price skimming**, a company charges the highest price that buyers who most desire the product will pay. **Penetration pricing** sets a price below the prices of competing brands in order to penetrate the market and produce a larger unit sales volume. Product line pricing establishes and adjusts the prices of multiple products within a product line. This strategy includes captive pricing, in which the marketer prices the basic product in a product line low but prices related items at a higher level; premium pricing, in which prices on higher-quality or more versatile products are set higher than those on other models in the product line; bait pricing, in which the marketer tries to attract customers by pricing an item in the product line low with the intention of selling a higher-priced item in the line; and price lining, in which the organisation sets a limited number of prices for selected groups or lines of merchandise.

Psychological pricing, encourages purchases that are based on emotional rather than rational responses. In referencing pricing marketers price a product at a moderate level and position it next to a more expensive model or brand. Bundle pricing is packaging together two or more complementary products that are sold for a single price. In multiple unit pricing, two or more identical products are packaged together and sold for a single price. Everyday low prices are employed by some companies to set a low price for products on a consistent basis. When using odd-even pricing, marketers try to influence buyers' perceptions of the prices of the product by ending the price with certain numbers. Customary pricing is based on traditional prices. With prestige pricing, prices are set at an artificially high level to project a quality image. Professional pricing, is used by people who have great skill or experience in a particular field. **Promotional pricing** is a pricing approach in which pricing is related to the short term promotion of a particular product. Price leaders, special event pricing and comparison discounting are examples of promotional pricing. Misleading pricing – in which consumers are intentionally misled about the true cost or value of a product or service – is increasingly monitored and tackled through consumer protection legislation.

The final stage in establishing a price is to determine the specific price to be asked for from customers. The basis for a price and the pricing strategy should direct and structure the selection of a final price. For the most part, pricing remains a flexible and convenient way to adjust the marketing mix. Pragmatism may require the marketer to revise pricing on an ad hoc basis in response to market developments. While such reactions are to some extent inevitable, marketers must never lose sight of the longer term implications for the brand or the fundamental relationship between demand, costs and profits.

Summary

*P*rice is the value placed on what is exchanged. The buyer exchanges buying power – which depends on the buyer's income, credit and wealth – for satisfaction or utility. *Financial price* is the basis of market exchanges – the quantified value of what is exchanged. However, price does not always involve a financial exchange; barter, the trading of products, is the oldest form of exchange.

❯❯ Price is a key element in the marketing mix because it relates directly to the generation of total revenue. The profit factor can be determined mathematically by first multiplying price by quantities sold to calculate total revenues and then subtracting total costs. Price is often the only variable in the marketing mix that can be adjusted quickly and easily to respond to changes in the external environment.

» A product offering can compete on either a price or a non-price basis. *Price competition* emphasises price as the product differential. Prices fluctuate frequently, and sellers must respond to competitors changing their prices. *EDLP*, everyday low pricing, is a budget saving passed on from the manufacturer to the consumer. *Non-price competition* emphasises product differentiation through distinctive product features, services, product quality or other factors. Establishing brand loyalty by using non-price competition works best when the product can be physically differentiated and when the customer can recognise these distinguishing characteristics and views them as desirable.

» *Pricing objectives* are overall goals that describe what a company wants to achieve through its pricing efforts. The most fundamental pricing objective is the organisation's survival. Price can easily be adjusted to increase sales volume to levels that match the company's expenses. Profit objectives, which are usually stated in terms of actual monetary amounts or percentage change, are normally set at a satisfactory level rather than at a level designed for profit maximisation. Pricing for return on investment (ROI) sets a specified rate of return as its objective. A pricing objective to maintain or increase market share is established in relation to total industry sales. Other types of pricing objective include cash flow, status quo and product quality.

» Nine factors affect pricing decisions: (1) organisational and marketing objectives, (2) pricing objectives, (3) costs, (4) other marketing mix variables, (5) channel member expectations, (6) buyers' perceptions, (7) competition, (8) legal and regulatory issues, and (9) perceived value. Thus, pricing decisions should be consistent with the organisation's goals and mission. Pricing objectives heavily influence price-setting decisions.

» When interpreting and responding to prices, customers compare prices with internal or external reference prices. An *internal reference price* is a price developed in the buyer's mind through experience with the product. When there is less experience, consumers rely more heavily on external reference prices. An *external reference price* is a comparison price provided by others, such as retailers, manufacturers or competing products. In the context of price, buyers can be characterised according to their degree of value consciousness, price consciousness and prestige-sensitivity. Marketers who understand these characteristics are better able to set pricing objectives and policies. *Value-conscious consumers* are concerned about both the price and the quality of a product. *Price-conscious consumers* strive to pay low prices. *Prestige-sensitive consumers* focus on purchasing products that signify prominence and status.

» Most marketers view a product's cost as the floor below which a product cannot be priced. Due to the interrelationship of the marketing mix variables, price can affect product, promotion, place/distribution and service-level decisions. The revenue that channel members expect for the functions they perform must also be considered when making price decisions.

» Buyers' perceptions of price vary. Some consumer segments are sensitive to price, but others may not be; before determining the price, therefore, a marketer needs to be aware of its importance to the target market. Knowledge of the prices charged for competing brands is essential so that a company can adjust its prices relative to those of competitors. Government regulations and legislation can also influence pricing decisions through laws to enhance competition and by invoking price controls – for example, to curb inflation.

» *Perceived value for money* is an important consideration when setting prices. Consumers do not regard price purely as the monetary value being demanded in exchange for a good or a service. The quality of the item, its brand image, purpose, usage and overall appeal – along with the consumer's previous experiences and certain tangible benefits such as interest-free credit and warranties – dictate the consumer's view of value for money.

» Unlike consumers, industrial or business buyers purchase products to use in their own operations or for producing other products. When adjusting prices, business sellers take into consideration the size of the purchase, geographic factors and transport requirements. Producers commonly provide *trade* or *functional discounts* off list prices to intermediaries. The five categories of discount include (1) trade, (2) quantity, (3) cash discounts, (4) seasonal discounts, and (5) allowances. A trade discount is a price reduction for performing certain functions. If an intermediary purchases in large enough quantities, the producer gives a *quantity discount*, which can either be *cumulative* or *non-cumulative*. A *cash discount* is a price reduction for prompt payment or payment in cash. Buyers who purchase goods or services out of season may be granted a *seasonal discount*. A final type of reduction from the list price is an *allowance*, such as a trade-in allowance.

» *Geographic pricing* involves reductions for transport costs or other costs associated with the physical distance between the buyer and the seller. An *FOB factory price* means that the buyer pays for shipping from the factory; an *FOB destination price* means that the producer pays for shipping the merchandise. When the seller charges a fixed average cost for transport, the practice is known as *uniform geographic pricing*. *Zone prices* take advantage of a uniform pricing system adjusted for major geographic zones as the transport costs increase. *Base point pricing* involves prices being adjusted for shipping expenses incurred by the seller from the base point nearest the buyer. A seller who absorbs all or part of the freight costs is using *freight absorption pricing*. *Transfer pricing* occurs when one company unit sells a product to another unit within the same company.

» When a *price discrimination* policy is adopted, different prices are charged in order to give a group of buyers a competitive edge. In some countries, price differentials are legal only in circumstances where competition is not damaged.

» The concept of *economic value to the customer (EVC)* is sometimes used in business markets to aid price setting. The underlying principle is that a premium price can be charged while still offering better value than the competition. This is because business-to-business organisations are driven by the need to reduce costs and increase revenue.

» The eight stages in the process of establishing prices are: (1) selecting pricing objectives; (2) assessing the target market's evaluation of price and its ability to buy; (3) determining demand; (4) analysing demand, cost and profit relationships; (5) evaluating competitors' prices; (6) selecting a basis for pricing; (7) developing a pricing strategy; and (8) determining a specific price to seek from intended customers.

» The three major dimensions on which prices can be based are cost, demand and competition. In using *cost based pricing,* a company determines price by adding a monetary amount or percentage to the cost of the product. *Demand based pricing* is based on the level of demand for a product and requires marketers to estimate the amounts of a product that buyers will demand at different prices, particularly if the company wishes to use *price differentiation* for a specific product. With *competition based pricing,* costs and revenues are secondary to competitors' prices. The fourth dimension, which is increasingly popular, is *marketing oriented pricing*, where a company takes account of a wide range of factors including marketing strategy, competition, value to the customer, price-quality relationships, explicability, costs, product line pricing, negotiating margins, political factors and the effect on distributors/retailers.

» A *pricing strategy* is an approach designed to achieve pricing and marketing objectives. The most common pricing strategies are differential pricing, new-product pricing, product-line pricing, *psychological pricing*, professional pricing, and *promotional pricing*. Two strategies used in new product pricing are price skimming and penetration pricing. With *price skimming*, a company charges the highest price that buyers who most desire the product will pay. *Penetration pricing* sets a price below the prices of competing brands in order to penetrate the market and produce a larger unit sales volume.

◉ *Key Links*

This chapter about pricing concepts should be read in conjunction with the rest of Part III, which summarises the marketing mix.

- Price impacts strongly on how businesses fare competitively. The concepts of competitive strategy and the competitive environment are explored in Chapters 2 and 3.
- Pricing impacts significantly on a brand's positioning, as described in Chapter 6.
- Price must reflect the expectations of the intended customer, as explored in Chapters 4 and 5.

Important Terms

Price
Financial price
Price competition
EDLP
Non-price competition
Pricing objectives
Internal reference price
External reference price
Value-conscious consumers
Price-conscious consumers
Prestige-sensitive consumers
Perceived value for money
Trade or functional discount
Quantity discounts
Cumulative discounts
Non-cumulative discounts
Cash discount
Seasonal discount
Allowance
Geographic pricing
FOB factory price
FOB destination price
Uniform geographic pricing
Zone prices
Base point pricing
Freight absorption pricing
Transfer pricing
Price discrimination
Economic value to the customer (EVC)
Cost based pricing
Demand based pricing
Price differentiation

Competition based pricing
Marketing oriented pricing
Pricing strategy
Price skimming
Penetration pricing
Psychological pricing
Promotional pricing

Discussion and Review Questions

1. Why are pricing decisions so important to an organisation?
2. Compare and contrast price and non-price competition. Describe the conditions under which each form works best.
3. How does a pricing objective of return on investment (ROI) differ from a pricing objective to increase market share?
4. Why is it crucial to consider both marketing objectives and pricing objectives when making pricing decisions?
5. In what ways do other marketing mix variables affect pricing decisions?
6. What types of expectation may channel members have about producers' prices, and how do these expectations affect pricing decisions?
7. How do legal and regulatory forces influence pricing decisions?
8. Why must marketers consider consumers' perceptions of value for money when setting prices?
9. What is the difference between a price discount and price discrimination?
10. Compare and contrast a trade discount and a quantity discount.
11. What is EDLP (everyday low pricing)? How does it work?
12. Why is the concept of EVC (economic value to the customer) important when setting prices in business-to-business markets?
13. Identify the eight stages that make up the process of establishing prices.

Recommended Reading

- Diamantopoulos, A. and Mathews, B.P., *Making Pricing Decisions: a Study of Managerial Practice* (London: Thomson Learning, 1995).

373

- Gijsbrechts, E., 'Pricing and pricing research in consumer marketing: some recent developments', *International Journal of Research in Marketing*, vol. 10, 1993, pp. 15–115.
- Monroe, B.K., *Pricing: Making Profitable Decisions*, (New York: McGraw-Hill, 2002).
- Morris, M.H., 'Separate prices as a marketing tool', *Industrial Marketing Management*, vol. 16, 1987, pp. 79–86.
- Nagle, T. and Holden, R.K., *The Strategy and Tactics of Pricing* (Englewood Cliffs, NJ: Prentice-Hall, 2005).

🌐 Internet Exercise

Whether interested in buying a used or a new car, buying it outright, on credit terms or by leasing, www.jamjar.co.uk offers car buyers a comprehensive website. Take a look at this online retailer at:
www.jamjar.co.uk

1 Find the lowest-priced VW Golf available today and list its features.
2 If you wanted to purchase this VW, what is the lowest monthly payment you could make and what would it cost if you were to buy this model outright?
3 Compare and contrast the relative benefits of leasing and buying this car outright.

🌐 Applied Mini-Case

Consumers can pay just 20 pence to write with a disposable biro, yet fancy fountain pens have become a common sight in the hands of influential businesspeople. Such pens have high price tags and are much more difficult to maintain than ballpoints, felt-tip pens or roller-ball pens. However, recent sales figures indicate that the semi-obsolete fountain pen is making a comeback as the writing instrument of choice for status-minded individuals. Of the premium-priced fountain pens, those produced by Montblanc are probably the most prestigious. Named after the highest mountain in Europe, these German-made fountain pens cost from about £100 to £5000 (for a solid gold one). The most popular model costs about £300. Prestige pricing has worked well for Montblanc, placing the pen in the same category as Rolex watches, BMW cars and Gucci luggage.

Sources: Chuck Tomkovick and Kathryn Dobie, 'Apply hedonic pricing models and factorial surveys at Parker Pen to enhance new product success', *Journal of Product Innovation Management*, vol. 12, no. 4, 1995, pp. 334–5; Allen Norwood, 'Pen offers status', *Charlotte Observer*, 20 November 1988, pp. 1c–3c; Parker Pen Co. sales literature, 1996.

❓ Question

A company competing in the same sector as Montblanc has asked you to prepare a report explaining the factors that influence the pricing decisions they should make for a new range of pens. What areas should your report include?

🌐 Case Study

Perfume Discounting – Classic Pricing Policies to Rattle the Leading Brands

For decades the leading perfume houses of Paris, London and New York have sought exclusive, premium brand positioning: Joy, Chanel No. 5 and Givenchy have been marketed as high-priced, deluxe lines available only from carefully selected retailers: leading department stores, fragrance houses and only those chemists with a genuine perfumery. Even a company as reputable as

Boots has failed to gain Chanel's permission to retail Chanel fragrances throughout its chain of stores. Chanel permits only certain branches of Boots to stock its brands, sometimes giving preference to an independent specialist fragrance house in a town to retail its products.

While these upmarket brands have controlled distribution, they have also prevented price discounting. The more mass market brands, such as Revlon, Max Factor and Boots' own No. 7, have been left to take the bulk of the market on volume, pricing way below Miss Dior, Chanel No. 5 or Givenchy. In this way, these more expensive, selectively distributed brands have nurtured an exclusive, premium image to support their higher prices.

The Superdrug chain, a discounter, caught the marketplace by surprise. It brought in full in-store pharmacies to rival Boots but kept its discounting focus by reducing the prices of proprietary medicines by around 10 per cent. Superdrug also looked to the perfume market, reducing the prices of the more mass market brands it stocked. Why, though, should Superdrug not create full perfumery sections in its larger branches and stock the more upmarket, exclusive brands? More importantly, why should Superdrug not discount the prices of these leading exclusive brands of perfume, in line with the chain's general trading philosophy as a discounter?

Shock waves were felt throughout the industry. The perfume producers had spent decades creating premium-priced, exclusive brands. Discounting by a retail chain was the antithesis of this strategy. Independent perfume retailers had been able to occupy prime pitch sites with high staffing levels and glamorous shop fittings on the basis of the higher margins offered by the slower-selling exclusive brands. The pricing and images of these brands had for decades protected them from the national retail chains and buying groups. The large department stores were less dependent on maintaining the premium pricing, but they similarly saw their sales decline as Superdrug followed through with its plans. EU and UK trading laws and anti-price fixing legislation seemed to be on Superdrug's side, too.

It was not easy going for Superdrug. Along with the other discounters, it was refused supplies from the perfume manufacturers; the company had to source from 'the grey market', mainly overseas wholesalers. The producers' PR mechanisms mobilised many industry players against the moves. Superdrug's first press advertising campaign for its discounting of fine fragrances was rejected by a string of upmarket colour supplements and publishing houses. According to the marketing press, the colour supplements of the *Independent on Sunday*, *The Sunday Times* and the *Observer* refused to carry the Superdrug advertisements for fear of provoking repercussions from the upmarket perfume houses, all leading advertisers in these newspapers' supplements.

Prior to Christmas, the peak selling season for all perfumes – including brands such as Joy, Chanel and Givenchy – leading department store operator House of Fraser, reduced the prices of many leading perfumes. Boots, too, retaliated against Superdrug's move. For example, in branches of Boots permitted to sell Chanel, a smaller Chanel No. 5 perfume dropped from around £28 to £21, a price still well ahead of the more mass market brands, but the largest discount for such a brand seen in one of its core retail outlets. Boots and House of Fraser admitted they were 'reviewing daily' their pricing policies.

Years of brand building and image cultivation were in jeopardy. More to the point, the retailers were to risk reducing sales of these still lucrative brands. Superdrug wanted to enter the upper echelons of the fragrance market, but not to let discounting devalue the worth of stocking some of these brands. There were no intentions to replicate the price discounting and tit-for-tat retaliations in the DIY or grocery sectors of retailing, or in the holiday industry. The fragrance market, though, witnessed quite dramatic upheavals in a very conservative market. The entry of Superdrug, with its aggressive pricing policy and discounting, caused changes in strategies throughout the industry, by perfume producers, retailers and the media.

Sources: 'Superdrug finds refuge in women's magazines', *Marketing Week*, 13 November 1992, p. 6; Helen Slingsby, 'House of Fraser reviews scent pricing', *Marketing Week*, 18 December 1992, p. 5; 'Stop press', *Marketing*, 19 November 1992, p. 7; 'Eau Zone expands with new name', *Marketing Week*, 6 November 1992, p. 8; Suzanne Bidlake, 'Givenchy TV ads "plug" discounters', *Marketing*, 17 December 1992, p. 6, Suzanne Bidlake, 'Perfume firms fear wrath of retailers', *Marketing*, 29 October 1992, p. 5; Suzanne Bidlake, 'Asda apes Superdrug with discount scent', *Marketing*, 22 October 1992, p. 5.

❷ *Questions for Discussion*

1 What were the pricing objectives of perfume manufacturers such as Chanel and Givenchy? Explain.

2 What impact could a price war have on brand loyalty in this market? Why?

3 On what criteria had competition in this market previously been based? Was the new focus on price a sensible development?

13
An Overview of Marketing Communications

> "Marketing communication is the art of seducing a consumer on his way to your competitor."

Patrick De Pelsmacker, University of Antwerp

Objectives

- To understand the role of promotion - marketing communications - in the marketing mix
- To examine the process of communication
- To understand the product adoption process and its implications for promotional efforts
- To understand the aims of promotion
- To explore the elements of the promotional mix
- To appreciate the nature of integrated marketing communications (IMC)
- To acquire an overview of the major methods of promotion
- To explore the factors that influence the selection of promotional mix ingredients

Introduction

Marketers spend large sums of money and significant amounts of time developing advertising campaigns, PR programmes, sales promotions and websites, to list only some of the activities grouped under promotional activity within the marketing mix. As discussed in Chapter 1, many lay people consider there to be little more to the role of marketing than the management of a company's marketing communications. In fact, there is much more to strategic marketing – as described in Chapters 1 and 2 – but the creation, execution and control of a company's marketing communications is indeed a significant task.

Communication is a sharing of meaning through the transmission of information. Marketing communication is the transmission of persuasive information about a good, service or an idea, targeted at key stakeholders and consumers or business customers within the target market segment. Marketing communications centre on the promotional mix, which comprises advertising, public relations, personal selling, sales promotion, direct mail, sponsorship and the Internet. Until relatively recently, each of these specialist areas was handled disparately within many companies. Integrated marketing communications (IMC) has emerged to coordinate and integrate all marketing communication tools, avenues and sources within a company into a seamless programme that maximises the impact on consumers and other end users, at minimal cost.

The 'target audience' is the marketing communications practitioner's term for those within the target market segment intended as the principal recipients of the promotional message. The product adoption process is awareness, interest, evaluation, trial and adoption. Marketing communications

377

play a key role in enticing customers to progress from awareness to adoption – consumption – of a product. In this context, there are five 'communications effects': category need, brand awareness, brand attitude, brand purchase intention and purchase facilitation. Marketers must be clear about their promotional objectives, and realistic about the likely returns.

Opener

End Cruelty to Children. FULL STOP.

The National Society for the Prevention of Cruelty to Children (NSPCC) exists to end cruelty to children. FULL STOP. The NSPCC wants you to join to fight to end cruelty to children. FULL STOP. 'Be the Full Stop . . . Join.' Child abuse happens in many situations: in the home, at school and sports facilities and in residential care and on vacations. The NSPCC's strategy is to protect children in all areas of their lives, through action programmes such as The Child in the Family, The Child in School and Child Protection. Someone to turn to is a key part of these programmes, collectively termed the 'Full Stop' campaign. The NSPCC estimates that the first phase of this innovative campaign requires £250 million. As a charity, this requires an extensive fundraising activity. FULL STOP.

In a multimedia campaign, the NSPCC pledged to raise £300 million in just 12 months. This figure was six times more than the charity's usual target of £50 million.

Through its Full Stop campaign, the NSPCC hopes to bring an end to child cruelty within a generation.

Following the trend for provocative charity advertising, the campaign began with a series of unsettling television advertisements. These depicted various toys and other children's icons, such as Action Man, Rupert Bear and the Spice Girls, covering their eyes against a soundtrack of shouting parents and crying children. At the same time, 3500 posters carrying the same message appeared, with the NSPCC website offering support (www.nspcc.org.uk). The mailing of leaflets to every UK household bearing the message, 'Together we can stop cruelty to children once and for all', followed. The intention was to capitalise on the awareness created by the advertising campaign. Through this mass targeting, the NSPCC was making clear its intention to mobilise everyone. At the centre of the campaign was a pledge document, through which the public and businesses were invited to donate funds to the charity.

The charity intended for 20 per cent of its target donations to come from businesses. There were many ways in which businesses could become involved. The NSPCC developed a special toolkit that explained some of the sponsorship opportunities and cause-related marketing possibilities. Microsoft, which sponsors NSPCC advertising and holds fundraising events for the charity, is one company that already had links with the NSPCC. The software company states it is happy to be associated with a cause that supports child welfare, particularly in view of its increasing emphasis on developing educational software for families and the young.

At the beginning of the NSPCC's campaign it was unclear whether or not the £300 million target could be met. However, the key was in the scale of the appeal and the fact that it combined a carefully constructed mix of different promotional tools and techniques. The target has not yet been met but, led by His Royal Highness the Duke of York as patron, the Full Stop campaign has so far raised a remarkable £140 million to help ease the suffering of abused children and lead the fight to end this terrible problem in society. In addition to the money raised, the Full Stop campaign, using most aspects of marketing communications, has helped raise awareness of the problem and has inspired others to help this worthy cause. Over 140,000 have signed up to help the NSPCC's campaign.

Sources: 'NSPCC aims to convert abuse anger into cash', *Marketing*, 25 March 1999, pp. 37–8; Jade Garrett, 'Charities snub shock tactics for subtle approach', *Campaign*, 26 March 1999, p. 10; 'Spotlight charity', *Marketing Week*, 17 December 1998, pp. 28–9; 'Charities unite in donor appeal', *Marketing*, 14 January 1999, p. 4. Advertisement: courtesy of the National Society for the Prevention of Cruelty to Children; www.nspcc.org.uk/html/home/newsandcampaigns, July 2004; http://www.nspcc.org.uk, January, 2008.

Organisations use various promotional approaches to communicate with target markets, as the NSPCC has with its Full Stop campaign. Practitioners generally refer to the use of the promotion ingredient of the marketing mix as 'marketing communications' or 'MarComms'. It is important not to confuse the promotion ingredient of the marketing mix with either sales promotion or price offer promotions. Promotion in the marketing mix incorporates all aspects of the promotional mix, including advertising, public relations, sponsorship, direct mail, sales promotion, personal selling and the use of the Internet to communicate with an organisation's target audiences. Increasingly, these elements of the promotional mix are coordinated in the guise of integrated marketing communications (IMC).

This chapter looks at the general dimensions of promotion, defining it in the context of marketing and examining the roles it plays. Next, to understand how promotion works, the chapter analyses the meaning and process of communication, as well as promotion's role within the product adoption process. The remainder of the chapter discusses the major types of promotional method and the factors that influence an organisation's decision to use specific methods of promotion: advertising, personal selling, publicity and public relations, sales promotion, sponsorship, direct mail, the Internet and direct marketing. The chapter includes an explanation of integrated marketing communications.

The Role of Promotion

People's attitudes towards promotion vary. Some hold that promotional activities, particularly advertising and personal selling, paint a distorted picture of reality because they provide the customer with only selected information.[1] Proponents of this view often suggest that promotional activities are unnecessary and wasteful, and that promotion costs are too high, resulting in higher prices. They may also argue that too much promotion has caused changes in social values, such as increased materialism. Others take a positive view. They believe that advertising messages often project wholesome values – such as affection, generosity or patriotism[2] – or that advertising, as a powerful economic force, can free countries from poverty by communicating information.[3] It has also been argued that the advertising of consumer products was a factor in the decline of communism and the move towards a free enterprise system in eastern Europe. However, none of these impressions is completely accurate.

Promotion

Communication with individuals, groups or organisations in order to facilitate exchanges by informing and persuading audiences to accept a company's products

The role of **promotion** in a company is to communicate with individuals, groups or organisations, with the aim of directly or indirectly facilitating exchanges by informing and persuading one or more of the audiences to accept the company's products.[4] PepsiCo, for example, recruited pop star Michael Jackson to communicate the benefits of its cola drink. Various brands currently employ David Beckham to help boost the appeal of their products. Rock Against Drugs (RAD), a not-for-profit organisation, employs popular rock musicians, such as Lou Reed, to communicate its anti-drug messages to teenagers and young adults. Like PepsiCo and RAD, marketers try to communicate with selected audiences about their company and its goods, services and ideas in order to facilitate exchanges.

Cause-related marketing
Links the purchase of a product to philanthropic efforts for a particular 'good' cause

Exchanges are facilitated by marketers ensuring that information is targeted at appropriate individuals and groups: potential customers, special interest groups such as environmental and consumer groups, current and potential investors and regulatory agencies. Some marketers use **cause-related marketing**, which links the purchase of their products to philanthropic efforts for a particular cause. Cause-related marketing often helps a marketer boost sales and generate goodwill through contributions to causes that members of its target markets want to support. For example, as this chapter's 'opener' explains, the NSPCC encourages organisations such as Microsoft to become involved in joint initiatives to raise funds. Similarly, Procter & Gamble has tied promotional efforts for some of its products to contributions to the Special Olympics.

Viewed from this wider perspective, promotion can play a comprehensive communications role.[5] Some promotional activities, such as publicity and public relations, can be directed towards helping a company justify its existence and maintain positive, healthy relationships between itself and various groups in the marketing environment.

Although a company can direct a single type of communication – such as an advertisement – towards numerous audiences, marketers often design a communication precisely for a specific target market. A company frequently communicates several different messages concurrently, each to a different group. For example, McDonald's may direct one communication towards customers for its Big Mac, a second message about its salads towards health-concerned consumers, a third message towards investors about the company's stable growth, and a fourth communication towards society in general regarding the company's Ronald McDonald Houses, which provide support to families of children suffering from cancer.

To gain maximum benefit from promotional efforts, marketers must make every effort to properly plan, implement, coordinate and control communications. As is explained later, the concept of integrated marketing communications helps to harmonise and coordinate an organisation's promotional activities. Effective promotional activities are based on information from the marketing environment (see Chapter 3), often obtained from an organisation's marketing information system (see Chapter 7). How effectively marketers can use promotion to maintain positive relationships depends largely on the quantity and quality of information an organisation takes in. For example, concerns about genetically modified (GM) foods have led certain supermarkets to improve in-store labelling, so that consumers are better informed about those products affected.

The basic role of promotion is to communicate, so it is important to analyse what communication is and how the communication process works.

The Communication Process

Communication
A sharing of meaning through the transmission of information

Marketing communication
The transmission of persuasive information about a good, service or an idea, targeted at key stakeholders and consumers within the target market segment

Communication can be viewed as the transmission of information.[6] For communication to take place, however, both the sender and the receiver of the information must share some common ground. They must share an understanding of the symbols used to transmit information, usually pictures or words. For instance, an individual transmitting the following message may believe he or she is communicating with readers of *Marketing Essentials*:

在工廠吾人製造化粧品, 在商店吾人銷售希望。

However, communication has not taken place, because few readers understand the intended message.[7] Thus **communication** is defined here as a sharing of meaning.[8] Implicit in this definition is the notion of transmission of information, because sharing necessitates transmission. Communication, therefore, is a sharing of meaning through the transmission of information. **Marketing communication** is the transmission of persuasive information about a good, service or an idea, targeted at key stakeholders and consumers within the target market segment. Marketing communications centre on the promotional mix, which comprises advertising, public relations, personal selling, sales promotion, direct mail, sponsorship and the Internet.

As Figure 13.1 shows, communication begins with a source. A **source** is a person, group or organisation that has an intended meaning it attempts to share with an audience. For example, a source could be a political party wishing to recruit new members or an organisation that wants to send a message to thousands of consumers through an advertisement. Developing a strategy can enhance the effectiveness of the source's communication. For example, a strategy in which a sales person attempts to influence a customer's decision by eliminating competitive products from consideration has been found to be effective.[9] A **receiver** is the individual, group or organisation that decodes a coded message. A **receiving audience** is two or more receivers who decode a message. The intended receivers, or audience, of an advertisement for MBA courses might be business executives wishing to broaden their managerial skills. The source may be a European business school, such as INSEAD.

To transmit meaning, a source must convert that meaning into a series of signs that represent ideas or concepts. This is called the **coding process**, or encoding. When encoding meaning into a message, a source must take into account certain characteristics of the receiver or receiving audience. First, to share meaning, the source should use signs that are familiar to the receiver or receiving audience. Marketers who understand this fact realise how important it is to know their target market and to make sure that an advertisement, for example, is written in language that the target market can understand. Thus when Lever Brothers advertises its Persil washing powder, it makes no attempt to explain the chemical reactions involved when the product removes dirt and grease, because this would not be meaningful to consumers. There have been some notable problems in the language translation of advertisements. For example, Budweiser has been advertised in Spain as the 'Queen of Beers' and the Chinese have been encouraged to 'eat their fingers off' when receiving KFC's slogan 'Finger-Lickin' Good'.[10]

Second, when encoding a meaning, a source should try to use signs that the receiver or receiving audience uses for referring to the concepts the source intends. Marketers should generally avoid signs that can have several meanings for an audience. For example, an international advertiser of soft drinks should avoid using the word soda as a general term for soft drinks. Although in some places soda is taken to mean 'soft drink', in others it may connote bicarbonate of soda, an ice cream drink, or something to mix with Scotch whisky.

To share a coded meaning with the receiver or receiving audience, a source must select and use a medium of transmission. A **medium of transmission** carries the coded message from the source to the receiver or receiving audience. Transmission media include ink on paper, vibrations of air waves produced by vocal cords, chalk marks on a chalkboard and electronically produced communication, as in radio, television, mobile phones and the Internet.

Source
A person, group or organisation that has an intended meaning it attempts to share with an audience

Receiver
An individual, group or organisation that decodes a coded message

Receiving audience
Two or more receivers who decode a message

Coding process
The process of converting meaning into a series of signs that represent ideas or concepts; also called encoding

Medium of transmission
The tool used to carry the coded message from the source to the receiver or receiving audience

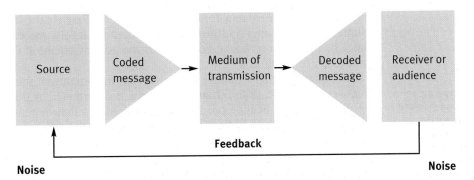

Figure 13.1
The communication process

Sometimes a source chooses an inappropriate medium of transmission. A coded message may reach some receivers, but not the right ones. For example, suppose a local theatre group spends most of its advertising budget on radio advertisements. If theatre-goers depend mainly on newspapers for information about local drama, then the theatre group will not reach its intended target audience. Coded messages may also reach intended receivers in an incomplete form because the intensity of the transmission is weak. For example, radio signals can be received effectively over a limited range that may vary depending on climatic conditions. Members of the target audience who live on the fringe of the broadcasting area may receive only a weak signal.

Decoding process
The process in which signs are converted into concepts and ideas

In the **decoding process**, signs are converted into concepts and ideas. Seldom does a receiver decode exactly the same meaning that a source encoded. When the result of decoding is different from what was encoded, **noise** exists. Noise has many sources and may affect any or all parts of the communication process. When a source selects a medium of transmission through which an audience does not expect to receive a message, noise is likely to occur. Noise sometimes arises within the medium of transmission itself. Radio static, faulty printing processes and laryngitis are sources of noise. Interference on viewers' television sets during an advertisement is noise and reduces the impact of the message. Noise also occurs when a source uses a sign that is unfamiliar to the receiver or that has a different meaning from the one the source intended. Noise may also originate in the receiver. As Chapter 4 discussed, a receiver may be unaware of a coded message because his or her perceptual processes block it out or because the coded message is too obscure.

Noise
A condition that exists when the decoded message is different from that which was encoded

Feedback
The receiver's response to a message

The receiver's response to a message is **feedback** to the source. The source usually expects and normally receives feedback, although it may not be immediate. During feedback, the receiver or receiving audience is the source of a message that is directed towards the original source, which then becomes a receiver. Feedback is encoded, sent through a medium of transmission – for example, a survey questionnaire – and then decoded by the receiver, the source of the original communication. It is logical to think of communication as a circular process.

During face-to-face communication, such as in personal selling or product sampling, both verbal and non-verbal feedback can be immediate. Instant feedback enables communicators to adjust their messages quickly to improve the effectiveness of their communication. For example, when a sales person realises through feedback that a customer does not understand a sales presentation, he or she adapts the presentation to make it more meaningful to the customer. This may be why face-to-face sales presentations create higher behavioural intentions to purchase services than do telemarketing sales contacts.[11] In interpersonal communication, feedback occurs through talking, touching, smiling, nodding, eye movements, and other body movements and postures.

When mass communication such as advertising is used, feedback is often slow and difficult to recognise. If Disneyland Paris increased its advertising in order to raise the number of visitors, it might be 6 to 18 months before the theme park could recognise the effects of the expanded advertising. Although it is harder to recognise, feedback does exist for mass communication. Advertisers, for example, obtain feedback in the form of changes in sales volume or in consumers' attitudes and awareness levels, monitored through tracking research. The coupon redemption rate for the advertisement in Figure 13.2 provides an opportunity for feedback.

Channel capacity
The limit on the volume of information that a particular communication channel can handle effectively

Each communication channel has a limit on the volume of information it can handle effectively. This limit, called **channel capacity**, is determined by the least efficient component of the communication process. Communications that depend on vocal speech provide a good illustration of this. An individual source can talk only so fast, and there is a limit to how much an individual receiver can take in aurally. Beyond that point, additional messages cannot be decoded; thus meaning cannot be shared. Although a radio announcer can read several hundred words a minute, a one-minute advertising message

Figure 13.2
This direct response advertisement provides an opportunity for feedback based on the coupon redemption rate
Source: The Advertising Archives

should not exceed 150 words because most announcers cannot articulate the words into understandable messages at a rate beyond 150 words per minute. This figure is the limit for both source and receiver, and marketers should keep this in mind when developing radio advertisements. At times, a company creates a television advertisement that contains several types of visual material and several forms of audio message, all transmitted to viewers at the same time. Such communication may not be totally effective, because receivers cannot decode all the messages simultaneously.[12]

Now that the basic communication process has been explored, it is worth considering more specifically how promotion is used in marketing communications to influence individuals, groups or organisations to accept or adopt a company's products. Although the product adoption process was touched upon briefly in Chapter 9, it is discussed more fully in the following section in order to provide a better understanding of the conditions under which promotion occurs.

Promotion and the Product Adoption Process

Marketers do not promote simply to inform, educate and entertain; they communicate to facilitate satisfying exchanges – products or services for money or donations. One long-run purpose of promotion is to influence and encourage buyers to accept or adopt goods, services and ideas. At times, an advertisement may be informative or entertaining, yet it may fail to entice the audience to purchase the product. For example, some advertisements seem to be weak in communicating benefits – they focus instead on getting customers to feel good about the product. The ultimate effectiveness of promotion is determined by the degree to which it affects product adoption among potential buyers or increases the frequency of current buyers' purchases.

To establish realistic expectations about what promotion can do, product adoption should not be viewed as a one-step process. Rarely can a single promotional activity cause an individual to buy a previously unfamiliar product. The acceptance of a product involves many steps. Although there are several ways to look at the **product adoption process**, it is commonly divided into five stages, as depicted in Figure 13.3 and explored in Chapter 9:

1 awareness,
2 interest,
3 evaluation,
4 trial
5 adoption.[13]

In the **awareness stage**, individuals become aware that the product exists, but they have little information about it and are not concerned about obtaining more. When Barclays launched b2 financial services, it used a provocative b2 flash teaser advertisement. Later, longer advertisements fully detailed the new portfolio of products. In Figure 13.4 JCB's teaser advertisement (left) did not reveal its innovative single-arm skid steer; later adverts did (right).

Consumers enter the **interest stage** when they are motivated to obtain information about the product's features, uses, advantages, disadvantages, price or location. During

Product adoption process
A series of five stages in the acceptance of a product: awareness, interest, evaluation, trial and adoption

Awareness stage
The beginning of the product adoption process, when individuals become aware that the product exists but have little information about it

Interest stage
The stage of the product adoption process when customers are motivated to obtain information about the product's features, uses, advantages, disadvantages, price or location

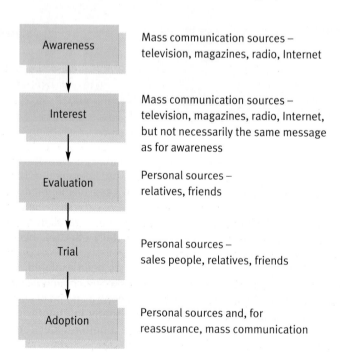

Figure 13.3
Effective promotional tools for reaching consumers in various stages of the product adoption process

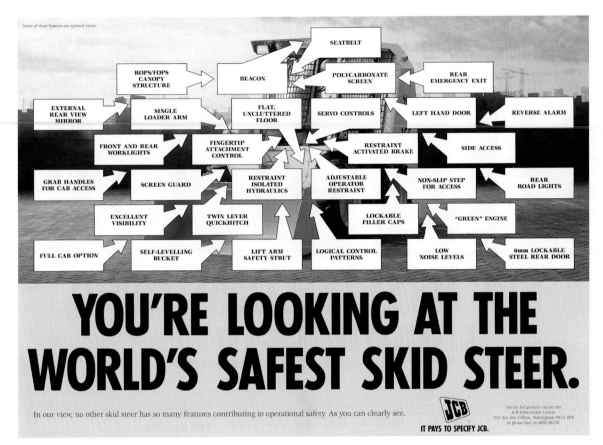

Figure 13.4
Building awareness. JCB launched its skid steer initially with this teaser advertisement (above) before running the second advertisement, which revealed the actual product (overleaf).
Source: Courtesy of JCB Design Works

(figure continued over page)

Evaluation stage
The stage of the product adoption process when customers decide whether the product will satisfy certain criteria that are crucial for meeting their specific needs

Trial stage
The stage of the product adoption process when individuals use or experience the product for the first time

the **evaluation stage**, individuals consider whether the product will satisfy certain criteria that are crucial for meeting their specific needs. In the **trial stage**, they use or experience the product for the first time, possibly by purchasing a small quantity, by taking advantage of a free sample or demonstration, or by borrowing the product from someone. Supermarkets, for example, frequently offer special promotions to encourage consumers to taste products such as cheese, cooked meats, snacks or pizza. During this stage, potential adopters determine the usefulness of the product under the specific conditions for which they need it.

Individuals move into the **adoption stage** by choosing the specific product when they need a product of that general type. It cannot be assumed, however, that because a person enters the adoption process she or he will eventually adopt the new product. Rejection may occur at any stage, including adoption. Both product adoption and product rejection can be temporary or permanent. Even if adoption occurs, as explored in Chapter 4, there is no guarantee of brand loyalty. Marketers must work hard to ensure repeat buying and an ongoing relationship.

For the most part, people respond to different information sources at different stages of the adoption process. Figure 13.3 illustrates the most effective sources for each stage. Mass communication sources, such as television advertising or the Internet, are often effective for moving large numbers of people into the awareness stage. Producers of consumer goods commonly use massive advertising campaigns when introducing new products.

SAFETY FIRST, SECOND, THIRD, FOURTH, FIFTH...

[1] Side access. [2] Left hand door. [3] Servo controls. [12] Self-levelling bucket. [13] Polycarbonate screen. patterns. [22] Front and rear worklights. [23] Reverse alarm. information on the world's safest skid steer, contact JCB [4] Adjustable operator restraint. [5] Restraint isolated [14] Screen guard. [15] 6mm lockable steel rear door. [24] Lift arm safety strut. [25] Beacon. [26] Rear road at the address below. First. hydraulics. [6] Restraint activated brake. [7] Seatbelt. [16] Lockable filler caps. [17] Grab handles for cab lights. [27] Non-slip step for access. [28] Single loader [8] ROPS/FOPS canopy structure. [9] "Green" engine. access. [18] Excellent visibility. [19] Flat, uncluttered arm. [29] Fingertip attachment control. [30] External [10] Low noise levels. [11] Twin lever quickhitch. floor. [20] Rear emergency exit. [21] Logical control rear view mirror. [31] Full cab option. For more detailed

JCB
IT PAYS TO SPECIFY JCB.

Write to: JCB Information Centre, P.O. Box 444, Clifton, Nottingham NG11 6PR. Or phone free on 0800 581761.

Figure 13.4 (continued)

Adoption stage
The final stage of product acceptance, when customers choose the specific product when they need a product of that type

They do so to create product awareness as quickly as possible within a large portion of the target market.

Mass communication sources may also be effective for people in the interest stage who want to learn more about a product. During the evaluation stage, individuals often seek information, opinions and reinforcement from personal sources – relatives, friends and associates. In the trial stage, individuals depend on sales people for information about how to use the product properly in order to gain the most out of it. Marketers must use advertising carefully when consumers are in the trial stage. If advertisements greatly exaggerate the benefits of a product, the consumer may be disappointed when the product does not meet expectations.[14] It is best to avoid creating expectations that cannot be satisfied, because rejection at this stage will prevent adoption. Friends and peers may also be important sources during the trial stage. By the time the adoption stage has been reached, both personal communication from sales personnel and mass communication through advertisements may be required. Even though the particular stage of the adoption process may influence the types of information source consumers use, marketers must remember that other factors – such as the product's characteristics, price and uses, as well as the characteristics of customers – also affect the types of information source that buyers desire and believe.

Because people in separate stages of the adoption process often require different types of information, marketers designing a promotional campaign must determine what stage of the adoption process a particular target audience is in before they can develop the message. Potential adopters in the interest stage will need different information from people who have already reached the trial stage. Often a campaign will include several different advertisements and promotional mix tools in order to appeal simultaneously to different consumers who are at different stages in the product adoption process.

When a company introduces a new product, people do not all begin the adoption process at the same time and they do not move through the process at the same speed. Of those people who eventually adopt the product, some enter the adoption process rather quickly, whereas others start considerably later. For most products, too, there is a group of non-adopters who never begin the process.

Product Adopter Categories

Adopter categories
Five groups into which customers can be divided according to the length of time it takes them to adopt a product: innovators, early adopters, early majority, late majority and laggards

Innovators
The first people to adopt a new product

Early adopters
People who choose new products carefully and are often consulted by people from the remaining adopter categories

Early majority
People who adopt products just prior to the average person

Depending on the length of time it takes them to adopt a new product, people can be divided into five major **adopter categories**: innovators, early adopters, early majority, late majority and laggards.[15] Figure 13.5 shows each adopter category and indicates the percentage of total adopters that it typically represents.

Innovators are the first to adopt a new product. They enjoy trying new products and tend to be venturesome. **Early adopters** choose new products carefully and are viewed as 'the people to check with' by those in the remaining adopter categories. People in the **early majority** adopt just prior to the average person; they are deliberate and cautious in trying new products. **Late majority** people, who are quite sceptical about new products, eventually adopt them because of economic necessity or social pressure. **Laggards**, the last to adopt a new product, are oriented towards the past. They are suspicious of new products or unable to afford them easily, and when they finally adopt the innovation, it may already have been replaced by a newer product. When microwave ovens first appeared, only 'technocrats' or 'food boffins' – the innovators – bought them. Then 'trend setters' – the early adopters – came into the market. After several years and prompted by many frozen food manufacturers' new product launches, many more consumers – the early majority – decided to adopt the microwave oven. Eventually, the rest of the masses – the late majority – decided that they, too, should have a microwave oven 'given that most people have one now'. There are, though, some households only now deciding to buy one – the laggards; and some – the non-adopters – never will. When developing promotional efforts, a marketer should bear in mind that people in different adopter categories often need different forms of communication and different types of information or message.

Aims of Promotion

Product adoption is a major focus for any promotional activity. There are, though, five basic communications aims, known as the **five communication effects**. These are:[16]

1 category need
2 brand awareness
3 brand attitude
4 brand purchase intention
5 purchase facilitation.

Figure 13.5
*Distribution of product adopter categories
Source: reprinted with the permission of The Free Press, a division of Simon & Schuster, Inc., from* Diffusion of Innovations, *3rd edn, by Everett M. Rogers. Copyright © 1962, 1971, 1983 by The Free Press*

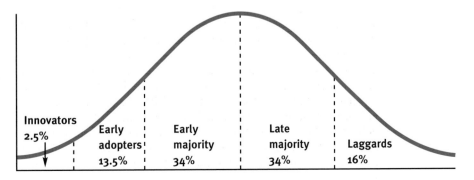

Innovators 2.5%

Early adopters 13.5%

Early majority 34%

Late majority 34%

Laggards 16%

Late majority
People who are quite sceptical about new products but eventually adopt them because of economic necessity or social pressure

Laggards
The last people to adopt a new product, suspicious of new products and oriented towards the past

Five communication effects
Communication aims that include category need, brand awareness, brand attitude, brand purchase intention and purchase facilitation

Category need
The consumer's perception of his or her need for a product in a certain category

Brand awareness
The consumer's ability to identify a manufacturer's or retailer's brand in sufficient detail to distinguish it from other brands

Brand attitude
A consumer's particular impression of a brand, formed by emotions and logic or cognitive beliefs

Brand purchase intention
The consumer's decision and efforts to purchase the particular product

Purchase facilitation
Circumstances that make it possible for the consumer to purchase the product: availability, location, price and familiarity of vendor

Category Need   The consumer must realise he or she wants a particular product – particularly for innovative new category product launches – and must perceive a **category need** in order to be motivated even to consider a product. When compact disc players were launched, many consumers had perfectly adequate album and/or cassette based hi-fi systems and did not see any need to purchase a compact disc player. CD producers had to create a category need. More recently, mobile phone networks have persuaded many users of the need for built-in cameras, web browsing or music downloads – eye-catching advertising has communicated the benefits of these cellphone attributes, creating category need.

Brand Awareness   The consumer must be able to identify – recognise or recall – a manufacturer's or retailer's brand within the category in sufficient detail to make a purchase. **Brand awareness** means that the manufacturer or retailer must make its brand stand out, initially through product attributes supported by distinctive promotional activity. Sony wants consumers to be aware of its compact disc or mp3 players rather than Aiwa or Creative players. In most marketing communications there is the objective of establishing brand awareness among target consumers.

Brand Attitude   Emotions and logic or cognitive beliefs combine to give the consumer a particular impression of a product. This **brand attitude** directs consumer choice towards a particular brand. Companies need customers to have a positive view of their brands. Much promotional mix activity and the creation of the promotional message relate to developing a favourable brand attitude, but other marketing mix ingredients also impact on these perceptions, notably product design, features and performance.

Brand Purchase Intention   Once a category need and brand awareness are established, if the consumer's brand attitude is favourable, he or she will decide to purchase the particular product and take steps to do so, showing **brand purchase intention**.

Purchase Facilitation   Having decided to buy, the consumer requires the product to be readily available at a convenient location, at a suitable price and from a familiar dealer: **purchase facilitation**. A manufacturer or supplier must ensure that other marketing mix factors – product, people, place (distribution) and price – do not hinder the purchase. Sony customers expect wide distribution from reputable retailers, with no budget pricing. Sony produces high-quality goods, but it has several well-respected competitors and must ensure product availability and continued product improvement to prevent brand switching.

To provide a better understanding of how promotion can move people closer to the acceptance of goods, services and ideas, the next section focuses on the major promotional methods available to an organisation–the promotional mix – and integrated marketing communications.

The Promotional Mix

Several types of promotional methods can be used to communicate with individuals, groups and organisations. When an organisation combines specific ingredients to promote a particular product, that combination constitutes the promotional mix for that product. The four traditional ingredients of a **promotional mix** are advertising, personal selling, publicity/public relations and sales promotion. Increasingly, sponsorship and direct mail are elements of the promotional mix in their own right (see Figure 13.6).[17] The Internet and direct marketing are recent additions to the promotional mix, as explored in the Marketing Insight box on page 390. For some products, organisations use all of these ingredients; for other products, two or three will suffice. This section analyses the major ingredients of a promotional mix and the chief factors that influence an organisation to include specific ingredients in the promotional mix for a specific product.

Figure 13.6
Possible ingredients of an organisation's promotional mix

Promotional Mix Ingredients

Promotional mix
The specific combination of ingredients an organisation uses to promote a product, traditionally including four ingredients: advertising, personal selling, publicity and public relations, and sales promotion

Advertising
A paid form of non-personal communication about an organisation and its products that is transmitted to a target audience through a mass medium

At this point consideration is given to some general characteristics of advertising, personal selling, publicity and public relations, sales promotion, sponsorship, direct mail, the Internet and direct marketing. The following chapters explore these tools in more detail.

Advertising **Advertising** is a paid form of non-personal communication about an organisation and its products that is transmitted to a target audience through a mass medium such as television, radio, newspapers, magazines, direct mail, public transport, outdoor displays, catalogues or the Internet. Individuals and organisations use advertising to promote goods, services, ideas, issues and people. Because it is highly flexible, advertising offers the options of reaching an extremely large target audience or focusing on a small, precisely defined segment of the population. For instance, McDonald's advertising focuses on a large audience of potential fast-food consumers, ranging from children to adults, whereas advertising for DeBeers' diamonds focuses on a much smaller and specialised target market. The main uses of advertising include the promotion of products or an organisation in order to create awareness among targeted audiences, the stimulation of demand, the off-setting of competitors' advertising, to support personal selling drives, for the education of a target market about a brand and its enhanced marketing mix or product benefits and attributes, to increase consumption and the perceived uses of a product, to remind and reinforce with intended customers, and to even-out seasonal sales fluctuations or manage production cycles.

Advertising offers several benefits. It can be an extremely cost-efficient promotional method because it reaches a vast number of people at a low cost per person. For example, if the cost of a four-colour, one-page advertisement in the *Sunday Telegraph* magazine is £7000, and the magazine reaches 700,000 readers, the cost of reaching 1000 subscribers is only £10 per person. Advertising also enables the user to repeat the message a number of times. Unilever advertises many of its products – cleaning products, foods, cosmetics – on television, in magazines and through outdoor advertising. Advertising repetition has been found to be especially effective for brand name extensions beyond the original product category.[18] In addition, advertising a product in a certain way can add to its value. For example, BMW cars are advertised as having more sophistication, style and technical innovation than Honda, Toyota and other Japanese companies' vehicles. The visibility that an organisation gains from advertising enhances the company's public image. There clearly is a link between a product's brand positioning and the role of marketing communications.

Advertising also has several disadvantages. Even though the cost per person reached may be low, the absolute monetary outlay can be extremely high, especially for advertisements

◇ Marketing Insight

Web Advertising Comes of Age

During the 1990s many corporate giants avoided using banners, buttons and other early forms of Internet advertising, believing them to be inefficient and ineffective. Now most large companies embrace Internet advertising. McDonald's uses websites, banners and buttons, instant messaging, online games and pop-up windows to engage with consumers through interactivity. As the company's director for media explains, 'We're not going to sell burgers online, but we can extend the experience of the brand online and bring McDonald's to life online.' Many web experts believe few consumer or business brands can now avoid harnessing wed-based advertising, particularly if – as in the case of McDonald's – the target audience is young and made up of frequent web users.

Nike has many websites, some of which promote specific brands, linking into its sponsorship of entertainers and sports stars. Guerrilla moves, such as mentioning its websites or celebrity tie-ins in chat room messages have been hugely successful for the company in attracting hundreds of thousands of visitors to its websites for specific online promotions and advertising campaigns. Sports-focused video clips, mp3 downloadable tracks, musical e-postcards suitable for personalisation, and e-mail games have proved a big hit with the youth market targeted by so many Nike products. The company encourages participation and repeat visits by inviting visitors to serve as DJs, rate the videos and register to receive daily game tips via e-mail.

Pepsi is harnessing the web to advertise its wares, but also to build its brand. Daily, a quarter of a million consumers log on to enjoy Pepsi.com's ever-changing mix of entertainment, promotions, games, merchandise offers and new product information. The company ties its web activity closely to its television advertising campaigns. For example, just hours before debuting a new advertisement on television featuring Britney Spears, Pepsi.com gave a sneak preview by posting it on Yahoo! – in the next four days, an incredible one million visitors viewed the Britney advert online. This combined use of media has become the norm for Pepsi's advertising, with online clips, interviews and footage of the advertising's stars behind the scenes. Pepsi's advertising agency believes this combined attack involves Pepsi consumers much more than when Pepsi only ran TV adverts.

The web has provided advertising executives with the opportunity to interact with the specific target audience for many brands. Initially, websites were developed at arm's length from a brand's advertising, but with the growing focus on fully integrated marketing communications, web advertising is now both very popular and increasingly linked with a brand's other advertising and promotional mix activity. Recently, viral advertising and the use of social networking websites have given the web more options.

Sources: McDonald's, Nike and Pepsi, with thanks to *Advertising Age* and *Campaign*.

shown during popular television programmes. These high costs can limit, and sometimes prevent, the use of advertising in a promotional mix. Moreover, advertising rarely provides rapid feedback. Measuring its effect on sales is difficult, and it ordinarily has a less persuasive impact on customers than, for example, personal selling.[19] With the growth in satellite channels, the creation of ever greater numbers of consumer and trade magazines, the role of the web for advertisers and interactive television, the choice of media for advertisers is growing increasingly complex and prone to error unless handled by specialist media buyers.

As illustrated in Figure 13.7, there are eight stages in creating an advertising campaign:

1 The identification and understanding of the advertising target, which relates to the company's target market strategy and a deep appreciation of targeted consumers' or business customers' expectations, perceptions, requirements and buying behaviour, as explored in Chapters 4 and 5.

2 The scoping of objectives for the campaign, such as sales levels, increased awareness of the brand, a specific impact on a competitor, or a change in the target audience's perceptions and attitudes.

Figure 13.7
General steps for developing and implementing an advertising campaign

3 The creation of the advertising platform which has relevance to the target audience and seeks to differentiate the brand from rivals, such as Andrex's puppies or BMW's The Ultimate Driving Machine.

4 Agreement on the available advertising budget, which is often a specific project amount, the percentage of sales approach or an amount set to match a specific competitor's activity.

5 The highly specialised act of establishing a media plan, which with the proliferation of TV channels, consumer magazines, local radio stations, e-channels and viral possibilities, has become far more flexible but much more complex.

6 The creation of the specific message, such as Tilda's *Indian Mum* proposition or flybe's value-led deals.

7 The execution of the campaign using the agreed platform, message, media and associated IMC activities.

8 The evaluation of the effectiveness of the campaign and assessment of its apparent benefits.

Personal Selling   Selling that involves informing customers and persuading them to purchase products through personal communication in an exchange situation is called **personal selling**. The phrase 'to purchase products' should be interpreted broadly to encompass the acceptance of ideas and issues. **Telemarketing**, described as direct selling over the telephone, relies heavily on personal selling.

Personal selling has both advantages and limitations when compared with advertising. Advertising is general communication aimed at a relatively large target audience, whereas personal selling involves more specific communication aimed at one person or several people. Reaching one person through personal selling costs considerably more than doing so through advertising, but personal selling efforts often have a greater impact on customers. Personal selling also provides immediate feedback, which allows marketers to adjust their message to improve communication. It helps them determine and respond to customers' needs for information.

When a sales person and customer meet face to face, they use several types of interpersonal communication. Obviously, the predominant communication form is language – both speech and writing. In addition, a sales person and customer frequently use **kinesic communication**, or body language, by moving their heads, eyes, arms, hands, legs or torsos. Winking, head nodding, hand gestures and arm motions are forms of kinesic communication. A good sales person can often evaluate a prospect's interest in a product or presentation by watching for eye contact and head nodding. **Proxemic communication**, a less obvious form of communication used in personal selling, occurs in face-to-face interactions when either person varies the physical distance that separates the two people. When a customer backs away from a sales person, for example, that individual may be indicating that he or she is not interested in the product or may be expressing dislike for the

Personal selling
The use of personal communication in an exchange situation to inform customers and persuade them to purchase products

Telemarketing
Direct selling over the telephone, relying heavily on personal selling

Kinesic communication
Body language, including winking, head nodding, hand gestures and arm movements

Proxemic communication
A subtle form of communication used in face-to-face interactions when either person varies the physical distance that separates the two

Tactile communication
Interpersonal communication through touching, including shaking hands

Publicity
Non-personal communication in news-story form about an organisation and/or its products that is transmitted through a mass medium at no charge

Public relations
Managing and controlling the process of using publicity effectively. It is the planned and sustained effort to establish and maintain goodwill and understanding between an organisation and its target publics

Sales promotion
An activity or material that acts as a direct inducement by offering added value to or incentive for the product to resellers, sales people or consumers

sales person. Touching, or **tactile communication**, can also be used; shaking hands is a common form of tactile communication in many countries. Management of sales people is very important in making this component of promotion effective. Sales people who are directly involved in planning sales activities develop greater trust in their company and have increased sales performance.[20]

Publicity and Public Relations   **Publicity** refers to non-personal communication in news-story form about an organisation or its products, or both, that is transmitted through a mass medium at no charge. Examples of publicity include magazine, newspaper, radio and television news stories about new retail stores, new products or personnel changes in an organisation. Although both advertising and publicity are transmitted through mass communication, the sponsor does not pay the media costs for publicity and is not identified. Nevertheless, publicity should never be viewed as free communication. There are clear costs associated with preparing news releases and encouraging media personnel to broadcast or print them. A business that uses publicity regularly must have employees to perform these activities, or obtain the services of a public relations consultancy or an advertising agency. Either way, the company bears the costs of the activities.

Publicity must be planned and implemented so that it is compatible with, and supportive of, other elements in the promotional mix.[21] However, publicity cannot always be controlled to the extent that other elements of the promotional mix can be. For example, just as Perrier's contamination problems appeared to be easing, a BBC television programme showed that the 'bottled at source' packaging was misleading because the bubbles were added during the bottling process. Sainsbury's, a major grocery retailer in the UK, refused for many months to restock Perrier until the wording on the packaging was altered, creating further adverse publicity for the mineral water company. The **public relations** mechanism manages and controls the process of using publicity.[22] As explored in the Marketing Insight box (see page 393), public relations is a powerful ingredient of the promotional mix.

Marketing public relations, now so important because of e-information availability, promotes products or brands, while corporate public relations focuses on the company and its impact on society, with all stakeholders and not just intended customers. Marketers make use of PR events, campaigns and programmes. In addition to using a company's web pages to communicate information, PR practitioners use press releases, feature articles, press conferences, interviews, visits and stunts. Third party endorsement of a product or company by trusted and respected independent authorities and personalities can prove very effective. In addition to creating product or brand awareness and generating interest, public relations is very important in handling crises and combating any negative publicity engineered by competitors or stemming from the media, regulatory bodies or public interest groups.

Sales Promotion   A **sales promotion** is an activity or material that acts as a direct inducement by offering added value to, or incentive for, the product to resellers, sales people or consumers.[23] Examples of sales promotion include coupons, on-pack deals, trade shows, bonuses and contests used to enhance the sales of a product. The term sales promotion should not be confused with promotion; sales promotion is but a part of the more comprehensive area of promotion that encompasses advertising, personal selling, publicity and public relations, sponsorship, direct mail, the Internet and direct marketing. Some sales promotions, however, are closely associated with additional elements of the promotional mix. Currently, marketers spend about half as much on sales promotion as they do on advertising. Sales promotion appears to be growing in use more than advertising.

Marketers frequently rely on sales promotion to improve the effectiveness of other promotional mix ingredients, especially advertising and personal selling. For example, some organisations allocate 25 per cent of their annual promotional budget to trade shows in order to introduce new products, meet key industry personnel and identify likely prospects.[24] For many business-to-business marketers, sales promotions are very important.

◇ Marketing Insight

Microsoft's Image Builders: PR Deflects Regulators' Criticisms

A monopoly and a bully, a champion of free enterprise or creative, inspired genius? Microsoft, the dominant software company and instigator of Windows, engenders many different images for various people. Image is important to Microsoft, which explains why the company employs a team of over 150 experts dedicated to public relations. Microsoft uses well-honed public relations skills to maintain favourable relationships with its stakeholders and to support new product introductions.

For example, in the weeks leading up to the launch of every major update of Windows, computer users are bombarded by media coverage in newspapers, magazines, television and radio, in web bulletins, and so forth. Customers receive direct mail and e-mail pop-ups. By the time the software update is released, such as Vista, a real buzz has been created.

Maintaining a positive image for Microsoft is another requirement of its publicity machine and public relations programmes. Bill Gates' charitable foundation has donated huge sums to medical research, higher-education establishments and schools. Software has been donated to libraries and schools, while computing equipment sponsored by Microsoft has found its way into many educational establishments around the world. These activities enable Microsoft to visibly support education, one of its stated goals, while simultaneously building brand equity. They also provide the PR managers at Microsoft with many positive news stories.

In the USA and in Europe, Microsoft has faced regulatory and legal pressures, being accused of overly aggressive tactics, monopoly power-broking and reducing consumer choice. Violations of US anti-trust law and fights with the EU Competition Commissioner generally receive huge media coverage, rarely favourable to the organisation accused. In Microsoft's situation, while costly to defend and in fines, the regulators' attacks have rarely either dented the image of the company in the eyes of users of Microsoft products or reduced the shareholder value of the business. Microsoft's PR people have been able to maintain a positive image for the company throughout the hearings and associated press coverage.

The celebrated status of founder Bill Gates has helped the company's PR executives. During the battles with regulators, Gates talked openly about his family, promoted more Microsoft products and increased his number of school visits. This visibility enabled Gates to air his views on technology and its impact on society, deflecting public attention from the regulators' criticisms of Microsoft. The company also commissioned research examining the value of technology in the workplace and in society. These studies' findings made the headlines, thanks to the company's PR department, rather than news stories about Microsoft's market size. The interest was in the valuable impact of its software, web browsers and future developments.

While the regulators have fined Microsoft and insisted on limitations to its market muscle, few computer users have negative views of this company. Far from it: most consumers and business people working with computers now feel Microsoft and Windows to be integral to their use of computers. Many members of the public simply watch in awe, awaiting the next 'big' software development from the company.

Source: Bill Pride and O.C. Ferrell, *Marketing*, Boston: Houghton Mifflin, 2003, pp. 485–6; BBC News 2008.

Marketers design sales promotion to produce immediate, short-run sales increases. For example, the major brewers, such as Heineken and Coors, use a continuous programme of sales promotion techniques to boost sales in the highly competitive beer and lager market: free drinks and prize competitions, scratch cards and trade incentives.

Generally, if a company employs advertising or personal selling, it either depends on them continuously or turns to them cyclically. However, a marketer's use of sales promotion tends to be irregular. Many products are seasonal. For example, Thomas Cook and First Choice promote summer package holidays predominantly in the winter and spring months. Qualcast pushes its lawn mowers and other gardening equipment from Easter onwards. On the whole, sales promotions are infrequent, ad hoc campaigns.

Consumer sales promotions encourage consumers to patronise a specific retail store or to try a particular product, or they strive to bring forward purchases by existing customers.

Techniques include coupons, free samples, demonstrations, competitions, frequent-user incentives and loyalty programmes, point-of-sale materials, money refunds, premiums, product bundling and price-off offers. Trade sales promotions encourage wholesalers, retailers or distributors to stock a product, increase display space and market the product. Popular techniques include buy-back allowances, buying allowances/temporary price reductions, count and re-count promotions, free merchandise, point-of-sales materials, merchandise allowances, cooperative advertising, dealer listings, money to incentivise sales personnel, sales competitions, and dealer loaders/gifts.

Sponsorship

The financial or material support of an event, activity, person, organisation or product by an unrelated organisation or donor

Sponsorship   The financial or material support of an event, activity, person, organisation or product by an unrelated organisation or donor is called **sponsorship**. Funds are made available to the recipient of the sponsorship in return for prominent public recognition of the benefactor's generosity, and display of the sponsor's name, products and brands. Sponsorship is no longer confined to the arts or the sporting world, although many galleries, theatrical companies, sports events and teams could not survive without sponsorship. Research and development, buildings, degree courses, charitable events – all often benefit from sponsorship. The donor or sponsor gains the benefits of enhanced company, brand or individual reputation and awareness, as well as, possibly, improved morale and employee relations. Note the number of prestigious or well-known brands sponsoring the Olympics or football's World Cup. It is important to select sponsorship partners with care, as negative publicity about one may in turn tarnish the reputation of the other.

Direct mail

A method of communication used to entice prospective customers or charitable donors to invest in products, services or worthy causes

Direct Mail   The direct mail industry takes a significant slice of the promotional budgets for many companies and organisations. Few households and companies fail to receive direct mail solicitations. **Direct mail** is used to entice prospective customers or charitable donors to invest in products, services or worthy causes. Throughout Europe, direct mail is used as a pre-sell technique prior to a sales call, to generate orders, qualify prospects for a sales call, follow up a sale, announce special or localised sales, and raise funds for charities and not-for-profit organisations. Good database management is essential, and the material must be targeted carefully to overcome the growing public aversion to 'junk mail'.

Internet

A network of computer networks stretching across the world, linking computers of different types

The Internet   From humble beginnings as a 'talking shop' for boffins and computer buffs, the **Internet** – a network of computer networks stretching across the world, linking computers of different types – is now firmly established in many office workers' daily routines and accessed in millions of households. Marketers have been quick to identify this additional medium as an opportunity for providing existing and potential customers with company, product and brand information. Most large companies now have their own websites, while the major Internet servers such as Microsoft and Yahoo! are targeting small businesses and providing e-commerce capability at affordable prices.[25] Web-based marketing is particularly important in many business-to-business markets. Use of the Internet is not uniform across all parts of society, although there is evidence to suggest that it is no longer the pastime of only the young, affluent and well educated. Scrambling of confidential information such as credit card and bank account details has enabled the recent explosion in the number of purchases made online.

As a promotional mix ingredient, the Internet provides a tool that can be interactive, updated or modified quickly, and that can produce material aimed at very tightly defined target groups or even individual consumers. From Interflora to Tesco to JCB, the Internet is increasingly part of the promotional mix and, for direct marketers, the actual point of the sales transaction. Many television and press advertisements for services or consumer goods now direct their target audience to associated websites for additional information. Consumers can then interact with these hosts, in many instances, via e-mail and interactive web page information request facilities. Websites must be tailored to match the target customer buying behaviour and expectations, and must be informative but not mesmerising, while reflecting the existing branding and product positioning already established by an organisation's marketers. They require expert design and updating, as with any ingredient in the promotional mix. Intranets – internal in-company Internet networks – have improved communications within many organisations, becoming an important facet of internal marketing.

Direct Marketing   First used in the 1960s, until recently direct marketing described the most common direct marketing approaches: direct mail and mail order. Currently experiencing a surge in popularity, direct marketing now encompasses all the communications tools that enable a marketer to deal directly with targeted customers: direct mail, telemarketing, direct response television advertising, door-to-door/personal selling and the Internet. **Direct marketing** is a decision by a company's marketers to both:

Direct marketing
A decision by a company's marketers to select a marketing channel which avoids dependence on marketing channel intermediaries and to focus marketing communications activity on promotional mix ingredients which deal directly with targeted customers

- select a marketing channel that avoids dependence on marketing channel intermediaries
- focus marketing communications activity on promotional mix ingredients that deal directly with targeted customers.

Direct marketing is now adopted by a host of organisations ranging from fast-moving consumer goods companies, business-to-business marketers, charities and even government departments.[26] Of all elements of the promotional mix, it is reported to be the fastest growing, but this is partly a reflection of the large number of promotional mix ingredients it includes.[27]

In terms of the promotional mix, there are several key implications. Direct mail is on the increase. Telemarketing has grown and will continue to do so, with more organisations turning to the direct marketing toolkit aided by advances in automated call centres. Door-to-door selling and leaflet dropping, visible forms of direct marketing encountered by most householders, are also on the increase. Direct response advertising – containing a call for action within the advertisement either by coupon or telephone – now makes up close to a third of all advertising as marketers turn to direct marketing, and as the growth in satellite and cable television channels enables more direct response television advertising. The Internet, too, is used by direct marketers to communicate with current and prospective customers. The deployment of any direct marketing campaign must strive to reflect targeted customer behaviour, needs and perceptions; provide a plausible proposition that is clearly differentiated from competitors' propositions; and match an organisation's corporate goals and trading philosophy. Direct marketing is not a substitute for the traditional promotional mix. Direct marketing is an increasingly popular deployment of marketing, resulting from marketers' choices regarding their preferred marketing channel and selection of promotional mix ingredients.

Integrated Marketing Communications (IMC)

Integrated marketing communications (IMC)
The coordination and integration of all marketing communication tools, avenues and sources within a company into a seamless programme that maximises the impact on consumers and other end users, at minimal cost

Currently popular is the concept of **integrated marketing communications (IMC)**. This is the coordination and integration of all marketing communication tools, avenues and sources within a company into a seamless programme of marketing communications activities. The intention of IMC is to maximise the impact on consumers or business customers and other target audiences, at minimal cost. IMC avoids the waste and duplication inherent in some organisations in which each element of the promotional mix is controlled by separate managers and may even be executed through different external agencies. There is nothing worse than when an advertising campaign on radio created by one agency has little resemblance to a television campaign running at the same time, and created by another advertising agency. This is often compounded by the public relations, sponsorship, packaging and sales promotions being implemented by yet more agencies in a poorly coordinated fashion. On one occasion, five different agencies were developing marketing communications for market-leading Gordon's Gin, each using different shades of green – the brand's famous identity – and adopting various typefaces for the logo.

IMC is the integration of the whole promotional mix, but also all business-to-business, marketing channel, customer-focused and internally directed communications. IMC as a concept is focused on complete coordination and harmonised execution of various campaigns across the elements of the promotional mix. Rather than treating all aspects of the promotional mix and internal marketing separately, often utilising many different departments and external agencies in an uncoordinated manner, the company instead opts to fully harmonise these activities. This does not have to result in only one supplying agency being commissioned: coordination ensures shared goals and common approaches to execution in a carefully scheduled manner. The benefits of IMC include greater clarity to customers, marketing channel members, employees and suppliers, as well as reduced costs, stronger impact in the marketplace and more effective branding.

Advertising, along with the rest of the promotional mix, exists to help implement a brand's target market strategy by communicating the product appeal and the brand positioning image to intended customers and other key stakeholders. Occasionally, a creative execution can be sufficiently memorable and strike a chord so well with the target audience, that an organisation rethinks its whole marketing mix for a brand or product. New KFC advertising agency BBH, renowned for its creativity, launched the 'Soul Food' campaign in an attempt to break away from standard fast-food chain advertising and to reflect recent menu changes at KFC. In 2003, KFC spent over £16 million on its UK advertising, depicting a soul food positioning through moody, relaxed and vivid advertisements that promoted the sharing of food. IMC built on the advertising concept to coordinate all of the brand's marketing communications activities, including website, in-store displays, sales promotions competitions, local press and radio advertising, publicity and new branch opening stunts. Now new-look interiors, using large refectory-style 'sharing' tables and atmospheric décor, are being introduced to the company's restaurants. The aim is to provide a relaxing, friendly, contemporary ambience in which to enjoy music, food and the company of family and friends. This positioning is quite different from the original no-frills, quick-meal-on-the-go imagery that the chain adopted in the past. The groundbreaking soul food advertising led to the reformulation of KFC's entire marketing mix. IMC was important in managing all of the soul food-linked marketing communications. Sainsbury's upturn owes much to its agency's use of chef Jamie Oliver in the company's advertising, but in-store demonstrations, point of sale promotions and displays, online activity and publicity also all featured the well known TV chef in a co-ordinated IMC programme.

Now that the basic components of an organisation's promotional mix have been discussed, it is important to consider how that mix is created. The factors and conditions that affect the selection of the promotional methods a specific organisation uses in its promotional mix for a particular product need to be examined.

Selecting Promotional Mix Ingredients

Marketers vary the composition of promotional mixes for many reasons. Although all ingredients can be included in a promotional mix, frequently a marketer chooses not to use them all. In addition, many organisations that market multiple product lines use several promotional mixes simultaneously.

An organisation's promotional mix (or mixes) is not an unchanging part of the marketing mix. Marketers can and do change the composition of their promotional mixes. The specific promotional mix ingredients employed and the intensity with which they are used depend on a variety of factors, including the organisation's promotional resources, objectives and policies; characteristics of the target market; characteristics of the product; and the cost and availability of promotional methods.

Promotional Resources, Objectives and Policies   The quality of an organisation's promotional resources affects the number and relative intensity of promotional methods that can be included in a promotional mix. If a company's promotional budget is extremely limited, the business is likely to rely on personal selling because it is easier to measure a sales person's contribution to sales than to measure the effect of advertising. A company must have a sizeable promotional budget if it is to use regional or national advertising and sales promotion activities. Organisations with extensive promotional resources can usually include more ingredients in their promotional mixes. However, larger promotional budgets do not necessarily imply that the companies will use a greater number of promotional methods.

An organisation's promotional objectives and policies also influence the types of promotion used. If a company's objective is to create mass awareness of a new convenience good, its promotional mix is likely to lean heavily towards advertising, sales promotion and possibly publicity. If a company hopes to educate consumers about the features of durable goods, such as home electrical appliances, its promotional mix may combine a moderate amount of advertising, possibly some sales promotion efforts designed to attract customers to retail stores and a great deal of in-store personal selling, this being an excellent way to inform customers about these types of product. If a company's objective is to produce immediate sales of consumer non-durables, such as paper products and many grocery goods, the promotional mix will probably stress advertising and sales promotion efforts. Business-to-business marketers often use detailed trade advertising, personal selling through sales representatives, sales promotions – often in the guise of bulk discounts and trade show exhibits – and direct mail of brochures and price lists.

Characteristics of the Target Market   The size, geographic distribution and socio-economic characteristics of an organisation's target market also help dictate the ingredients to be included in a product's promotional mix. To some degree, market size determines the composition of the mix. If the size is quite limited, the promotional mix will probably emphasise personal selling, which can be quite effective for reaching small numbers of people. Organisations that sell to industrial business markets, and companies that market their products through only a few wholesalers, frequently make personal selling the major component of their promotional mixes. When markets for a product consist of millions of customers, organisations use advertising and sales promotion because these methods can reach masses of people at a low cost per person. The Coca-Cola Company attempted to reach consumers through a non-traditional vehicle when it placed an advertisement for Diet Coke in the introduction to the home video version of the blockbuster *Batman*. Warner Home Video, the distributor of *Batman*, believed that it would sell more than 10 million copies of the video cassette, exposing millions of consumers to the Diet Coke message at a low cost per person.[28]

The geographic distribution of a company's customers can affect the combination of promotional methods used. Personal selling is more feasible if a company's customers are concentrated in a small area than if they are dispersed across a vast region. When the company's customers are numerous and dispersed, advertising may be more practical.

The distribution of a target market's socio-economic characteristics, such as age, income or education, may dictate the types of promotional technique that a marketer selects. For example, personal selling may be much more successful than print advertisements for communicating with poorly educated people, because it allows meaning or product attributes to be explained face to face.

Characteristics of the Product   Generally, promotional mixes for industrial business products concentrate on personal selling and the web. In promoting consumer goods, on the other hand, advertising plays a major role. This generalisation should be treated with caution, however. Industrial goods producers do use some advertising to promote their goods, particularly in the trade press. Advertisements for computers, road-building equipment and aircraft are not altogether uncommon, and sales promotion is deployed to promote industrial goods. Personal selling is used extensively for services and consumer durables, such as insurance, leisure and education, home appliances, cars and houses, and consumer convenience items are promoted mainly through advertising and sales promotion. Publicity appears in promotional mixes for industrial goods, consumer goods and services. Many organisations use direct mail, and more are now examining the growing use of corporate sponsorship. Most organisations are also developing websites and embracing e-marketing.

Marketers of highly seasonal products are often forced to emphasise advertising, and possibly sales promotion, because off-season sales will not support an extensive year-round salesforce. Although many toy producers have salesforces to sell to resellers, a number of these companies depend to a large extent on advertising to promote their products.

The price of a product also influences the composition of the promotional mix. High-priced products call for more personal selling because consumers associate greater risk with the purchase of such products and usually want the advice of a sales person. Few consumers, for example, would be willing to purchase a refrigerator or personal computer from a self-service establishment. For low-priced convenience items, marketers use advertising rather than personal selling at the retail level. The profit margins on many of these items are too low to justify the use of sales people, and most customers do not need advice from sales personnel when buying such products.

A further consideration in creating an effective promotional mix is the stage of the product life cycle (see Chapter 8). During the introduction stage, a good deal of advertising may be necessary for business-to-business and consumer products to make potential users aware of a new product. For many products, personal selling and sales promotion are also helpful at this stage. In the case of consumer non-durables, the growth and maturity stages call for a heavy emphasis on advertising. Business products, on the other hand, often require a concentration of personal selling and some sales promotion efforts during these stages. In the decline stage, marketers usually decrease their promotional activities, especially advertising. Promotional efforts in the decline stage often centre on personal selling and sales promotion efforts.

The intensity of market coverage is yet another factor that affects the composition of the promotional mix. When a product is marketed through intensive distribution, the organisation depends strongly on advertising and sales promotion. A number of convenience products – such as lotions, cereals and coffee – are promoted through samples, coupons and cash refunds. Where marketers have opted for selective distribution, marketing mixes vary considerably in terms of amount and type of promotional method. Items handled through exclusive distribution frequently demand more personal selling and less advertising. Expensive watches and high-quality furniture are products that are typically promoted heavily through personal selling. Intensive, selective and exclusive distribution are discussed in Chapter 11.

A product's use also affects the combination of promotional methods. Manufacturers of highly personal products, such as non-prescription contraceptives, feminine hygiene products and haemorrhoid treatments, count on advertising for promotion because many users do not like to talk to sales personnel about such products.

Cost and Availability of Promotional Methods   The cost of promotional methods is a major factor to analyse when developing a promotional mix. National advertising and sales promotion efforts require large expenditures. For example, some detergent brands have annual advertising budgets of £15 to £20 million. Tesco and Morrisons each spent £18 million in the run up to Christmas. However, if the efforts are effective in reaching extremely large numbers of people, the cost per individual reached may be quite small, possibly a few pence per person. Moreover, not all forms of advertising are expensive. Many small, local businesses advertise their products through local newspapers, magazines, radio stations, outdoor signs, public transport and the web.

Another consideration that marketers must explore when formulating a promotional mix is the availability of promotional techniques. Despite the tremendous number of media vehicles, a company may find that no available advertising medium reaches a certain market effectively. For example, a product may be banned from being advertised on television, as are cigarettes in many countries. A stockbroker may find no suitable advertising medium for investors in Manchester United Football Club – should the stockbroker use financial publications, sports magazines or general media?

The problem of media availability becomes even more pronounced when marketers try to advertise in other countries. Some media, such as television, simply may not be available to advertisers. Television advertising in Scandinavia is minimal. In the UK only seven and a half minutes of advertising are permitted per average hour of terrestrial television, with a maximum of 12 minutes in any one 'real' hour.[29] The media that are available may not be open to certain types of advertisement. For example, in Germany, advertisers are forbidden to make brand comparisons in television advertisements. Other promotional methods have limitations as well. An organisation may wish to increase the size of its salesforce but be unable to find qualified personnel. In the United States, some state laws prohibit the use of certain types of sales promotion activities, such as contests. Such prohibited techniques are thus 'unavailable' in those locations.

Push Policy versus Pull Policy

Push policy
A promotional policy in which the producer promotes the product only to the next institution down the marketing channel

Pull policy
A promotional policy in which an organisation promotes directly to consumers in order to develop a strong consumer demand for its products

Another element that marketers should consider when they plan a promotional mix is whether to use a push policy or a pull policy. With a **push policy**, the producer promotes the product only to the next institution down the marketing channel. For instance, in a marketing channel with wholesalers and retailers, the producer promotes to the wholesaler, in this case the channel member just below the producer (see Figure 13.8). Each channel member in turn promotes to the next channel member. A push policy normally stresses personal selling. Sometimes sales promotion, direct mail and advertising are used in conjunction with personal selling to push the products down through the channel.

As Figure 13.8 shows, a company using a **pull policy** promotes directly to consumers with the intention of developing a strong consumer demand for the products. It does so through advertising, sales promotion, direct mail, the web, sponsorship, and packaging that helps manufacturers build and maintain market share.[30] Because consumers are persuaded to seek the products in retail stores, retailers will in turn go to wholesalers or the producer to buy the products. The policy is thus intended to 'pull' the goods down through the channel by creating demand at the consumer level.

A push policy can be combined with a pull policy. Mars, for example, has a pull policy aimed at the consumer: sponsorship of events and advertising create awareness; packaging, sales promotions – such as competitions or discounts – and direct mail prompt product trial and adoption. Simultaneously, the company's push policy of trade advertising, sales promotions and personal selling persuades channel members to stock and retail its products.

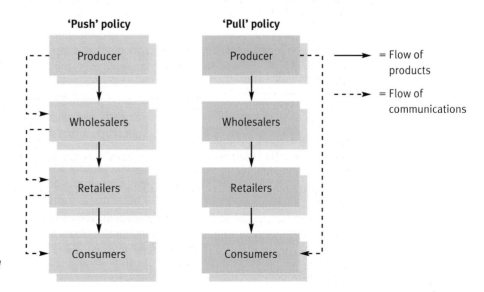

Figure 13.8
Comparison of push and pull promotional policies

Summary

The primary role of *promotion* is to communicate with individuals, groups or organisations with the aim of directly or indirectly facilitating exchanges. Promotion is commonly known as marketing communications.

» *Communication* is a sharing of meaning through the transmission of information. The communication process involves several steps. Using the *coding process*, the *source* first converts the meaning into a series of signs that represent concepts. The source should employ signs that are familiar to the *receiver* or *receiving audience*, and choose signs that the receiver or receiving audience uses for referring to the concepts or ideas being promoted. The coded message is sent through a *medium of transmission* to the receiver or receiving audience. The receiver or receiving audience then uses the *decoding process* to convert the signs into concepts and usually supplies *feedback* to the source. When the decoded message differs from the encoded one, a condition called noise exists. Occasionally, *channel capacity* is reached when the volume of information can no longer be handled effectively.

» *Marketing communication* is the transmission of persuasive information about a good, service or an idea, targeted at key stakeholders and consumers within the target market segment. Marketing communications centre on the promotional mix, which comprises advertising, public relations, personal selling, sales promotion, direct mail, sponsorship and the Internet. Cause-related marketing links product purchases to a 'good' cause.

» One long-run purpose of promotion is to influence and encourage customers to accept or adopt goods, services and ideas. The ultimate effectiveness of promotion is determined by the degree to which it affects product adoption or increases the frequency of current buyers' purchases. The *product adoption process* consists of five stages: (1) in the *awareness stage*, individuals become aware of the product; (2) people move into the *interest stage* when they seek information about the product; (3) in the *evaluation stage*, individuals decide whether the product will meet certain criteria that are crucial for satisfying their specific needs; (4) during the *trial stage*, the consumer actually uses or experiences the product for the first time; (5) in the *adoption stage*, the consumer decides to use the product on a regular basis. Product rejection may occur at any stage. People can be divided into five major *adopter categories* – *innovators*, *early adopters*, *early majority*, *late majority* and *laggards* – according to how long it takes them to start using a new product.

» There are *five communication effects*. A manufacturer or retailer must establish a *category need* for a product. Consumers must have *brand awareness* and a favourable *brand attitude* towards the products. If the consumer decides to make a purchase – *brand purchase intention* – the company's overall marketing policy must guarantee distribution, suitable product quality and attributes, and set the relevant price points – *purchase facilitation*.

» The *promotional mix* for a product traditionally included the four major promotional methods – advertising, personal selling, publicity/public relations and sales promotion. Now it is usually defined as also including sponsorship, direct mail and the web. The Internet and direct marketing are currently very popular additions to companies' promotional mixes. *Advertising* is a paid form of non-personal communication about an organisation and its products that is transmitted to a target audience through a mass medium. *Personal selling* is a process of informing customers and persuading them to purchase products through personal communication in an exchange situation. *Telemarketing* often supports personal selling. *Kinesic*, *proxemic* and *tactile communication* are important in personal selling. *Publicity* is non-personal communication in news-story form about an organisation or its products, or both, that is transmitted through a mass medium at no charge, and controlled by the *public relations* mechanism. *Sales promotion* is an activity or material that acts as a direct inducement by offering added value to, or incentive for, the product to resellers, sales people or consumers. *Sponsorship* involves financial or material support of an event, activity, person, organisation or product in return for prominent public recognition and display of the sponsor's name, products and brands. *Direct mail* is used to entice prospective customers or charitable donors to invest in products, services or worthy causes. The *Internet*, networked independent computers, through organisations' websites is a growing part of promotional activity. Many businesses are turning to *direct marketing*, which is a decision to avoid the use of marketing channel intermediaries and to focus marketing communications activity on promotional mix ingredients that deal directly with targeted customers, such as personal selling, direct mail, direct response advertising, telemarketing and the Internet.

❯❯ Currently popular is the concept of *integrated marketing communications (IMC)*. IMC is the coordination and integration of all marketing communication tools, avenues and sources within a company into a seamless programme that maximises the impact on consumers and other end users at a minimal cost. It is integration of the whole promotional mix but also all business-to-business, marketing channel, customer-focused and internally directed communications. Rather than treating all aspects of the promotional mix and internal marketing separately, often utilising many different departments and external agencies in an uncoordinated manner, a company instead opts to fully harmonise these activities. The benefits of IMC include greater clarity, reduced costs, stronger impact in the marketplace and more effective branding.

❯❯ There are several major determinants of what promotional methods to include in a promotional mix: the organisation's promotional resources, objectives and policies; the characteristics of the target market; the characteristics of the product; and the cost and availability of promotional methods. Marketers must also consider whether to use a push policy or a pull policy, or a combination of the two. With a *push policy*, the producer promotes the product only to the next institution down the marketing channel. Normally, a push policy stresses personal selling. A company that uses a *pull policy* promotes directly to consumers, with the intention of developing a strong consumer demand for the products. Once consumers are persuaded to seek the products in retail stores, retailers in turn go to wholesalers or the producer to buy the products.

◈ Key Links

This chapter overviews the role of promotion – marketing communications – within the marketing mix. It should be read in conjunction with:

- Chapter 9, which features the product adoption process in developing products.
- Chapter 6, which examines brand positioning.
- Chapter 14, which covers branding.

Important Terms

Promotion
Cause-related marketing
Communication
Marketing communication
Source
Receiver
Receiving audience
Coding process
Medium of transmission
Decoding process
Noise
Feedback
Channel capacity
Product adoption process
Awareness stage
Interest stage
Evaluation stage
Trial stage
Adoption stage
Adopter categories
Innovators
Early adopters
Early majority
Late majority
Laggards
Five communication effects
Category need
Brand awareness
Brand attitude

Brand purchase intention
Purchase facilitation
Promotional mix
Advertising
Personal selling
Telemarketing
Kinesic communication
Proxemic communication
Tactile communication
Publicity
Public relations
Sales promotion
Sponsorship
Direct mail
Internet
Direct marketing
Integrated marketing communications (IMC)
Push policy
Pull policy

Discussion and Review Questions

1 What is the major task of promotion?
2 What is communication? Describe the communication process. Is it possible to communicate without using all of the elements in the communication process? If so, which ones can be omitted?
3 Identify several causes of noise. How can a source reduce noise?
4 Describe the product adoption process. In certain circumstances, is it possible for a person to omit one or more of the stages in adopting a new product? Explain your answer.
5 Describe a product that many people are in the process of adopting. Have you begun the adoption process for this product? If so, what stage have you reached?
6 What is category need? Illustrate your answer with examples.

7 Identify and briefly describe the major promotional methods that can be included in an organisation's promotional mix. How does publicity differ from advertising?
8 What forms of interpersonal communication in addition to language can be used in personal selling?
9 List the communications tools that direct marketing encompasses and explain the recent surge in popularity of this promotional tool.
10 How do target market characteristics determine which promotional methods to include in a promotional mix? Assume that a company is planning to promote a cereal to both adults and children. Along what major dimensions would these two promotional efforts have to be different?
11 How can a product's characteristics affect the composition of its promotional mix?
12 Explain the difference between a pull policy and a push policy. Under what conditions should each be used?

Recommended Reading

- Belch, G. and Belch, M., *Advertising and Promotion: An Integrated Marketing Communications Perspective with Powerweb* (New York: McGraw-Hill, 2006).
- Fill, C., *Marketing Communications* (Harlow: Prentice-Hall, 2006).
- FitzGerald, M. and Arnott, D., *Marketing Communications Classics* (London: Thomson Learning, 2000).
- Percy, L. and Elliott, R., *Strategic Advertising Management* (Oxford: Oxford University Press, 2005).
- Rapp, S. and Collins, T., *New Maximarketing* (New York: McGraw-Hill, 1999).
- Shimp, T.A., *Advertising, Promotion and Other Aspects of Integrated Marketing Communications* (Cincinnati, OH: South Western, 2006).

⊗ Internet Exercise

Most leading brands embrace a mix of promotional techniques, including advertising, sales promotions, publicity, the web and the rest of the promotional mix. Pepsi is no exception.

Pepsi's *Pepsi World* award-winning website is an important part of the company's promotional activity, integrating advertising, sales promotions activity and publicity releases with customer involvement. Brand information, TV advertisements, music links, sports, promotions and street motion – there is much on offer on Pepsi's web pages. Log on to www.pepsi.com/home.

1 In what ways and with what messages is Pepsi engaging with customers through the pages of its website?
2 How do these approaches support the brand's positioning?
3 How do the web pages relate to the brand's television advertising?

🎯 Applied Mini-Case

By now, most consumers are familiar with 'chip and pin', the e-solution to 'signing' when paying by credit or debit card. Despite regulations forcing retailers to adopt this technology, less that 10 months before the full launch of the system, under 10 per cent of retailers had made arrangements to install the required keypads and make modifications to their till systems. Leading payment processing business Barclaycard Merchant Services, whose customers include many high-street retailers, joined forces with IT vendor Fujitsu to offer a one-stop off-the-shelf solution to retailers' requirement to install chip and pin. Despite the ramifications of chip and pin, take up by retailers was slow. The very largest retail groups had their own in-house solutions, but most independents and even some large retail chains had no chip and pin provision. In cases of fraud, previously the processing banks, such as Barclaycard Merchant Services, assumed liability and reimbursed the retailer for the fraud. Under the new system, liability rests with the retailers, so it is in their interests to adopt the latest technology and prepare their staff in advance of the changeover from signature to PIN code.

❓ Question

As marketing manager for Barclaycard Merchant Services, how would you promote the need for chip and pin installations to your retail clients? What would be the core messages and what ways could be used to communicate these messages to these retailers?

🎯 Case Study

Häagen-Dazs: Promoting an Adult Ice Cream

Häagen-Dazs makes the best-selling super-premium ice cream in North America. Its luscious ingredients include chocolate from Belgium, vanilla from Madagascar, coffee from Brazil, strawberries from Oregon, and nuts from Hawaii. The packaging serenely asserts that it is the world's best ice cream.

London's Leicester Square shop served close to one million ice cream lovers in its first year. The success of the Victor Hugo Plaza shop in Paris, now the company's second busiest, led to the establishment of its first European factory in France. Häagen-Dazs shops have opened in Italy, Spain, Benelux and Scandinavia, among other countries. The appealing flavours can now be found not only in the company's shops but also at airports, in cafés and in carefully selected delicatessens, with rapidly growing popularity.

The product's high quality has been essential in maintaining a loyal customer following, but it was promotional work that led to the successful take-off of what was previously an unheard-of brand in Europe. Sales promotion in the guise of free tasting was a major part of the promotional mix: over 5 million free cupfuls of ice cream were given away during the company's European launch. Thousands of retailers, cafés and delis were supplied with branded freezers both to display and carefully look after the new premium ice cream. As part of its European launch, Häagen-Dazs spent £30 million on advertising, stressing the deluxe ingredients, unusual flavours and novelty of its product. Europeans currently eat 25 per cent of the 3 billion gallons of ice cream each year consumed worldwide. Häagen-Dazs plans to increase consumption by appealing to more than traditional ice cream-loving children.

The summer afternoon stroll with an ice cream cornet, the family trip to a fun park or beach, a snack during a film or concert, the sticky climax of a birthday party feast had long been the core market for Wall's and Nestlé. Ice Cream Mars changed all that by creating an ice cream bar suitable for any occasion and particularly attractive to adults. Häagen-Dazs went further. Award-winning press adverts, artistically shot, often in black and white, featured lithe, semi-nude couples entwined in exotic poses while feeding each other Häagen-Dazs ice cream. The appeal of vanilla ice cream bars hand-dipped in Belgian chocolate and rolled in roasted almonds now seems hard to resist for adults everywhere. The advertising imagery promotes an adult, upmarket, glamorous positioning for this superpremium ice cream.

The Häagen-Dazs range has grown, expanding to include frozen yoghurts, sorbets and now ice cream novelties, such as the ice cream sandwich made with cookies. Product development and quality controls are important to Häagen-Dazs' brand positioning as an upmarket, indulgent treat for adults, but so is the company's innovative promotional mix and the messages at the heart of its advertising. Industry observers suggest that despite the exceptional quality and novel flavours, without marketing communications Häagen-Dazs would not have been so successful.

Sources: Sainsbury's, 2004–8; 'Dairy produce', *Campaign*, 15 March 1996, p. 34; 'Häagen-Dazs cinema first', *Campaign*, 26 March 1995, p. 5; 'Pillsbury's global training plan', *Crossborder Monitor*, 19 April 1995, p. 9; G. Mead, 'Sex, ice and videod beer', *Financial Times*, 26 September 1992, p. 5; 'Saucy way to sell a Knicker-bocker Glory – Häagen-Dazs' new ice cream campaign', *Financial Times*, 8 August 1991, p. 8; 'Häagen-Dazs is using sex to secure an up market niche in Britain's £400m ice cream market', *Observer*, 4 August 1991, p. 25; M. Carter, 'The luxury ice cream market', *Marketing Week*, 22 May 1992, p. 30; www.haagen-dazs.com, July 2004 and January, 2008.

❷ Questions for Discussion

1 Why did the London launch of Häagen-Dazs utilise more than just advertising?

2 Why did Häagen-Dazs target the adult market rather than families or children?

3 Was the 'adult' positioning and promotional execution risky? Why did Häagen-Dazs deploy this positioning strategy?

14
Branding

*"*Brands are at the very heart of marketing. When a company creates a strong brand it attracts customer preference and builds a defensive wall against competition.*"*

Peter Doyle, formerly of Warwick Business School

Objectives

- To recognise the importance of brands and brand equity

- To understand the types and benefits of brands and how to select, name, protect and license them

- To appreciate the best practice guidelines for creating strong brands

- To examine the roles of brand attributes, brand values and brand personality in brand development

- To understand the role of branding at the corporate level

- To become aware of the major packaging functions and packaging design considerations

- To consider the ways in which packaging is used in marketing strategies

- To examine the functions of labelling and the legal issues associated with labelling

Introduction

Effective marketing requires product or service differentiation. Differentiation entails product design, features and attributes, customer service, branding and the other ingredients of the marketing mix. Branding is seen as a core activity of a company's marketing function.

Brands enable customers to readily identify their favoured products and marketers to more easily communicate their advantages. Marketers invest vast sums in persuading targeted customers to prefer their products over and above those supplied by competitors, as they strive to create brand loyalty. Effectively creating a well-differentiated and memorable image for the brand is a core requirement for a marketing-oriented organisation.

Brand equity is increasingly important in many boardrooms and results from the financial and marketing value that can be placed on a brand owing to its market position and standing. Brand awareness, brand loyalty, perceived brand quality and brand associations create brand equity. An effective brand has what is termed 'brand strength', and generally marketers will have defined brand attributes, values and personality.

Packaging and labelling are also part of the marketing process. Packaging includes the immediate container (the primary packaging) and the shipping packaging (the secondary packaging). Both need to exhibit functionality in order to protect and convey the product inside, and facilitate its easy use and storage. Additionally, packaging should support the product's branding and differentiation.

Labelling is integral to packaging, but must increasingly conform to regulations and ethical controls. Labelling should be informative, truthful and – to assist in product differentiation – distinctive.

Opener

Polos: No Longer Just in a Tube

At a factory in York, each day a mountain of thumbnail-sized tyre-shaped white mints is deemed slightly imperfect: chipped, broken or improperly moulded. The sight is awe-inspiring, but gives a clue as to the volume of perfectly formed Polo mints manufactured: millions are produced, packaged and shipped daily; 147 Polos are consumed every second, with more than 100 million polo mints eaten every week in the UK alone. Nestlé's take-over of Rowntree assured the world domination of Polo, 'the mint with the hole'.

Polo is the UK's top-selling mint, with sales of £35 million per annum, and has established leadership in many other countries, too. It was not too long before trial flavours and strengths were tested by product developers at Nestlé. In India there is a cinnamon flavoured Polo to 'spice things up, while being refreshing'. However, the end of 1998 saw one of the most successful spin-offs from the original Polo concept: the sugar-free Polo Supermint, for 'instant refreshment'. This was not only a masterful brand extension of the Polo name but also proved to be an inspired packaging execution.

The Polo Supermint from Nestlé was even awarded 'Millennium Products' status by the Design Council, an accolade reserved for just a few new designs. The new mini-mints 'with the hole' weigh only a tenth of the original, yet contained four times the amount of peppermint oil in relation to their size. This super-strength mint not only appealed to traditional Polo mint buyers, but also enabled the brand to compete head to head with the plethora of extra-strong mints produced by rival manufacturers such as Trebor.

The new size and extra-strong Polo would inevitably have caught the eye of confectionery buyers on the back of the Polo heritage and the extensive distribution network established by the mighty Nestlé. Marketers at Nestlé wanted to ensure a successful launch and were determined to make the new item distinctive and appealing in its own right. The innovative packaging design and eye-catching styling of the new item made an immediate impact in a rather crowded marketplace. The Supermints were packed in plastic dispensers, developed by RPC Market Rasen, which were themselves shaped as giant versions of the original and very familiar Polo mint. The pack housed a pop-up hatch that enabled it to dispense individual mini-Polos and to be resealed easily. The regular user soon developed the ability to dispense one-handed and in suitable quantities to appease friends also requiring a refreshing treat. The plastic dispenser was itself packaged in a cool blue, square container with eye-catching graphics, permitting easy stocking and shelf displays.

Nestlé says that while the mini-Polos were launched to celebrate the Polo brand's 50th birthday, the new item emerged as one of the company's greatest successes ever. Nestlé believes this demonstrates that it is possible to innovate with a 50-year-old brand. The new item, though, matched the brand values and positioning of the original Polo mint: an effective brand extension must have an affinity with existing brand values. This, and other related Polo product developments, reflected competitor moves and responded to consumer tastes. With the Polo Supermint, the combination of astute branding and clever packaging certainly created a very successful product for Nestlé and a welcome alternative for Polo fans. More importantly, the successful brand extension demonstrates that Nestlé's marketers are, rightly, seeking to leverage further sales from this long-term brand, first launched in 1948.

Sources: Nestlé Rowntree, York, 1999; One Stop, 2004; *Marketing*, 4 February 1999, p. 22; www.nestle.co.uk, May 2004 and January, 2008; www.nestle.in, January, 2008. Photo: mediablitzimages (uk) Limited/Alamy

Brands and packages are part of a product's tangible features, the verbal and physical cues that help customers identify the products they want and influence their purchase choices. For Nestlé's Polo Supermints, branding and packaging have been central to the product's success. A good brand is distinctive and memorable; without one, companies could not differentiate their products and shoppers' choices may, essentially, be arbitrary. A good package design is cost effective, safe, environmentally responsible and valuable as a promotional tool.

This chapter first defines branding and explains its benefits to customers and sellers; it then examines the importance of brand equity, brand attributes, values and personality, strong brands and the various types of brand. The next section explores how companies choose brands, how they protect them, the various branding policies that companies employ, and brand licensing. The chapter goes on to discuss how organisations manage brands and how they ensure that they contribute effectively to a company's fortunes. Packaging is then the focus, as part of the product and how it is marketed: the functions of packaging, issues to consider in packaging design, packaging development and how the package can be a major element in marketing strategy. After considering criticisms of packaging, the chapter concludes with a brief discussion of labelling.

Branding

Most marketers believe a key focus for their activity is the differentiation of their product proposition vis-à-vis competing products and services. For many consumer, service or business products, such differentiation entails a mix of product design, features and attributes with the creation of a distinctive image. This generally involves creating a brand and brand identity for products or services. Indeed, without distinctive branding, many service products in particular would struggle to differentiate themselves against rivals (see Chapter 10).

In addition to making decisions about actual products, as described in Chapter 8, marketers must make many decisions associated with branding, such as brands, brand names, brand marks, trademarks and trade names. A **brand** is a name, term, design, symbol or any other feature that identifies one seller's good or service as distinct from those of other sellers. A brand may identify one item, a family of items or all items of that seller.[1] A **brand name** is that part of a brand that can be spoken – including letters, words and numbers – such as Coca-Cola or Channel Four. A brand name is often a product's only distinguishing characteristic. Without the brand name, a company could not identify its products. To consumers, brand names are as fundamental as the product itself. Brand names simplify shopping, guarantee a specific level of quality and allow self-expression. Table 14.1 details the world's most valuable brands. For many marketers, establishing a distinctive brand, which is easily remembered and recognised by targeted customers, is one of the primary activities of effective marketing management.

The element of a brand that is not made up of words but is often a symbol or design is called a **brand mark**. One example is the symbol of a baby on Procter & Gamble's Fairy Liquid detergent. Occasionally, brand marks are modified for local markets. For example, Microsoft tops its brand name with a butterfly in France, a fish in Portugal and a sun in Spain. A **trademark** is a legal designation indicating that the owner has exclusive use of a brand or a part of a brand, and that others are prohibited by law from using it. To protect a brand name or brand mark a company must register it as a trademark with the appropriate patenting office. Finally, a **trade name** is the full and legal name of an organisation, such as Ford Motor Company, rather than the name of a specific product.

Brand
A name, term, design, symbol or any other feature that identifies one seller's good or service as distinct from those of other sellers

Brand name
That part of a brand that can be spoken, including letters, words and numbers

Brand mark
The element of a brand that cannot be spoken – often a symbol or design

Trademark
Legal designation indicating that the owner has exclusive use of a brand

Trade name
The full and legal name of an organisation

Benefits of Branding

Branding provides benefits for both buyers and sellers.[2] Brands help buyers identify specific products that they do and do not like, a process that in turn facilitates the purchase of

TABLE 14.1 WORLD'S MOST VALUABLE BRANDS

2007 Rank	Brand	Brand Value (US $m)	Country of origin
1	Coca-Cola	65,324	USA
2	Microsoft	58,709	USA
3	IBM	57,091	USA
4	GE	51,569	USA
5	Nokia	33,696	Finland
6	Toyota	32,070	Japan
7	Intel	30,954	USA
8	McDonald's	29,398	USA
9	Disney	29,210	USA
10	Mercedes	23,568	Germany
11	Citi	23,443	USA
12	Hewlett-Packard	22,197	USA
13	BMW	21,612	Germany
14	Marlboro	21,283	USA
15	American Express	20,827	USA
16	Gillette	20,415	USA
17	Louis Vuitton	20,321	France
18	Cisco	19,099	USA
19	Honda	17,998	Japan
20	Google	17,837	USA
21	Samsung	16,853	Korea
22	Merrill Lynch	14,343	USA
23	HSBC	13,563	UK
24	Nescafé	12,950	Switzerland
25	Sony	12,907	Japan
26	Pepsi	12,888	USA
27	Oracle	12,448	USA
28	UPS	12,013	USA
29	Nike	12,004	USA
30	Budweiser	11,652	USA

Sources: 'Best Global Brands 2007', *The Marketing Pocket Book 2008*, p. 253.

items that satisfy their needs and reduces the time required to purchase the product. Without brands, product selection would be quite random, because buyers could have no assurance that they were purchasing what they preferred. Imagine the chaos in a supermarket if every shopper entered not knowing which products and brands to purchase! Research indicates, however, that the bulk of supermarket shoppers are highly brand loyal. So much so, that in-store redesigns and new shelf-space allocations cause significant distress and generate high levels of customer complaints.

A brand also helps buyers evaluate the quality of a product, especially when they are unable to judge its characteristics. In other words, a purchaser for whom a brand symbolises a certain quality level will transfer that perception of quality to the unknown item. A brand thus helps to reduce a buyer's perceived risk of purchase. In addition, it may offer the psychological reward that comes from owning a brand that symbolises status. Certain brands of watches (Rolex) and cars (Rolls-Royce) fall into this category.[3]

Sellers benefit from branding because each company's brands identify its products, which makes repeat purchasing easier for consumers. Branding helps a company introduce a new product that carries the name of one or more of its existing products, because buyers are already familiar with the company's existing brands. For example, Heinz regularly introduces new tinned products. Because consumers are used to buying the brand and have a high regard for its quality, they are likely to try the new offerings. The same applies to Tesco's quickly growing *Finest* range. Branding also facilitates promotional efforts because the promotion of each branded product indirectly promotes all other products that are similarly branded.

Branding helps sellers by fostering brand loyalty. **Brand loyalty** is a strongly motivated and long-standing decision to purchase a particular product or service. To the extent that buyers become loyal to a specific brand, the company's market share for that product achieves a certain level of stability, allowing the company to use its resources more efficiently.[4] Loyal customers are highly desirable and much marketing activity is aimed at reassuring existing customers and canvassing their ongoing support and interest. When a company succeeds in fostering some degree of customer loyalty to a brand, it can charge a premium price for the product. For example, brand loyal buyers of Anadin aspirin are willing to pay two or three times more for Anadin than for a generic brand of aspirin with the same amount of pain-relieving agent.

However, brand loyalty is declining, partly because of marketers' increased reliance on discounted sales, coupons and other short-term promotions, and partly because of the sometimes overwhelming array of similar new products from which consumers can choose. In the brand-dominated US, a *Wall Street Journal* survey found that 12 per cent of consumers are not loyal to any brand, whereas 47 per cent are brand loyal for one to five product types. Only 2 per cent of the respondents were brand loyal for more than 16 product types. To stimulate loyalty to their brands, some marketers are stressing image advertising, mailing personalised catalogues and magazines to regular users, and creating membership clubs for brand users, for example, Tesco's ClubCard or Sainsbury's Nectar points. Sometimes consumers make repeat purchases of products for reasons other than brand loyalty. Spurious loyalty is not stable and may result from non-availability of alternative brands or the way in which products are displayed in retail outlets.

There are three degrees of brand loyalty: recognition, preference and insistence.

Brand loyalty
A strongly motivated and long-standing decision to purchase a particular product or service

Brand recognition
A customer's awareness that a brand exists and is an alternative to purchase

Brand Recognition **Brand recognition** exists when a customer is aware that a brand exists and views it as an alternative to purchase if the preferred brand is unavailable or if the other available brands are unfamiliar to the customer. This is the mildest form of brand loyalty. The word loyalty is clearly being used very loosely here. One of the initial objectives of a marketer introducing a new brand is to create widespread awareness of the brand in order to generate brand recognition. This theme is considered in Chapter 13.

Brand preference
The degree of brand loyalty in which a customer prefers one brand over competitive offerings

Brand Preference **Brand preference** is a stronger degree of brand loyalty in which a customer definitely prefers one brand over competitive offerings and will purchase this brand if it is available. However, if the brand is not available, the customer will accept a substitute brand rather than expend additional effort finding and purchasing the preferred brand. A marketer is likely to be able to compete effectively in a market when a number of customers have developed brand preference for its specific brand.

Brand insistence
The degree of brand loyalty in which a customer strongly prefers a specific brand and will accept no substitute

Brand Insistence **Brand insistence** is the degree of brand loyalty in which a customer strongly prefers a specific brand, will accept no substitute and is willing to spend a great deal of time and effort to acquire that brand. If a brand-insistent customer goes to a store and finds the brand unavailable, rather than purchasing a substitute brand, he or she will seek the brand elsewhere. Brand insistence is the strongest degree of brand loyalty. It is a marketer's dream. However, it is the least common type of brand loyalty. Customers vary considerably regarding the product categories for which they may be brand insistent.

Brand Equity

Brand equity
The marketing and financial value associated with a brand's strength in a market

A well-managed brand is an asset to an organisation. The value of this asset is often referred to as brand equity. **Brand equity** is the marketing and financial value associated with a brand's strength in a market. Besides the actual proprietary brand assets, such as patents and trademarks, four major elements underlie brand equity. These components are brand name awareness, brand loyalty, perceived brand quality and brand associations, as shown in Figure 14.1.[5]

Being aware of a brand leads to brand familiarity, which in turn results in a level of comfort with the brand. A familiar brand is more likely to be selected than an unfamiliar brand because often the familiar brand is viewed as reliable and of acceptable quality compared to the unknown brand. The familiar brand is likely to be in a customer's evoked set (see Chapter 4), whereas the unfamiliar brand is not.

Brand loyalty is a valued component of brand equity because it reduces a brand's vulnerability to competitors' actions. Brand loyalty allows an organisation to keep its existing customers and avoid having to spend enormous amounts of resources gaining new ones. Loyal customers provide brand visibility and reassurance to potential new customers. And because customers expect their brand to be available when and where they shop, retailers strive to carry the brands known for their strong customer following.

Customers associate a certain level of perceived overall quality with a brand. A brand name itself actually stands for a certain level of quality in a customer's mind and is used as a substitute for actual judgement of quality. In many cases, customers cannot actually judge the quality of the product for themselves and instead must rely on the brand as a quality indicator. Perceived high brand quality helps to support a premium price, allowing a marketer to avoid severe price competition. Also, favourable perceived brand quality can ease the introduction of brand extensions, as the high regard for the brand is likely to translate into high regard for the related products.

The set of associations linked to a brand is another key component of brand equity. At times a marketer works to connect a lifestyle, or in some instances a certain personality type, with a particular brand. For example, customers associate Volvo cars with protecting family members; a De Beers diamond with a loving, long-lasting relationship (a diamond is for ever); and Drambuie liqueur with a unique taste. These types of brand association contribute significantly to the brand's equity.

Figure 14.1
Major elements of brand equity
Source: Adapted with the permission of The Free Press, a division of Simon & Schuster, Inc., from Managing Brand Equity: Capitalizing on the Value of a Brand Name *by David A. Aaker. Copyright © 1991 by David A. Aaker*

Although difficult to measure, brand equity represents the value of a brand to an organisation. An organisation may buy a brand from another company at a premium price because outright brand purchase may be less expensive and less risky than creating and developing a brand from scratch – for example, IKEA's purchase of Habitat. Brand equity helps to give a brand the power to capture and maintain a consistent market share, which provides stability to an organisation's sales volume. The top brands with the highest economic value are shown in Table 14.1. Any company that owns a brand listed in Table 14.1, such as Nestlé with Nescafé, would agree that the economic value of that brand is likely to be the greatest single asset in the organisation's possession. A brand's overall economic value rises and falls with the brand's profitability, brand awareness, brand loyalty, perceived brand quality and strength of positive brand associations.

Brand Personality, Values and Attributes

Brand attributes
The bullet-point specific benefits to the customer from purchasing or using the brand

Brand values
The emotional benefits and less tangible identifiers attached to the brand, providing reassurance and credibility for targeted consumers, supplementing the specific brand attributes in making the brand attractive

Brand personality
The psychological cues and less tangible desirable facets of a well-presented brand

Most companies have identified specific attributes that may be linked to their brands. **Brand attributes** are the bullet-point selling-type features listed in brochures or in an advertisement: the specific benefits to the customer from purchasing or using the brand. A decade or so ago, it became fashionable to also identify brand values to help differentiate a brand and build its appeal to target audiences, particularly those within an organisation. **Brand values** are the emotional benefits and less tangible identifiers attached to the brand, creating a sense of identity and purpose within the organisation, providing reassurance and credibility for targeted consumers, supplementing the specific brand attributes in making the brand attractive to current or potential purchasers. For example, IT services company Fujitsu has many brand attributes, including its ability to manage business clients' IT infrastructure, offer the latest technology and thinking, and be cost effective and reliable. Its brand values are defined as offering knowledge, dependability, technical excellence, reassurance and passion, but to staff the message is that 'we tell it as it is'. These values are far more emotional than the brand attributes. Together, the brand values and brand attributes constitute a more compelling proposition in the marketplace and help staff understand for what the brand stands.

Many branding experts argue that in addition to brand attributes and brand values, an effective brand strategy should identify brand personality variables in order to facilitate greater differentiation in relation to competitors' products and to form a stronger affinity with customers. **Brand personality** traits are the psychological cues and less tangible desirable facets of a well-presented brand. In Fujitsu's case, the brand personality variables include having friendly, customer-focused personnel who are confident, technically savvy and passionate about assisting clients to improve their organisations. In the market for IT services to large corporations, these are desirable traits. Many companies readily identify the brand attributes and, after a little deliberation, they are able to scope out a few brand values. However, the identification of an attractive set of brand personality traits is often more difficult, yet once developed, such emotive sentiments often 'bring the brand to life' and help to establish differentiation vis-à-vis rivals. The Marketing Tools and Techniques box below illustrates this approach to effective branding.

🖐 Marketing Tools and Techniques

Practitioners' Use of the Brand Development Theory: the Brand Personality Grid

Leading branding exponents, such as Prophet (David Aaker) and Interbrand, suggest that organisations identify core values that are reflected in their business capabilities and their brands' positionings, and in the perceptions of their target stakeholders. In addition, specific features or attributes that can be construed as brand benefits should be defined. In order to truly make a brand 'come alive' and be distinctive in the marketplace, leading branding experts argue that a *brand personality* should be specified and communicated to stakeholders. Such personality traits are the emotive characteristics of the brand, whereas the brand benefits are more tangible and specific attributes, as outlined opposite.

1 *Personality*
What sets the company apart/describes its character and personality

2 *Values*
The heart of the organisation's ethos.

3 *Brand benefits/attributes*
Detailed/specific features of benefit to the customer

Fujitsu's evolving branding is a good example of this.

Japanese-based Fujitsu is one of the world's biggest businesses, focusing mainly on electronics and IT services. The company had traded under different names across the world and in the UK was familiar to business clients as ICL. Fujitsu decided to maximise its global standing under the Fujitsu name and looked to create a leading brand. Globally, Fujitsu is the world's number three IT services company, is growing and is increasingly successful. In the UK, Fujitsu handles IT outsourcing and management for major banks and retailers, central and local government, the Post Office and many manufacturers.

The old brand in the UK was somewhat staid: hardware-led, overly 'techy', 'grey' and stood for ICL's old values from when the company focused on producing mainframe computers rather than offering innovative IT solutions and management options to leading-edge businesses. The new-look Fujitsu is a dynamic, progressive, forward-thinking business, partnering other leading-edge suppliers to

address clients' fast-changing IT requirements and to help clients to transform their business practices.

There are many providers of IT support and many may be able to offer the brand benefits stated above, in the right-hand column. However, fewer B2B companies could claim to have a reputation for being caring, passionate, likeable, dependable and knowledgeable about clients' business issues. In IT services, interpersonal relationships between the supplier and the client are of paramount importance. Clients also perceive high risks in handing over their IT – on which the success of their operations may depend – to a third party. The brand values and brand personality suggested in this analysis would be highly attractive to many senior executives in current or potential business clients.

Having developed a brand proposition – personality, values and attributes – as hypothesised in the example above, the marketing challenges are then to ensure that both:

- all promotional activity reflects this overall message
- any interface with clients and suppliers or partners conveys these sentiments, whether in print format, e-communications, broadcast media or even with any personnel meeting and working with clients.

In addition to developing suitable marketing communications materials, therefore, there is a core requirement to ensure that a company's workforce understands and utilises the brand proposition developed, not only a company's marketers. There is a requirement for internal marketing.

The brand personality grid for Fujitsu could easily look like this:*

Fujitsu
The Possibilities are Infinite

Brand Personality	Brand Values	Brand Benefits
Friendly People	**Knowledge** Customers business Across sectors	**Infrastructure Management**
Customer-focused	**Dependability** Trusted to deliver 30/40 year track record	**Free-up Resources**
Confident	**Technical Excellence** At forefront of change Tap into Fujitsu's huge R&D	**Operational Efficiency**
Dynamic		**Customers Enabled to Focus on *Their* Business Imperatives**
Future-focused	**Passion** Staff are passionate Deliver for customers	**Latest Technology**
Passionate	**Collaboration** Working together Networking with partners	**Total Solutions**
Likeable Staff		**Leading-edge Partnerships**
Global		**Reliable**
		Cost Effective

© Dibb/Simkin

* The suggested brand personality grid for Fujitsu is an external observer's view and does not necessarily reflect the company's own analyses or intended brand strategy.

Implicit in this discussion is the need to determine a strong and relevant brand image that is managed effectively. As explained in Chapter 6's examination of brand positioning, a management team must determine the desired brand proposition and manage its portfolio of brands in order to ensure that the target market recognises the specified brand attributes, values and personality. Targeted customers should never be left to deduce for themselves a brand's proposition and messages. The role of the brand manager and the management of portfolios of brands are examined in Chapter 9.

Types of Brand

There are three categories of brand: manufacturer brands, own label brands (also called private brands, store brands or dealer brands) and generic brands.

Manufacturer brands
Brands initiated by producers to ensure that they are identified with their products at the point of purchase

Manufacturer Brands   **Manufacturer brands** are initiated by producers and ensure that they are identified with their products at the point of purchase – for example, Green Giant, Apple and Wall's ice cream. A manufacturer brand usually requires a producer to become involved in distribution, promotion and, to some extent, pricing decisions. Brand loyalty is encouraged by promotion, quality control and guarantees; it is a valuable asset to a manufacturer. The producer tries to stimulate demand for the product, which tends to encourage middlemen to make the product available.

Figure 14.2
There are many examples of retailer own-label brands, but Boots deliberately created a stand-alone brand for its own, highly popular, range of No. 7 cosmetics, emulating the major manufacturer brands
Photo: Courtesy of Karen Beaulah

Own label brands
Brands initiated and owned by resellers – wholesalers or retailers

Own label Brands   **Own label brands** are initiated and owned by resellers (wholesalers or retailers). The major characteristic of own-label brands is that the manufacturers are not identified on the products. Retailers and wholesalers use these brands to develop more efficient promotion, to generate higher gross margins and to improve store images. Own label brands give retailers or wholesalers freedom to purchase products of a specified quality at the lowest cost without disclosing the identity of the manufacturer. Wholesale brands include Roca, Family Choice, Happy Shopper and Lifestyle. Familiar retailer brand names include St Michael and Per Una (Marks & Spencer), Yessica (C&A) and George (ASDA). Many successful own label brands are distributed nationally. Matsui domestic appliances (Currys) are as well known as most name brands. Sometimes retailers with successful distributor brands start manufacturing their own products to gain more control over product costs, quality and design in the hope of increasing profits. While one might think that store brands appeal most strongly to lower-income shoppers or to upmarket shoppers who compare labels, studies indicate that buyers of own label brands have characteristics that match those of the overall population.[6] One reason for the growth of store brands is that retailers advertise the manufacturer brands, which brings customers to their stores, but sell the store brands, especially to price-sensitive customers.[7] Another reason is that retailers with store labels negotiate better prices from producers of manufacturer brands.[8]

Generic brand
A brand that indicates only the product category and does not include the company name or other identifying terms

Generic Brands   Some marketers of products that have traditionally been branded have embarked on a policy of not branding, often called generic branding. A **generic brand** indicates only the product category – such as aluminium foil – and does not include the company name or other identifying terms. Usually generic brands are sold at prices lower than those of comparable branded items. Although at one time generic brands may have represented as much as 10 per cent of all retail grocery sales, today they account for less than 1 per cent.[9] They are popular for pharmaceuticals and in some discount grocery stores.

The Battle of the Brands   Competition between manufacturer brands and own label brands – sometimes called 'the battle of the brands' – is intensifying in several major product categories, particularly tinned foods, breakfast cereal, sugar and soft drinks. Own label brands now account for around 45 per cent of all supermarket sales.[10] Both men and women are quite favourable towards own label brands of food products, with women – still the major grocery purchasers – even more favourable than men. For manufacturers, developing multiple manufacturer brands and distribution systems has been an effective means of combating increased competition from own label brands. By developing a new brand name, a producer can adjust various elements of a marketing mix to appeal to a different target market. For example, Scott Paper has developed lower-priced brands of paper towels; it has tailored its new products to a target market that tends to purchase own label brands.

Manufacturers find it hard to ignore the marketing opportunities that come from producing own label brands for resellers. If a manufacturer refuses to produce an own label brand for a reseller, a competing manufacturer will. Moreover, the production of own label brands allows the manufacturer to use excess capacity during periods when its own brands are at non-peak production. The ultimate decision whether to produce an own label or a manufacturer brand depends on a company's resources, production capabilities and goals.

Choosing a Brand Name

Marketers should consider a number of factors when they choose a brand name. The name should be easy for customers – including foreign buyers, if the company intends to market its products in other countries – to say, spell and recall. Short, one-syllable names such as

Mars or Tide satisfy this requirement. The brand name should indicate the product's major benefits and, if possible, should suggest in a positive way the product's uses and special characteristics: negative or offensive references should be avoided. For example, a deodorant should be branded with a name that signals freshness, dryness or long-lasting protection, as do Sure, Right Guard and Arrid Extra Dry. The brand should be distinctive, to set it apart from competing brands. If a marketer intends to use a brand for a product line, it must be compatible with all products in the line. Finally, a brand should be designed so that it can be used and recognised in all of the various types of media.

Finding the right brand name has become a challenging task, because many obvious product names have already been used. The Marketing Tools and Techniques box opposite outlines the role played by brand name consultancies in the naming process.

How are brand names derived? Brand names can be created from single or multiple words – for example, Bic or Apple iPod Nano. Initials, numbers or sometimes combinations of these are used to create brands such as IBM. At times, words, numbers and initials are combined to yield brand names such as Mazda MX5 or Mitsubishi 3000GT. To avoid terms that have negative connotations, marketers sometimes use fabricated words that have absolutely no meaning at the time they are created – for example, Kodak and Esso. Occasionally, a brand is simply brought out of storage and used as it is or modified. Companies often maintain banks of registered brands, some of which may have been used in the past. Cadillac, for example, has a bank of approximately 360 registered trademarks. The LaSalle brand, used in the 1920s and 1930s, may be called up for a new Cadillac model soon to be introduced. Possible brand names are sometimes tested in focus groups or in other settings to assess customers' reactions.

Who actually creates brand names? Brand names can be created internally by the organisation. Sometimes a name is suggested by individuals who are close to the development of the product. Some organisations have committees that participate in brand name creation and approval. Large companies that introduce numerous new products annually are likely to have a department that develops brand names. Increasingly, outside consultants are used in the process of developing brand names. An organisation may also hire a company that specialises in brand name development.

Even though most of the important branding considerations apply to both goods and services, services branding has some additional dimensions. The brand of the service is usually the same as the company name. For example, American Express, Vidal Sassoon, ProntoPrint, and Sheraton are names of companies and the services that they provide. Whereas companies that produce tangible goods (such as Procter & Gamble) can use separate brand names for separate products (such as Daz, Head & Shoulders, Flash and Camay), service providers (such as British Airways) are perceived by customers as having one brand name, even though they offer multiple products (first class, business class and economy). Because the service brand name and company name are so closely interrelated, a service brand name must be flexible enough to encompass a variety of current services, as well as new ones that the company may offer in the future. For example, British Airways (BA) has Club World or Eurotraveller (economy) services, each separately branded, but both strongly branded as BA. Geographical references like 'western' and descriptive terms like 'trucking' limit the scope of associations that can be made with the brand name. Northwest Airlines becomes less of a good name as the company begins to fly south and east more regularly.[11] Frequently, a service marketer will employ a symbol along with its brand name to make the brand distinctive and to communicate a certain image.

Protecting a Brand

Marketers need to design brands that can be protected easily through registration. Among the most difficult to protect are generic words, such as aluminium foil, surnames, and descriptive geographic or functional names.[12] Research shows that, overall, consumers prefer descriptive and suggestive brand names, and find them easier to recall than fanciful and arbitrary

⬢ Marketing Tools and Techniques

Who Thought of That Name?!

Burger King, Coca-Cola, JCB, Nike, Sony or Virgin – no matter what the brand, someone, somewhere, sometime created the names now recognised instantly by millions of loyal customers. David Rivett of Design Bridge, responsible for many new product development projects and the creation of brand names, believes that all too often clients focus on the physical properties of their new products – features, size, colours, quality, operation – at the expense of name consideration, which is 'tacked on' to the new product development process just prior to launch. Branding consultancies believe that creating the right atmosphere and having a very clear understanding of both client culture and target market characteristics are fundamental to the creation of a suitable brand name. Very often a creative workshop is used by the consultancy to probe the minds of the client personnel in order to establish buzzwords or emotive trigger descriptions for the new product that may be incorporated into the brand name. The name for Anchor's So Soft new spreadable butter was created in this way.

The real difficulty comes not from creating a suitable name, but in registering the preferred choice. Intellectual property lawyers now specialise in trademark registration and searching. Qualitative research, such as focus groups, often throws up many brand names consumers believe might be appropriate. Marketing strategy workshops amongst managers in a company frequently do the same. The result is that some organisations compile extensive lists of names with potential for their types of product, which are then registered, even though at the time there is no expectation of using these names. Companies such as Cadbury's and Ford have large lists of already registered brand names which at some time they may use but that are no longer available to any other company. This is not 'sharp practice', merely a logical extension of marketers hearing good suggestions from colleagues, distributors and consumers and marking them down for possible future use.

Another consideration for branding consultancies is how the new product's name will work alongside the client's umbrella brand. For example, Novon is given independence from owner Sainsbury's, and Cap Colombie from Nescafé; whereas the Focus, Mondeo and Fiesta names are very much tied to the Ford umbrella brand. There is no right or wrong in this dilemma. Some companies, such as Sainsbury's with Novon, want to create sub-brands that, in the eyes of target consumers, are apparently free-standing. For Ford, the logic of cross-promotion and economies of scale in creating brand awareness have persuaded senior marketers to always utilise the Ford brand alongside the individual model name.

Most brand names are, at some point in the creation process, tested out on consumers, but according to leading branding consultancy Interbrand Newell & Sorrell, such tests have to be carefully constrained so as not to allow consumer suggestions to set the process back to square one. The research, argues Interbrand, should identify profoundly incorrect name suggestions, rather than present consumers with a blank sheet of paper for totally new suggestions. Interbrand's Nometrics testing methodology is well respected in the branding fraternity. First, names are tested in isolation of any product or service. Consumers are invited to nominate likely products to be associated with the suggested names. In the second stage of the Nometrics process, names are linked overtly to specific products, and the research gauges the views of consumers and the likelihood that they will purchase products that are so named. Ultimately, a good name cannot overcome product deficiencies, poor distribution, ineffectual promotion, incorrect pricing or inferior customer service, nor can it combat the superiority of a competitor's marketing strategy. A poor, inappropriate, confusing, unmemorable or misleading name can, though, do much harm to an otherwise good product offering.

Sources: Peter Doyle, 2001; Tom Blackett, Interbrand Newell & Sorrell; Deborah Carter, Dragon; David Rivett, Design Bridge; Colin Mechan, FLB; Paul Gander, 'Generation game', *Marketing Week*, 22 October 1998, pp. 45–8; Prophet, 2004; Interbrand, 2004–8.

names.[13] Because of their designs, some brands can be legally infringed upon more easily than others. Although registration provides trademark protection, a company should develop a system for ensuring that its trademarks will be renewed as needed. To protect its exclusive rights to a brand, the company must make certain that the selected brand is not likely to be considered an infringement on any existing brand already registered with the relevant patent office. This task may be complex because infringement is determined by the courts, which base their decisions on whether a brand causes consumers to be confused, mistaken or deceived about the source of the product. McDonald's is one company that aggressively protects its trademarks against infringement; it has brought charges against a number of companies with 'Mc' names because it fears that the use of the 'Mc' will give consumers the impression that these companies are associated with or owned by McDonald's.

If possible, marketers must guard against allowing a brand name to become a generic term used to refer to a general product category.[14] Generic terms cannot be protected as exclusive brand names. For example, names such as aspirin, escalator and shredded wheat – all brand names at one time – were eventually declared generic terms that refer to product classes; thus they could no longer be protected. To keep a brand name from becoming a generic term, the business should spell the name with a capital letter and use it as an adjective to modify the name of the general product class, as in Kellogg's Rice Krispies.[15] Including the word 'brand' just after the brand name is also helpful. An organisation can deal with this problem directly by advertising that its brand is a trademark and should not be used generically. The company can also indicate that the brand is a registered trademark by using the symbol ®.

Companies that try to protect a brand in a foreign country frequently encounter problems. In many countries, brand registration is not possible; the first company to use a

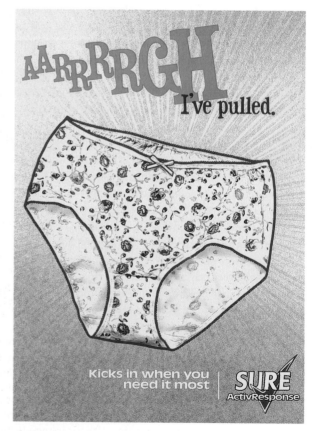

Figure 14.3
Unilever opts to develop individual brands, in this case for its range of Sure deodorants
Source: SURE is a registered trade mark of Unilever

brand in such a country has the rights to it. In some instances, a company has actually had to buy its own brand rights from a company in a foreign country because the foreign company was the first user in that country.

Marketers trying to protect their brands must also contend with brand counterfeiting. In many countries, for instance, it is possible to buy fake General Motors parts, fake Rolex watches, fake Chanel perfume, fake Microsoft software, fake Walt Disney character dolls and a host of other products illegally marketed by manufacturers that do not own the brands. Many counterfeit products are manufactured overseas – in South Korea, Italy, Taiwan and China, for example – but some are counterfeited in the countries in which they are sold. The International Anti-Counterfeiting Coalition estimates that roughly $70 billion in annual world trade involves counterfeit merchandise. The sale of this merchandise obviously reduces the brand owners' revenues from marketing their own legitimate products.

Brand counterfeiting is particularly harmful because the usually inferior counterfeit product undermines consumers' confidence in the brand and their loyalty to it. After unknowingly purchasing a counterfeit product, the buyer may blame the legitimate manufacturer if the product is of low quality or – even worse – if its use results in damage or injury. Since counterfeiting has become such a serious problem, many companies are taking legal action against counterfeiters. Others have adopted such measures as modifying the product or the packaging to make counterfeit items easier to detect, conducting public awareness campaigns, and monitoring distributors to ensure that they stock only legitimate brands.

Branding Policies

Before it establishes branding policies, a company must first decide whether to brand its products at all. If a company's product is homogeneous and similar to competitors' products, it may be difficult to brand. Raw materials – such as coal, salt, sand and milk – are hard to brand because of the homogeneity of such products and their physical characteristics. Marketers must also consider the degree to which consumers differentiate among brands of a product. For example, while brand may be an important factor in the purchase of coffee, snacks and frozen foods, it is not usually so important a consideration in buying light bulbs, cheese and cling film.

If a company chooses to brand its products, it may opt for one or more of the following branding policies: individual, overall family, line family and brand extension branding.

Individual branding
A policy of naming each product differently

Individual Branding

Individual branding is a policy of naming each product differently. Procter & Gamble relies on an individual branding policy for its line of fabric washing products, which includes Tide, Bold, Daz and Dreft. There are several Procter & Gamble brands in the UK's top 50 biggest consumer brands, including Pampers, Ariel, Oral B and Pringles – Table 14.2.

A major advantage of individual branding is that if an organisation introduces a poor product, the negative images associated with it will not contaminate the company's other products. An individual branding policy may also facilitate market segmentation when a company wishes to enter many segments of the same market. Separate, unrelated names can be used, and each brand can be aimed at a specific segment.

Overall family branding
A policy of branding all of a company's products with the same name, or at least part of the name

Overall Family Branding

In **overall family branding**, all of a company's products are branded with the same name, or at least part of the name, such as Kraft, Heinz, Microsoft or Ford. In some cases, a company's name is combined with other words to brand items. Heinz uses its name on its products along with a generic description of the item, such as Heinz Salad Cream, Heinz Baked Beans, Heinz Spaghetti and Heinz Tomato Soup. The quality image of its products increases consumer confidence in what they are buying. This brand consistency is stressed in Heinz advertisements (see Figure 14.4). Unlike individual branding, overall family branding means that the promotion of one item with the family brand promotes the company's other products.

TABLE 14.2 THE UK'S BIGGEST GROCERY BRANDS

Rank	Brand	Rank	Brand
1	Kelloggs	26	L'Oreal
2	Heinz	27	Robinsons
3	Walkers Crisps	28	Felix
4	Cadbury	29	Persil
5	Birds Eye	30	Princes
6	Coca-Cola	31	Pedigree
7	Muller	32	Carling
8	Warburtons	33	Colgate
9	McVitie's	34	Hardys
10	Hovis	35	Pepsi
11	Stella Artois	36	Walls Ice Cream
12	Nescafe	37	Nivea
13	Danone	38	Weetabix
14	Weight Watchers	39	Fosters
15	Bernard Matthews	40	Lurpak
16	Nestle Cereals	41	Ariel
17	Andrex	42	Aunt Bessies
18	Kingsmill	43	Gallo
19	Gillette	44	Johnson & Johnson
20	Pampers	45	Cathedral City
21	Flora	46	Huggies
22	Fairy	47	Oral B
23	Youngs	48	Tropicana
24	Whiskas	49	Smirnoff
25	McCain	50	Pringles

Source: TNS World Panel, 'Top 50 Take-Home Grocery Brands, 2006/7', *The Marketing Pocketbook 2008*, p. 99

Line family branding
A policy of using family branding only for products within a single line

Line Family Branding   Sometimes an organisation uses family branding only for products within a single line. This policy is called **line family branding**. Colgate-Palmolive, for example, produces a line of cleaning products that includes a cleanser, a powdered detergent and a liquid cleaner, all with the name Ajax. Colgate also produces several brands of toothpaste, none of which carries the Ajax brand name.

Brand extension branding
A company's use of one of its existing brand names as part of an improved or new product, usually in the same product category as the existing brand

Brand Extension Branding   **Brand extension branding** occurs when a company uses one of its existing brand names as part of a brand for an improved or new product that is usually in the same product category as the existing brand. The makers of Timotei shampoo extended the name to hair conditioner and skincare products. There is one major difference between line family branding and brand extension branding. With line family branding, all products in the line carry the same name, but with brand extension branding this is not the case. The producer of Arrid deodorant, for example, also makes other brands of deodorant. Waterford, an upmarket Irish brand of crystal, extended its name to writing instruments when seeking sales growth beyond closely related product categories, such as china, cutlery and table linens.[16]

Choice of Branding Policy   An organisation is not limited to a single branding policy. Instead, branding policy is influenced by the:

- number of products and product lines the company produces
- characteristics of its target markets

Figure 14.4
Overall family branding. Heinz uses its name on its products, along with a generic description of the item
Source: mediablitzimages (uk) Limited/Alamy

- number and type of competing products available
- size of its resources.

Anheuser-Busch, for example, uses both individual and brand extension branding. Most of the brands are individual brands; however, the Michelob Light brand is an extension of the Michelob brand. Sometimes companies must update brands so that they remain fresh and interesting.

Brand Licensing

A recent trend in branding strategies involves the licensing of trademarks. By means of a licensing agreement, a company may permit approved manufacturers to use its trademark on other products for a licensing fee. Royalties may be as low as 2 per cent of wholesale revenues or higher than 10 per cent. The licensee is responsible for all manufacturing, selling and advertising functions, and bears the costs if the licensed product fails. Not long ago, only a few companies licensed their corporate trademarks but today the licensing business is worth billions of pounds and is growing. Harley-Davidson, for example, has authorised the use of its name on non-motorcycle products such as cologne, wine coolers, gold rings and shirts. Disney also licenses its brand for use on a range of products. JCB and Coca-Cola both now license ranges of clothing sold in high-street stores.

The advantages of licensing range from extra revenues and low cost to free publicity, new images and trademark protection. For example, Coca-Cola has licensed its trademark for use on glassware, radios, trucks and clothing in the hope of protecting its trademark. Similarly, Jaguar has licensed a range of leisure wear. However, brand licensing is not without its drawbacks. The major disadvantages are a lack of manufacturing control, which could hurt the company's name, and the undesirability of bombarding consumers with too many unrelated products bearing the same name. Licensing arrangements can also fail because of poor timing, inappropriate distribution channels or mismatching of product and name.

Managing Brands

With the need for brands to create product differentiation, assist in establishing a competitive edge and encourage product awareness, marketers must manage their brands with care.[17] This involves understanding when a brand requires repositioning, modifying, deleting or simply being left alone. Most companies operate with a portfolio of separate brands and products, and must make difficult decisions in terms of which are to receive support and the bulk of an organisation's marketing resource, and which are to be killed off or given only minimal support. Chapter 9 explores these strategic choices.

As explained in Chapter 4's discussion of consumer buying behaviour, without an understanding of brand loyalty and brand switching, it is difficult to manage an organisation's brands effectively. It is essential, therefore, for companies to make an effort to research brand loyalty and brand perceptions to help them make sensible decisions that accurately reflect consumers' views.

Research shows that to create **successful brands**, a company must:

- prioritise quality – the top brands are all high quality in their product fields
- offer superior service – less easily copied by competitors than pure product attributes
- get there first – not necessarily technologically but, in the minds of targeted customers, by
  - exploiting new technology (Rank Xerox, Sony)
  - new positioning concepts (Body Shop, First Direct)
  - new distribution channels (Argos, Direct Line)
  - new market segments (Orange, Ocado)
  - using gaps resulting from environmental change (Ecover, Daz Ultra)
- differentiate its brands – so that consumers perceive the brands on offer as being different
- develop a unique positioning concept – making the brand and its differentiating characteristics stand out with a clear image and positioning message against rival brands
- support the brand and its positioning with a strong communications programme – so that target consumers are aware of the brand and its positioning proposition
- deliver consistency and reliability over time – keeping the brand's values trustworthy as perceived by target consumers.

Branding expert Peter Doyle[18] stated that, to build effective brands, it is essential for an organisation to understand that there is more to a brand than simply a catchy name and visible logo. Doyle argued that **brand strength** is a function of the product's attributes and functionality, its differentiation, plus any demonstrable added value to the purchaser or user. For example, Nike sports shoes are designed for serious running and are fit for this core purpose, but Nike has a reputation for innovation and progression, so the brand is perceived as a 'first mover', providing differentiation versus rival brands. For the purchaser, the reputation of the brand for being state-of-the-art and highly desirable, provides 'street cred', which is the added value to the consumer.

There are, in fact, four **levels of brands**: the tangible product, the 'basic' brand, the 'augmented' brand and the 'potential' of the brand. Level 1, the tangible product, is the degree of quality, performance, features and actual attributes. Level 2, the 'basic' brand, is the identity, differentiation and positioning. Level 3, the 'augmented' brand, is the aggregated impact from including supplementary products and service support. Level 4, the 'potential' of the brand, is reached when customers will not willingly accept substitutes and are unhappy to switch to rival brands; psychological benefits and barriers in the minds of target customers are important determinants of brand potential.

There are three essential acid tests for determining whether a brand is successful. Although most companies consider only the overall profit contribution to the end-of-year

Successful brands
Brands for which a company must prioritise quality, offer superior service, get there first, differentiate brands, develop a unique positioning concept, have a strong communications programme, and be consistent and reliable

Brand strength
A function of the product's attributes and functionality, its differentiation, plus any demonstrable added value to the purchaser or user

Levels of brands
The tangible product, the 'basic' brand, the 'augmented' brand and the 'potential' of the brand

financial annual report and accounts, when determining a brand's success they should ask the following three fundamental questions:

1 Has the brand captured the leading share in its market segment or distribution channel?
2 Does the brand command prices sufficiently high enough to produce a large profit margin?
3 Will the brand sustain its strong share of profits when rival and generic versions of the product enter the market?

Using these core criteria, many brands are relatively unsuccessful. For marketers, managing brands must include knowing when a brand is succeeding, when it is faltering but may be saved, and when a brand is a lost cause and should be deleted from the company's range of brands. Chapter 9 examines this difficult issue in more detail.

Corporate Branding

Corporate branding
The application of product branding at the corporate level, reflected visibly through the company name, logo and visual presentation, and in the organisation's underlying values

Corporate image
Reflects the perceptions that external audiences hold about an organisation

Corporate identity
Overlapping with the corporate branding concept: branding at the corporate level

Corporate branding involves applying the principles of product branding at the corporate level. Corporate branding is reflected in visible manifestations such as the company name, logo and visual presentation, and also in the organisation's underlying and guiding values. Thus British Airways, McDonald's, Wal-Mart and Manchester United Football Club each has a corporate brand that is based around the organisation itself. Sometimes the terms **corporate image** and **corporate identity** are also used in relation to corporate branding. The concepts of corporate identity and corporate branding overlap: both referring to what the company transmits about itself.[19] Corporate image reflects the perceptions that external audiences hold about the organisation.[20]

Corporate branding plays a role in guiding all of a company's marketing activities. The corporate brand is transmitted through tangible and intangible features. The tangible dimensions include visual features of the corporate brand, such as corporate logo and symbols, typography, colour, buildings, staff uniforms, vehicles and stationery. For example, Unilever has recently overhauled its corporate identity to fit with the company's mission: 'to add vitality to life'. The corporate brand is reflected in a new logo featuring flowers, animals and stars, which will be carried by the organisation's products.[21] Less tangible features include how the corporate brand is portrayed through what people inside and outside the organisation believe and say about it.

To be effective, the corporate brand should be embedded in all company actions. This means that all aspects of the company's communication, including internal communication with employees and external marketing activities ranging from the annual report through to its advertising and PR, must convey a consistent message about the corporate brand. Corporate branding is particularly important for services organisations, because customers look for help in understanding and visualising the services product. A strong corporate brand can therefore help buyers to overcome the intangibility of some of these products. For example, First Direct bank has worked hard to build a corporate image based on service quality, which reflects the company's reliability and flexible approach to meeting customer needs. This has helped to build a corporate image based around the notion of good service. The fact that this image is also reflected in research examining service in the financial services sector adds credibility to the bank's offering.

Packaging and Labelling

Packaging and labelling are also part of the marketing process. They impact upon the image of the product, its functionality and, ultimately, upon the customer's perception of satisfaction. At times, they create differentiation vis-à-vis rival products. For example, Coca-Cola introduced limited-edition packaging for its iconic glass bottle to appeal to upmarket consumers. Working with fashion designer Matthew Williamson, the designer bottle was available in three wrap-around prints, each taken from Williamson's summer clothing collection. The bottles were retailed only through selected style bars and restaurants.[22]

Packaging
The development of a product's container and label, complete with graphic design

Packaging involves the development of a container and label, complete with graphic design for a product. A package can be a vital part of a product, making it more versatile, safer or easier to use. Like a brand name, a package can influence customers' attitudes towards a product and thus affect their purchase decisions. For example, several producers of sauces, salad dressings and ketchups have packaged their products in squeezable containers to make use and storage more convenient. Package characteristics help shape buyers' impressions of a product at the time of purchase or during use. This section examines the main functions of packaging and considers several major packaging decisions. The role of the package in marketing strategy is also analysed.

Packaging Functions

Effective packaging means more than simply putting products into containers and covering them with wrappers. First of all, packaging materials serve the basic purpose of protecting the product and maintaining its functional form. Fluids such as milk, orange juice and hairspray need packages that preserve and protect them; the packaging should prevent damage that could affect the product's usefulness and increase costs. Since product tampering has become a problem for marketers of many types of goods, several packaging techniques have been developed to counter this danger. Some packages are also designed to foil shoplifters.

Another function of packaging is to offer convenience for consumers. For example, small, sealed packages – individual sized boxes or plastic bags that contain liquids and do not require refrigeration – appeal strongly to children and young adults with active lifestyles. The size or shape of a package may relate to the product's storage, convenience of use or replacement rate. Small, single-serving tins of fruit, such as Del Monte's Fruitini, may prevent waste and make storage easier. Low, regular-shaped packets may be easier to stack and use cupboard space more efficiently. A third function of packaging is to promote a product by communicating its features, uses, benefits and image. At times, a reusable package is developed to make a product more desirable. For example, some ice-cream containers can be used again as food storage containers.

Major Packaging Considerations

Packaging must support a product's brand image and positioning, helping develop differentiation vis-à-vis rival products. When developing packages, marketers must take many factors into account. Some of these factors relate to consumers' needs; others relate to the requirements of resellers. Retailers, wholesalers and distributors will be required to handle and stock the products, and in many instances to display and deliver them. Packaging solutions must reflect the needs of these channel members in addition to the requirements of end-user customers. Obviously, one major consideration is cost. Although a variety of packaging materials, processes and designs are available, some are rather expensive. In recent years buyers have shown a willingness to pay more for improved packaging, but there are limits. Marketers should try to determine, through research, just how much customers are willing to pay for packages.

Developing tamper-resistant packaging is very important. Although no package is totally tamper-proof, marketers can develop packages that are difficult to tamper with and that also make any tampering evident to resellers and consumers. Because new, safer packaging technologies are being explored, marketers should be aware of changes in packaging technology and legislation, and prepared to make modifications that will ensure consumer safety. One packaging innovation includes an inner pouch that displays the word 'open' when air has entered the pouch after opening. Marketers now also have an obligation to inform consumers of the possibilities and risks of product tampering by educating them to recognise possible tampering and by placing warnings on packaging.[23] For example, the tops of many sauce and condiment bottles now have plastic seals around them, so that consumers can be confident they have not been opened. Baby food manufacturers, such as Cow & Gate and Heinz, have taken this protection method one step further by using special metal jar tops with pop-up discs showing when a jar has been opened. This move followed cases of tampering in which foreign bodies were introduced into baby foods. Now the special tops expressly warn consumers to watch out for tampering. Although effective tamper-resistant packaging may be expensive to develop, when balanced against the costs of lost sales, loss of consumer confidence and a company's reputation, and potentially expensive product liability lawsuits, the costs of ensuring consumer safety are minimal.[24]

Marketers should consider how much consistency is desirable in a company's package designs. The best policy may be not to attempt consistency, especially if a company's products are unrelated or aimed at vastly different target markets. To promote an overall company image, a company may decide that all packages are to be similar or include one major element of the design. This approach is called **family packaging**. Sometimes it is used only for lines of products, as with Campbell's soups, Weight Watchers foods and Planters nuts.

Family packaging
An approach in which all of a company's packages are similar or include one major element of the design

A package's promotional role is an important consideration. Through verbal and non-verbal symbols, the package can inform potential buyers about the product's content, features, uses, advantages and hazards. A company can create desirable images and associations by its choice of colour, design, shape and texture. Many cosmetics manufacturers, for example, design their packages to create impressions of richness, luxury and exclusiveness. A package performs a promotional function when it is designed to be safer or more convenient to use, if such characteristics help stimulate demand.

To develop a package that has a definite promotional value, a designer must consider size, shape, texture, colour and graphics.[25] Beyond the obvious limitation that the package must be large enough to hold the product, a package can be designed to appear taller or shorter. For instance, thin vertical lines make a package look taller; wide horizontal stripes make it look shorter. A marketer may want a package to appear taller because many people perceive something that is taller as being larger.

Colours on packages and in branding are often chosen to attract attention. People associate specific colours with certain feelings and experiences, as outlined below.

Blue is soothing, it is also associated with wealth, trust and security.
Grey is associated with strength, exclusivity and success.
Orange can stand for low cost.
Red has connotations of excitement, stimulation and danger.
Yellow is associated with cheerfulness and joy.
Purple is linked with dignity and stateliness.
Black is associated with being strong and masterful.[26]

For example, BMW always uses the blue and grey colour palettes in its advertising and brochures, while easyJet's planes famously are adorned in orange. Uncle Ben's rice is familiar in its orange packaging as it emphasises convenience and value for money, while more up-market competitor Tilda – focusing on premium quality and superior taste – utilizes blue in its branding and smart new packaging.

When selecting packaging colours, marketers must decide whether a particular colour will evoke positive or negative feelings when it is linked to a specific product. Rarely, for example, do processors package meat or bread in green materials, because customers may associate green with mould. However, recent concern about the state of the environment has, in general, led to an increase in the use of green-coloured packaging. Marketers must also decide whether a specific target market will respond favourably or unfavourably to a particular colour. Cosmetics for women are more likely to be sold in pastel-coloured packaging than are personal care products for men. Packages designed to appeal to children often use primary colours and bold designs.

Packaging must also meet the needs of resellers. Wholesalers and retailers consider whether a package facilitates transportation, storage and handling. Packages must allow these resellers to make maximum use of storage space, both in transit and in the shops. Products should be packed so that sales staff can transfer them to the shelves with ease. The shape and weight of packaging are also important. Resellers may refuse to carry certain products if their packages are cumbersome. Figure 14.5 shows how these factors have been taken into consideration in developing Cuprinol's Castlepak woodcare varnish container.

A final consideration is whether to develop packages that are environmentally responsible. A Cable News Network (CNN) report on the growing refuse disposal problem in the USA stated that nearly 50 per cent of all rubbish consists of discarded plastic packaging, such as polystyrene containers, plastic soft drink bottles, carrier bags and other packaging items. Plastic packaging material does not biodegrade, and using paper requires the destruction of valuable forest lands. Consequently, a number of companies are recycling more materials and exploring packaging alternatives, helped by packaging experts such as Tetra Pak. Heinz, for example, is looking for alternatives to its plastic squeezable ketchup bottles.

Companies that decide to develop environmentally responsible packaging have not always received a positive response. For example, customers' responses to US burger chain Wendy's paper plates and coffee cups were mixed; some customers prefer the old non-biodegradable foam packaging. Other companies searching for alternatives to environmentally harmful packaging have experienced similar problems. Thus marketers must carefully balance society's desires to preserve the environment against consumers' desires for convenience. Green concerns are forcing changes to packaging.

Packaging development
A mix of aesthetic considerations and structural necessities to guarantee the functionality of the design

Packaging Development

Packaging development requires a mix of aesthetic considerations and structural necessities to guarantee the functionality of the design. There are cartons, bottles, tubes, cans, tubs and jars, multipacks, clamshells and blister packs, CD boxes, gift packs, plus many innovative formats for storing, displaying and dispensing products in a manner that is

Easy-open features

Single pack material for ease of recycling

Brush wipe to aid product application

Effective point of sale presentation and stackability

Efficient pallet utilisation

Figure 14.5
Cuprinol's Castlepak™ woodcare varnish container highlights how environmental consumer usage and operation needs can be incorporated into a single packaging solution
Source: Courtesy of Marketing Magazine, *London*

ahead of the competition. Material selection is an important stage in the design process, as are the specification and application of surface graphics and typography. Decisions must be made concerning information layout and the hierarchy of messages, front-of-pack versus back-of-pack detailing, choice of language and jargon, the photography and images to be selected, illustrations and use of colour, deployment of symbols and icons, final finishes and effects. There are often practical requirements to consider, such as weights, measures, ingredients, nutritional information and barcoding to display.

Packaging and Marketing Strategy

Packaging can be a major component of a marketing strategy. A new cap or closure, a better box or wrapping, or a more convenient container may give a product a competitive edge. The right type of package for a new product can help it gain market recognition very quickly. In the case of existing brands, marketers should periodically re-evaluate packages. Particularly in the case of consumer convenience products, marketers should view packaging as a major strategic tool. Tilda re-launched its *Rizazz* microwavable rice pouches as *Tilda Steamed Basmati* rice in smarter, more up-market packaging with improved graphics so as to adequately reflect the superiority of the recipes and ingredients, with significant success in terms of appealing to its target market consumers. This section examines ways in which packaging can be used strategically.

Altering the Package   At times, a marketer changes a package because the existing design is no longer in style, especially when compared with competitive products. Smith & Nephew redesigned its Simple range of toiletries to show that the products have evolved with the times. A package may also be redesigned because new product features need to be highlighted on the package, or because new packaging materials have become available. A company may decide to change a product's packaging to make the product more convenient or safer to use, or to reposition the product. A major redesign of a simple package costs about £25,000, and the redesign of a line of products may cost up to £300,000. Choosing the right packaging material is an important consideration when redesigning. Different materials vary in popularity at different times. For example, glass is becoming more popular as views on the environment and the need for recyclability come to the fore.

Secondary use package
A package that can be reused for purposes other than its initial use

Secondary Use Packaging   A **secondary use package** is one that can be reused for purposes other than its initial one. For example, a margarine container can be reused to store leftovers, a jam jar can be used as a drinking glass, and shortbread tins can be reused for storing cakes and biscuits. Secondary use packages can be viewed by customers as adding value to products. If customers value this type of packaging, then its use should stimulate unit sales.

Category-consistent packaging
The packaging of a product according to the packaging practices associated with a particular product category

Category-consistent packaging   **Category-consistent packaging** means that the product is packaged in line with the packaging practices associated with a particular product category. Some product categories – for example, mayonnaise, mustard, ketchup and jam – have traditional package shapes. Other product categories are characterised by recognisable colour combinations – red and white for soup; red and yellow for tea; red, white and blue for Ritz-type crackers. When a company introduces a brand in one of these product categories, marketers will often use traditional package shapes and colour combinations to ensure that customers will recognise the new product as being in that specific product category.

Innovative Packaging   Sometimes, a marketer will employ a unique cap, design, applicator or other feature to make the product competitively distinctive, as illustrated in Figure 14.6. Such packaging can be effective when the innovation makes the product safer or easier to use, or when the unique package provides better protection for the product. In some instances, marketers use innovative or unique packages that are inconsistent with traditional packaging practices, to make the brand stand out relative to its competitors. Procter & Gamble, for example, used an innovative, crush-proof cylinder to package its Pringles potato crisps. Innovative packaging generally requires considerable resources, not only for the package design itself but also to make customers aware of the unique package and its benefit. Sometimes, innovative

Figure 14.6
Leading packaging supplier Tetrapak promotes the functionality and applicability of its cartons
Source: Courtesy of Ian Bilbey/CIA, Abbott Mead Vickers. BBDO

packaging can change the way in which consumers use a product. The introduction of cardboard-boxed, single serving soft drinks made it easier for consumers to have a drink while travelling by car, train and plane. Even cyclists can drink with ease while on the move.

Multiple Packaging   Rather than packaging a single unit of a product, marketers sometimes use twin packs, tri-packs, six-packs or other forms of **multiple packaging**. For certain types of product, multiple packaging is used to increase demand because it increases the amount of the product available at the point of consumption – in consumers' houses, for example. However, multiple packaging does not work for all types of product. Consumers would not use additional table salt simply because an extra box was in the cupboard. Multiple packaging can make products easier to handle and store, as in the case of six-packs for soft drinks; it can also facilitate special price offers, such as two-for-one sales. In addition, multiple packaging may increase consumer acceptance of the product by encouraging the buyer to try the product several times.

> **Multiple packaging**
> Packaging that includes more than one unit of a product, such as twin packs, tri-packs and six-packs

Handling Improved Packaging   Packaging of a product may be changed to make it easier to handle in the distribution channel – for example, changing the outer carton, special bundling, shrink wrapping or palletising. In some cases the shape of the package may need to be changed. For example, an ice cream producer may switch from a cylindrical package to a rectangular one to facilitate handling. In addition, at the retail level, the ice cream producer may be able to get more shelf facings with a rectangular package as opposed to a round one. Outer containers for products are sometimes changed so that they will proceed more easily through automated warehousing systems.

428

As package designs improve, it becomes harder for any one product to dominate because of packaging. However, marketers still attempt to gain a competitive edge through packaging. Skilled artists and package designers who have experience in marketing research, test out packaging to see what sells well, not just what is aesthetically appealing. Since the typical large store stocks 15,000 items or more, products that stand out are more likely to be bought.

Criticisms of Packaging

The last few decades have seen a number of improvements in packaging. However, some packaging problems still need to be resolved. Some packages simply do not work well. The packaging for flour and sugar is, at best, often not much better than poor. Both grocers and consumers are very much aware that these packages leak and are easily torn. Can anyone open and close a bag of flour without spilling at least a little bit? Certain packages, such as biscuit tins, milk cartons with fold-out spouts and potato crisp bags, are frequently difficult to open. The traditional shapes of packages for products such as ketchup and salad dressing make the products inconvenient to use. Have you ever questioned, when slapping a ketchup bottle, why the producer did not put the ketchup in a mayonnaise jar?

Certain types of packaging are being questioned with regard to their recyclability and biodegradability. For example, throw-away bottles take considerably more resources to produce than do reusable glass bottles. Social concerns and regulatory pressures are bringing green issues to the fore, with significant implications for marketers and packaging designers.

Although many steps have been taken to make packaging safer, critics still focus on health and safety issues. Containers with sharp edges and easily broken glass bottles are sometimes viewed as a threat to safety. Certain types of plastic packaging and aerosol containers represent possible health hazards.

At times, packaging is viewed as being deceptive. Package shape, graphic design and certain colours may be used to make a product appear larger than it actually is. The inconsistent use of certain size designations – such as 'giant', 'economy', 'family', 'king' and 'super' – can certainly lead to customer confusion. Although customers have traditionally liked attractive, effective, convenient packaging, the cost of such packaging is high. For some products, such as cosmetics, the cost of the package is higher than the cost of the product itself.

Labelling

Labelling
Packaging information that can be used for a variety of promotional, informational and legal purposes

Labelling is very closely related to packaging and can be used for a variety of promotional, informational and legal purposes. The label can be used to facilitate the identification of a product by presenting the brand and a unique graphic design. For example, Heinz's ketchup is easy to identify on a supermarket shelf because the brand name is easy to read and is coupled with a distinctive, crown-like graphic design. Labels have a descriptive function. For certain types of product, the label indicates the grade of the product, especially for tinned fruit. Labels can describe the source of the product, its contents and major features, how to use the product, how to care for the product, nutritional information, type and style of the product, and size and number of servings. The label can play a promotional function through the use of graphics that attract attention. The food and drug administrations and consumer protection agencies in different countries have varying requirements concerning warnings, instructions, certifications and manufacturers' identifications. Increasingly, however, the EU is demanding similar standards in all member countries. Despite the fact that consumers have responded favourably to the inclusion of this type of information on labels, evidence as to whether they actually use it has been mixed. Several studies indicate that consumers do not use nutritional information, whereas other studies indicate that the information is considered useful. Labels can also promote a manufacturer's other products or encourage proper use of products, resulting in greater customer satisfaction with them.

Universal product code (UPC) or barcode
A series of thick and thin lines that identifies the product, and provides inventory and pricing information readable by an electronic scanner

The label for many products includes a **universal product code (UPC) or barcode** – a series of thick and thin lines that identifies the product, and provides inventory and pricing information that can be read by an electronic scanner. The UPC is read electronically at the retail checkout counter. This information is used by retailers and producers for price and inventory control purposes.

Colour and eye-catching graphics on labels overcome the jumble of words – known to designers as 'mouse print' – that have been added to satisfy government regulations. Because so many similar products are available, an attention-getting device or 'silent sales-person' is needed to attract interest. As one of the most visible parts of a product, the label is an important element in a marketing mix.

Labelling is an integral part of packaging that can be used effectively to convey product information and benefits to customers, and to promote a brand's positioning image. There are increasing legal considerations that marketers must address, such as EU regulations in terms of food sourcing, ingredient content, nutritional information, weights and measures, as well as cooking or application instructions. Ethical marketing requires that consumers are not misled or 'over-sold' owing to the information provided on labels. In 2004, Coca-Cola had to withdraw its 'pure still water' Dasani after a batch was contaminated with an excess of the cancer-causing mineral, bromate. Just before Dasani's withdrawal from the market, the Food Standards Agency in the UK had been examining the manufacturer's claim that the product – heavily filtered tap water – was 'pure'. Partly in response, the members of the Natural Mineral Water Association, including Danone Waters, Nestlé Waters, Spadel and Highland Spring, launched an over-arching symbol to appear on the packing of their respective brands, indicating their products as pure, natural mineral water: 'Natural Mineral Water Certified'. This 'purity' symbol is intended to signify which brands are unadulterated pure mineral water, in a highly competitive and fast-evolving market, with a plethora of flavoured and modified waters now widely available.[27] Concerns about obesity and diabetes are forcing manufacturers of foods to include nutritional and healthy-eating information on their packaging. This provides a window of opportunity for healthier brands to compete with many leading brands whose domination was once viewed as impregnable. *Innocent* smoothies have stolen market share from the colas in most supermarkets, and *Innocent*'s humorous packaging stresses its wholesome and healthy qualities.

Summary

A *brand* is a name, term, design, symbol or any other feature that identifies one seller's good or service as distinct from those of other sellers. A *brand name* is that part of a brand that can be spoken, including letters, words and numbers; the element that cannot be spoken – often a symbol or design – is called a *brand mark*. A *trademark* is a legal designation indicating that the owner has exclusive use of a brand or part of a brand, and that others are prohibited by law from using it. A *trade name* is the legal name of an organisation.

❯❯ Branding helps buyers identify and evaluate products, helps sellers facilitate repeat purchasing and product introduction, and fosters *brand loyalty* – a customer's strongly motivated and long-standing decision to purchase a particular product or service. The three degrees of brand loyalty are recognition,

preference and insistence. *Brand recognition* exists when a customer is aware that a brand exists and views it as an alternative to purchase if the preferred brand is unavailable. *Brand preference* is the degree of brand loyalty in which a customer prefers one brand over competing brands and will purchase it if it is available. *Brand insistence* is the degree of brand loyalty in which a customer will accept no substitute. *Brand equity* is the marketing and financial value associated with a brand's strength in a market. It represents the value of a brand to an organisation. The four major elements underlying brand equity are brand name awareness, brand loyalty, perceived brand quality and brand associations.

❯❯ Branding experts believe that well-managed, strong and desirable brands should identify a set of specific tangible benefits to attach to the brand, known as *brand attributes*, a set of reassuring and more emotive *brand values* which help develop a unified sense of purpose among staff as well as support differentiation with external audiences, plus a set of appealing and desirable *brand personality* traits. Implicit in this view is the importance of effectively creating a well-differentiated and memorable image for the brand that is carefully controlled.

» A *manufacturer brand*, initiated by the producer, makes it possible to associate the company more easily with its products at the point of purchase. An *own label brand* is initiated and owned by a reseller, such as a retailer. A *generic brand* indicates only the product category and does not include the company name or other identifying terms. Manufacturers combat the growing competition from own label brands by developing multiple brands.

» When selecting a brand name, a marketer should choose one that is easy to say, spell and recall, and that alludes to the product's uses, benefits or special characteristics. Brand names are created inside an organisation by individuals, committees or branding departments, or by outside consultants. Brand names can be devised from words, initials, numbers, nonsense words or a combination of these. Services as well as products are branded, often with the company name and an accompanying symbol that makes the brand distinctive or conveys a desired image.

» Producers protect ownership of their brands through patent and trademark offices. Marketers at a company must make certain that their selected brand name does not infringe on an already-registered brand by confusing or deceiving consumers about the source of the product. In many countries, brand registration is on a first-come, first-served basis, making protection more difficult. Brand counterfeiting, increasingly common, has potential for undermining consumer confidence in, and loyalty to, a brand.

» Companies brand their products in several ways. *Individual branding* designates a unique name for each of a company's products; *overall family branding* identifies all of a company's products with the same name; *line family branding* assigns all products within a single line the same name; and

brand extension branding applies an existing name to a new or improved product. Trademark licensing enables producers to earn extra revenue, receive low cost or free publicity, and protect their trademarks. Through a licensing agreement, and for a licensing fee, a company may permit approved manufacturers to use its trademark on other products.

» *Successful brands* tend to prioritise quality, offer superior service, get to market or the targeted segment first, be clearly differentiated from rival brands, have a unique positioning concept supported by a strong communications programme and be consistent over time. *Brand strength* is a function of the product's attributes and functionality, its differentiation, plus any demonstrable added value to the purchaser or user. Strong brands usually create product differentiation, help establish a competitive edge, encourage product awareness and demand a significant amount of management and control. Four *levels of brands* need to be addressed: the tangible product, the 'basic' brand, the 'augmented' brand and the 'potential' of the brand. To be successful, a brand should capture the leading share in its market segment or distribution channel, command prices sufficiently high to offer high profit margins and be likely to maintain its profit position after more brands and generic versions enter the market. Many companies should be more effective in managing their brands, many of which do not live up to these success criteria.

» *Corporate branding* involves applying the principles of product branding at the corporate level. Corporate branding is reflected in visible manifestations such as the company name, logo and visual presentation, and also in the organisation's underlying and guiding values. Sometimes the terms *corporate image* and *corporate identity* are also used in relation to corporate branding. Corporate branding plays a role in guiding all of a company's marketing activities. Corporate branding is transmitted through tangible and intangible features and, to be effective, should be embedded in all company actions.

» *Packaging* involves the development of a container and label, complete with graphic design for a product. Effective packaging offers protection, economy, safety and convenience. It can influence the customer's purchase decision by promoting a product's features, uses, benefits and image. When developing a package, marketers must consider costs relative to how much the target market is willing to pay. Other considerations include how to make the package tamper-resistant; whether to use *family packaging, secondary use packaging, category-consistent packaging* or *multiple packaging*; how to design the package as an effective promotional tool; how best to accommodate resellers; and whether to develop environmentally responsible packaging.

» *Packaging development* involves aesthetic and structural choices. Other considerations include: material selection, surface graphics, typography, information layout and hierarchies, front-of-pack versus back-of-pack detailing, language and jargon, photography and illustrations, use of colour, symbols and icons, final finishes and effects, labelling practicalities and barcoding/tracking. There are numerous primary packaging options: cartons, bottles, tubes, cans, tubs and jars, multipacks, clamshells, blister packs, CD boxes, gift packs and a host of innovative solutions for storing, displaying and dispensing products.

» Packaging can be a major component of a marketing strategy. Companies choose particular colours, designs, shapes and textures to create desirable images and associations. Producers alter packages to convey new features or to make them safer or more convenient. If a package has a secondary use, the product's value to the consumer may be increased. Category-consistent packaging makes products more easily recognised by consumers, and innovative packaging enhances a product's distinctiveness. Consumers may criticise packaging that doesn't work well, is not biodegradable or recyclable, poses health or safety problems, or is deceptive in some way.

» *Labelling* is an important aspect of packaging that can be used for promotional, informational and legal purposes. Because labels are attention-getting devices, they are significant features in the marketing mix. Various regulatory agencies can require that products be labelled or marked with warnings, instructions, certifications, nutritional information and the manufacturer's identification. Increasingly, most products – even cars – have a *universal product code (UPC) or barcode*. There are ethical considerations for marketers as customers should not be misled or mis-sold owing to the information conveyed on a product's packaging.

◈ *Key Links*

- This chapter, about effective branding, should be read in conjunction with the section of Chapter 6 that addresses the linked concept of brand positioning.
- The branding strategy must reflect the characteristics of the product too, as explored in Chapter 8.
- Many companies operate a portfolio of brands and often must select some for priority investment and marketing spend, as described in Chapter 9.

Important Terms

Brand
Brand name
Brand mark
Trademark
Trade name
Brand loyalty
Brand recognition
Brand preference
Brand insistence
Brand equity
Brand attributes
Brand values
Brand personality
Manufacturer brands
Own-label brands
Generic brand
Individual branding
Overall family branding
Line family branding
Brand extension branding
Successful brands
Brand strength

Levels of brands
Corporate branding
Corporate image
Corporate identity
Packaging
Family packaging
Packaging development
Secondary use packaging
Category-consistent packaging
Multiple packaging
Labelling
Universal product code (UPC) or barcode

Discussion and Review Questions

1 What is the difference between a brand and a brand name? Compare and contrast the terms brand mark and trademark.
2 How does branding benefit customers and organisations?
3 What are the advantages associated with brand loyalty?
4 What are the distinguishing characteristics of own label brands?
5 Given the competition between own label brands and manufacturer brands, should manufacturers be concerned about the popularity of own label brands? How should manufacturers fight back in the brand battle?
6 Identify and explain the major considerations consumers take into account when selecting a brand.
7 The brand name Xerox is sometimes used generically to refer to photocopying machines. How can Xerox Corporation protect this brand name?
8 Identify and explain the four major branding policies and give examples of each. Can a company use more than one policy at a time? Explain your answer.
9 What are the major advantages and disadvantages of licensing?
10 Why is there more to a brand than its name? Explain your response.
11 What are the most commonly found foundations for successful brands? Illustrate your response with brand examples.
12 What constitutes brand strength?
13 What are the differences between brand attributes, brand values and brand personality?
14 What is brand equity and why is this notion increasingly important?
15 What are the three core criteria for assessing the success of a brand?
16 Describe the functions that a package can perform. Which function is most important? Why?
17 When developing a package, what are the major issues that a marketer should consider?
18 In what ways can packaging be used as a strategic tool?
19 What are the major criticisms of packaging?
20 What are the major functions of labelling?

Recommended Reading

- Aaker, D., *Building Strong Brands* (New York: Free Press, 2002).
- Aaker, D.A. and Joachimsthaler, E., *Brand Leadership* (New York: Free Press, 2002).
- Calver, G., *What is Packaging Design?* (Mies, Switzerland: RotoVision SA, 2004).
- De Chernatony, L. and McDonald, M., *Creating Powerful Brands* (Oxford: Butterworth-Heinemann, 2004).
- Doyle, P., *Marketing Management and Strategy* (Harlow: Pearson/FT, 2002).
- Kahn, K., *The PDMA Handbook of New Product Development* (New York: John Wiley, 2004).
- Keller, K.L., *Strategic Brand Management* (Englewood Cliffs, NJ: Prentice-Hall, 2007).
- Lehmann, D. and Winer, R., *Product Management* (Boston, Mass: McGraw-Hill, 2004).
- Macrae, C., *The Brand Chartering Handbook* (London: Thomson, 1999).
- Ries, A. and Ries, L., *The 22 Immutable Laws of Branding: How to Build any Product or Line into a World Class Brand* (London: HarperCollins, 2002).

Internet Exercise

Packaging has to reflect manufacturers' requirements and also evolving consumer issues. Log on to: www.tetrapak.com
Consider the information on this leading packaging company's website, notably the information offered about the company, its ethos, Core Values, innovation and new product development.
1 To what extent and in what ways is Tetra Pak addressing changing and evolving manufacturer and consumer issues?
2 What innovative packaging solutions is Tetra Pak currently developing?

● Applied Mini-Case

In the 1980s, one of Europe's retailing success stories was the creation by George Davies of fashion chain Next. Leading out-of-town grocery retailer ASDA persuaded Davies to rekindle the fortunes of its clothing range. The result was the George range of men's, women's and children's clothing, positioned as a low price, high style fashion brand. 'Styles straight off the catwalk' at affordable prices, targeted at ASDA's value-conscious shoppers, proved incredibly successful. In the highly competitive clothing market, in 2004 the George range in ASDA grocery superstores overtook Debenhams to become the UK's third biggest retailer of clothing. A few years ago, George Davies moved on and, to the surprise of many onlookers, was approached by erstwhile arch-rival Marks & Spencer to help improve the former market leader's fortunes. The result for Marks & Spencer was the recently launched highly successful range of stylish fashion, branded Per Una.

Both ASDA, with George, and Marks & Spencer, with Per Una, decided to utilise newly created brands for their new clothing ranges. In the case of Marks & Spencer, this was even more remarkable, as previously all of its merchandise retailed under the St Michael retailer own label brand, familiar to generations of shoppers. It is believed that without brand identities so deliberately far removed from the host retailers' own brands, neither George nor Per Una would have been so successful. Both brands have themselves enabled their owners to extend their operations: George is available by catalogue, and both George and Per Una have now been given fashion-only high-street branches.

Sources: George/ASDA, 2004; Marks & Spencer stores, 2003/2004; Rachel Barnes, 'ASDA to highlight style in George repositioning', *Marketing*, 25 March 2004, p. 4.

● Question

Why did ASDA and Marks & Spencer both opt to launch clothing ranges with new brand identities that were different to the host retailers' brands?

● Case Study

3D and Environmentally Friendly Packaging Design

Three-dimensional packaging does much more than protect products and make them easy to distribute, handle and use. For marketers, 3D packaging can help differentiate a brand, add value or simply aid consumer recognition. The distinctive shape of the Coca-Cola bottle, recognised worldwide, is synonymous with the brand. The importance of creative packaging design is well established. Maximising packaging design benefits requires an integrated approach that considers financial, manufacturing, distribution and marketing requirements. In some companies this total business approach is achieved by forming staff teams with representatives from all business areas. The teams will consider all aspects of packaging design: materials, size and shape, opening and closure features, material conversion efficiency, retail storage and display, transportability, disposability, filling speed and costs.

Research shows that for some products, innovative packaging is seen to add value in the eyes of target consumers. There is the sensual pleasure of handling the product, a perception of creativity and added prestige from the purchase, as well as the implication that the manufacturer 'cares' about the consumer.

Growing consumer concern about the environment and government targets for recycling are putting new pressures on packaging design and development, in addition to all the other marketing and operational requirements of the process. As they look for ways to increase the environment-friendliness of their packaging, companies need to ask a series of questions.

- Can the amount of material in the package be reduced?
- Can the size of the package be reduced?
- Is recyclable material a possibility?
- Are the necessary recycling processes available?
- Are the raw materials used easy to replenish?

Environmental concerns are causing companies to reconsider the appropriateness of traditional packaging materials. For example, glass is coming back to supermarket shelves, while new developments in the use of plastics and paper/board are leading to improvements in recyclability. Even when companies are able to move towards more ecologically sympathetic packaging, there may be hidden problems. For example, the process of recycling itself may waste energy and create pollution. To ensure that the disadvantages of changing packaging design do not outweigh the benefits, a company should undertake a 'cradle to grave' analysis of the proposed packaging, looking at all aspects of its manufacture, distribution, use and disposal.

In the rush to meet consumer demands and regulatory requirements, companies are in danger of introducing ineffective packaging solutions. For example, manufacturers have recently introduced flexible refill pouches as a replacement for plastic bottles. To the consumer, who sees rigid plastic bottles as bulky and difficult to dispose of, this seems to be a positive step. The lightweight alternative may look better but in practice is awkward to distribute, problematic to stock, hard to open and difficult to recycle. Packaging must be sensible and capable of adding to the brand's image.

These concerns led to Lever Brothers adopting a novel packaging solution for its best-selling Comfort fabric conditioner. In 1998 it launched crushable refill containers, which are easier to stock, display and keep at home than refill pouches. On-pack instructions explain to consumers that the concentrated liquid and thinner packaging save 60 per cent of packaging material versus regular fabric conditioner bottles, and that this bottle 'is crushable and can be recycled'.

With BMW setting up plants to recycle and dispose of old BMW cars, PC World retailing reused inkjet cartridges and Sainsbury's encouraging the reuse of carrier bags, Lever Brothers is not alone in seeking and promoting environmental solutions. Packaging is increasingly a concern, though, for 'Green' consumers. For Lever Brothers, it does appear that the crushable container has overcome consumer aversion to the flimsy refill pouches tried out in the mid-1990s.

As ever, packaging is an evolutionary process and no doubt by the time this book hits the bookshops, a more innovative technique will have been deployed.

Sources: Sainsbury's, May 2004; Lever Brothers, 1999; CGM, *Marketing Guide 14: 3D Packaging Design*, Haymarket Publishing Services Ltd, 1992; John S. Blyth, 'Packaging for competitive advantage', *Management Review*, May 1990, p. 64; Dagmar Mussey and Juliana Kanteng, 'Packaging strict Green rules', *Advertising Age*, 2 December 1991, p. S-10; Katrina Carl, 'Good package design helps increase consumer loyalty', *Marketing News*, 19 June 1995, p. 4; Andy Gilgrist, 'The shape of things to come', *Marketing Week*, 16 September 1994, pp. 43–7; DTI, 1999; www.tetra.pak.com, May 2004 and June 2008.

❓ *Questions for Discussion*

1 What are the functions and benefits of 3D packaging?
2 How does innovative packaging add value to products?
3 In what ways are companies such as Lever Brothers addressing environmental concerns regarding packaging materials?

Part III Strategic Case

Napster
Napster's Creation

Napster was the brainchild of Shawn Fanning, a 17-year-old fresher at Northeastern University who left college to develop a technology to trade music over the Internet. The technology was commercialised through Napster, which allowed computer users to share high quality digital recordings – MP3s – of music via the Internet using its proprietary MusicShare software. Napster did not actually store the recordings on its own computers, but instead provided an index of all the tracks available on the computers of members who were logged onto the service. In other words, it functioned as a sort of clearing house where members could search by artist or track title and identify MP3s of interest so that they could be downloaded from another member's hard drive. Napster quickly became one of the most popular US sites on the Internet, with 15 million users in little more than a year. Indeed so many college students were downloading tracks from Napster that many universities were forced to block the site from their systems in order to regain bandwidth.

From the beginning, Napster's service was as controversial as it was popular. Barely a year after its 1999 launch, Napster was sued by the Recording Industry Association of America (RIAA), which represents major recording companies such as Universal Music, BMG, Sony Music, Warner Music Group and EMI. RIAA claimed that Napster's service violated copyright laws by allowing users to swap music recordings for free. RIAA also sought an injunction to stop the downloading of copyrighted tracks, as well as damages for lost revenue. RIAA argued that track swapping via Napster and similar companies had cost the music industry more than $300 million in lost sales. Metallica and rap star Dr. Dre filed separate lawsuits accusing Napster of copyright infringement and racketeering. Lars Ulrich, Metallica's drummer, told a Senate committee that he felt that Napster users are basically stealing from the band every time they download one of its tracks.

The Fall of Napster

On July 26, 2000, US District Judge Marilyn Patel granted the RIAA's request for an injunction and ordered Napster to stop making copyrighted recordings available for download, which would have effectively destroyed the company by pulling the plug on its most popular feature. However, on July 28 – just nine hours before Napster would have shut down – the 9th Circuit Court of Appeals 'stayed' that order, granting Napster a last minute reprieve until the lawsuits could be tried in court. Despite the brief reprieve, Napster was ultimately found guilty of direct copyright infringement of the RIAA members' musical recordings and that ruling was upheld on appeal on February 12, 2001. The District Court of Appeals refuted all of Napster's defence tactics and ordered the company to stop allowing its millions of users to download and share copyrighted material without properly compensating the owners of the material.

In late September 2001, Napster agreed to pay $26 million for past distribution of unauthorized music and made a proposal that would enable songwriters and musicians to distribute their music on Napster for a fee. This settlement would have covered as many as 700,000 tracks, but Napster still needed an agreement before the company could legally distribute the music. However, with failed attempts to reach a suitable compromise with the recording industry and litigation expenses mounting, the company entered Chapter 11 bankruptcy proceedings in June 2002 as a last ditch effort to try and reach a deal with Bertelsmann AG, Napster's strategic partner.

The end for Napster came on September 3, 2002 when a Delaware bankruptcy judge blocked the sale of the company to Bertelsmann, ruling that negotiations with the German media company had not been made at arm's length and in good faith. Bertelsmann had agreed to pay creditors $8 million for Napster's assets. According to the bankruptcy petition, the company had assets of $7.9 million and debts of $101 million as of April 30, 2002. Shortly after the judge's ruling, Napster laid off nearly all of its 42 staff and proceeded to convert its Chapter 11 reorganisation into a Chapter 7 liquidation. At the time, it seemed like the end of Napster.

The Digital Music Revolution

The music industry has changed beyond recognition. Predictions are that sales of traditional music, in the form of CDs, will decline by between 15 per cent and 20 per cent per annum, with some compensation coming in the form of DVD sales, which are forecast to increase by around 4 per cent per annum. One major reason for the decline in music sales is changing consumer preferences. Although consumers value CDs because they provide 'long-term' entertainment, surveys find that many feel that CDs cost too much. RIAA's research indicates that a significant number of consumers do not fully understand the variables that play a role in the overall pricing of a CD. Consumers say that they resent paying £9–£14 for a CD to attain only one or two favourite tracks. Many consumers, therefore, find downloading music an appealing alternative to high CD prices.

With Napster out of the picture and the RIAA bringing lawsuits against individual downloaders of music online, other online music providers were rapidly 'getting their houses in order'. One of the first was AOL, which launched MusicNet in February 2003 with 20 music streams and 20 downloads for $3.95 per month. Apple's iTunes, which inaugurated in April 2003, was by far the heaviest hitter to join the foray into online music. Other services were available as well. Rhapsody, a division of RealNetworks, whose RealPlayer is ubiquitous on millions of PCs offered 400,000 tracks for download. MusicMatch, a major partner with Dell, which preinstalled MusicMatch Jukebox on all new PCs, offered 200,000 tracks for download. Amazon, too, entered the market for music downloads.

To everyone involved with the music downloading controversy, it is clear that online music distribution is here to stay. It was only a matter of time until a compromise could be reached among the recording studios, the artists and the various online music providers. A few bands now only release their new tracks via the web, shunning disk formats. Some thorny issues remained to be resolved, however. First, because even pay-for-download services are not immune to piracy, the recording industry wanted to develop technology that would prevent downloaders from swapping files on their own even after making a legitimate purchase. The industry also wanted to limit the number of times a track can be downloaded and copied in order to protect the artists. Suggestions included using the MD5 hash – a digital fingerprint – or using software that monitors sound patterns to detect illegal copies. A second issue was the development of a revenue model. Should MP3 files be available individually, as one file in a complete album, or both? Should pricing be based on a per-download basis or on an unlimited basis for a monthly subscription fee?

The Rise of Napster 2.0

In late 2002, Napster's name and assets were purchased by Roxio, a company well known for its CD 'burning' software. After much fanfare and excitement, Roxio revived Napster as Napster 2.0 on 29 October 2003. The new fee-based service offered 750,000 tracks for download, giving it the largest online catalogue currently available in the industry.

The new Napster launched in the UK in early 2004, stating:

> Napster is the legal, safe and easy way to discover and share the most music. With critically acclaimed Napster you can listen to over 750,000 songs, get advert-free radio stations or personalise your own, collect your favourite music along with new releases every Monday.

The re-born Napster offered users the opportunity to burn a CD and transfer tracks to a portable device for £1.09 per track or starting at £9.95 for an album. Subscribers saved over 10 per cent – making the cost as low as 88p per track – when they bought multiple tracks at a time.

There was also a second service available – *Napster Light*. This service permitted users to search and browse 30-second clips within Napster's catalogue of 750,000 tracks for free. Selected full tracks were then purchased for 99p, or £9.95 for albums or Napster Custom Compilations.

Napster's relaunch came with the blessing of five major record labels. Napster also developed a number of partnerships with Microsoft, Gateway, Yahoo!, and Samsung, that provided advantages during its relaunch. Napster's partnership with Samsung led to the creation of the Samsung YP-910GS, a 20 gigabyte digital audio player that was fully integrated with Napster 2.0. The device allowed users to transfer tracks from Napster directly to the unit via a USB connection. The player also boasted an integrated FM transmitter, which allowed users to broadcast MP3 playback through their home or car stereo system. Additionally, Napster subscribers received the industry's leading CD creation software package, developed by parent company Roxio, as a bonus. A major tie-up was with Ericsson, to create Napster Mobile. Other MP3 players followed, from a host of manufacturers.

Although the re-born Napster offered the largest catalogue of tracks, it continued to face competition from a growing number of companies, particularly MusicNet and iTunes. MusicNet was marketed by AOL, the world's largest Internet Service Provider (ISP). In addition to its massive potential user base, AOL's diverse business operations granted it the ability to offer music at a lower price than Napster. AOL could afford to take a volume-based approach to pricing, rather than a profit-based approach. Because MusicNet was also heavily supported by advertisers and sponsors, it offered many different promotional packages to bolster sales.

Despite MusicNet's potential size advantages, Apple's iTunes posed the biggest threat to Napster. iTunes initially offered over 400,000 tracks, but is now colossal, adding thousands of tracks weekly. It also offers a wide selection of audio books. The popularity of Apple's iPod MP3 player also confers on Apple the distinct advantage of the iPod providing customers with a perfect vehicle to attain the music they desire. The iTunes software application works for both Macintosh and Windows operating systems. The service is easy to use and boasts fewer restrictions than MusicNet and other brand competitors. As a result, iTunes has developed a high customer satisfaction rating.

Other competitors include the thousands of offline and online music record stores that offer CDs and other merchandise. However, given the movement in the industry to online downloading of music, these competitors may soon become less of a threat. There are also still websites where music can be downloaded free of charge, albeit illegally. Some potential customers would rather chance getting caught than pay for the music. The mighty Microsoft launched a download service of its own. Given existing competition and the likelihood of future competitive threats, it is imperative that the Napster brand becomes a significant player with a loyal customer base. Napster's pricing strategy is fundamental to attracting sufficient customers quickly enough and to creating routinised re-buying in order to combat the expected new entrants in this growing market sector.

Currently, Napster offers 6,000,000 music tracks, all of the latest releases every week, eighty advertising-free radio stations, hand-picked playlists, live sessions and pre-release parties from the hottest bands, plus digital music videos, to consumers in the US, Canada, UK, Germany and Japan. All legally. All for £9.95 per month. 'Listen to and download unlimited music from the mainstream to the obscure. Amazing features let you create any mood and discover the new.'

Current content and pricing information is available at http://trial.napster.co.uk.

Questions for Discussion

1 What factors seem to have the greatest influence on Napster 2.0's pricing decisions? Explain.
2 Assess the level of price competition in the music industry as a whole and within the online music distribution business specifically.
3 In what ways has Napster attempted to differentiate its proposition vis-à-vis its competitors?
4 How best should Napster communicate its proposition to its target audiences?

References

Chapter 1

1 Ajay Kohli and Bernard J. Jaworski, 'Market orientation: the construct, research propositions and managerial potential', *Journal of Marketing*, April 1990, pp. 1–18.

2 Jim Lynch in *Effective Industrial Marketing*, Norman Hart, ed. (London: Kogan Page, 1994).

3 Sally Dibb, Lyndon Simkin and John Bradley, *The Marketing Planning Workbook* (London: International Thomson Business Publishing, 1996).

4 Hugh J. Munro, Roderick J. Brodie and Nicole E. Coviello, 'Understanding contemporary marketing: development of a classification scheme', *Journal of Marketing Management*, vol. 13, no. 6, August 1997, p. 501(22).

5 Philip Kotler, *Marketing Management: Analysis, Planning, Implementation, and Control*, 6th edn (Englewood Cliffs, N.J.: Prentice-Hall, 1988), p. 6.

6 O.C. Ferrell and George Lucas, 'An evaluation of progress in the development of a definition of marketing', *Journal of the Academy of Marketing Science*, Fall 1987.

7 Christian Gronoos, 'Defining marketing: a market-oriented approach', *European Journal of Marketing*, vol. 23, no. 1, January 1989, p. 52(9); and Rajendra K. Srivastava, Tasaddug Shervani and Liam Fahey, 'Market-based assets and shareholder value: a framework for analysis', *Journal of Marketing*, vol. 62, no. 1, January 1998, pp. 2–18.

8 Lisa M. Wood, 'Added value: marketing basics?' *Journal of Marketing Management*, vol. 12, no. 8, November 1996, p. 735(21); and Thomas Robert-son, 'New developments in marketing: a European perspective', *European Management Journal*, vol. 12, no. 4, p. 362(4).

9 Jagdish N. Sheth and Rajendras Sisodia, 'More than ever before, marketing is under fire to account for what it spends', *Marketing Management,* Fall 1995, pp. 13–14.

10 Christian Gronoos, 'From marketing mix to relationship marketing; towards a paradigm shift in marketing', *Management Decision*, 32(2), 1994, pp. 4–20; Adrian Payne, Martin Christopher, Moira Clark and Helen Peck, *Relationship Marketing for Competitive Advantage* (Oxford: Butterworth-Heinemann, 1998).

11 Gene R. Laczniak and Robert F. Lusch, 'Environment and strategy in 1995: a survey of high-level executives', *Journal of Consumer Marketing*, Spring 1986, p. 28.

12 Sally Dibb and Lyndon Simkin, *The Marketing Segmentation Workbook* (London: Thomson, 1996).

Chapter 2

1 B. A. Weitz and R. Wensley, *Readings in Strategic Marketing* (Chicago: Dryden, 1988).

2 P. Rajan Varadarajan, 'Strategy content and process perspectives revisited', *Journal of the Academy of Marketing Science*, vol. 27, no. 1, Winter 1999, pp. 88–100.

3 G. Homas, M. Hult, David W. Cravens and Jagdish Sheth, 'Competitive advantage in the global marketplace: a focus on marketing strategy', *Journal of Business Research*, January 2001, pp. 1–3.

4 Sally Dibb, Lyndon Simkin and John Bradley, *The Marketing Planning Workbook* (London: Thomson, 1996).

5 Derek F. Abell and John S. Hammond, *Strategic Market Planning* (Englewood Cliffs, N.J.: Prentice-Hall, 1979), p. 10.

6 P. Rajan Varadarajan, Terry Clark and William Pride, 'Determining your company's destiny', working paper, Texas A&M University, 1990.

7 J. Paul Peter and James H. Donnelly, Jr., *A Preface to Marketing Management*, 5th edn (Homewood, Ill.: Irwin, 1991), p. 9.

8 Adapted from Peter and Donnelly, *A Preface to Marketing Management*, pp. 8–12.

9 Zachary Schiller, with Russell Mitchell, Wendy Zellner, Lois Therrien, Andrea Rothman and Walecia Konrad, 'The great American health pitch', *Business Week*, 9 October 1989, p. 116.

10 Derek F. Abell, 'Strategic windows', *Journal of Marketing*, July 1978, p. 21.

11 Abell and Hammond, p. 213.

12 Liam Fahey, William K. King and Vodake K. Naraganan, 'Environmental scanning and forecasting in strategic planning – the state of the art', *Long Range Planning*, February 1981, p. 38.

13 David M. Georgaff and Robert G. Mundick, 'Managers' guide to forecasting', *Harvard Business Review*, January–February 1986, p. 120.

14 "Energy efficient house design', *House Builder Magazine*, September 1986.

15 Philip Kotler, 'Strategic planning and the marketing process', *Business*, May–June 1980, pp. 6–7.

16 Nigel Piercy, *Market-Led Strategic Change* (Oxford: Butterworth-Heinemann Ltd, 1992).

17 C. Anthony Di Benedetto, 'The relationship between strategic type and firm capabilities in Chinese firms', *International Marketing Review*, 20 (5), 2003, pp. 514–534.

18 Roger A. Kerin, Vijay Majahan and P. Rajan Varadarajan, *Contemporary Perspectives on Strategic Marketing Planning* (Boston: Allyn & Bacon, 1990).

19 Ronald Grover, 'When Columbia met Sony ... a love story', *Business Week*, 9 October 1989, pp. 44–45.

20 Graham Hooley and John Saunders, *Competitive Positioning: The Key to Market Success* (London: Prentice-Hall, 1993).

21 P. Rajan Varadarajan, 'Marketing strategy and the Internet: an organizing framework', *Journal of the Academy of Marketing Science*, Fall 2002, pp. 296–313.

22 Al Ries and Jack Trout, *Marketing Warfare* (New York: McGraw-Hill, 1986); John Saunders, 'Marketing and competitive success', in Michael Baker, ed., The *Marketing Book* (London: Heinemann, 1987).

23 Hirokazu Takada, 'Multiple time series analysis of competitive marketing behavior', *Journal of Business Research*, October 1998.

24 Peter Doyle, *Marketing Management and Strategy* (London: Prentice-Hall, 1994).

25 David A. Aaker, *Strategic Market Management*, 2nd edn (New York: Wiley, 1988), p. 35.

26 John Saunders, 'Marketing and competitive success', Michael J. Baker, ed., in *The Marketing Book* (London: Heinemann, 1987), pp. 10–28.

Chapter 3

1 Richard C. Becherer and John G. Maurer, 'The moderating effect of environmental variables on the entrepreneurial and marketing orientation of entrepreneur-led firms', *Entrepreneurship Theory and Practice*, vol. 22, no. 1, Fall 1997, pp. 47–58; Ravi S. Achrol, 'Changes in the theory of interorganizational relations in marketing: toward a network paradigm', *Journal of the Academy of Marketing Science*, vol. 25, no. 1, Winter 1997, pp. 56–71.

2 Philip Kotler, 'Megamarketing', *Harvard Business Review*, March–April 1986, pp. 117–124.

3 *Britain 1990: An Official Handbook* (London: Central Office of Information, 1990).

4 Joseph Plummer, 'The concept of application of life style segmentation', *Journal of Marketing*, January 1974, p. 34.

5 *The IBA Code of Advertising Standards and Practice* (London: Independent Broadcasting Authority, December 1977), p. 3. (The IBA is now the ITC.)

6 Brian Bremner, 'A new sales pitch: the environment', *Business Week*, 24 July 1989, p. 50.

7 Robin Knight, with Eleni Dimmler, 'The greening of Europe's industries', *U.S. News & World Report*, 5 June 1989, pp. 45–46.

8 Reprinted by permission from Herbert Simon, 'Technology and environment', *Management Science*, 19 (10), June 1973. Copyright 1973, The Institute of Management Sciences.

9 Wroe Alderson, *Dynamic Marketing Behavior* (Homewood, Ill.: Irwin, 1965), pp. 195–197.

10 Michael Porter, *Competitive Strategy* (New York: The Free Press, 1980).

11 P. Kotler, G. Armstrong, J. Saunders and V. Wong, *Principles of Marketing* (Hemel Hempstead: Prentice-Hall, 1999).

12 D. Abell, *Defining the Business: The Starting Point of Strategic Planning* (Englewood Cliffs, N.J.: Prentice-Hall, 1980).

13 P. Doyle, *Marketing Management and Strategy* (Hemel Hempstead: Prentice-Hall, 1998).

14 I. Ansoff and E. McDonell, *Implementing Strategic Change* (Englewood Cliffs, N.J.: Prentice-Hall, 1990).

15 D. Brownlie, 'Environmental Analysis', in M. Baker (ed), *The Marketing Book* (Oxford: Butterworth-Heinemann, 1987).

16 Sally Dibb, Lyndon Simkin and John Bradley, *The Marketing Planning Workbook* (London: Thomson, 1996).

17 J. Diffenbach, 'Corporate environmental analysis in large US corporations', *Long Range Planning*, 16 (3), 1983, pp. 107–116.

Chapter 4

1 James F. Engel, Roger D. Blackwell and Paul W. Miniard, *Consumer Behavior*, 7th edn (Hinsdale, Ill.: Dryden Press, 1993), p. 4.

2 John A. Howard and Jagdish N. Sheth, *The Theory of Buyer Behavior* (New York: Wiley, 1969), pp. 27–28.

3 Roy F. Baumeister and David Glen Mick, 'Yielding to temptation: self-control failure, impulsive purchasing, and consumer behavior', *Journal of Consumer Research*, March 2002, pp. 670–677.

4 G. Foxall, 'Consumer decision-making', in *The Marketing Book*, 3rd edn, M. Baker, ed. (London: Heinemann/ Chartered Institute of Marketing, 1995).

5 Kevin L. Keller and Richard Staelin, 'Effects of quality and quantity of information on decision effectiveness', *Journal of Consumer Research*, September 1987, pp. 200–213.

6 Gabriel Biehal and Dipankar Chakravarti, 'Con-sumers' use of memory and external information in choice: macro and micro perspectives', *Journal of Consumer Research*, March 1986, pp. 382–405.

7 Bobby J. Calder and Brian Sternthal, 'Television commercial wearout: an information processing view', *Journal of Marketing Research*, May 1980, pp. 173–186.

8 Michael J. Houston, Terry L. Childers and Susan E. Heckler, 'Picture-word consistency and the elaborative processing of advertisements', *Journal of Marketing Research*, November 1987, pp. 359–369.

9 Robert A. Westbrook, 'Product/consumption-based affective responses and postpurchase processes', *Journal of Marketing Research*, August 1987, pp. 258–270.

10 Roger Bougie, Rik Pieters and Marcel Zeelenberg, 'Angry customers don't come back: the experience and behavioral implications of anger and dissatisfaction in services', *Journal of the Academy of Marketing Science*, Fall 2003, 31 (4), pp. 377–394.

11 Anthony J. Capraro, Susan Broniarczyk and Rajendra K. Srivastava, 'Factors influencing the likelihood of customer defection: the role of consumer knowledge', *Journal of the Academy of Marketing Science*, March 2003, pp. 164–176.

12 Neil Denny, 'Why complaining is our new hobby', *Marketing*, 26 November 1998, p. 16.

13 Patricia Sellers, 'The ABC's of marketing to kids', *Fortune*, 8 May 1989, p. 115.

14 Judith Waldrop, 'Inside America's households', *American Demographics*, March 1989, pp. 20–27.

15 Houston, Childers and Heckler, pp. 359–369.

16 Thomas S. Robertson and Hubert Gatignon, 'Competitive effects on technology diffusion', *Journal of Marketing*, July 1986, pp. 1–12.

17 Robertson and Gatignon, pp. 1–12.

18 Al Ries and Jack Trout, *Positioning the Battle for Your Mind* (New York: McGraw-Hill Book Co., 1986).

19 James R. Bettman, *An Information Processing Theory of Consumer Choice* (Reading, Mass.: Addison-Wesley, 1979), pp. 18–24.

20 David Aaker and Douglas Stayman, 'Implementing the concept of transformational advertising', *Psychology and Marketing*, May and June 1992, pp. 237–253.

21 James H. Myers, 'Determinant buying attitudes: meaning and measurement', *Marketing Manage-ment*, Summer 1997.

22 Joseph W. Alba and J. Wesley Hutchinson, 'Dimensions of consumer expertise', *Journal of Consumer Research*, March 1987, pp. 411–454.

23 Akshay R. Rao and Kent B. Monroe, 'The moderating effect of prior knowledge on cue utilization in product evaluations', *Journal of Consumer Research*, September 1988, pp. 253–264.

24 Ibid.

25 Hans Baumgartner, 'Towards a personology of the consumer', *Journal of Consumer Research*, September 2002, pp. 286–293.

26 John L. Lastovika and Erich A. Joachimsthaler, 'Improving the detection of personality-behavior, relationships in consumer research', *Journal of Consumer Research*, March 1988, pp. 583–587.

27 Martha T. Moore, 'Spring break: brand names chase sales', *USA Today*, 17 March 1989, p. B1.

28 Angela Donkin, Yuan Huang Lee and Barbara Toson, 'Implications of changes in the UK social and occupational classifications in 2001 for vital statistics', *National Statistics*, Spring 2002, pp. 23–29.

29 Emily Rogers, 'Adland takes up fat challenge', *Marketing*, 11 March 2004, p. 19.

30 Marieke De Mooij, 'Convergence and divergence in consumer behavior: implications for global advertising', *International Journal of Advertising*, 2003, 22 (2), pp. 183–203.

31 Leonard L. Berry, 'The time-sharing consumer', *Journal of Retailing*, Winter 1979, p. 69.

32 Mona Doyle, 'The metamorphosis of the consumer', *Marketing Communications*, April 1989, pp. 18–22.

33 Randolph E. Bucklin, 'Determining segmentation in sales response across consumer purchase behaviours', *Journal of Marketing Research*, May 1998.

Chapter 5

1 J. Carlos Jarillo and Howard H. Stevenson, 'Co-operative strategies: the payoffs and the pitfalls', *Long Range Planning*, February 1991, pp. 64–70.

2 John I. Coppett, 'Auditing your customer service activities', *Industrial Marketing Management*, November 1988, pp. 277–284; Thomas L. Powers, 'Identify and fulfill customer service expectations', *Industrial Marketing Management*, November 1988, pp. 273–276.

3 Mary Jo Bitner, Bernard H. Booms and Mary Stanfield Tetreault, 'The service encounter: diagnosing favorable and unfavorable incidents', *Journal of Marketing*, 54, January 1990, pp. 71–84.

4 Weld F. Royal, 'Cashing in on complaints', *Sales & Marketing Management*, May 1995, pp. 88–89.

5 Moin Uddin, 'Loyalty programmes: the ultimate gift', *Dsn Retailing Today*, 5 March 2001, p. 12.

6 Jim Shaw, Joe Giglierano and Jeff Kallis, 'Marketing complex technical products: the importance of intangible attributes', *Industrial Marketing Management*, 18, 1989, pp. 45–53.

7 Frederick E. Webster and Yoram Wind, 'A general model for understanding organizational buyer behaviour', *Marketing Management*, Winter/Spring 1996, pp. 52–57.

8 E. Gummesson, 'The new marketing: developing long-term interactive relationships', *Long Range Planning*, vol. 20, issue 3, 1987, pp. 10–20.

9 H. Hakansson, *International Marketing and Purchasing of Industrial Goods* (Chichester: Wiley, 1982).

10 M. Christopher, A. Payne and D. Ballantyne, *Relationship Marketing* (Oxford: Butterworth-Heinemann, 1991).

11 David Ford, *Understanding Business Marketing and Purchasing* (London: Thomson Learning, 1982).

12 Regis McKenna, *Relationship Marketing* (Reading, Mass.: Addison-Wesley, 1991).

13 Nigel C. G. Campbell, John L. Graham, Alan Jolibert and Hans Gunthe Meissner, 'Marketing negotiations in France, Germany, the United Kingdom and the United States', *Journal of Marketing*, 52, April 1988, pp. 49–62.

14 J. Carlos Jarillo and Howard H. Stevenson, 'Co-operative strategies: the payoffs and the pitfalls', *Long Range Planning*, February 1991, pp. 64–70.

15 *Standard Industrial Classification Revision* (London: Central Statistical Office, 1979).

16 Peter Doyle and John Saunders, 'Market segmentation and positioning in specialized industrial markets', *Journal of Marketing*, Spring 1985, p. 25.

Chapter 6

1 P. Doyle, 'Marketing in the New Millennium', *European Journal of Marketing*, 29, 1995, pp. 23–44; N. Piercy, *Market-Led Strategic* Change (Oxford: Butterworth-Heinemann, 1997).

2 A. Weinstein, *Handbook of Market Segmentation: Strategic Targeting for Business and Technology Firms* (New York: Haworth Press, 2004).

3 David W. Stewart, 'Segmentation and positioning for strategic marketing decisions', *Journal of Marketing Research*, vol. 35, no. 1, February 1998, pp. 128–129.

4 R. Frank and Y. Wind, *Market Segmentation* (Englewood Cliffs, N.J.: Prentice-Hall, 1972); Yoram Wind, 'Issues and

advances in segmentation research', *Journal of Marketing Research*, August 1978, pp. 317–327.

5 Catherine M. Schaffer and Paul E. Green, 'Cluster-based market segmentation: some further comparisons of alternative approaches', *Journal of the Market Research Society*, vol. 40, no. 2, April 1998, pp. 155–163.

6 M. Wedel and W. Kamakura, *Market Segmentation: Conceptual and Methodological Foundations* (Boston: Kluwer Academic Publications, 2000).

7 D. Peppers and M. Rogers, *The One-to-One Manager* (New York: Currency Doubleday, 1999).

8 P. Postma, *The New Marketing Era: Marketing to the Imagination of a Technology-Driven World* (New York: McGraw-Hill, 1998).

9 J. H. Sheth, R. S. Sisodia and A. Sharma, 'Customer-centric marketing', *Journal of the Academy of Marketing Science*, 28 (1), 2000, pp. 55–66.

10 D. Peppers and M. Rogers, *The One-to-One Manager* (New York: Currency Doubleday, 1999).

11 D. Chaffey, R. Mayer, K. Johnston and F. Ellis-Chadwick, *Internet Marketing* (Harlow: Pearson Education, 2000).

12 J. Saunders, 'Cluster analysis', *Journal of Marketing Management*, 10, 1994; pp. 13–28; J. Saunders, 'Cluster analysis for market segmentation', *European Journal of Marketing*, 14, 1980, pp. 422–435.

13 James U. McNeal, *Kids Marketing: Myths and Realities* (Ithaca, NY: Paramount Market Publishing, 1999).

14 Joseph G. Albonetti and Luis V. Dominguez, 'Major influences on consumer goods marketers' decision to target US Hispanics', *Journal of Advertising Re-search*, February–March 1989, pp. 9–11.

15 HMSO, *Social trends*, 1998.

16 John L. Lastovicka and Erich A. Joachimsthaler, 'Improving the detection of personality-behavior relationships in consumer research', *Journal of Consumer Research*, March 1988, pp. 583–587.

17 Joseph T. Plummer, 'The concept and application of life style segmentation', *Journal of Marketing*, January 1974, p. 33.

18 James F. Engel, Roger D. Blackwell and Paul W. Miniard, *Consumer Behavior* (Orlando, Fla.: Dryden Press, 1990), pp. 348–349.

19 Russell I. Haley, 'Benefit segmentation: a decision-oriented research tool', *Journal of Marketing*, July 1968, pp. 30–35.

20 Yoram Wind and Richard Cardoza, 'Industrial market segmentation', *Industrial Marketing Management*, vol. 3, 1974, pp. 153–166.

21 T. P. Beane and D. M. Ennis, 'Market segmentation: a review', *European Journal of Marketing*, vol. 21 (5), 1987, pp. 20–42.

22 Thomas Bonoma and B. P. Shapiro, *Segmenting the Industrial Market* (Lexington, Mass.: Lexington Books, 1983).

23 Donald F. Blumberg, 'Developing service as a line of business', *Management Review*, vol. 76, February 1987, p. 61.

24 A. Diamantopoulos and B. Schlegelmilch, *Taking the Fear out of Data Analysis* (London: Dryden Press, 1997); J. Saunders, 'Cluster analysis', *Journal of Marketing Management*, 10, 1994, pp. 13–28; J. Saunders, 'Cluster analysis for market segmentation', *European Journal of Marketing*, 14, 1980, pp. 422–435.

25 G. L. Lilien and P. Kotler, *Marketing Decision-Making: A Model Building Approach* (New York: Harper & Row, 1983); P. Naert and P. Leeflang, *Building Implementable Marketing Models* (Leiden: Martinus Nijhoff, 1978).

26 J. Maier and J. Saunders, 'The implementation of segmentation in sales management', *Journal of Personal Selling and Sales Management*, 10 (1), 1990, pp. 39–48.

27 J. Saunders, 'Cluster analysis', *Journal of Marketing Management*, 10, 1994, pp. 13–28; J. Saunders, 'Cluster analysis for market segmentation', *European Journal of Marketing*, 14, 1980, pp. 422–435.

28 A. Diamantopoulos and B. Schlegelmilch, *Taking the Fear out of Data Analysis* (London: Dryden Press, 1997); J. Saunders, 'Cluster analysis', *Journal of Marketing Management*, 10, 1994, pp. 13–28; J. Saunders, 'Cluster analysis for market segmentation', *European Journal of Marketing*, 14, 1980, pp. 422–435.

29 M. McDonald, *Marketing Plans* (Oxford: Butterworth-Heinemann, 1995).

30 S. Dibb and L. Simkin, 'Marketing and marketing planning: still barriers to overcome', *EMAC*, Warwick, May 1997.

31 Peter Doyle, John Saunders and Veronica Wong, 'A comparative study of Japanese marketing strategies in the British market', *Journal of International Business Studies*, 17 (1), 1986, pp. 27–46.

32 Y. Wind, 'Going to market: new twist for some old tricks', *Wharton Magazine*, 4, 1980.

33 T. Harrison, *A Handbook of Advertising Techniques* (London: Kogan Page, 1987), p. 7.

34 A. Ries and J. Trout, Positioning: *The Battle for Your Mind* (New York: McGraw-Hill, 1981); Jack Trout with Steve Rivkin, *The New Positioning: The Latest on the World's #1 Business Strategy* (New York: McGraw-Hill, 1996).

35 Philip Kotler, *Marketing Management: Analysis, Planning, and Control*, 6th edn (Englewood Cliffs, N.J., Prentice-Hall, 1988), p. 257.

Chapter 7

1 David Birks, chapter 10 in *The Marketing Book*, M. Baker, ed. (Oxford: Butterworth-Heinemann, 1994).

2 "Research" is accredited by The Market Research Society (Great Britain). Reprinted by permission.

3 'Pizza Hut studies effects of "pizza deprivation" on college and high school students', *PRNewswire*, via AmericaOnline, 30 May 2001.

4 Jerry Wind, 'Marketing research forum: state of the art in quantitative research', *Marketing Research*, Winter 1997.

5 Sally Dibb and Lyndon Simkin, *The Marketing Case-book* (London: Routledge, 1994).

6 http://www.esomar.org/print.php?a=6&p=1140.

7 'Research league tables top 65', *Marketing*, 14 July 2004, pp. 37–46.

8 Johny K. Johansson and Ikujiro Nonaha, 'Market research the Japanese way', *Harvard Business Review*, May–June 1987, pp. 16–22.

9 Donald Tull and Del Hawkins, *Marketing Research* (New York: Macmillan, 1990).

10 Vikas Mittal and Wagner A. Kamakura, 'Satisfaction, repurchase intent, and repurchase behavior: investigating the moderating effects of customer characteristics', *Journal of Marketing Research*, February 2001, pp. 131–142.

11 'Internal secondary market research', *Small Business Owner's Toolkit*, www.lycos.com/business/cch/guidebook.html?lpv=1&docNumber=P03_3020, 23 June 2001.

12 Ronald L. Vaughn, 'Demographic data banks: a new management resource', *Business Horizons*, November–December 1984, pp. 38–42. See also Chapter 5.

13 Jeffrey S. Conant, Denise T. Smart and Bruce J. Walker, 'Main survey facilitation techniques: an assessment and proposal regarding reporting practices' (working paper, Texas A&M University, 1990).

14 Riche, p. 8.

15 Stephen M. Billing, 'Go slow, be wary when considering switch to computer assisted interviewing system', *Marketing News*, 26 November 1982, secl. 2, p. 2.

16 Tull and Hawkins.

17 Yorkshire Television's *The Marketing Mix* series.

18 Hal Sokolow, 'In-depth interviews increasing in importance', *Marketing News*, 13 September 1985, p. 26.

19 Alan J. Bush and A. Parasuraman, 'Mall intercept versus telephone interviewing environment', *Journal of Advertising Research*, April–May 1985, p. 42.

20 Alan J. Bush and Joseph F. Hair, Jr, 'An assessment of the mall intercept as a data collecting method', *Journal of Marketing Research*, May 1985, p. 162.

21 Jagdip Singh, Roy D. Howell and Gary K. Rhoads, 'Adaptive designs for Likert-type data: an approach for implementing marketing surveys', *Journal of Marketing Research*, August 1990, pp. 304–321.

22 Norman Hart and John Stapleton, *Glossary of Marketing Terms* (Oxford: Butterworth-Heinemann), 1981.

23 'Closer encounters', *Marketing*, 14 July 2004, pp. 48–49.

24 Peter Jackson, Adsearch, Richmond.

25 A. Diamantopoulos and B. Schlegelmilch, *Taking the Fear out of Data Analysis* (London: Dryden Press, 1997).

26 Michael J. Olivette, 'Marketing research in the electric utility industry', *Marketing News*, 2 January 1987, p. 13.

27 Deborah Utter, 'Information-driven marketing decisions: development of strategic information systems', *Journal of the Academy of Marketing Science*, Spring 1998.

28 Laurence N. Goal, 'High technology data collection for measurement and testing', *Marketing Research*, March 1992, pp. 29–38.

29 Kathleen Cholewka, 'Tiered CRM: serving pip-squeaks to VIPS', *Sales & Marketing Management*, April 2001, pp. 25–26.

30 O. C. Ferrell and Steven J. Skinner, 'Ethical behavior and bureaucratic structure in marketing research organizations', *Journal of Marketing Research*, February 1988, pp. 103–104.

31 Michael Kavanaugh, 'Masked Brawl', *Marketing Week*, 15 October 1998, p. 65.

32 Lynn Colemar, 'It's selling disguised as research', *Marketing News*, 4 January 1988, p. 1.

33 Brandt Allen, 'Make information services pay its way', *Harvard Business Review*, January–February 1987, p. 57.

Chapter 8

1 Part of this definition is adapted from James D. Scott, Martin R. Warshaw and James R. Taylor, *Introduction to Marketing Management*, 5th edn (Homewood, Ill.: Irwin, 1985), p. 215.

2 Theodore Levitt, 'Marketing intangible products and product intangibles', *Harvard Business Review*, May–June 1981, pp. 94–102.

3 Robert W. Haas, *Industrial Marketing Management*, 3rd edn (Boston: Kent Publishing, 1986), pp. 15–25.

4 Peter Doyle, *Marketing Management and Strategy* (London: Prentice-Hall, 1994).

5 William P. Putsis Jr and Barry L. Bayus, 'An empirical analysis of firms' product line decisions', *Journal of Marketing Research*, February 2001, pp. 110–118.

6 M. J. Thomas, 'Product development management', in *The Marketing Book*, M. Baker, ed. (London: Heinemann/ The Chartered Institute of Marketing, 1987).

7 Sonja Radas and Steven M. Shugan, 'Seasonal marketing and timing new product introductions', *Journal of Marketing Research*, vol. 35, no. 3, August 1998, pp. 296–315; Marjorie E. Adams, 'Enhancing new product development performance: an organisational learning perspective', *The Journal of Product Innovation Management*, September 1998.

8 Brian A. Lukas and O. C. Ferrell, 'The effect of market orientation on product innovation', *Journal of the Academy of Marketing Science*, February 2000, pp. 239–47.

9 Gary Lynn and Richard Reilly, 'How to build a blockbuster', *Harvard Business Review*, October 2002, vol. 80, no. 10, pp. 18–20.

10 David Benady, 'Chopping brands', *Marketing Week*, 10 June 2004, pp. 22–25.

11 Gerald Tellis and Peter Golder, 'First to market, first to fail? Real causes of enduring market leadership', *Sloan Management Review*, Winter 1996, pp. 65–75.

12 'Guinness in facelift as volume dips', *Marketing Week*, 20 May 2004, p. 8.

13 Caroline Parry, 'Cadbury axes Trebor 24-7 after poor sales', *Marketing Week*, 15 April 2004, p. 5.

14 Levitt, 'Marketing intangible products and product intangibles', p. 96.

15 Christopher W. L. Hart, 'The power of unconditional service guarantees', *Harvard Business Review*, July–August 1988, pp. 54–62.

Chapter 9

1 Rajesh Sethi, 'New product quality and product development', *Journal of Marketing*, April 2000, pp. 1–14.

2 Roger C. Bennet and Robert G. Cooper, 'The product life cycle trap', *Business Horizons*, September–October 1984, pp. 7–16.

3 'Product development: where planning and marketing meet', *Journal of Business Strategy*, September–October 1990, pp. 13–16.

4 Lee G. Cooper, 'Strategic marketing planning for radically new products', *Journal of Marketing*, January 2000, pp. 1–16.

5 Lisa C. Troy, David M. Szymanski and P. Rajan Varadarajan, 'Generating new product ideas: an initial investigation of the role of market information and organizational characteristics', *Journal of the Academy of Marketing Science*, January 2001, pp. 89–101.

6 Peter F. Drucker, 'The discipline of innovation', *Harvard Business Review*, May–June 1985, pp. 67–68; Wu Couchen, 'A proposed method for the design of consumer products', *Journal of International Marketing and Marketing Research*, February 1999.

7 Jonathan B. Levine, 'Keeping new ideas kicking around', *Business Week*, Innovation 1989 issue, p. 128.

8 Aric Rindfleisch and Christine Moorman, 'The acquisition and utilization of information in new product alliances: a strength-of-ties perspective', *Journal of Marketing*, April 2001, pp. 1–18.

9 Joshua Hyatt, 'Ask and you shall receive', *Inc.*, September 1989, pp. 90–101.

10 Christine Moorman and Anne S. Miner, 'The convergence of planning and execution: improvisation in new product development', *Journal of Marketing*, vol. 62, no. 3, July 1998, pp. 1–20; V. Padmanabhan, Surendra Rajiv and Kannan Srinivasan, 'New products, upgrades, and new releases: a rationale for sequential product introduction', *Journal of Marketing Research*, vol. 34, no. 4, November 1997, pp. 456–472.

11 Barry L. Bayus, Sanjay Jain and Ambar G. Rao, 'Truth or consequences: an analysis of vaporware and new product announcements', *Journal of Marketing Research*, February 2001, pp. 3–13.

12 Cyndee Miller, 'Little relief seen for new product failure rate', *Marketing News*, 21 June 1993, p. 5.

13 Chung K. Kim, Anne M. Lavack and Margo Smith, 'Consumer evaluation of vertical brand extensions and core brands', *Journal of Business Research*, March 2001, pp. 211–222.

14 Ian Grime, Adamantios Diamantopoulos and Gareth Smith, 'Consumer evaluations of extensions and their effects on the core brand: key issues and research propositions', *European Journal of Marketing*, November 2002, pp. 1415–1438.

15 Adapted from Everett M. Rogers, *Diffusion of Innovations* (New York: Macmillan, 1962), pp. 81–86.

16 Graham J. Hooley and John Saunders, *Competitive Positioning: The Key to Market Success* (Englewood Cliffs, N.J.: Prentice-Hall, 1993).

17 F. Stewart DeBruicker and Gregory L. Summe, 'Make sure your customers keep coming back', *Harvard Business Review*, January–February 1985, pp. 92–98.

18 Geoffrey L. Gordon, Roger J. Calantone and Anthony di Benedetto, 'Mature markets and revitalization strategies: an American fable', *Business Horizons*, May–June 1991, p. 42.

19 Kim B. Clark and Takahiro Fujimoto, 'The power of product integrity', *Harvard Business Review*, November–December 1990, pp. 108–118.

20 Lynn W. Phillips, Dae R. Chang and Robert D. Buzzell, 'Product quality, cost position and business performance: a test of some key hypotheses', *Journal of Marketing*, Spring 1983, pp. 26–43.

21 Douglas M. Lambert and Jay U. Sterling, 'Identifying and eliminating weak products', *Business*, July–September 1988, pp. 3–10.

22 Joseph P. Guiltinan and Gordon W. Paul, *Marketing Management: Strategies and Programmes* (New York: McGraw-Hill, 1982), p. 31.

23 George S. Day, 'Diagnosing the Product Portfolio', *Journal of Marketing*, April 1977, pp. 30–31.

24 Sally Dibb and Lyndon Simkin, *The Market Segmentation Workbook* (London: Thomson, 1996).

25 Robert Jacobson, 'Distinguishing among competing theories of the market share effect', *Journal of Marketing*, October 1988, pp. 68–80.

26 George S. Day, *Analysis for Strategic Market Decisions* (St. Paul, Minn.: West, 1986), pp. 117–118.

27 Robert D. Buzzell and Bradley T. Gale, *The PIMS Principles: Linking Strategy to Performance* (New York: Free Press, 1987).

28 Day, *Analysis for Strategic Market Decisions*, p. 10.

29 David W. Cravens, 'Strategic marketing's new challenge', *Business Horizons*, March–April 1983, p. 19.

Chapter 10

1 Leonard L. Berry and A. Parasuraman, *Marketing Services: Competing Through Quality* (New York: Free Press, 1991), p. 5.

2 Glenn B. Voss, A. Parasuraman and Dhruv Grewal, 'The roles of price, performance, and expectations in determining satisfaction in service exchanges', *Journal of Marketing*, vol. 64, no. 4, October 1998, pp. 46–61; Jochen Wirtz and John E. G. Bateson, 'Consumer satisfaction with services: integrating the environment perspective in services marketing into the traditional disconfirmation paradigm', *Journal of Business Research*, vol. 44, no. 1, January 1999, pp. 55–66.

3 Donald Cowell, *The Marketing of Services* (London: Heinemann, 1984).

4 Based on K. Douglas Hoffman and John E. G. Bateson, *Essentials of Services Marketing* (Fort Worth, Texas: Dryden Press, 1997), pp. 25–28; and Valerie A. Zeithaml, A. Parasuraman and Leonard L. Berry, *Delivery Quality Service: Balancing Customer Perceptions and Expectations* (New York: Free Press, 1990).

5 John E. G. Bateson, 'Why we need service marketing', in O. C. Ferrell, S. W. Brown and C. W. Lamb, Jr, eds, *Conceptual and Theoretical Development in Marketing* (Chicago: American Marketing Associa-tion, 1979), pp. 131–146.

6 Valarie A. Zeithaml, 'How consumer evaluation process-es differ between goods and services', in James H. Donnelly and William R. George, eds, *Marketing of Services* (Chicago: American Marketing Association, 1981), pp. 186–190.

7 Leonard L. Berry, Valarie A. Zeithaml and A. Parasuraman, 'Responding to demand fluctuations: key challenge for service businesses', in Russell Belk et al., eds, *AMA Educators' Proceedings* (Chicago: American Marketing Association, 1984), pp. 231–234.

8 Brian Moores, *Are They Being Served?* (Oxford: Philip Allan, 1986).

9 J. Paul Peter and James H. Donnelly, *A Preface to Marketing Management* (Burr Ridge, Illinois: McGraw-Hill/ Irwin, 2000), p. 203.

10 Randi Priluck, 'Relationship marketing can mitigate product and service failures', *Journal of Services Marketing*, March 2003, pp. 37–52.

11 Dennis B. Arnett, Steve D. German and Shelby D. Hunt, 'The identity salience model of relationship marketing success: the case of nonprofit marketing', *Journal of Marketing*, April 2003, pp. 89–106.

12 James Reardon, Chip Miller, Ronald Hasty and Blaise J. Waguespack, 'A comparison of alternative theories of ser-vices marketing', *Journal of Marketing Theory and Practice*, vol. 4, no. 4, Fall 1996, pp. 61–71.

13 Christopher H. Lovelock, 'Classifying services to gain strategic marketing insights', *Journal of Marketing*, Summer 1983, p. 15.

14 Christopher H. Lovelock, *Services Marketing* (Englewood Cliffs, N.J.: Prentice-Hall, 1984), pp. 46–64.

15 Yoram Wind, 'Financial services: increasing your market-ing productivity and profitability', *Journal of Services Marketing*, Fall 1987, p. 8.

16 Cathy Goodwin, 'Marketing strategies for services: glob-alization, client-orientation, deregulation', *International Journal of Research in Marketing*, July 1997.

17 Lovelock, *Services Marketing*, pp. 279–289.

18 Ibid.

19 Berry, Zeithaml and Parasuraman, pp. 231–234.

20 Valarie A. Zeithaml, A. Parasuraman and Leonard L. Berry, *Delivering Quality Service: Balancing Customer Perceptions and Expectations* (New York: Free Press, 1990).

21 A. Parasuraman, Leonard L. Berry and Valarie A. Zeithaml, 'An empirical examination of relationships in an extended service quality model', *Marketing Science Institute Working Paper Series*, Report no. 90–122 (Cambridge, Mass.: Marketing Science Institute, 1990), p. 29.

22 Valarie A. Zeithaml, Leonard L. Berry and A. Parasuraman, 'Communication and control pro-cesses in the delivery of service quality', *Journal of Marketing*, April 1988, pp. 35–48.

23 Valarie A. Zeithaml, Leonard L. Berry and A. Parasuraman, 'The nature and determinants of customer expectations of service', *Journal of the Academy of Marketing Science*, Winter 1993, pp. 1–12.

24 Hartline and Ferrell, 'Service quality implementation', p. 36.

25 Mary Jo Bitner, 'Evaluating service encounters: the effects of physical surroundings and employee responses', *Journal of Marketing*, April 1990, p. 70.

26 Hartline and Ferrell, 'Service quality implementation', pp. 17–19.

27 Myron Glassman and Bruce McAfee, 'Integrating the personnel and marketing functions: the challenge of the 1990s', *Business Horizons*, May–June 1992, pp. 52–59.

28 Keith J. Blois, 'Marketing for non-profit organisations', in Michael J. Baker (ed.), *The Marketing Book* (London: Heinemann, 1994), p. 405.

29 J. Whyte, 'Organisation, person and idea marketing as exchange', *Quarterly Review of Marketing*, January 1985, pp. 25–30.

30 John Garrison, 'Telethons – the positive story', *Fund Raising Management*, November 1987, pp. 48–52.

31 Philip Kotler, *Marketing for Non-profit Organisations*, 2nd edn (Englewood Cliffs, N.J.: Prentice-Hall, 1982), p. 37.

32 Ibid.

33 Meryl Davids, 'Doing well by doing good', *Public Relations Journal*, July 1987, pp. 17–21.

34 Leyland F. Pitt and Russell Abratt, 'Pricing in non-profit organisations – a framework and conceptual overview', *Quarterly Review of Marketing*, Spring–Summer 1987, pp. 13–15.

35 Kelly Walker, 'Not-for-profit profits', *Forbes*, 10 September 1984, p. 165.

Chapter 11

1 Erin Anderson, George S. Day and V. Kasturi Rangan, 'Strategic channel design', *Sloan Management Review*, vol. 38, no. 4, Summer 1997, p. 59.

2 Mitzi M. Montoya-Weiss, Glenn B. Ross and Dhruv Grewal, 'Determinant of online channel use and overall satisfaction with a relational, multichannel service provider', *Journal of the Academy of Marketing Science*, Fall 2003, pp. 448–459.

3 O.C. Ferrell and William M. Pride, national sample of 2,042 households.

4 Wroe Alderson, *Marketing Behavior and Executive Action* (Homewood, Ill.: Irwin, 1957), pp. 201–211.

5 Lester E. Goodman and Paul A. Dion, 'The determinants of commitment in the distributor–manufacturer rela-tionship', *Industrial Marketing Management*, April 2001, pp. 287–300.

6 James D. Hlavacek and Tommy J. McCuistion, 'Industrial distributors: when, who, and how?' *Harvard Business Review*, March–April 1983, p. 97.

7 S. Altan Erdem and L. Jean Harrison-Walker, 'Managing channel relationships: toward an identification of effec-tive promotional strategies in vertical marketing

systems', *Journal of Marketing Theory and Practice*, vol. 5, no. 2, Spring 1997, pp. 80–87.

8 Jordan D. Lewis, 'Using alliances to build market power', *Planning Review*, September–October 1990, pp. 4–9, p. 48.

9 Leo Aspinwall, 'The marketing characteristics of goods', in *Four Marketing Theories* (Boulder: University of Colorado Press, 1961), pp. 27–32.

10 Allan J. Magrath, 'Differentiating yourself via distribution', *Sales & Marketing Management*, March 1991, pp. 50–57.

11 David W. Cravens, Thomas N. Ingram and Raymond W. LaForge, 'Evaluating multiple sales channel strategies', *Journal of Business and Industrial Marketing*, Summer–Fall 1991, pp. 3–4.

12 Bert Rosenbloom, *Marketing Channels: A Management View* (Hinsdale, Ill.: Dryden, 1987), p. 160.

13 Ibid., p. 161.

14 Donald J. Bowersox and M. Bixby Cooper, *Strategic Marketing Channel Management* (New York: McGraw-Hill, 1992), pp. 177–178.

15 Wroe Alderson, *Dynamic Marketing Behavior* (Homewood, Ill.: Irwin, 1965), p. 239.

16 Tony Seideman, 'Get with the program', *Inbound Logistics*, September 1998, p. 29.

17 Steven J. Skinner, Julie B. Gassenheimer and Scott W. Kelley, 'Cooperation in supplier-dealer relations',*Journal of Retailing, Summer* 1992, pp. 174–193; H. Hakansson, *International Marketing and Purchasing of Industrial Goods* (Chichester: Wiley, 1982).

18 J. Joseph Cronin Jr., Thomas L. Baker and Jon M. Hawes, 'An assessment of the role performance measurement of power-dependency in marketing channels', *Journal of Business Research*, vol. 30, no. 3, July 1994, pp. 201–210.

19 Nirmalya Kumar, Lisa K. Scheer and Jan-Benedict Steenkamp, 'Interdependence, punitive capability, and the reciprocation of punitive actions in channel relationships', *Journal of Marketing Research*, vol. 35, no. 2, May 1998, pp. 225–235; Robert F. Lusch, 'Interdependency, contracting, and relational behavior in marketing channels', *Journal of Marketing*, October 1996.

20 Jonathan D. Hibbard, Nirmalya Kumar and Louis W. Stern, 'Examining the impact of destructive acts in marketing channel relationships', *Journal of Marketing Research*, February 2001, pp. 45–61.

21 Adel I. El-Ansary, 'Perspectives on channel system performance', in *Contemporary Issues in Marketing Channels*, ed. Robert F. Lusch and Paul H. Zinszer (Norman: University of Oklahoma Press, 1979), p. 50.

22 Kenneth G. Hardy and Allan J. Magrath, 'Ten ways for manufacturers to improve distribution management', *Business Horizons*, November–December 1988, p. 68.

23 Ronald D. Michman and Stanley D. Sibley, *Marketing Channels and Strategies* (Columbus, Ohio: Grid Publishing, 1980), pp. 412–417.

24 Janet E. Keith, Donald W. Jackson and Lawrence A. Crosby, 'Effect of alternative types of influence strategies under different dependence structures', *Journal of Marketing*, July 1990, pp. 30–41.

25 John F. Gaski and John R. Nevin, 'The differential effects of exercised and unexercised power sources in a marketing channel', *Journal of Marketing Research*, July 1985, p. 139.

26 Rosenbloom, *Marketing Channels*, p. 98.

27 Ibid., pp. 96–97.

Chapter 12

1 John Gourville and Dilip Soman, 'Pricing and the psychology of consumption', *Harvard Business Review*, September 2002, pp. 91–96.

2 Donald Lichtenstein, Nancy M. Ridgway and Richard G. Netemeyer, 'Price perceptions and consumer shopping behavior: a field study', *Journal of Marketing Research*, May 1993, pp. 234–245.

3 Ramarao Desiraju, 'Strategic service pricing and yield management', *Journal of Marketing,* January 1999.

4 Bruce L. Alford and Brian T. Engelland, 'Advertised reference price effects on consumer price estimates, value perception, and search intention', *Journal of Business Research*, May 2000, pp. 93–100.

5 Philip Buxton, 'Can marketing save falling retail giants?', *Marketing Week*, 28 January 1999, pp. 19–20.

6 Stephen J. Hoch, Xavier Dreze and Mary Park, 'EDLP – hi-lo, and margin arithmetic', *Journal of Marketing*, 58 (4), 1994, pp. 16–22; Allan Mitchell, 'Two sides of the same argument', *Marketing Week*, 16 February 1996, pp. 26–27.

7 Saeed Samier, 'Pricing in marketing strategies of U.S. and foreign based companies', *Journal of Business Research*, 1987, pp. 15–23.

8 J. Winkler, 'Pricing', M. Baker, ed., in *The Marketing Book* (London: Heinemann, 1987).

9 JCB company literature, 1992.

10 Joseph P. Guiltinan, 'The price-bundling of services: a normative framework', *Journal of Marketing*, April 1987, pp. 74–85.

11 George S. Day and Liam Fahey, 'Valuing market strategies', *Journal of Marketing*, July 1988, pp. 45–57.

12 Valerie A. Zeithaml, 'Consumer perceptions of price, quality and value: a means-end model and synthesis of evidence', *Journal of Marketing*, July 1988, pp. 2–22.

13 Eric Anderson and Duncan Simester, 'Mind your pricing cues', *Harvard Business Review*, September 2003, pp. 97–103.

14 David E. Griffith, 'The price of competitiveness in competitive pricing', *Journal of the Academy of Marketing Science*, Spring 1997; K. Sivakumar, 'Quality tier competition: how price change influences brand choice and category choice', *Journal of Marketing*, July 1997.

15 James B. Wilcox, Roy D. Howell, Paul Kuzdrall and Robert Britney, 'Price quantity discounts: some implications for buyers and sellers', *Journal of Marketing*, July 1987, pp. 60–61.

16 Robert G. Eccles, 'Control with fairness in transfer pricing', *Harvard Business Review*, November–December 1983, pp. 149–161.

17 Michael H. Morris, 'Separate prices as a marketing tool', *Industrial Marketing Management*, 16, 1987, pp. 79–86.

18 Jack Trout, 'Prices: simple guidelines to get them right', *The Journal of Business Strategy*, vol. 19, no. 6, November/December 1998, pp. 13–16.

Chapter 13

1 Richard W. Pollay, 'On the value of reflections on the values in "The distorted mirror"', *Journal of Marketing*, July 1987, pp. 104–109.

2 Morris B. Holbrook, 'Mirror, mirror, on the wall, what's unfair in the reflections on advertising', *Journal of Marketing*, July 1987, pp. 95–103.

3 Richard N. Farmer, 'Would you want your granddaughter to marry a Taiwanese marketing man?' *Journal of Marketing*, October 1987, pp. 111–116.

4 Colin Coulson-Thomas, *Marketing Communications* (London: Heinemann, 1986); Kusum L. Ailawadi and Scott A. Neslin, 'The effect of promotion on consumption: buying more and consuming it faster', *Journal of Marketing Research*, vol. 35, no. 3, August 1998, pp. 390–398.

5 James Engel, Martin Warshaw and Thomas Kinnear, *Promotional Strategy: Managing the Marketing Communications Process* (Boston: Irwin, 1994).

6 John Rossiter and Larry Percy, *Advertising and Promotion Management* (New York: McGraw-Hill, 1987).

7 In case you do not read Chinese, this says, 'In the factory we make cosmetics, and in the store we sell hope'. Prepared by Chih Kang Wang.

8 Terence A. Shimp and M. Wayne Delozier, *Promotion Management and Marketing Communication* (Hinsdale, Ill.: Dryden Press, 1986), pp. 25–26.

9 Judy A. Wagner, Noreen M. Klein and Janet E. Keith, 'Selling strategies: the effects of suggesting a decision structure to novice and expert buyers', *Journal of the Academy of Marketing Science*, 29 (3), 2001, pp. 289–306.

10 John S. McClenahen, 'How can you possibly say that?', *Industry Week*, 17 July 1995, pp. 17–19.

11 David M. Szymanski, 'Modality and offering effects in sales presentations for a good versus a service', *Journal of the Academy of Marketing Science*, 29 (2), 2001, pp. 179–189.

12 David Jones, 'Setting promotional goals: a communications' relationship model', *Journal of Consumer Marketing*, 11 (1), 1994, pp. 38–49.

13 Adapted from Everett M. Rogers, *Diffusion of Innovations* (New York: Free Press, 1962), pp. 81–86, 98–102.

14 Lawrence J. Marks and Michael A. Kamins, 'Product sampling and advertising sequence, belief strength, confidence and attitudes', *Journal of Marketing Research*, August 1988, pp. 266–281.

15 Rogers, pp. 247–250.

16 Rossiter and Percy.

17 J. Richard Shannon, 'The new promotions mix: a proposed paradigm, process, and application', *Journal of Marketing Theory and Practice*, Winter 1996.

18 Vicki R. Lane, 'The impact of ad repetition and ad content on consumer perceptions of incongruent extensions', *Journal of Marketing*, April 2000, pp. 80–91.

19 M. Flandin, E. Martin and L. Simkin, 'Advertising effectiveness research: a survey of agencies, clients and conflicts', *International Journal of Advertising*, 11 March 1992, pp. 203–214.

20 Scott B. MacKenzie, Philip M. Podsakoff and Gregory A. Rich, 'Transformational and transactional leadership and sales person performance', *Journal of the Academy of Marketing Science*, 29 (2), 2001, pp. 115–134.

21 Todd Hunt and James Grunig, *Public Relations Techniques* (Fort Worth: Harcourt Brace, 1994).

22 Sally Dibb, Lyndon Simkin and Adam Vancini, 'Competition, strategy, technology and people: the challenges facing PR', *International Journal of Advertising*, 15 (2), 1996, pp. 116–127.

23 This definition is adapted from John F. Luick and William L. Ziegler, *Sales Promotion and Modern Merchandising* (New York: McGraw-Hill, 1968), p. 4.

24 Roger A. Kerin and William L. Cron, 'Assessing trade show functions and performance: an exploratory study', *Journal of Marketing*, July 1987, pp. 87–94.

25 Michael Kavanagh, 'Free ISPs spur Net market growth', *Marketing Week*, 11 March 1999, pp. 30–31.

26 M.J. Evans, L. O'Malley and M. Patterson, 'Direct marketing communications in the UK: a study of growth, past, present and future', *Journal of Marketing Communications*, 2, 1996, pp. 51–65.

27 Lisa O'Malley, Maurice Patterson and Martin Evans, *Exploring Direct Marketing* (London: ITBP, 1999), p. 9.

28 Marcy Magiera, 'Holy Batvideo! Christmas already?', *Advertising Age*, 11 September 1989, p. 6.

29 *Marketing Week*, 5 July 1996, p. 13.

30 Alvin A. Achenbaum and F. Kent Mitchel, 'Pulling away from push marketing', *Harvard Business Review*, May–June 1987, p. 38.

Chapter 14

1 Peter D. Bennett, ed., *Dictionary of Marketing Terms* (Chicago: American Marketing Association, 1988), p. 18.

2 Peter Doyle, 'Building successful brands: the strategic options', *The Journal of Consumer Marketing*, vol. 7, no. 2, 1993, pp. 5–20.

3 James Bell, 'Brand management for the next millennium', *The Journal of Business Strategy*, vol. 19, no. 2, March/April 1998, pp. 7–10; Joseph Arthur Rooney, 'Branding: a trend for today and tomorrow', *The Journal of Product and Brand Management*, vol. 4, no. 4, 1995, pp. 48–56.

4 Henry Assael, *Consumer Behaviour and Marketing Action*, 4th edn (Boston: PWS-Kent, 1992).

5 David A. Aaker, *Managing Brand Equity: Capitalizing on the Value of a Brand Name* (New York: Free Press, 1991), pp. 16–17.

6 Chip Walker, 'What's in a name?' *American Demographics*, February 1991, pp. 54–57.

7 'British retailing: chemistry upset,' *The Economist*, 24 February 2001, p. 68.

8 Marcel Corstjens and Rajiv Lal, 'Building store loyalty through store brands', *Journal of Marketing Research*, August 2000, pp. 281–291.

9 Alan Miller, 'Gains share in dollars and units during 1990 third quarter', *Private Label*, January–February 1991, pp. 85–89.

10 Taylor Nelson, Sofres Superpanel, 1999.

11 Leonard L. Berry, Edwin E. Lefkowith and Terry Clark, 'In services, what's in a name?" *Harvard Business Review*, September–October 1988, pp. 2–4.

12 Dorothy Cohen, 'Trademark Strategy', *Journal of Marketing*, January 1986, p. 63.

13 Chiranjev Kohli and Rajheesh Suri, 'Brand names that work: a study of the effectiveness of different brand names', *Marketing Management Journal*, Fall/Winter 2000, pp. 112–120.

14 Zeynep Gurhan-Canli and Durairaj Maheswaran, 'The effects of extensions on brand name dilution and enhancement', *Journal of Marketing Research*, vol. 35, no. 4, November 1998, pp. 464–473.

15 "Trademark Stylesheet", U.S. Trademark Association, no. 1A.

16 Vicki R. Lane, 'The impact of ad repetition and ad content on consumer perceptions of incongruent extensions', *Journal of Marketing*, April 2000, pp. 80–91.

17 Graham Hurrell, 'Solpadol – a successful case of brand positioning', *Journal of the Market Research* Society, July 1997.

18 Peter Doyle, *Marketing Management and Strategy* (London: Prentice-Hall, 1994) and chapter 20 in M. Baker, ed., *The Marketing Book* (Oxford: Butterworth-Heinemann, 1995).

19 Lesley de Chernatony, 'Brand management through narrowing the gap between identity and brand reputation', *Journal of Marketing Management*, 15 (1–3), 1999, pp. 157–179.

20 Claudia Simoes and Sally Dibb, 'Rethinking the brand concept: new brand orientation', *Corporate Communications: An International Journal*, November/December 2001, pp. 217–224.

21 Samuel Solley, 'Unilever in radical identity overhaul', *Marketing*, 19 February 2004, p. 1.

22 Emily Rogers, 'Coca-Cola introduces designer glass bottles', *Marketing*, 25 March 2004, p. 19.

23 Fred W. Morgan, 'Tampered goods: legal developments and marketing guidelines', *Journal of Market-ing*, April 1988, pp. 86–96.

24 Ibid.

25 Brian Wansink, 'Can package size accelerate usage volume?', *Journal of Marketing*, vol. 60, no. 3, July 1996, pp. 1–14.

26 Thomas J. Madden, Kelly Hewett and Martin S. Roth, 'Managing images in different cultures: a cross national study of color meanings and preferences', *Journal of International Marketing*, Winter 2000, p. 90.

27 Branwell Johnson, 'Mineral water companies to launch 'purity' symbol', *Marketing Week*, 29 April 2004, p. 8.

Index